Safeguarding Personal Information

National Standards for Data Privacy

snova
New York

Privacy and Identity Protection Series

Guidelines for Digital Identity Verification
Damon Solis (Editor)
ISBN: 979-8-88697-838-4
eBook ISBN: 979-8-88697-929-9

Information Security: Cyberattacks, Data Breaches and Security Controls
Paul Scholz (Editor)
ISBN: 978-1-53615-880-9
eBook ISBN: 978-1-53615-881-6

More information about this series can be found at
https://novapublishers.com/product-category/series/privacy-and-identity-protection/

Margaret K. Derosa
Editor

Safeguarding Personal Information

National Standards for Data Privacy

snova
New York

Library of Congress Cataloging-in-Publication Data

ISBN: 979-8-89530-698-7 (Hardcover)
ISBN: 979-8-89530-870-7 (eBook)

Published by Nova Science Publishers, Inc. † New York

Contents

Preface

In the 21st century, consumer information provides businesses with the ability to make informed decisions, develop products in response to customer feedback, and deliver goods and services to consumers. More generally, various types of information facilitate consumers' ability to make financial decisions, enable medical professionals to treat symptoms and provide critical health care, and enable educational institutions to facilitate a child's learning.

In each of these cases involving specific information about individuals, sector-specific laws protect and limit the purposes for which such information can be collected, used, or shared. This book examines the gaps in the protection of consumers' personal information, how businesses navigate compliance with sectoral laws, and why a comprehensive privacy and data security law must be enacted.

Chapter 1

Promoting U.S. Innovation and Individual Liberty Through a National Standard for Data Privacy*

Committee on Energy and Commerce

February 24, 2023

TO: Members, Subcommittee on Innovation, Data, and Commerce
FROM: Committee Majority Staff
RE: Hearing Entitled "Promoting U.S. Innovation and Individual Liberty through a National Standard for Data Privacy"

I. Introduction

The Subcommittee on Innovation, Data, and Commerce will hold a hearing on Wednesday, March 1, 2023, at 8:30 AM in Rayburn 2123. The hearing is entitled "Promoting U.S. Innovation and Individual Liberty through a National Standard for Data Privacy."

II. Witnesses

- Alexandra Reeve Givens, President and CEO, Center for Democracy & Technology
- Graham Mudd, Founder and Chief Product Officer, Anonym
- Jessica Rich, Of Counsel and Senior Policy Advisor for Consumer Protection, Kelley Drye & Warren, LLP

* This is an edited, reformatted and augmented version of Committee on Energy and Commerce, Subcommittee on Innovation, Data, and Commerce, dated March 1, 2023.

In: Safeguarding Personal Information: National Standards for Data Privacy
Editor: Margaret K. Derosa
ISBN: 979-8-89530-698-7

III. Background

A. Legislative Action Around the World

Data is central to commerce in the 21st century economy. It provides opportunities for businesses to make informed decisions and develop products responsive to customer feedback. Due to the digitization of our society, data has become more readily available to collect and use, and as a result more difficult for the individual whose data is collected and used to ultimately track. As a result, countries across the globe have enacted privacy and data security legislation dictating how businesses and entities can collect, use, and transfer data as well as providing their citizens with more control over their data.

In 1970, a German state enacted the world's first Data Protection Act and other states followed suit, creating the impetus for the first German Federal Data Protection Act in 1978.[1] Forty years later, the European Union enacted the General Data Protection Regulation (GDPR), which became the leading model for the world.[2] As of 2021, 137 out of 194 countries have put in place legislation to secure the protection of data and privacy within the bounds of their country.[3]

While other countries have led to provide protections for their citizens' data privacy, the United States has failed to enact the same broad protections.[4] While Congress has enacted sectoral laws for specific industries, for instance, the Gramm Leach Bliley Act (GLBA), which regulates financial institutions,[5] many of these sectoral laws are limited to notices on how user data is used and grant limited opportunities for consumers to opt out. In the absence of Federal action on comprehensive privacy and data security legislation, five States have enacted broad privacy and data security laws that vary in scope, protections, obligations, and enforcement mechanisms.[6] To ensure all Americans receive strong privacy and data security protections, and all businesses have clear rules of the road to operate within, the U.S. must enact a comprehensive and preemptive privacy and data security law so that it can maintain its leadership on the world stage.

This hearing will examine how personal data is currently treated and handled in today's digital ecosystem and the dangers facing the U.S. if Congressional inaction continues.

---

[1] Germany has given rise to two political systems in which the surveillance of its own people played a fundamental part in their control, manipulation and oppression – this history has made data privacy critically important for Germans. *See*, Olga Stepanova et al., *The Privacy, Data Protection and Cybersecurity Law Review: Germany*, The Law Reviews (October 27, 2022).

[2] Bahrain, Israel, Qatar, Turkey, Kenya, Mauritius, Nigeria, South Africa, Uganda, Japan, New Zealand, South Korea, Argentina, Brazil, Uruguay, and Canada have all enacted national legislation similar to GDPR. *See*, Mike Woodward, *16 Countries with GDPR-like Data Privacy Laws,* Security Scorecard (July 8, 2021). *See also*, *Adequacy decisions*, European Commission (Accessed February 17, 2023).

[3] *Data Protection and Privacy Legislation Worldwide*, UNCTAD (December 14, 2021).

[4] The French data privacy regulator, the CNIL, labeled the U.S. as a country that does not ensure an adequate level of data protection recognized by the EU. *See*, *Data protection around the world*, CNIL (November 15, 2022).

[5] Gramm-Leach-Bliley Act, available at: https://www.congress.gov/bill/106th-congress/senate-bill/900.

[6] Rajesh De et al., *Connecticut Passes Comprehensive Privacy Law: Comparing to Other States*, Mayer Brown (May 11, 2022).

B. The Problem

Without a comprehensive federal standard governing how companies can collect, process, and transfer data, Americans find it challenging to know which entities have their data and how their data is being used, in many cases, for purposes beyond what they expect. With each passing year, privacy policies have become so convoluted and extensive that the average American may not fully comprehend what they are agreeing to or even take the time to read. Additionally, without a comprehensive federal standard, there are insufficient limits to what types of data companies may collect, process, and transfer.

This problem is exacerbated when companies provide or sell data to data brokers.[7] Data brokers are companies whose primary business is collecting personal data from various sources ranging from traffic tickets to property data to purchase history. They process, aggregate and analyze the personal data to make inferences about specific consumers. These consumer insights are then sold or licensed to individuals or companies for purposes such as marketing products or verifying an individual's identity.[8] Significantly, data brokers do all this without interacting with the consumer directly. Therefore, consumers have little awareness of the marketplace for their personal data.[9]

The data broker industry is a multibillion-dollar economy selling consumers' data with virtually no restrictions or oversight.[10] The biggest brokers tout the details of their data on millions or even billions of people,[11] which powers their ability to create remarkably specific and rich consumer profiles with enough information to link sensitive data to real people. Numerous websites populate the internet where someone may go to purchase this data, without any regard to the verification on how they may use the information.

C. Data Security

For the last decade, Americans have been flooded by reports and breaking news related to ransomware attacks perpetrated by both private entities and state sponsored entities. When American's data is in the hands of nefarious actors it can be used for a variety of harmful purposes. For example, consumer data can be used to steal someone's identity. Identity theft can allow nefarious actors to gain access to a consumer's secure accounts, set up credit cards using the consumers name, or otherwise use the victim's identity to benefit themselves and wreak havoc on the consumer's life.[12] Nefarious actors can also sell consumer data on black

---

[7] Yael Grauer, *What are 'Data Brokers,' and Why Are They Scooping Up Information About You?*, Vice (March 27, 2018).

[8] Edith Ramirez et al., *Data Brokers A Call for Transparency and Accountability*, Federal Trade Commission (May 2014).

[9] Apple ran a commercial that does a good job presenting the mostly invisible consumer data marketplace. *See, Privacy on iPhone | Data Auction*, Apple via YouTube (May 18, 2022).

[10] Justin Sherman, *Data Brokers Are a Threat to Democracy*, Wired (April 13, 2021).

[11] For example, CoreLogic advertises its real estate and property information contains 99.9% of the U.S. population. *See, Property Data Solutions*, CoreLogic (Accessed February 17, 2023).

[12] *What is data theft and how to prevent it*, Kaspersky.

market websites where data is illegally bought and sold.[13] This data can be bought by cybercriminals or state actors and government entities.[14]

To protect American's data effectively, any comprehensive federal standard must include rigorous data security protections and privacy by design requirements for businesses to consider how they are collecting, processing, and transferring personal data. Data minimization requirements can also assure that companies are not collecting more information than they need, which guarantee less personal information is available for cybercriminals to breach.

D. Digital Advertising Ecosystem

American's data in the hands of companies can be used for a variety of purposes. As advertising has given birth to innovation in support of new business models, companies can use consumer data to make products better by incorporating user behaviors into product design to make the consumer experience better.[15] Conversely, companies can use the data they collect to monetize their customers as an additional revenue stream, or for companies that operate a "freemium" business model,[16] monetizing consumer data can be their primary revenue stream.

Companies primarily monetize American's data through digital advertising, utilizing two main categories of digital advertisements. The first method companies may use is contextual advertising, a technique which creates and ensures the content on an advertisement depends on or relates to the content on a webpage.[17] The second method is targeted advertising, a practice which involves the use of previously collected data on a consumer, whether that be from historical online activity or real world interactions, to deliver specific advertisements.[18] With no regulation to disincentivize what information a company can collect, they have been able to collect vast amounts of data on Americans.

In 2006, the digital advertising ecosystem transformed through the advent of social media, which provided advertisers looking to reach specific demographics and users with a rich data profile and method to do so. This led to the current digital advertising ecosystem and online environment where consumers receive more targeted advertisements as opposed to the traditional contextual advertisements.[19] The more data collected from Americans translated directly to the increase in hyper specialized ads, which to many Americans, felt like an invasion of privacy.[20]

---

[13] Robert Elgart, *The Data Black Market: Where Hackers Take Stolen Data*, Turn-Key Technologies (August 5, 2019).

[14] Senator Wyden has been investigating the U.S. government's purchase of American's data without judicial authorization for several years. *See*, Ron Wyden, *Letter to Inspector Generals of DHS, DOJ & DOD*, United States Senate (September 21, 2022).

[15] Anne Taylor, 4 ways to create better customer experiences with data, CIO (August 1, 2022).

[16] "Freemium" is a combination of "free" and "premium". It has become the dominant business model among internet start-ups and smartphone app developers. Users get basic features at no cost and can access richer functionality for a subscription fee. *See*, Vineet Kumar, *Making "Freemium" Work*, Harvard Business Review (May 2014).

[17] *Contextual vs Behavioral vs Audience Targeting: A Full Comparison*, AdButler (July 25, 2022).

[18] Id.

[19] Karla Hesterberg, *A brief History of Online Advertising*, HubSpot (November 29, 2021).

[20] *New Survey Reveals that Consumers want Digital Ads to Carry a "Privacy Guaranteed" Seal*, Businesswire (December 15, 2021).

This invasion feels worse when the same targeted ad follows you around the internet in a practice known as retargeting – a form of targeted advertising that serves ads to people who have already visited a website or are in a company's database. There are two main types of retargeting: pixel-based and list-based.[21] The pixel-based retargeting practice starts when a consumer enters a website, a cookie is added to the consumer's browser to remember which pages the consumer has viewed.[22] When the consumer leaves the website to surf the web, that cookie notifies retargeting platforms to serve specific ads based on the specific pages the consumer visited on other websites, allowing ads to retarget consumers immediately after they leave the original website, giving the consumer a feeling that they are being followed. A company will upload a list of email addresses or phone numbers to a retargeting campaign, usually on a social network, and the platform will identify users on that network who have the same email address or phone number and serve retargeting ads just to them.

Advertising in the digital age has prompted Americans to question how their information is collected, processed, and transferred. Many Americans certainly appreciate the ease of shopping online that comes with different advertising practices. However, the American people deserve more transparency into the ways in which theses targeted advertising practices exploit their data and should be granted more autonomy to decide how they want to participate in the digital advertising ecosystem.

E. Americans Support Data Privacy Legislation

Despite not having a complete understanding of all the ways in which digital devices and services track consumers,[23] a majority of Americans still believe their online and offline activities are being tracked and monitored by companies and the government with some regularity.[24] It is such a common condition of modern life that roughly six-in-ten U.S. adults say they do not think it is possible to go through daily life without having data collected about them by companies or the government.[25]

Due to the ubiquitous, insidious, and pervasive nature of data collection and Americans' increasing awareness of these practices, data privacy and security has become a major concern. A recent study reveals that nearly all Americans surveyed (92%) believe it is important for

Congress to pass new legislation to protect consumers' personal data, and 4 in-5 voters (81%) support a national standard that outright prohibits harmful ways of collecting, using and sharing personal data.[26]

---

[21] Dan Hecht, *What Is Retargeting? How To Set Up an Ad Retargeting Campaign*, HubSpot (August 5, 2021).

[22] Katie Broida, *What Is Cookie Tracking*?, HubSpot (May 9, 2018).

[23] Natasha Singer et al., *Americans Flunked This Test on Online Privacy*, The New York Times (February 7, 2023).

[24] Brooke Auxier et al., *Americans and Privacy: Concerned, Confused and Feeling Lack of Control Over Their Personal Information*, Pew Research Center (November 15, 2019).

[25] Ibid.

[26] *New Data Reveals Americans' Overwhelming and Bipartisan Support for Federal Privacy Legislation*, Privacy for America (November 18, 2021).

F. Privacy Enhancing Technologies

In a world where Americans value their privacy and data security, businesses need to explore new and innovative technologies that can both provide value for their business in addition to protecting the privacy of their customers and users. Previously this proposition was a trade-off that needed to be made but with the advent of privacy enhancing technologies (PETs) companies can do both - extract value from American's data while maintaining their privacy.

PETs are a growing suite of tools that can help maximize a company's use of data by reducing risks inherent to data use, especially data related to consumers. Some PETs provide new tools for anonymization, while others enable collaborative analysis on privately held datasets, allowing data to be used without disclosing copies of data.[27] PETs can play an important role in privacy by design approaches to data governance and are already being used in a variety of commercial applications.

G. Relevant Committee Action and Previous Legislation

The American Data Privacy and Protection Act

Reps. Pallone (D-NJ), Rodgers (R-WA), Schakowsky (D-IL), and Bilirakis (R-FL) introduced H.R. 8152, the "American Data Privacy and Protection Act" (ADPPA) on June 21, 2022, and subsequently passed it out of Committee by a 53-2 vote. ADPPA is the first bipartisan, bicameral national comprehensive privacy and data security proposal with support from leaders on the House Energy and Commerce Committee and the Senate Commerce, Science, and Transportation Committee.

The legislation establishes a preemptive national consumer privacy and data security framework built around limitations for collecting, processing, and transferring individuals' information, obligations for covered entities and service providers, and providing individuals with control with respect to their personal information. Certain covered data is considered sensitive and subject to additional restrictions and there are further protections for Americans under 17 years old. Covered entities may not use covered data in any manner that discriminates or makes unavailable the equal enjoyment of goods or services on the basis of protected classes. Large businesses are subject to additional requirements, while small and midsize businesses are exempted from certain provisions and eligible to participate in certain technical compliance programs. H.R. 8152 provides for federal, state, and private enforcement.

H. Issues

- How will the emerging patchwork of state data privacy laws impact business that operate in the digital economy?
- Should a federal standard preempt state laws that would not be covered within such standard?

---

[27] Alison Noble, *From Privacy to Partnership – the role of privacy enhancing technologies in data governance and collaborative analysis*, The Royal Society (January 2023).

- What is the difference between a company using first party data for advertising and transferring such data to a third party for advertising?
- Why are safe harbors important for complying with federal law?
- What aspects of other countries data privacy laws are too restrictive?
- Why should Congress enact legislation that would establish comprehensive privacy and data security protections as opposed to rulemakings, or a continued state by state approach?

Staff Contacts

- Tim Kurth, Chief Counsel
- Teddy Tanzer, Senior Counsel
- Brannon Rains, Professional Staff Member
- Michael Cameron, Professional Staff Member
- Lacey Strahm, Technology Fellow
- Jessica Herron, Clerk

Promoting U.S. Innovation and Individual, Liberty through a National Standard for Data Privacy, Wednesday, March 1, 2023, House of Representatives, Subcommittee on Innovation, Data, and Commerce, Committee on Energy and Commerce, Washington, D.C.

The subcommittee met, pursuant to call, at 8:34 a.m., in Room 2123, Rayburn House Office Building, Hon. Gus Bilirakis [chairman of the subcommittee] presiding.

Present: Representatives Bilirakis, Bucshon, Walberg, Duncan, Dunn, Lesko, Pence, Armstrong, Allen, Fulcher, Harshbarger, Cammack, Rodgers (ex officio), Schakowsky, Castor, Dingell, Kelly, Soto, Trahan, Clarke, and Pallone (ex officio).

Also Present: Representatives Carter and Obernolte.

Staff Present: Sarah Burke, Deputy Staff Director; Michael Cameron, Professional Staff Member, Consumer Protections & Commerce; Jessica Herron, Clerk, CPAC; Nate Hodson, Staff Director; Tara Hupman, Chief Counsel; Peter Kielty, Counsel; Emily King, Member Services Director; Tim Kurth, Chief Counsel, CPAC; Brannon Rains, Professional Staff Member, CPAC; Hannah Anton, Minority Staff Assistant; Ian Barlow, Minority FTC Detailee; Waverly Gordon, Minority Deputy Staff Director and General Counsel; Daniel Greene, Minority Professional Staff Member; Tiffany Guarascio, Minority Staff Director; Perry Hamilton, Minority Member Services and Outreach Manager; Lisa Hone, Minority Chief Counsel, Innovation, Data, and Commerce; Mackenzie Kuhl, Minority Digital Manager; Joe Orlando, Minority Senior Policy Analyst; Greg Pugh, Minority Staff Assistant; and Andrew Souvall, Minority Director of Communications, Outreach and Member Services.

Mr. Bilirakis. Good morning. The Subcommittee on Innovation, Data, and Commerce will come to order.

The chair recognizes himself for 5 minutes for an opening statement.

Good morning, again. I appreciate y'all being here. We got an early jump start on the day to accommodate our friends across the aisle who have a issues conference later this afternoon. So I am confident we will make the most of our time this morning.

We made great strides last Congress, as you know, with the leadership of this committee, demonstrating that we can come together in a bipartisan fashion for the American people. I look forward to continuing and completing that important work this Congress.

Earlier this week, the House passed H.R. 538, the Informing Consumers about Smart Devices Act, from Representatives Curtis and Moulton, with broad bipartisan support. I want to recognize Chair Cantwell and Ranking Member Cruz in the Senate for sponsoring the Senate companion bill, which I take as a strong sign that the Senate cares about American's privacy. I hope I am right. I thank these Members for working on legislation that complements this committee's broader privacy goals and provides great transparency to Americans about the ability for devices to secretly record them.

This is just one of many examples of why congressional action on broader comprehensive privacy and data security is desperately needed and why we are holding this hearing today, the second in a series of three.

With that, I want to express my gratitude to our panelists for being here. We appreciate you very much, not only for bearing with us with the early start time, but also for sharing your expertise today. Each of you bring important insights that will help our committee advance comprehensive privacy and data security legislation this Congress.

Americans need and deserve more transparency over how their information is collected, processed, and transferred. In the past several years, our constituents have likely noticed the internet becoming more personalized for them, whether they are seeing more targeted advertisements, showing items that they recently viewed on another website, or experiencing content on social media that matches what they have interacted with elsewhere. Sometimes it is scary stuff.

To some, these practices may be viewed as more convenient for their shopping or useful for how they digest information. But others may find this practice is invasive and unsolicited. So let's give Americans the right to choose if they want this or not. Why not?

Mr. Mudd, thank you, again, for being here to walk us through how legislation can work for businesses operating in the digital ecosystem and to share your expertise about how we can both protect innovation in our economy and still give Americans freedom to choose what to do with their personal and sensitive data. I know we can get this done. I appreciate you being here, sir.

We also need to ensure legislation works for everyone and doesn't adversely impact our constituents or impede on the basic liberties that every American deserves.

Ms. Givens, I want to thank you for your expertise on these matters, as well as for your support over the last year in advancing comprehensive legislation. Thank you so much.

Lastly, we need to ensure responsible government approach to enforcing clear rules for businesses to comply. Companies, especially small startups, shouldn't be subject to random or punitive letters in the mail notifying them that certain practices could be unfair or deceptive. It is essential that the FTC enforce the laws so that we as a Congress enact and, specifically, authorize but not go rogue beyond the rules of the road we provide. This type of regulatory certainty is needed for businesses to comply. They must comply but, again, it has got to be fair.

Ms. Rich, thank you for testifying today again. You have great insights regarding the role of the FTC in enforcing laws but doing so in a way that doesn't unduly burden legitimate business activity. I look forward to continuing to work with you on achieving the right balance for the FTC to enforce a national privacy and data security law to protect Americans of all ages, while at the same time ensure that businesses that follow the rules aren't subject to government overreach and frivolous litigation. The committee appreciates your deep institutional knowledge and insight. Thank you so much.

Again, thanks again to our panel for being here, and I look forward to your testimony.

The chair now recognizes the subcommittee ranking member, Ms. Schakowsky, for her 5 minutes for an opening statement. Good morning.

[The prepared statement of Mr. Bilirakis follows:]

Opening Statement of Chair Gus Bilirakis, as Prepared for Delivery, Committee on Energy and Commerce Subcommittee on Innovation, Data, and Commerce, Hearing Entitled "Promoting U.S. Innovation and Individual Liberty through a National Standard for Data Privacy," March 1, 2023

Good morning everyone. We got an early jump start on the day to accommodate our friends across the aisle who have a retreat later today. I'm confident we'll make the most of our time this morning.

We made great strides last Congress with the leadership of this Committee demonstrating that we can come together in a bipartisan fashion for the American people. I look forward to continuing and completing that important work this Congress.

Earlier this week, the House passed H.R. 538, the Informing Consumers about Smart Devices Act from Representatives Curtis and Moulton, with broad bipartisan support. I want to recognize Chair Cantwell and Ranking Member Cruz in the Senate for sponsoring the Senate Companion bill, which I take as a strong sign that the Senate cares about Americans' privacy. I thank these Members for working on legislation that compliments this Committee's broader privacy goals and provides greater transparency to Americans about the ability for devices to secretly record them. This is just one of many examples why Congressional action on broader comprehensive privacy and data security is desperately needed and why we are holding this hearing today, the second in a series of three.

With that I want to express my gratitude to our panelists not only for bearing with us for the early start time, but also for sharing your expertise today. Each of you bring important insights that will help our Committee advance comprehensive privacy and data security legislation this Congress.

Americans need and deserve more transparency over how their information is collected, processed, and transferred. In the past several years, our constituents have likely noticed the internet becoming more personalized for them – whether they are seeing more targeted advertisements showing items that they've recently viewed on another website, or experiencing content on social media that matches what they've interacted with elsewhere. To some, these practices may be viewed as more convenient for their shopping or useful for how they digest information. But others may find this practice invasive and unsolicited. So let's give Americans the right to choose if they want this or not.

Mr. Mudd, thank you for being here to walk us through how legislation can work for businesses operating in the digital ecosystem and to share your expertise about how we can both protect innovation in our economy and still give Americans freedoms to choose what to do with their personal and sensitive data.

We also need to ensure legislation works for everyone and doesn't adversely impact our constituents or impede on the basic liberties that every American deserves. Miss Givens, I want to thank you for your expertise on these matters, as well as for your support over the last year in advancing comprehensive legislation.

Lastly, we need to ensure responsible government approach to enforcing clear rules for businesses to comply. Companies, especially small startups, shouldn't be subject to random or punitive letters in the mail notifying them that certain practices could be unfair or deceptive. It is essential that the FTC enforce the laws that we as a Congress enact and specifically authorize, but not go rogue beyond the rules of the road we provide. This type of regulatory certainty is needed for businesses to come into compliance.

Miss Rich, thank you for testifying. You have great insights regarding the role of the FTC in enforcing laws but doing so in a way that doesn't unduly burden legitimate business activity. I look forward to continuing to work with you on achieving the right balance for the FTC to enforce a national privacy and data security law to protect Americans of all ages, while at the same time ensure that businesses that follow the rules aren't subject to government overreach and frivolous litigation. The Committee appreciates your deep institutional knowledge and insight.

Thank you again to our panel for being here and I look forward to your testimony.

* * *

Ms. Schakowsky. Good morning, everyone. Thank you so much, Mr. Chairman.

And I really want to begin by saying how proud I am of the work that this subcommittee has done really over the years, particularly in the last session of Congress, in a bipartisan way. And I am really looking forward, as you said in your beginning remarks, that we can do this together, that we can go forward.

We were almost there. We were able to pass in a unanimous way, almost, the American Data Privacy and Protection Act, again, working together.

We heard the cry of the vast majority of Americans who are really tired of feeling helpless online. We heard from stakeholders from every corner of government and civic society – civil society and industry at six different roundtables that we had. But absent any action by the – by the Congress, big tech is collecting evermore information about us, our personal information, intimate data. And these companies know our habits, they know our finances, where we are, where we live, where we are going. And when you browse the web or wear a smartwatch, a tech company is tracking you.

So they use this data to manipulate us, to addict us, and to keep us on their platforms so that they can provide even more ads to us, or they sell the data to the highest bidder so that companies that you don't even know what their names are or who they are can build a profile about you.

Harmful targeting of advertising on social media has exacerbated the mental health problems that we face, particularly among our young people. Our adolescents, our kids are the most vulnerable. Our teenagers, we have to make sure that we are protecting them.

All this is in the name of profit. It is time – it is time, and the time has really passed, I think, for us to do a data privacy law, and I really, really look forward to working together. Our past effort I think provides, once again, the guidelines for how we can move together, and I absolutely look forward to building on the momentous gains that we have made.

And so I think it is time for us to roll up our sleeves in a bipartisan way to get to work. The United States is far behind, and we need to catch up with states that are beginning to introduce their own privacy laws, many different ones from around the country, and to give consumers what they want.

And, with that, I yield back.

[The prepared statement of Ms. Schakowsky follows:]

Committee on Energy and Commerce, Opening Statement as Prepared for Delivery of Subcommittee on Innovation, Data, and Commerce, Ranking Member Jan Schakowsky, Hearing on "Promoting U.S. Innovation and Individual Liberty through a National Standard for Data Privacy," March 1, 2023

We made it almost to the finish line on data privacy by working together. A majority of Americans agree: consumers need comprehensive federal data privacy protections.[28]

That's because the internet is not living up to its promise. The early internet promised more social connections, new communities, and more innovation and economic opportunity. But these benefits have come at the expense of our privacy.

Big Tech has become dependent on collecting ever more personal and intimate data about us. Data on our habits, our finances, who we love, where we live, and our most sensitive health data. Every time you browse the web or wear a smart watch, a tech company is tracking you.

They use this data to manipulate us, to addict us, and to keep us on their platforms so we can be fed more ads. Or they sell the data to the highest bidder so that companies you've never heard of can build profiles of you. Social media has become like cigarettes, addicting in the name of profit.

Like with cigarettes, our teenagers are particularly affected. Harmful targeted advertising on social media has exacerbated the mental health crisis plaguing our young people. Americans are tired of feeling helpless online. It is time to pass data privacy legislation that protects consumers and promotes innovation.

I'd like to acknowledge, with immense gratitude, the years of tireless work on both sides of the aisle. Our efforts prove, once again, that privacy is not a partisan or an extreme issue. The "American Data Privacy and Protection Act" represented a groundbreaking milestone and is inspiring privacy advocates across the country. Just last summer, it overwhelmingly passed the Energy & Commerce Committee 53-2.

I look forward to today's bipartisan hearing to build on our momentum, years in the making, to pass transformational privacy protections for all Americans. It's time to return control of their data back to the American people, and to finish what we started last year.

---

[28] https://iapp.org/news/a/poll-55-of-registered-us-voters-want-federal-privacy-law/.

* * *

Mr. Bilirakis. I thank the ranking member.

The chair now recognizes the chair of the full committee, Ms. Rodgers, for 5 minutes for her opening statement.

The Chair. Good morning. Thank you to the witnesses for being here this morning. Really appreciate this panel. Your testimony is essential as we keep the momentum going, as Ms. Schakowsky was just mentioning, for a strong data privacy and security and those protections for all Americans.

This subcommittee's first hearing this year focused on data privacy and security to ensure America's global competitive edge against China. Today's second hearing in our series will consider what a strong national data privacy standard will mean in our everyday lives to rein in big tech, protect kids online, and put people in charge of their data. These discussions build on the bipartisan, bicameral ADPPA, which moved through this committee last year with a vote of 53 to 2. That was the first time this committee reached such a milestone, and no other committee has come close on a national privacy and data security standard with bipartisan support necessary to clear the House and make the Senate take notice.

This is a new Congress with new considerations, so we much continue to improve on the legislation from last Congress, build consensus among stakeholders. Bringing together experience in business, civil society, and government is the three-legged stool that will support our efforts in developing bipartisan, comprehensive privacy, and data security legislation. We must continue our work so individuals can exercise their rights, businesses can continue to innovate, and the government's role is clearly defined.

Today turns that conversation inward so we are preserving the engine of innovation while ensuring that we aren't just dollar signs for data brokers and big tech.

They are harvesting people's data, selling or sharing it without their knowledge, and not keeping it secure. We need a national data privacy standard that changes the status quo regarding people's data.

Right now, there are no robust protections. Americans have no say over whether and where their personal data is sold and shared. They have no guaranteed way to access, delete, or correct their data. And they have no ability to stop the unchecked collection of their sensitive personal information. This isn't acceptable.

Data brokers' and big techs' day of operating in the dark should be over. People should trust their data is being protected.

We are at an inflection point to ensure our personal information is responsibly collected so artificial intelligence is developed with our values. We need to ensure that the metaverse doesn't become the next frontier of exploitation for our kids. That requires a broad, comprehensive bill that will address all American's data and put even stronger guardrails around our kids. That is why the American Data Privacy and Protection Act included the strongest internet protections for children of any legislation last Congress. And its protections did not stop with kids. ADPPA gave everyone data protections no matter where they live and no matter their age.

We will continue to build on ADPPA this Congress and get these strong protections for our kids and all Americans signed into law.

I want to thank the ranking member, Ranking Member Pallone, other colleagues, ranking member of this subcommittee, Jan Schakowsky, as well as the chairman of this subcommittee, Gus Bilirakis, and colleagues on this committee across the aisle for working together on this legislation. We have a shared goal here, and we are going to continue this work, and we are going to get it done in this Congress.

I look forward to today's hearing and for our privacy series to continue on March 23, when TikTok's CEO is before this committee.

Thank you, and I yield back.

[The prepared statement of Chair Rodgers follows:]

Opening Statement of Chair Cathy McMorris Rodgers, as Prepared for Delivery, Committee on Energy and Commerce, Subcommittee on Innovation, Data, and Commerce, Hearing entitled "Promoting U.S. Innovation and Individual Liberty through a National Standard for Data Privacy," March 1, 2023

Good morning.

Thank you to our panel of witnesses here this morning.

Your testimony today is essential, as we keep the momentum going for strong data privacy and security protections for all Americans.

This subcommittee's first hearing this year focused on data privacy and security to ensure America's global competitive edge against China.

Today's second hearing in our series will consider what a strong national data privacy standard will mean in our everyday lives to rein in Big Tech, protect kids online, and put people in charge of their data.

These discussions build on the bipartisan, bicameral ADPPA, which we moved through the committee last year with a vote of 53-2.

That was the first time this committee reached such a milestone, and no other committee has come close on a national privacy and data security standard with the bipartisan support necessary to clear the House and make the Senate take notice.

This is a new Congress, with new considerations, so we must continue to improve on the legislation from last Congress and build consensus amongst stakeholders.

Bringing together experience in business…. civil society…. and government…. is the three-legged stool that will support our efforts in developing bipartisan comprehensive privacy and data security legislation.

We must continue our work so that individuals can exercise their rights…. businesses can continue to innovate…. and the government's role is clearly defined.

Today turns that conversation inward so we are preserving the engine of innovation while ensuring that we aren't just dollar signs for data brokers and Big Tech.

They are harvesting people's data, selling or sharing it without their knowledge, and not keeping it secure.

We need a national data privacy standard that changes the status quo regarding people's data. Right now, there are no robust protections.

Americans have no say over whether and where their personal data is sold and shared…

… they have no guaranteed way to access, delete, or correct their data…

… and they have no ability to stop the unchecked collection of their sensitive personal information.

This isn't acceptable. Data brokers' and Big Tech's days of operating in the dark should be over. People should trust their data is being protected.

We are at an inflection point to ensure our personal information is responsibly collected so artificial intelligence is developed with our values.

We need to ensure that the metaverse doesn't become the next frontier of exploitation for our kids.

That requires a broad comprehensive bill that will address all Americans' data, and puts even stronger guardrails around our kids.

That's why the American Data Privacy and Protection Act includes the strongest internet protections for children of any legislation last Congress.

And its protections does not stop with kids.

ADPPA gives everyone data protections—no matter where they live and no matter their age.

We will continue to build on ADPPA this Congress and get these strong protections for kids and all Americans signed into law.

Thank you, Ranking Member Pallone and my colleagues across the aisle, for continuing to work with us.

We share the goal for strong bipartisan consensus like we had last year on ADPPA.

I look forward to today's hearing... and for our privacy series to continue on March 23rd when Tik Tok's CEO is before the Committee.

Thank you, I yield back.

* * *

Mr. Bilirakis. Thank you. I want to thank the chair. And again, as you said, we got to get it across the finish line this time, but we did our job last Congress under your leadership, Madam Chair, and the leadership of the ranking member. So we can make a good bill even better. So we appreciate that very much.

With that, the chair recognizes the ranking member of the full committee, my friend, Mr. Pallone, for his 5 minutes.

Mr. Pallone. Thank you, Chairman Bilirakis.

Last Congress, when I chaired the committee, I was proud to work with then Ranking Member Rodgers and now Chair Rodgers and the other subcommittee leaders on the American Data Privacy and Protection Act. And that was the first bipartisan and bicameral comprehensive data privacy legislation in decades. And this was a historic achievement with a 53 to 2 vote out of committee.

In this subcommittee's first hearing of this Congress, I was pleased, but not surprised, to hear Chair Rodgers reaffirm her commitment to advancing this bill.

Simply put, as we will hear from today's witnesses, we need comprehensive Federal data privacy legislation, and we need it urgently. Today, many of our essential consumer products, especially those offered by the largest tech companies, require consumers, including children and teens, to trade their personal data for services. And this is not a real choice. People can't thrive in our digital economy without access to websites, mobile applications, email services, and other forms of online communication.

Members of both parties talk a lot about holding big tech accountable, and I firmly believe that the way to do that is by adopting a strong national privacy standard that limits the excesses of big tech and makes the digital world safer.

The testimony we will hear today will illustrate the fact that the lack of a national privacy standard doesn't just hurt consumers, it also hurts small and emerging businesses by favoring big providers at the expense of new competitors. Providing certainty to all consumers, businesses, and markets about fair and appropriate data collection and use is crucial for continued American innovation. We simply cannot go another Congress without passing comprehensive privacy legislation.

Our legislation last Congress includes input from many of you on this subcommittee and countless other stakeholders. It directly confronts and reaches important compromises on the sticking points which derailed earlier congressional efforts. The American Data Privacy and Protection Act will put people back in control of their personal data, stop data collection abuses by big tech, provide important protections for kids, rein in the shadowy world of data brokers, and establish strong Federal data security standards.

The legislation achieves all this by starting with the fundamental shift in how data is collected, used, and transferred. It rejects the coercive notice and consent system that has failed to protect Americans' data privacy and security. Instead, the bill adopts a data minimization obligation. It requires companies to limit the personal information they collect. They will only be able to collect what is reasonably necessary and proportionate to providing the services that consumers are requesting.

At this subcommittee's first hearing this year, we heard testimony that data minimization protects consumer privacy and is critical for cybersecurity and national security, and that is exactly what our bill did. And again, the American Data Privacy and Protection Act also protects kids from big tech. It bans targeted advertising to children under 17, and covered entities will not be able to transfer covered data belonging to children without consent. To help enforce these protections for kids, the bill establishes a youth privacy and marketing division at the Federal Trade Commission.

Our legislation also shines a light on the shadowed world of data brokers that profit from buying and selling our personal data. These companies don't interact with consumers directly, but they do collect and sell massive amounts of consumer data, including sensitive personal data like health information and precise geolocation data that identifies a consumers location within 18 feet. We must stop these data brokers from collecting, using, and selling consumers' data without their knowledge or permission.

The American Data Privacy and Protection Act will require data brokers to register with the FTC and will provide consumers with a single mechanism to opt out of data collection by all registered brokers.

Now, while Congress has stalled on privacy for years, the rest of the world has not, ceding American leadership on technological regulation. The European Union has passed comprehensive privacy laws, and this bill would immediately reset the global landscape.

So I want to thank the witnesses for being here today to shed even more light on the need for a national privacy standard. I want to thank Chairwoman Rodgers, Ranking Member Schakowsky, Chairman Bilirakis, and the members of this subcommittee for their really tireless efforts and their unwavering commitment to move a comprehensive data privacy bill across the finish line this Congress. I know that we can do it. So thank you again.

I yield back to the chairman.

[The prepared statement of Mr. Pallone follows:]

Committee on Energy and Commerce, Opening Statement as Prepared for Delivery of Ranking Member Frank Pallone, Jr., Innovation, Data, and Commerce Subcommittee Hearing on "Promoting U.S. Innovation and Individual Liberty through a National Standard for Data Privacy," March 1, 2023

Last Congress, when I Chaired this Committee, I was proud to work with then-Ranking Member Rodgers and this Subcommittee's leaders on the American Data Privacy and Protection Act (ADPPA) - the first bipartisan and bicameral comprehensive data privacy legislation in decades. This was a historic achievement, with a 53-2 vote out of Committee. In this Subcommittee's first hearing of this Congress, I was pleased, but not surprised, to hear Chair Rodgers reaffirm her commitment to advancing that bill.

Simply put, as we will hear from today's witnesses, we need comprehensive, federal data privacy legislation. And we need it urgently.

Today, many of our essential consumer products—especially those offered by the largest technology companies—require consumers, including children and teens, to trade their personal data for services. This is not a real choice. People cannot thrive in our digital economy without access to websites, mobile applications, email services, and other forms of online communication.

Members of both parties talk a lot about holding big tech accountable. I firmly believe that the way to do that is by adopting a strong national privacy standard that limits the excesses of Big Tech and makes the digital world safer.

The testimony we will hear today will illustrate the fact that the lack of a national privacy standard doesn't just hurt consumers. It also hurts small and emerging businesses by favoring big providers at the expense of new competitors. Providing certainty to all consumers, businesses, and markets about fair and appropriate data collection and use is crucial for continued American innovation.

We simply cannot go another Congress without passing comprehensive privacy legislation. Our legislation last Congress includes input from many of you on this Subcommittee and countless other stakeholders. It directly confronts—and reaches important compromises—on the sticking points which derailed earlier Congressional efforts.

The American Data Privacy and Protection Act will put people back in control of their personal data, stop data collection abuses by Big Tech, provide important protections for kids, rein in the shadowy world of data brokers, and establish strong federal data security standards.

The legislation achieves all this by starting with a fundamental shift in how data is collected, used, and transferred. It rejects the coercive "notice and consent" system that has failed to protect Americans' data privacy and security.

Instead, the ADPPA adopts a data minimization obligation. It requires companies to limit the personal information they collect. They will only be able to collect what is reasonably necessary and proportionate to providing the services consumers are requesting. At this Subcommittee's first hearing this year, we heard testimony that data minimization protects consumer privacy and is critical for cybersecurity and national security, and that's exactly what our bill did.

The American Data Privacy and Protection Act also protects kids from Big Tech. It bans targeted advertising to children under 17. And covered entities will not be able to transfer covered data belonging to children without consent. To help enforce these protections for kids, the bill establishes a Youth Privacy and Marketing Division at the Federal Trade Commission (FTC).

Our legislation also shines a light on the shadow world of data brokers that profit from buying and selling our personal data. These companies don't interact with consumers directly, but they do collect and sell massive amounts of consumer data, including sensitive personal data like health information and precise geolocation data that identifies a consumer's location within 18 feet.

We must stop these data brokers from collecting, using, and selling consumers' data without their knowledge or permission. The American Data Privacy and Protection Act will require data brokers to register with the FTC and will provide consumers with a single mechanism to opt out of data collection by all registered brokers.

While Congress has stalled on privacy for years, the rest of the world has not, ceding American leadership on technological regulation. The European Union has passed comprehensive privacy laws. This bill would immediately reset the global landscape.

I want to thank the witnesses for being here today to shed even more light on the need for a national privacy standard. I thank Chair Rodgers, Ranking Member Schakowsky, Chair Bilirakis and the members of this Subcommittee for their tireless efforts and their unwavering commitment to move comprehensive data privacy legislation across the finish line this Congress.

Thank you and I yield back.

* * *

Mr. Bilirakis. I thank the ranking member.

We have now concluded with member opening statements. The chair would like to remind members that pursuant to the committee rules, all members' opening statements will be made part of the record.

We would like to, again, thank all of our witnesses for being here, again, earlier than normal, to testify before the committee.

Today's witnesses will have 5 minutes to provide oral testimony, which will be followed by a round of questions from members.

Our witness panel for today's hearing will include Mr. Graham Mudd, who is the founder and chief product officer of Anonym. I asked him yesterday if he was related to the late Roger Mudd, was a great journalist, and he said yes, distantly. That is pretty cool. If you don't ask, you don't get the answer.

And then Ms. Alexandra Reeve Givens, who is the president and CEO of Center for Democracy and Technology. And Ms. Jessica Rich, of counsel and senior policy advisor for consumer protection, Kelley, Drye & Warren, LLP.

So, Mr. Mudd, you are recognized for 5 minutes. We appreciate you being here again, sir.

Statements of Graham Mudd, Founder and Chief Product Officer, Anonym; Alexandra Reeve Givens, President and CEO, Center for Democracy & Technology; Jessica Rich, of Counsel and Senior Policy Advisor for Consumer Protection, Kelley Drye & Warren, LLP

Statement of Graham Mudd

Mr. Mudd. [Inaudible.] My apologies.

Chairman Bilirakis, Ranking Member Schakowsky, Chair Rodgers, Ranking Member Pallone, and distinguished members of this committee, thank you for the opportunity to testify at this important hearing.

My name is Graham Mudd, and I am cofounder and chief product officer of Anonym, a privacy technology company. I want to begin by thanking you for pushing forward ADPPA. I am looking forward to the passage of strong Federal privacy legislation along with strong enforcement authority.

We are here to talk about creating a more privacy safe internet for Americans. The collection, sharing, and use of data for advertising is at the heart of the digital privacy challenge facing our country and the world. We started Anonym because we believed the notion that you can't have both privacy and an efficient digital advertising ecosystem is a false dichotomy. While we are focused on building technologies that support privacy, we are also convinced that strong Federal privacy legislation is necessary if we want to make progress on this issue.

We have been part of the development of internet advertising since the early days. We spent more than 10 years helping to develop Meta's data-driven advertising business. Over the years, consumer data has become an increasingly powerful asset. The companies we work for and competed with adopted increasingly aggressive approaches in how they used data to improve their advertising products. To be frank, we helped develop these methods.

But in the past few years, we, and many others, have become increasingly uncomfortable with the privacy implications of the practices we helped pioneer. And so we started Anonym with a simple goal: to provide technically guaranteed privacy protections to consumers while enabling effective digital advertising.

Today, digital advertising is supported by the wholesale and unregulated sharing of individual level data between advertisers and the companies that run ads for them. The mechanics are fairly complex, so I will just use a recent personal example.

My wife and I are doing a few renovations at our home, so I have been spending a lot of time on home improvement sites, like Home Depot. Not surprisingly, I see ads for products I researched, and some I haven't but might find interesting. Most of you and most Americans are familiar with this experience. Sometimes it is useful. Oftentimes it is a bit unsettling. So how did this come to be?

Well, the majority of companies who run digital ads, including The Home Depot, have added tracking software from dozens of ad platforms that they do business with. These trackers are from ad tech companies most of you have never heard of, in addition to large tech companies like Google and Meta, Pinterest, et cetera. Now, these trackers collect information about my browsing and buying at sites like Home Depot, and they share that data with ad platforms. This data allows platforms to effectively target ads to me, and it allows advertisers like Home Depot to measure how well those ads work so they can spend their ad dollars efficiently. But at scale, this approach allows ad platforms to build tremendously rich profiles of people's browsing and buying behavior across millions of websites.

Now, does the average American expect and appreciate that their internet behavior on millions of sites is being beamed to dozens of advertising companies so they can build a profile on them? Of course they don't. We call this the profiling problem, and we believe the profiling problem is at the heart of the privacy challenge we should all be focused on. The solution to this challenge, we believe, requires two ingredients.

First, strong Federal privacy legislation. Legislation that ensures that Americans' data is collected and, importantly, shared only in ways they would reasonably expect or with their explicit consent. Legislation that increases protection for children beyond COPPA. Legislation that unifies the current protections that exist at the State level to provide protections for all Americans. Legislation that provides for strong and clear enforcement authority. And we believe that enlightened legislation like ADPPA has all of these components.

The second critical ingredient is technology. After all, technology got us into this problem, so it stands to reason it can help get us out of it. Privacy enhancing technologies are used in many other industries – in financial services, in pharmaceuticals, and in government – to extract value from data without compromising the privacy of individuals. A number of companies, ours included, are working to apply these technologies to make digital advertising more private by default. These technologies can, in effect, reduce the cost of improving privacy.

So while technology can help, ultimately, we have got to be clear-eyed about the incentives at play. We would all love for ad platforms and publishers to proactively adopt more privacy preserving technologies, but doing so alone means putting oneself at a massive competitive disadvantage. A strong regulatory backstop is critical in addressing this incentive problem.

With regulation in place, I am confident that we and others will find innovative ways to leverage privacy enhancing technologies to support business growth while guaranteeing the privacy of all Americans.

[The prepared statement of Mr. Mudd follows:]

Written Testimony of: Graham Mudd, Founder & Chief Product Officer Anonym, Inc., Hearing: Promoting U.S. Innovation and Individual Liberty through a National Standard for Data Privacy, House Subcommittee on Innovation, Data, and Commerce, March 1, 2023, at 8:30 AM

Chairman Bilirakis, Ranking Member Schakowsky, and distinguished Members of this Committee, thank you for the opportunity to testify at this important hearing.

My name is Graham Mudd, and I am co-founder and chief product officer of Anonym, Inc., a privacy-technology company that is focused on solving the privacy challenges facing digital advertising. My colleague and fellow cofounder, Brad Smallwood, who also is here with us today, is our chief executive officer. We're here, however, not to pitch our company–although we hope to talk a bit about what we're doing in privacy tech–but to show our support for reintroduction of the bicameral, bipartisan American Data Privacy Protection Act (ADPPA), which we believe would create a comprehensive privacy framework that would benefit all American consumers.

So, I want to begin by thanking you all–and particularly Chair Rodgers and Ranking Member Pallone of the Energy and Commerce Committee for their groundbreaking work in the last Congress–for introducing this comprehensive framework designed to set higher standards for protecting American data privacy. We at Anonym share your belief that the ADPPA has the potential to mark a historical watershed in privacy law and policy. This legislation, we believe, will reform data-privacy practices – and at the same time it will promote the ethical use of data that supports the evolution of stronger digital services.

My co-founder and I have been part of the development of the internet advertising ecosystem since the first wave of the internet in the late 1990s. Prior to Anonym, we both worked at Meta for more than 10 years, where we helped build and run the advertising business. We ran teams responsible for building the products that marketers leveraged to deliver and measure their advertising. Prior to that, we worked in product and analytics roles at Yahoo and other firms.

In all of our roles over the past 25-plus years, consumer behavioral data was an incredibly powerful asset in building more relevant products for people and more effective advertising solutions for businesses. As a result, acquiring data and putting it to use in increasingly sophisticated ways was always a strategic imperative. However, over the years, a tension began to emerge – the development of the rich consumer profiles that were so powerful in improving products of all kinds came at the cost of individuals' privacy. This trade-off is why we're here today.

We started Anonym with a simple goal – to provide technical privacy protections to consumers while at the same time ensuring that businesses continue to have the tools they need to grow. In effect, our goal is to reduce the trade-off cost of becoming a more privacy-safe digital ecosystem.

But technical protections alone are not sufficient. That's because without regulation and strong enforcement there is little incentive for companies to stop leveraging individuals' data to enhance their business.

How Did We Get Here?

To chart a path forward, it's often useful to reflect on what led to the status quo. Media companies have always strived to put the right information in front of their consumers. This competition for relevance – whether focused on content or advertising – has benefited consumers tremendously. Until the explosion of the internet at the turn of the century, almost all media were broadcast. Producers and editors curated content to ensure that it was relevant to the audience they were serving. Advertisers used audience research to understand the demographic makeup of these audiences so they could place their ads where their target customers were likely to see them.

Digital advertising initially relied on the same approach. Advertisers used audience research to understand the demographics of the visitors to web sites or sections of sites, like Yahoo Sports. Just as with TV, radio and print, advertisers ran ad campaigns based on informed generalizations. There were of course exceptions, like dircct mail, which has always harnessed individual-level data. In fact, political campaigns were among the earliest users of detailed data for content and advertising delivery.

But then internet search changed everything. Search-based advertising for the first time allowed companies to segment their audience at scale efficiently, and importantly, match the advertising to a consumer's interests and behaviors. The opportunity to use the information about what a consumer searched for to target advertising was game changing to advertisers, consumers, and search providers alike.

Other digital publishers and ad platforms that served display advertising (e.g., banner ads) weren't as naturally blessed with the rich consumer data search providers had. To compensate, display platforms sought ways to generate and aggregate consumer data from as many sources as possible and build rich consumer profiles with it. Ad networks collected browsing and ad-click data from tens of thousands of publishers. Data brokers, who had previously focused on direct mail, began selling data to digital display-ad platforms Finally, social media companies began accumulating vast user bases – and since their users were required to log in, building rich profiles was much easier, given their access to highly accurate consumer identity data. To further extend their ability to collect, measure, and improve ad performance, many major ad platforms begin using "pixels" to collect data from across the web.

A Pixel Is Worth a Thousand Words

Pixels, and their mobile-app equivalent, tracking SDKs, are an elegantly simple yet massively powerful set of technologies, so they're important to understand. At the most basic level, pixels are small pieces of code that look for a "cookie" to identify a device or user. They are deployed by a specific ad platform to many websites and apps that they don't own or control. When a person visits a website with a pixel installed, the pixel sends data about the user's behavior on that website back to the ad platform, where it is then typically associated with that user's profile.

I'll share a recent personal example to make this all a bit more concrete. My wife and I are in the process of completing a few home renovations. As a result, I've spent a fair bit of time on home improvement sites like Home Depot. For the past few weeks, I've seen ads across the web for products I've researched (and sometimes bought) as well as many I haven't but might be interested in. Behind the scenes, pixels are at work. Home Depot has more than a dozen tracking pixels on its web site.

Those pixels pass my browsing and buying behavior to ad platforms. Those platforms then use that data in their ad products. This pixel-based approach to data sharing creates value for a number of parties:

- First, and most obviously, Home Depot wins because they measure the performance of their ads by understanding which ads led to purchases on their site. Home Depot can also improve the performance of its campaigns by running highly targeted ads.
- Ad platforms win because they earn more for ads that work better. They're also able to enrich their profile of me, which allows their machine learning algorithms to deliver more effective ads for not just Home Depot, but for all of their advertising customers.
- I'm arguably a winner too, because ad platforms show me ads that are more likely to be relevant to me. Thanks to the exchange of data about my interests, I will now see more home improvement ads instead of ads for products and services that either seem

randomly selected, or that may be cued by something less relevant, like the particular content of the page I happen to be visiting.

Of course it's not all upside. While most Americans quite reasonably haven't spent the time to understand the mechanics at play, they know full well that their data is being shared – and most people are uncomfortable with this fact. While it may be the case that no laws have been broken, it's fair to say that the data sharing underpinning this discomfort is a violation of people's reasonable expectation of privacy.

The scale of data collection and transfer using these mechanics is difficult to comprehend. Millions of web sites and apps have dozens of trackers installed. As a result, my behavioral data is collected by hundreds, perhaps thousands, of companies. Once data about my particular interests, activities and transactions is captured by entities that may or may not have a relationship with me, and have no particular loyalty to me, it's totally out of my control.

The unfortunate by-product of a system like this is at the heart of the central privacy problem plaguing digital advertising. We can call this "the profiling problem." In the model I've just described, ad platforms and advertisers have strong economic incentives to participate in this digital advertising system – and are disadvantaged compared to their competitors if they don't participate. As a result of this system, ad platforms are able to build tremendously rich profiles about their user base including most of your browsing and buying behavior.

To be clear, I'm not calling out the ad platforms categorically for having bad motives. I believe there are many good actors in the ad tech ecosystem that understand the potential harms caused by the development of these profiles. The challenge is this: without clear rules (e.g., laws and regulations) ad tech companies are highly incentivized to gather and use data as aggressively as possible. Proactively eliminating the collection and use of third party data (e.g., pixel data) would put a platform at a massive disadvantage because ads that are data driven are just far more effective than those that are informed only by context or broad demographics. To address this incentive problem, we need to level the playing field by establishing clear criteria for what is and isn't acceptable.

Creating this level playing field requires a combination of efforts from legislators, regulators, advocates and technology companies. We believe there are three critical components that must come together to produce sustainable progress on digital privacy:

1. *Federal privacy legislation,* and supporting regulations, to provide baseline protections for all Americans and put an end to the race to the bottom in terms of data collection and use
2. *Strong enforcement authority* and action to make sure good actors aren't unduly disadvantaged when they take the initiative to improve their privacy practices
3. *Privacy enhancing technologies,* which, which will support massive advances in consumer privacy while ensuring advertising can continue to help businesses grow and keep content free

We've covered the importance of regulations and enforcement, given the incentives at play in the ad tech ecosystem, so now I'll focus on the technologies that can support a transition to a far more private approach to advertising.

How Privacy Enhancing Technologies Work

Privacy enhancing technologies (PETs) are a fairly broad class of technologies that enable confidential and private computing. PETs are used in many other industries and contexts. Financial services firms use them to collaboratively build fraud models without compromising individuals" data by sharing it directly with other companies. Pharmaceutical companies use PETs to bring together disparate data sets to conduct clinical trials while ensuring no party has access to sensitive healthcare information.

The Census Bureau uses PETs to support research on census data without compromising individuals' privacy. In the context of advertising, PETs can be employed to support three key use cases:

- Measurement: Understanding how ads lead to outcomes like purchases
- Targeting: Serving ads to individuals likely to have specific characteristics or interests, such as runners, mothers of young children or university students
- Optimization: Improving the relevance and effectiveness of advertising by using algorithms to make ad delivery decisions in an automated manner

To support these use cases, one must match two sets of data, one from the ad platform with information about who saw the ads and the other from an advertiser with information about actions on the advertiser's site or app.

Historically, the advertiser information has been sent directly to the ad platform, which is what creates "the profiling problem" I discussed earlier. With a PET-ba sed approach, however, the profiling proble m can be nipped in the bud – instead of one party directly sharing data with the other, the data is processed by an intermediary that its elf has no access to unencrypted data. All computation happens in a fully safe and encrypted environment.

Inside this secure system the two data sets are joined and computations take place – including measurement and correlations that create aggregated data and statistics (in the example above, an advertiser like Home Depot might learn that 4% of men my age who saw the ad ended up buying the product).

Importantly, however, after completing the computation and generating trusted aggregated results, the individual-level data used to generate those results is deleted. The aggregated results of these computations are then further anonymized by using privacy mechanisms such as Differential Privacy, which adds noise (effectively random data) to limit the likelihood that individuals can be re-identified using the aggregated results.

The aggregated and anonymized results are then shared with the advertiser and the ad platform. The end result is that everyone gets what they need, but no party has learned anything new about any individual. This is the promise of privacy enhancing technologies, and this is the model we have been building at Anonym.

Summary

In summary, we believe the notion that you cannot have both privacy and an efficient digital advertising ecosystem that support businesses of all sizes is a false dichotomy. We believe in a win-win set of solutions that includes (but is not limited to) the following:

- Increased protections for children and older minors beyond COPPA, which was enacted in an earlier era when the internet and its content was frequently analogized to television – hence the focus on age 13.
- A single federal statutory scheme that provides a baseline for how data is treated and that strongly limits or prohibits sharing of individual consumer data directly between companies.
- Unified protections that operate the same way in all states to provide protections to all Americans. We support ADPPA because it provides these unified consistent protections.
- Strong and clear enforcement authority for privacy regulators.
- Technology that guarantees privacy while still empowering businesses to operate efficiently, find customers and grow.
- Im portantly, to keep incentives clean and encourage competition, these technology solutions should be open and transparent and operated by companies that do not sell data or advertising.

Bringing these critical elements together will be a powerful demonstration of how government, citizens, businesses, and advocates can work together to establish a law-driven, technology-backed baseline for data privacy protection. We believe this will provide a global roadmap for how regulation and technology can work hand in hand to respect people's fundamental right to privacy while enabling quality consumer experiences and supporting economic growth.

Thank you again, Chairman Bilirakis, Ranking Member Schakowsky, and the other honorable members of this committee for your time and attention. I look forward to answering any questions you may have about my testimony or about these issues generally.

Mr. Bilirakis. Thank you. Thank you, Mr. Mudd. Appreciate it very much.

Ms. Givens, you are recognized for 5 minutes.

Statement of Alexandra Reeve Givens

Ms. Givens. Thank you, Mr. Chair, and thank you, committee members, for the opportunity to testify on the importance of data privacy and the urgent need for Congress to pass a meaningful Federal privacy law to protect consumers, create certainty for businesses, and restore trust in the online ecosystem that is so essential to our economy and our society.

I am Alexandra Reeve Givens, and I have the privilege of leading the Center for Democracy and Technology, a nonprofit, nonpartisan organization that defends civil rights, civil liberties, and democratic values in the digital age.

For over two decades, CDT has advocated for Congress to adopt strong privacy protections, and we are grateful for the work of this committee and its jurisdictional counterparts in raising public understanding of privacy harms.

By our count, this is the 31st hearing in the U.S. Congress on consumer privacy in just the past 5 years, substantive hearings that have built a rigorous and detailed record about the overwhelming need for a comprehensive Federal privacy law. We commend the committee's focus on this issue early this session because it is long past time for Congress to act.

Looking for information on your device can feel very private, but with every click and scroll, companies collect information about your activities, typically using, sharing, or selling that information to make inferences about you or so you can be targeted with ads. A visit to a single web page can involve hundreds or even thousands of cookies or beacons tracking your activities on that site. Websites you have visited and search queries you have entered can be collected and shared.

In addition to your cell phone provider knowing your general whereabouts, apps on your phone can track and my share your location with anyone willing to pay a price, revealing where you live and work, where you socialize, what doctors you visit, and where you pray.

Consumers also share an incredible amount of personal and private information with different apps and online services, whether it be details about our physical health, our sleep cycles, our mental health, or social messages and family photographs.

In addition to direct collection by companies, all of that data can now be shared with third parties, such as data brokers, which are companies that aggregate information about users and market it, primarily for targeting ads. The huge variety and scale of data points gathered by data brokers allows precise inferences to be drawn about individual users.

A 2013 report by the Senate Commerce Committee details how data brokers assign profiles to people, including categories like "suffering seniors," "rural and barely making it," and "ethnic second-city strugglers." A report published by researchers at Duke University just last month revealed that data brokers were selling mental health information, including, for example, a list titled, "Consumers with Clinical Depression in the United States." This committee published a report on privacy concerns raised by data brokers as early as 2006, but these practices haven't been reined in.

When consumers learn about companies lax data practices, they are offended, but the issue is about more than just offensive stereotyping or privacy leakage. It can lead to social, psychological, and economic harm. It might not seem all that important if a person is targeted with particular clothing ads, but it matters when predatory lenders can hyper-target an audience that is vulnerable to payday loans and exploitative interest rates, as has happened with veterans and families navigating medical crises. It matters when scammers can target their ads to seniors who are more likely to fall for schemes hawking low-cost medical devices. It matters when inferences about people are used to unfairly target ads for jobs, housing, or credit, the gateways to economic and social opportunity.

My written testimony details how loose data practices can also raise national security harms.

The lack of a comprehensive Federal privacy law is leaving consumers open to exploitation and to abuse. Under current law, Americans' main privacy protections rely on a theory of notice and consent under which companies can set their own privacy rules and collect whatever data they like, provided they disclose it to their customers in their lengthy terms of service.

Any modern user of technology knows why this notice and consent model is broken. Even if a consumer could feasibly read and understand these labyrinths in privacy policies, they often have no real choice but to consent. Many online services are such an important part of everyday life, that quitting is effectively impossible. We have to move on from this broken regime of notice and consent to one that establishes baseline safeguards for consumers' information, clear rules of the road for businesses, and meaningful enforcement of the law. This must include specific protections for sensitive information and protections for civil rights.

The bipartisan American Data Privacy and Protection Act is the place to start. Last year, this committee did admiral work forging a bipartisan compromise that offers strong protections for consumers while also accommodating business realities. To be clear, CDT and other consumer groups wished the bill offered stronger protections in places. This is not our perfect bill, but this committee put in the work to achieve meaningful compromise. Respectfully, we urge you to build on that momentum by taking up the bill without delay.

I thank the committee again for your leadership, and I look forward to answering your questions.

[The prepared statement of Ms. Givens follows:]

Testimony of Alexandra Reeve Givens, President & CEO, Center for Democracy & Technology, for the U.S. House of Representatives Energy & Commerce Committee, Subcommittee on Innovation, Data, & Commerce, Hearing Entitled "Promoting U.S. Innovation and Individual Liberty through a National Standard for Data Privacy," March 1, 2023

Thank you Chair Bilirakis, Ranking Member Schakowsky, and Chair Rodgers and Ranking Member Pallone of the full committee for the opportunity to testify on the importance of data privacy, and the urgent need for Congress to pass a meaningful federal privacy law to protect consumers, create certainty for businesses, and restore trust in the online ecosystem that is so essential to our economy and our society.

I am Alexandra Reeve Givens, President and CEO of the Center for Democracy & Technology, a nonprofit, nonpartisan organization that defends civil rights, civil liberties and democratic values in the digital age. For over two decades, CDT has advocated for Congress to adopt strong privacy protections. We were one of the first organizations to propose a comprehensive privacy framework in the aftermath of the Cambridge Analytica scandal, when it was revealed that the data of almost 90 million Facebook users was collected without their consent by a political consulting firm to create profiles of people to more precisely target political advertising. Even in the short time since then, the public understanding of privacy harms has changed significantly, in part thanks to the work of this Committee and its Senate counterpart. By our count, this is the 31st hearing held in the U.S. Congress on consumer privacy in just the past five years: substantive hearings that have built a rigorous and detailed record about the overwhelming need for a comprehensive federal privacy law. We commend the Committee's focus on this issue early in the new Congress, because it is long past time for Congress to act.

This morning, I plan to briefly describe how the current commercial data ecosystem is harming consumers, how the current legal regime governing online privacy has failed to keep up with innovation, and why the U.S. needs a significant shift in how we protect consumer privacy and the use of consumers' data through passage of a meaningful federal privacy law.

I. How Current Commercial Data Practices Harm Consumers

Looking for information on your device can feel very private, but with every click and scroll, companies collect information about your activities, typically using, sharing or selling that information to make inferences about you or so you can be targeted with ads. A visit to a single webpage can involve hundreds or even thousands of cookies or beacons tracking your activities on that site, both from the company you are visiting ("first party" tracking) and from mostly unknown third parties ("third party tracking").[29] Websites you have visited and search queries you have entered can be collected and shared. In addition to your cellphone provider knowing your general whereabouts, apps on your phone can track and may share your location with anyone willing to pay a price – revealing where you live and work, where you socialize, what doctors you visit, and where you pray to people and companies you have never heard of or interacted with.[30] Those apps may have no business collecting that information except to target advertising. Apps and websites are even fingerprinting your device and web browser to more precisely identify you and to circumvent both technical protections and consent requirements for cookies.[31] Consumers also share an incredible amount of personal and private information with different apps and online services, whether it be details about our physical health, our sleep cycles, our mental health, or social messages and family photographs.[32]

All of that data (and inferences companies make about consumers based on that data) can be collected and stored indefinitely by companies, and they can share it with third parties such as data brokers, which are companies that aggregate information about users and market it for, among many things, targeting ads.[33] The huge variety and scale of data points gathered by data brokers allows precise inferences to be drawn about individual users. A 2014 report by the Federal Trade Commision described how data brokers assigned profiles to people based on the detailed information collected across the web, assigning users to categories like "Expectant

---

[29] Dan Rafter, *Tracking Cookies: What Are Tracking Cookies and How Do They Work?*, Norton (May 6, 2021), https://us.norton.com/blog/privacy/what-are-tracking-cookies.

[30] Stuart A. Thompson & Charlie Warzel, *Twelve Million Phones, One Dataset, Zero Privacy*, N.Y. Times (Dec. 19, 2019), https://www.nytimes.com/interactive/2019/12/19/opinion/location-tracking-cell-phone.html.

[31] Chiara Castro, *Web trackers: What they are and how to protect from them*, TechRadar (June 21, 2022), https://www.techradar.com/features/web-trackers-what-they-are-how-to-protect-from-them ("Browser fingerprint: With cookies getting more regulated - in some countries websites *must* allow users to choose to enable them or not - new tracking techniques are rising. Every browser connected to a certain device brings with it some unique data, including device model, screen resolution, operating system, language, browsing history, and so on. That defines its own browser fingerprint, which can then be used to track down your online activities every time you open the browser.").

[32] Mozilla, *Top Mental Health and Prayer Apps Fail Spectacularly at Privacy, Security* (May 2, 2022), https://foundation.mozilla.org/en/blog/top-mental-health-and-prayer-apps-fail-spectacularly-at-privacy-security (detailing how apps that deal with private consumer information, such as health ailments, routinely have poor privacy practices).

[33] Companies also use the data for fraud detection and credit check services, and sell data to law enforcement. *See* Carey Shenkman, Sharon Bradford Franklin, Greg Nojeim, and Dhanaraj Thakur, *Legal Loopholes and Data for Dollars*, Center for Democracy & Technology (Dec. 2021), https://cdt.org/wp-content/uploads/2021/12/2021-12-08-Legal-Loopholes-and-Data-for-Dollars-Report-final.pdf.

Parent," "Diabetes Interest" and "Smoker in Household."[34] A 2013 report by the Senate Commerce Committee detailed how dataset titles included categories like "Suffering Seniors," "Rural and Barely Making It," "Ethnic Second-City Strugglers" and "Rough Start: Young Single Parents."[35] This Committee explored these concerns in a report as early as 2006, and also held a hearing that addressed data broker practices in 2019.[36]

These data broker practices have not been reined in. A report published by researchers at Duke University just last month revealed that data brokers were selling mental health information, in some cases tied to consumer identities, including whether someone has depression, insomnia, or ADHD, among other medical conditions.[37] Data brokers made available 28 types of medical data, and 42 types of non-medical data about consumers. These categories include data from wearable medical devices, specific medications, income, credit score, Social Security Numbers, and information about children.[38] Data brokers are still grouping people and selling those lists, including specifically a list entitled "Consumers with Clinical Depression in the United States."[39] The logic, said one data broker, is to exploit that data to specifically target people with medical ads based on their illnesses: "households with ailments are more likely to be interested in targeted offers about medical needs."[40]

In addition, advertising trackers can detect specific and often personal information that users share with any given site. Last December, *The Markup* found that, out of the 50 telehealth websites they analyzed, 13 of them contained at least one tracker that collected patients' answers to medical intake questions.[41] Trackers on 25 sites told at least one big tech platform that the user had added an item like a prescription medication to their cart, or checked out with a subscription for a treatment plan.[42] Since then, the U.S. Department of Health and Human Services has clarified that use of tracking technologies like cookies by entities covered by the

---

34 Federal Trade Commission, *Data Brokers: A Call for Transparency and Accountability* (May 2014), at 42-43, https://www.ftc.gov/system/files/documents/reports/data-brokers-call-transparency-accountability-report-federal-trade-commission-may-2014/140527databrokerreport.pdf.

35 Staff Report, *A Review of the Data Broker Industry: Collection, Use, and Sale of Consumer Data for Marketing Purposes*, S. Committee on Commerce, Science & Transportation (Dec. 18, 2013), https://www.commerce.senate.gov/public/_cache/files/0d2b3642-6221-4888-a631-08f2f255b577/AE5D72CBE7F44F5BFC846 BECE22C875B.12.18.13-senate-commerce-committee-report-on-data-broker-industry.pdf.

36 *See* Internet Data Brokers: Who Has Access to Your Private Records?, Hearings Before the Subcomm. on Oversight and Investigations of the H. Comm. on Energy and Commerce, 109th Cong. (2006); Protecting Consumer Privacy in the Era of Big Data, Hearing Before the Subcomm. on Consumer Prot. and Commerce of the H. Comm. on Energy and Commerce, 116th Cong. (2019). https://www.congress.gov/event/116th-congress/house-event/108942.

37 Joanne Kim, *Data Brokers and the Sale of Americans' Mental Health Data*, Duke University Sanford Cyber Policy Program (Feb. 2023), at 9, https://techpolicy.sanford.duke.edu/wp-content/uploads/sites/4/2023/02/Kim-2023-Data-Brokers-and-the-Sale-of-Americans-Mental-Health-Data.pdf ("some firms clearly advertised data already directly linked to individuals, as they offered individual names, addresses, and various forms of contact information (such as phone numbers and emails) in a dataset.").

38 *Id.* at 20, app'x. B.

39 *Id.* at 14.

40 *Id.*

41 Todd Feathers, Katie Palmer, & Simon Fondrie-Teitler, *"Out of Control": Dozens on Telehealth Startups Sent Sensitive Health Information to Big Tech Companies*, The Markup (Dec. 13, 2022), https://themarkup.org/pixel-hunt/2022/12/13/out-of-control-dozens-of-telehealth-startups-sent-sensiti ve-health-information-to-big-tech-companies.

42 *Id.*

Health Information Portability and Accountability Act (HIPAA) are subject to the HIPAA privacy and HIPAA security rules.[43]

When consumers learn about these practices and how careless companies are with consumer data, they are often gravely offended. But the issue is about more than just offensive stereotyping or privacy leakage – it can lead to social, psychological, and economic harm. It might not seem that important if a person is targeted with particular clothing ads. But it does matter when predatory lenders, for example, can hyper-target an audience that is vulnerable to payday loans and exploitative interest rates, as has happened with veterans and families navigating medical crises.[44] It matters when ads for diets and dangerous weight loss medications can persistently target people with histories of disordered eating, leading to depression and self-harm.[45] It matters when scammers can target their ads to seniors who are more likely to fall for schemes hawking low-cost medical devices.[46] It matters when inferences about people are used to unfairly target ads for jobs, housing or credit, the gateways to economic and social opportunity.[47]

Even when online platforms prevent advertisers from targeting audiences on their platform using explicit protected categories such as race, gender or age, research has shown how easily "interest categories" and other means of audience targeting can serve as proxies for those characteristics.[48] We have long known that zip code can be a proxy for race,[49] but so can a person's identified interest pages, the websites they have visited, or their likes. To give just one example, it is easy to determine someone's religion from the Facebook pages they have liked, which will often denote the church or faith community to which they belong.

Other harms can result from loose commercial data practices. In 2018, it was revealed that a fitness app was inadvertently revealing secret information about the location and layouts of

---

[43] *See* Department of Health and Human Services, *Use of Online Tracking Technologies by HIPAA Covered Entities and Business Associates* (Dec. 2022), https://www.hhs.gov/hipaa/for-professionals/privacy/guidance/hipaa-online-tracking/index.html (HHS/OCR December Bulletin highlighting the important privacy obligations health providers - such as doctor's offices and hospitals - are required to follow when using apps and websites, under the Health Information Portability and Accountability Act, which limits how your doctor or insurer can share patient health information).

[44] Office of Representative Katie Porter, *AWOL: How Watchdogs are Failing to Protect Servicemembers from Financial Scams* (2021), https://porter.house.gov/uploadedfiles/va_home_loans_final.pdf; Justin Sherman, *Data Brokers and Sensitive Data on U.S. Individuals*, Duke U. Sanford Cyber Policy Program (2021), https://techpolicy.sanford.duke.edu/wp-content/uploads/sites/4/2021/08/Data-Brokers-and-Sensitive-Data-on US-Individuals-Sherman-2021.pdf. *See also* Coulter Jones, Jean Eaglesh, & AnnaMaria Andriotis, *How Payday Lenders Target Consumers Hurt by Coronavirus*, Wall Street Journal (June 3, 2020), https://www.wsj.com/articles/how-payday-lenders-target-consumers-hurt-by-coronavirus-11591176601.

[45] Liza Gak, Seyi Olojo, & Niloufar Salehi, *The Distressing Ads That Persist: Uncovering The Harms of Targeted Weight-Loss Ads Among Users with Histories of Disordered Eating* (2022), https://doi.org/10.48550/arXiv.2204.03200.

[46] AARP, *Medical Equipment Scams* (Mar. 2022), https://www.aarp.org/money/scams-fraud/info-2019/medical-equipment.html.

[47] *See* Dept. of Justice, *Justice Department Secures Groundbreaking Settlement Agreement with Meta Platforms, Formerly Known as Facebook, to Resolve Allegations of Discriminatory Advertising* (June 2022), https://www.justice.gov/opa/pr/justice-department-secures-groundbreaking-settlement-agreement-meta-platforms-formerly-known.

[48] Till Speicher *et al.*, *Potential for Discrimination in Online Targeted Advertising*, Proceedings of Machine Learning Research, Conference on Fairness, Accountability, and Transparency (2018), http://proceedings.mlr.press/v81/speicher18a/speicher18a.pdf.

[49] Madeline St. Amour, *ZIP Codes and Equity Gaps*, Inside Heigher Ed (July 2020), https://www.insidehighered.com/news/2020/07/09/report-finds-racial-equity-gaps-college-attendance-debt-and-defaults-based-zip-codes.

U.S. military bases because personnel were recording their exercise regimes and sharing it with the application. Following a public outcry, the company made changes to its platform, and I am sure military personnel now receive stronger briefings on privacy protections. But the example illustrates the revealing nature of location information, and the inadequacy of requiring users to be the sole guardians of their privacy, when it is often hard for users to know how an app will collect, use, or share their data with the world.

Security experts and members of this Committee have raised additional concerns over the national security effects of sharing data with other countries, including China. The permissive nature of the current U.S. privacy framework allows for data to be collected and shared by companies with impunity, which could be helped by imposing substantive guardrails on commercial data practices through federal privacy reform.

II. The Need for Comprehensive Federal Privacy Legislation

While some companies have taken important steps to protect their users' privacy, the lack of a comprehensive federal privacy law is leaving consumers open to exploitation and abuse. Under current law, Americans' primary comprehensive privacy protections are based on the Federal Trade Commission's limited Section 5 authority over unfair and deceptive practices. Under Section 5, the primary mode of enforcement has relied on a theory of notice and consent, under which companies can set their own privacy rules and collect whatever data they like provided they disclose it to their customers.

Any modern user of technology can understand why this "notice and consent" approach is inadequate. Companies typically give notice to consumers through long privacy policies, often buried deep within the fine print of their terms of service. One academic study showed that a person would need to spend 244 hours to read all the privacy policies they encounter in a single year.[50] Even if a consumer does read and understand the privacy policies, their choices are limited: either accept the service's terms, or do not use it. But many online services like internet service providers and social media companies are such an important part of everyday life that quitting is effectively impossible—and often there are few, if any, alternatives to use instead. If a social media service is the only way a consumer stays in touch with family and friends, asking them to quit is unreasonable.

Nor are countless pop-up windows asking a user to "accept or reject" a company's privacy practices the answer, as Europeans have found after the European Union's passage of the largely consent-based General Data Protection Regulation (GDPR). Users find these pop-up windows annoying and hard to navigate, and companies often establish default settings that funnel users into accepting less privacy-protecting options.[51] There is a rich academic literature about dark patterns, the ways in which privacy notices, consent boxes, and other design

---

[50] Aleecia M. Mcdonald & Lorrie Faith Cranor, *The Cost of Reading Privacy Policies*, I/S: A Journal of Law and Policy for the Information Society (2008), https://kb.osu.edu/bitstream/handle/1811/72839/ISJLP_V4N3_543.pdf; Geoffrey A. Fowler, *I Tried to Read All My App Policies. It Was 1 Million Words*, Wash. Post (May 31, 2022), https://www.washingtonpost.com/technology/2022/05/31/abolish-privacy-policies/.

[51] Colin M. Gray *et al.*, *The Dark (Patterns) Side of UX Design*, Proceedings of the 2018 CHI Conf. on Human Factors in Computing Systems, Paper 534, at 5 (2018), https://dl.acm.org/doi/pdf/10.1145/3173574.3174108 ("Nagging behaviors may include pop-ups that obscure the interface, audio notices that distract the user, or other actions that obstruct or otherwise redirect the user's focus.").

elements of a website or app can nudge consumers to accept certain policies through design choices intended to induce consent, even when the consumer would otherwise take the more privacy-protective action.[52] Dark patterns include misleadingly positive language, omitting details of how a person's data will be used or shared, or adding friction to privacy interfaces that make it hard for users to find how to change their settings.[53]

Against this backdrop, it is no surprise that consumers have lost trust in online companies.[54] Consumers are worried about their data and their privacy online, but are powerless to control that privacy.[55] They know they are being tracked by companies.[56] Consumers also have little confidence that companies will admit when they misuse data.[57]

This lack of trust is bad for the economy, for businesses, and for consumers, as they feel powerless and like their only recourse is to simply stop using certain products and services—which many have.[58] But it doesn't have to be that way. Consumers have been asking for years for the government to protect their privacy.[59] It is time to heed that call.

---

[52] *See, e.g.,* Jamie Luguiri & Lior Jacob Strahilevitz, *Shining a Light on Dark Patterns*, 13 J. Legal Analysis 43 (2021), https://academic.oup.com/jla/article/13/1/43/6180579; Lauren E. Willis, *Deception by Design*, 34 Harvard J. L. Tech 116 (2020), https://jolt.law.harvard.edu/assets/articlePDFs/v34/3.-Willis-Images-In-Color.pdf; Johanna Gunawan, Amogh Pradeep, David Choffness, Woodrow Hartzog, and Christo Wilson, *A Comparative Study of Dark Patterns Across Mobile and Web Modalities*, Proceeding of the ACM on Human-Computer Interaction, https://www.ftc.gov/system/files/ftc_gov/pdf/PrivacyCon-2022-Gunawan-Pradeep-Choffnes-Hartzog-Wilson-A-Comparative-Study-of-Dark-Patterns-Across-Mobile-and-Web-Modalities.pdf.

[53] Federal Trade Commission, *Bringing Dark Patterns to Light* (Sept. 2022), https://www.ftc.gov/system/files/ftc_gov/pdf/P214800%20Dark%20Patterns%20Report%209.14.2022%20-%20FINAL.pdf.

[54] *See, e.g.*, Orson Lucas, *Corporate Data Responsibility: Bridging the Consumer Trust Gap*, KPMG (Aug. 2021), at 1, https://advisory.kpmg.us/articles/2021/bridging-the-trust-chasm.html (stating that 40% of consumers do not trust companies to use their data ethically).

[55] *See e.g.*, Brooke Auxier, Lee Rainie, Monica Anderson, Andrew Perrin, Madhu Kumar, & Erica Turner, *Americans and Privacy: Concerned, Confused and Feeling Lack of Control Over Their Personal Information*, Pew Research Center (Nov. 2019), https://www.pewresearch.org/internet/2019/11/15/americans-and-privacy-concerned-confused-and-feel ing-lack-of-control-over-their-personal-information/ (81% of consumers say they lack control over what types of data companies collect; 81% say the risks of companies collecting data outweigh the benefits, 59% say they lack understanding of how companies use data); *Most Americans say it is increasingly difficult to control who can access their online datai,* Ipsos (Jan. 2022), https://www.ipsos.com/en-us/news-polls/data-privacy-2022 ("Seven in ten (70%) Americans agree that controlling who can access their online personal information has become more challenging").

[56] Brooke Auxier, Lee Rainie, Monica Anderson, Andrew Perrin, Madhu Kumar, & Erica Turner, *Americans concerned, feel lack of control over personal data collected by both companies and the government*, Pew Research Center (Nov. 2019), https://www.pewresearch.org/internet/2019/11/15/americans-concerned-feel-lack-of-control-over-perso nal-data-collected-by-both-companies-and-the-government/ (72% think all or mostly all of what they do online is tracked by companies).

[57] Brooke Auxier, Lee Rainie, Monica Anderson, Andrew Perrin, Madhu Kumar, & Erica Turner, *Americans and Privacy: Concerned, Confused and Feeling Lack of Control Over Their Personal Information*, Pew Research Center (Nov. 2019), https://www.pewresearch.org/internet/2019/11/15/americans-and-privacy-concerned-confused-and-feel ing-lack-of-control-over-their-personal-information/ (79%).

[58] *Most Americans Say it is Increasingly Difficult to Control Who Can Access Their Online Data*, Ipsos (Jan. 7, 2022), https://www.ipsos.com/en-us/news-polls/data-privacy-2022 (36%).

[59] Privacy for America, *New Data Reveals Americans' Overwhelming and Bipartisan Support for Federal Privacy Legislation* (Nov. 18, 2021), https://www.privacyforamerica.com/new-data-reveals-americans-overwhelming-and-bipartisan-support-for-federal-privacy-legislation/ (stating 92% of voters want a privacy law).

III. Elements of a Comprehensive Federal Privacy Law

Congress can make the U.S. a global leader by passing meaningful comprehensive privacy legislation, building on the foundational work of this Committee, its Senate counterpart, and Republican and Democratic administrations over more than a dozen years.[60] The most important thing Congress can do is free consumers from a regime that primarily relies on notice-and-consent as a privacy protection. We need privacy laws that work in the 21st century digital economy, that give consumers the baseline protections they need and create clear rules of the road for businesses. As discussed below, we also need to ensure any privacy law can be effectively enforced.

There are several elements of a federal privacy law that would address the harms I have discussed today and significantly increase consumer trust:

- Data minimization requirements that restrict companies to collecting and using only data that is necessary for the services they perform,
- Specific protections for sensitive data such as biometric information, location information, health information, or information revealing someone's race, religion, sexual orientation, and similar factors,
- Civil rights protections and algorithmic transparency and assessment provisions to prevent companies from discriminating against people based on protected characteristics,
- Data security requirements ensuring that companies take steps to avoid data breaches and other unauthorized access to data,
- The rights for consumers to access, correct, delete, and port data pertaining to them that is held by a company,
- Effective, easy-to-use mechanisms for consumers to opt-out of targeted advertising,
- Children's protections that take into account the inability of children to protect themselves against exploitative data practices, Limits on sharing or selling data with third parties, including a national registry for data brokers and the right for consumers to delete data about them held by a data broker, and Meaningful enforcement by the Federal Trade Commission, state Attorneys General, and a private right of action.

Last year, this committee passed in an overwhelmingly bipartisan fashion the American Data Privacy and Protection Act (ADPPA), which includes all of these protections and more. CDT commends the Committee for its tireless work on that bill. To be clear, it is not a perfect bill. For instance, we would like to see narrower preemption of state laws and a broader private right of action, and higher penalties for data brokers failing to register. But we recognize that to ensure bipartisanship, compromise is necessary. ADPPA represents a reasonable middle ground for protecting privacy and civil rights online, and we encourage this Committee to take it up again without delay.

---

[60] Congressional Research Service, *Privacy Protections for Personal Information Online* (April 2011), https://www.everycrsreport.com/files/20110406_R41756_d4893c5a84e54603899b9471b9d853219c034 24a.pdf. ("Beginning with the 109th Congress, every Congress has held numerous privacy-related hearings. The current Congressional privacy agenda is broad and includes items that Congress has worked on for several years, new issues posed by advances in technology, and items related to efforts to update the electronic surveillance laws for advances in technology.").

IV. Ensuring Meaningful Enforcement

It is essential that any privacy law passed by Congress can be meaningfully enforced and can keep up with rapidly changing innovations in commercial data practices. Given the complexity and scale of the modern digital ecosystem, this can be achieved only through a complementary approach that empowers the Federal Trade Commission, State Attorneys General, and a private right of action for consumers to enforce their rights.

The expert staff of the FTC is well positioned to bring cases involving data privacy harms. Congress should ensure, however, that the FTC is properly resourced to handle enforcement of a new privacy law. Investing in the FTC is good for consumers who receive more money in refunds from FTC enforcement,[61] and good for the federal government because, according to an analysis from the Congressional Budget Office, every dollar invested in the FTC reduces the deficit by over three dollars.[62] Congress should also ensure the Commission provides resources to help businesses understand their obligations and pursue responsible data practices, for example by staffing a resource center.

Even with greater resources, federal enforcers cannot possibly keep up with the entire ecosystem of commercial data practices. State Attorneys General can and should play an essential role in protecting consumers' privacy, building on the existing expertise many have demonstrated in fraud, privacy, data security, and digital civil rights. In addition to bringing enforcement actions, Attorneys General frequently work with business leaders and advocacy organizations to identify concerns about products and services and to develop best practices, playing a vital role in protecting consumers' interests.[63] Finally, a private right of action is essential. Even with multiple levels of government enforcers, resource constraints will limit effective application of the law. Consumers should have the ability to be made whole through the court system if their issues are not taken up by government enforcers. A private right of action would help ensure that people's wrongs can be made right.

V. Why Congress Must Also Address AI and Automated Decision-Making

A final issue I would like to highlight is the need to address artificial intelligence and automated decision-making. Increasingly, AI systems that leverage large amounts of data are being used in decisions about employment, lending, tenant screening and other settings that can

[61] Since 2018, for every dollar invested in the FTC, consumers have been refunded $2.44. *See* Federal Trade Commission, FTC Appropriation and Full-Time Equivalent (FTE) History, https://www.ftc.gov/about-ftc/bureaus-offices/office-executive-director/financial-management-office/ftc-appropriation (showing FTC funding betwee 2018 and 2022 at $1.675 billion); Federal Trade Commission, *Data on Refunds to Consumers*, https://public.tableau.com/app/profile/federal.trade.commission/viz/Refunds_15797958402020/Refun dsbyDate (showing total refunds between 2018 and 2022 at $4.1 billion).

[62] Congressional Budget Office, *Estimated Budgetary Effects of Title III, Committee on Energy and Commerce, H.R. 5376, the Build Back Better Act* (Nov. 18, 2021), https://www.cbo.gov/publication/57623 (showing that a $1 billion investment in the FTC over the course of ten years equates to a reduction in the deficit by $3.1 billion).

[63] Danielle Keats Citron, *The Privacy Policymaking of State Attorneys General*, 92 Notre Dame L. Rev. 747, 759 (2016). *See also* Senate Commerce Committee, Testimony of Laura Moy (Oct. 10, 2018), at 12-13, https://www.commerce.senate.gov/services/files/baf68751-c9bc-4b15-ab0f-d4a5f719027c.

dramatically impact people's lives.[64] These tools raise significant risks of bias, lack of transparency, and unfair decision-making. In particular, these issues come up when tools evaluate people based on factors that do not actually relate to the decision in question (causing hidden errors and unfair outcomes), or when they make inferences about people that approximate protected characteristics such as race, gender, religion, or disability status (perpetuating bias and discrimination).

The ADPPA takes a meaningful step in the right direction. It increases transparency into algorithmic systems, used by large data holders, to help people, regulators, legislators, and others to understand what the purpose of the AI system is, how it was designed, and the steps the company has taken to mitigate various foreseeable harms. More public and detailed information will better inform policymaking going forward.

Thank you very much for your time and I look forward to your questions.

Mr. Bilirakis. Thank you so very much. Appreciate it.

Ms. Rich, you are recognized for 5 minutes.

Statement of Jessica Rich

Ms. Rich. Thank you, Chairman Bilirakis and Ranking Member Schakowsky, and the rest of the members of the committee. I am Jessica Rich, of counsel and senior policy advisor for consumer protection at Kelley Drye & Warren. I am pleased to be here today testifying on the need for Federal privacy legislation.

I really want to thank this committee for its bipartisan leadership on this important issue over the course of years. I also want to make clear that my remarks today are my own, based largely on my years of government service.

As background, I worked for over 26 years at the Federal Trade Commission, the last 4 as director of the Bureau of Consumer Protection. Much of my FTC career was devoted to data privacy and security. I was the first manager of the FTC's privacy program, and continued to lead its expansion as I rose through the ranks at the agency.

In my various roles, I developed or oversaw enforcement against hundreds of companies that failed to protect consumers' personal information, rule makings to implement privacy laws, such as the Children's Online Privacy Protection Act, and dozens of FTC workshops and reports on emerging issues.

During my time there, I also wrote or oversaw multiple recommendations to Congress, seeking stronger legal authority and remedies for privacy and security. The years have come and gone with multiple hearings and privacy bills. And as we all know, there is still no Federal privacy law over two decades later.

Today, the need for a Federal privacy standard has never been greater, and there is no substitute for congressional action here. Federal privacy legislation is simply the best way to create a consistent set of rules for consumers and businesses, fill in the many gaps in our privacy

---

[64] *See, e.g.*, Emmanuel Martinez & Lauren Kirchner, *The Secret Bias Hidden in Mortgage-Approval Algorithms*, The Markup (Aug. 25, 2021), https://themarkup.org/denied/2021/08/25/the-secret-bias-hidden-in-mortgage-approval-algorithms; Pranshu Verma, *AI is Starting to Pick Who Gets Laid Off*, Wash. Post (Feb. 20, 2023), https://www.washingtonpost.com/technology/2023/02/20/layoff-algorithms/.

patchwork, enlist multiple enforcement in policing the marketplace, and provide much needed credibility abroad. Although I could expand on every single one of those points, I am going to focus today on a related issue, which is why the FTC needs a Federal privacy law.

As much as the FTC has been able to do with the tools it has, it needs more authority from Congress to be a truly effective privacy enforcer. In fact, under current law, the FTC's legal authority is limited, whether it is pursuing case-by-case enforcement under the FTC Act or attempting to develop a privacy regulation. I will explain why briefly here, but I refer you to my written remarks for more details.

First, because there is no comprehensive Federal privacy law, the FTC has had to bring most of its privacy enforcement under section 5 of the FTC Act, a general purpose consumer protection law enacted long before the internet existed or was even thought about. Section 5 prohibits unfair or deceptive practices, and each of these standards has a three-part legal test.

Sometimes the legal tests simply don't work for privacy because they weren't written with privacy in mind. For example, to prove unfairness, the FTC must show that a practice causes or is likely to cause substantial consumer injury, which can be very difficult in privacy where injury can be very subjective and there is a range of different types of harms.

In addition, section 5 doesn't establish clear standards for companies to follow before a problem occurs. It is mostly reactive allowing the FTC to challenge data practices afterwards.

Finally, the FTC Act doesn't authorize civil penalties for first-time violations, and it doesn't even cover nonprofit entities or companies engaged in common carrier activities. Now, the FTC is attempting to plug at least some of these holes by developing a privacy regulation, and in theory, an FTC privacy regulation could set forth practices that companies must follow – do this, don't do that – and also pave the way for civil penalties.

But this approach faces even more obstacles in case-by-case enforcement, and it will use up the FTC's limited resources too. That is because without specific direction from Congress to develop a privacy rule, the FTC must rely on its rulemaking authority under the FTC Act, which is also called Magnuson-Moss rulemaking.

The Mag-Moss process – we all have a nickname for it – is extremely cumbersome and time consuming, as compared with the usual rulemaking process under the Administrative Procedures Act. For example, Mag-Moss requires the FTC to prove that each practice it seeks to regulate is not only unfair or deceptive, but prevalent.

Mag-Moss also includes an extra round of public comments, public hearings, and a more rigorous standard for judicial review. Rules developed under this process have typically taken years to complete, and with all the controversy surrounding privacy, we can also expect legal challenges here. There is simply no substitute for Federal privacy legislation.

Congress can write a law that says do this, don't do that. It can plug the holes in the FTC Act, as well as in the U.S. privacy patchwork that we all know overall, and only Congress can resolve the thorniest issues here and put them to rest, preemption and the privacy right of action.

Thank you very much. I look forward to your questions.

[The prepared statement of Ms. Rich follows:]

Statement of Jessica Rich, of Counsel and Senior Policy Advisor for Consumer Protection, Kelley Drye & Warren LLP, before the Subcommittee on Innovation, Data, and Commerce, Committee on Energy and Commerce, United State House of Representatives, on "Promoting U.S. Innovation and Individual Liberty through a National Standard for Data Privacy," March 1, 2023

I. Introduction and Background

Chair McMorris Rodgers, Ranking Member Pallone, Chairman Bilirakis, Ranking Member Schakowsky, and members of this Subcommittee, I am Jessica Rich, Of Counsel and Senior Policy Advisor for Consumer Protection at Kelley Drye & Warren, and a Distinguished Fellow at Georgetown University. I am pleased to be here today, testifying before this Subcommittee on setting a national standard for data privacy. I want to thank this Committee for its leadership and ongoing efforts on data privacy issues. I also want to make clear that my remarks today are my own, based largely on my years of experience in government service.

My background is as a lawyer and law enforcement official. I worked for over 26 years at the Federal Trade Commission (FTC), the last four as Director of the Bureau of Consumer Protection, overseeing the agency's efforts to protect consumers from harmful marketing, advertising, and data privacy and security practices. Much of my FTC career was devoted to data privacy and security. I was the first manager of the FTC's privacy program, starting in the late 1990s, and led its expansion as a division manager, and later as Deputy Director and then Director of the Bureau of Consumer Protection. In my various roles, I developed or oversaw enforcement against hundreds of companies that failed to protect consumers' personal information; rulemakings to implement privacy laws such as the Gramm-Leach-Bliley Act (GLBA),[65] the Children's Online Privacy Protection Act (COPPA),[66] and the Fair and Accurate Credit Transactions Act (FACTA);[67] and educational and policy initiatives to highlight emerging issues and promote best practices.

I also wrote or oversaw multiple recommendations to Congress seeking stronger legal authority and remedies for privacy, starting in 2000[68] and then echoed and refined in subsequent years.[69] I left the agency in 2017, but I have continued to press for a federal privacy law in Congressional testimony, op-eds, and speeches because of its importance to consumers, businesses, the FTC, and my longtime commitment to the issue.[70]

---

[65] 15 U.S.C. § 6801 et seq.

[66] 15 U.S.C. § 6501 et seq.

[67] 15 U.S.C. § 1681 et seq.

[68] *Privacy Online: Fair Information Practices in the Electronic Marketplace: A Report to Congress* (May 2000) ("2000 Report"), https://www ftc.gov/sites/default/files/documents/reports/privacy-online-fair-information-practices-electronic-marketplace-federal-trade-commission-report/privacy2000.pdf.

[69] See, e.g., *Protecting Consumer Privacy in an Era of Rapid Change: Recommendations for Businesses and Policymakers* (March 2012), https://www.ftc.gov/reports/protecting-consumer-privacy-era-rapid-change-recommendations-businesses-policymakers.

[70] See, e.g., *Give the FTC Some Teeth to Guard our Privacy*, New York Times Op-Ed (August 2019), https://www.nytimes.com/2019/08/12/opinion/ftc-privacy-congress html.

II. The Need for a Comprehensive Federal Privacy Law

I am here today to plead the same case yet again. The need for a federal privacy law has never been greater, and there is no substitute for Congressional action here. For over two decades, Congress has debated the issue. While Congress did pass some sector-specific legislation like COPPA and GLBA, it has repeatedly failed to act on comprehensive legislation. Meanwhile, Europe and countries all over the world moved ahead with detailed data protection laws, as have five U.S. states, with more in the pipeline.[71] All states now have data breach notification laws;[72] about half have data security laws;[73] and many also have sector-specific laws, like Illinois' Biometric Information Privacy Act.[74]

This "patchwork" (as it is so often called) is confusing and costly for consumers and businesses alike, and getting more so. Consumers need a strong and consistent law to protect them across jurisdictions and market sectors, and to clarify what privacy rights they should expect and demand as they navigate the marketplace. Businesses – especially small and medium sized ones – need to know what the rules are without having to spend millions of dollars on attorneys and overly complex compliance schemes. We have just the opposite now – a rolling wave of new and disparate privacy laws that confuse everyone and require an armada of experts to interpret.

Federal privacy legislation is the best way – and indeed the only way – to create a consistent set of rules that protect consumers nationwide. It will bring clarity for consumers and businesses; level the playing field between large and small companies; cast a wide net of protection that can address issues like discrimination and the misuse of kids' and teens' data; significantly boost enforcement and remedies for violations; and provide much-needed credibility abroad.

Although I could expand on each of the above points, my testimony today will focus on a related issue that is just as important – which is why *the FTC* needs a federal privacy law. As much as the FTC has been able to do with the tools that it has, it needs more authority from Congress to be a truly effective privacy enforcer. That's why the FTC has asked Congress so many times to pass federal privacy legislation. That's also likely why all three of the FTC's Democratic Commissioners, even as they launched their Section 18 (a/k/a "Mag-Moss") rulemaking on Commercial Surveillance and Data Security[75] (hereinafter "Privacy Rulemaking"), stated or implied that they would back away from the rulemaking if Congress were to pass a comprehensive privacy law.[76]

Indeed, under current law, the FTC's authority is limited, whether pursuing case-by-case enforcement or attempting a Mag-Moss rulemaking. Only Congress can establish the kind of

---

[71] See *IAPP State Privacy Legislation Tracker*, https://iapp.org/resources/article/us-state-privacy-legislation-tracker/.

[72] See *Security Breach Notification Laws* (National Conference of State Legislatures or "NCSL"), https://www.ncsl.org/technology-and-communication/security-breach-notification-laws.

[73] See *Data Security Laws – Private Sector* (NCSL), https://www ncsl.org/technology-and-communication/data-security-laws-private-sector.

[74] 740 ILCS 14.

[75] See *Commercial Surveillance and Data Security Rulemaking*, https://www.ftc.gov/legal-library/browse/federal-register-notices/commercial-surveillance-data-security-rulemaking.

[76] Despite her support for stronger federal privacy mandates, Republican Commissioner Wilson dissented from the rulemaking, stating that Congressional action is the best course. All of the Commissioners' statements can be found at https://www.ftc.gov/news-events/news/press-releases/2022/08/ftc-explores-rules-cracking-down-commercial-surveillance-lax-data-security-practices.

broad-based protections contained in recent privacy bills such as the ADPPA. And only Congress can put to rest the issues that have been debated for years – notably whether to preempt state privacy laws and/or grant a private right of action, and how much discretion the FTC should have to shape the requirements (i.e., through rulemaking). Below, I provide more details about some of the strengths and limits of the FTC's privacy authority.

III. The FTC's Privacy Authority

Background on the FTC's Privacy Program

The FTC built its privacy program almost entirely around Section 5 of the FTC Act, a law that was written long before the arrival of the Internet.[77] That's because, in the mid-1990s, when the Internet did arrive, there were very few U.S. laws (federal or state) that specifically addressed privacy. After holding hearings on what the Internet would mean for consumers and competition, the FTC quickly recognized that privacy would be a serious concern. It therefore sought to use Section 5, its general law prohibiting "unfair or deceptive" practices, to address this issue.[78]

Since then, the FTC has used Section 5 to challenge the data practices of a wide range of companies, including retailers, data brokers, mortgage companies, pharmacies, software companies, mobile apps, and most of the major tech companies.[79] The cases have spanned a wide range of fact patterns, too – false or misleading data privacy and security statements or settings,[80] including about children's data;[81] breaches of financial[82] and health information,[83] and even personal data about extramarital affairs;[84] spyware in people's homes;[85] and a wide range of other alleged violations.

---

[77] 15 U.S.C. Sec. 45.

[78] See *2000 Report*, supra at n. 4, for discussion of the FTC's early privacy efforts.

[79] See *Privacy and Security Enforcement,* https://www.ftc.gov/news-events/topics/protecting-consumer-privacy-security/privacy-security-enforcement. There is a misperception that the FTC shied away from using unfairness until recently. In fact, many of the FTC's data privacy and security cases have been based on unfairness.

[80] See, e.g., *FTC Imposes $5 Billion Penalty and Sweeping New Privacy Restrictions on Facebook ("Facebook Settlement"),* https://www.ftc.gov/news-events/news/press-releases/2019/07/ftc-imposes-5-billion-penalty-sweeping-new-privacy-restrictions-facebook.

[81] See, e.g., *FTC Sues Failed Website, Toysmart.com, for Deceptively Offering for Sale Personal Information of Website Visitors*, https://www ftc.gov/news-events/news/press-releases/2000/07/ftc-sues-failed-website-toysmartcom-deceptively-offering-sale-personal-information-website-visitors.

[82] See, e.g., *Agency Announces Settlement of Separate Actions Against Retailer TJX, and Data Brokers Reed Elsevier and Seisint for Failing to Provide Adequate Security for Consumers Data,* https://www.ftc.gov/news-events/news/press-releases/2008/03/agency-announces-settlement-separate-actions-against-retailer-tjx-data-brokers-reed-elsevier-seisint.

[83] See, e.g., *Electronic Health Records Company Settles FTC Charges It Deceived Consumers About Privacy of Doctor Reviews*, https://www.ftc.gov/news-events/news/press-releases/2016/06/electronic-health-records-company-settles-ftc-charges-it-deceived-consumers-about-privacy-doctor.

[84] See, e.g., *Operators of AshleyMadison.com Settle FTC, State Charges Resulting From 2015 Data Breach that Exposed 36 Million Users' Profile Information*, https://www.ftc.gov/news-events/news/press-releases/2016/12/operators-ashleymadisoncom-settle-ftc-state-charges-resulting-2015-data-breach-exposed-36-million.

[85] See, e.g., *FTC Halts Computer Spying*, https://www ftc.gov/news-events/news/press-releases/2012/09/ftc-halts-computer-spying.

The FTC has bolstered this enforcement, and increased its influence and visibility, with frequent use of the "bully pulpit" – including workshops and reports highlighting emerging issues and recommending best practices; consumer and business guidance; and testimony and recommendations to Congress.[86] Often, the FTC faced strong headwinds from industry and members of Congress, who opposed, not only the FTC's efforts, but any attempts to strengthen federal privacy laws.

Although Congress passed some sectoral privacy laws in the late 1990s and early 2000s (including COPPA, GLBA, and FACTA), the FTC Act continues to serve as the agency's core legal authority in privacy, given its broad scope relative to the sectoral laws. Most of the cases brought against the large tech companies, for example, were based on Section 5.[87]

Significantly, though, virtually all of the FTC's privacy and data security cases are settlements. That means that many of the legal theories advanced, as well as the remedies obtained, have never been tested in court.[88]

2. Limits of Section 5

The FTC's success in building a substantial and influential data privacy and security program can sometimes mask the limits of its legal authority in this area. In fact, Section 5 was not designed for privacy and is ill-suited for it in various ways. On the one hand, it has provided the FTC with substantial flexibility to tackle a wide array of practices. But on the other, the concepts of "deception" and "unfairness" contain many gaps and shortcomings when it comes to privacy. These shortcomings have become increasingly problematic as data use has proliferated and become more complex.

As a reminder, to prove deception, the FTC must show that there is a material representation, omission, or practice that is likely to mislead a reasonable consumer.[89] To prove unfairness, the FTC must show that a practice causes or is likely to cause substantial injury to consumers that cannot reasonably be avoided by consumers, and is not outweighed by countervailing benefits to consumers or competition.[90]

One challenge is that Section 5 (and associated case law) was developed with traditional commercial transactions in mind – such as when a company sells, and a consumer purchases, a product or service (such as a sweater, tractor part, or investment) for a particular purpose and the consumer does not receive the goods or services intended or expected. In such situations, privacy may not be top-of-mind for consumers as they consider the transaction, even if they care about it in a general sense. In the case of the sweater, consumers may be thinking about its appearance, fit, or fabric, not whether the company stores credit card numbers securely, or sells

---

[86] See *FTC Policy Work on Privacy and Data Security*, https://www ftc.gov/news-events/topics/protecting-consumer-privacy-security/ftc-policy-work.

[87] See, e.g., *Facebook Settlement*, supra at n. 16; *Google Will Pay $22.5 Million to Settle FTC Charges it Misrepresented Privacy Assurances to Users of Apple's Safari Internet Browser*, https://www.ftc.gov/news-events/news/press-releases/2012/08/google-will-pay-225-million-settle-ftc-charges-it-misrepresented-privacy-assurances-users-apples.

[88] One notable exception is the *Wyndham* case, in which the 3rd Circuit upheld the FTC's authority to challenge lax data security practices as unfair. *FTC v. Wyndham Worldwide Corp.*, 799 F. 3d 240 (2015).

[89] *Policy Statement on Deception*, https://www.ftc.gov/legal-library/browse/ftc-policy-statement-deception.

[90] 15 U.S.C. § 45(n). The statutory test, enacted by Congress in 1994, superseded the FTC's Policy Statement on Unfairness ("Unfairness Statement"), https://www.ftc.gov/legal-library/browse/ftc-policy-statement-unfairness. However, the FTC and the courts still refer to portions of the Policy Statement, especially its discussion of consumer harm, and many of its principles are baked into FTC case law.

consumer data to third parties. This can make it difficult to show that privacy was *material* to a consumer's decision to purchase the product or service.

Another challenge is that proving a practice "causes or is likely to cause" substantial injury for purposes of unfairness has always been a conundrum in privacy, especially since the concept of privacy injury can be so subjective. Is emotional or reputational injury sufficient? Is the mere release of data (even sensitive data) enough? How sensitive must data be to have its sale or compromise rise to the level of "likely" substantial injury? The FTC's Unfairness Statement (which courts still cite in their opinions) says that "emotional impact" and other "subjective" types of harm will not ordinarily make a practice unfair, but might do so in "extreme cases" when "tangible injury" can be shown.[91] Similarly, the Supreme Court has held that "concrete harm," and not the "mere risk of future harm," is necessary to confer standing to plaintiffs in privacy class actions.[92] The FTC must continuously navigate the issue of harm when it comes to privacy.

Yet another problem is that Section 5 does not establish clear standards for companies to follow before problems occur – it is almost wholly reactive. It does not tell businesses, for example, what privacy disclosures and choices they need to provide to consumers, or what data uses are so inherently risky or harmful that they should be avoided or modified. Instead, it allows the FTC to evaluate a company's practices after the fact, to determine whether they meet the unfairness and/or deception tests. (The FTC is trying to fix this problem by promulgating its Privacy Rule, but that faces obstacles of its own, as discussed below.)

In addition, certain requirements that appear in existing privacy laws and bills are an especially poor fit for Section 5. Is the failure to provide access or deletion rights to consumers, without more, deceptive or unfair? What about a company's failure, without more, to audit its practices using certain criteria, or to have its executives attest to the audit? Certainly, companies have agreed to these types of requirements in settlements (as so-called "fencing-in" to prevent the companies from committing additional violations in the future) but that doesn't mean that failure to take these steps meets the deception and/or unfairness tests, or that a court would make that determination.

Finally, the FTC Act does not cover non-profits or companies engaged in common carrier activities – limitations that have long created an obstacle to even-handed FTC enforcement. Nor does it authorize civil penalties for first time violations or, since *AMG*, allow the FTC to seek consumer redress in federal court under Section 13(b).[93] (A rulemaking would lay the groundwork for monetary relief, but cannot alter the FTC's jurisdictional limits).

3. Magnuson-Moss Rulemaking

The FTC is well aware of the limits discussed above. That's why it has repeatedly, on a bipartisan basis, asked Congress to pass a federal privacy law that includes specific privacy mandates; authority to obtain civil penalties; and jurisdiction over nonprofits and common carriers.[94]

---

[91] See *Unfairness Statement*, supra at n. 26.

[92] *TransUnion LLC v. Ramirez*, 141 S. Ct. 2190 (2021).

[93] Given the difficulty of quantifying many types of privacy injuries, penalties are often the better remedy.

[94] See, e.g., *FTC Report to Congress on Privacy and Security* (September 2021), https://www.ftc.gov/system/files/documents/reports/ftc-report-congress-privacy-security/report to congress on privacy and data security 2021.pdf; *Prepared Remarks of Chairman Joseph J. Simons on "Oversight of the Federal Trade Commission:*

Congress has not acted, which is frustrating for many. So after two decades of asking, the FTC has moved ahead on its own, by launching its Privacy Rulemaking under Mag-Moss.

The Mag-Moss process is more cumbersome than "normal" rulemaking under the Administrative Procedures Act (APA). That's because Congress deliberately added provisions to make it so, due to perceived overreach by the FTC in the 1970s (especially its proposal to ban TV food advertising to kids – known as "kid vid").[95] Of particular note, Mag-Moss requires the FTC to prove that each practice it seeks to regulate is unfair or deceptive, as well as prevalent. In other words, the FTC is confined to the very same legal standards that, as discussed above, create obstacles for privacy – and must prove prevalence, too.

Mag-Moss also includes an extra round of public comments, public hearings as requested by stakeholders, and a more rigorous standard for judicial review.[96] According to a professor who analyzed FTC rules developed under Mag-Moss, the average time it took to complete them was almost six years, versus less than a year for APA rules.[97]

In addition, a sometimes-forgotten Mag-Moss provision limits the FTC's authority to develop rules regarding kids' advertising. This provision, now found in Section 18(h) of the FTC Act, prohibits the FTC from promulgating "any rule in the children's advertising proceeding pending on May 28, 1980" (i.e., 'kid vid") or in any "substantially similar proceeding" based on unfairness.[98]

In July 2021, an FTC majority voted to simplify the Mag-Moss rulemaking procedures, to the extent that it could, by stripping away some steps that the FTC had previously added to the process through its own internal rules.[99] However, most of the cumbersome requirements appear in the law, which the FTC cannot change. In addition, the Commission appears to be charting an ambitious path forward in the Privacy Rulemaking, one that portends a very long process. In its first request for comment (the Advance Notice of Proposed Rulemaking, or ANPRM), the FTC discussed dozens of privacy topics, posed 95 questions, and touched on many controversial issues. Not surprisingly, the agency received over 11,000 comments from the public.

The obstacles here are enormous. To develop a rule of the breadth that Congress considered in the bipartisan ADPPA, the FTC would need to prove that many dozens of practices are both prevalent and unfair or deceptive, with all of the associated challenges discussed above. It must review and analyze thousands of comments (twice) and hold public hearings with numerous stakeholders clamoring to be heard. Even if the FTC is able to complete the rulemaking, litigation seems likely, whether based on the particular issues regulated or bigger picture questions about the FTC's legal authority here.[100]

Strengthening Protections for American's Privacy and Data Security," https://www.ftc.gov/legal-library/browse/prepared-remarks-chairman-joseph-j-simons-oversight-federal-trade-commission-strengthening.

95 See, e.g., *The FTC as National Nanny* (Washington Post Editorial, March 1, 1978, at A22).

96 15 U.S.C. § 57a.

97 Jeffrey Lubbers, *It's Time to Remove the 'Mossified' Procedures for FTC Rulemaking* (G.W. Law Review, February 2015), https://papers.ssrn.com/sol3/papers.cfm?abstract id=2560557.

98 15 U.S.C. § 57a(h).

99 *FTC Votes to Update Rulemaking Procedures, Sets Stage for Stronger Deterrence of Corporate Misconduct,* https://www.ftc.gov/news-events/news/press-releases/2021/07/ftc-votes-update-rulemaking-procedures-sets-stage-stronger-deterrence-corporate-misconduct. Among other things, the changes eliminated the need for a staff report analyzing the rulemaking record, and gave the Chair more authority to control the public hearings process.

100 Multiple comments on the FTC's ANPRM argue that the FTC's proposal raise concerns under the "Major Questions" doctrine recently discussed by the Supreme Court in *West Virginia v. EPA*, 142 S. Ct. 2587 (2022).

Additionally, the FTC cannot resolve (or should not be the one to resolve) the most controversial issues in the privacy debate – whether to preempt state laws,[101] grant a private right of action, and/or impose limits on its own rulemaking discretion. Nor can it address the data practices of common carriers and non-profits – those entities would not be covered by an FTC rule.

IV. Conclusion

There is simply no substitute for federal privacy legislation. No other U.S. privacy regime or proposal can create the broad protections and consistent standards that the U.S. sorely needs. Congress must finally pass a federal privacy law to protect and reassure the American public.

* * *

Mr. Bilirakis. Thank you very much. I appreciate it.

I thank all of the witnesses for their testimony today. Excellent testimony, by the way.

We will now move into the question and answer portion of the hearing. I will begin the questioning and recognize myself for 5 minutes.

Thank you again to the panel. We have made clear the American people deserve to have more control over their data, and we are hard at work to pass comprehensive privacy and data security legislation to do just that. But we are also committed to this effort, because businesses, especially small and medium sized businesses, need certainty. They should not live in fear of spending their time and resources to legal compliance to survive in the digital economy.

Unfortunately, the opposite is occurring, and the growing state patchwork is unsustainable for the American economy. And California is still adding more layers to the regulation.

Ms. Rich, you referenced the FTC's current privacy rulemaking in your testimony. I want to highlight that their rulemaking would not preempt State laws, meaning more regulatory uncertainty. How will adding another layer to the current patchwork lead to negative economic impact and a disruption for small and medium sized businesses to operate?

Ms. Rich. I agree that that would be problematic, especially since the FTC can't work through the difficult issues related to preemption that this committee and Congress can.

Mr. Bilirakis. Thank you very much.

Mr. Mudd, would you like to comment on this, please?

Mr. Mudd. Sure. You know, I think it is absolutely the case, Congressman, that a patchwork of State legislation really does hurt smaller businesses and particularly smaller publishers more than it does larger ones. Larger tech companies have armies of engineers that can adjust their technologies State by State, jurisdiction by jurisdiction. That is just not possible for smaller publishers and companies.

Mr. Bilirakis. Thank you.

Ms. Rich, protecting all Americans from unfair and deceptive acts is no small undertaking. As you may know, the ADPPA included a section for FTC-approved compliance mechanisms

---

[101] In theory, the FTC could try to preempt state privacy laws, or set its Privacy Rule as floor that the state laws could exceed (as it has proposed to do in its rulemaking to ban non-compete clauses). See e.g., *Fidelity Savings & Loan Assn. v. De La Questa,* 458 U.S. 141 (1982). However, any such proposal would likely draw legal challenge.

for small businesses who may have difficulty complying with a law. I know safe harbors have also helped the FTC in their ability to enforce laws.

Can you speak more on that, and explain why safe harbors would be helpful to the FTC and legislation such as the ADPPA?

Ms. Rich. Thank you. If done right, safe harbors or compliance programs can increase compliance overall while also providing the certainty and the flexibility that certain – that businesses, especially small and medium sized businesses, need. The idea is that an independent organization can create a compliance program that meets or exceeds the standards in the law. And then the FTC approves them using a rigorous process, and then companies that need this kind of structure and guidance and help can join the program and be evaluated and certified for compliance, and thus comply with the law. If the requirements are rigorous, which they are in the ADPPA, it expands both compliance, while also providing certainties for the companies that joined these programs.

Mr. Bilirakis. Very good. Thank you very much. I will yield back.

And now we will ask the ranking member of the subcommittee, I give her 5 minutes for her questions. Thank you.

Ms. Schakowsky. First of all, let me just say how cheered I am by the consensus that we have. You know, we have got a practitioner, we have got a not for profit, we have got government. We have got, it seems, Republicans and Democrats, so let's move forward.

So the question – let me start with Ms. Givens. So it seems to me that the current notice and consent privacy regime really doesn't work very well for consumers. So is there a better approach, and how would you describe that?

Ms. Givens. Thank you for the question. And you are absolutely right that the current model of notice and consent is broken. And I think any person that uses the internet or a device today knows that, right? We are forced to click through long terms of service that many people do not stop and take the time to read. And even if we could take the time to read them, consumers don't feel like they have a choice. Often we need to be able to access a service to communicate with friends or family, for example.

So instead, what we need is the model pursued in the ADPPA, which is strong baseline protections for consumers' data that don't rely on somebody clicking through on whatever a company has chosen to disclose in its terms of service, but instead provide baseline protections and rules of the road. These include things like protections for data minimization. So the assumption that companies can only collect, process, and share data in the course of delivering the service that the user expects, as well as heightened protections for sensitive areas of data which can include anything from precise location information to health data, for example, to other biometric information.

Those are the types of rules that we need to give customers confidence again in the online ecosystem and also help businesses know how to govern their practices.

Ms. Schakowsky. Thank you.

So, Mr. Mudd, I also want to talk to you about the burden that I think is really right now on the consumer themselves, the notice and consent regime, but how does this play in the ad tech world? I mean, do you know anybody who reads all of the – I mean, I once brought in the pages and pages of the terms of service and all of that. So I just wondered how you would comment on what we need to do better. And I don't want to see more burdens than saying the consumer has to do more to protect themselves.

Mr. Mudd. I couldn't agree more. I do believe that the current approach is wholly insufficient in protecting consumers. And I think your assumption that the vast majority of people do not read privacy policies or terms of service is, of course, correct and, therefore, that consumers do not understand how data that they admit is being used, transferred, collected, et cetera.

Ms. Schakowsky. So what do you do to help the consumers? How is your business different?

Mr. Mudd. As Ms. Givens pointed out, I think the whole point of the technologies that we and others are developing is to just raise the baseline, to not allow the kinds of data sharing that have taken place in the past, as opposed to asking consumers, putting the work on them to make decisions that they are not well informed to make and they certainly don't have the time or inclination to focus on. And so it is all about privacy by default, data minimization, moving the bar up, instead of putting the work on the consumer.

Ms. Schakowsky. Yeah. And let me ask you, Ms. Rich. So what you are talking about is that we have the tools or we can have the tools through the Federal Trade Commission. And how important, then, do you think is the role of the FTC as our regulator?

Ms. Rich. Oh, the FTC as the regulator here is critical. They have been doing this work for 25 years. They have enormous sophistication about the issues. They have the will to protect consumers, and they just need better tools, stronger legal tools to protect consumers across the marketplace.

Ms. Schakowsky. You know, I do have time, but I want to say that the witnesses that we have today I think can really be helpful to us as we move forward to make sure that the law that we did pass can be improved, can be made better, so that we can, during this Congress, get across the line that I think we have really come close to right now. And, you know, the United States of America really owes it, I think, to our consumers. We are just too far behind. We owe it to our children. We owe it to our families. We owe it to legitimate businesses to make sure that we – that we move forward.

So let me just say thank you very much. And I yield back.

Mr. Bilirakis. The gentlelady yields back. And I would like to say to the ranking member, you are right, we are too far behind, too far behind. That is the bottom line.

Okay. Now I will recognize the vice chairman of the subcommittee, Mr. Walberg, for his 5 minutes of testimony.

Mr. Walberg. Thank you, Mr. Chair. And I would certainly concur that we are far behind, but we take an early start here, and that is a good thing, as we have already talked about the patchwork of competing laws that are out there in the State level. And now we are working on something I think we can come together. We have shown that.

One area I think we can all agree is the need to address children's privacy. Republicans in the House are committed to putting parents back in the driver seat, and even grandparents back in the driver seat. Being a little personal there. It includes providing more tools to protect them online.

Kids' privacy has long been a priority for me. In past Congresses, I introduced bipartisan legislation that would update COPPA for our increasingly digital world, and the ADPPA included additional protections for those under the age of 17.

Ms. Givens, how should children's privacy protections be addressed differently than those for adults in the comprehensive privacy law?

Ms. Givens. Thank you for the question, and thank you for your leadership on this issue to protect children across the country.

The ADPPA includes some important protections for children, and it is specific in calling them out. One is the additional division created at the FTC to focus on this issue. But additionally there are protections, for example, prohibiting the targeting of ads to children and teenagers under the age of 17, and also express limits on the sharing of their information without expressed opt-in consent.

This matters because our children are being targeted online and, unfortunately, COPPA right now is not up to the job in addressing abusive data practices. But what is critically important is that we can't just focus on the privacy needs of kids. We need to do this in a comprehensive way that protects all consumers. And the reason we need to do that is, when you only focus on protecting the interests of children, you actually create new obligations, for example, to test for people's ages, that can sometimes undermine people's privacy.

So what we need to do is the approach that is followed in ADPPA today, which is to lift up privacy protections for all consumers, and then charge those additional resources to protecting kids in additional ways, to make sure that we really are living up to what our children need online.

Mr. Walberg. Okay. What is good for one can be good for all in a great way as we do it comprehensively.

COPPA currently includes an actual knowledge standard for information, Ms. Rich, collected on those under age of 13. The law was passed in 2000, and the FTC last made rule changes in 2013.

How has the landscape changed since then, and is an actual knowledge standard still appropriate?

Ms. Rich. You went right to the heart of the issues, didn't you?

Mr. Walberg. Sometimes I do it right.

Ms. Rich. Yeah, yeah. The FTC has not updated COPPA, and a lot of people wonder why. In remarks, public remarks, there was some suggestion that they are waiting to see if Congress updates the law so that, you know, they don't have to do it twice, but I can't fully understand why they are not using the tools that they have.

COPPA is very outdated. Information collection has just exploded even since 2013, and it was pretty considerable then, and all sorts of new practices in the marketplace. And we really do need special protections for kids and teens as is included in the ADPPA.

Mr. Walberg. Okay. Ms. Givens, in your testimony, you referenced a report by Duke University, which was interesting, which revealed that data brokers were selling mental health information to advertisers. This included whether someone has depression, insomnia, Alzheimer's disease, other medical conditions. I read the same report or read the same report and am extremely concerned.

HIPAA was created to protect our medical information, but with the explosion of health apps, that data is no longer just held by your doctor's office. What gaps are there in protecting medical privacy, and how do we fill them?

Ms. Givens. Thank you for the question because this is an urgent problem. You are right that HIPAA does protect data, but it is only when it is held by a covered entity, which doesn't include any of the commercial apps or services that users interact with every day. Sometimes sharing really important mental health insights, if you are using an app to kind of do, you know, journaling. And in addition, inferences that companies can make about you based on your behavior, from which they might be inferring some of the medical conditions that we just described, which is why we have to have –

Mr. Walberg. True or untrue, yeah.

Ms. Givens. Yeah. So which is why we have to have a comprehensive privacy law to fill those gaps for all of the non-HIPAA covered entities that are still making inferences and deductions about people's mental health status, as well as other medical conditions as well.

Mr. Walberg. Thank you. My time has expired.

Mr. Mudd, I have another question, the best question you could ever have had, but I will submit it for the record.

Mr. Mudd. Sounds good.

Mr. Bilirakis. Thank you very much. I appreciate that.

And now we will recognize the gentleman from Florida, Mr. Soto, for his 5 minutes. Florida is very well represented on both sides of the aisle in this committee. It is just a coincidence, right?

Thank you. You are recognized. Go ahead.

Mr. Soto. Thank you, Chairman. You are making Florida proud.

You know, it is nothing short of a mild miracle last term when we saw both parties come together to pass out of the committee the America Data Privacy and Protection Act. When you look at some of these key sections, like the sensitive covered data section, it reads really like an internet privacy bill of rights. Information that everyday Americans would think would already be protected is still subject to risk of being distributed and used for – in commerce, like people's Social Security numbers and health information, financial account information, debit card information, biometric information, genetic information, your precise geolocation at this very moment, your private communications like voice mails, emails, text messages, and mail, account logins and passwords, identifying people's different behaviors socially, as well as calendar information, address book information, so many of the things that we would all shudder to know that could be sold and used for profit to help target people in a really intimate way that violates our notions of privacy in the Nation.

You know, Florida does not have internet privacy laws, even though we have a privacy amendment in our constitution. It is failed a couple times over enforcement disputes. So our State and 22 million Floridians are left vulnerable by not having rights, which is why it is time for us to step up to create a national standard. Not to mention that I can't think of anything more related to interstate commerce than the internet. So it is a really important time for us.

Ms. Givens, it would be great to get your opinion on this list of basic data covered, on these basic rights that we have, and do you think there should be any others added?

Ms. Givens. In my opinion, the ADPPA did an excellent job capturing many of the major categories of sensitive data. You listed many of them. And to the point that you made, these are things Americans already expect to be protected. They are horrified when they find out that it is not protected, and they want baseline safeguards in place to make sure that they can trust the services they consult online.

While the list is strong and good now, there needs to be ongoing flexibility to add to it in the future, because we know that the marketplace will continue to innovate. We cannot foresee what data uses may arise in the next 5, 10, 15, 20 years, which is how long, of course, this law would likely be in place in governing user behavior.

And so one of the important innovations in the bill is to leave some room for the FTC to fill in the gaps where needed and be responsive to emerging cases, which the FTC can do based on rulemaking procedures, stakeholder consultation as new norms evolve. And that, I think, is the right approach that the bill takes today.

Mr. Soto. So do you believe that already is included, that kind of flexibility is already enough in the ADPPA already for the FTC to recognize these new types of information?

Ms. Givens. I do think so. I think the covered list that we have now, the fact that it includes both the data itself and inferences that may reveal that information, coupled with the ability to fill in gaps in the future, is a really important combination.

Mr. Soto. Thank you.

And, Ms. Rich, we know how important enforcement is. We saw in Florida that was the key sticking point that kept our State from actually having a new law. And I am very concerned that we don't end up having a toothless tiger here. The bill we already passed out of the committee last year had both a role for the FTC, a private right of action, and rules for state attorney generals.

How critical is it to have all three of these mechanisms in place, and can you give us any guidance on that?

Ms. Rich. Well, having been part of this debate for over 20 years, I would say, whatever it takes for you guys to agree on a law is what I support. But I do think that some level of consistency is important and – which is why I do support some level of preemption and some limits on private litigation, especially since private litigation sometimes benefits attorneys more than consumers.

But I actually think the model in the ADPPA is very good because it empowers the FTC, it empowers not just all the state attorney generals, but other officers in the State that might have a role in privacy. And so given that the state attorneys general have been very active in privacy, I think this new tool would empower them even more, and we have a lot of cops on the beat.

Mr. Soto. Well, thanks for that opinion. You know, many tech companies are running circles around government enforcement right now. And so very important to have a balance, in my opinion, between FTC or state attorney generals and having some private right of action. Thank you for your opinions.

And I yield back.

Mr. Bilirakis. Thank you, sir. Appreciate it very much

Now I will recognize the gentleman from South Carolina. Mr. Duncan, for his 5 minutes.

Mr. Duncan. Thank you, Mr. Chairman. And this has been an informative hearing. I am an energy guy, so this isn't in my wheelhouse, but it is educating me on the issue.

So just one real quick question, because, Ms. Rich, we have heard a lot from downtown over the preemption clause in the ADPPA, namely that it doesn't go far enough, especially with respect to overly restrictive provisions coming out of California.

While the previous Speaker of the House disagreed with that sentiment, I understand there are concerns over certain carve-outs that are not otherwise addressed in the bill.

Could you speak to that?

Ms. Rich. Well, as I said, I do think that there is some level of preemption that should be in the bill so we get as much consistency as possible. I would also note that by the measure of many consumer advocacy groups who are reading all of these bills and laws very carefully, the ADPPA is stronger than existing State laws, for the most part. It may be one provision here and there and stronger. But, you know, in an effort to compromise, this committee carved out certain things, including the California private right of action.

So as I said, whatever it takes, but I do believe the ADPPA is the strongest law we have seen – the strongest bill we have seen anywhere on privacy.

* * *

Mr. Duncan. Thank you for that.

I think some sort of uniformity where States know how to comply with a lot of different things, the ADPPA being an example of that.

Mr. Chairman, legislative hearings and hearings like this are very informative. I appreciate you doing that.

I don't have another question. I yield back.

Mr. Bilirakis. I appreciate that very much. Thank you.

And now I will recognize the ranking member of the full committee, Mr. Pallone, for his 5 minutes.

Mr. Pallone. Thank you, Mr. Chairman.

I am concerned about data brokers collecting and selling massive and detailed amounts of information about consumers who have never interacted with these data brokers.

So let me start with Mr. Mudd. In your written testimony, you point out that the scale of data collection and transfer using online mechanics is difficult to comprehend. Based on your experience working in advertising technology, could you tell us what types of information data brokers have about consumers, how they collect that information, and what they do with it in about a minute or so?

Mr. Mudd. I will do my best.

So, in terms of the types of data that are collected by data brokers, it is, again, difficult to be comprehensive here. Certainly basic demographics: your age, your gender, your household composition and so forth. But certainly also well beyond that: your profession, the makeup of your household, the age of your children, the location, of course, of your household, oftentimes also your workplace, oftentimes even your real-time location, your income, and other financial statistics about you.

And then, of course, your behaviors. Your behaviors on the web through, you know, pixels, cookies, and so forth, as well as off the web in the real world. Retailers oftentimes will sell data about your shopping behavior to data brokers, who will then resell that data onward to others.

And then, as others have pointed out, health conditions are oftentimes also gathered and inferred as well.

Now, where do they get this information? Well, as of right now, there is very little constraint on how they can go about gathering it, and so they, of course, gather it from everywhere they possibly can. That means public databases. That means the websites that we interact with and so forth. It means, as I mentioned, real world, you know, retailers.

And then there are even, you know, specialty location companies that try to understand where you are in the physical world and share that data with brokers.

Mr. Pallone. Thank you.

Well, let me have some followup on that with Ms. Givens.

Ms. Givens, are consumers aware of these data brokers? And do consumers have any practical options to tell data brokers to stop collecting or to delete their information? And does the American Data Protection and Privacy Act that we, you know, passed out of committee last Congress, does that take the right approach on data brokers?

Ms. Givens. So consumers are largely unaware of data broker practices and I think would be extremely hard pressed to name any. Part of the problem is that they operate in an opaque layer of the digital ecosystem and don't have to interact directly with consumers, which means they don't need to earn consumer trust.

Some data brokers allow users to opt out, and some States are beginning to require that they make this option available, but it is incredibly hard to exercise. First of all, you need to know who the data brokers are, and there are thousands of them. So even knowing where to go to opt out is a challenge.

Second, even if one is able to go through that interface, and often it involves many steps, you have to keep going back to do it again and again because the settings might change. They might collect new data over time.

So the ADPPA has some really important provisions on this. One is the data brokers need to disclose who they are, and they need to register with the FTC. So there is a one-stop shop for users to go and see who data brokers are.

Data brokers also need to comply if you opt out of sharing your information with them, and they need to have a centralized mechanism that allows opting out across the entire data broker ecosystem. That is hugely important for consumers to actually be able to influence and operate their rights.

Mr. Pallone. All right. Thank you so much.

I have got a little over a minute left.

Let me ask Ms. Rich. Can you tell me about some of the most egregious practices you saw by data brokers in your time at the FTC?

Ms. Rich. Well, this is going to seem kind of old fashioned since companies can do so much more with data even than when I left the FTC in 2017. But selling data to con artists with reason to know it could be used for fraud. We had a bunch of cases like that.

Failing to secure sensitive data, leading to massive breaches. Many of the breach cases, especially in the early days, involved data brokers who would amass all of this sensitive information, leading to identity theft when the data was breached.

Failing to vet buyers, leading to significant access to sensitive information by, you know, anyone that could pay. And, again, identity theft.

So these are – this is what we saw all the time, and, again, the market place is so much more sophisticated that, you know, I am sure there are all sorts of – a litany of other things that we could list that are even worse.

Mr. Pallone. Thank you very much.

Thank you, Mr. Chairman.

Mr. Bilirakis. Thank you very much. I appreciate it.

I next will recognize the ranking member – excuse me – the chairman of the committee. She is wearing her E&C? colors today.

The Chair. That is right.

Mr. Bilirakis. Well, we appreciate all of your great work.

And I recognize you for 5 minutes. Thank you.

The Chair. Thank you. Thank you very much, Mr. Chairman.

And, again, thank you to the panel for being here.

I wanted to start with an issue that we have been focusing on, debating over the last few years around targeted advertising.

Mr. Mudd, there is a particular line in your testimony which I think really hit the mark. And you said: Over the years, a tension began to emerge. The development of the rich consumer profiles that were so powerful in improving products of all kinds came at the cost of individuals' privacy. This tradeoff is why we are here today.

And I believe that you are right on that assessment, even if the online advertising industry doesn't want to admit its reliance on personal information and freely flowing, following Americans as they browse the internet.

So the question is, do they really need personally identifiable information in order to facilitate the e-commerce? And you are suggesting that there is a middle ground here. So I just wanted to ask, would your privacy-enhancing technologies, also called PETs, permit innovation in the digital advertising ecosystem to continue? And how can PETs be used to help small businesses advertise to their customers without customers feeling that the businesses know too much about them?

Mr. Mudd. Thank you, Chair Rodgers.

Yes, we do believe that this is a reasonable middle ground and that it would protect from the flow and sharing of personally identifiable information from one company directly to another, which leads, as I mentioned, to the development of these very rich profiles, which we have talked a lot about today.

And the way that that happens is, you know, reasonably straightforward. What we need to do is ensure that only the aggregated anonymized insights that are required to understand how ads work and to improve their relevance are shared, not the individual-level data. That is not required.

To give an example in another industry, pharmaceutical trials. They need to bring data together from, you know, the drug companies, as well as the practicing physicians, but they don't want to share individual-level data. They can use these exact same privacy-enhancing technologies to understand whether the drug worked or didn't work, but they don't need the user-level data to do that. That is not important for the case.

The Chair. Thank you. Thank you.

Ms. Rich, you mentioned in your statement the importance of creating a regulatory climate that is conducive for businesses to be able to comply, and, you know, there is a lot that has been said about the negotiation that took place on ADPPA.

We included a right to cure in the private right of action to ensure businesses are able to comply with the law, and this is important so businesses are not buried underneath piles of demand letters seeking payments without the opportunity to cure an alleged violation because I don't think any of us want to be there.

So would you speak to the benefits of a right to cure for businesses who face an alleged allegation?

Ms. Rich. Well, when I was at the FTC, I wouldn't have supported a right to cure because it does give people a second bite of the apple to, you know, violate the law, but when it comes to a private right of action and their concerns about the effect on, you know, companies that aren't the largest companies and can't afford all of this litigation, I think the right to cure is a very reasonable response to make sure that, instead of a private right of action leading to a lot of litigation, companies have a chance to get it right, one chance, and then comply and have the protections in place for consumers.

And I would note that other privacy regimes include rights to cure both for private right of actions and for government enforcement.

The Chair. Thank you.

Ms. Givens, I know that we may not see eye to eye on every aspect of ADPPA, but I do want to thank you for your support of our work.

A private right of action is a tough nut to crack in the scope of a bill like ADPPA. You highlight some of the boundaries of where FTC can enforce harms. In your testimony, you state the FTC's unfairness statement, which courts still cite in their opinion, says that emotional impact and other subjective types of harm will not ordinarily make a practice unfair but might do so in extreme cases when tangible injury can be shown.

So I am sympathetic for why there is strong desires to include a private right of action in such an instance when Big Tech may harm someone, especially a child. However, I also want to make sure that it is not abused by the plaintiffs' attorneys who would rather laws be so stringent so businesses are more likely to be out of compliance in order to sue.

Would you be willing to work with us to ensure that there are parameters for how the private right of action operates for businesses, especially businesses of different sizes?

Ms. Givens. Yes, Madam Chair. Of course, we are always happy to work with this committee.

A private right of action really is essential because the FTC and State AGs alone won't be able to keep up with the pace of commercial activity, and consumers deserve the right to be able to vindicate their rights when State enforcement aren't stepping in.

But, respectfully, the ADPPA already puts in a lot of protections to help small businesses and others from this risk of litigation, sometimes over the objection of consumer advocates in the negotiations. But the committee did an awful lot of work to get there.

Just to give a couple of examples, the private right of action only applies to some portions of the law and cannot be used against small businesses. In addition to that, there are limits on the damages that can be pursued. So right now the private right of action can only be used for compensatory damages and injunctive relief, not for statutory damages, which might remove a lot of the incentives for more speculative litigation.

In addition, you already mentioned the right to cure. There is also an obligation for any plaintiffs before they file suit or even send a demand letter to give notice to the FTC and to State Attorneys General in case either the FTC or State AGs want to bring the enforcement action instead. And there is a 60-day waiting period for that to happen as well.

When you couple that with restrictions the courts have already brought on standing, making it hard for consumer groups and class actions to be filed, there are a lot of protections that I think address the concerns that you have raised, coupled, finally, with the reporting obligation in the bill for the FTC to assess the impact on small businesses.

So, again, what we see here is the hard-fought compromise, but it is one that helps make sure consumers can vindicate their rights in some circumstances while mitigating the risks of abuse against small businesses or extraneous litigation.

The Chair. Thank you.

And, just to clarify, that was a quote. I was asking – I said it was from Ms. Rich, but I appreciate you addressing and answering my question. Thank you.

Ms. Givens. I will take credit for her testimony any time.

The Chair. Thank you, Mr. Chairman. I yield back.

Mr. Bilirakis. I thank the chair. I appreciate it very much.

Next we have Mrs. Trahan. I recognize you for your 5 minutes of questioning.

Mrs. Trahan. Great.

Thank you, Mr. Chairman, Ranking Member Schakowsky, for organizing today's important hearing.

You know, like many of my colleagues on the dais, I am disappointed that we failed to pass the American Data Privacy and Protection Act in the full House last Congress, and I urge my colleagues, particularly those who are new to the committee, to continue working in a bipartisan way to pass a comprehensive privacy law that meets the needs of the families we represent.

Mr. Chairman, the Federal laws that govern our privacy today, in March of 2023, are the same ones that were in place when we had a hearing on holding Big Tech accountable a year ago in March 2022. They are the same laws that were on the books when the CEOs of Google, Meta, and Twitter testified before this same committee a year prior to that in March 2021.

In fact, they are the same laws that for decades have permitted companies to harvest our sensitive data. Things like medical symptoms that we look up on a search engine or our location that paints a picture of where we work, where we send our kids to school, and where we pray, and sell that data to third parties or use it in ways that are contrary to what any of us would reasonably expect.

Many of us have been sounding the alarm about this for a while. In the past 2 years, I have sent inquiries to phone and messaging apps asking about the misuse and sale of messaging metadata to data brokers, about the sale of geolocation data, and to online gaming companies about their treatment of data collected on our teens. These companies can and should be doing better, but without comprehensive privacy legislation like ADPPA, they won't act.

And it doesn't stop there. One type of product I want to highlight the desperate need for an update is education technology. According to a 2021 study from Center For Democracy and Technology, 85 percent of teachers and 74 percent of parents believe EdTech is very important to students' education, and more teachers are becoming aware of the need to thoughtfully consider students' privacy.

However, a majority of parents still have concerns about student privacy, and a significant number of teachers still have not had training on privacy policies and procedures.

So, Ms. Givens, with the Family Educational Rights and Privacy Act, or FERPA, having passed nearly a half century ago, back in 1974, and still being the law of the land when it comes to student data, can you describe to what extent companies that offer EdTech software are or are not covered by FERPA?

Ms. Givens. Thank you for the question and for citing our report.

We spend a lot of time with educators, teachers in the classroom, as well as students and their families, and so we see firsthand the level of concern about how kids' data is being used in this environment.

To answer your question, FERPA applies to personal information from education records that are maintained by covered entities. That basically means public K through 12 schools, colleges, and universities that accept Federal student aid. When EdTech software vendors work with those covered entities, they have to comply with FERPA.

But, really importantly, FERPA falls short in all of the other ways in which EdTech vendors might be engaging and receiving information about students. So, first, it doesn't contemplate harms that might result from other types of information, like when the vendor interacts directly with the student and gathers that type of record.

Second, FERPA doesn't address any of the civil rights issues that can stem from algorithmic harms, as we are seeing increasing use of AI systems deployed in education settings.

And, third, FERPA's enforcement mechanisms fall directly on schools and not on the vendors, and the punishments are draconian. You lose your Federal funding.

We need the burden for privacy compliance to sit not just with the schools, which are so overwhelmed, but with vendors in this space as well. And so complementing FERPA with strong comprehensive privacy protections for those commercial uses of this technology is really important as well.

Mrs. Trahan. Thank you.

You know, in some cases, EdTech software is, as you mentioned, not offered through business to school contracts. Instead, they may be a free online game or an educational app, and the data collected while on these cites or apps can later be used to target ads or sold to third parties, particularly on our students who are 13 and older.

So the idea of consent gets murky, as you mentioned, when we are talking about a student or their parents deciding between participating in class while being tracked versus not participating at all. Can you speak to how the duty of loyalty and data minimization and ADPPA would be applied to these types of sites and apps?

Ms. Givens. You are exactly right. So FERPA only applies to vendors when they are processing education records, which doesn't include many of the many other ways that students are interacting with technology today.

I think about the experience with my own children, and they download apps, not going through those official channels. They are sharing a lot of information, and they are doing it to be able to have an educational experience. Again, this shows why notice and consent is broken as a model because there isn't a question of consent. You want to be able to access these platforms.

And, sadly, COPPA is falling short here, too; although, of course, it does offer some protection to services targeting children under the age of 13. That, too, essentially, rests on the notice and consent regime that is really hard to operationalize in practice.

So that is why we need the broader comprehensive privacy protection is to regulate those additional uses and create baseline protections for students.

Mrs. Trahan. Thank you. Thank you so much for your testimony.

I yield back.

Mr. Bilirakis. Thank you. Thank you very much.

Next we will recognize Dr. Dunn from the great State of Florida.

Mr. Dunn. Thank you very much, Mr. Chairman.

I appreciate the opportunity to discuss the importance of advancing a bipartisan national privacy and data security bill. For years the FTC and the industry has been calling on Congress to enact a uniformed data privacy bill, and it is high time we did that. A national standard will provide all Americans certainty that their data is protected while providing clear rules for the road for businesses to follow.

But I know that this topic is incredibly complex, and it has to be carefully crafted to make sure that we protect Americans without stifling our innovation and our industry. Fortunately, the chairman and the ranking member have assembled a stellar panel of witnesses with outstanding qualifications in just exactly this very difficult area. So we are counting on the three of you to make this happen. No pressure.

During my time on the China Task Force last year, it became clear that the Chinese Communist Party poses a huge threat to the free world. All these digital areas they cheerfully sabotage freedom democracy everywhere they go, and this mentality permeates all of their corporations, including those that operate in America.

Ms. Givens, the Center for Democracy and Technology promotes civil liberties and democratic values in the digital age to help provide context and clarity for our committee. Can you briefly summarize the difference in the civil liberties and the fundamental values in the digital area, you know, between the CCP authoritarian system and our own system?

Ms. Givens. So I will admit that I am not a China expert, and I know that this committee had an important hearing last month that dove even deeper into these issues.

But I will tell you why we fight for privacy legislation as a question of American democracy, and the reason is, when consumers are trying to access information, when they are trying to communicate with their loved ones, when they are trying to find and share information and express themselves, they deserve a right to not be tracked and surveilled with every step, click, and scroll that they take.

People often talk about the right to privacy being the gating item that protects all of our other fundamental rights, our rights to expression, our right to access information, our right to associate with other people, and I deeply believe in that. We need those baseline protections for people to be able to exercise their democratic rights, and that is what makes this bill an important aspect for American values.

Mr. Dunn. I thank you for that.

In your testimony, you highlight the ways that data brokers assign profiles to people based on information they compile from multiple sources. I am concerned, by the way, that CCP could take advantage of this system to build highly individualized profiles on our Americans in general.

What would you say that current threat assessment is of the CCP accessing American citizens' data?

Ms. Givens. Well, the problem with the current digital ecosystem today is that consumers have no idea where that data is going, and it could be accessed by anybody, third parties, foreign intermediaries, foreign entities.

Mr. Dunn. So this is threat level orange or higher?

Ms. Givens. And we need controls on that, and the way to do it is by minimizing the amount of data that companies have and putting restrictions on what data can be shared so that people actually can have confidence that, when they share something, it is not being accessed by those unknown third parties.

Mr. Dunn. Let me ask you another. So the ADPPA would require companies to notify individuals whether or not their data is collected by – and that is whether it is processed and transferred to, stored in any way accessible to China, in addition to a few other concerning countries.

Is this an adequate protection? Or should we be fencing this data just into America alone? I mean, how would we control data once it is outside our borders, whether it is in China or in a great ally like Canada? I mean, how does that happen?

Ms. Givens. Right. So I think the idea of fencing data is incredibly problematic.

It is hard to operationalize. It raises much bigger questions.

Here the regime that you talked about in ADPPA provides notice about when data is being transferred to some particular named countries, but more important than that in my opinion are the data minimization provisions in the bill, which say that, for everyone, let's be careful about how much data is collected in the first place, and then let's impose restrictions on how that data is shared.

And that is the way to help rein in this unfettered sharing and access to information to any type of unknown party, including foreign entities.

Mr. Dunn. Excellent. Excellent.

Mr. Mudd, would you like to comment on the potential benefits of greater transparency by data collection for individuals? And does that represent challenges to the businesses in terms of complying with more transparency requirements?

Mr. Mudd. I think transparency is an important element of the solution, but by no means is it sufficient. I think it is important for consumers to certainly understand and have the access to the data that is collected about them, to control it and so forth, but as we have talked about at length here, it is really important to raise the baseline instead of just putting the work and the burden on consumers to understand the data collected and how they might use it.

Mr. Dunn. Thank you very much for your answers.

Mr. Chairman, thank you very much.

And, Ranking Member, thank you very much for this meeting. I yield.

Mr. Bilirakis. My pleasure. Thank you very much. The questions.

We will recognize now Ms. Kelly from the State of Illinois. You are recognized, ma'am, for 5 minutes.

Ms. Kelly. Thank you, Mr. Chair, and Ranking Member Schakowsky for holding this hearing this morning.

I am encouraged that my colleagues on both sides of the aisle who agree that we must continue working on a national standard for data privacy for American consumers. Although I had hoped to get something in this space done last Congress, as we know, it is never too late to discuss such an important topic impacting all of our constituents' lives.

As we all know, almost everyone uses a smartphone, tablet, or laptop to complete mundane daily tasks to order food, shop online, or simply search the web for entertainment. So I am especially interested in how data practices, which include companies sharing or selling consumer information, can be used to harm Americans.

Ms. Givens, you address this very concern at the top of your witness testimony. Can you explain some of the specific harms resulting from companies and data brokers using, sharing, or selling consumer information?

Ms. Givens. Absolutely. And thank you for the question.

As I outlined in my testimony, there are examples of how data brokers gather all of these different pieces of information across the web to create very detailed profiles on people and to lump them into categories, which is used for targeting of ads and other types of inference-based behavior. When we look at what some of those categories are, you can instantly see what the nefarious harm might be.

Ethnic, second-city dwellers, you know, struggling seniors, this is offensive, but it also is showing why those ads might be targeted to particular vulnerable populations, and that is the type of consumer harm that we need to be careful about, and we really need to try to rein in.

The other part is when ads are being targeted to people based on protected characteristics. That can be race, gender, religious, you know, religious identity, and many other factors or approximations of those factors. And that is another instance where we are seeing live instances of economic and social harm.

Ms. Kelly. Also, I am the founder of the Tech Accountability Caucus, and I want to dig into this issue around data purpose and use limitation. So I am interested in making it easy for consumers to understand when their personal information is being collected, how it is used and when and for what purpose it shared.

So, Ms. Givens, toward that end, in addition to requiring data minimization, do you think it would be beneficial to consumers for a Federal privacy framework to include a provision directing the creation of a list of standardized privacy categories and symbols aimed at providing simple, clear indications to consumers about how their data is being treated?

Ms. Givens. So we need baseline rules about how data can be used, but there also, of course, need to be elements about clarifying notices to consumers. We don't want to rely on notice alone because consumers can't keep up, but we do want consumers to better understand what practices are. And when there are moments to exercise their rights, to agree to a particular instance of data sharing, to be able to do that in an educated way and in an efficient way.

There is language in ADPPA now that talks about what their short form notices are called. That is the term of art in the bill. But I do think that real guidance there about what that looks like, some standardized way of talking about this, perhaps the use of symbols to help people understand particular practices could go a long way in boosting consumer education and, therefore, having consumers feel more empowered.

Ms. Kelly. Thank you.

Lastly, as a Black woman and member of the Congressional Black Caucus, I am deeply concerned with the prevalence of discriminatory digital marketing and advertising. We know companies use different data points to discriminate against consumers and cause real harm.

Ms. Givens, I am going to give you a break.

Mr. Mudd and Ms. Rich, if you could answer this question: Are there certain use limitations, for example, that can curb discrimination and help protect civil rights, especially as it relates to protecting communities of color?

Ms. Rich. Absolutely. And the ADPPA, as you well know, includes antidiscrimination provisions that are remarkably powerful given where we have been in this debate, as well as assessment and auditing provisions to create greater transparency and accountability.

And I would note that many of those provisions – I mean, the FTC has stated that it can reach discrimination, but many of the provisions like accountability, assessment, executive accountability, the restrictions on targeted advertising, the data broker registry, all these things we have been talking about would be very hard for the FTC to reach. Congress needs to do it.

Ms. Kelly. Thank you.

Mr. Mudd. I would agree wholeheartedly. I would say that it is absolutely reasonable and critical for sensitive data, race, gender, sexual orientation and so forth, to be treated very differently from, you know, other types of behavioral data, not just in its use but also its collection and sharing.

Ms. Kelly. Anything you want to quickly throw in? I am running out of time.

Ms. Givens. No. I will let me colleagues do the talking. Thank you.

Ms. Kelly. Thank you so much.

And I yield back my time.

Mr. Bilirakis. Thank you very much.

Next we will recognize the gentlelady from Arizona, my good friend Ms. Lesko.

Mrs. Lesko. Thank you, Mr. Chairman.

And thank you to all the witnesses for being here today.

In-home connectivity has become a major selling point for homeowners, and voice-controlled personal assistance, such as Apple's Siri, Amazon's Alexa, and Google's Google Assistant have been designed to serve as the control center for our homes.

In Google's case, it allows consumers to use their voice to control Smart Home devices around their home that are third-party Smart Home products. This functionality requires specific data sharing between the connected device and the Google Assistant device to carry out a simple command.

Google is making a change in June of this year to how these integrations work which will significantly expand the breadth and frequency of data sharing and increase the rate at which data is collected and transferred to Google for their analysis.

My question to Mr. Mudd: What changes, if any, should be made to the American Data Privacy and Protection Act passed out of the committee last Congress to put consumers in control of data shared through their Smart Home systems?

Mr. Mudd. Thank you, Representative.

I cannot profess to be an expert in Smart Home data collection, but I will say that the collection of data not just online but offline certainly must be in scope for this legislation, and I am happy to get back to you with some suggestions, if helpful, on how the legislation might be improved.

I am also happy to defer to my fellow panelists here.

Mrs. Lesko. And, Ms. Rich, do you have any thoughts on that?

Also, Ms. Rich, should certain types of Smart Home data be subject to higher standards of privacy controls and sharing limits? For example, data about a door lock or a security system?

Ms. Rich. I would have to review the long list of sensitive information detailed in the ADPPA to see if it already captures that, but certainly when there are sensitive categories of information that might be captured by an Internet of Things, technology, those should have special levels of protection.

Certainly, kids' information also should have special levels of protection. Mrs. Lesko. Thank you.

For Ms. Givens, how do we strike the right balance between protecting consumers' data while not creating loopholes for criminals? We have had law enforcement have some concerns about the legislation.

Ms. Givens. Yes. So, to speak to those concerns, the bill as it stands today does not limit law enforcement's ability to pursue its investigations, to access information from companies. I understand there have been some concerns raised that by reining in the sheer extreme volume of data that data brokers are able to gather, that might impede law enforcement's ability to do kind of one-stop shopping and go to those data brokers as a source of resources for their investigations.

I would say on that point we have to reach a balance here, and when we look at the unfettered collection and the additional harms being perpetrated by data brokers, I think that that is an important balance to strike, and we need to weigh those harms.

The bill also includes some really important provisions that already consider law enforcement concerns. So, for example, users' rights to delete their information or to opt out of data brokers' information on them are limited when it might impact a law enforcement investigation. So the committee has already given careful conversation to this. I think they have landed in the right place, and it cannot be that we allow the unfettered, widespread sharing of data purposes just because of this law enforcement concern when law enforcement can still access the vital records that it needs from the first-party holders of that information. For example, credit card companies, et cetera.

Mrs. Lesko. Thank you.

Mr. Mudd, do you believe it is possible to protect personal data while also allowing businesses, especially small businesses, to efficiently digitally advertise? I mean, a number of businesses have been worried that they won't be able to advertise.

Mr. Mudd. Thank you for the question.

Yes, I do. I won't pretend that there is zero cost to business from moving to a more private approach to digital advertising, but I do believe that it will not be and should not be a catastrophic change and that the tradeoff is well worth it.

The technologies that we and others are developing, as I mentioned earlier, are employed in many other industries. They have found ways to complete what they need to do using privacy enhancing technologies, and I think with legislation in place, we can apply the innovation that has currently been focused on extracting data from as many places as possible to instead using it in as private a way as possible.

And so my general answer to your question is, yes, I do believe it is very possible for businesses to thrive with this legislation in place.

Mrs. Lesko. Thank you.

My time has expired, and I yield back. Mr. Bilirakis. I thank the gentlelady.

And I now recognize the gentlelady from Michigan, Mrs. Dingell.

Mrs. Dingell. Thank you, Chairman Bilirakis and Ranking Member Schakowsky for holding this important hearing today and all of you for testifying.

I am hoping that this is going to be the Congress we get this done because this subject is so important. I look forward to this discussion as a continuation of this committee's very strong bipartisan work to enact comprehensive data privacy legislation.

We have got, I think, total agreement that self-regulation is not sufficient and that it has created a multibillion dollar industry through the transfer and sell of consumer data mostly without the consent or knowledge of the consumer.

We want to empower the consumer to be the ultimate arbiter of their data while allowing companies to perform any action that consumers should reasonably expect from the use of a platform device or other technology. Any legislation that this committee supports must protect personally identifiable information, including geolocation, sensitive health data; provide what everybody has talked about today, additional protections for minors and teenagers, who to this day do not have robust protections online; minimize the necessary data captured to perform operations and promote innovation.

This topic is important and has significant ramifications on public health and safety, our economy, national security, and competitiveness. So your being here and our work really matters.

I am going to focus on data and how much is being collected and people not realizing it.

Mr. Mudd, in your testimony you mentioned the significant amount of data companies collect to develop profile of users, which I will respectfully say again nobody has any idea how much is being collected on them.

On average, how many pixels would you estimate that these companies collect on average on one individual? And are there categories of data captured that the user may not have explicitly consented to sharing while using a platform device or being tracked?

Mr. Mudd. Thank you for the question.

In terms of, you know, estimates of the prevalence of pixels and data collection, there are many out there, but, frankly, the scale of the use of these is so large that it is actually quite difficult to study them comprehensibly. I would estimate that there are well over 3- to 400, if not into the thousands of companies that are actually deploying these pixel technologies to collect data.

Now, for the average consumer, as you visit any given website, you are likely to encounter numerous of these. For a given retailer, my estimate would be somewhere on the order of 5 to 15 different pixels that are sharing data with various ad platforms. So, you know, you multiply that by the number of websites that you visit over the course of a week or month, and the ability to collect a very rich profile is certainly there.

Mrs. Dingell. Thank you.

And, by the way, subject to misinterpretation, I always tell the committee I do a lot of my own research before committees. And I was doing opioids and within 2 hours started getting opioid drug addiction treatment ads.

I have only got a minute and forty. So I am going to ask for a yes or no from everybody on the panel. To the panel: Do you believe that, absent a national data privacy law, tech companies and others are incentivized to maximum their collection of data to participate in the digital economy and data marketplace?

Yes or no, Mr. Mudd?

Mr. Mudd. Yes.

Ms. Givens. Yes.

Ms. Rich. Yes.

Mrs. Dingell. Thank you.

As we have seen at events like the Cambridge analytical scandal, data breaches present a very real threat to consumers and companies participating in the data economy.

To the panel, yes or no again: Without a national data privacy law, can companies be expected to enact stringent standards to ensure that consumers' data is secure?

Mr. Mudd. No.

Ms. Rich. No.

Ms. Givens. No.

Mrs. Dingell. I got no from all three.

Last question to the panel again: Yes or no, do you believe that without a national privacy law, the amount of data that these companies acquire presents a risk to consumers and children using the platforms or devices?

Mr. Mudd. Yes.

Ms. Rich. Yes.

Ms. Givens. Yes.

Mrs. Dingell. Thanks again to all of you for being here today.

Robust data protections in this space will provide safety and security for consumers' children, survivors of domestic violence, which I care about a lot, protected classes while offering businesses and industries the expectations, regulations, and the tools necessary to operate, innovate, and also, the most important thing, mitigate risk from dangerous data breaches.

Thank you to all of you for your work.

I yield back, Mr. Chairman, 10 seconds.

Mr. Bilirakis. I appreciate it. Thank you very much. We appreciate that. It all counts.

Next we will have Representative Pence from the State of Indiana. You are recognized for 5 minutes, sir.

Mr. Pence. Thank you, Chairman. Thank you for holding this meeting.

Thank you to the witnesses for being here today.

You know, you are hearing the same thing from everybody because we all feel the same way. Our constituents all feel the same way. I can tell you feel the same, the data privacy.

And, Ms. Givens, when you said that we have had 21 hearings in 5 years, I took all of my comments and I threw them out because I thought, well, here we go again. It is almost like we are just déjà vu, doing the same thing over and over and over.

And Mr. Mudd, in your testimony, which with Ms. Dingell you were making this point again, and I am going to quote, the scale of data collection and transfer using these mechanisms is difficult to comprehend how big, how much data you are collecting from me.

I walked in this morning, and I have a letter from Privacy for America. I don't know anything about them really, but here they say that consumers' incomes have been enhanced to the tune of $30,000 because of all of this data collection. And I think that is great.

So my question gets to the money. I have been a businessman all my life, and if data collectors – and they are sitting in this room – are providing me $30,000 in services, how much are they making to give me that much value?

And since it is incomprehensible the amount of data being taken from me, and I am going to ask you each of this, can I be compensated for this incomprehensible amount of data that is being taken from me? Starting with you, Mr. Mudd.

Mr. Mudd. Sure. Thank you for the question.

Whether users can be directly compensated or not I think certainly is an interesting question, one that has been posed many times in the past and should be further explored.

I will say that the notion that the only way that businesses can leverage digital advertising effectively is through this incomprehensible collection of data is absolutely false and that there are other ways through this problem that do not sacrifice the privacy of individuals and that those technologies, as I have mentioned earlier, are employed elsewhere in a proven fashion.

Mr. Pence. You know, if I can go off on that, I have done a lot of digital advertising in business, okay? And we have thrown out the baby with the bath water when it comes to mail, radio, and TV. And I am not doing an advertisement for the other mediums or the other venues, okay? But I have found that digital advertising for a small business is not very effective.

But back to the same question. Can I make money off my data that everybody has taken from me?

Ms. Givens. Like my colleague, I will say it is an interesting question, but I don't think it gets to the heart of how we protect consumers going forward. But discussions about monetization and compensating users doesn't actually get them the protections they – Mr. Pence. Okay. I can see where you are going with that, Ms. Givens, but if 21 committee hearings in 5 years isn't moving the ball forward and in a sense there is almost a sense of delay, keep talking about the same thing, why wouldn't finding a way to monetize, for me to get paid for my information, why wouldn't that maybe change the trajectory?

Ms. Givens. Well, it is my job to be an optimist, and I think this committee has made progress as a result of those 31 hearings, and we are close.

But what is important and I think what needs to be addressed here is that really, in the advertising world, we have market failure. Right now the only incentive is a race to the bottom, to hyper-target as much as you can.

And for the digital advertising companies that offer the most specific profiles on people, they are the ones that win the race, and there is no incentive for them to innovate into privacy-protecting ways of delivering ads that matter. That is the innovation we want to encourage.

Mr. Pence. Thank you.

And I will move on to the last witness.

You know, if I get to opt in because I will get paid for it, maybe that will change their behavior, too.

Okay. And then, finally, last witness?

Ms. Rich. Oh, you are asking me?

Mr. Pence. Yes, ma'am.

Ms. Rich. You are asking me the same question?

Mr. Pence. Yes, Ms. Rich.

Ms. Rich. Well, one of the problems with that idea of an even exchange is that it hasn't worked in terms of notice and choice where consumers have to individually, you know, supposedly negotiate with each company. So I think it is putting the burden – Mr. Pence. Well, I was in the banking industry, and we had Truth in Lending where you had to make it real simple what you were agreeing to when you clicked "yes." But, with that, I have run out of time. Mr. Chair, I yield back.

Mr. Bilirakis. I appreciate that very much.

Now we will have the gentlelady, my good friend, from the Tampa Bay area, Representative Castor. We will recognize her for her five minutes.

Ms. Castor. Well, thank you, Mr. Chairman and my good friend.

And thanks to the ranking member.

And, to the witnesses, thank you. You have been very strong and have provided very clear expert advice to the committee. We need it.

This is really our kick start to our privacy effort, this session, and it is heartening to understand that it is a priority for us across the aisle here.

I was very proud to contribute to the committee's efforts in the last Congress for the American Data Privacy and Protection Act, particularly the provisions relating to children's online safety because ADPPA included elements of my Kids PRIVCY, such as the targeted advertising ban, age-appropriate design provisions, enhanced limitation on sharing children's personal information with third parties, special protections for personally identifiable information about children, a dedicated youth and privacy in marketing division at the FTC, and increase oversight of COPPA safe harbors.

I really urge my colleagues to act with urgency here. The harms to kids online are now very clear, and we really shouldn't take too much longer to act. We need to do this for all Americans, but I think there is a special threat to children's online privacy and safety.

The Children's Online Privacy Protection Act, COPPA, is wholly outdated. It has been many years since the Congress has acted. Can you all take a look at that, at what has happened since the adoption of COPPA and give us some examples of what you see as a growing online harm to children and all Americans?

Ms. Rich. Well, for one thing, COPPA is limited to children under 13, and as this committee and other work done in other committees has shown, there were a lot of harms at least to people who are, you know, under 16 or 17. You could go higher, too, but all the things we have seen with social media. So, if this committee and the public is seeking greater protections for teens, COPPA doesn't do it.

COPPA also is very basic, and the FTC, even in the 2013 rule review, which was the last one, did summersaults to try to get at the platforms, to try to protect information that wasn't listed in the original COPPA statute, like location data and IP addresses. And so it absolutely needs to be updated to reflect what has happened since COPPA was passed in 1998.

Ms. Castor. And you highlighted the fact that the FTC hasn't been using some of its tools. Now, in response to language I offered in the fiscal year 2022 omnibus, the FTC published a report providing details about its work on COPPA. In that report, the FTC stated that the Commission dedicates approximately 9 to 11 staff and has opened 80 investigations of potential COPPA violations in the past 5 years.

That is woefully inadequate, and even the FTC says as much in the conclusion of their report. They stated: With more resources, however, the FTC could do more.

And we need them to do more.

Do you think the FTC should have more resources and authority to protect kids online?

Ms. Rich. Absolutely. It is shocking how few resources the FTC has for privacy.

It is a fairly large proportion of the consumer protection mission, but it is about 50 dedicated people to privacy, which if you consider that to other countries that are much smaller and the kind of staff they have to police privacy, it is just woefully inadequate.

The FTC absolutely needs more resources, but it also needs more authority because the authority is thin.

Ms. Castor. Ms. Givens?

Ms. Givens. The one point I would add on the FTC resources is that all of the research shows that it is an excellent investment of taxpayer dollars. The Congressional Budget Office has shown that for every dollar invested in the FTC, taxpayers get $3 in return because of the enforcement power that it would add to the agency.

So I think it is incredibly important when we think not only about protecting consumers but good governance as well.

Ms. Castor. I want to thank – my time is running out. I want to be sure that I take time to thank Ranking Member Schakowsky for being a leader on giving the FTC more resources to protect consumers, and I hope we will continue this Congress.

And I want to thank the chair, Ms. McMorris Rodgers. I heard her clarion call at the beginning of this hearing loud and clear, and I appreciate her outreach to my office, and we are going to continue working to make ADPPA strong for all consumers, especially our kids.

Thanks. I yield back.

Mr. Bilirakis. I thank the gentlelady.

Now I recognize the gentleman from the State of Georgia. Mr. Allen, you are recognized for 5 minutes, sir.

Mr. Allen. Thank you, Mr. Chairman and Ranking Member for holding this hearing on the need for a national privacy standard.

I think today we are getting closer than ever to enacting some type of nationwide privacy and data security framework, which will give businesses the certainty they need to innovate while providing Americans more control over their data.

I appreciate the hard work done by Chair Rogers and Ranking Member Pallone last Congress to get to this point, and I look forward in engaging and getting this done in this Congress.

Mr. Mudd, as a former employee of Meta and now as chief product officer of Anonym, you have seen both sides of the advertising ecosystem. Kind of help us understand exactly how they make the money that they make in using our information.

Mr. Mudd. Certainly.

So the collection of data I described earlier, you know, it is based on your behavior on websites and often is then shared with the ad platform that any given advertiser is using to find their customers.

Now, how do those ad platforms make money using that data? I think that was your question.

Well, effectively, the better the ads work, that is, the more effective they are in identifying specific individuals who are likely to be customers of any given company, the more those ad platforms can charge for those ads. And so their incentive, of course, is to improve the relevance of the advertising. Nothing wrong with that incentive in and of itself. It is the means by which they do it that we have talked about that is oftentimes very problematic.

And so that incentive challenge, gather more data to become more relevant in order to charge higher prices for ads, is at really the heart of the vicious cycle that we are faced with today.

Mr. Allen. Yes, and as I see it, there is certain information that, obviously, I just want maybe me and my family to know about me, and they like to get that information. Does it bring the highest price?

Mr. Mudd. It is a good question. You know, the value of data, you know, is certainly, you know, variable based on who the advertiser is, right. Location data is very important to an offline retailer who wants to find customers that are near their outlet whereas healthcare data is very valuable to different types of advertisers.

Mr. Allen. What role do the data brokers play in this?

Mr. Mudd. Data brokers oftentimes enrich, as the term of art is called, the profiles of ad platforms that might not be able to collect that information themselves.

So to give an example, maybe a newspaper site doesn't have any real insight into, you know, your financial history and so forth, but they would love to be able to sell advertising to credit card companies. And so they go to the data broker, buy that data about your financial situation, and, therefore, can sell to a credit card company more effective advertising.

Mr. Allen. And any idea how much this information is being held and used by data brokers?

Mr. Mudd. I don't know that I could find a way to quantify that for you. All I can say, as I said earlier, is that it is incomprehensible to any ordinary citizen, and the scale is quite massive.

Mr. Allen. Well, you know, my State has been ranked as the number one State to do business in, in the last 10 years, and in my younger days, I started a company, a small business, and I was a small business owner until I was elected to Congress.

I know a lot of small companies can unintentionally bear the brunt of regulations if protections aren't carefully crafted. How can companies like yours enable small businesses without sacrificing the privacy of consumers?

Mr. Mudd. Thank you for the question.

I think there are a number of ways. First of all, I would say that we want to encourage competition in the digital advertising ecosystem, and to do that, what we need to do is level the playing field so that smaller publishers and ad platforms can compete with the largest ones more effectively.

By enacting legislation like ADPPA, we take a meaningful step forward in making the digital advertising ecosystem I believe more competitive, which will serve small businesses in providing them more options for promoting their business, you know, and competing with larger businesses.

Mr. Allen. And, Ms. Rich, I have got 21 seconds, but why is it essential that any data privacy law protect all Americans regardless of age?

Ms. Rich. Because all Americans, regardless of age, need privacy protections and haven't had it.

And, by the way, it hasn't been 31 hearings. It has probably been several hundred since I have been participating in this debate.

In addition to the kids' provisions, though, the ADPPA would provide – not only would it provide targeted protections for kids of the kind that we have already talked about, but even the adult, even the general provisions – data minimization, data security, privacy by design – would also protect kids, which is why we need to do it all together.

Mr. Allen. Thank you.

And I yield back.

Mr. Bilirakis. Thank you very much. I appreciate it.

Now I will recognize Ms. Clarke from the State of New York for her 5 minutes of questioning. Thank you.

Ms. Clarke. I thank you very much, Mr. Chairman, and I thank our Ranking Member Schakowsky for holding this very important hearing.

I also want to thank our witnesses for testifying here today. You have really enriched the debate and conversation in this space.

I was encouraged that major pieces of my bill, the Algorithmic Accountability Act, were included in the ADPPA that this committee marked up last year. I hope to continue working with members on this committee to ensure any national data privacy standard requires algorithmic transparency and risk mitigation.

AI systems are often trained on the datasets that replicate human biases, and, thus, bias is built into the technology itself. I am concerned that, without proper transparency and explicit steps to mitigate against bias, the use of artificial intelligence and critical decisions could erode essential civil rights protections in the digital realm.

Discrimination, whether done by a person or an algorithm, cannot and must not be tolerated.

Ms. Givens, in your testimony, you highlighted how AI and automated decisionmaking is already used in a wide range of decisions like employment, lending, and tenant screening. Could you elaborate on why requiring transparency with algorithmic use and algorithmic impact assessments are a critical part of comprehensive consumer data privacy legislation?

Ms. Givens. I can. And I have to start by thanking you for your incredible leadership on these issues over the past few years, really shining a light on these concerns and how we can move forward to address them.

Tools that use algorithmic decisionmaking are increasingly being used in ways that significantly impact people's lives. To give just one example in the employment context, we are seeing the increasing use of vendor-created tools to screen resumes, to conduct video-based interviews and analyze those interviews, to have people play online games.

And the way in which these are AI-driven is that those tests are automatically looking for traits that match the traits of existing people in the company, which is an automatic recipe for perpetuating existing systems of discrimination and also raise questions about fitness for purpose in the first place. Are you actually measuring things that really are indicative of someone's likelihood to succeed on the job?

And there has been important research done in the field to show that often these tools actually are not fit for purpose. One of the most notorious examples analyzed an AI resume tool where there was weighted factors in favor of a candidate if their name was Jared and if they had played lacrosse in either high school or college.

The reason this matters is not just for the employees who are being screened out but also for the businesses that are relying on these tools based on commitments from vendors that they have been screened, that they are appropriately designed, and they are bias free.

How can businesses actually trust that these tools are doing what the vendors say they do and that they are complying with existing law?

So transparency really matters, and what ADPPA does, lifting many of the important provisions from your legislation on this issue, is say we need to have companies, number one, disclose how these tools work, what data they are based on, do it in a way that protects trade secrets and doesn't overwhelm but analyze this, and the company's need to show they have gone through a rigorous internal process of detecting potential bias and assessing fitness for purpose.

The reason that matters is that we need to inculcate a company culture of asking those questions before we put these tools out into the world, and that is what ADPPA will help do.

Ms. Clarke. Well, thank you. As a member of the Committee on Homeland Security, I am particularly concerned with what can happen when companies collecting our sensitive information are not adequately protecting that information.

Ms. Givens, if companies are largely free to collect, possess, and transfer user data that is not necessary to provide a specific product or service, does that increase the risk or a consequence of a data breach?

Ms. Givens. It does absolutely, because without those purpose limitations or minimization requirements, it leads to the unfettered sharing of additional information solely for the purposes of helping to target ads, and that is what leads to these massive data sets that can be so vulnerable to abuse.

Ms. Clarke. Thank you.

Ms. Rich, how would you – how would a comprehensive national policy framework increase the FTC's ability to protect the American public from data breaches?

Ms. Rich. Oh, there are so many ways. First of all, there are the data security provisions in the order that would require data security to protect the data, but also many of the core provisions would serve the same function – data minimization. So many data breaches happen to data that is sitting there and shouldn't be. And same with protections for sensitive information. If people can prevent their sensitive information from being overcollected and stored, it is less likely to be breached.

So there are so many ways in which this helps the FTC and, you know, not even – in addition to giving them civil penalty authority, which they do not have for first-time violators to increase deterrence.

Ms. Clarke. Mr. Chairman, I thank you, and I yield back.

Mr. Bilirakis. Thank you so very much.

Okay. Now what we will do is we have votes on the floor, and we will recess and come back 10 minutes after the final vote, because I have several members on our side, on the Republican side, that haven't had the opportunity to ask questions, whether it is sitting on the committee, but we have had several that have waived on as well. And I really think we need to give them an opportunity.

I appreciate the witnesses for their patience. Thank you so much. So we will go ahead and – without objection, we will recess. [Recess.]

* * *

Mr. Bilirakis. All right. The meeting will come to order.

I want to thank y'all. I thank the witnesses. Y'all were outstanding, by the way, okay, and the consensus is really good for us to know that we – I mean, we knew it anyhow, but to know that we passed a good bill last session and we can improve upon it, and y'all are contributing factors, there is no question.

So why don't I recognize my good friend from east Tennessee, Ms. Harshbarger, who is our – what is it, the – yeah, the youngest pharmacist.

Mrs. Harshbarger. Yeah.

Mr. Bilirakis. The youngest pharmacist on the committee.

Mrs. Harshbarger. Youngest. Buddy can still claim the oldest.

Mr. Bilirakis. Recognize you for 5 minutes.

Mrs. Harshbarger. Thank you, sir. Thank you, Mr. Chairman. Thank you for the witnesses.

My first question, sir, is for Mr. Mudd. One of the reasons that America has such a robust economy is because startups are able to establish themselves in the marketplace. What safeguards should authors of the Federal privacy legislation build in specifically for the protection of the small and medium sized businesses?

Mr. Mudd. Thank you for the question. You know, I do believe, and I am no expert, that there are some provisions that safeguard the, you know, smaller businesses and their use of data, and I think those are very much appropriate. I would say that it is – it is important to level the playing field between smaller companies that are trying to establish a publishing presence and an advertising business online and the very large ones. And I think this bill goes a long way towards leveling that playing field and raising the bar across the board so that it is not just the largest tech companies that have access to the data that is so powerful in advertising business and that have such an incumbent advantage.

Mrs. Harshbarger. Okay. Very good. That kind of leads me into my next question. You know, I am thrilled we are working to draft a privacy framework that appropriately balances data privacy for our constituents while also helping businesses receive more clarity about the rules of the road. Black and white clarity of what is and isn't permissible is especially important for these small and medium sized businesses who don't have dedicated compliance departments and lack the resources to survive endless lawsuits from predatory attorneys.

And I can say that because I have been a small business owner of independent pharmacies for over 30 years and, believe me, I know that it is incredibly difficult to navigate the rules, the privacy rules, the data rules, the healthcare rules, from State to State. And then you have to outsource that to be compliant to somebody who knows the rules and, therefore, you run the risk of having that data compromised and used.

You know, healthcare fraud is very prevalent, as you mentioned.

My question is: What can be done to ensure there is clarity for all these businesses to thrive under a Federal privacy framework? And I will open that up to all three of you, whoever wants to go first.

Mr. Mudd. I will mention one thing and then I will pass it to my colleagues here, and that is just that I think a State-by-State patchwork is particularly onerous to small businesses who are trying to comply with different rules, as you mentioned, and that even just establishing a single benchmark and compliance program would go a long way toward supporting small business and innovation.

Ms. Givens. In addition, the ADPPA has a number of protections to help small businesses. So some provisions don't apply to small businesses or they have a lesser burden. For example, access rights for users to access and understand the data that is held about them, and the private right of action as well. So small businesses are shielded from that.

In addition, there are provisions like making sure the FTC provides a business resource center to help businesses actually comply and understand their obligations, which is really important, as well as some of the other provisions to address these concerns about excessive litigation or runaway litigation. There are limits on the damages provisions that can be sought. There is this notice and cure opportunity that the chair was talking about. So other more measures to make sure the consumers can vindicate their rights, which is so important and what Congress is focused on, while also making sure that businesses aren't overly burdened.

Mrs. Harshbarger. Okay. Very good.

Ms. Rich. I would add one thing to what my splendid co-panelists have just said, which is what we discussed with Chair Bilirakis, which is the compliance programs. If you have a rigorous compliance program and small and medium businesses can join and get some certainty and help in their compliance, it benefits everybody.

Mrs. Harshbarger. Exactly. I keyed in on that point when you were talking previously.

I guess another question – and this will be to each one of you too – can you think of an example of an unintended consequence with a Federal privacy legislation?

And I say that because, you know, when you poll this across the country, across businesses, across citizens, they want one policy so it is easy to navigate. But would there be any unintended consequences for businesses or individuals?

Ms. Givens. So I will chime in that States have a really important and legitimate role in protecting their citizens, and we need to make sure that at the same time it is fighting for consistency for businesses and how they think about consumer privacy. We are not infringing on States' rights to protect their citizens and the values that they care about. And thinking about things like consumer protection laws of general applicability, civil rights laws.

A number of States have been really important first movers on things like child exploitation online, antispam laws, data breach notification laws which are in place in all States around the country. And people have gotten used to those. They have been on the books for a long time, and States have played a really important role. So we need to strike a balance here of creating that certainty for businesses but still allowing the States to provide that traditional function they have had of protecting their citizens, and that is the balance the ADPPA is trying to strike.

Mrs. Harshbarger. Anybody else?

Ms. Rich. I will just quickly add research. We need to incentivize research using data, and the ADPPA does it while also having protections. So that is very important.

Mrs. Harshbarger. Yes, ma'am. I agree. Well, with that – go ahead, sir.

Mr. Mudd. Oh, the only thing I would add to that is I do think a potential unintended consequence of a privacy law is to constrain, you know, unnecessarily at least, the use of data for very productive reasons by small businesses. And so I think technology, again, can really help to bridge that gap, but it would be all the more helpful if, to the degree possible, the law is very clear about what does constitute reasonable privacy and what doesn't, so that technology companies know how to, you know, sort of navigate the solution.

Mrs. Harshbarger. Absolutely. That goes back to clarity.

Mr. Mudd. That is right.

Mrs. Harshbarger. Thank you. And, with that, I yield back, sir.

Mr. Bilirakis. Thank you. The gentlelady yields back.

No one on Democrat side, so we will recognize the gentlelady that represents Gator Nation, Ms. Cammack, who is a great friend of mine.

Mrs. Cammack. Thank you, Mr. Chairman. And, yes, we do represent the Gator Nation, home to one of the best damn football teams in all of the Nation, as well as a wonderful research institution.

So, Mr. Chairman, thank you for your support, not just of the Gator Nation, but of this issue. I think it is critically important that we address this issue, and I feel like we have hit on all of the topics really in some way or another.

So I do want to give you all the opportunity to narrow in on something that hasn't been addressed here yet today. But before I do, while you are thinking of that, I would like to ask you guys, particularly when we are seeing Federal agencies collect data from various companies and then using that data in ways that may or may not – I am not going to say ethical, but there is a bit of a gray area in how that data is being used, what are some of the national security implications for that data collection and then the subsequent breaches that we have seen?

And I will start with you, Ms. Rich, and then we will go down the line.

Ms. Rich. Well, there are so many ways this has international implications.

That is a big piece of this. For one thing – well – for one thing, you know, U.S. companies are having serious problems in Europe, because Europe believes that the U.S. doesn't have strong enough laws. It affects trade. It affects companies' ability to process European data. And then, in the U.S., because they are not allowed to transfer it, which creates a lot of inefficiencies. So that is a serious trade and credibility issue we have.

As we deal with issues of hacking and surveillance from other countries, there is – not only is the data exposed, but we have very little credibility as we deal with those other countries. And, you know, it comes up, you know, in the TikTok situation, people talking about banning TikTok. Well, I think we would have more credibility talking about that if we had a privacy law of our own. And then there is the costs of disproportionate costs on U.S. companies of complying with multiple laws.

Mrs. Cammack. And I appreciate it. I want to make sure to give Ms. Givens and Mr. Mudd an opportunity as well, as quickly as you can.

Ms. Givens. So I agree with my colleague, and I do think the biggest risk to all of this is the unfettered collection, storage, and sharing of data. And that creates cybersecurity risks. It creates national security risks. And so that is why we have to pursue a framework that minimizes the amount of data that companies are collecting and storing and puts limits on how they can share that information.

Mrs. Cammack. Mr. Mudd?

Mr. Mudd. Very much agree with that. And, you know, in the tech world, we call that surface area, right? The more the data is out there, the bigger the risk, right? Data is intimately replicable and can be stored, you know, forever. And so to the degree that we are able to limit it through technology, through regulation, then we reduce the risk, national security and otherwise.

Mrs. Cammack. Do you think that we should require or have a way to incentivize that data servers be housed here in the United States as part of the national security framework when we are talking about housing our data, Ms. Givens?

Ms. Givens. I think that gets you into risky territory really quickly, and part of the reason is we need the global flow of information around the world. It is how the global internet functions. It is how we are able to communicate and do business with other nations. It is the way in which the U.S. is being a leader, and innovation around the world is through that free flow of information.

So instead of just throwing up firewalls, what we need is strong data protections across the board to make sure that everyone is following the same rules, as opposed to having to impose these really hard to enforce laws on data localization.

Mrs. Cammack. Something that I haven't heard yet today is the emergence of AI, ChatGPT, how AI is going to essentially revolutionize the data collection models, and what are some of the implications of using AI with some of these algorithms and these platforms? We can go down the line, and then I will open it to you in the 1 minute and 7 seconds that I have left.

Ms. Rich.

Ms. Rich. One implication is this is an area where technology has become so sophisticated, and the FTC laws, basic laws, can't get at it in the way they were able to get at issues earlier.

Mrs. Cammack. Thank you.

Ms. Givens. Congress is going to be grappling with this issue for a long time as AI transforms our society. One of the first things we need to do is just get a handle on which companies are using these tools and making sure that they are going through a responsible process when they are deciding how to design them and how to deploy them to impact assessments. And that is one of the provisions in the ADPPA and why it matters.

Mrs. Cammack. Excellent. Thank you.

Mr. Mudd.

Mr. Mudd. Would make two points. First, that regulating the use is really important, as Ms. Rich mentioned, and flexibility to adapt, you know, to further use cases along the way is really important. The second is I think that explicit bias detection can play a really meaningful role in this. And then the last would just be around transparency, right, understanding when AI is used and so consumers have some understanding of the end result.

Mrs. Cammack. Excellent. My time has expired, so I will have to yield back, so sorry.

Mr. Bilirakis. I thank the gentlelady.

Mrs. Cammack. Maybe Mr. Obernolte will give you a few moments. Thank you.

I yield back.

Mr. Bilirakis. Okay. Very good. Now we will recognize – there is no Democrat. They are all getting ready for their issues conference. So we are going to go with Representative Armstrong, the vice chair of the full committee, from the great State of North Dakota.

You are recognized for 5 minutes.

Mr. Armstrong. Thank you, Mr. Chairman.

And before we had to recess, Ms. Givens, you had an interaction with Congresswoman Lesko, and you talked about the balance of law enforcement and primary source versus secondary source data. I think it is important to point out the biggest difference, at least in most cases, between secondary source data and primary source data, one requires a warrant, one doesn't. And I personally think the privacy portion of this is a feature, not a buck.

Are you familiar with the September 26, 2022, letter to the House from various law enforcement associations expressing concern with potential data privacy legislation? There is a quote that it has major negative consequences that would make it harder to investigate criminal activity.

Ms. Givens. Not the specifics of that letter, but I am with the general set of issues raised.

Mr. Armstrong. Well, the letter continues and it says: will likely complicate the private sector's ability to continue its ongoing efforts to cooperate and voluntarily share certain information with law enforcement.

Essentially, the letter addresses the warrantless purchase of consumer data from brokers to generate investigatory leads.

Are you familiar with the Center for Democracy and Technology report from December of 2021?

Ms. Givens. I am. My team and colleagues wrote it.

Mr. Armstrong. Legal Loopholes and Data for Dollars: How Law Enforcement and Intelligence Agencies Are Buying Your Data from Brokers.

Would you mind briefly summarizing the general conclusion of that document?

I will let you weigh in too, Mr. Mudd, because you have been pretty fired up about some of this stuff.

Ms. Givens. So yes, one of the major concerns about data brokers is that they aggregate these vast amounts of information. And in addition to selling it to target ads, it does become a target for law enforcement. And law enforcement is able to buy that data on the open market, like any other person, and in doing so, circumvent their Fourth Amendment obligations.

So CDT and other civil society organizations have been vocal in raising the constitutional concerns that that raises and the protections for people's freedoms and civil liberties. We are not saying that law enforcement work shouldn't happen – of course it should – but it needs to be subject to reasonable oversight in the constraints of the Constitution and the law.

Mr. Armstrong. Well, I want to be perfectly clear. Law enforcement should use every tool. Good law enforcement officers are going to use every single tool that exists for them to solve crimes, to do all of those things. It is our job to set the guardrails on this, and it is the Federal Government's job to set the guardrails on this, because it actually implicates what I think is maybe the most existential conversation of the 21st century and what the actual right to privacy means as we continue to move forward.

The report cites DOJ's use of commercially aggregated data for prosecutions related to January 6th. Grand jury information states location data history for thousands of devices were present inside the Capitol, were essentially obtained from several sources.

I was at the Capitol that day. I was performing a constitutionally and statutory mandated function. You think DOJ had access to my data?

Ms. Givens. Sir, I wouldn't want to speculate on a particular fact pattern, but –

Mr. Armstrong. I think they did, so – Ms. Givens, hundreds of journalists were at the Capitol that day. They were performing activities expressly protected by the First Amendment. And you wouldn't want to speculate, but that information existed as well. And I am more than willing to guess that locator systems and toll records were collected from around the beltway. There are lots of other commercially available data that was probably accessed.

Mr. Mudd, are you familiar with the majority in U.S. v. Carpenter?

Mr. Mudd. I am not.

Mr. Armstrong. Okay.

Ms. Rich, are you?

Ms. Rich. Yes.

Mr. Armstrong. So the time-stamped data referring to cell site location information provides an intimate window into a person's life, revealing familial, political, professional, religious, and sexual associations. And I think the court has – this particular court, and even the previous iteration of the court, has been willing to reexamine what privacy looks like in the form of the government in the digital age. And we have talked a lot about data collection and data brokers. And I think I will just be more blunt really quickly.

Data brokers say this will put them out of business, which means, not only will law enforcement not have access to this, but other people won't. But I think we don't spend enough time talking about – I mean, data collection is just the first part. Representative Cammack just talked about AI, talked about all this. The ability to analyze that data in real time is advancing at an incredibly rapid rate, which makes it very much different than having a drug dog search a box at a post office.

And how do we deal with this and continue towards constitutionally protected activity when the Federal Government has what I think is an incred – all law enforcement has this end-run around the Fourth Amendment by being able to purchase this data on the civilian market?

Ms. Rich. That is exactly right. If our rights exist for a certain reason, you shouldn't be able to just go to another company and get the same data and not abide by those rights. It is an end-run. That is exactly what it is.

Mr. Armstrong. With that, I will yield back. And I apologize to Mr. Mudd. I kind of wasn't totally honest with him.

Mr. Bilirakis. Thank you. The gentleman yields back.

No one on the Democratic side. So we will recognize Representative Fulcher for his 5 minutes, from the great State of – right, Idaho?

Mr. Fulcher. Idaho, yes. Thank you, Mr. Chairman.

And to our panelists, thank you for your participation today and for your testimonies. And as I have said in previous sessions, please understand that some of us have dueling responsibilities, and so the fact that we are not here the entire time doesn't mean we don't care what you have to say. To the contrary, very much so, and for your written testimony as well.

I want to focus on two things, and I am going to ask Ms. Rich to start this, please. Transparency and algorithms and what those relay, what those do is something I am very interested in. I think that there needs to be some exposing of that and some increased improved transparency.

My question for you: Is it possible to have transparency without exposing secrets necessary to operate a business?

Ms. Rich. Are you referring to the algorithms?

Mr. Fulcher. I am referring to the algorithms used.

Ms. Rich. Yes. Assessments. Yes.

Mr. Fulcher. Yes. And expand on that if you would, please.

Ms. Rich. So the FTC can seek a lot of information right now that would be used to create those assessments. The assessments, though, create even more transparency so that an agency can look to see if laws are being violated and being adhered to. The FTC already has a model for this, because in all of its data security orders and its investigations too, it gets very, very sensitive information and even audits in those orders, which it evaluates. So it can do this, and there are procedures for protecting trade secrets and keeping the confidential information in those reports private. There is extensive confidentiality procedures.

Mr. Fulcher. If I could ask you to take that same analysis and direct it towards, what about the end user of that information, of that – you are talking about the FTC, I think.

Ms. Rich. Yeah.

Mr. Fulcher. What about for the transparency by the user?

Ms. Rich. I think that is more difficult because I am not sure that consumers are really going to understand all the details disclosed about algorithms. The information that the FTC gets is probably pretty complex and they need technologists to help them evaluate it and figure out whether discrimination is going on. So while there could be some mechanisms for explaining the algorithms to consumers, I am not sure we would want to give it to them. I don't think it would mean much, and it would be very difficult then to protect it.

Mr. Fulcher. My personal concern is the use of the data, who owns that data, how that data gets used. Mr. Mudd has talked about that. I caught a piece of that. I am going to do a follow-up question with him. But that is – this is a big complicated issue.

And so one followup to you, if I may. Is the FTC the best entity to be the regulator of that, the monitor of that?

Ms. Rich. Yes, it is the most experienced, but it would need to get help. It needs more technologists. It needs more resources if it is going to be evaluating algorithms.

Mr. Fulcher. Statutory changes as well?

Ms. Rich. Excuse me?

Mr. Fulcher. Statutory changes as well?

Ms. Rich. It totally needs statutory changes. It needs the ADPPA or something like it.

Mr. Fulcher. Okay.

Ms. Givens. Mr. Fulcher, if I may, there are provisions in the ADPPA that protects trade secrets. And so the vision is that those impact assessments are performed by companies, submitted to the FTC, that can then look further into them if they want to. Disclosure to the public is optional by a company, and there is specific language in there to protect trade secrets while still making sure companies are going through that assessment process of really making sure they are being honest and thoughtful about the – Mr. Fulcher. In your opinion, is that language sufficient?

Ms. Givens. Yes, I think it is well drafted.

Mr. Fulcher. All right. Thank you.

Mr. Mudd, shifting gears a little bit. I want to talk about GDPR. Maybe I am not shifting gears all that much.

My perception of what has transpired in Europe over that is that it has been helpful to large companies, not so helpful to small companies.

First of all, is that your perception as well? And secondly – we have only got about 50 seconds left – is – what is the primary component or components that need to be different when we embark on that path?

Mr. Mudd. Sure. My perception matches yours, that it has likely been more – easier for larger business to adjust to that regulation and to comply with it, and therefore probably more difficult for smaller businesses.

In terms of what we got to learn from GDPR and potentially do differently, I think one of the challenges with GDPR, putting my sort of consumer hat on, is that it really does put a lot of work on the consumer to read and understand many, many, many consent dialogues. And instead, I would hope that we can find a way to sort of raise the bar, as we have talked about, instead of asking consumers to navigate very difficult choices, in some cases no choice at all, if they want to access content.

Mr. Fulcher. So the answer is get rid of the complexity?

Mr. Mudd. I think reduce complexity, but more importantly, focus on data minimization and technologies that support that, as opposed to asking consumers to say yes or no to answers they have very little understanding of.

Mr. Fulcher. Okay. Thank you.

Mr. Chairman, I yield back.

Mr. Bilirakis. Thank you very much. I appreciate that.

Now we will recognize – he waived onto the committee, appreciate it, one of the hardest workers in Congress. I am not even going to mention the pharmacy thing. It has been overblown.

Mr. Carter. Thank you.

Mr. Bilirakis. Yeah, I am not going to do that. But in any case, I will yield 5 minutes to my friend from the State of Georgia.

Mr. Carter. Thank you, Mr. Chairman, and thank you for having this hearing.

And thank y'all for being here. As was indicated, I am pharmacist. I am not an IT technician, but I will tell you I am a consumer, and I am concerned. And, you know, I have experienced it myself. I have experienced – I have a truck. I have got a Toyota Tundra, 478,000 miles on it, and I am going to get to 500, I am sure.

But, you know, I had a cover on the back and it dry-rotted, and I needed to get a replacement for it. And I just searched for it, and then all of a sudden, I started getting all these ads for this. And I thought, how in the world? So it is real. This is real and this is something – and this is why I wanted to waive on, because this is so vitally important to us. And it is just fascinating to me because I know we need to do something, but I want to do the right thing. I don't want to suppress freedom of speech. I don't want to suppress innovation. But when you don't do something, you are doing something. And if we don't do something, then we are going to be in a mess.

Mr. Chairman, to begin with, according to the Information Technology and Innovation Foundation, over the next 10 years, it is estimated that the growing patchwork of State privacy laws that we are experiencing will cost over a trillion dollars, with at least $200 billion hitting small businesses. And I know about small businesses because I ran one for 32 years. So I am – I do have some expertise there.

But, Mr. Chairman, I would like to ask unanimous consent to include this report from the ITIF in the record.

Mr. Bilirakis. Without objection, so ordered. [The information follows in the submitted files as a report entitled "The Looming Cost of a Patchwork of State Privacy Laws";]

Mr. Carter. Okay. Ms. Rich, I want to start with you and get right to it.

Mr. Bilirakis hit on this earlier in the hearing, but the FTC rulemaking won't be preempting the five States with the enacted laws, nor any succeeding legislation. So I agree with you, we, this committee, we have the responsibility to pass a national standard, and that is going to be extremely important.

But I want to dig into the FTC rulemaking a little bit more. I understand there is a difference between the FTC's APA rulemaking authority and their Mag-Moss rulemaking authority. I have heard there may not be legal authority for the FTC to do their own privacy rule under Mag-Moss, but their authority is pretty clear-cut.

Can you put on your FTC expertise hat right now and give us your thoughts on whether they have a legal standing to promulgate this rule?

Ms. Rich. Yes. And thanks for the question. So the FTC Act explicitly authorizes the FTC to develop rules under this so-called Mag-Moss process to hold and remedy unfair deceptive practices. It even tells the FTC what process to use. And the FTC has used Mag-Moss to develop other rules. So I think the FTC is on pretty solid ground, generally, doing rulemaking using this tool. The problem is it is very cumbersome, and it is limited so that, you know, given the breadth and significance of the privacy issues here, the FTC may not – can't do so much of what is in the law that you guys have been, you know, writing and grappling with.

Mr. Carter. Absolutely. Absolutely. Even more reason why we need to pass a national standard.

Ms. Rich. Yes.

Mr. Carter. Mr. Mudd, I want to go to you. In your opinion, do you think overly restrictive rules that stymy innovation – because I am concerned about freedom of speech. I am concerned about stymying innovation as well. I don't want to do that. The internet is one of the greatest inventions of our lifetime. I get it. And I understand that, but at the same time, as I said earlier, if we don't do something, you are doing something. You know, we have got to address this. And it is incumbent upon us, us here in Congress. That is our responsibility, and we are responsible people. I know that some people would disagree with that, but I don't. We are. We need to do something.

But just let me ask you, do you think that overly restricted rules that would stymy innovation and the data-driven economy harm America's competitiveness with respect to our global competitors?

Mr. Mudd. I think there is potential, but I don't believe the ADPPA will have that effect. I believe that what technology companies big and small need is clarity. And the idea of trying to adjust to multiple jurisdictions across the country is extremely taxing and probably a bigger tax on innovation than would be clarity across the board.

The second point I would make is that there are technologies, again, that are deployed in many other verticals that allow you to process data in privacy compliant ways, and if these rules – if this legislation takes effect, the innovation will shift towards using those technologies. And I think that is a really good thing for consumers and a really good way for this country to lead on innovation in this space.

Mr. Carter. Well, you know, look, all of that put together – the fact that I don't want to suppress freedom of speech, I don't want to suppress innovation, I don't want us to get behind our global competitors – that is why this is a heavy lift. We need y'all's help.

Mr. Chairman, I am out of time, and I will yield back. Thank y'all again for being here.

Mr. Bilirakis. Appreciate it. The gentleman yields back.

Now I will recognize, certainly last but not least – certainly not least. He has got a lot of experience in this area. So we will recognize Representative Obernolte from the great State of California. Five minutes.

Mr. Obernolte. Thank you, Mr. Chair. Thank you, sir.

Ms. Rich, you said something at the end of your testimony that really resonated with me. You said that one of the primary reasons why Congress needs to act to establish data privacy standards at a Federal level is because the FTC is unable to, through rulemaking, resolve the primary controversies of data privacy, those being preemption and also private right of action. I couldn't agree with you more.

So I know that Mr. Duncan asked you about preemption, and you said some level of preemption is necessary, but I wanted to tunnel down on that. Should we completely preempt away from the States this space or should we allow the States to create standards that might be more stringent than those created at the Federal level?

Ms. Rich. Well, as I have said, I think that some level of preemption is necessary for consistency. I also think we are beyond in the debate total preemption because, clearly, compromises need to be made. And I am in awe of this committee's work for making some of those hard cuts, at least attempting to.

So, you know, I think the ADPPA strikes – attempts to strike a good balance of partially preempting to create as much consistency as possible, but allowing – first of all, allowing all the state AGs and other State agencies to enforce, which is incredibly important, and then leaving certain things in place.

There is a third issue that is really controversial too that I think Congress needs to resolve, which is how much discretion the FTC should have to its own rulemaking. And so if the FTC does its rulemaking that it is doing, it has total discretion. But this body has tried to make decisions about when the FTC should be able to do rulemaking and when Congress' decisions should be the law of the land.

Mr. Obernolte. Yeah. Well, talking about this issue of preemption, I am going to partially agree with you. I am of the opinion we need to totally federally preempt it. And the reason that I feel that way is one of the primary justifications for preempting at all, I think, is to avoid creating this patchwork quilt of 50 different State regulations, which as has been pointed out in the testimony, very destructive to entrepreneurialism, very difficult for small businesses to deal with. And unfortunately, if we only partially preempt, we leave that problem out there, because small companies, you know, two guys in a garage in Cupertino, they are still going to have to navigate this space.

And by the way, before this I served in the California legislature. I was one of the leads in the drafting and passage of the California Consumer Privacy Act. So I am one with the vested interest of saying, no, no, don't touch my baby. But, you know, I really firmly believe that this is something that we need to preempt. If we are going to do it, we need to do it all the way.

Mr. Mudd, we have been talking about private right of action. And let me ask you – because I know opinions have varied in the testimony here – who do you think should be responsible for enforcing whatever privacy protections we put in place?

Should it be the FTC? Should it be state attorney generals? The Federal attorney generals? Should there be a private right of action? What do you think about enforcement?

Mr. Mudd. Representative, I apologize, it is not in the area of my expertise, and I would be reluctant to offer an opinion like that.

Mr. Obernolte. Okay. We will go back to Ms. Rich then. I know she has an opinion on this subject.

Ms. Rich. Again, I support as much consistency as possible. And so even – you know, when I was at the FTC and then at Consumer Reports, I had worries about the private right of action and some of the incentives there. I do think that between the FTC and all of the state attorneys general and all of the other agencies within the State, that is a lot of enforcers on the beat, plus the FTC really needs more resources. But we are a little bit beyond barring the entire, you know, private right of action.

Again, a lot of this is a political decision that you all need to make, and compromises have been made. And my hat is off to you guys for being able to do so.

Mr. Obernolte. Sure. Well, and I think that we are all interested in getting this across the finish line. You know, the bill that we had last year, we didn't quite get it there. And so we are trying to figure out how to tweak it to get it the rest of the way to passage, which I think is a goal we all support. I, myself, though, have some very serious concerns about private right of action. And one need look no further than other domains that we have implemented it in to find out the truth of, you know, what you said in your testimony earlier, which was sometimes, in fact, quite often, it benefits attorneys more than plaintiffs.

In California, we have – I mean, obviously, we have the Americans with Disabilities Act. I am sure we are all familiar with those abuses. But in California, we have had the Private Attorney General Act for the last few years that creates a private right of action for the enforcement of California labor laws. And every single one who – person who represents any piece of California can testify to the number of abusive lawsuits that have been brought, you know, clearly without the intention of actually forcing compliance with the labor law, but only through a profit motive on the part of a law firm. So that is why I think this is really difficult to navigate, and I really think that we have sufficient authority through the FTC and the state AGs to be able to enforce this.

But I see my time has expired. I want to thank you all for your testimony, and hopefully we will be able to get this across the finish line this time around.

I yield back, Mr. Chairman.

Mr. Bilirakis. Thank you. And the gentleman yields back.

So seeing that there are no further members wishing to be recognized, I would like to thank all the witnesses for being here. Thank you so much for your patience.

Y'all did an amazing job, you really did. I appreciate it. Very informative. So you guys don't have to stay. I have got some business to take care of. But thank you so very much.

Pursuant to the committee rules, I remind members that they have 10 business days to submit questions for the record, and I ask the witnesses to respond to the questions promptly. If you kindly will respond, we would appreciate that. Members should submit their questions by the close of business on March 15.

So, let's see, I have got some documents that need to be entered into the record.

So pursuant to the committee rules, I ask unanimous consent to enter the following documents into the record: A letter from the Institute of Electrical and Electronics Engineers USA; a letter from the Insights Association; a letter from the Privacy for America; a letter from Teknek; a letter from the Health Innovation Alliance; a letter from the Credit Union National Association; a letter from Engine; a letter from the Confidentiality Coalition; a letter from the National Association of Federally Ensured Credit Unions; a letter from Mr. Brandon Pugh of the R Street Institute; a letter from the National Multifamily Housing Council and the National Apartment Association; a letter from the Main Street Privacy Coalition; a letter from the Electronic Transactions Association; a letter from the BSA, the Software Alliance; a letter from the commissioner, Peter A. Feldman, of the Consumer Protection Safety Commission; a letter from ACT, The App Association and the Connected Health Initiative; a letter from the U.S. Chamber of Commerce; a report from the Information Technology and Innovation Foundation, entitled "The Looming Cost of a Patchwork of State Privacy Laws"; a letter from the National Association of Manufacturers; a letter from the Leadership Conference on Civil and Human

Rights; a letter from the law enforcement stakeholders; and finally, a letter from the Fraternal Order of Police and the International Association of Chiefs of Police.

Without objection, so ordered.

[The information follows:]

28 February 2023

Representative Cathy McMorris Rodgers,
Chair
House Committee on Energy and Commerce
Washington, DC 20515

Representative Frank Pallone, Jr.,
Ranking Member
House Committee on Energy and Commerce
Washington, DC 20515

Representative Gus Bilirakis, Chair
Subcommittee on Innovation, Data, and Commerce
House Committee on Energy and Commerce
Washington, DC 20515

Representative Jan Schakowsky,
Ranking Member
Subcommittee on Innovation, Data, and Commerce
House Committee on Energy and Commerce
Washington, DC 20515

Dear Rep. McMorris Rodgers, Pallone, Bilirakis, and Schakowsky,

Thank you for conducting the Subcommittee's March 1st hearing on the role of standards in protecting the online privacy of Americans, in particular children. IEEE, as a leading global standards developer, believes that the standardization process is important to both promoting innovation and, as rapidly growing technologies change the way we interact and expose our personal data, ensuring that technologies do not harm users.

The U.S. has for decades consistently, and in our opinion appropriately, promoted the principles of consensus-based standards developed in a decentralized direct-participation model. These principles have contributed greatly to advancing U.S. innovations and technological competitiveness. We encourage the federal government to continue to engage actively and effectively with standards setting bodies as a means of strengthening data privacy governance.

The U.S. should lead discussions on global technical standardization and establishment of a national data privacy standard. Below are listed the IEEE standards and related programs that are most relevant to the protection of online privacy, including IEEE 2089™, a standard that establishes a framework for developing age-appropriate digital services for situations where users are children.

IEEE-USA is the American component of the global IEEE (Institute of Electrical and Electronics Engineers), the world's largest technical professional society. We represent technology professionals in all parts of our 21st century technology-based society – from space exploration to biotech, cryptocurrency to power generation. IEEE has more than 150,000 individual members across the United States. The IEEE Standards Association (IEEE SA) is one of the world's largest global standard setting bodies with a catalog of more than 2100 standards and projects, including many at the heart of our modern economy.

If you have any questions, please do not hesitate to contact Erica Wissolik at (202) 530-8347 or e.wissolik@ieee.org.

Sincerely,

Eduardo F. Palacio
President

IEEE Standards and Related Information

Name/Title	Description	Link
IEEE 7002™ Standard for Data Privacy Process	Defines requirements for a systems/software engineering process for privacy-oriented considerations regarding products, services, and systems utilizing employee, customer, or other external user's personal data.	https://standards.ieee.org/ieee/7002/6898/ The PDF of this standard is provided at no cost in the IEEE GET Program at https://ieeexplore.ieee.org/browse/standards/get-program/page/series?id=93)
IEEE 2410™ Standard for Biometric Privacy	This standard provides for private identity assertion, and includes a formal specification for privacy and biometrics such that a conforming system will meet GDPR, CCPA, BIPA, or HIPAA privacy requirements.	https://standards.ieee.org/ieee/2410/7746/
IEEE P1912 Standard for Privacy and Security Framework for Consumer Wireless Devices	This standard project (in development) defines a privacy scale for data that is defined as personal identifiable information, which is collected, retained, processed, or shared on networked edge, fog, or cloud computing devices. This privacy scale will provide input to assessment tools that developers or users of these applications employ to develop, discover, recognize, or implement appropriate privacy settings for the personal data resident on these devices.	https://standards.ieee.org/ieee/1912/10174/
IEEE 2089™ Standard for Age Appropriate Digital Services Framework – Based on the 5Rights Principles for Children.	This standard establishes a framework for developing age-appropriate digital services for situations where users are children. The framework centers around the following key areas: a) recognition that the user is a child, b) considers the capacity and upholds the rights of children, c) offers terms appropriate to children, d) presents information in an age-appropriate way and e) offers a level of validation for service design decisions.	https://standards.ieee.org/ieee/2089/7633/

Name/Title	Description	Link
IEEE P2876™ Recommended Practice for Inclusion, Dignity and Privacy in Online Gaming.	This standard project (in development) defines a set of recommended practices for inclusion, dignity, and privacy in online gaming. It includes a descriptive taxonomy to enable clear and concise communication between stakeholders, and a set of best practices designed to help game developers build more inclusive online communities. A reference model defining common concerns, challenges, and remediation methods across all online games is also included.	https://standards.ieee.org/ieee/2876/10184/
IEEE 802E™ Recommended Practice for Privacy Considerations for IEEE 802® Technologies	This recommended practice helps promote a consistent approach by IEEE 802 protocol developers to mitigate privacy threats identified in the specified privacy threat model, and to provide a privacy guideline.	https://standards.ieee.org/ieee/802E/6242/
IEEE P2933™ Standard for Clinical Internet of Things (IoT) Data and Device Interoperability with TIPPSS – Trust, Identity, Privacy, Protection, Safety and Security.	A set of guidelines and standards is necessary to standardize the use of clinical Internet of Things (IoT) devices for precision medicine, data sharing, interoperability, and security, with a goal of improved and measurable healthcare outcomes and protection of patient data. This standard project will establish that framework, with the incorporation of TIPPSS principles. It will encompass wearable device interoperability with healthcare systems such as electronic health records (EHR), electronic medical records (EMR), other clinical IoT devices, hospital devices, and with future devices and connected healthcare systems.	https://standards.ieee.org/ieee/2933/7592/
IEEE 2883-2022™ Standard for Sanitizing Storage	This standard covers methods of sanitizing logical storage and physical storage, as well as providing technology-specific requirements and guidance for the elimination of recorded data.	https://standards.ieee.org/ieee/2883/10277/
IEEE 1619.1-2018™ Standard for Authenticated Encryption with Length Expansion for Storage Devices	This standard specifies requirements for cryptographic units that provide encryption and authentication for data contained within storage media.	https://ieeexplore.ieee.org/do cument/8637991
IEEE 1619.2-2021™ Standard for Wide-Block Encryption for Shared Storage Media	EME2-AES and XCB-AES wide-block encryption with associated data (EAD) modes of the NIST AES block cipher, providing usage guidelines and test vectors, are described.	https://standards.ieee.org/ieee/1619.2/1025 2/
IEEE 2089™ Standard for an Age Appropriate Digital Services Framework Based on the 5 Rights Principles for Children	This standard establishes a set of processes by which organizations seek to make their services age appropriate. It sets out processes through the life cycle of development, delivery and distribution that will help organizations ask the right relevant questions of their services, identify risks and opportunities by which to make their services age appropriate and	https://standards.ieee.org/ieee/2089/7633/

(Continued)

Name/Title	Description	Link
	take steps to mitigate risk and embed beneficial systems that support increased age appropriate engagement.	
IEEE 2890™ Recommended Practice for Provenance of Indigenous Peoples' Data	This recommended practice details the rules by which the provenance of Indigenous Peoples' data should be described and recorded.	https://standards.ieee.org/ieee/2890/10318/
IEEE SA Industry Connection Program on Cybersecurity for Next Generation Connectivity Systems	A pre-standardization initiative addressing cyber security issues and rethinking architectures to address critical market needs. IEEE SA proposes five architecture principles or baseline realities that will be used to explore new architectures to create more secure and trusted digital platforms: passwords, phishing, data breaches, privacy erosion and surveillance, and misinformation and unverified sources.	https://standards.ieee.org/ industry-connections/cyber-security-for-next-generation-connectivity-systems/
IEEE SA Industry Connections Program on Cybersecurity in Agile	A pre-standardization addressing cloud remote access security, including performing a gap analysis of existing	https://standards.ieee.org/indu stry-connections/cybersecurit y-agile-cloud-computing/
Cloud Computing	cloud standards and certifications and evaluating the need for extending them for secured remote access. Emphasizes defense organizations which have more restricted security requirements and may require more restricted security on remote access to their data.	

IA letter on federal privacy hearing (2/27/23) 1.

February 27, 2023
The Honorable Gus Bilirakis
Chairman

The Honorable Jan Schakowsky
Ranking Member
House Subcommittee on Innovation, Data, and Commerce

RE: March 1, 2023 subcommittee hearing on "Promoting U.S. Innovation and Individual Liberty through a National Standard for Data Privacy"

Dear Chair Bilirakis and Ranking Member Schakowsky,

The Insights Association (IA), the leading nonprofit trade association for the market research and data analytics industry (also known as the insights industry), is heartened by the March 1, 2023 hearing in the House Energy and Commerce Committee Innovation, Data, And Commerce Subcommittee on federal privacy legislation and your commitment to continue to try to craft a preemptive national privacy law.

IA needs to highlight three key points for the Subcommittee to consider during this hearing and as you continue work on such legislation: market research should be allowed to function;

Congress should set a national privacy standard; and the Privacy for America framework provides a model approach for legislation.

1. *Market research needs to be permitted to function.* Our more than 7,100 members are the world's leading producers of intelligence, analytics and insights measuring and defining the needs, attitudes and behaviors of consumers, organizations and their employees, students and citizens. With that essential understanding, leaders can make intelligent decisions and deploy strategies and tactics to build trust, inspire innovation, realize the full potential of individuals and teams, and successfully create and promote products, services and ideas. Any legislation you consider should not unnecessarily restrict companies and organizations from using data to better the products, services and ideas they offer to consumers or conduct research on the markets for their offerings (and public policies). Innovation and developments in products, services and ideas work to benefit consumers and citizens.
2. *Congress should set a national privacy standard, not the Federal Trade Commission (FTC).* The regulation of the modern economy, which is data-driven in every way, should be a matter left to the democratically-accountable legislative branch. Agencies like the FTC should act only when directly instructed to do so by Congress through specific authorities contained in legislation. A national standard for data collection and processing should be set at the federal level, through the clear authority granted by the American people and the Constitution in Congress.
3. *The Privacy for America Framework provides a model approach for privacy legislation.* The Subcommittee can look to the Privacy for America Principles of Privacy Legislation[102] as an example of how to strike an appropriate balance for national data standards. The Framework would designate certain uses of personal information to be reasonable and others to be per se unreasonable (and thus prohibited). The Framework prioritizes consumer protection while still preserving beneficial uses of data and access to a vibrant online ecosystem.

Thank you for your consideration of these points for your March 1st hearing. IA anticipates working closely with Congress as it continues to evaluate and develop approaches to preemptive, comprehensive, privacy legislation. Please reach out with any questions or concerns.

Sincerely,
Howard Fienberg
Senior VP, Advocacy
Insights Association

CC: House Innovation, Data, And Commerce Subcommittee members

[102] Privacy for America, Principles for Privacy Legislation (2019).

March 1, 2023

The Hon. Cathy McMorris Rodgers
Chair
House Energy & Commerce Committee
2125 Rayburn House Office Building
Washington, D.C. 20515

The Hon. Gus Bilirakis C
hairman
House Energy & Commerce
Subcommittee on Innovation, Data, and Commerce
2306 Rayburn House Office Building
Washington, D.C. 20515

The Hon. Frank Pallone
Ranking Member
House Energy & Commerce Committee
2322 Rayburn House Office Building
Washington, D.C. 20515

The Hon. Jan Schakowsky
Ranking Member
House Energy & Commerce
Subcommittee on Innovation, Data, and Commerce
2408 Rayburn House Office Building
Washington, D.C. 20515

Dear Chair Rodgers, Chairman Bilirakis, Ranking Member Pallone, and Ranking Member Schakowsky:

Privacy for America is a coalition of trade organizations and companies representing a broad cross-section of the American economy. Our membership includes companies and trade associations in the advertising, travel, hospitality, media, financial services, data services, market research, and many other industries. We have long supported the creation of a comprehensive, preemptive national standard for consumer privacy. We are encouraged by the House Energy and Commerce Committee Innovation, Data, And Commerce Subcommittee's ("Subcommittee") decision to hold a hearing and continue to work on the creation of a preemptive national privacy law. We write to highlight several facts that the Subcommittee should consider during this hearing and its work going forward.

- *Responsible data-driven practices deliver over $30,000 in value to consumers per year.* Studies found that data-driven practices used by companies supplemented consumer incomes to the tune of $30,000 per year in free and discounted entertainment, information, and other services.[103] Congress should not create a new $30,000 tax on consumers by disrupting the engine that drives that value.

- *Research proves that data-driven advertising is valued by consumers.* Data-driven advertising allows consumers to access near-endless free and low-cost content and services, such as research, music, news, videos, games, and more. According to a study of consumer attitudes towards data-driven advertising, more than half of consumers desire relevant ads, which are facilitated by such advertising, and a substantial majority (over 85 percent) desire personalized discounts for online products and services.[104]
- *Data-driven advertising creates opportunities for new, small, and growing businesses to access and thrive in the market.* Data-driven advertising fosters a competitive marketplace where small and mid-size businesses, as well as self-employed individuals, which are overwhelmingly minority-owned businesses, can compete with the economy's largest players.[105] Companies of all sizes use data-driven advertising, but smaller firms and new market entrants depend on it for a significantly greater portion of their revenue.[106]
- *Congress should set a national standard, not the Federal Trade Commission.* The regulation of the modern economy, which is data-driven in every way, should be a matter left to the democratically accountable legislative branch. Agencies like the Federal Trade Commission should act only when directly instructed to do so by Congress through specific authorities contained in legislation. A national standard for data collection and processing should set once, through the clear authority granted by the American people and the Constitution in Congress.
- *Private companies should follow the law, not create their own.* When Congress speaks and sets a national framework for data practices all companies should follow that law. No company, just because of its position in the marketplace as the intermediary between consumers and publishers, should be able to interfere in the legitimate, responsible, data practices of others. This is especially true when those private actors do so to further their own financial goals to the detriment of their competitors. A federal law should prohibit such meddling.
- *The Privacy for America Framework provides model approach for privacy legislation.* The Subcommittee can look to the Privacy for America *Principles of Privacy*

---

[103] J. Howard Beales & Andrew Stivers, *An Information Economy Without Data*, 2 (2022), https://www.privacyforamerica.com/wp-content/uploads/2022/11/Study-221115-Beales-and-Stivers-Information-Economy-Without-Data-Nov22-final.pdf.

[104] Mark Sableman, Heather Shoenberger & Esther Thorson, *Consumer Attitudes Toward Relevant Online Behavioral Advertising: Crucial Evidence in the Data Privacy Debates* (2013), located at https://www.thompsoncoburn.com/docs/default-source/Blog-documents/consumer-attitudes-toward-relevant-online-behavioral-advertising-crucial-evidence-in-the-data-privacy-debates.pdf?sfvrsn=86d44cea 0.

[105] Nora Esposito, *Small Business Facts, Spotlight on Minority-Owned Employer Businesses*, U.S. SMALL BUSINESS ADMINISTRATION (May 2019), https://cdn.advocacy.sba.gov/wp-content/uploads/2019/05/31131339/Small-Business-Facts-Spotlight-on-Minority-Owned-Employer-Businesses.pdf.

[106] Digital Advertising Alliance, *Study: Online Ad Value Spikes When Data Is Used to Boost Relevance* (Feb. 10, 2014), located here; Deloitte, *Dynamic Markets: Unlocking Small Business Innovation And Growth Through The Rise Of The Personalized Economy* at 27 (May 2021), https://scontent-bos5-1.xx.fbcdn.net/v/t39.8562-6/10000000430307876974354472376030503739935470 n.pdf? nc cat=109&ccb=1-7& nc sid=ad8a9d& nc ohc=diYsZTH66PEAX 6cORb& nc ht=scontent-bos5-1.xx&oh=00 AfAIdldtTvwNhD6amBfDnljWEW3VTNTzhgjXULbzMJn1mg&oe=63FB1089.

Legislation ("Framework") as an example of how to strike an appropriate balance for national data standards.[107] The Framework would designate certain uses of personal information to be reasonable and others to be *per se* unreasonable and thus prohibited.[6] The Framework prioritizes consumer protection while also preserving beneficial uses of data and access to a vibrant online ecosystem.

* * *

Thank you for your consideration of this letter on this important topic. We look forward to working with the Congress as it continues to evaluate and develop approaches to preemptive, comprehensive, privacy legislation. Please contact us with any questions.

Sincerely,
Privacy for America

February 28, 2023

The Honorable Cathy McMorris Rodgers
Chair
House Committee on Energy and Commerce
2188 Rayburn House Office Building
Washington, D.C. 20515

The Honorable Frank Pallone
Ranking Member
House Committee on Energy and Commerce
2322 Rayburn House Office Building
Washington, D.C. 20515

Dear Chair McMorris Rodgers and Ranking Member Pallone:

In advance of this week's Subcommittee on Innovation, Data, and Commerce hearing titled "Promoting U.S. Innovation and Individual Liberty through a National Standard for Data Privacy," I am writing to highlight TechNet's support for enactment of comprehensive federal privacy legislation and share TechNet's privacy policy principles as you work to advance this legislation in the 118th Congress.

TechNet is the national, bipartisan network of technology CEOs and senior executives that promotes the growth of the innovation economy by advocating a targeted policy agenda at the federal and 50-state level. TechNet's diverse membership includes dynamic American businesses ranging from startups to the most iconic companies on the planet and represents more than five million employees and countless customers in the fields of information technology, e-commerce, the sharing and gig economies, advanced energy, cybersecurity, venture capital, and finance.

---

[107] Privacy for America, *Principles for Privacy Legislation* (2019) https://www.privacyforamerica.com/overview/principles-for-privacy-legislation/. [6] Framework at Part 1, Sec. 1(Y); Sec. 3: Sec 6(G)(c).

The need to pass a federal privacy law has never been greater. The global nature of data impacts every industry across our economy and demands a federal approach. Instead, we're seeing a growing patchwork of state privacy laws that are confusing consumers and hurting businesses, especially small businesses. Since 2018, 154 comprehensive privacy bills have been considered across 43 states, including 28 bills filed in 16 states just this year. By the end of the year, consumers and businesses in California, Colorado, Connecticut, Utah, and Virginia will all be regulated by different privacy laws. As more states pass their own privacy laws, failure by Congress to take action will cost our economy more than $1 trillion over 10 years, with more than $200 billion being paid by small businesses.

This week's Subcommittee hearing is an important step to building continued momentum for the enactment of comprehensive federal privacy legislation in the 118th Congress and examining the best ways to protect consumers and promote America's global leadership in innovation. TechNet has long believed that for the data-driven economy to remain strong, we must always put the consumer first. In addition, we believe federal privacy legislation must provide harmonized, consistent, tech- and sector-neutral standards throughout the United States to provide regulatory certainty for all businesses, including new entrants, small businesses, as well as underserved and under-resourced innovators. We encourage the Committee to examine the cost and operational impact of the patchwork of state privacy laws on small- and medium-sized businesses and evaluate the rapid emergence of nuisance lawsuits impacting these same job creators in the absence of a federal data privacy law.

Your efforts to craft comprehensive federal privacy legislation during the 117th Congress demonstrated that there is bipartisan support in Congress to protect the privacy of all Americans and provide regulatory certainty for businesses. Polls overwhelmingly show that Americans across the ideological spectrum want Congress to come together to act on privacy legislation, with four in five voters in support of Congress prioritizing the passage of privacy legislation.

We stand ready to assist you in protecting American consumers, helping small businesses, and propelling our economy forward. We thank you for your commitment to advancing a federal data privacy law and look forward to working with you on this important issue. Please don't hesitate to reach out if we can be a resource on this issue or if you have any questions. I can be reached at cholshouser@technet.org or (210) 286-6276.

Sincerely,

Carl Holshouser
TechNet Senior Vice President

February 28, 2023
The Honorable Cathy McMonis Rodgers, Chair
House Energy & Commerce Committee
2125 Rayburn House Office Building
Washington, DC 20515

The Honorable Frank Pallone, Ranking Member
House Energy & Commerce Committee
2322 Rayburn House Office Building
Washington, DC 20515

Dear Chairwoman McMonis Rogers and Ranking Member Pallone,

The Health Innovation Alliance (HIA) appreciates your continued leadership on improving consumer privacy protections for people across the countiy. HIA is a diverse coalition of patient advocates, healthcare providers, consumer organizations, employers, technology companies, and payers who suppo l l the commonsense use of data and technology to improve health outcomes and lower costs.

As you consider modernizing our nation's p l ivacy framework, we urge you to explicitly caive out existing healthcare laws and regulations in any legislation considered by the Committee. Health info l mation exchange is vital to the practice of medicine and its regulation, and Congress has worked for years to facilitate the access, exchange, and use of health data for eve l ything from preventing malpractice and improving patient cai·e to advancing medical research.

Privacy of sensitive health info l mation is necessaiy to establish t l l lst to deliver cai·e, enhance quality, and pay for se l vices and products. This necessity is one reason there ai·e so many existing laws to protect patient p l ivacy while ensming health data is available to those who need it.

Congress should ensure that any policies intended to rein in inappropriate use, disclosure, or sale of info l mation do not thwait advances in medicine or stop medical reseai·ch. Legislators in California had to amend the state's privacy law to avoid shutting down effo l l s to advance patient care and conduct clinical tiials. Any federal legislation in this area should avoid this problem by caiving out existing healthcai·e protections. The Health Innovation Alliance has already shai·ed legislative text with the Energy and Commerce Committee to achieve this goal.

Additionally, health care is a complicated industiy, and the regulation of health info l mation is as well. As the Committee considers advancing consumer p l ivacy protections and ca l ving out existing regulations in health cai·e, HIA urges consideration of the Health Data Use and Plivacy Commission Act (S. 3620, 117th Congress). This legislation would establish a commission of expe l l s to analyze whether health data privacy regulation should be updated, and if so, how. The Health Data Use and PI·ivacy Commission Act would info l m the Energy and Commerce Committee and the rest of Congress on how best to navigate healthcai·e regulation and modernize privacy for patients and consumers.

HIA stands ready to fmther assist the Committee in its impo l tant work to better protect consumer and health data. Thank you for your consideration.

Sincerely,
Brett Meeks
Executive Director

March 1, 2023

The Honorable Gus Bilirakis
Chairman
Energy and Commerce Subcommittee
on Innovation, Data and Commerce
United States House of Representatives
Washington, DC 20515

The Honorable Jan Schakowsky
Ranking Member
Energy and Commerce Subcommittee
on Innovation, Data and Commerce
United States House of Representatives
Washington, DC 20515

Dear Chairman Bilirakis and Ranking Member Schakowsky:

On behalf of America's credit unions, I am writing about your hearing "Promoting U.S. Innovation and Individual Liberty through a National Standard for Data Privacy." CUNA represents America's credit unions and their more than 130 million members.

Credit unions strongly support the enactment of a national data security and data privacy law that includes robust security standards that apply to all who collect or hold personal data and is preemptive of state laws. We firmly believe that there can be no data privacy until there is strong data security. Securing and protecting consumer data is important not only for their individual financial health but as a further safeguard against rogue international agents and interference by foreign governments.

Data privacy and data security are major concerns for Americans given the frequency of reports of misuse of personally identifiable information (PII) data by businesses and breaches by criminal actors, some of which are state sponsored. Since 2005, there have been more than 10,000 data breaches, exposing nearly 12 billion consumer records. These breaches have cost credit unions, banks, and the consumers they serve hundreds of millions of dollars, and they have compromised the consumers' privacy, jeopardizing their financial security.

Stringent information security and privacy practices have long been part of the financial services industries' business practices and are necessary as financial institutions are entrusted with consumers' personal information. This responsibility is reflected in the strong information security and privacy laws that govern data practices for the financial services industry as set forth in the Gramm Leach Bliley Act ("GLBA"). GLBA's protection requirements are strengthened by federal and state regulators' examinations for compliance with the GLBA's requirements and robust enforcement for violations. Several of these significant regulatory requirements and internal safeguards include:

- *Federal Requirements to Protect Information:* Title V of the GLBA and its implementing rules and regulations require credit unions to protect the security, integrity, and confidentiality of consumer information.
- *Federal Requirements to Notify Consumers:* Credit unions are required to notify their members whenever there is a data breach where the misuse of member information has occurred or where it is reasonably likely that misuse will occur.
- *Strong Federal Oversight and Examination:* Under their broad-based statutory supervisory and examination authority, the National Credit Union Administration (NCUA) and the Consumer Financial Protection Bureau (CFPB) regularly examine credit unions for compliance with data protection, privacy, and notice requirements.
- *Strong Federal Sanction Authority:* Under numerous provisions of federal law, credit unions are subject to substantial sanctions and monetary penalties for failure to comply with statutory and regulatory requirements.

While this extensive legal and regulatory examination and enforcement framework ensures that credit unions robustly protect consumers' personal financial information, this safety net only extends to financial institutions. As consumers' personal information is disseminated to third parties, those protections end and credit unions and their members are adversely impacted by the lax data security standards at other businesses. These loopholes must end and a comprehensive data security and privacy framework that covers all entities that that collect consumer information and is preemptive of state laws must be established and this standard must hold those who jeopardize that data accountable through enforcement.

With that in mind, we ask the committee to consider the following data security and privacy principles for any comprehensive framework:

1. *New Privacy and Data Security Laws Should Keep GLBA Intact:* Congress should leave financial services' robust data and privacy requirements in place. Financial services and the healthcare industry are subject to federal data privacy laws. The GLBA and the Health Insurance Portability and Accountability Act (HIPAA) have protected American's PII for over two decades and should be left in place as financial services and healthcare and their respective regulators have developed regulations, guidance, and procedures for compliance.
2. *Data Privacy and Data Security Are Hand in Glove:* Any new privacy law should include both data privacy and data security standards. Simply put, data cannot be kept private unless it is also secured. Congress should enact robust data security standards to accompany and support data privacy standards.
3. *Every Business Not Already Subject to Federal Law Should Follow the Same Rules:* The new law should cover all businesses, institutions, and organizations. Consumers will lose if Congress focuses only on tech companies, credit-rating agencies, and other narrow sectors of the economy because any company that collects, uses, or shares personal data or information can misuse the data or lose the data through breach.
4. *There Should Be One Rule for the Road:* Any new law should preempt state requirements to simplify compliance and create equal expectation and protection for all consumers. We understand that some states have strong security and privacy requirements. Congress should carefully examine those requirements and take the best approaches from state law, as appropriate. A patchwork of state laws with a federal standard as a floor will only perpetuate a security system littered with weak links. The federal law should be the ceiling and the ceiling should be high. Just like moving away from the sector specific approach, the goal should be to create a strong national standard for all to follow.
5. *Breach Disclosure and Consumer Notification Are Important, But These Requirements Alone Won't Enhance Security or Privacy:* Breach notification or disclosure requirements are important, but they are akin to sounding the alarm after the fire has burned down the building. By the time a breach is disclosed, harm could already have befallen hundreds of thousands, if not millions, of individuals.
6. *Hold Entities that Jeopardize Consumer Privacy and Security Accountable Through Regulatory Enforcement:* The law should provide mechanisms to address the harms that result from privacy violations and security violations, including data breach. Increasingly, courts are recognizing rights of action for individuals and companies (including credit unions). However, individuals and companies should be afforded a

private right of action to hold those that violate the law accountable, and regulators should have the ability to act against entities that violate the law.

7. *Recognize This Issue For What It Is – A National Security Issue:* More and more, data breaches that expose consumer PII are perpetrated by foreign governments and other rogue international entities. The proceeds from these attacks are being used to fund illicit activity. The nature of these breaches alone calls for a strong federal response that ensures all involved in collecting, holding, and using PII do so with the security of the information of paramount concern. You simply cannot have data privacy unless there is data security.

On behalf of America's credit unions and their more than 130 million members, thank you for your consideration of our views and for holding this important hearing.

Sincerely,
Jim Nussle
President & CEO

* * *

February 28, 2023

Committee on Energy and Commerce
Subcommittee on Innovation, Data, and Commerce
2125 Rayburn House Office Building
Washington, D.C. 20515

Honorable Members of the Subcommittee on Innovation, Data, and Commerce:

Engine is a non-profit technology policy, research, and advocacy organization that bridges the gap between policymakers and startups. Engine works with government and a community of thousands of high-technology, growth-oriented startups across the nation to support the development of technology entrepreneurship. Data-driven innovation plays a central role in technology development and entrepreneurship, and Engine accordingly appreciates the subcommittee's longstanding interest in and work toward a federal privacy framework, including by holding tomorrow's hearing on "Promoting U.S. Innovation and Individual Liberty through a National Standard for Data Privacy."

The attached document contains high-level takeaways from forthcoming research about the impacts of the current data privacy landscape upon startups. The research is to be published in full in the coming weeks, but we wanted to share with the subcommittee because it speaks to several of the questions highlighted in the "Issues" section of the hearing memo. We hope the subcommittee finds this information useful and takes into account the experiences of startups as it explores a national standard for data privacy. Engine is committed to being a resource for the subcommittee on these and other issues impacting technology entrepreneurship.

Sincerely, Engine
700 Penn Ave SE; Washington D.C. 20003

Startups need a federal privacy framework that works for them

Startups need a federal privacy framework that creates uniformity, promotes clarity, limits bad-faith litigation, accounts for the resources of startups, and recognizes the interconnectedness of the startup ecosystem.

Startups care about the privacy of their users and invest heavily in data privacy and security.

$100,000 – $300,000+

Amount individual startups have invested in their data privacy infrastructure and compliance with current or soon effective privacy laws

"We care a great deal about privacy and we want to be compliant, but it can be very expensive and complex."

Ben Brooks, Founder & CEO, PILOT, New York, NY

"Working with children, our priority is protecting their data."

Katherine Grill, Co-Founder & CEO, Neolth, Walnut Creek, CA

A patchwork of privacy laws creates confusion and duplicative costs for startups.

Five states have passed and enacted comprehensive data privacy legislation and already this year more than a dozen states have introduced at least three dozen privacy laws. The rapidly shifting landscape of state privacy laws makes compliance difficult for startups leads them to spend considerable time and resources navigating these disparate, complex frameworks.

$15,000 – $60,000+

Costs individual startups spend per each additional state added to the patchwork

"The rules can vary significantly on a state-by-state level. On top of that, our attorneys keep telling us that they're still changing fast, which means it's hard to have a stable, up-to-date privacy policy you feel confident is fully compliant."

Camila Lopez, Co-Founder, People Clerk, Miami, FL

"In the U.S., many states have their own rules—or no rules—and we have to approach compliance in every state on a case-by-case basis...trying to figure out how to build a business in an environment with differing rules about the same issue becomes hard and expensive."

Aditya Vishwanath, Co-Founder & CEO, Inspirit VR, Palo Alto, CA

$55,000

Average monthly resources of a venture-backed, seed-stage startup

"As a high-growth and early-stage startup trying to grow fast, you're at a major competitive disadvantage...I would have to raise an entire second Series A to navigate many of these frameworks."

Sam Caucci, Founder & CEO 1Huddle, Newark, NJ

Startups need Congress to act.

"It would be helpful to have a nationwide standard when it comes to data privacy policy, especially since we're looking to expand into new states"

Andrew Prystai, CEO & Co-Founder, EventVesta, Omaha, NE

"One uniform, consistently enforced federal policy framework could help make running RAVN easier."

Tani Chambers, Co-Founder & CEO, RAVN, New York, NY

February 28, 2023

The Honorable Gus Bilirakis
Chair
House Committee on Energy & Commerce
Subcommittee on Consumer Protection
& Commerce
Washington, D.C. 20515

The Honorable Jan Schakowsky
Ranking Member
House Committee on Energy & Commerce
Subcommittee on Consumer Protection
& Commerce
Washington, D.C. 20515

RE: March 1 "Promoting U.S. Innovation and Individual Liberty through a National Standard for Data Privacy" Hearing

Dear Chair Bilirakis and Ranking Member Schakowsky:

The Confidentiality Coalition thanks you for holding a hearing on, "Promoting U.S. Innovation and Individual Liberty through a National Standard for Data Privacy."

The Confidentiality Coalition is composed of a broad group of hospitals, medical teaching colleges, health plans, pharmaceutical companies, medical device manufacturers, vendors of electronic health records, biotech firms, employers, health product distributors, pharmacies, pharmacy benefit managers, health information and research organizations, and others, committed to advancing effective patient privacy and security protections. Our mission is to advocate policies and practices that safeguard the privacy and security of patients and healthcare consumers while, at the same time, enabling the essential flow of patient information that is critical to the timely and effective delivery of healthcare, improvements in quality and safety, and the development of new lifesaving and life-enhancing medical interventions.

Accessing and appropriately sharing health data allows healthcare providers to deliver quality care and enables patients to become more engaged in their health decisions. While the Health Insurance Portability and Accountability Act (HIPAA) safeguards a specific subset of "protected health information" (PHI) and applies only to specific healthcare entities and their business associates, a vast amount of health-related information does not fall within the HIPAA regulatory framework and is largely unprotected from misuse. Today, a significant amount of personal health information is collected outside the HIPAA regulatory structure. This information should be afforded privacy and security protections that align with HIPAA. Creating protections for this information will build public trust in data collection and sharing so that the information can be used to improve health outcomes and improve the patient healthcare experience.

The Confidentiality Coalition thanks the Committee for its work on the bipartisan, bicameral "American Data Privacy and Protection Act." This bill provides a meaningful step to ensure that patients and healthcare consumers receive robust privacy protections for all their personal health information, and we look forward to working with the Committee on the safeguarding of this sensitive data. As the Committee continues its work on this important legislation, we are pleased to share the Confidentiality Coalition's "Beyond HIPAA" principles, which focus on health information not protected by the HIPAA privacy rule. These principles emphasize harmonization with HIPAA's privacy and security rules. They also advocate for individual authorization processes (including revocation of authorization) for use and disclosure of identifiable health information not covered by HIPAA. Furthermore, Coalition members support limits on the use of identifiable data beyond the expressed purpose for which authorization was given. Developing legislative and regulatory solutions to protect consumers' health information not covered by the HIPAA rules will build trust in data collection, give stakeholders better certainty about how to protect such information, and ultimately help improve health outcomes.

The Confidentiality Coalition looks forward to working with you on steps to improve privacy protections for non-HIPAA health data. Please contact me at tgrande@hlc.org or 202-306-3538 with any questions.

Sincerely,

Tina O. Grande
Chair, Confidentiality Coalition and
Executive VP, Policy, Healthcare Leadership Council

* * *

February 28, 2023

The Honorable Gus M. Bilirakis
Chairman
Committee on Energy and Commerce
Subcommittee on Innovation, Data, and Commerce
U.S. House of Representatives
Washington, DC 20515

The Honorable Janice D. Schakowsky
Ranking Member
Committee on Energy and Commerce
Subcommittee on Innovation, Data, and Commerce
U.S. House of Representatives
Washington, DC 20515

Re: Tomorrow's Hearing, "Promoting U.S. Innovation and Individual Liberty through a National Standard for Data Privacy"

Dear Chairman Bilirakis and Ranking Member Schakowsky:

I write to you today on behalf of the National Association of Federally-Insured Credit Unions (NAFCU) ahead of Wednesday's hearing, "Promoting U.S. Innovation and Individual Liberty through a National Standard for Data Privacy." NAFCU advocates for all federally-insured not-for-profit credit unions that, in turn, serve over 135 million consumers with personal and small business financial service products. NAFCU and our members welcome the Subcommittee's review of this important issue.

As NAFCU has previously communicated to Congress, we believe there is an urgent need for comprehensive federal data privacy legislation that protects consumer data, establishes data safeguards, and recognizes the standards that have been in place for over two decades with the Gramm-Leach-Bliley Act (GLBA). In 2019, recognizing the importance of data privacy and the ongoing privacy debate, NAFCU issued a series of data privacy principles that calls for a comprehensive federal cybersecurity standard, the harmonization of existing federal data privacy laws, and the preemption of state privacy laws. As the Subcommittee works to develop much-needed comprehensive federal data privacy legislation, NAFCU recommends you include the following elements as key aspects in any such proposal:

- *A comprehensive federal cybersecurity standard covering all entities that collect and store consumer information.* Uniformly strong cybersecurity is necessary to ensure Americans' data is adequately protected across the economy. Existing strong federal cybersecurity standards, like that contained in the GLBA, should be extended to the activities of all data collectors and processors exceeding certain reasonable thresholds.
- *Harmonization of existing federal laws and preemption of any state privacy law related to the privacy or security of personal information.* The current patchwork of federal and state data privacy laws generates incredible consumer confusion and significant compliance burdens while failing to address the most significant data privacy risks to Americans—those risks posed by unregulated or inconsistently regulated entities that collect, control, and process vast amounts of our data. Comprehensive federal data privacy legislation should responsibly build on the successes of robust, time-tested federal laws by extending the same high data privacy standards across the economy and ensuring that already well-regulated entities, like credit unions, may confidently operate within their existing federal frameworks without fear of being subject to more than 50 different data privacy and security standards.
- *Delegation of enforcement authority to the appropriate sectoral regulator.* The National Credit Union Administration (NCUA) should be federal credit unions' sole data privacy and cybersecurity regulator. Allowing the NCUA, which is well-versed in the unique nature of federal credit unions and their operations, to continue to examine and enforce any privacy and cybersecurity requirements is the most efficient option for both credit unions and American taxpayers. Exposing credit unions and other already well-regulated entities to suits by states' attorneys general and private rights of action will dramatically increase compliance costs without providing a corresponding increase in consumer protection.
- *A safe harbor for businesses that take reasonable measures to comply with the privacy standards.* Comprehensive federal data privacy legislation should adopt principles-based requirements based on an organization's specific operations and risk profile and include a safe harbor for organizations that design and implement appropriate measures.

- *Notice and disclosure requirements that are easily accessible to consumers and do not unduly burden regulated entities.* Providing multiple data privacy disclosures and opt-out mechanisms across multiple channels creates consumer confusion and unreasonable burdens for subject entities. A new privacy law should avoid conflicting or duplicative disclosure requirements by incorporating easy to understand language, like that consistent with the GLBA's disclosure requirements.
- *Scalable civil penalties for noncompliance imposed by the sectoral regulator that seek to prevent and remedy consumer injury.* Actual damages to consumers are too difficult to establish by evidence, and statutory damages for violations are incredibly ripe for frivolous lawsuits. Sectoral regulators alone should have the power to assess scalable civil penalties, which can then be used to remedy and prevent consumer harm in a meaningful way.

While NAFCU supports a national data security and privacy standard, we had some concerns about the American Data Protection and Privacy Act (ADPPA) that the Committee considered in the last Congress, including:

- *GLBA Exemption.* Through the GLBA, Congress defined robust federal data privacy and information security standards for the financial services industries and provided the NCUA and other federal financial regulators the means with which to create and maintain strong privacy and data safeguards. The ADPPA did not recognize the long-standing requirements by providing a GLBA exemption. Congress should recognize the strength and successes of the GLBA and other time-tested federal sectoral data privacy regulation, and the value of regulator-led regulation, by wholly exempting credit unions and other already closely-regulated entities.
- *Private Right of Action.* This legislation provided a private right of action that would allow individuals or states' attorneys generals to sue covered entities over potential violations, allowing courts to determine the law. This means that different judicial interpretations will allow a consumer in California to have different privacy protections than a consumer in South Carolina, and credit unions will find themselves immediately and unnecessarily exposed to new and substantial compliance and legal risks.
- *Preemption of State Laws.* The ADDPA would preempt many state laws but then subsequently provided exceptions that undermine the preemption. This would perpetuate a patchwork of state and federal data privacy legislation and regulation. We believe Congress must leverage comprehensive federal data privacy legislation to expressly preempt all state data privacy legislation and regulation.

As your colleagues on the House Financial Services Committee tackle the Financial Data Privacy Act of 2023 within its jurisdiction to improve the GLBA for financial services entities, we urge the Subcommittee to craft a workable GLBA expansion to cover those outside of financial services that may be handling consumer financial data. The GLBA has successfully served consumers, credit unions, and other covered financial institutions for nearly a quarter-century. Changes to the GLBA for those already covered by it must be viewed with a cautionary eye. While some modernization of the GLBA for financial institutions may be in store, the system has generally been a success and should be a model for other areas. Making the system work best means expanding financial data protection requirements outside of just financial services. Retailers, merchants, and others that handle financial data should be subject to new requirements similar to those standards adopted for financial institutions. We urge the Subcommittee to work with your counterparts on the House Financial Services Committee to ensure a balance that recognizes existing law and the concerns of credit unions as Congress tackles the important issue of privacy reform.

NAFCU looks forward to continuing to work with you to address these concerns with consumer privacy. On behalf of our nation's credit unions and their more than 135 million members, we thank you for your attention to this important matter. Should you have any questions or require any additional information, please contact me or Amber Milenkevich, NAFCU's Senior Associate Director of Legislative Affairs, at 703-842-2238 or amilenkevich@nafcu.org.

Sincerely,

Brad Thaler
Vice President of Legislative Affairs

cc: Members of the Subcommittee on Innovation, Data, and Commerce

1212 New York Ave. NW
Suite 900
Washington D.C. 20005
202-525-5717

February 26, 2023

Representative Gus Bilirakis, Chairman Innovation, Data, and Commerce Subcommittee House Energy and Commerce Committee

Re: Comments for the Record - "Promoting U.S. Innovation and Individual Liberty through a National Standard for Data Privacy" Hearing on March 1, 2023

Dear Chairman Bilirakis,

I would like to thank you again for the opportunity to testify at the Feb. 1, 2023, hearing "Economic Danger Zone: How America Competes to Win the Future Versus China." I am thrilled to see that the March 1, 2023, hearing "Promoting U.S. Innovation and Individual Liberty through a National Standard for Data Privacy" will focus on a comprehensive data privacy and security law. Such a law is needed now more than ever. Data privacy and security is a central part of the R Street Institute's Cybersecurity and Emerging Threats team's work. I respectfully submit a series of resources as "comments for the record" to aid the subcommittee as it considers a federal data privacy and security law.

For background, we published a report last year in conjunction with the Harvard Kennedy School's Belfer Center to provide recommendations to address some of the most challenging aspects of a federal data privacy and security law, including preemption, a private right of action and the role of the Federal Trade Commission. Our research included consultations with over

125 entities of varying ideologies, and we also held multiple events and Hill briefings. We were thrilled to see many of the recommendations make it into the bipartisan, bicameral American Data Privacy and Protection Act (ADPPA) last congress. We believe that a federal data privacy and security law will require consensus and compromise to become a reality.

One key aspect of our ongoing work is the intersection of privacy and security, including how national security and data security should be key drivers in passing a federal law. That was the subject of my Feb. 1 testimony.[108] However, consumers and industry would also directly benefit from a federal law. Notably, some proposals are only targeted toward protecting children's privacy. While protecting children is a laudable goal, we believe that a comprehensive law that protects all Americans regardless of age is critical.

Thank you for your consideration of these materials. Please do not hesitate to let me know if I can be a resource to you or any member of the subcommittee.

Respectfully,
Brandon J. Pugh
Brandon Pugh
Policy Director & Senior Fellow
Cybersecurity & Emerging Threats Team
bpugh@rstreet.org

Material Overview:

1. Brandon Pugh, "If the president is genuine on data privacy and security, specifics would help," February 2023.
2. Steven Ward, "Data Privacy and Security Lessons from the Latest Law Enforcement Data Exposure," January 2023.
3. Brandon Pugh, "Readout from a Congressional Data Privacy and Security Briefing," September 2022.
4. Tatyana Bolton et al., "The Path to Reaching Consensus for Federal Data Security and Privacy Legislation," May 2022. – Intro article with three components:
   4a. Intro Article
   4b. Preemption in Federal Data Security and Privacy Legislation
   4c. The Role of the Federal Trade Commission in Federal Data Security and Privacy Legislation
   4d. Limiting a Private Right of Action in Federal Data Security and Privacy Legislation

Real Solutions: If the President Is Genuine on Data Privacy and Security, Speciics Would Help

BY BRANDON PUGH
FEB 8, 2023
Issues: Cybersecurity Policy, Data Security and Data Privacy

[108] Brandon Pugh and Steven Ward, "House Subcommittee on Innovation, Data, and Commerce Hearing," Feb. 1, 2023. https://www.rstreet.org/commentary/house-subcommittee-on-innovation-data-and-commerce-hearing-overview-featuring-r-streets-brandon-pugh.

The 2023 State of the Union address brought about mixed results for data privacy followers and for all Americans. On one hand, privacy and data collection got shout-outs, but it was not more than we have already heard from the White House. If the president is genuine about acting on data privacy and security, he must move beyond generic calls for action and offer a concrete position. The president called for bipartisan legislation to stop Big Tech from collecting personal data on kids, a ban on targeted ads to kids and stricter limits on personal data collection. There was no mention of the historic bipartisan privacy legislation introduced last Congress, the American Data Privacy and Protection Act (ADPPA), nothing concrete on how to move forward, and no mention of the data privacy and security risk holistically.

It is helpful to review what the president said in the 2022 State of the Union address to get a fuller picture of his stance. Last year, President Joe Biden essentially called for the same as this year: strengthening privacy protections, banning targeted ads to kids and demanding tech companies to stop collecting personal data on kids. While strengthening privacy protections was mentioned, it was in a section dedicated to kids. There was no call for federal legislation and no direct connection to privacy concerns facing all Americans. The only real difference in the 2023 address was that bipartisan privacy legislation was flagged and all Americans were considered.

Against the 2022 stance, the president's op-ed in the Wall Street Journal, "Republicans and Democrats, Unite Against Big Tech Abuses," became one of the first and loudest statements from the administration on data privacy and security. This shifted the view to risks posed for "ordinary Americans" and highlighted potential issues with data misuse. The direct call for "serious federal protections for Americans' privacy" was a good step, although combining it with a slew of anti-Big-Tech rhetoric and broader controversial tech measures reduced the effectiveness of this call and overshined the privacy focus.

A hopeful sign that the 2023 address might have contained a strong privacy stance was the White House's "Fact Sheet" released before the speech. In that, the president expanded in the greatest detail yet on his desire to "protect kids online" and "strengthen data privacy and platform accountability for all Americans." Specifically, he flagged the data collection risk and the need for strict limits on collection, use and transfer of data.

How, then, do we move forward in 2023?

First, the president should more closely work with Congress to find a solution. In an ideal world, he would support moving the ADPPA forward and help break down challenges experienced in the 117th Congress. For example, we did not see consensus between key leaders in the Senate and House and a California versus the United States trend developed over whether a federal law should override state privacy laws. The support from members of Congress is there, evidenced recently by member comments in a House Energy and Commerce subcommittee hearing and applause for privacy in the State of the Union.

Second, we need to remember that action is not just a matter of helping consumers. While that is important, there are broader benefits. This includes helping industry like small- and medium-sized businesses, advancing America's competitive stance on the global stage and strengthening national security.

Third, we need to move away from the notion that data privacy and security risks are caused solely by Big Tech. Data privacy and security risks do not depend on company size. There are countless examples of small and medium-sized companies, and even large non-tech companies, employing terrible data privacy and security practices involving highly sensitive data. Relatedly, we should keep action on privacy focused on privacy. Adding in other controversial measures, like antitrust, content moderation and Section 230, are sure ways to stall progress. This means acting on legislation that protects the data privacy and security of all Americans, not just kids.

While it is always great to hear data privacy get mentioned by the president, hopefully it appears next year as a bipartisan accomplishment.

Real Solutions: Data Privacy and Security Lessons from the Latest Law Enforcement Data Exposure

BY STEVEN WARD
JAN 26, 2023
ISSUES: CYBERSECURITY POLICY, DATA SECURITY AND DATA PRIVACY, FEDERAL GOVERNMENT AFFAIRS

When agencies decide to use third-party vendors, they must be aware of any and all potential issues that could arise from the convenience of the service. Recently, a security flaw discovered in SweepWizard, an app developed by ODIN Intelligence to assist law enforcement agencies in managing multi-agency raids, illustrated a prime example of the risks associated with third-party vendors. SweepWizard permitted unauthorized access to sensitive data, including over 1,000 suspects' social security numbers; law enforcement officers' names, phone numbers and email addresses; pre-raid briefing locations; and raid locations. Law enforcement agencies were using a free trial of SweepWizard, which claimed to be Criminal Justice Information Services (CJIS) compliant. Later, unknown hackers claimed to possess 16 gigabytes of data from ODIN Intelligence.

SweepWizard is a kind of intelligence sharing, which refers to the collection and dispersion of sensitive data with agencies and third-party vendors to prevent and solve crime. When an agency shares data with a third-party vendor, it must assess whether that shared data will be secured from non-authorized users, foreign adversaries or malicious cyber actors, like ransomware hackers plotting to exploit security vulnerabilities. But an assessment is not foolproof.

The privacy implications of SweepWizard's data exposure could devastate officers and suspects. Some states provide special protection to law enforcement officers' personal information because disseminating an officer's personal information can have dire consequences. Further, the suspects' names and locations were exposed, which may put people at risk. The suspects could find themselves an internet search away from employment and housing opportunity denial or in the mob justice and vigilantes' crosshairs, like Richard Jewels and Steven Hatfill.

There are operational implications to consider, too. Raids are most successful when each suspect's residence is raided simultaneously to prevent the raid details from being leaked. If revealed, officer safety and evidence are severely compromised, and the opportunity to secure incriminating evidence for current or future investigations vanishes. Potential investigative leads vanishing could have devastating consequences, and crime victims will bear that cost. In online child sexual exploitation cases, for example, one suspect can help bring down an entire criminal organization dedicated to exploiting children. An investigator can assume a suspect's vetted online identity and infiltrate exclusive groups and organizations, which might otherwise be impossible to access.

The Need for a Comprehensive Data Privacy Law

To safeguard public trust and community safety, agencies must apply data privacy and security protection principles to data collected and shared with other agencies or third-party vendors. Generally, there are law enforcement and/or government exceptions from most comprehensive privacy laws. However, agencies must comply with the Federal Bureau of Investigation's (FBI) CJIS Security Policy if accessing the FBI's CJIS databases, like fingerprint identification data. The CJIS Security Policy guides law enforcement agencies nationwide to secure and protect criminal justice information from unauthorized access, dissemination and transmission. However, CJIS compliance—even when subject to audits—can fail. That is why we need a comprehensive federal data privacy and security law that third-party vendors must adhere to.

A comprehensive federal data privacy and security law, like the American Data Privacy and Protection Act (ADPPA) proposed in the 117th Congress, is one of the best ways that we can secure our data. In 2022, the ADPPA made significant progress, but ultimately stalled out. Many privacy professionals and groups supported the comprehensive bipartisan privacy bill. It would have brought stability to the legal privacy landscape currently hampered by state-by-state privacy patchwork laws. Multiple provisions in the ADPPA could help prevent breaches like the one that SweepWizard experienced. For example, Section 208 of the ADPPA requires non-exempt entities to implement and maintain security measures adequately to protect data against unauthorized access and acquisition. Section 208 also provides specific requirements that certain entities must meet, including security system vulnerabilities, taking preventive and corrective action, evaluating their systems, retention and disposal schedule, training and an organization's incident response.

In addition, a fundamental privacy principle conveyed in ADPPA was data minimization, which limits what data an entity may collect, process or transfer. This helps limit the amount of data collected in the first place. Another ADPPA strength was its inclusion of essential privacy principles, like a data retention and disposal schedule that requires ".... the deletion of covered data when such data is required to be deleted by law or is no longer necessary…." While some privacy frameworks touch on data minimization, the ADPPA expanded data minimization with specific and detailed restrictions.

In the SweepWizard data breach, several police investigations from as far back as 2011 were accessed without authorization. Whether that data needed to be retained is unknown—but it seems unlikely. Decade-old multi-agency raid data holds minimal value and should have been deleted from the SweepWizard's database.

Passing a comprehensive federal privacy and security law and demanding better privacy and security policies from law enforcement agencies will improve community trust and safety. Only then can we work together to secure our data from those who wish to do us harm.

Analysis: Readout from a Congressional Data Privacy and Security Briefing

By Brandon Pugh
Sept 26, 2022
Issues: Cybersecurity, Cybersecurity Policy, Data Security and Data Privacy, Federal Government Affairs

On Sept. 21, 2022, R Street's Cyber team, in partnership with Public Knowledge and The Leadership Conference on Civil and Human Rights, hosted a briefing geared toward Hill staffers on data privacy and security legislation. The briefing focused on the American Data Privacy and Protection Act (ADPPA), which was released by the House Energy and Commerce Committee in July by a 53-2 vote. We sought to provide an overview on the legislation, explore specific aspects and highlight the broader need for action.

House Energy and Commerce Chairman Rep. Frank Pallone (D-N.J.), one of the main sponsors of the ADPPA, opened the program with introductory remarks. He emphasized several provisions in the bill, including additional protections for consumers and children. He also highlighted the legislation's bipartisan backing and movement on key areas that have been obstacles in the past.

The briefing featured a panel of diverse experts, including Brandon Pugh of the R Street Institute, Paul Lekas of the Software & Information Industry Association (SIIA), Sara Collins of Public Knowledge and Yosef Getachew of Common Cause. The panel was moderated by Lauren Zabierek of the Harvard Kennedy School's Belfer Center, who helped lead an earlier effort at reaching consensus on privacy legislation.

Highlights are shared below.

Reasons to Support the ADPPA

Each panelist began by sharing reasons their organization supports the ADPPA and highlighting the need for data privacy and security legislation more broadly. While there was some overlap, each speaker raised a different aspect. These reasons included ensuring the United States remains competitive on the global stage; providing rules of the road for how data can be used and shared; increasing protections for marginalized communities; allowing Congress to act on privacy policy questions instead of federal agencies; and increasing national security and data security.

Discussions also touched on the current landscape of privacy legislation, which includes laws in five states, federal laws in different sectors like health and finance, and international frameworks, among others. Some panelists conveyed that this structure supports legislative action itself because it leaves a gap in protections for individuals and leads to a patchwork of laws that impacts businesses.

The Necessity of Compromise for the ADPPA

Panelists shared historical efforts at passing legislation along with traditional points of contention like a private right of action, preemption and the role of the Federal Trade Commission (FTC) in rulemaking and enforcement. Some highlighted the important role of compromise in the ADPPA since some members of Congress and external groups have moved on specific areas in the spirit of passing a federal law. For instance, some traditionally opposed to broad preemption are supportive of a bill with it because other parts were included, like a private right of action, and vice versa. However, support for the bill does not revolve solely around these key areas because the substance and fundamental provisions are still important.

An attendee raised California's concerns with preemption, especially as House Speaker Nancy Pelosi (D-Calif.) said work is needed to address outstanding concerns. Panelists' responses to this included reflecting on the changes to the ADPPA to account for the California Privacy Protection Agency; providing a role in enforcement for states; the ADPPA being stronger in multiple areas like civil rights; and providing rights for all Americans.

Possible Adjustments to the ADPPA

While panelists all expressed support for the progress so far, each shared ways the ADPPA can be fine-tuned, and not all agreed with each change mentioned. Some suggestions included clarifying the distinction between Federal Communications Commission (FCC) and FTC in privacy enforcement; revising the applicability and scope of algorithmic impact assessments; tailoring specific definitions for algorithms and sensitive covered data categories; ensuring the ability to use publicly available information in the public interest; and revisiting the applicability of sections to some entities like nonprofits and small businesses. Even broader changes are possible, but they could impact the delicate attempt at consensus.

Panelists explored a variety of other questions, such as how provisions apply to communities of color and the benefits and challenges with the provisions surrounding children.

Overall, the panel showed how groups with different ideologies and constituencies are coming together in the spirit of compromise to help make data privacy and security legislation a reality given the overarching need for action. The ADPPA still has barriers ahead, like the timing of the election and some outstanding concerns, but it is the most significant step in the U.S. privacy journey thus far.

Real Solutions: The Path to Reaching Consensus for Federal Data Security and Privacy Legislation

By Tatyana Bolton, Brandon Pugh, Sofia Lesmes, Lauren Zabierek, Cory Simpson
Issues: Cybersecurity Policy, Data Security and Data Privacy
May 26, 2022

This is a joint project between the R Street Institute's Cyber Team, led by Tatyana Bolton, the Belfer Center's Cyber Project, led by Lauren Zabierek, and Cory Simpson, a senior advisor on the Cyberspace Solarium Commission.

Data privacy is one of the nation's most pressing issues. The current lack of federal privacy legislation affects the economy, national security and consumer safety and is—at its most basic level—not a controversial issue for most Americans. Multiple leaders of top-tier tech companies have, in recent weeks, called for privacy legislation. The major bills on the table are mostly aligned.

Where they differ, however, and where Congress must find consensus, is on the most contentious issues: preemption, private right of action (PRA) and the role of the Federal Trade Commission (FTC). Our goal in developing this series is to offer recommendations on the best way to find agreement on these key issues.

The United States is one of the industrialized countries that lacks a single, national data privacy law, which affects our global competitiveness. In the vacuum left by the lack of federal government progress, state laws are passing quickly. But this isn't the best path forward. Studies have shown that a patchwork of state privacy laws could cost the United States over $1 trillion in out-of-state costs over 10 years. In addition, this patchy landscape would be difficult for businesses to navigate, especially small and medium companies.

Moreover, many countries want to take our data and weaponize it. For example, China—the most significant of these threats—is working to overtake the United States in the technology sector and is actively using our weak cybersecurity and data privacy protections to gather our data and use it against us. This can have many consequences, from blackmailing U.S.-based critics to identifying intelligence agents. Thus, the United States stands to gain significant competitive and national security advantages if our companies keep data private and secure.

The majority of Americans want data privacy regulation. Without a federal standard, consumers are left with unequal protections, or none at all.

We have drafted three articles, each of which focuses on one of the main areas of federal privacy law debate, identifies a variety of options for consensus and offers initial recommendations for compromise.

Our articles on preemption, PRA and the role of the FTC are intentionally framed differently than standard academic and think tank products. Our goal is to provide key members who are debating privacy legislation with a guide to the most challenging issues national legislation has faced, offering succinct options for bipartisan consensus. Although we present these topics separately, we recognize that these issues overlap, and progress toward consensus on one may mean a tradeoff on another.

Our work, which is the result of over 130 engagements across a full range of stakeholders, including Congress, the private sector, consumer groups and privacy advocates, builds off of the efforts of other experts, such as the Brookings Institution, Privacy for America and Duke University. Varied perspectives—even if conflicting—were crucial to understanding what an effective, passable bill could look like.

A federal data security and privacy law has never been more necessary, and we are closer to realizing that goal than ever before. For the sake of our economy, national security and consumer rights, the United States must act now rather than continue to hold out for the perfect law.

PART 1 – Preemption in Federal Data Security and Privacy Legislation
PART 2 – The Role of the Federal Trade Commission in Federal Data Security and Privacy Legislation
PART 3 – Limiting a Private Right of Action in Federal Data Security and Privacy Legislation
EXPLAINER – Answer to Tough Questions: The Framework of a Federal Data Security and Privacy Law

Real Solutions: Preemption in Federal Data Security and Privacy Legislation

By Tatyana Bolton, Brandon Pugh, Sofia Lesmes, Lauren Zabierek, Cory Simpson
Issues: Cybersecurity Policy, Data Security and Data Privacy
May 31, 2022

Preemption is the ability of the federal government to overrule or replace state law in favor of federal law. It is rooted in the U.S. Constitution's Supremacy Clause, and it remains a central challenge in passing federal data security and privacy legislation.

Five U.S. states have passed comprehensive data privacy laws. In 2021, at least 25 states introduced comprehensive legislation, along with even more that introduced less-comprehensive legislation to address specific privacy issues. In fact, in the span of time it took us to write this article, the United States went from three to five states with comprehensive data privacy laws. State laws could all be affected by a preemptive federal law, so determining whether and how existing and future state laws should operate with federal law is an essential part of developing federal privacy legislation.

This has fueled a debate on whether federal privacy legislation should allow for stronger state privacy frameworks or whether it should prevent states from having their own frameworks at all. On one side of the debate, a federal law could set minimum requirements and allow states to make new or stricter laws. Proponents of this approach believe that states are best suited to account for their unique needs and to innovate. On the other side, a federal law could displace state frameworks and serve as the uniform standard, with or without carve-outs for state action and existing federal law. Proponents of this strong preemption approach assert that it would end the current patchwork of laws that have led to inconsistent protections for consumers and avoid the industry-related compliance challenges that would come with meeting the requirements of 50+ frameworks.

Fortunately, the preemption debate does not need to be resolved by taking one side or the other. The solution exists along a spectrum, depending on how much Congress wants to allow state laws to complement federal law. A balance can be achieved by having a uniform federal privacy law that can preempt states on substantive provisions covered at the federal level but also preserve existing privacy-related federal frameworks and carve out areas for traditional state authority and emerging areas.

This publication—the first in a series of three main articles—explores the various forms preemption can take and provides recommendations to reach consensus among these options. For more, read our explainer about tough questions and answers here.

Considerations and Options

Consideration #1: Preemption and Savings Clauses

Preemption allows federal law to overrule or replace state law in a field or topic, but a savings clause, which is referred to as a carve-out for simplicity, can be added to prevent certain areas of state law from being preempted. Such a clause determines how federal law interplays with state law. Of note, preemption and savings clauses often arise with regard to federal legislation so they are not unique to privacy legislation. In certain situations, preemption is impermissible and considered commandeering (e.g., *Murphy v. NCAA*). Congress should be aware of these limitations as they craft preemption for privacy legislation.

Consideration #2: Carve-Outs for State Action

At least 10 areas could be considered for carve-outs in federal privacy legislation to keep existing state law intact, and statutory language should address how carve-outs involving covered data are handled. Doing so would result in uniform legislation while allowing states to retain control over certain areas. The areas that should be considered for carve-outs broadly fall into two categories: areas of traditional state control and emerging areas/gap-fillers.

Areas of traditional state control to consider include, but are not limited to:

- Civil Rights Laws—Establishing carve-outs for these laws helps avoid canceling protections in states with more robust civil rights laws. If a federal data privacy law contains a civil rights clause, it may address some of these restrictions, but states still may provide additional protections.
- State Statutes Surrounding Unfair and Deceptive Acts and Practices— Every state has a consumer protection law that prohibits deceptive practices, and many others prohibit unfair or unconscionable practices. The effectiveness, strength and applicability of these laws vary widely across the country.
- State Constitutional Law—States may offer their denizens additional rights under their state constitution that are not offered at the federal level.
- State Laws Relating to Tort, Contract and Property in Statute or Common Law—These areas have evolved at the state level over time and often reflect a state view.
- State Criminal Law—All 50 states have computer crime laws of varying scope, from unauthorized access to targeting specific types of crime.
- Laws Governing Specific Relationships—Common examples in state statute include landlord-tenant, employer-employee relationships, library patrons and student privacy.
- State Laws Pertaining to Government Activities—States often regulate state government agencies or state government employee actions relating to privacy, including prohibiting or permitting certain actions. For example, a state may regulate the collection and preservation of public records.

Emerging areas and gap-fillers to consider include, but are not limited to:

- State Cybersecurity Laws—Some states have laws that require businesses to follow rules related to encryption, data breaches, incident reporting, ransomware and other cybersecurity practices that could go further than the provisions in a federal data privacy bill.

- State Versions of Federal Laws That Allow for Stronger Provisions— Multiple federal privacy laws do not preempt stricter privacy protections at the state level like the Health Insurance Portability and Accountability Act (HIPAA) and the Cable Communications Policy Act of 1984, among others. In fact, some federal laws preempt "contrary" state laws but include an exception for state laws providing greater protections.
- State Laws Governing an Area the Federal Law Does Not Address or Contemplate— Federal privacy legislation is unlikely to account for certain privacy concerns unique to certain states, so states should retain the ability to legislate in these areas to avoid gaps, such as anti-paparazzi laws and audio recordings between parties.
- Biometrics—This area requires special consideration because aspects such as definitions, collection versus use and enforcement mechanisms are still widely debated. While some bills do contain biometric definitions and provisions already, and one state—Illinois—has passed a law governing this particular data, this hotly debated topic should be considered outside of existing debates on comprehensive data security data privacy legislation.

Consideration #3: Carve-Outs for Existing Federal Laws

Multiple pieces of current, privacy-related federal law could be explicitly carved out so they are not modified by a new law. Statutory language should address how data is treated when it may be subject to a sectoral privacy law and a comprehensive privacy law, including whether compliance with a sectoral law satisfies requirements set by a new comprehensive law. Existing privacy-related federal laws already have regulatory frameworks in place, and any changes should be addressed through different legislation or amendments to the original statute. These broadly fall into six categories, including but not limited to:

- Student Privacy—Family Educational Rights and Privacy Act (FERPA)
- Health Privacy—HIPAA and Health Information Technology Economic and Clinical Health (HITECH) Act
- Financial Privacy—Gramm-Leach-Bliley Act (GLBA), Fair Debt Collection Practices Act (FDCPA) and Fair Credit Reporting Act (FCRA)
- Children's Privacy—Children's Online Privacy Protection Act (COPPA)
- Federal Government Practices—Privacy Act of 1974 and E-Government Act of 2002
- Other Laws—Communications Assistance for Law Enforcement Act (CALEA), Communications Act of 1934, Electronic Communications Privacy Act (ECPA), *Driver's* Privacy Protection Act of 1994, Controlling Assault of *Non*-Solicited Pornography and Marketing Act, Restore Online Shoppers' Confidence Act, part C of title XI of the Social Security Act, Telemarketing and Consumer Fraud and Abuse Prevention Act, Telephone Consumer Protection Act, Genetic Information Nondiscrimination Act and Federal Aviation Act of 1958

Consideration #4: Other Aspects: The scope of preemption is important, but there are other aspects to consider when including preemption language. These include:

- Language and definitions need clear meaning—Otherwise, uncertainty can be introduced in the laws and regulations, which could lead to litigation and force courts to decide what is and is not preempted or additional agency action may be required. For example, if new legislation has language targeting laws that "directly conflict," a debate could ensue on what falls under that provision. To ensure that clear language and definitions are established, a federal agency like the FTC could be empowered to review cases of preemption as either an advisory body for federal courts or with decision-making authority. In addition, Congress could leave certain provisions open to states or a federal agency like the *FTC* to define (e.g., the federal law may not establish a uniform age of consent to define minors and teens).
- Grandfather existing state privacy laws—Specific state laws could be grandfathered in or each one enacted *prior to* federal legislation to allow them to continue despite a new federal law. For example, California's privacy legislation could be allowed to remain in effect, while others are preempted.
- Enforcement by state governments—State attorneys general or other state agencies could be empowered to assist in enforcing federal legislation, including bringing civil actions on behalf of residents of their state and/or investigating violations. This could be helpful in enforcement against largely local bad actors. They already play a role in enforcing other pieces of federal privacy legislation. Specific considerations would need to include whether notification needs to be made to the *FTC* first, whether the *FTC* has a right of first refusal, where actions can be brought, and the role of state-level data protection authorities.

Recommendations

Taking these options into consideration, we offer three main recommendations related to preemption in federal data security and privacy legislation: preemption should not be approached as all-or-nothing, rights and provisions of a federal law should be compared to existing and proposed state laws, and state governments should have a role in enforcement.

Recommendation #1: Preemption Should Not Be Approached as All-or-Nothing

A federal privacy law should preempt states on substantive provisions covered by the federal law but should also include carve-outs. It is important to prohibit states from making stricter or additional protections, as failure to restrict this action would inevitably result in returning to the existing patchwork of state restrictions. Federal legislation must also be strong enough to provide adequate privacy and security protections to consumers while taking into account the needs of businesses and groups that will be tasked with complying with it.

This allows for a uniform approach for both consumers and industry while protecting areas of state concern through carve-outs. It will prevent entities from having to follow various state frameworks and any subsequent amendments, which would result in large compliance costs, uncertainty on what is needed to comply and the need to monitor all 50 states regularly. A single standard also produces greater trust and ensures that all individuals enjoy the same protections regardless of where they reside or travel.

Specifically, we suggest that federal privacy legislation include:

- Clear Statutory Language That Explicitly Preempts States from Making Their Own Privacy Laws, but That Includes Carve-Outs for Certain Areas—This would prevent states from making distinct, inconsistent frameworks. Select carve-outs are important, however, because they respect and uphold the long history of states having control over unique issues that affect their area, they account for areas that are best addressed by having a local approach instead of a national one and they can help fill gaps not covered by federal law.

We recommend carve-outs for areas of traditional state concern (civil rights laws; state statutes surrounding unfair and deceptive acts and practices; state constitutional law; state laws relating to tort, contract, and property in statute or common law; state criminal law; laws governing specific relationships; and state laws pertaining to government activities) and for emerging areas and gap-fillers (state cybersecurity laws, state versions of federal laws that allow for stronger provisions and state laws governing an area the federal law does not address or contemplate; biometrics require special consideration, as highlighted above).

We also recommend that carve-out implementation be considered in statute in the following ways:

- If an issue area has been addressed by federal statute, the statute should preempt any state level law covering the same topic. For example, if biometric provisions are substantively included in a federal law, states should not be able to make additional or stricter standards.
- If state laws regulate the collection, use, maintenance or other handling of covered data addressed by federal legislation, then those provisions of state law should be preempted, even if that state law encompasses a carve-out enumerated above.
- State laws should not be used to litigate claims related to violations of the federal data security and privacy law.
- Actions by states should be monitored to ensure that additional or new protections are not being created under a carve-out, including under unfair and deceptive acts and practices statutes. For example, a new privacy protection could be created by a state as a tort or an unfair and deceptive practice as a way to expand provisions and get around preemption.
- A Prohibition of Grandfathering Existing State Frameworks or Laws Outside of Those Covered as Carve-Outs—One or multiple existing state laws, such as California's, should not be singled out and allowed to stand while preempting others. A basic premise of the U.S. legal system and our constitutional framework is that all states are equal. Selective preemption of some states' laws would undermine that concept. Furthermore, allowing some existing frameworks to persist would result in inconsistencies from the outset.
- Clear Statutory Language That Explicitly Excludes Select Federal Laws from Being Affected—Certain existing laws have agreed-upon regulatory frameworks that have

existed for years. If these current frameworks were affected by a new law, it would result in burdensome compliance actions and costs for companies and would weaken data security by subjecting unique data to a broader law instead of a sector-specific law. Although this means that some entities would have to follow multiple frameworks, the challenges of making changes to existing laws would outweigh the benefits of a single framework. Therefore, any changes suggested to these existing frameworks should be considered through separate legislation or amendments to their original statute.

The federal carve-outs we recommend excluding from a federal privacy law are 11 of the statutes previously mentioned. They pertain to student privacy, health privacy, financial privacy, children's privacy and other categories. These include FERPA, HIPAA, HITECH Act, GLBA, FCRA, COPPA, CALEA, ECPA, Communications Act of 1934 (except as noted below), *Driver's* Privacy Protection Act of 1994, and the Federal Aviation Act of 1958. Specifically, data covered by and used in accordance with these existing federal privacy laws should be excluded, but if a covered entity collects data not subject to the other laws, it should follow the provisions in the comprehensive federal legislation for that other data. This will help avoid dual systems for the same data.

Also, we recommend that a data privacy federal law aims to have entities covered by the statute be regulated by only one agency for data privacy and security, rather than multiple. In the area of data security and privacy, specifically, Congress could consider allowing the FTC to solely regulate the area to avoid confusion and duplication with the Federal Communications Commission. Of note, certain provisions of existing statutes currently prevent the *FTC* from regulating data security and privacy fully, such as those related to common carriers; therefore, existing statues may need to be amended or superseded to allow for this approach.

Recommendation #2: Rights and provisions of a federal law should be compared to existing and proposed state laws.

The substance of a final privacy bill will reflect how the politics surrounding preemption are addressed. For example, advocates of California's privacy framework may be less likely to oppose broader preemption if the rights and structures currently in place are comparable or stronger in a federal law. On the other hand, if federal law offers fewer protections and still preempts state laws, many are likely to see the federal law as a step backward.

This means that preemption is directly related to other areas of disagreement in the privacy debate like a private right of action (PRA), rulemaking authority and enforcement mechanisms. For example, if the *FTC* has rulemaking authority, there is an increased likelihood of conflict with state laws and regulations in the absence of broader preemption.

Recommendation #3: State Governments Should Have a Role in Enforcement

Permitting state attorneys general, consumer protection officials, or other state officials to share in enforcement will amplify enforcement efforts and make sure local concerns are being addressed. States should be able to conduct investigations into violations affecting their state and bring civil suits in federal court. However, the *FTC* or a designated federal agency should have the right to be heard in any case brought to help ensure consistency and expertise.

In addition, states should be permitted to maintain state-level data protection authorities, like the California Privacy Protection Agency. However, the agencies should not be permitted to take action that is inconsistent with federal legislation or that is exclusively granted to a federal agency. Sample roles could include serving as a subject-matter expert for implementation, addressing previously mentioned carve-outs, training and raising awareness.

About this series: This is part of a series considering the major stumbling blocks of federal data security and data privacy efforts. It draws upon existing research and interview data to identify the most salient issues within data security and data privacy and recommend the most appropriate courses of action in an effort to fnd compromise on federal legislation.

INTRODUCTION – The Path to Reaching Consensus for Federal Data Security and Privacy Legislation

PART 1 – Preemption in Federal Data Security and Privacy Legislation

PART 2 – The Role of the Federal Trade Commission in Federal Data Security and Privacy Legislation

PART 3 – Limiting a Private Right of Action in Federal Data Security and Privacy Legislation

EXPLAINER – Answer to Tough Questions: The Framework of a Federal Data Security and Privacy Law

(Image credit: "The Era of Oversharing (pt.3)" by is licensed under CC BY 4.0)

Real Solutions: The Role of the Federal Trade Commission in Federal Data Security and Privacy Legislation

By Tatyana Bolton, Brandon Pugh, Sofia Lesmes, Lauren Zabierek , Executive Director, Cyber Project at Harvard Kennedy School's Belfer Center, Cory Simpson, Senior Advisor, Cyberspace Solarium Commission, May 31, 2022

Issues: Cybersecurity Policy, Data Security and Data Privacy

The Federal Trade Commission (FTC) is the nation's primary consumer protection body, and while some have called for a new data protection agency, most believe the FTC should be the body responsible for data security and privacy. Indeed, the FTC already enforces some privacy legislation and seeks to expand on its role in data privacy. As federal data and privacy bills are considered, it is therefore critical that we understand the role the FTC might play in overseeing and enforcing such legislation as well as the important role that lawmakers will have in setting parameters for the FTC.

The issues related to rulemaking and enforcement authority are especially important and complex. Unchecked or overly prescriptive authority risks unwieldy regulation that could harm innovation and business, but too little authority risks insufficient protection from privacy harms and overly rigid protections that cannot adapt to rapidly changing technology. We must work to avoid both ends of this spectrum and, instead, strike a balance that ensures that the FTC is appropriately resourced to deliver on the agency's promise to protect citizens and their data.

As a result of our engagement with stakeholders, we believe the key to striking the right balance lies in "guided FTC rulemaking" in a federal law, echoed by privacy experts and private sector companies alike. With such an approach, Congress would be tasked with establishing clear guardrails and definitions around the type of rulemaking authority the FTC could use, the targeted areas in which that authority could be applied, and the means by which such efforts could be undertaken. Parameters for assessing penalties would also be key in ensuring that the enforcement of violations is carried out in a way that upholds compliance rather than conveying a perception of unguided fining.

This publication—the second in a series of three main articles—explores these issues and provides recommendations for what we consider to be the most reasonable solutions.

Considerations and Options

This section addresses the key question and options available to lawmakers in considering the FTC's role in federal privacy legislation. There are four categories of questions:

- What type of rulemaking authority should the FTC be given and under which laws should that authority be granted?
- For which aspects of a data security and privacy law should the FTC be granted targeted rulemaking authority?
- How will the FTC handle the enforcement of federal privacy legislation (e.g., assessing violations, determining whether a warning is warranted, determining fines) and should the FTC provide regular guidance to companies beyond enforcement?
- How should these efforts be funded and organized (e.g., budget amount, personnel needed, phased funding, new FTC bureau)?

Below, we explore these considerations and options, bringing together our assessments of four major federal privacy bills (two Democratic, two Republican), interviews with stakeholders, and a review of existing research.

Consideration #1: Current Authorities under Which the FTC Can Operate

The FTC is the nation's consumer protection body and it generally operates under the FTC Act and additional rules that it promulgates pursuant to the Magnuson-Moss Warranty Act (MMWA) of 1975. This differs from other federal agencies in that the Administrative Procedures Act (APA) is more commonly the primary rulemaking authority.

Although Section 18 of the FTC Act authorizes the Commission to create rules specifying and governing unfair and deceptive acts or practices (currently the Commission's key tool for addressing data privacy and security), MMWA rulemaking requires a much more lengthy and cumbersome process (to include publishing an Advanced Notice of Proposed Rulemaking, publishing a Notice of Proposed Rulemaking for public comment, holding informal hearings, publishing the final rule, and—after all of this—any person may seek judicial review within 60 days), which is largely why the authority has rarely been used since its inception in 1975.

The APA is the standard authority granted to most federal agencies to create, amend, or appeal rules. The authority, which is known as "notice and comment," requires agencies to publish a notice of proposed rulemaking in the federal register and provide ample time for public comment, among other requirements. APA authority must be specifically granted to the FTC by Congress in legislation; currently, the FTC has been directed to use this authority for specific laws, such as the Children's Online Privacy Protection Act (COPPA) and the Telemarketing and Consumer Fraud and Abuse Prevention Act. According to the U.S. Chamber of Commerce, rules promulgated under APA authority on average took less than a year to adopt versus five years for those under MMWA.

To address the lengthy rulemaking procedures of MMWA, the FTC recently worked to streamline the process; however, it must be noted that, despite the changes (including as the Commissioner's statement notes: "providing the Commission with greater accountability and control over Section 18 rulemaking, deciding the final list of disputed material facts to be resolved, deciding who will make oral presentations to the Commission and who will cross examine or present rebuttals submissions"), the requirements are still difficult to meet and may not eliminate many of the obstacles that held up previous attempts at rulemaking under the authority. However, the FTC has stated that it intends to use these updated procedures in new rulemakings on privacy issues—an approach encouraged by the Biden Administration to address privacy and security because Congress has not yet been able to. This has drawn concern with regard to the lack of oversight and the agency's capacity to enforce such rules.

Consideration #2: Areas for Rulemaking

Under the current MMWA rulemaking procedures, the FTC is theoretically free (notwithstanding its resource limitations) to create multiple rules to address "unfair and deceptive practices." In its Statement on Regulatory Priorities, the Commission indicated that it intends to create, among other areas, rules to curb lax security practices, limit surveillance abuses and ensure that algorithmic decision-making does not result in unlawful discrimination. This has caused some concern among stakeholders across the spectrum. On one end, companies fear unchecked rulemaking and enforcement; on the other, advocates fear the inability to oversee and enforce these rules broadly.

Four of the main legislative proposals—Sen. Maria Cantwell's (D-Wash.) Consumer Online Privacy Act (COPRA), Sen. Roger Wicker's (R-Miss.) SAFE Data Act, Sen. Sherrod Brown's (D-Ohio) DATA 2020 (which would create a Data Accountability and Transparency Agency rather than place principal enforcement and rulemaking authority with the FTC) and Sen. Jerry Moran's (R-Kan.) Consumer Data Privacy and Security Act (CDPSA)—have collectively identified the following areas for FTC rulemaking:

- Determining which data elements qualify for enhanced protections under the term "sensitive covered data" (COPRA, SAFE Data Act and CDPSA)
- Designating approved processes for covered entities to implement to allow individuals to opt out of transfers of covered data (COPRA)
- Identifying circumstances that would require organizations to obtain individuals' explicit consent for processing personal data (CDPSA and SAFE Data Act)
- Setting requirements for covered entities to adequately respond to individuals' rights requests in a timely fashion, including requests to access, correct and delete personal data (CDPSA)
- Establishing regulations for biometric data (COPRA)

- Identifying unlawful, unfair, deceptive or abusive acts or practices in connection with the collection, use or sharing of personal data (under a new data protection agency; DATA 2020)
- Identifying processes (in consultation with the National Institute of Standards and Technology [NIST]) for receiving and assessing information regarding vulnerabilities to the security of covered data that are reported to the covered entity (SAFE Data Act)

Consideration #3: Enforcement

The FTC's role in the enforcement of the law and subsequent rules is also important to navigate smoothly. Legislation from both sides of the aisle generally aligns on the scope of FTC enforcement: With the exception of Brown's DATA 2020 Act (which calls for an entirely new agency), each of the four main bills described above provides that a violation of the privacy law (or a regulation promulgated under the privacy law) "shall be treated as a violation of a rule." These provisions would allow the agency to seek monetary relief "to redress injury to consumers," including refunds, damages and "public notification respecting the" underlying violation. Such authority would supplement—not replace—other FTC enforcement mechanisms, including penalty authority.

Here, we present the most controversial and intractable issues of FTC enforcement: the collection of penalties and associated frameworks, the right to cure, the role of state attorneys general and how fines would be used.

- Collection of penalties—As with the other provisions described in this document, the aim of robust enforcement is compliance and protection, not lawsuits and collection of penalties. If left undefined, the parameters of first-time fining authority could be viewed as controversial by businesses, resulting in overly burdensome fines on well-meaning companies on one end and insufficient mechanisms for halting egregious and continuing harms on the other.

Each of the four main bills grants the FTC (or another future data protection agency) the authority to collect civil penalties in violation of the law (or rules promulgated under the law) and to treat violations as unfair and deceptive practices under the FTC Act. Historically, business groups have balked at this, claiming that the FTC has failed to provide specific, detailed guidance on what is deemed "unfair and deceptive."

The CDPSA is more prescriptive in the authority it would grant the FTC; it limits penalties per violation "up to $42,530 multiplied by the number of individuals affected" and designates a number of considerations for the FTC in determining penalties, such as the degree of harm; intent in committing the violation; size, complexity and resources of a covered entity; reasonable expectations; degree of compliance; self-reporting; and steps taken to address the violation. This is similar to how COPPA determines its penalties but differs from the current enforcement of unfair and deceptive practices for general privacy violations. However, it must be noted that many experts have commented on the difficulty of translating privacy harms into quantitative amounts.

Although the CDPSA is more specific in outlining how the FTC may seek penalties, it does not determine where penalties would go or how they would be used. The other main bills identify the creation of a victims' relief fund, which the Commission could draw from to issue payments to victims of harmful data practices. Some have stated that the funds should be deposited into the general U.S. Treasury and be usable by the federal government for general public good. Others have suggested that the funds not only go toward victims' relief but also toward helping small and medium businesses bolster their data privacy and security compliance. We present the following options:

- Penalties obtained by the FTC and the attorney general could be deposited into a Data Privacy and Security Victims' Relief Fund which would provide redress, payments or compensation, or other monetary relief to individuals.
- Funds could also be used "for the purpose of consumer or business education relating to data privacy and security or for the purpose of engaging in technological research that the Commission considers necessary to enforce."
- Funds could also be used to help with data privacy and security compliance for small- and medium-sized businesses, especially in the early years of the law, and could be shared with the Cybersecurity and Infrastructure Security Agency (CISA) to assist with their outreach and services.

Consideration #4: Capacity

Most stakeholders agree that the FTC is not appropriately resourced (in either staff or budget) to regulate or enforce privacy. The Commission's current annual budget is approximately $351 million, but in its privacy mission, it employs 61 people at $13 million. For context, the United Kingdom's Information Commissioner's Office has a budget of approximately $90 million with 822 permanent staff, and Ireland's Data Protection Commission has a budget of approximately $18 million with 138 permanent staff. Both countries have more data privacy officers than the United States but have significantly fewer citizens to protect. The U.S.'s capacity to address data security and privacy is out of sync with the degree of potential harms and threats.

In a letter written to Representative Frank Pallone (D-N.J.) in 2019, then-FTC Commissioner Joe Simons laid out what he could do with additional funding: With $50 million of funding per year, the FTC could hire and retain 160 more staff members; with $75 million, the FTC could hire and retain 260 more staff members; and with $100 million, the FTC could hire and retain 360 more staff members. Those staff members would join the 40 current (at that time) staff members in the Division of Privacy and Identity Protection, expanding the Commission's capacity to bring approximately 20 cases per year to 180 cases per year and enabling the agency to enforce not only any future federal data privacy and security law but also COPPA and the Fair Credit Reporting Act. Simons also estimated that he would need an additional 10 to 15 technologists to join the 5 on staff at that time and cited the need for additional infrastructure, such as office space.

Although the major federal bills (with the exception of DATA 2020, which argues for the creation of a new data protection agency) designate the FTC as the enforcement body and note that the FTC is currently under-resourced, they differ on the approaches they recommend to bolster those resources. The CDSPA grants the FTC the ability to grow to 440 personnel but doesn't authorize specific funding to get there (though it does note the need for additional experts like technologists). The CDPA also directs the FTC in its regulation and enforcement authority but designates no specifics for its growth in funding or personnel. COPRA directs the creation of a new FTC bureau but leaves out specifics on budgetary and personnel needs. Of note, the Build Back Better (BBB) infrastructure bill also proposed $500 million over seven years for the development and growth of a new FTC bureau to enhance its ability to work on data privacy and security matters.

Recommendations

After assessing the many considerations and options for the role of the FTC above, below we list our recommendations and rationales. Of note, we do not recommend safe harbor provisions or the right to cure. Our goal is to strike a balance between ensuring safety for the consumer; preserving the ability to innovate and deliver services to businesses; and protecting our national security. We acknowledge that we cannot satisfy every stakeholder's wish, but we have taken key interests into account and offer below what we believe to be the most prudent courses of action.

Recommendation #1: Authority—A Federal Privacy Bill Should Grant the FTC Targeted Rulemaking Authority under Section 5, Administrative Procedure Act

A bill should grant authority under Section 5 of the Administrative Procedure Act. Targeted rulemaking under the APA allows Congress to provide necessary oversight while not slowing the process—thus allowing the FTC to be agile and responsive to changing technological conditions and privacy harms. We recommend the following additional considerations:

- As a prerequisite to rulemaking, the FTC must demonstrate any harm brought about by new technology and business models.
- The law should specify ample time for stakeholders to comment (no less than 90 days).

Recommendation #2: Targeted Rulemaking Areas—Rules Must Be Made Clear with Limited Interpretation Left to Organizations

It is impossible to enumerate all the areas for which the FTC should create rules without having a bill—or a crystal ball—to consult. But the point of rulemaking is to ensure that the law can keep up with evolving technology, business models and the harms that develop with them. Therefore, targeted rulemaking means that the FTC should be allowed to update regulatory provisions as defined by Congress that it has deemed inadequate to address the new harms brought about by technological change, but the agency must clearly demonstrate the need to do so through its rulemaking procedures. As such, a federal privacy law must determine the standard for proof of harm. Furthermore, to ensure the best enforcement of data security, the FTC should be directed to work in coordination and consultation with the relevant security agencies (e.g., CISA, NIST, Office of the National Cyber Director).

Recommendation #3: Enforcement—The Aim of a Federal Law Should Be for Broad Compliance and Increased Consumer Data Security and Privacy, Not to Collect Fines

To move toward improvements and ensure a balanced bill, Congress should designate the FTC as the primary federal enforcer and allow state attorneys general to bring suit on behalf of that state's constituents—but not in parallel. Congress should also grant the FTC and state attorneys general the authority to collect civil penalties for violations of a data privacy and security law and rules promulgated as part of that law. However, the following conditions should be met:

- Congress should give covered entities two years to comply with the basic provisions laid out in legislation once the law is signed before the FTC is authorized to enforce it.
- Clear penalty criteria and explanatory framework should be developed based on the type of covered entity, the intent and actions to correct, and the measure of harm as defined by Congress (such as how Sen. Moran's CDPSA bill does).

As a matter of practice to ensure broad compliance, the FTC should use warning and remediation letters and should issue and update best-practice guidance regularly. Specific recommended tactics include:

- Warning letters describing violations and steps for remediation should be issued to covered entities when needed.
- Congress should require the FTC to release regular and specific guidance around the law and subsequent rules to help covered entities understand and comply, especially small and medium businesses and nonprofits with limited means.
- Fines should go into a victims' relief fund mirroring COPRA and CDPA and a data privacy and security fund (a split that Congress should determine).

Recommendation #4: Capacity—The FTC Needs Staffing and Budget Increases to Be Fully Effective

Continuing with the status quo will result in little-to-no increase in resources for the FTC to carry out its duties, especially if federal privacy legislation is passed. Failure to provide more resources to the FTC would hamstring its ability to protect consumers by limiting its capacity to investigate suspected or alleged violations and enforce rules.

Therefore, Congress should allocate an additional $500 million for a new FTC Bureau of Data Security and Privacy, allowing it to grow to 360 personnel over the next five years, which is in line with former FTC Commissioner Joe Simons' recommendations. We also recommend an additional $100 million for capital infrastructure and technology upgrades. It's worth noting the need to focus on hiring diverse staff to address the varied nature of privacy threats and harms. Therefore, we recommend that bills require the hiring of technologists, privacy experts and other experts from varying fields to appropriately identify harms and ways to combat them. Although different stakeholders are advocating for both lower and higher resource and staff allotments for FTC privacy functions, our recommendation reflects the middle ground in the debate.

About this series: This is part of a series considering the major stumbling blocks of federal data security and data privacy efforts. It draws upon existing research and interview data to identify the most salient issues within data security and data privacy and recommend the most appropriate courses of action in an effort to fnd compromise on federal legislation.

INTRODUCTION – The Path to Reaching Consensus for Federal Data Security and Privacy Legislation

PART 1 – Preemption in Federal Data Security and Privacy Legislation

PART 2 – The Role of the Federal Trade Commission in Federal Data Security and Privacy Legislation

PART 3 – Limiting a Private Right of Action in Federal Data Security and Privacy Legislation

EXPLAINER – Answer to Tough Questions: The Framework of a Federal Data Security and Privacy Law

(Image credit: "Tracking" by Ifrah Yousuf is licensed under CC BY 4.0)

Real Solutions: Limiting a Private Right of Action in Federal Data Security and Privacy Legislation

By Tatyana Bolton, Brandon Pugh, Sofia Lesmes, Lauren Zabierek, Executive Director, Cyber Project at Harvard Kennedy School's Belfer Center, Cory Simpson, Senior Advisor, Cyberspace Solarium Commission, June 7, 2022

Issues: Cybersecurity Policy, Data Security and Data Privacy

Enforcing national data security and privacy legislation presents challenges in both scope and scale. Congress's decision regarding who they choose to empower—be it individuals, state attorneys general, one or more federal agencies, or a combination thereof—will dictate the true shape of the law, once passed. If individuals are empowered with an enforcement role—that is, if a private right of action (PRA) is established—it is important to outline the structure, procedures and limits to craft a fair and functional law.

But reaching a consensus on whether federal data security and privacy legislation should even include a PRA has been particularly challenging. Many advocates of a PRA see it as a necessary component to a meaningful enforcement regime, as a properly drafted PRA could fulfill at least three strategic goals: empowering consumers to advocate for themselves, incentivizing the compliance of covered entities and allowing consumers to be made whole for damages—a supplement to potential Federal Trade Commission (FTC) authority to order monetary relief or impose fines. On the other hand, opponents warn that a PRA in federal data security and privacy legislation would likely result in widespread litigation, including frivolous lawsuits and overly broad legal exposure for the private sector. These skeptics believe enforcement by a federal agency or by a combination of a federal agency and state attorneys general would result in a more effective, cohesive and predictable enforcement regime.

In deciding whether to create a PRA, Congress must balance the diverse priorities and perspectives of different stakeholders. It must consider industry and consumer concerns, the adequacy of remedies, the role of states, and regulatory capability and capacity. While a PRA has its drawbacks, the consensus position that takes these issues into account has settled around a limited PRA as a backstop against shifting political winds and executive branch control over privacy enforcement. Just as in other areas, however, Congress should avoid an all-or-nothing approach in striking this balance, taking into account the role of enforcement by the FTC and state attorneys general under state laws and any new federal privacy law. In addition, if Congress chooses to create a PRA, it should empower everyday Americans to assist in the enforcement of the new law in a clear, confined and meaningful way that protects both the American consumer and innovation.

This publication—the last in a series of three main articles—explores the various considerations and options for structuring such an enforcement mechanism and then presents our key recommendations for reaching a consensus.

Considerations and Options

Consideration #1: Applicability of a PRA

A PRA could either apply broadly in statute or exclusively to specific provisions. The broadest approach would allow a PRA for any individual alleging a violation of the federal law or regulation to be brought in either state or federal court. This could permit suits for violations of all provisions from a right to access to data breaches. However, a PRA could be limited to apply to specific violations of the statute like a data breach. For example, California's privacy legislation permits a PRA only in the case of a data breach, whereas other enforcement mechanisms permit broader action (e.g., the state attorney general is empowered to address all violations of the statute).

Consideration #2: Consumer Standing

The Constitution requires that individuals have "standing" in order to bring a civil suit. This means they must have suffered a real and individualized harm to bring a successful lawsuit. Demonstrating such harm as a result of privacy violations can be challenging because the harm may not be direct or apparent and would therefore present a constitutional standing challenge. This challenge would be exacerbated by the fact that traditional legal concepts are hard to apply to the digital world.

Indeed, in Spokeo, Inc. v. Robins, the U.S. Supreme Court held that demonstrating a violation of the statute alone, without showing a real and individualized harm, is insufficient to meet the constitutional standing requirement. Of note, there is one prominent instance in privacy law in which individuals can bring suit without alleging harm beyond a violation of their rights under the statute; it is in the case of one particular type of data (biometrical) in one specific state (Illinois).

In determining whether an individual has standing, courts are required to look to traditional harms for comparisons, like those caused by defamation and theft. The Court noted in Spokeo that Congress can play a role in assisting the courts by clarifying the harm in privacy violations that may give an individual standing. Subsequently, in TransUnion LLC v. Ramirez, the Court underscored that "Congress's creation of a statutory prohibition or obligation…does not relieve courts of their responsibility to independently decide whether a plaintiff has suffered a concrete harm…any more than, for example, Congress's enactment of a law regulating speech relieves courts of their responsibility to independently decide whether the law violates the First Amendment."

Concrete harm appears to be a constitutional standing requirement, and the court has continued to look to traditional harms when determining whether a harm has occurred in a particular case. The Spokeo and TransUnion holdings create uncertainty in terms of the harms that may be sufficient to give an individual standing to bring suit for privacy violations. Future court decisions to clarify this issue are necessary and likely. While this area of the law develops, Congress could articulate a harm in statute, specifically considering the violations the harm would apply to, what traditional harms would be similar, and what alternative enforcement mechanisms would exist if standing were inadequate. Thankfully, legislative bodies and academic institutions across the country have identified practical frameworks under which privacy harms can be better understood.

Some of these frameworks have attempted to articulate what harms should be legally cognizable (i.e., sufficient) to provide an individual standing to bring suit. Recent literature categorizes the harms into seven areas: physical, economic, reputational, psychological, autonomy, discrimination and relationship. Some of these have a clear basis in existing law and might help future courts consider harm in the privacy context.

Other frameworks see a duty of loyalty as being a solution to standing issues, where entities should act in the best interest of those who expose their data, and the integrity of the relationship guides the duties. A breach of a duty of loyalty is the injury itself and has long been recognized by courts as a legally cognizable harm. In contrast, a duty of care is not based solely on the relationship, and specific harm is needed.

In the Consumer Online Privacy Rights Act (COPRA), privacy harms are included under the duty of loyalty provisions, covering the definitions of deceptive data practices and harmful data practices. Under harmful data practice, five injuries are established: physical; financial; reputational; physical or other offensive intrusion upon the solitude or seclusion of the individual; and "other" substantial injury. The former acting chair of the FTC, Maureen Ohlhausen, discussed injury similarly—the five types of injury she identified through cases brought by the FTC were financial; health and safety; reputational; unwarranted intrusion; and deception injury and subverting consumer choice.

Consideration #3: Advocacy Groups as Enforcers

Groups could be designated at the state level to bring lawsuits in lieu of consumers. If groups were empowered to bring lawsuits instead of consumers, this would lower the number of potential litigants and most likely reduce litigation. Some Senate bills have included provisions permitting a protection and advocacy (P&A) organization to bring a civil action against a covered entity, allowing each state to designate one organization. Of note, there is precedent in federal law for this approach: The Developmental Disabilities Assistance and Bill of Rights Act of 1975, for example, established state P&A systems to advocate, investigate abuses and ensure enforcement. That system also permits class litigation in some cases.

Consideration #4: Sunrise and Sunset Provisions

Sunrise and sunset provisions can impact when a PRA would become effective and how long it would last. A sunrise provision allows for a portion of a law to apply to a specific period of time before the main body of the law becomes active. A sunset clause, on the other hand, provides that an entire statute or portion thereof ceases to exist after a fixed amount of time or certain statutory conditions are satisfied. These mechanisms could be a way to keep legislation in check by timing more aggressive enforcement and incentivizing lawmakers to assess the law's effectiveness continually. The mechanics of such provisions would be important to outline, including: whether time alone triggers the provision; whether certain conditions in the statute need to be met; what other provisions in the legislation might have a sunrise and/or sunset provision; or whether additional congressional approval is needed.

Consideration #5: A Right to Cure

A right to cure, also known as an opportunity to cure, refers to an opportunity for entities to address complaints by consumers before litigation. This process can be managed by a federal agency or court and, when an individual files a complaint, the agency or court is responsible for ensuring that the complaint is addressed; if it is not sufficiently addressed, a PRA could commence. A recent report suggests this could go hand in hand with a right to recourse—an entity's internal process through which a consumer can resolve potential violations and/or privacy concerns. For either to work, standards would need to address what is "corrected enough," whether it should apply to all companies or just smaller ones, how much time should be allowed to resolve the issue and what entity makes and enforces these rules.

Consideration #6: Filing of Complaints with Particularity

Filing complaints "with particularity" means that a plaintiff must provide "in great detail, all the relevant facts forming the basis of her belief" with facts for any malice, intent, knowledge and other conditions of a person's mind that may be alleged generally. Some argue that privacy claim pleadings now are not mapped to harms, and, after the passage of a federal bill, should be mapped to statutorily granted harms. This is similar to the process undertaken for Securities and Exchange Commission filings or for fraud claims under the Federal Rules of Civil Procedure.

Consideration #7: Feasibility Review

Frivolous lawsuits present a challenge to a PRA. Suit under a PRA could address this concern by being subject to a screening before proceeding to the courts. A review could answer questions of legitimacy, basic adequacy and motivation.

Multiple existing state and federal bodies could serve as a model for this type of board, including the Massachusetts Medical Malpractice Tribunal, federal administrative review boards and the U.S Equal Employment Opportunity Commission. Any screening model selected would need to set specifications for duration of review, impartiality, sufficiency standards and resource determinations.

Consideration #8: Injunctive Relief

Injunctive relief is mandated legal action that forces an individual or entity to stop or start a behavior or to carry out a certain action. Injunctive relief could mandate that behavior that is causing harm to an individual or group of individuals be stopped. If enforcement encompasses injunctive relief, it could help reduce lawsuits motivated by financial reasons. However, despite injunctive relief's potential usefulness as an enforcement tool, its effectiveness depends on the specific harm in question. For example, injunctive relief could be granted to require a company to improve its security controls to prevent future similar attacks, but it would not offer other remedies available to litigants in traditional litigation.

Consideration #9: Tiered Rights and Damages

Damages could be structured in several ways to account for the potentially competing variables at play, which include how to make harmed individuals whole, ensure that punishments are appropriate for specific violations and prevent excessive judgments. One proposed concept suggests that dynamic standards be tied to the different provisions in legislation. It would require harms be recognized as invasions of privacy, discrimination or financial loss in one way; violations that affect privacy be recognized in another way; and that all other types of violations be recognized a third way, with a different level of knowledge or intention to be subject to different degrees of liability.

Other considerations related to tiered rights and damages include capping damages to limit exposure; escalating enforcement for willful and repeated violations; determining the types of damages to be awarded like statutory damages and/or punitive damages; and covering other expenses like attorney fees and litigation costs.

Consideration #10: Limiting Legal Exposure

Measures could be implemented to help covered entities limit their legal exposure. There are two common ways of approaching this issue: establishing a safe harbor and making a breach by a nation-state actor an affirmative defense.

A safe harbor, or an affirmative defense, can provide legal protection for a covered entity against a data breach claim if certain steps are taken. By following an established data protection and security framework, such as the standards set out by the National Institute of Standards and Technology, covered entities can be shielded entirely or have their liability limited in precise and predictable ways. A safe harbor serves as an incentive for covered entities to implement data protection measures in favor of incurring litigation expenses and damages. Some states, like Ohio and New Jersey, have already begun the process of framing safe harbors in their respective state laws. To ensure adherence, covered entities can make a certification that is subject to penalties if later proven to be false and/or be subject to independent assessment by a government agency.

A breach caused by a nation-state actor could also be an affirmative defense to prevent companies from being liable. For example, if a company is breached by a Russian advanced persistent threat, lawsuits arising out of that breach would be reserved for governmental prosecution. This could be useful, as some insurance companies are already excluding coverage for hacks and breaches from nation-state actors. Of note, a safe harbor established under similar motivation was enacted after the September 11 attacks with the Terrorism Risk Insurance Act and has been proposed by the Cyberspace Solarium Commission for systemically important critical infrastructure entities.

Consideration #11: Arbitration

An alternative method of resolving disputes is using an arbitrator or a panel of arbitrators instead of litigating in court—a process that would require most cases to be settled outside of court. There is ongoing debate, however, as to whether arbitration should be considered within the confines of a data security and privacy law.

Recommendations

If Congress decides to include a PRA in federal legislation, it must balance an individual's right to be made whole for a privacy violation with a covered entity's concern over excessive lawsuits. If included, it must also strive to create more consistency in enforcement and avoid disparities between courts.

Opponents to a PRA cite drawbacks such as frivolous class-action lawsuits and high costs to businesses, which are concerns we share. Therefore, to achieve a consensus on this issue, we believe a more limited PRA is the solution for addressing these concerns and breaking the deadlock of an all-or-nothing approach. A limited PRA can be viewed as a backstop against the politicization of federal and state enforcement of individual damages, especially for marginalized communities that may be underserved by enforcement agencies. Below, we present our three key recommendations for balancing these objectives and finding a path forward.

Recommendation #1: The Structure of a PRA Needs to Be Carefully Crafted to Ensure It Is Workable

If Congress decides to include a PRA in legislation, it should address the mechanics for how a PRA will operate, including specific methods to address standing uncertainty, a delayed start and automatic termination.

- Specify a right to bring suit in statute, but vary outcomes based on the type of harm—Demonstrating harm has been a challenge in privacy cases, and recent Supreme Court cases create even more uncertainty as to what level and type of harm is sufficient to bring suit. Congress has a role in defining injuries that can help form the basis of a case, although that does not automatically satisfy standing requirements. Still, Congress could create statutory procedures to allow an individual to sue if, for example, their individual data was unlawfully disclosed—with a one-year statute of limitations from the period the individual knew or should have known about the breach. Congress could also specify the type of data that could constitute sufficient harm. For example, it could be all data covered by the definition of data, or it could be narrowed to a smaller subset.

In addition, individuals should be permitted to exercise a PRA in cases where actual harm can be demonstrated. This accounts for scenarios in which data was shared or disclosed in violation of the statute outside of a data breach and resulted in a measurable harm.

Permitting a PRA for other violations covered by federal legislation may present standing issues, including for a right to opt-in or access data. Congress should include statutory procedures to allow for a suit for these violations, but injunctive relief—after a statutorily required compliance period—should be the default instead of monetary damages. This would help reduce the risk of future harm.

There are at least two exceptions to this recommendation: FTC fines and civil rights litigation. The FTC should maintain its right to levy fines in cases it deems necessary. Likewise, in civil rights litigation, individuals should maintain their rights to file suit under civil rights statutes.

- Privacy harms should be specific, substantive, measurable and enforceable—As Ohlhausen said in her speech on consumer injury, "Government does the most good with the fewest unintended side effects when it focuses on stopping substantial consumer injury instead of expanding resources to prevent hypothetical injuries." The seven harms identified in recent literature (physical, economic, reputational, psychological, autonomy, discrimination and relationship)—while informative—are too expansive and are not ready to be used as the framework for privacy legislation. Because this list of harms does not have clear recognition and support by courts or consensus policy support, a narrower list of eligible harms should be enumerated by Congress.

Based on the position taken by the FTC and the definition of harms in COPRA, consensus exists around at least five harms: physical, financial, reputational, deception and unwarranted intrusion. These should form the basis of the data security and data privacy law harm provisions.

Congress should also consider the implications of injury constraint provisions and ensure that decisions on privacy harms in this bill do not negatively impact common law understandings of harms in areas such as property and contracts. Moreover, Congress should make these determinations with the understanding that any standards established for harms are bound by the inherent checks on the ability to use a PRA in the First Amendment, Section 230 and the rules of standing.

- Do not allow sunrise or sunset provisions—A sunrise provision would create a window for covered entities to revisit internal compliance structures ahead of enforcement and allow courts the necessary preparation time. However, this also means that consumers would have limited recourse for addressing violations because agency enforcement will initially be slow, given the need to hire additional staff and establish procedures. This makes PRA even more essential at the outset of a federal law.

A sunset provision would provide covered entities with security that a PRA would be revisited after a certain period or it would end. However, if the PRA were to end abruptly, it could harm consumer recourse, and there is no guarantee that Congress would again revisit the statute to pass updates to the legislation. Congress should instead revisit the legislation holistically after a period of time and revise the PRA as needed.

Recommendation #2: Procedural Steps Should Be Implemented before a PRA Can Be Exercised

This approach will help reduce the number of lawsuits and allows for fixes to be made before litigation. Important aspects of this approach include:

- Establish a right to cure as a step to solve issues before litigation—

Consumers and covered entities should have a way to address privacy concerns and make complaints before exercising a PRA. As some argued was the case after the passage of the American with Disabilities Act of 1990, initial compliance can create crushing and antagonistic suits without doing much in the way of improving compliance. It can also threaten to put some companies out of business. Addressing initial compliance and creating a cure period can help achieve the aims of consumers (who want to ensure the security and privacy of their data) and of covered entities (who need to use data as a function of their business). There are, however, limits to the usefulness of a right to cure. In cases where the harm was done already, such as a data breach or publication of private images, a right to cure would offer little utility. The focus should therefore remain on the majority of instances where a right to cure is both feasible and useful.

The ultimate end goal of any enforcement approach is to ensure compliance. A right to cure paired with injunctive relief would likely result in that goal, as the cure period would require a company to implement data protection and privacy safeguards with some immediacy. This has an overall broader beneficial effect on individual consumers as a whole, with faster action and compliance, rather than the limited effect of relief for individual litigants that may come before the court.

Specifically, for a five-year period after enactment, companies should be given a 30-day window to fix violations before a lawsuit should proceed to allow for a transition period. Courts should be the arbiters in cases of whether a company cured a violation (i.e., instead of federal agencies), and companies should be encouraged to develop an internal process to address violations by working with consumers. This is advantageous because informal resolution may be possible before escalating the issue.

- Privacy complaints should be filed with particularity—Filing with particularity is a common-sense solution to address the concern that privacy claims could be overly broad. More specifically, in privacy legislation, Congress should include language that specifies that in any private action, the complainant should be required to specify allegations, each violation alleged, and the reasons they believe that to be the case. In cases in which the plaintiff makes allegations against a company (i.e., that it violated the act, made an untrue statement of a material fact, committed a harmful data practice, conducted a deceptive data practice or violated the rights set forth in the act), the complaint should specify each violation alleged and the reason why the claimant believes it to be a violation. In addition, if an allegation regarding the behavior is made on information and belief, the complaint shall state with particularity all facts on which that belief is formed.

Moreover, in any private action in which the plaintiff may recover monetary damages only on proof that the defendant acted with a particular state of mind, the complaint should state with particularity facts giving rise to a strong inference that the defendant acted with that state of mind.

- A review process should be a future consideration—Having a process in place for a federal agency or state attorney general to screen potential lawsuits would be a way to prevent those without merit from proceeding. Of course, specific safeguards would be necessary to ensure that consumers have access to courts in appropriate situations without being limited by a federal or state entity. This is not recommended at the present time because there are inadequate resources at the federal level to accomplish it. If such a federal screen were to be conducted by the FTC, additional resources would be needed. In the case of the passage of federal privacy legislation, the FTC's resources would all go to establishing the privacy bureau and would not be available to establish another new process.

Recommendation #3: Limits Should Be Established for a PRA

A PRA needs to be restricted with the goal of limiting lawsuits with inconsistent and excessive monetary awards while still providing relief to consumers. Specific ways to limit a PRA include:

- Incorporate injunctive relief to avoid or mitigate further harm—The specifics of injunctive relief will depend on the final provisions of a federal privacy bill. Injunctive relief is especially warranted when a consumer alleges that their rights under federal legislation were violated, but a breach has not occurred.

A challenge is that injunctive relief is not always effective after a breach has occurred and works most effectively in situations where immediate remedy is necessary. After a breach, an individual's data has already been disclosed. In such cases, injunctive relief could serve to prevent greater disclosure, but it would not correct what has already transpired in the same way that monetary damages could.

- Place limitations on damages—Having constraints on damages would prevent uncapped legal exposure for companies, create more consistent results and interpretation across the courts, and help reduce financially motivated lawsuits. For data breaches and cases where actual harm is demonstrated, individuals should be entitled to actual damages without statutory damages. If the harm is caused by willful behavior, punitive damages should be permitted up to a cap. As has been typical in recent years, courts should also have the authority to order a company to pay for credit monitoring for those who have been affected. For all other violations of federal privacy law, the actions of the company should be willful or repeated to be recoverable. Those cases should be eligible for actual damages and discretionary punitive damages up to a capped amount.
- Establish a safe harbor—Entities that take proactive steps or experience a breach from exceptional circumstances should not face the same liability as those who have failed to take affirmative measures to comply with statutory requirements, remain susceptible to known attacks or fail to address longstanding and known vulnerabilities. First, there should be a safe harbor for entities that voluntarily conform to a stated security framework. This would incentivize stronger cybersecurity programs by potentially limiting legal costs. The challenge will be assessing compliance beyond certifications by industry actors. A federal agency should evaluate compliance if a company seeks a proactive evaluation, which would serve as evidence for review by a court. However, a court needs to be able to reject that evaluation and independently evaluate it should an entity not go through agency review first.

In addition, liability for data breaches caused by nation-state actors should not be the responsibility of covered entities. Safe harbor for covered entities does not preclude those entities from their responsibilities to protect their networks, but it does acknowledge that nation-state, adversary-caused incidents are beyond the normal scope of network defense and liability. In such situations, proof should be required that the breach was caused by a nation-state. With such proof, the company should be able to have an affirmative defense and should not be subjected to monetary penalties.

About this series: This is part of a series considering the major stumbling blocks of federal data security and data privacy efforts. It draws upon existing research and interview data to identify the most salient issues within data security and data privacy and recommend the most appropriate courses of action in an effort to nd compromise on federal legislation.

INTRODUCTION – The Path to Reaching Consensus for Federal Data Security and Privacy Legislation

PART 1 – Preemption in Federal Data Security and Privacy Legislation

PART 2 – The Role of the Federal Trade Commission in Federal Data Security and Privacy Legislation

EXPLAINER – Answer to Tough Questions: The Framework of a Federal Data Security and Privacy Law

Image: fizkes

* * *

February 27, 2023

The Honorable Guy Bilirakis
Chairman
Subcommittee on Innovation, Data and Commerce
U.S. House Committee on Energy and Commerce
2125 Rayburn House Office Building
Washington, DC 20515

The Honorable Jan Schakowsky
Ranking Member
Subcommittee on Innovation, Data and Commerce
U.S. House Committee on Energy and Commerce
2107 Rayburn House Office Building
Washington, DC 20515

Dear Chairman Bilirakis and Ranking Member Schakowsky:

On behalf of the members of the National Multifamily Housing Council (NMHC) and the National Apartment Association (NAA)[109], we applaud the bipartisan, bicameral work done to

[109] For more than 25 years, the National Multifamily Housing Council (NMHC) and the National Apartment Association (NAA) have partnered to provide a single voice for America's apartment industry. Our combined memberships are engaged in all aspects of the apartment industry, including ownership, development, management, finance and suppliers partners/service providers. NMHC represents the principal officers of over 1,500 firms that own, develop, manage and finance apartments. As a federation of more than 145 state and local affiliates, NAA encompasses over 95,000 members, 141 affiliates, and more than 11.6 million apartment homes globally. The apartment industry today plays a critical role in housing this nation's households by providing apartment homes to 40.1 million residents, contributing $3.4 trillion annually to the economy while supporting 17.5 million jobs.

establish a long-overdue federal data privacy standard that protects consumers and American businesses, including apartment firms. As the House Energy and Commerce Subcommittee on Innovation, Data, and Commerce holds a hearing entitled "Promoting U.S. Innovation and Individual Liberty through a National Standard for Data Privacy" and renews the discussion on the American Data Privacy and Protection Act (ADPPA), NMHC and NAA wish to thank you for the bipartisan leadership on these critical issues.

Apartment owners and operators, and their service providers, rely heavily on highly sensitive, personal data about apartment applicants, residents and employees to run their day-to-day business. Therefore, they are actively engaged in these issues. Given the sensitivity of the information that apartment operators rely on and the ever-expanding cyber threat landscape we face, our industry has placed a high priority on strengthening defenses against vulnerabilities and protecting sensitive data and consumer privacy. In fact, apartment firms are committing tremendous resources to this cause.

As the Subcommittee on Innovation, Data and Commerce Subcommittee discusses the need for a national privacy standard and the ways in which the American Data Privacy and Protection Act (ADPPA) would better protect consumers, NMHC and NAA would like to share our perspective. Outlined below are NMHC and NAA's priorities in this space, many of which are included as part of ADPPA. We believe that these priorities should serve as a starting point for any federal data privacy and security measure:

- *Federal Preemption:* ADPPA outlines a federal preemption for most existing state data privacy and security laws. NMHC and NAA believe a clear federal preemption is necessary to provide clarity for apartment firms. The current patchwork of state laws creates a significant compliance burden for apartment firms and leaves consumers vulnerable to myriad of mistakes and unintended consequences. This is particularly true given the constantly evolving nature of state data privacy and security laws.
- *Flexible and Scalable National Standard:* ADPPA reflects a need to take into consideration the data collected and the size of the company. NMHC and NAA believe any enforcement regime must provide for a flexible and scalable national standard for data security, privacy and breach notification that takes into account the needs and available resources of small businesses, as well as large firms and the sensitivity of the data in question.
- *The Ability to Continue to Perform Essential Business Functions:* ADPPA encourages data collection minimization and also rightfully acknowledges that entities may have an essential business need to engage with consumer data. Apartment firms must maintain the right to collect, use and retain sensitive information necessary for business operations. This is particularly important to ensure the safety and security of apartment residents and employees through prospective resident screening while also ensuring compliance with regulatory requirements such as reporting under the Fair Housing Act.
- *Reasonable Time Frame to Respond to Consumers:* ADPPA directs the Federal Trade Commission (FTC) to promulgate regulations for compliance by covered entities. Given the complexities of verifying any privacy or protection request and responding accurately, apartment firms need sufficient time to carry out any request, with the option for an extension if necessary.

- *Third-Party/Service Provider Responsibilities:* ADPPA makes an important distinction between covered entities, service providers and third parties. We believe that service providers must hold responsibility for their own security and privacy safeguards. Liability for any third-party/service provider security lapse or privacy violation must not shift to apartment firms or other primary consumer relationship holders. Often, businesses of all sizes are faced with the reality of being forced to accept boilerplate contractual language when contracting with a service provider or supplier. For example, while one large company may have the market share and financial leverage to negotiate and demand certain security protocols, the vast majority of American businesses do not. The responsibility for overseeing a third party's data security program and consumer privacy safeguards should remain with the party that is collecting, using and retaining sensitive information—not with apartment companies or other firms that rely on third party services.
- *Assignment of Financial and Legal Liability:* ADPPA establishes the need to differentiate between a covered entity, their service provider or a third-party data collector. We support a clear assignment of financial and legal liability to the entity that actually suffered the data breach or caused the consumer privacy violation, particularly in the case of third-party breaches or security incidents. NMHC and NAA encourage apartment operators to ensure that service provider contracts include strong and specific language governing data security, incident response and breach notification. Unfortunately, this can often be a significant challenge, especially for smaller property owners. For this reason, the law should be clear on this point.
- *Clarity in FTC's Role in Rulemaking and Enforcement:* ADPPA designates enforcement will be carried out by the FTC. Should the FTC take on the role as regulator of data privacy and security laws, the scope of their rulemaking and enforcement role should be clarified to allow for entities to have a reasonable amount of time to respond to FTC and consumer inquiries. Additionally, entities that must comply with new data privacy and security regulations stemming from this legislation will need education, flexibility and the right to cure when the FTC notifies the entity of a possible violation before any enforcement action is taken.

We thank you for the opportunity to present the views of the apartment industry as you continue deliberations to enhance consumer privacy and data security standards. NMHC and NAA stand ready to work with Congress to create a federal data privacy and protection standard that recognizes the unique nature and needs of the apartment industry while ensuring the data that our members collect, use and maintain is secure.

Sincerely,

Sharon Wilson Géno
President
National Multifamily Housing Council

Robert Pinnegar
President & CEO
National Apartment Association

* * *

February 28, 2023

The Honorable Cathy McMorris Rodgers
Chairman
U.S. House Committee on Energy and Commerce
Washington, D.C. 20515

The Honorable Gus Bilirakis
Chairman
U.S. House Subcommittee on Innovation, Data, and Commerce
Washington, D.C. 20515

The Honorable Frank Pallone
Ranking Member
U.S. House Committee on Energy and Commerce
Washington, D.C. 20515

The Honorable Jan Schakowsky
Ranking Member
U.S. House Subcommittee on Innovation, Data, and Commerce
Washington, D.C. 20515

RE: Hearing on "Promoting U.S. Innovation and Individual Liberty through a National Standard for Data Privacy"

Dear Chairman Rodgers, Ranking Member Pallone, Chairman Bilirakis, and Ranking Member Schakowsky:

We appreciate your hosting the hearing entitled, "Promoting U.S. Innovation and Individual Liberty Through a National Standard for Data Privacy" on March 1. As the first subcommittee hearing held by the Energy and Commerce Committee on data privacy in the 118th Congress, the Main Street Privacy Coalition (MSPC) wishes to introduce ourselves to the new committee members as we look forward to continuing to work collaboratively with you and your staff to enact a preemptive federal data privacy law that establishes a uniform national standard for data privacy that protects all American consumers and requires all businesses handling consumers' personal information to protect that data and honor consumers' rights requests with respect to it.

The MSPC is comprised of 19 national trade associations that together represent more than a million American businesses—a broad array of companies that line America's Main Streets[110]. From retailers to Realtors®, hotels to home builders, grocery stores to restaurants, gas stations to travel plazas, self-storage to convenience stores, including franchise establishments, MSPC member companies interact with consumers day in and day out. Our

---

110 The Main Street Privacy Coalition website and member list may be accessed at: https://mainstreetprivacy.com.

members' businesses can be found in every town, city, and state, providing jobs, supporting our economy, and serving Americans as a vital part of their communities.

Collectively, the industries that MSPC member associations represent directly employ approximately 34 million Americans and constitute over one-fifth of the U.S. economy by contributing $4.5 trillion (or 21.8%) to the U.S. gross domestic product (GDP). Our success depends on maintaining *trusted* relationships with our customers and clients: trust that goods and services we provide are high quality and offered at competitive prices; and trust that information customers provide to us while we are serving them is kept secure and used responsibly. For these reasons, our associations are actively engaged in the discussions by policy makers surrounding data privacy protections in U.S. legislation and regulations.

MSPC firmly believes that consumers across the country should be empowered to control their personal data. Having data privacy and security laws that create clear protections for Americans while allowing our members' businesses to serve their customers in the ways they have come to rely upon is a key goal. Achieving that goal, however, has been elusive. One of the challenges central to this legislative effort is that the overwhelming focus on the data practices of so-called "big tech" companies in public policy debates can blind us to the fact that privacy law must also work for Main Street businesses interacting with consumers daily.

American businesses have no higher priority than earning and maintaining trusted relationships with their customers. To preserve those relationships, businesses must protect and responsibly use the personal information that customers share with them. As policymakers consider legislative and regulatory solutions to address data privacy concerns, our coalition urges adoption of federal privacy legislation that meets the following core principles:

- *Establishing Uniform Nationwide Rules and Enforcement for Data Privacy* – We should have a sensible, uniform federal framework for data privacy legislation that benefits consumers and businesses alike by ensuring that sensitive consumer information is protected in a consistent manner regardless of the state in which a consumer resides. Preempting state laws by enacting a set of nationwide rules for all businesses handling consumers' personal data is necessary to achieve the important, national public policy goal of establishing uniform consumer privacy protections.
- *Industry Neutrality and Equal Protection for Consumers Across Business Sectors* – Federal data privacy frameworks should apply requirements to all industries that handle personal data and not place a disproportionate burden on certain sectors of the economy while simultaneously alleviating other sectors from providing equal protection of consumer data. An equivalent data privacy standard should apply, regardless of whether a business directly collected data from a consumer or obtained it in a business-to-business transaction.
- *Direct Legal Obligations (Rather than Contractual Requirements Alone) for All Entities that Handle Consumer Data* – Effective consumer protection law cannot be achieved by relying on some businesses to regulate the conduct of other businesses through contracts alone. Data service providers and other third parties need direct statutory obligations to ensure they comply with the relevant privacy scheme, particularly those offering transmission, storage, analytical processing or other consumer data services for thousands of businesses.

- *Preservation of Customer Rewards and Benefits* – Any federal data privacy framework should preserve the ability of consumers and businesses to voluntarily establish mutually beneficial business-customer relationships and set the terms of those relationships. Legislation should include safe harbors to ensure that consumers can purchase, or otherwise obtain, the goods and services they want by taking advantage of benefits, incentives, or enhanced services they earn from being loyal customers, even if other customers choose not to engage in such programs.
- *Transparency and Customer Choice* – Consumers deserve to know what categories of personal data businesses collect and how that data is generally used. These policies should be clearly disclosed in company privacy policies and readily accessible to consumers. These obligations should apply to all businesses handling consumers' personal data, including service providers, third parties, and financial services businesses.
- *Accountability for Business's Own Actions* – Privacy legislation should not include terms that could potentially expose businesses, including contractors and franchises, to liability for the actions or noncompliance of a business partner. Those business partners should be responsible for their own compliance and any resulting liability. In particular, consumer-facing businesses should not be unfairly saddled with liability if other types of businesses do not fulfill their own obligations under the regulation.
- *Data Security Standards* – A federal data privacy law should include a reasonable data security standard for all businesses handling consumer data, as well as a uniform process for businesses suffering a data security breach to notify affected individuals. Currently, consumer-facing industry sectors are required to comply with 54 state and U.S. territorial laws on data breach notification requirements, and nearly half of the states have enacted data security laws. However, financial institutions and service providers are often exempt from these state breach notice requirements. All businesses handling consumers' data should be statutorily required to protect personal data and provide notice of their own security breaches when they occur.

We appreciate the Committee's work with MSPC last year to address our concerns within the American Data Privacy and Protection Act (ADPPA) such as strengthening the obligations for service providers handling controllers' customer information and preserving customer loyalty, rewards, and benefits programs. We would like to continue to work with the Committee this Congress to address MSPC's remaining concerns by strengthening the preemption language to ensure consistent rules to protect privacy across the nation and by adding protections to ensure that good actors complying with the law do not face abusive lawsuits (and threats of lawsuits).

Finally, we note that the House Committee on Financial Services today marked up H.R. 1165, the "Data Privacy Act of 2023," to update current privacy requirements for the financial sector regulated by the Gramm-Leach-Bliley Act. We shared our concerns in a letter to the Committee ahead of its markup addressing the inconsistencies between H.R. 1165 and the ADPPA that create significant concerns for Main Street businesses. Ultimately, MSPC would like to work with both committees to ensure the bills reported by each are harmonized in a way that creates consistent rules across industry sectors and does not cause unwarranted liability on businesses in one sector for privacy practices that businesses in another sector control.

The guiding principle should be the American consumer herself, who expects her data to be protected by all businesses handling it in an equivalent way and that her privacy rights with respect to her data will be honored to the same extent by all of them. After all, the consumer's data is the same, and the protections should be the same regardless of who handles it.

Members of the MSPC – many of whom struggled to remain open to serve consumers during the COVID-19 pandemic and are facing historic pressures from the confluence of inflation, supply chain constraints, and labor shortages – look forward to collaborating with you to meet our shared goals of effectively protecting privacy in a uniform way that works for both consumers and Main Street businesses alike.

Sincerely,
Main Street Privacy Coalition

cc: Members of the U.S. House Committee on Energy and Commerce

* * *

March 1, 2023

The Honorable Gus Bilirakis
Chairman
Subcommittee on Innovation, Data,
and Commerce
Washington, DC 20515

The Honorable Jan Schakowsky
Ranking Member
Subcommittee on Innovation, Data,
and Commerce
Washington, DC 20515

Dear Chairman Bilirakis and Ranking Member Schakowsky:

On behalf of the Electronic Transactions Association (ETA), I appreciate the opportunity to submit this statement for the record before the Subcommittee's hearing, "Promoting U.S. Innovation and Individual Liberty through a National Standard for Data Privacy."

ETA is the world's leading advocacy and trade association for the payments industry. Our members span the breadth of significant payments and fintech companies, from the largest incumbent players to the emerging disruptors in the U.S and in more than a dozen countries around the world. ETA members make commerce possible by processing approximately $44 trillion annually in purchases worldwide and deploying payments innovation to merchants and consumers.

ETA and its members support U.S. and international efforts to strengthen privacy laws in ways that help the industry combat fraud and help consumers understand how their data is being used. As lawmakers and regulators explore additional ways to protect consumers, it is critical that the government coordinates with the payments industry to combat fraud and cybercrime so that all consumers have access to safe, convenient, and affordable payment options and other financial services.

A robust financial system is integral to the economy because it enables the fundamental functions of economic activity, including connecting borrowers with savers, facilitating investments, processing payments, and safekeeping financial assets. For the U.S. financial system to remain competitive in the global economy, the U.S. must continue to prioritize consumer protection, safety, and reliability, while also continuing to lead in innovation.

ETA looks forward to encouraging a collaborative approach and believes a framework should include the following principles:

Permissible Use to Fight Fraud

The payment industry has a long commitment and history of fighting fraud and is constantly developing and deploying new technology to detect, deter, and eliminate fraud. New and enhanced technologies have amplified the payments industry's ability to offer new fraud solutions and strengthen our on-going efforts. Any privacy or data protection standard should include provisions for permissible uses of data to prevent fraud and protect consumers.

Creating a Uniform National Standard and Enforcement

Consistent protections provided by a uniform national law will benefit consumers and businesses. A federal uniform standard will provide certainty and consistency for businesses and consumers in lieu of having to navigate a complex patchwork of state laws and regulation. A uniform standard – that is a ceiling – would also reduce the complexity and costs of compliance and enforcement.

To protect consumer rights and provide responsibility, enforcement needs to be consistent and coordinate between the federal government and the state's regulatory agencies. Collaboration between the appropriate federal agency and state attorney generals should be followed to avoid duplicate or conflicting enforcement actions. However, a privacy law should not provide a private right of action for enforcement.

Industry and Sector Neutrality

A national privacy framework should be applied to all industry sectors that handle consumer data and such protections should be consistent for companies across products and services. It should also be technology neutral and allow organizations to adopt privacy protections that are appropriate to specific risks. Protections shouldn't interfere with innovation and economic competitiveness in an evolving technology landscape.

Keeping Pace with Innovation

ETA supports a privacy framework that applies to financial services in a manner that is consumer centered and risk-focused while encouraging innovation. To that, ETA supports policymakers setting principles-based guidelines for industry-led standards to meet. This would permit flexibility over time to accommodate the technology capabilities of various stakeholders and satisfy consumer expectations.

Access to Data

Individuals must have a reasonable right to access the personal information they have provided to a company and, where practical, the right to have that information corrected. Individuals should also have the ability to request the deletion of personally identifiable information provided to companies, unless there is a legitimate or legal obligation to retain that information.

* * *

The payments industry never rests — we are working tirelessly to fight fraud and protect consumers by developing new tools to prevent or identify fraud data analysis as well as by frequently introducing new fraud-fighting solutions. Privacy laws should continue to recognize these goals and the important role the payments industry plays in combating fraud. By working together, lawmakers, regulators, and industry participants can protect consumers while providing them with access to the safest and most convenient payments system in the world.

ETA would like to thank the Subcommittee for this opportunity to provide this statement for the record on this important topic. We appreciate your leadership on this important issue. If you have any questions, please contact me or ETA's Senior Vice President of Government Affairs, Scott Talbott, at stalbott@electran.org.

Sincerely,

Jeff Patchen
Director of Government Affairs
Electronic Transactions Association

* * *

March 1, 2023

The Honorable Gus Bilirakis
Chairman
Innovation, Data, and Commerce Subcommittee
2306 Rayburn House Office Building
Washington, DC 20515

The Honorable Jan Schakowsky
Ranking Member
Innovation, Data, and Commerce Subcommittee
2408 Rayburn House Office Building
Washington, DC 20515

RE: Hearing on a National Standard for Data Privacy

Dear Chairman Bilirakis and Ranking Member Schakowsky:

Thank you for convening today's hearing on establishing a national standard for data privacy. Every day, American consumers share their personal information with countless businesses just by using routine products and services. Consumers deserve to know that their data is being used responsibly. As more states consider or advance comprehensive privacy legislation, consumers and businesses alike face the possibility of fragmented regulatory regimes that could prove to be difficult to both navigate and enforce. A strong national data privacy standard will provide consumers and businesses the certainty they deserve.

BSA | The Software Alliance is the leading advocate for the global software industry.[111] Our members are enterprise software companies that create the business-to-business technology products and services that power the digital transformation of companies in every industry. BSA members provide cloud storage services, customer relationship management software, human resource management programs, identity management services, and remote collaboration software, along with a range of other enterprise technology products.

BSA commends the Energy and Commerce Committee's efforts and progress towards advancing a strong federal privacy law in the 117th Congress through the bipartisan committee passage of H.R. 8152, The American Data Privacy and Protection Act (ADPPA). Additionally, we appreciate the Committee's engagement with a broad range of stakeholders, including industry, to ensure that any federal privacy law is both effective and workable.

This Congress has a real opportunity to enact a comprehensive federal privacy law on a bipartisan basis. Passing a strong federal privacy law is a pillar of BSA's National Agenda for Digital Transformation,[112] and today's hearing represents an opportunity to build upon the momentum developed last Congress. Specifically, BSA urges Congress to enact a federal privacy law that (1) establishes consumers' rights in their personal data; (2) imposes strong obligations on companies that require them to handle consumers' data responsibly; and (3) provides strong and consistent enforcement. A federal privacy standard should:

- *Establish Consumer Rights.* A federal privacy law should create new rights for consumers, including the rights to access, correct, and delete their personal data, as well as the right to opt out of the sale and sharing of their personal information. These rights can help provide consumers control over their information and increase their ability to both trust and verify how their data is used.

---

[111] BSA's members include: Adobe, Alteryx, Atlassian, Autodesk, Bentley Systems, Box, Cisco, CNC/Mastercam, Databricks, DocuSign, Dropbox, Graphisoft, IBM, Informatica, Juniper Networks, Kyndryl, MathWorks, Microsoft, Okta, Oracle, Prokon, PTC, Salesforce, SAP, ServiceNow, Shopify Inc., Siemens Industry Software Inc., Splunk, Trend Micro, Trimble Solutions Corporation, TriNet, Twilio, Unity Technologies, Inc., Workday, Zendesk, and Zoom Video Communications, Inc.

[112] https://www.bsa.org/files/policy-filings/01182023uspolicyagendaltr.pdf.

- *Create Clear Obligations for Businesses to Handle Data Responsibly.* A federal privacy law should place meaningful limits on businesses that handle consumers' personal data and require them to handle consumers' data responsibly. Those limits should also reflect a business's role in handling consumer data, including whether a company decides why and how to collect a consumer's personal data, or instead acts as a service provider that processes a consumer's data on behalf of another company and pursuant to that company's instructions. The distinction between these two types of companies is critical to a host of privacy laws worldwide, which recognize that both types of businesses have important responsibilities and obligations to safeguard consumers' personal data and that those obligations must reflect how the company interacts with consumers' data to avoid creating new privacy and security risks for consumers.[113]
- *Provide Strong and Consistent Enforcement.* Effective enforcement is important to protecting consumers' privacy, ensuring that organizations meet their commitments and legal obligations, and deterring potential violations. A federal privacy law should not be enforced by a single regulator, but by federal and state agencies working together. We support enforcement of a federal privacy law not only by the FTC but also all state Attorneys General, to create consistent and effective enforcement.

* * *

BSA supports strong privacy protections for consumers, and we appreciate the opportunity to provide these comments. We welcome and look forward to further engagement with the Committee on these important issues.

Sincerely,

Craig Albright
Vice President, US Government Relations

CC:
The Honorable Cathy McMorris Rodgers
The Honorable Frank Pallone

* * *

March 1, 2023

The Honorable Gus Bilirakis
Chairman
Subcommittee on Innovation, Data, and Commerce
United States House of Representatives
Washington, DC 20510

---

113 *See* BSA, Controllers and Processors: A Longstanding Distinction in Privacy, *available at* https://www.bsa.org/files/policy-filings/10122022controllerprodistinction.pdf.

The Honorable Jan Schakowsky
Ranking Member
Subcommittee on Innovation, Data, and Commerce
United States House of Representatives
Washington, DC 20510

Dear Chairman Bilirakis and Ranking Member Schakowsky:

I write to thank you for holding today's hearing on "Promoting U.S. Innovation and Individual Liberty through a National Standard for Data Privacy," and to thank you for your efforts to craft a strong national data privacy law that will advance consumer interests and interstate commerce.

As the House Energy and Commerce Committee develops legislation in this area, I hope it will also consider the impact of certain privacy provisions on the ability of retailers, manufacturers, and others to conduct efficient recalls of hazardous consumer products. I am concerned with "Right to Delete"-style provisions, for example, the one contained in the the California Consumer Privacy Act (CCPA), which limit the ability of firms to collect and use consumer data for direct notice recalls.[114]

The U.S. Consumer Product Safety Commission (CPSC) is an independent federal regulatory agency responsible for protecting the public from unreasonable risks of injury and death associated with consumer products. Because CPSC is not a privacy regulator, I take no official position on the merits of broader consumer privacy considerations. However, given CPSC's extensive work on consumer product recalls, I would like to call your attention to the ways in which CPSC and recalling firms rely on industry-collected personally identifiable information (PII) of customers purchasing consumer products to advance safety.

CPSC is currently exploring innovative ways to effect consumer notification.[115] These efforts would be severely limited without access to the consumer data such "Right to Delete" provisions seek to restrict.

To improve recall effectiveness, CPSC compliance staff works with manufacturers, distributors, and retailers to develop mutually acceptable programs that include a variety of notification methods to alert affected consumers about product recalls. Research shows, and the CPSC has long recognized, a powerful positive relationship between direct notification of consumers and recall success.[116] Direct notification is not possible without affected consumers' PII. Often, CPSC will encourage a recalling firm to use the information it collects through registration cards, sales records, catalog orders, retailer loyalty cards, or other means, to effect direct notification.[117] In other situations, companies may purchase commercially-available

---

[114] California Consumer Privacy Act of 2018, ch. 55, 2018 Cal. Stat. 91 (codified at Cal. Civ. Code tit. 1.81.5); Cal. Civ. Code § 1798.105 (effective Jan. 1, 2020); Cal. Civ. Code § 1798.120 (effective Jan. 1, 2020).

[115] Sean Oberle, *Innovative Consumer Notification is a CPSC Theme at ICPHSO,* 52 PROD. SAFETY LTR., Feb. 27, 2023, https://productsafetyletter.com/Content/8802.aspx.

[116] *See e.g.,* Dennis R. Murphy & Paul H. Rubin, *Determinants of Recall Success Rates*, 11 J. OF PROD. LIAB. 17, 17-28 (1988); *and see* U.S. CONSUMER PROD. SAFETY COMM'N, RECALL EFFECTIVENESS WORKSHOP REPORT 5 (2018), *available at* https://www.cpsc.gov/s3fs-public/Recall_Effectiveness_Workshop_Report-2018.pdf?R1VyLltrl8M_id.2vkAklHoUZjaSCab (last visited Mar. 1, 2023) (CPSC staff finding that "[d]irect notice recalls have proven to be the most effective recalls").

[117] *See* U.S. CONSUMER PROD. SAFETY COMM'N, RECALL HANDBOOK 19 (2012), https://www.cpsc.gov/s3fs-public/8002.pdf (last visited Mar. 1, 2023).

mailing lists of consumers who are likely to use a particular product.[118] Industry-collected consumer PII, and the direct notification it enables, is an important tool to locate and remove hazardous product as quickly as possible.

Because existing state "Right to Delete" provisions could result in the deletion of this critical consumer PII, it is my hope that you will consider the importance of preserving the ability of firms to conduct efficient transmission of recall notifications. To that end, the Committee should consider language that provides a national and uniform federal framework that recognizes product recalls as a legitimate use of consumer PII. Also, federal privacy legislation should include an exemption for consumer safety and recall efficiency.

Thank you for your attention to this matter. As always, I am available to assist you in any way I can.

Sincerely,

Peter A. Feldman
Commissioner

cc: The Honorable Cathy McMorris Rodgers
Chair
Committee on Energy and Commerce
U.S. House of Representatives

The Honorable Frank Pallone
Ranking Member
Committee on Energy and Commerce
U.S. House of Representatives

Hearing: Promoting U.S. Innovation and Individual Liberty through a National Standard for Data Privacy, House Committee on Energy and Commerce Subcommittee on Innovation, Data, and Commerce, Statement for the Record of Morgan Reed, President, ACT | The App Association and Connected Health Initiative

Dear Chairman Bilirakis, Ranking Member Schakowsky, and members of the Subcommittee:

Thank you for the opportunity to provide input for this hearing on data privacy, one of the most important pillars of the internet age. ACT | The App Association's (the App Association's) Connected Health Initiative (CHI), is a multistakeholder coalition with a shared interest in ensuring the public policy landscape enables and encourages the use of digital health tools that improve outcomes and help control the costs of care. CHI's interest in federal privacy law under the Subcommittee on Innovation, Data and Commerce's (IDC's) jurisdiction has grown in

[118] Because such lists are generally available from business that sell personal information about consumers to third parties, the CCPA "Right to Opt-Out" provision raises additional concerns with respect to the commercial availability, accuracy, and completeness of consumer PII for these purposes. *See* Cal. Civ. Code § 1798.120 (effective Jan. 1, 2020).

concert with the expansion of digital health information that is created or transferred outside the scope of the Health Insurance Portability and Accountability Act (HIPAA). In the latter days of a global pandemic that forced virtual care adoption and in the middle of a crushing physician shortage set to increase to up to 122,000 by 2032,[119] digital health tools like remote monitoring and telehealth platforms are playing a more important role than ever.

Patients, providers, and consumers must be able to trust that innovators in this space are protecting the security and privacy of sensitive personal information.

Introduction

The App Association has long called for a strong national data privacy law, and CHI has also put forth principles for a federal privacy law of general applicability. The biggest problem with the privacy landscape is the mismatch between consumers' expectations of their privacy and the reality of how many entities buy, sell, and use their data. We have all experienced the phenomenon of discussing a topic with friends and getting served a targeted ad shortly after. While we feel as though our phones are spying on us, companies are actually using our online behavioral data to predict other things in which we might be interested. We willingly consent to the collection and use of our data in this way through the terms and conditions of signing up for nearly any online account—for rideshare apps, social media sites, online retail, and web-enabled consumer health products, to name just a few. And we rarely think about the implications of these conditions afterward.

A comprehensive national privacy policy would help consumers understand where their data is located, who has access to it, and what their rights are surrounding the sale or use of it. Especially in the health care space, consumers need to be protected from actors looking to misuse their data and expose them to risk. Many consumers misunderstand the protections afforded to them by existing laws like HIPAA or Federal Trade Commission (FTC) regulations. Instead of modifying or expanding these existing laws and regulations, Congress should create a new, privacy-focused law that covers all kinds of consumer data.

Consumers and Companies Alike Usually Misunderstand HIPAA

At its core, HIPAA focuses on the portability and interoperability of health data. Congress designed it to ensure that consumers can change insurance providers or primary care physicians without having their data hoarded by those entities. The original text of the law did not include a privacy requirement, but instead required the Department of Health and Human Services (HHS) to promulgate a rule on privacy standards three years after enactment if Congress failed to pass a national set of privacy requirements for entities regulated under HIPAA.[120] Since HHS promulgated the Privacy Rule under the existing, limited authorities granted to it under the original HIPAA statute, it could break no new ground on protecting privacy and only worked

---

[119] Assoc. of American Medical Colleges, "New Findings Confirm Predictions on Physician Shortage," press release (Apr. 23, 2019), *available at* https://www.aamc.org/news-insights/press-releases/new-findings-confirm-predictions-physician-shortage.

[120] *Health Insurance Portability and Accountability Act of 1996* (P.L. 104-91).

within its interoperability-driven mandate. This legislative and regulatory history helps explain why the HIPAA Privacy Rule exhibits otherwise surprising levels of permissiveness and interoperability rather than protection and patient control of personal health data. And now, the explosion of health data held by a wide variety of entities not covered under HIPAA means that much of our health data is not covered by a Privacy Rule that is not a good fit for it in the first place.

Most consumers do not understand this misalignment. A 2019 Pew Research study found that 63 percent of Americans say they understand very little or nothing at all about the laws and regulations that are currently in place to protect their data privacy.[121] To complicate the picture further, there are many cases that consumers might think are covered but are not because of the construction of the HIPAA Privacy Rule. For example, HIPAA rules mostly do not apply to vendors of public health records (like fitness trackers), payment processors (like banks), and even some doctors who do not bill through electronic claims to insurance plans.[122] These are all instances where Americans without an understanding of the limitations of the HIPAA privacy rule could reasonably expect their data to be protected, but it is not.

HIPAA regulations are difficult for companies to understand as well. The definitions of "covered entity" and "business associate" have many nuances, and it is often hard for small businesses like App Association members to determine whether they are subject to the regulations. To help our members and other similar organizations, the App Association created a resource to check for whether they are a covered entity or a business associate. If a business focused on healthcare data has difficulty in understanding its legal obligations, it is not reasonable to expect consumers to understand their rights and protections under the law.

Any national privacy legislation Congress passes must avoid overly burdensome, duplicative, and even unsafe requirements for those entities already required to comply with HIPAA and the Health Information Technology for Economic and Clinical Health (HITECH) Act. The patient-provider relationship makes some of the general privacy provisions in the major bills under consideration inappropriate for HIPAA covered entities and business associates. For example, deletion of data may pose a safety hazard to patients and staff in the context of clinical care. Thus, Congress should keep HIPAA and HITECH in place and carve a general federal privacy law around them. However, we recommend that such a law adopt an approach to sensitive data, including health data, that is roughly consistent with HIPAA's requirements.

Notwithstanding its shortcomings as a federal privacy law of general applicability, HIPAA requires robust protections for patients tailored to healthcare that should be maintained. Patients have come to rely on a federal healthcare regime that generally keeps their health records out of circulation. However, despite its interoperability roots, HIPAA's de-emphasis on patient control over health records helped contribute to a situation where, perversely, patients have struggled to bring their records with them to new providers efficiently. But more relevantly here, it also rendered patients essentially unable to port their health information outside the HIPAA umbrella. Responding to this unintended consequence, Congress enacted the 21st Century Cures Act, which required the sub-agency that enforces HIPAA, the Office of Civil Rights (OCR), to prohibit "information blocking" by HIPAA covered entities and business

[121] https://www.pewresearch.org/internet/2019/11/15/americans-and-privacy-concerned-confused-and-feeling-lack-of-control-over-their-personal-information/.

[122] HIPAA Privacy Rule, 45 CFR 160 and 45 CFR 164 subparts A and E.

associates. Although OCR is not yet enforcing the information blocking rule, it is already applying additional pressure on Congress to establish a privacy framework to address risks to health information once a patient requests its transfer to non-HIPAA entities as the information blocking rules contemplate. To help orient patients, providers, and consumers to those risks—and to bolster FTC enforcement in these scenarios—CHI suggested that the information blocking rules require any non-HIPAA covered entities receiving health information on behalf of patients make a few high-level attestations as to their privacy and data security practices. This approach is no substitute for a federal privacy law. However, it would help address the perceived and actual privacy and security disparities between the HIPAA environment and the rest of the American economy. For the information blocking rules to work as intended, Congress should enact a federal privacy framework.

Some advocates have proposed that, instead of working out compromise general privacy protections, Congress should expand HIPAA to cover health-related data collection and processing activities across the rest of the economy. However, as alluded to above, policymakers would need to rework HIPAA extensively to support such an expansion. Rules around covered entities, business associate agreements, types of data covered, and reasons for triggering coverage would all need to be radically altered. In addition, the HIPAA Privacy Rule is not law but an agency rule and could be changed if the agency chooses. HHS also does not have the budget, personnel, or authority to oversee a large expansion of the scope of the HIPAA Privacy Rule. Because of the permissiveness of the original law, the limited circumstances covered by it, and the difficulty in understanding requirements, expanding HIPAA—and OCR—to police the entire economy is not likely to be the best approach. We need a comprehensive privacy law that would protect all kinds of data, including sensitive health information. Similarly, a federal law of general applicability should avoid accidentally imposing its requirements on Protected Health information (PHI) subject to HIPAA, which would result in unintended consequences explored in more detail below.

Data Use Disclosures Do Not Work for Consumers

While not federally required (except in the case of users under 13 years of age), many websites and apps have privacy policies and terms and conditions of data collection and use. They notify consumers of those policies primarily through long documents, sometimes hiding the fact that many companies generate significant revenue through the sale and collection of data. Sometimes, apps or websites will push a shorter notification to a user's device to inform them of the applicability of a certain part of the policy. While none of the available methods is a perfect way of conveying dense information quickly, the in-time notices tend to be more effective since they appear more seamlessly in the context of the consumer's engagement with an online service.

However, there is no easy way to increase the usefulness of such notices without a clear and universal privacy law that would outline the basic requirements of such disclosures. To operate in an increasingly online world, consumers should understand how their data is being collected, what it is being used for, and who has access to it. A national privacy law would take steps toward ensuring this future.

We Need Strong Federal Privacy Protections

This Committee has made significant progress in negotiations toward a compromise federal privacy bill over the past few years. The remaining disagreements are understandable, but I urge you to find a middle ground on these issues in order to establish long-overdue protections for patients and consumers for the processing and collection of their health data. Although the FTC takes an active role in enforcing the prohibition on unfair or deceptive acts or practices (UDAP), other agencies also have jurisdiction, such as the Department of Health and Human Services (HHS), to enforce industry-specific privacy and security requirements. Left to its own devices and with incomplete authorities from Congress, the FTC is working with limited resources, such as interpreting its data breach notification requirements to cover privacy harms.[123] Although this may have some of the deterrent effects the FTC intended, it is ultimately a confusing interpretation of rules Congress drafted to apply in instances of unauthorized access to data—as opposed to situations where health apps share data purposefully with third parties.[124] A more fundamental question is how government should regulate the aggregation and monetization of sensitive health information outside HIPAA's scope and the FTC's limited ability to directly address the associated risks.

Consumers, patients, and innovators in connected health deserve a more certain and comprehensive legal framework for regulations applied to digital health companies to guide their collection and processing activities involving sensitive information like health data. Similarly, explicit privacy prohibitions would better equip the FTC to prevent likely privacy harms involving health data, instead of waiting until harmful conduct has occurred and then seeking to prohibit the activity under its UDAP authority. As you work toward a compromise, we encourage you to keep the following guiding principles in mind with respect to healthcare privacy:

1. *Individual Rights.* Where practicable, legislation should require covered companies to provide individuals access to their data, the ability to amend incorrect information, and to direct entities to not sell their health data that those companies collect or maintain. In some situations, a right to data deletion may be allowed, unless patient safety or other risks are likely. Accordingly, we agree with the drafters of the major privacy bills under consideration in Congress that the obligation to honor data deletion requests should not extend to HIPAA covered entities or business associates, underscoring the need for legislation to carefully exclude data subject to HIPAA and associated privacy requirements. Privacy rights should be honored unless they are waived by an individual in a meaningful way.
2. *Transparency and Consent.* Where appropriate, legislation governing electronic data in apps should require covered companies to obtain affirmative, opt-in consent for sensitive information, including health data, informed by clear disclosures as to how covered companies collect, use, store, protect, and share health data, and for what purpose a covered company collects or processes such data. Terms should be clearly

[123] Fed. Trade Comm'n, Statement of the Commission on Breaches by Health Apps and Other Connected Devices, (Sept. 15, 2021), *available at* https://www.ftc.gov/system/files/documents/rules/health-breach-notificationrule/statement_of_the_commission_on_breaches_by_health_apps_and_other_connected_devices.pdf.

[124] See letter from Morgan Reed, president, ACT | The App Association, to United States House of Representatives Committee on Energy and Commerce, Re: *Flo Health, Inc.*, Fed. Trade Comm'n complaint (Feb. 17, 2021).

defined and unambiguous, and this should be more than a "check the box" process to use an app.

3. *Civil Rights.* Legislation should clarify the FTC's role in assisting other federal agencies tasked with enforcing discrimination laws, where appropriate, against entities that process health data in a manner that results in harmful bias or discrimination. The FTC should, in collaboration with those federal agencies, protect individuals' civil rights and work to evaluate the potential risks posed by algorithms, particularly as inferences are drawn from individuals' sensitive health data.
4. *Data Security.* Legislation should require covered companies to maintain a comprehensive security program that is designed to protect the security, privacy, confidentiality, and integrity of health data against risks—such as unauthorized access or use, or unintended or inappropriate disclosure—through the use of reasonable administrative, technological, risk management, and physical safeguards built into the design of their applications, products, or services to appropriately protect the data. These programs should be scalable and technology neutral.
5. *Data Minimization and Access Restrictions.* Legislation should require companies to limit health data processing, transfer, and collection to those activities that are reasonably necessary, proportionate, and limited to provide a product or service specifically requested by an individual, reasonably anticipated within the context of a company's ongoing relationship with an individual, or meeting a particular purpose identified publicly on a company's website or marketing materials. Legislation should also require companies to limit internal access to health data to only those employees or third-party service providers whose access is necessary to provide or improve products or services to the individual to whom the data pertains, within the context of the company's ongoing relationship with the individual.
6. *More Resources.* A federal privacy law should include increased funding authorization levels for the FTC to carry out its expanded obligations and better position itself to address healthcare privacy issues under such a framework.
7. *Rulemaking Authority.* Legislation should provide the FTC with limited, clearly defined Administrative Procedure Act rulemaking authority, enabling the FTC to define needed privacy and security guardrails where they are not already covered by existing laws (e.g., HIPAA and HITECH).

The App Association believes American Data Privacy and Protection Act (ADPPA, H.R. 8152, 117th Cong.) strikes a reasonable balance on several of its main provisions. I hope that my testimony has made it clear that modification of the existing laws at the expense of a national statute would lead only to additional complications. Congress should act on a strong, bipartisan, national framework for data privacy that draws from our evolving understanding of the needs of businesses and consumers.

March 1, 2023
The Honorable Gus Bilirakis
Chair
Subcommittee on Innovation, Data & Commerce
Committee on Energy and Commerce

U.S. House of Representatives
Washington, DC 20515

The Honorable Jan Schakowsky
Ranking Member
Subcommittee on Innovation, Data & Commerce
Committee on Energy and Commerce
U.S. House of Representatives
Washington, DC 20515

Dear Chairman Bilirakis and Ranking Member Schakowsky:

In advance of your Subcommittee's hearing entitled "Promoting U.S. Innovation and Individual Liberty Through a National Standard for Data Privacy," the U.S. Chamber of Commerce reiterates our support for a preemptive privacy standard that protects all Americans equally.

A Single National Privacy Standard

For the United States to continue to reap the benefits of the 21st century digital economy and enable a thriving ecosystem that facilitates small business growth, Congress must pass a single *preemptive* national privacy standard. Simply adopting a national privacy law without strong preemption would enable a state patchwork of laws that will be confusing to both consumers and potentially impossible for small businesses to comply.

A recent report from ITI highlighted that a national patchwork of privacy laws would cost the United States economy $1 trillion and disproportionately impact small businesses with a $200 billion economic burden.[125]

To provide the strongest preemption, according to a Congressional Research Service report, Congress should use words like preemption "related to" certain subjects.[126]

Congress should avoid merely preempting what a proposed bill is "covering" or "covered by," because such clauses are considered by the Supreme Court to be less restrictive on states than phrases like "related to."[127] According to the Supreme Court, "'Covering' is a more restrictive term which indicates that preemption will lie only if the federal regulations substantially subsume the subject matter of the relevant state law."[128] A national privacy law that merely preempts what is "covers" and then provides for exceptions to that preemption would likely be taken by many as evidence that Congress has not intended to "substantially subsume" regulation.

In recent years, legislation has been authored by Republican and Democrats that would provide strong preemption:

---

[125] https://itif.org/publications/2022/01/24/50-state-patchwork-privacy-laws-could-cost-1-trillion-more-single-federal/.

[126] https://crsreports.congress.gov/product/pdf/R/R45825.

[127] *Id.* at 10.

[128] *CSX Transportation, Inc. v. Easterwood*, 507 U.S. 663 (1993).

- In the 117th Congress, H.R. 1816, the Information Transparency and Personal Data Control Act provided that, "No State or political subdivision of a State may adopt, maintain, enforce, or continue in effect any law, regulation, rule, requirement, or standard *related to* the data privacy or associated activities of covered entities."[129]
- Also in the 117th Congress, Rep. Armstrong proposed an amendment to the American Data Privacy and Protection Act that would have provided, "No law, rule, regulation, requirement, prohibition, standard, or other provision having the force and effect of law *relating to* any subject matter regulated under this Act…"[130]
- In the 118th Congress, House Financial Services Committee Chairman Patrick McHenry has proposed the "Data Privacy Act of 2023," which provides that legislation "supersedes any statute or rule of a State."[131]

Balanced Enforcement

Compliance should be collaborative and reside with appropriate regulators and enforcers like the Federal Trade Commission (FTC) and state attorneys general and not the trial bar through the use of private rights of action.[132]

Agency Enforcement

FTC has historically been the agency with the expertise in data privacy matters in the federal government for companies not regulated by sectoral data protection laws. The Chamber believes that FTC remains the appropriate agency to continue to regulate and enforce data protection—but with appropriate guardrails.

In light of FTC Commissioner Christine Wilson's recent resignation in protest, the Chamber has called for oversight of the Commission's mismanagement and called for a moratorium on granting the agency further rulemaking authority until appropriate safeguards were placed upon the agency to protect due process.[133]

In particular, we call to your attention FTC's recent Advanced Notice of Proposed Rulemaking in which it appears to replace Congress and develop comprehensive privacy rules. Former Commissioner Noah Phillips who dissented against the proposal stated what the privacy rulemaking "does accomplish is to recast the Commission as a legislature, with virtually limitless rulemaking authority where personal data are concerned."[134]

We believe FTC's actions to exceed its authority run afoul of the Supreme Court's "Major Questions Doctrine," which holds that in matters of "political and economic significance" Congress must grant clear authority to an agency to regulate.[135]

---

129 https://www.congress.gov/bill/117th-congress/house-bill/1816/text (emphasis added).

130 https://docs.house.gov/meetings/IF/IF17/20220623/114958/BILLS-117-8152-A000370-Amdt-6.pdf (emphasis added).

131 https://financialservices.house.gov/uploadedfiles/glb 2023 xml 2.24 934.pdf.

132 https://www.uschamber.com/assets/archived/images/9.6.18 us chamber - ctec privacy principles.pdf.

133 https://www.uschamber.com/assets/documents/230216FTC-Oversight Sen.-CST-House-EC.pdf.

134 https://www.ftc.gov/system/files/ftcgov/pdf/Commissioner%20Phillips%20Dissent%20to%20Commercial%20Surveillance%20ANPR%2008112022.pdf.

135 https://www.uschamber.com/assets/documents/221121CommentsCommercialSurveillanceDataSecurityFTC.pdf.

The Commission is subject to rulemaking requirements under the Magnuson-Moss Act regarding its mandate to enforce against "unfair and deceptive trade practices."[136] The Magnuson Moss Act did not delegate authority to the FTC but imposed heightened procedural safeguards on the agency. Knowing the FTC is flouting the procedural constraints placed upon it, Congress should not delegate broad new rulemaking authority to the Federal Trade Commission.

For example, Congress should refrain from granting the Commission Administrative Procedure Act-style rulemaking authority to broadly define types of data that are prohibited from collection without exceptions like consumer consent. If the Commission were to determine that broad categories of data are prohibited from collection it would be harmful to small businesses. According to a recent report from the Chamber, 80 percent of small businesses stated that technology platforms like payments apps, digital advertising, and delivery help them compete with larger companies.[137] 80 percent of small business also say that limiting access to data will harm their business operations.[138] One small business owner of a coffee shop stated in response to the FTC being able to have this kind of authority said[139]:

> *This is very unfortunate as it would essentially be another "pandemic" for us.* Not having customer data means that we would go back to the early 1980's where we would market our products to a generic list, which in turn would be extremely costly and not a good customer experience. Having customer data helps us customize our marketing so the end result is more meaningful to the customer.

The Commission should narrowly tailer rulemaking authorities that it gives the Federal Trade Commission.

Private Rights of Action

Comprehensive privacy legislation should leave enforcement to agencies like the Federal Trade Commission and state attorneys general and not empower the private trial bar at the expense of business innovation and viability. Frivolous, non-harm-based litigation in particular has been used in the past to extract costly settlements from companies, even small businesses, based on privacy law provisions granting a private right of action. Private rights of action are ill-suited in privacy laws because:[140]

- Private rights of action undermine appropriate agency enforcement and allow plaintiffs' lawyers to set policy nationwide, rather than allowing expert regulators to shape and balance policy and protections. By contrast, statutes enforced exclusively by agencies are appropriately guided by experts in the field who can be expected to

---

[136] 15 U.S.C. § 45.

[137] https://americaninnovators.com/wp-content/uploads/2022/08/Empowering-Small-Business-The-Impact-of-Technology-on-U.S.-Small-Business.pdf.

[138] *Id.*

[139] https://www.uschamber.com/technology/small-business-owners-credit-technology-platforms-as-a-lifeline-for-their-business (emphasis added).

[140] https://instituteforlegalreform.com/wp-content/uploads/2020/10/Ill-Suited-Private RIghts of Action and Privacy Claims Report.pdf.

understand the complexities of encouraging compliance and innovation while preventing and remediating harms.

- They can also lead to a series of inconsistent and dramatically varied, district-by-district court rulings. Agency enforcement can provide constructive, consistent decisions that shape privacy protections for all American consumers and provide structure for companies aiming to align their practices with existing and developing law.
- Combined with the power handed to the plaintiffs' bar in Federal Rule of Civil Procedure 23, private rights of action are routinely abused by plaintiffs' attorneys, leading to grossly expensive litigation and staggeringly high settlements that disproportionally benefit plaintiffs' lawyers rather than individuals whose privacy interests may have been infringed.
- They also hinder innovation and consumer choice by threatening companies with frivolous, excessive, and expensive litigation, particularly if those companies are at the forefront of transformative new technologies.

Private rights of action would be particularly devastating for business under a privacy law that does not have a strong preemptive effect. Not only would states be able to continue passing their own laws, but individual judicial district precedent could also create further confusion and conflict.

Harmonizing State Trends

Congress should incorporate principles from good state legislation into a national privacy law because companies are already operationalizing requirements in five states. It has been more than 1,700 days since the California Consumer Privacy Act (CCPA) was signed into law. Since then, four other states have passed comprehensive privacy laws and another 20 are considering their own bills. The map provided below[141] illustrates that states are looking at diverging privacy proposals which further emphasizes the need for a preemptive national privacy standard.

When framing a national privacy law, Congress should assess where trends are developing. For example, all state privacy laws that have been enacted provide some form of transparency requirement and grant consumers access, deletion, correction, and opt out rights in the case of things like data sales. No state privacy law has created a private right of action for privacy violations. Rather, these laws have granted state attorneys general or other relevant agencies enforcement powers. No state privacy law has strict opt-in or broad data collection prohibitions that as described above could harm small businesses. As a general trend, red and purple states like Texas, Indiana, Maryland, Iowa, and Montana are considering legislation that resemble variants of Virginia's new privacy law. Traditionally blue states are considering legislation that resembles either CCPA, the American Data Privacy and Protection Act, or strictly opt-in consent regimes with private rights of action.

---

[141] For detailed summaries of the state proposals visit https://americaninnovators.com/2023-data-privacy/.

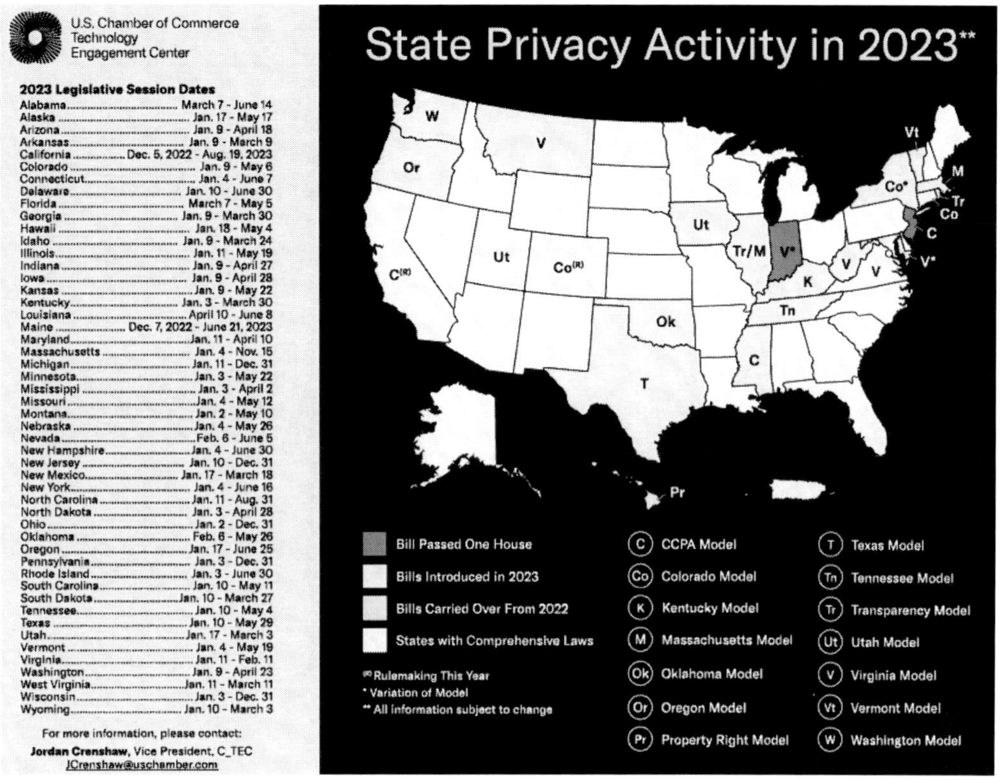

Conclusion

It is urgent that Congress pass preemptive national privacy legislation that provides strong protections for all Americans equally. Additionally, agencies like the FTC should be given narrow grants of authority with appropriate guardrails. Enforcement should not be exercised through private rights of action. We also urge Congress to build operational harmony into a national privacy law by drawing upon workable provisions of state privacy laws that protect consumers and provide certainty.

Sincerely, Jordan Crenshaw
Vice President
Chamber Technology Engagement Center
U.S. Chamber of Commerce

cc: House Energy & Commerce Committee

The Looming Cost of a Patchwork of State Privacy Laws

DANIEL CASTRO, LUKE DASCOLI, AND GILLIAN DIEBOLD | JANUARY 2022

In the absence of a federal privacy law, a growing patchwork of state laws burdens companies with multiple, duplicative compliance costs. The out-of-state costs from 50 such laws could exceed $1 trillion over 10 years, with at least $200 billion hitting small businesses.

Key Takeaways

- Since 2018, 34 states have passed or introduced 72 privacy bills regulating the commercial collection and use of personal data.
- These laws create significant compliance costs for in-state businesses and confusion for consumers while also raising costs for out-of-state businesses that increasingly find themselves subject to multiple, duplicative rules.
- State privacy laws could impose out-of-state costs of between $98 billion and $112 billion annually. Over a 10-year period, these out-of-state costs would exceed $1 trillion.
- Small businesses would bear $20–23 billion of this out-of-state burden annually.
- Congress should pass federal privacy legislation that preempts states, protects consumers, and promotes innovation.

Summary

In the absence of a comprehensive federal law, a handful of large states, including California, Colorado, and Virginia, have passed or begun to enact data privacy legislation. More states are likely to pass similar laws in the coming years, which would create a patchwork of different and sometimes conflicting state privacy laws regulating the commercial collection and use of personal data. Not only do these laws create significant costs for in-state businesses, both in terms of direct compliance costs and decreases in productivity, but they also raise costs for out-of-state businesses that can find themselves subject to multiple and duplicative rules and create confusion for consumers.

The Information Technology and Innovation Foundation (ITIF) has estimated that, in the absence of Congress passing privacy legislation, state privacy laws could impose out-of-state costs of $98 billion and $112 billion annually. Over a 10-year period, these costs would exceed $1 trillion. The burden on small businesses would be substantial, with U.S. small businesses bearing $20– 23 billion annually.

ITIF's economic model also shows the impact of privacy laws on each state. For example, ITIF has estimated that California's privacy law will cost $78 billion annually, with California's economy bearing $46 billion and the rest of the U.S. economy bearing the other $32 billion. California small businesses will bear $9 billion of in-state costs, while out-of-state small businesses face $6 billion of costs.

These estimates highlight the high costs of states creating a patchwork of privacy laws and the need for Congress to move quickly to pass legislation to create a national privacy framework that streamlines regulation, preempts state laws, establishes basic consumer data rights, and minimizes the impact on innovation.

Introduction

Over the past few years in the United States, there has been a growing interest in establishing a new "omnibus" data protection law that would apply to a broad spectrum of organizations and go beyond the nation's many sectoral data protection laws. While members of Congress have introduced multiple proposals, none have yet to gather widespread bipartisan support. Without federal action, multiple states have proposed or enacted their own data protection laws. Unless Congress acts quickly, states will continue to erect a patchwork of potentially conflicting privacy laws that will not only confuse consumers but also impose significant costs on organizations, as they will have to comply with differing laws from multiple states.

In addition, many of the states advancing data protection legislation are modeling their proposals on the European Union's General Data Protection Regulation (GDPR)—one of the most restrictive data protection regimes in the world—which means businesses in the United States will be subject to significant regulatory costs that will ultimately be passed on to consumers. However, few of these states seem to understand that one of the primary purposes of the GDPR was to harmonize data protection laws across EU member states, and by enacting competing, and potentially contradictory, state data protection laws, state legislatures are creating the exact type of fragmentation in the United States that the EU created the GDPR to solve.

Congress should pass legislation to create a national privacy framework that streamlines regulation, establishes basic consumer data rights, and minimizes the impact on innovation. Ideally, such legislation should protect and promote innovation by minimizing compliance costs and restrictions on data use, such as by allowing consumers to generally opt out of data collection (rather than requiring them to opt in) and avoiding data-minimization requirements, purpose-specification requirements, limitations on data retention, and privacy-by-design requirements. But even in the absence of such an optimal bill, two priorities stand out: First, Congress should preempt state data protection laws to ensure that there is one uniform national standard; and second, Congress should avoid creating a private right of action that would open a floodgate of expensive, and unnecessary, lawsuits against organizations subject to the new law. With President Biden signaling that his administration will be taking a more active role on data privacy, Congress may finally find the momentum it needs to move forward with comprehensive privacy legislation.[142]

Brief Overview of Proposed U.S. Data Privacy Laws

Historically, the United States has embraced a light-touch regulatory approach to the digital economy. Rather than create a single data protection law, as the EU has done with the GDPR, the United States has a series of sectoral laws such as the Health Insurance Portability and Accountability Act (HIPAA), the Gramm-Leach-Bliley Act (GLBA), and the Family Educational Rights and Privacy Act (FERPA) to regulate data in the health, financial, and educational sectors, respectively.

Over the past few years, federal and state lawmakers have proposed various privacy laws to regulate the collection and use of personal data. While these proposals have stalled in Congress, states have begun to enact new data protection laws that will have a significant impact on consumers and businesses, including those outside their respective states.

---

[142] Margaret Harding McGill, "Biden administration makes first move on data privacy," *Axios*, November 30, 2021, https://www.axios.com/biden-administration-data-privacy-commerce-department-65c99433-f7ac-49a8-88ce-b377e7e72382.html.

Federal Laws

Members of Congress introduced dozens of bills relating to privacy in 2021. While most of these bills addressed specific privacy issues, such as rules for contact tracing apps, vaccine passports, or social media, a handful of bills propose a broader federal privacy framework.[143] Some of these bills focus on businesses providing online services or engaging in e-commerce, while others include any organization processing personal data. Key bills introduced in 2021 include:

- *H.R. 1816, Information Transparency & Personal Data Control Act:* Introduced by Rep. DelBene (D-WA), this legislation directs the Federal Trade Commission (FTC) to establish requirements for how data controllers collect, transmit, store, process, and use sensitive personal information, including rules for obtaining affirmative consent, publishing an understandable privacy policy, and conducting regular privacy audits, as well as providing users with the ability to opt out of sharing nonsensitive information.[144] The legislation would preempt states from creating or enforcing their own competing privacy laws. The bill has 20 cosponsors and no companion bill in the Senate.
- *S. 113, BROWSER Act:* Introduced by Sen. Blackburn (R-TN), the Balancing the Rights of Web Surfers Equally and Responsibly (BROWSER) Act requires broadband providers and online service providers to obtain opt-in consent from users to use or share their sensitive personal information and allows users to opt out of the use and sharing of nonsensitive personal information.[145] This legislation would preempt states from creating or enforcing their own competing privacy laws. It has no cosponsors, but it does have a companion bill in the House with five cosponsors.[146]
- *S. 919, Data Care Act of 2021:* Introduced by Sen. Schatz (D-HI), the Data Care Act imposes specific obligations on online service providers, including a duty to secure information from unauthorized access, a duty to refrain from using data in ways that might harm end users, and a duty to not disclose data to a third party unless that third party is also bound by these same obligations.[147] This legislation would not preempt states from creating or enforcing their own privacy laws. It has 18 cosponsors and no companion bill in the House.
- *S. 1494, Consumer Data Privacy and Security Act of 2021:* Introduced by Sen. Moran (R-KS), the Consumer Data Privacy and Security Act requires most businesses and nonprofit organizations to follow certain rules when collecting and processing personal data, including adhering to notice and consent requirements, providing users with an easy-to-understand privacy policy, and offering users the ability to access, transfer,

---

143 Müge Fazlioglu, "Privacy Bills in the 117th Congress," Privacy Tracker, August 24, 2021, https://iapp.org/news/a/privacy-bills-in-the-117th-congress/.

144 Information Transparency & Personal Data Control Act, H.R. 1816, 117th Congress (2021), https://www.congress.gov/bill/117th-congress/house-bill/1816.

145 BROWSER Act of 2021, S.133, 117th Congress (2021), https://www.congress.gov/bill/117th-congress/senate-bill/113/text.

146 BROWSER Act of 2021, H.R. 4659, 117th Congress (2021), https://www.congress.gov/bill/117th-congress/house-bill/4659.

147 Data Care Act of 2021, S. 919, 117th Congress (2021), https://www.congress.gov/bill/117th-congress/senate-bill/919.

correct, or delete their personal data.[148] This legislation would preempt states from creating or enforcing their own competing privacy laws. It has no cosponsors and no companion bill in the House.

- *S. 2134, Data Protection Act of 2021:* Introduced by Sen. Kirsten Gillibrand (D-NY), this legislation would establish a new Data Protection Agency tasked with enforcing the nation's laws around the processing and use of personal data and preventing and remediating privacy harms. The bill would not preempt states from creating or enforcing their own privacy laws. It has one cosponsor and no companion bill in the House.
- *S. 2499, SAFE DATA Act:* Introduced by Sen. Wicker (R-MS), the Setting an American Framework to Ensure Data Access, Transparency, and Accountability (SAFE DATA) Act requires most businesses and nonprofit organizations to implement a broad range of measures, including minimizing data collection, processing, and retention to what is reasonably necessary; conducting regular privacy impact assessments; appointing a data privacy officer and data security officer; and granting consumers the right to access, transfer, correct, or delete their data.[149] This legislation would preempt states from creating or enforcing their own competing privacy laws. It has one cosponsor and no companion bill in the House.

State Laws

States have passed a number of data privacy laws in recent years. Three states—California, Virginia, and Colorado—have passed comprehensive privacy legislation that gives consumers in those states new rights regarding the collection of their personal information and imposes new obligations on businesses. Many other states are looking to enact similar privacy laws. Since California passed its first law in 2018, the number of privacy bills introduced each year in state legislatures has increased. As shown in Figure 1, over the past three years, state legislatures have introduced 72 bills in a total of 34 states, with these bills reaching various stages of the legislative process.[150] This privacy patchwork will continue to expand unless federal lawmakers pass legislation that preempts state privacy laws.

States have also passed laws regulating specific data privacy issues. For example, the Illinois Biometric Information Privacy Act (BIPA) and the Texas Capture or Use of Biometric Identifier Act (CUBI) regulate the use of biometric data. BIPA is the more stringent of the laws, requiring written, informed consent for the collection and use of any biometric data and imposing serious penalties on companies that fail to comply with the rules. As of 2021, 5 states had biometric privacy laws modeled after the Illinois law, and 27 have similar legislation pending.[151]

---

[148] Consumer Data Privacy and Security Act of 2021, S.1494, 117th Congress (2021), https://www.congress.gov/bill/117th-congress/senate-bill/1494/.

[149] SAFE DATA Act, S.2499, 117th Congress (2021), https://www.congress.gov/bill/117th-congress/senate-bill/2499.

[150] "The Growth of State Privacy Legislation," IAPP, last modified November 2021, https://iapp.org/resources/article/the-growth-of-state-privacy-legislation-infographic/.

[151] Christopher Ward and Kelsey C. Boehm, "Developments in Biometric Information Privacy Laws," Foley & Lardner, LLP, accessed December 2021, https://www.foley.com/en/insights/publications/2021/06/developments-biometric-information-privacy-laws.

The following summarizes key provisions of the comprehensive privacy laws that have passed in each of those three states.

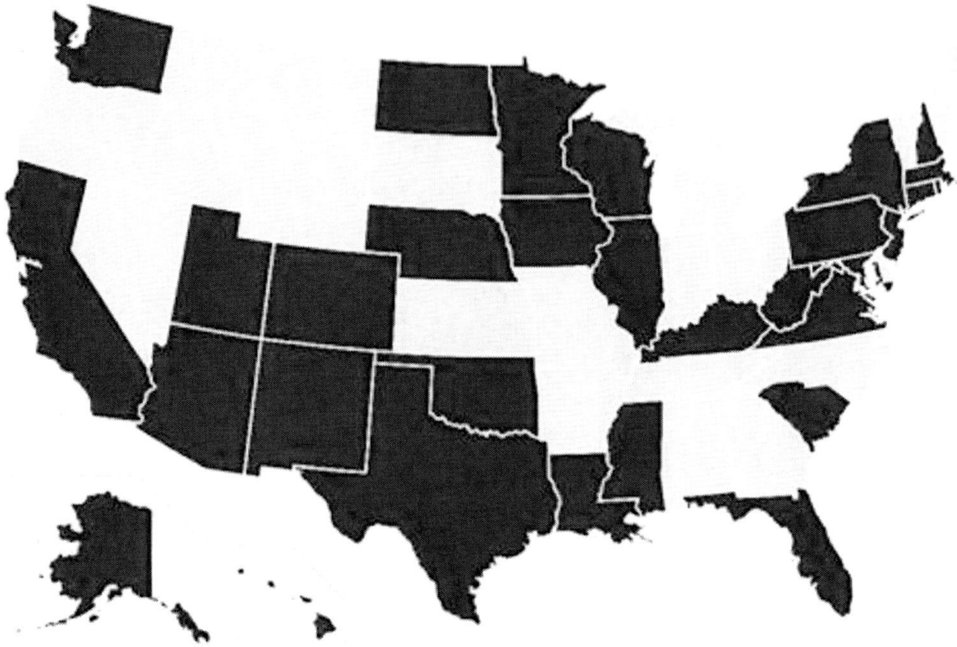

Source: IAPP.

Figure 1. States (in blue) that have passed or introduced privacy legislation, 2018–2021.

California

The California Consumer Privacy Act (CCPA) is the most sweeping state privacy law in the United States. Legislators passed the law in June 2018, and it took effect in January 2020. The CCPA creates four new rights for California consumers: the right to know about the collection and use of personal information; the right to delete collected personal information; the right to opt-out of the sale of personal information; and the right to nondiscrimination for exercising CCPA rights.[152]

The CCPA applies to businesses operating in California or working with the data of California residents. To fall under the scope of the CCPA, a business must have a gross annual revenue greater than $25 million, buy or sell the personal information of more than 50,000 California residents, or derive more than 50 percent of its annual revenue from selling personal information.[153] It does not apply to nonprofit organizations or government agencies.

The California Property Rights Act (CPRA) is a ballot provision amending the CCPA that passed in November 2020. The provision, also known as Proposition 24, amends and expands on the rights and obligations of the CCPA. It establishes the California Privacy Protection Agency, a body specifically dedicated to privacy regulation enforcement. It creates a new

[152] State of California Department of Justice, California Consumer Privacy Act (CCPA), https://oag.ca.gov/privacy/ccpa.

[153] State of California Department of Justice, California Consumer Privacy Act (CCPA), https://oag.ca.gov/privacy/ccpa#:~:text=The%20CCPA%20requires%20business%20privacy,the%20Right%20to%20Non%2D Discrimination.

definition of "sensitive data" and expands data breach liability for businesses processing and collecting personal information. The CPRA also gives consumers the right to correct personal information held by a business, the right to obtain meaningful information about the logic used in automated decision-making technology, and the right to opt out of the use of their personal information in automated decision-making.

Virginia

Passed in March 2021, the Virginia Consumer Data Protection Act (CDPA) is another comprehensive state privacy law. The law applies to businesses both in and outside Virginia that target Virginia consumers, and it excludes nonprofits and small businesses. To be subject to the CDPA, a business must collect and process the data of over 100,000 consumers, or over 25,000 consumers if more than half the firm's revenue derives from data sales.[154] The CDPA sets a threshold for revenue and does not apply to businesses that only engage in data sales in a small way. Businesses must obtain consent before processing personal data and perform data impact assessments. The bill also creates new consumer rights: the right to access, correct, delete, and move data, along with the right to opt out of the processing of personal data for purposes of targeted advertising.[155]

Colorado

The Colorado Privacy Act (CPA) establishes rules for businesses operating in Colorado regarding the collection and use of personal data and creates a new set of rights for Colorado consumers, such as the rights of deletion and data portability. The CPA applies to Colorado businesses that produce or deliver products or services targeted at Colorado residents and control the personal data of at least 100,000 Colorado residents or control the data of 25,000 residents and derive revenue from the sale of that data.[156] These requirements cast a wider net than the CDPA does, but are narrower than California's criteria.

The CPA does not create a private right of action, a right of restriction, or a right to opt-out of automated decision-making.[157] Notably, Colorado is the first state to mandate an "easy to use" appeals process that can be used whenever a data controller denies a consumer request.[158] The CPA is also the only comprehensive state privacy law that does not exempt nonprofit organizations. Information maintained by state institutions, financial institutions covered by the Gramm-Leach-Bliley Act (GBLA), higher education institutions regulated by FERPA, and information covered by the Fair Credit Reporting Act (FCRA), HIPAA, and the Children's Online Privacy Protection Act (COPPA) is exempt if in compliance with federal law.

---

154 Virginia Consumer Data Protection Act, H.B. 2307, https://lis.virginia.gov/cgi-bin/legp604.exe?212+sum+HB2307.

155 Virginia Consumer Data Protection Act, SB 1392, https://lis.virginia.gov/cgi-bin/legp604.exe?211+sum+SB1392.

156 Colorado Privacy Act, SB21-190, https://leg.colorado.gov/bills/sb21-190.

157 "US State Privacy Legislation Tracker," IAPP, last modified January 3, 2022, https://iapp.org/media/pdf/resource_center/State_Comp_Privacy_Law_Chart.pdf.

158 "Colorado Privacy Act becomes law," The Privacy Advisor, July 8, 2021, https://iapp.org/news/a/colorado-privacy-act-becomes-law/.

Methodology

Data protection laws impose costs on firms through both compliance costs and market inefficiencies. When firms are subject to multiple laws from more than one state, these costs can increase further as firms must comply with conflicting and overlapping regulations. Even when the laws are similar, small differences in definitions or scope, as well as divergent implementation of regulations, can create significant compliance costs as firms hire lawyers and engineers to ensure their systems comply fully with each state.

To estimate the economic impact state privacy laws have on businesses both within and outside those states, ITIF designed a model to observe empirical change in the earnings of a state's industries due to the passage of state-level privacy. While this type of econometric analysis can only provide a rough cost projection and is limited by data availability, it helps illustrate the negative effects of creating a patchwork of 50 separate state privacy laws, as opposed to a single federal law, to regulate the collection and use of consumer data by firms.

The Economic Impact of a Patchwork of State Privacy Laws

ITIF's model calculates a composite index—the privacy restrictiveness linkage (PRL)—in order to quantify the extent a given industry is restricted by a particular state's privacy laws. Therefore, this model assumes that data-intensive industries are more impacted by privacy laws than non-data-intensive ones are. ITIF also conducted an econometric exercise to determine the relationship between industry earnings and the composite index scores of privacy restrictiveness. ITIF also produced estimates of aggregate costs for individual states' industries associated with privacy laws passed within those states, as well as the costs imposed on other states' economies due to passing such laws. For example, a privacy law in California would impact both California businesses as well as the many non-California businesses outside the state that wish to conduct business with California consumers.

ITIF's overall quantitative model aims to estimate the costs for each U.S. state, as well as the country at large, in the increasingly likely scenario of all 50 states establishing their own unique privacy laws. It is informed by ITIF's previous 2019 work on assessing the costs of privacy laws at the federal level.[159] This report differs from previous studies in that it incorporates econometric evidence on gross operating surplus (GOS), or earnings by industry, and uses such analysis to assess out-of-state costs associated with state privacy laws. Appendix A elaborates in greater detail on the data and methodology used.

State Restrictiveness Scores

ITIF established a scoring system to measure the extent of U.S. states' privacy restrictiveness over a period between 2003 to 2021. A higher state restrictiveness score (SRS) conveys a stricter privacy law set in that state in the given year. To quantify privacy restrictiveness, ITIF first recorded SRS as the unweighted cumulative sum of the number of unique privacy restrictions passed in a given state *x* observed in year *y*. ITIF used a combination of existing legislation trackers alongside state government sites to compile a list of 15 different privacy restrictions passed between 2003 and 2021.

---

[159] Alan McQuinn and Daniel Castro, "The Costs of an Unnecessarily Stringent Federal Data Privacy Law" (ITIF, August 5, 2019), https://itif.org/publications/2019/08/05/costs-unnecessarily-stringent-federal-data-privacy-law.

However, SRS is a function of both in-state restrictions passed as well as out-of-state restrictions observed in other states. This model assumes that the larger a state's share of the nation's data-concerned industries is, the greater the impact of that state's privacy restrictions on businesses in other states. For example, California's privacy laws would expectedly impact businesses across the country far more than privacy laws set in a smaller-share state such as South Dakota would. Since there is no single decisive measurement of data-concerned industries, ITIF employs a proxy-calculation to supplement this measurement. To control for issues of endogeneity, a state's share of the nation's data-concerned industries is observed for the year 2019 and used as a constant in calculating SRS in all other years. The formula of the proxy calculation *d* for the share of the nation's data-concerned industries held by state *x* is below.

$$1.\quad d_x = \frac{(Consumer\ Products\ Share_x + Consumer\ Finance\ Share_x + Advertisement\ Share_x)}{3}$$

A state's share *d* is observed as the unweighted mean of its share of national gross domestic product (GDP) in the consumer products, consumer finance, and advertising industries. We obtained state shares for the consumer products and consumer finance GDP from the U.S. Bureau of Economic Analysis (BEA) and state shares of national advertising from Statista.[160] Using *d* as a state-specific coefficient to scale the relevance state privacy laws have on the rest of the country, the formula of SRS for state *x* in year *y* is below.

$$2.\quad SRS_{xy} = \sum_{n=2003}^{y}(State\ Privacy\ Restriction_{xn}) + \sum_{j\neq x} d_j * \sum_{n=2003}^{y}(State\ Privacy\ Restriction_{jn})$$

This notation for the calculation of SRS reflects an in-state privacy restriction impacting all applicable business within that state, whereas an out-of-state privacy restriction impacts only a fraction of the applicable businesses, since not every business is a multi-state operation impacted by other states' restrictions on consumer data. Further, not every industry within a state is equally impacted by restrictions on consumer privacy. For example, the insurance and retail sectors are more reliant on consumer data than are agriculture and mining industries. To measure more precisely how state privacy laws impact downstream industries differently, ITIF calculates the data-intensity modifier (DIM) to measure how data intensive each industry is. Data intensity is approximated by measuring the software usage per worker in each U.S. industry. The model further controls for endogeneity by using national-level data in the base year 2013 to calculate DIM, as opposed to calculating state- and year-specific DIMs. This control, however, assumes equal technology among states and over time. The calculation of DIM for industry *z* is below.

$$3.\quad DIM_z = \ln\left(\frac{Intangible\ Software\ Expenditure_z}{Employment_z}\right)$$

---

[160] Bureau of Economic Analysis, Regional Data (GDP and Personal Income; accessed November 2021), https://apps.bea.gov/itable/iTable.cfm?ReqID=70&step=1&acrdn=1; "Advertising spending in the United States from 2010 to 2019, by state," Statista, 2015, https://www.statista.com/statistics/652235/ad-spend-state-usa/.

Data for intangible software expenditure per industry is taken as noncapitalized software expenditures listed in the 2013 U.S. Census Information and Communication Technology Survey. This data is divided by the number of workers in each corresponding industry as provided by the U.S. Bureau of Labor Statistics (BLS) for the same reference year of 2013. DIM is taken as a natural log to align with previous literature on factor intensity.

Privacy Restrictiveness Linkage

Data-intensive industries should be noted as being more susceptible to changes in privacy restrictions than non-data-intensive industries are. Therefore, this model provides a score of privacy restrictiveness for a given industry within a state by linking SRS values with DIM ratios. ITIF draws this linkage as the product of SRS for state *x* in year *y* with the DIM for industry *z* in order to calculate the PRL for that state's given industry. The formula for PRL of industry *z* in state *x* during year *y* is below.

$$1.\quad PRL_{xyz} = SRS_{xy} * DIM_z$$

The Econometric Model

The composite index of state-industry-year privacy restrictiveness serves as the final independent variable to compare in econometric analysis how changes in state privacy laws impact in-state and out-of-state economies. The dependent variable chosen to measure economic costs incurred by states from state privacy laws is GOS, which is the total profit of enterprises in an industry minus intermediate costs and workers (GOS = Output – Intermediate Expenses – Compensation of Employees). GOS is selected as the dependent variable because it is a residual, meaning its value is the difference between an industry's output and costs. Therefore, a decrease in GOS can be caused by a loss in output or a rise in intermediate expenses or compensation of employees.

This makes GOS a highly useful variable in observing how privacy laws impact the economy, as change in GOS captures both compliance costs and market inefficiencies associated with increased privacy laws. For example, compliance costs from privacy laws requiring more data personnel or legal expenses would increase compensation and intermediate expenses, lowering GOS. Market inefficiencies due to privacy laws making data less usable and transferable would lower output, lowering GOS. Change in GOS would also be driven by privacy laws of multiple states incurring duplicative costs, and by in-state regulatory efforts distorting commerce out of state. Using the income approach to GDP, a loss in GOS is an equivalent loss in GDP. The final regression equation in the model is below.

$$1.\quad \widehat{GOS}_{xyz} = \hat{\beta}_0 + \hat{\beta}_1 * PRL_{xyz} + \hat{\beta}_2 * GDP_{xy} + \alpha_y + \gamma_z + \varepsilon_i$$

This regression model adds controls via state-year GDP to control for differences in economic size, as well as controlling for fixed effects for both year and industry. Fixed effects control for the many unobservable factors that undoubtedly impact industry performance over time, such as various economic shocks and supply shortages. α_y represents year fixed effects, γ_z represents industry fixed-effects, and ε_i represents the error term. This model implements no time lag, as it aims to also capture how GOS changes due to firms anticipating new policies in the same year of a law's passing.

Findings

The model described yields three primary insights:

- Without Congress passing privacy legislation, state privacy laws could impose out-of-state costs of $98 billion to $112 billion annually.
- Over a 10-year period, these out-of-state costs would exceed $1 trillion.
- The burden on small businesses would be substantial, with U.S. small businesses bearing $20 billion to $23 billion annually.

Each of these findings is discussed ahead in more detail.

The Economic Impact of Privacy Restrictions

The regression equation (formula 5) yields the regression table shown in Figure 2. All coefficient estimates are found statistically significant above the 95 percent confidence level (all estimated p-values are less than 0.05). The independent variable of interest, PRL, has a significant negative relationship to GOS. Interpreting the model's negative coefficient estimate on PRL, an additional state privacy restriction (a 1.0 unit increase in PRL) is associated on average with a 0.39 percent decrease in GOS among its private industries.

	Coefficient Estimate	Standard Error	t-value	Pr(>ltl)
Intercept	13.27	0.10	132.8	< 2e-16
PRL	-0.00389	0.00115	-3.78	0.000737
GOP	1.025e-09	2.6e-11	39.4	< 2e-16

R-Squared: 0.734, Number of Observations: 3,984.

Figure 2. Regression Table.

To further test the validity of ITIF's econometric model in measuring the cost of state privacy laws, we consider the predicted cost of the CCPA. ITIF's list of state privacy laws between 2003 and 2021 (see appendix B) shows that the CCPA adds 10 new privacy restrictions for the State of California. Using the model's findings, the CCPA would convey nearly a 3.9 percent loss in California's $1.19 trillion 2020 GOS of private industry. Therefore, the CCPA's total costs between compliance costs and market inefficiencies borne in California would be approximately $46 billion annually. ITIF estimates an additional $32 billion a year in costs borne by businesses outside the state of California that seek to comply with the CCPA. In total, the CCPA will create a $78 billion annual economic burden on the U.S. economy.

ITIF's estimated in-state costs of $46 billion for the CCPA compare favorably to the cost estimate produced by Berkeley Economic Advising and Research, LLC in 2019.[161] The California Attorney General-sanctioned report found that the CCPA would cost the Californian

[161] Berkeley Economic Advising and Research, LLC, "Standardized Regulatory Impact Assessment: California Consumer Privacy Act of 2018," September 2019, https://iapp.org/media/pdf/resource_center/standardized_regulatory_impact_assessment_CCPA.pdf.

economy upwards of $55 billion annually. Their methodology, however, focuses only on the cost impacts borne in California and considers no out-of-state effects in the analysis. It also relies heavily on survey data from firms required by law to self-report forecasted costs. The 2019 report also clarifies that their methodology yielding the final $55 billion in annual costs oversamples large- sized firms and thus overestimates costs faced by small firms, indicating that their $55 billion estimate in annual costs is likely overestimated in some small part. Comparing the two model estimates and their nuances, the fact that ITIF's estimate of California's in-state annual costs due to the CCPA is similar to findings from the California Attorney General's Office shows the accuracy of this report's econometric findings used to model the costs of state privacy laws.

Cost-Modeling a 50-State Scenario over 15 Years

To understand the impact of states continuing to enact their own privacy laws in the absence of federal law, ITIF modeled a scenario in which all 50 states would enact their own privacy law. We assumed not all states would implement identical laws and early adopters would likely favor stricter policies, whereas laggard states would expectedly favor less-stringent consumer privacy laws. ITIF's 50-state scenario models a time horizon of 15 years, where over that time, all 50 states would enact their own state privacy law. The length of this time horizon was based on the rate at which all the states enacted their own data breach laws between 2003 and 2018. During this period, 32 states adopted data breach laws in the first 5 years, 13 states adopted between years 6 and 10, and the final 5 states passed laws between years 11 and 15. And since they are not assumed to have set equally stringent laws, states are modeled in th is exercise to set one of three possible levels of restrictiveness in privacy laws. At "high strictness," states' SRS = 10, at "medium strictness," states' SRS = 4, and at "low strictness," states' SRS = 2. Using regression findings quantifying the negative relationship between state privacy restrictions and GOS, this time-horizon model can estimate costs borne by each state over the 15-year span. Further, this model can discern between costs borne by each state incurred through its own state privacy laws as well as those incurred by privacy laws passed in other states.

	Year 5	Year 10	Year 15
Number of States with Privacv Laws	32	45	50
Total U.S. Economy Costs	$2098	$2308	$2398
In-State Costs	$1128	$1228	$1278
Out-of-State Costs	$988	$1078	$1128
Total U.S. Small Business Costs	$438	$488	$508
In-State Costs	$238	$258	$268
Out-of-State Costs	$208	$228	$238

*Note: Total costs in the table may not equal the sum of corresponding in-state and out-state costs due to rounding.

Figure 3. Annual costs of a SO-state privacy law patchwork.

State	Expected Privacy Law Strictness	Expected Year of Adoption	Total Costs of 50-state Privacy Laws	Costs of Out-of-State Privacy	Costs of In-State Privacy	Total Costs on Small Business	In-State Costs on Smal Business	Out-ot-State Costs on Small Business
Alabama	Low	15	$1.98	$1.28	$0.68	$0.48	$0.18	$0.38
Alaska	Low	10	$0.48	$0.38	$0.18	$0.18	$0.08	$0.18
Arizona	Low	5	$3.18	$2.18	$1.18	$0.68	$0.28	$0.48
Arkansas	Low	5	$1.18	$0.78	$0.48	$0.28	$0.18	$0.28
California	High	5	$58.98	$12.58	$46.48	$11.88	$9.38	$2.58
Colorado	High	5	$7.48	$2.08	$5.48	$1.78	$1.28	$0.58
Connecticut	Low	5	$2.58	$1.78	$0.98	$0.58	$0.28	$0.38
Delaware	Low	5	$0.98	$0.68	$0.38	$0.28	$0.18	$0.18
Florida	Low	15	$9.58	$6.28	$3.38	$2.08	$0.78	$1.38
Georgia	Low	5	$5.88	$3.88	$2.08	$1.18	$0.48	$0.78
Hawaii	Low	5	$0.78	$0.48	$0.28	$0.28	$0.18	$0.18
Idaho	Low	5	$0.78	$0.58	$0.38	$0.28	$0.18	$0.18
Illinois	Medium	5	$9.88	$4.88	$5.18	$1.98	$1.08	$0.98
Indiana	Low	5	$3.58	$2.38	$1.28	$0.78	$0.28	$0.48
Iowa	Low	10	$2.08	$1.38	$0.78	$0.48	$0.18	$0.38
Kansas	Low	5	$1.78	$1.18	$0.68	$0.48	$0.18	$0.28
Kentucky	Low	15	$1.88	$1.28	$0.68	$0.38	$0.18	$0.28
Louisiana	Low	5	$2.28	$1.58	$0.88	$0.58	$0.28	$0.38
Maine	Low	5	$0.58	$0.48	$0.28	$0.28	$0.18	$0.18
Maryland	Medium	10	$4.28	$2.18	$2.18	$0.98	$0.58	$0.58
Massachusetts	Medium	5	$6.48	$3.18	$3.38	$1.28	$0.68	$0.68
Michigan	Low	5	$4.48	$2.98	$1.58	$0.98	$0.38	$0.68
Minnesota	Medium	5	$4.38	$2.18	$2.28	$0.88	$0.48	$0.48
Mississippi	Low	10	$0.98	$0.68	$0.38	$0.28	$0.18	$0.18
Missouri	Low	10	$2.88	$1.88	$0.98	$0.58	$0.28	$0.48
Montana	Low	5	$0.58	$0.38	$0.28	$0.28	$0.18	$0.18
Nebraska	Low	5	$1.48	$0.98	$0.58	$0.38	$0.18	$0.28
Nevada	Low	10	$1.58	$1.08	$0.58	$0.38	$0.18	$0.28
New Hampshire	Low	5	$0.78	$0.58	$0.28	$0.28	$0.18	$0.18
New Jersey	Low	5	$5.18	$3.48	$1.78	$1.18	$0.48	$0.78
New Mexico	Low	15	$0.78	$0.58	$0.28	$0.28	$0.18	$0.18
New York	Medium	5	$21.28	$9.88	$11.48	$4.18	$2.28	$1.98
North Carolina	Medium	10	$7.18	$3.48	$3.68	$1.48	$0.78	$0.78
North Dakota	Low	5	$0.58	$0.38	$0.28	$0.18	$0.08	$0.18
Ohio	Medium	5	$8.18	$3.98	$4.28	$1.58	$0.88	$0.78
Oklahoma	Low	10	$1.68	$1.08	$0.58	$0.48	$0.18	$0.28
Oregon	Low	5	$2.18	$1.48	$0.78	$0.58	$0.28	$0.38
Pennsylvania	Medium	5	$8.98	$4.38	$4.68	$1.78	$0.98	$0.88
Rhode Island	Low	5	$0.58	$0.38	$0.28	$0.18	$0.08	$0.18
South Carolina	Low	10	$2.08	$1.38	$0.78	$0.48	$0.18	$0.38
South Dakota	Low	15	$0.68	$0.48	$0.28	$0.28	$0.18	$0.18
Tennessee	Low	5	$3.38	$2.28	$1.18	$0.68	$0.28	$0.48
Texas	Low	10	$15.38	$10.08	$5.38	$2.98	$1.08	$1.98
Utah	Low	5	$1.88	$1.28	$0.68	$0.48	$0.18	$0.28
Vermont	Low	10	$0.28	$0.28	$0.18	$0.18	$0.08	$0.08
Virginia	High	10	$9.68	$2.68	$7.08	$3.18	$2.38	$0.88
Washington	Low	5	$5.38	$3.58	$1.88	$1.18	$0.48	$0.78
West Virginia	Low	10	$0.68	$0.48	$0.28	$0.18	$0.08	$0.18
Wisconsin	Low	5	$2.88	$1.98	$1.08	$0.68	$0.28	$0.48
Wyoming	Low	5	$0.38	$0.28	$0.18	$0.18	$0.08	$0.08
USA	—	—	$239.38	$112.28	$127.18	$49.58	$26.48	$23.18

Figure 4. State-by-state costs of a SO-state privacy patchwork.

Privacy laws can have a significant and detrimental impact on small businesses, which may be less able to weather the compliance burden. To understand the impact on small businesses (defined here as enterprises employing fewer than 50 workers), we further break down the state-by-state cost estimates for a 50-state patchwork of privacy laws. Using U.S. Census County Business Patterns payroll data on enterprises by size, the time-horizon model captures a state's share of total payroll paid from small businesses.[162] This share is used to proxy a state's share of GOS held by small businesses. Thus, we estimate costs of state privacy laws borne by small businesses as a state's share of GOS loss from small businesses.

A state's privacy law has a significant impact outside that state. ITIF estimates that state privacy laws could impose out-of-state costs of $98 billion to $112 billion annually. As a point of comparison, the United States spends around $100 billion on police every year.[163] Over a 10-year period, these annual costs would exceed $1 trillion, cumulatively. U.S. small businesses would also face a heavy burden, paying $20 billion to $23 billion in annual costs from out-of-state privacy laws. For both the economy at large and small businesses, a 50-state privacy patchwork levies greater costs through a system of duplicative compliance and enforcement than through in-state costs alone. Below the national level, states vary in their economic burdens coming from in state or out of state based on economic size and restrictiveness. The table ahead elaborates each state's estimated costs from a 50-state privacy patchwork absent any one unifying federal policy on consumer privacy.

Direct and Indirect Costs of State Privacy Laws

The prior analysis shows the magnitude of the potential economic impact of a patchwork of 50 different state privacy laws. However, it is also important to understand the sources of many of these costs. This section discusses some of the primary ways privacy laws impose costs on firms either directly through compliance costs or indirectly by creating market inefficiencies. Notably, duplicative state privacy laws create redundant costs, which means firms spend more on compliance and are subject to additional market inefficiencies while not increasing privacy safeguards for consumers.

Compliance Costs

There are several compliance costs associated with data privacy legislation, including hiring data protection officers, conducting privacy audits, and building and maintaining information systems to facilitate various user rights (e.g., data access, deletion, portability, and correction). Firms must devote resources to regulatory compliance, either by reducing investment in existing products and services or by passing on some of the costs to consumers. While initial compliance costs may be highest, because of certain fixed costs, as this report shows, many of the compliance costs are recurring expenses. Moreover, the costs associated with data privacy laws adversely affect small businesses, often more so than their larger counterparts, because the high costs represent a larger proportion of their revenue. Larger firms are also more likely

---

[162] 2018 SUSB Annual Data Tables by Establishment Industry (census.gov).

[163] David Cloud, "On Life Support"; "Rethinking The Blues: How We Police in The U.S. And at What Cost," Justice Policy Institute, 2012, https://justicepolicy.org/wp-content/uploads/justicepolicy/documents/rethinking theblues_executive_summary.pdf.

to have in- house regulatory expertise and to be in compliance with privacy laws outside the United States.

Data Protection Officers

Some data privacy laws require organizations to designate a data protection officer, data privacy officer, or information security officer to be responsible for compliance. For most organizations, this requirement would compel them to hire additional personnel to handle data protection compliance issues, retain a law firm or similar service provider to handle this responsibility, or divert existing staff to reallocate their time away from other activities.

The GDPR, which many states have cited as a model for their own privacy laws, requires businesses of all sizes and sectors to have a dedicated data protection officer to guarantee compliance with the law.[164] For a small business, hiring a data protection officer would be a significant endeavor likely involving a trade-off between hiring for compliance purposes and hiring for expanding a business's product or service.[165]

Privacy Audits

Some privacy laws require organizations to submit to periodic compliance audits, administered by either their organization or a third party. The GDPR requires some organizations to participate in periodic audits, and even direct inspections by data protection authorities.[166] Similarly, HIPAA requires covered entities to meet certain requirements, which they must prove through periodic audits. These audits create both direct costs and costs of employee time and range in scope depending on the types of data collected and the protections required. According to the health care compliance company Datica, a full HIPAA audit costs between $30,000 and $60,000 in both employee and direct costs.[167]

Data Impact Assessments

Some state privacy legislation requires businesses to perform risk assessments similar to the data protection impact assessments (DPIA) required by the GDPR. These assessments examine the costs and benefits to both the business and user of collecting personal data. While the specific conditions for assessment vary from state to state, they typically apply to the processing of sensitive data. Because these obligations are similar to the GDPR's DPIA requirements, larger companies are more likely to be familiar with the process and complete routine assessments.

Consumer Privacy Rights

State privacy laws often establish new consumers rights over their personal data. Examples of common rights include the right to access personal data stored by an organization, the right to move their personal data to other services, the right to delete their personal data, and the right

---

[164] "Data Protection Officer," European Data Protection Supervisor, n.d., https://edps.europa.eu/data-protection/data-protection/reference-library/data-protection-officer-dpo_en.

[165] "How startups can ensure CCPA and GDPR compliance in 2021," *TechCrunch*, April 15, 2021, https://techcrunch.com/2021/04/15/how-startups-can-ensure-ccpa-and-gdpr-compliance-in-2021/.

[166] "Processor," Regulation (EU) 2016/679 (General Data Protection Directive), Art. 28, https://gdpr-info.eu/art-28-gdpr/.

[167] Travis Good, "What is the Cost of a HIPAA Audit?" Datica, January 23, 2019, accessed July 23, 2019, https://datica.com/blog/what-is-the-cost-of-a-hipaa-audit/.

to correct their personal data. State privacy laws obligate firms to respond to consumer requests, so in order to comply with these requests, firms must account for three types of costs. First, companies must build and maintain information systems that allow them to store, find, delete, and update requested personal information. These are often fixed costs on the back end to allow them to respond to such queries in a timely manner. It may involve, for example, linking multiple disparate systems together so that all consumer data can be queried from a single interface.

Second, businesses must create mechanisms and processes to authenticate and document when consumers make those requests. Without sufficient authentication protocols in place, firms may inadvertently expose personal data to bad actors seeking to exploit privacy rights in order to gain access to consumer data.[168] Authentication tools can range in complexity from something as simple as requiring a username and password to access an online service to requiring users to submit government identification that a third-party authentication service reviews to verify an individual's identity. Costs vary depending on complexity, but they can be quite significant. For smaller businesses, the additional requirement of costly authentication tools can quickly add up. Lastly, each new privacy right comes with processing costs that vary depending on the number and types of requests they receive. Although many of these requests come through digital portals, businesses still need some type of human processing, which can significantly increase labor costs.

Differences in state laws can also create confusion among consumers about their individual data privacy rights. For example, consumers may not understand why firms must process their data one way if they are a resident of one state and another way if they are a resident of another one. These differences between states can also make it harder for businesses, the media, and others to educate consumers about their data rights because they have to tailor their messages to people depending on where they live. Similarly, since different state privacy laws may have unique provisions or require specific disclosures, businesses have to create different privacy policies for each state. With a patchwork of state privacy laws, privacy policies and related notices on apps and websites will likely become even longer, more complex, and harder for consumers to understand.

Market Inefficiencies and Lawsuits

While privacy laws come with clear compliance costs, they also include several indirect costs that adversely impact innovation and limit an organization's ability to do business in a given locale. A patchwork of multiple state privacy laws exacerbates these market inefficiencies because businesses must navigate competing regulations, which can limit their ability to use data effectively. ITIF previously estimated that overly restrictive privacy regulations in the United States could generate $104 billion in market inefficiencies, which would manifest as higher costs, lower productivity (for both organizations and consumers), and decreased innovation.

Privacy laws can constrain businesses from collecting and using data, thereby limiting data-driven innovation and adversely affecting consumers. For example, some biometric laws have

---

[168] Alec Stapp, "Against Privacy Fundamentalism in the United States" (Niskanen Center, November 2018), accessed July 23, 2019, https://niskanencenter.org/blog/against-privacy-fundamentalism-in-the-united-states/.

prevented businesses from selling certain products and services in those jurisdictions.[169] Other privacy rules, such as data minimization requirements, can prevent firms from collecting more data than necessary for a particular service, even though businesses often do not know what insights they might derive from data until after they have had an opportunity to analyze it.

Likewise, purpose specification requirements, found in many privacy laws, mandate that businesses both inform users why they are collecting their personal information and not use that data for any other reason. These restrictions prohibit firms from using the data they have for new purposes, thereby limiting innovation.

Privacy legislation that inhibits the collection and use of personal data can reduce the effectiveness of targeted advertising, thereby hurting not only advertisers that can no longer efficiently access specific audiences, but also app developers, media companies, and content creators that obtain revenue from targeted ads. For consumers, this means a worse Internet experience with less-relevant ads, lower-quality online content and services, and more paywalls.[170]

Beyond general market inefficiencies from less-efficient use of data, a patchwork of state privacy laws also opens the door to inefficiencies from litigation on multiple fronts, especially if some states create a private right of action that allows individuals to file lawsuits against companies for potential violations. Privacy litigation has grown rapidly in recent years, with certain laws clearing the way for a proliferation of class action lawsuits. A patchwork of state laws with varying definitions and standards creates a complex regulatory minefield for businesses to navigate, especially if potential violations risk costly litigation.

BIPA, for example, demonstrates the potential for costly litigation. It was designed to regulate the collection of biometric data by companies operating in a given state or whose products reach consumers in that state. The state privacy law includes a private right of action that allows both consumer class action lawsuits and employer lawsuits. Although BIPA passed into law in 2008, most lawsuits have occurred more recently after the Illinois Supreme Court held in 2019 that individuals are not required to show harm and instead can file lawsuits even when there has only been a technical violation of BIPA.[171] Likewise, a ruling by the U.S. Court of Appeals for the Ninth Circuit found that plaintiffs had legal standing for filing lawsuits alleging technical violations of BIPA.[172] Since then, a definitive trend has taken hold, as the Illinois courts have ruled in favor of plaintiffs in most class action suits.

Since 2019, the number of BIPA lawsuits has skyrocketed, with many high-profile cases. In March 2021, Facebook paid $650 million in a case filed over the social media platform's use of facial recognition technology for tagging in photos.[173] As a result, almost 1.6 million Illinois

---

[169] "Privacy Law Prevents Illinoisans From Using Google App's Selfie Art Feature," Illinois Policy, January 23, 2018, https://www.illinoispolicy.org/privacy-law-prevents-illinoisans-from-using-google-apps-selfie-art-feature/.

[170] Benjamin Mueller and Daniel Castro, "The Value of Personalized Advertising in Europe" (Center for Data Innovation, November 22, 2021), https://www2.datainnovation.org/2021-value-personalized-ads-europe.pdf.

[171] "The BIPA Litigation Landscape and What Lies Ahead," Woodruff Sawyer, April 1, 2021, https://woodruffsawyer.com/cyber-liability/bipa-litigation-landscape/.

[172] Patel v. Facebook, Inc., 932 F.3d 1264 (9th Cir. 2019), https://cdn.ca9.uscourts.gov/datastore/opinions/2019/08/08/18-15982.pdf.

[173] "Judge approves $650 million settlement of Facebook privacy lawsuit linked to facial photo tagging," *Business Insider*, February 27, 2021, https://www.businessinsider.com/facebook-settlement-pay-650-million-privacy-lawsuit-biometrics-face-tagging-2021-2.

residents will receive $345 or more.[174] Similarly, in April 2021, security company ADP paid a $25 million settlement for supplying equipment and support to employers that required workers to scan their fingerprints. Over 40,000 residents filed claims.

There have also been BIPA lawsuits against employers. Walmart settled for $10 million in June 2021 due to the company's use of palm-scanning technology.[175] Over 20,000 employees were involved in the case—which stemmed from Walmart giving employees that needed to take out their cash-register drawers at the end of their shifts the option of using a biometric scanner, rather than entering a PIN code, to verify their identities—due to their use of the technology without giving written consent, although no actual injury was involved. Walmart subsequently deleted all data and ended the scanning option in Illinois.

The number of lawsuits filed under BIPA has grown over time. In 2019, there were around 300 lawsuits, and the number of cases referencing BIPA doubled in 2020.[176] The legal specifics, such as the private right of action and the grounds for standing make taking legal action for biometric data collection all too easy in Illinois. The consequences of BIPA have implications not only for Illinois but other states considering stringent biometrics laws as well. As there is currently no such federal data privacy law, states must consider the collective cost of class action litigation on their economies. Some companies, such as Clearview AI, have pulled out of Illinois altogether, while others limit the technology available to consumers.[177] For example, Nest (smart home devices) will not include facial recognition features for Illinois consumers. Similarly, Google never released its Arts and Culture app outright in Illinois due to BIPA-compliance concerns.

BIPA is not alone in creating a wave of privacy litigation. As the standard for privacy legislation in the United States, the CCPA has been the focus of over 190 lawsuits since it was enacted in 2020.[178] Regulating any firm that "does business in California," the law even applies to those without a physical presence in the state. With a private right of action for those wherein consumer information "is subject to an unauthorized access and exfiltration, theft, or disclosure," many cases have emerged that argue businesses have failed to maintain necessary security procedures. The number of cases increases each year, with 125 claims filed in 2021.[179]

Class action lawsuits can lead to major settlements, thereby threatening the viability of smaller businesses. Even if a business can prevail in a lawsuit, the costs of the lawsuit are often significant, especially in state courts that are often more favorable for plaintiffs in class action litigation compared with federal courts and allow for expensive discovery processes, such as

---

[174] "Facebook privacy settlement approved: Nearly 1.6 million Illinois users will 'expeditiously' get at least $345," *Chicago Tribune*, February 26, 2021, https://www.chicagotribune.com/business/ct-biz-facebook-privacy-settlement-approval-20210227-okljqhsiargl7ijvzzfcotpyby-story.html.

[175] "Nearly 22,000 Illinois Walmart workers could get share of $10 million privacy settlement," *Chicago Tribune*, January 19, 2021, https://www.chicagotribune.com/business/ct-biz-walmart-biometric-palm-scan-lawsuit-20210119-parcawurhzcshir2naurw5pccu-story.html.

[176] "Illinois Supreme Court Finds Insurer Has Duty to Defend BIPA Suit," *Bloomberg Law*, June 18, 2021, https://news.bloomberglaw.com/privacy-and-data-security/illinois-supreme-court-finds-insurer-has-duty-to-defend-bipa-suit.

[177] "Clearview AI Has Promised To Cancel All Relationships With Private Companies," *BuzzFeed News*, May 7, 2020, https://www.buzzfeednews.com/article/ryanmac/clearview-ai-no-facial-recognition-private-companies.

[178] "CCPA Litigation Tracker, Updated as of December 2021," Perkin Coie, n.d., https://www.perkinscoie.com/en/ccpa-litigation-tracker.html (accessed January 10, 2022).

[179] "2021 Year in Review: CCPA Litigation," *The National Law Review*, December 31, 2021, https://www.natlawreview.com/article/2021-year-review-ccpa-litigation.

requesting documents and witness interviews, that can drive up the costs of litigation very quickly.

Conclusion

Poorly designed data privacy laws can impose a substantial toll on the economy through both direct compliance costs and indirect costs from lower productivity and constraints on innovation; and when multiple states subject businesses to conflicting privacy laws, they increase these costs. To avoid conflicting laws and unnecessary costs, Congress should act swiftly to pass comprehensive privacy legislation that preempts state laws, streamlines regulation, establishes basic consumer data rights, and minimizes the impact on innovation (e.g., by avoiding requirements for data minimization, universal opt-in, purpose specification, limitations on data retention, or privacy-by-design). This legislation should not include a private right of action and instead rely on federal and state regulators for enforcement. Establishing a comprehensive federal privacy law would also simplify compliance for businesses, especially small businesses working across multiple U.S. jurisdictions, as well as help consumers better understand their privacy rights and avoid the confusion resulting from a patchwork of state laws.

Appendix A: Detailed Methodology

This analysis is informed by best practices in modeling the effects of data regulation between nations as demonstrated by the Organization for Economic Cooperation and Development (OECD) and the European Center for International Political Economy (ECIPE).[180]

State Restrictiveness Scores

SRSs are calculated as a function *f* of both in-state and out-of-state privacy restrictions on consumer data.

SRS = f(in-state restriction, out-state restriction)

The table on state privacy laws shown in appendix B is the source document referenced in calculating SRS. States occupying larger shares of national data-concerned industries are

[180] Martina F. Ferracane and Erik van der Marel, "Do Data Policy Restrictions Inhibit Trade in Services?" (ECIPE), https://ecipe.org/publications/do-data-policy-restrictions-inhibit-trade-in-services/; Martina F. Ferracane and Erik van der Marel, "Do Data Policy Restrictions Impact the Productivity Performance of Firms and Industries?" (ECIPE), https://ecipe.org/publications/do-data-policyrestrictions-impact-the-productivity-performance-of-firms-and-industries/; "The 2018 edition of the OECD PMR indicators and database: Methodological improvements and policy insights" (OECD, March 23, 2020), https://www.oecd-ilibrary.org/economics/the-2018-edition-of-the-oecd-pmr-indicators-and-database-methodological-improvements-and-policy-insights_2cfb622f-en; "Trade and cross-border data flows" (OECD, December 21, 2018), https://www.oecd.org/officialdocuments/publicdisplay documentpdf/?cote=TAD/TC/WP(2018)19/FINA L&docLanguage=En.

assumed to be of greater weight in the composition of a state's contribution of SRS resulting from out of state. Since all applicable businesses within a state would require direct compliance with their own state's laws, in-state restrictions are taken as unweighted. Out-of-state restrictions would only impact multistate operations complying in those other states, which would be a smaller fraction than all businesses based within the state. To provide a weight to the contribution of out-of-state restrictions into the calculation of SRS, ITIF's model uses deflator *d* as a state-specific coefficient for out-of-state restrictions. The equation for deflator *d* of state *x* is below.

$$d_x = \frac{(Consumer\ Products\ Share_x + Consumer\ Finance\ Share_x + Advertisement\ Share_x)}{3}$$

A state's deflator is the unweighted average of its share of U.S. GDP in the consumer products, consumer finance, and advertising industries. *d* is calculated using only 2019 data for all states and is applied to all years' calculations of SRS to control for issues of endogeneity. Data on a state's share of the national consumer products industry is taken from BEA's Regional Data table on retail trade as a percentage of the U.S. industry's GDP. Data on a state's share of the national consumer finance industry is taken from BEA's Regional Data table on finance and insurance as the state's percentage of the U.S. industry's GDP. Lastly, data on a state's share of national advertising spending is taken from a 2019 Statista dataset and study of U.S. total advertisement spending. Using *d* to deflate the value of out-of-state laws in the calculation of SRS, the equation for SRS of state *x* during year *y* is below.

$$SRS_{xy} = \sum_{n=2003}^{y} (State\ Privacy\ Restriction_{xn}) + \sum_{j \neq x} d_j * \sum_{n=2003}^{y} (State\ Privacy\ Restriction_{jn})$$

SRS is equal to the unweighted cumulative sum of state privacy restrictions passed up to year *y* in state *x*, plus the cumulative sum of deflated state privacy restrictions across states other than *x* passed up to year *y*. These scores provide a common quantitative scale to measure the level of restrictiveness imposed onto a state's consumer data, wherein higher SRS means stricter compliance/enforcement regarding data privacy. While some privacy restrictions are undoubtedly of higher economic cost than others (e.g., laws requiring rights to access, deletion, data portability, and rectification would levy higher compliance costs than laws requiring privacy audits would), this model provides no weighting to the value of state privacy restrictions in the calculation, in order to simplify methodology.

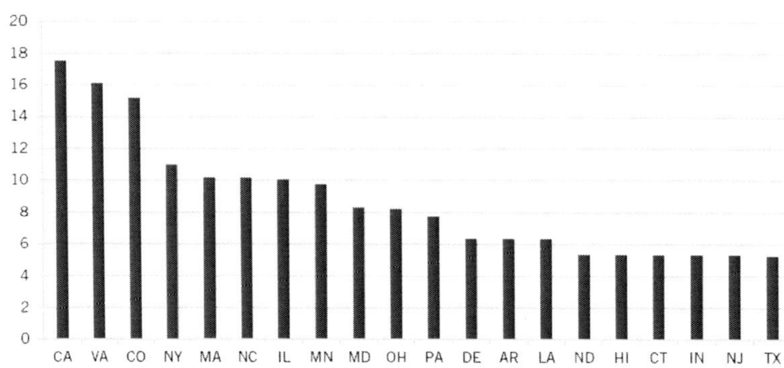

Figure 5. Highest SRSs in 2021.

Data-Intensity Modifiers

ITIF's model assumes that restrictions on consumer data have greater effects on industries that are more reliant on data and data-related tools and services. To best weigh state-level measurements of SRS at the precision of industry-specific scores, a DIM is calculated to help correct for bias in the proxy SRS by weighting each downstream industry's linkage with state privacy restrictiveness for every industry within the North American Industry Classification System (NAICS) categorization. Furthermore, this model selects U.S. national data as a reference in a given baseline year for computing industry-specific measurements of DIM to be applied to states in the sample. However, this approach assumes that all U.S. states have technologies equal to the national estimated for the United States. U.S. Census ICT 2013 Survey data on intangible software expenditure and BLS data of employment by industry in the same year are gathered to compute the ratios of data-related service expenditures per worker in each industry. ITIF's methodology for calculating DIM is based on best practice as demonstrated by ECIPE's studies on data localization. Employment is recorded in number of workers employed, and noncapitalized software expenditure is recorded in millions of U.S. Dollars. DIM is taken as a natural log to align with previous literature on factor intensity.

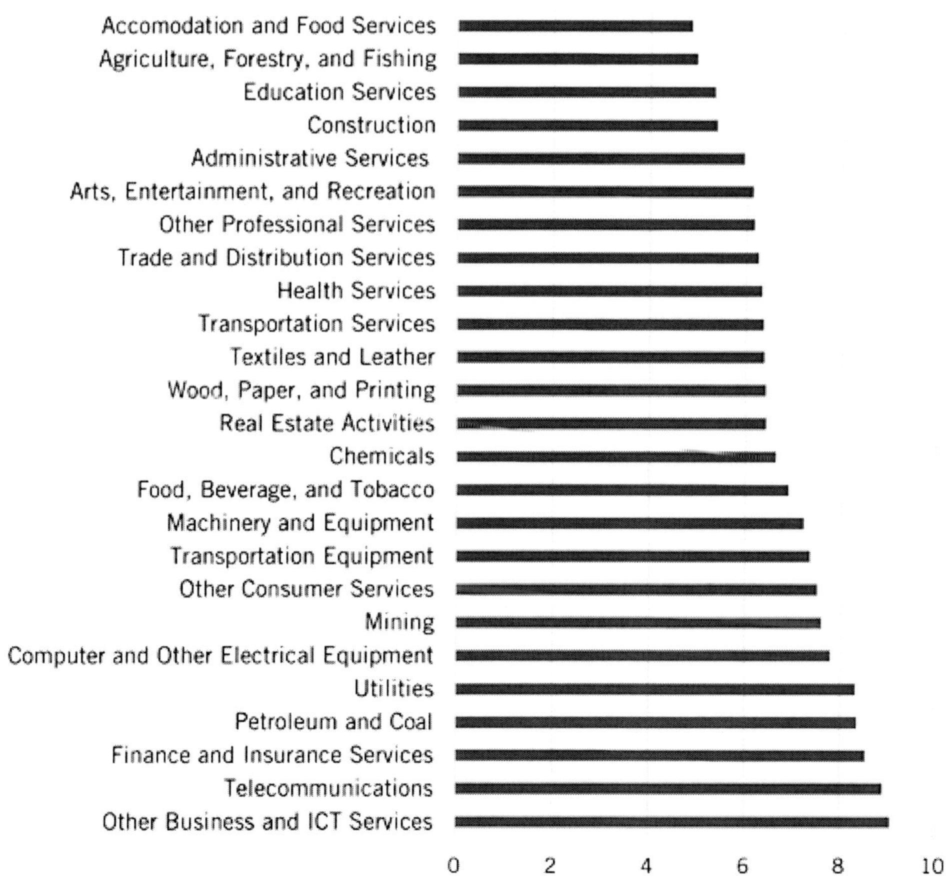

Figure 6. Data intensity by Industry (as a log of noncapitalized software expenditures per worker).

The proxies SRS by state and DIM by industry function as components of a composite index at the state-industry level. This composite index links the level of privacy restrictiveness within a state to the level of data reliance faced by an industry in order to provide measurement on the level of effective restrictiveness faced by a state's industries due to privacy restrictions passed by that state. This PRL is the composite index and final independent variable observed to analyze the economic impact of privacy laws on industries. Conducting this analysis at the level of state-industry-year rather than just state-year provides greater precision in identifying a statistical relationship between privacy laws and economic performance. Since not every industry relies on data equally, not every industry within a state will be equally impacted by its privacy law changes. The product of a state's SRS with an industry's DIM gives the PRL of that industry within the state. The equation for PRL of state-year-industry x, y, and z is below.

$$PRL_{xyz} = SRS_{xy} * DIM_z$$

PRL is recorded over a panel between years 2003 to 2021 for 50 U.S. states among 25 NAICS industries included by the U.S. BEA's Regional Data tables on industry GDP in order to be compatible with response variable data. Note that total number of observations will not equal the total number of entries recorded for PRL due to missing responses and control variables. Since most states so far do not impose privacy laws to similar levels of stringency found in California, most PRL in early years in the panel data is accounted for by out-of-state restrictions in the calculation of SRS. Further, since most states have not yet determined their privacy law, distribution of PRL will be skewed by early actors. As a result, the distribution of PRL in years 2018 and on yield the following histogram. The distribution of PRL is positively skewed above the normal. While still skewed and dealing with imperfect data, correcting for variation in data intensity among industries helps normalize the predictor variable, whereas a vector of SRS values would otherwise be irregularly distributed and thus less suitable for regression.

This econometric exercise is informed by best econometric practices in modeling the effects of data regulation between nations as demonstrated by OECD and ECIPE.[181] ITIF's econometric model selects GOS as its main response variable based on economic theory and statistical convenience. GOS is the residual earnings among corporations within an industry after subtracting their total intermediate expenses and compensation of employees. GOS can therefore be understood as a measurement of an industry's net economic performance. This makes GOS a fitting response variable since this model's purpose is to examine how a state's industry earnings are impacted by a rise in state privacy laws adopted across 50 U.S. states.

Further, GOS has direct implications for GDP. GDP can be calculated by three main approaches, and while it is chiefly calculated by the production approach (the sum of all domestically created goods and services), the income approach to GDP relies in part on GOS to calculate GDP. The income approach calculates GDP as the sum of total incomes, including total net corporate earnings. Net corporate earnings are often represented in this calculation with GOS, meaning that a change to a state's GOS, by the income approach to GPD, marks an equivalent change in GDP.

---

[181] Ibid.

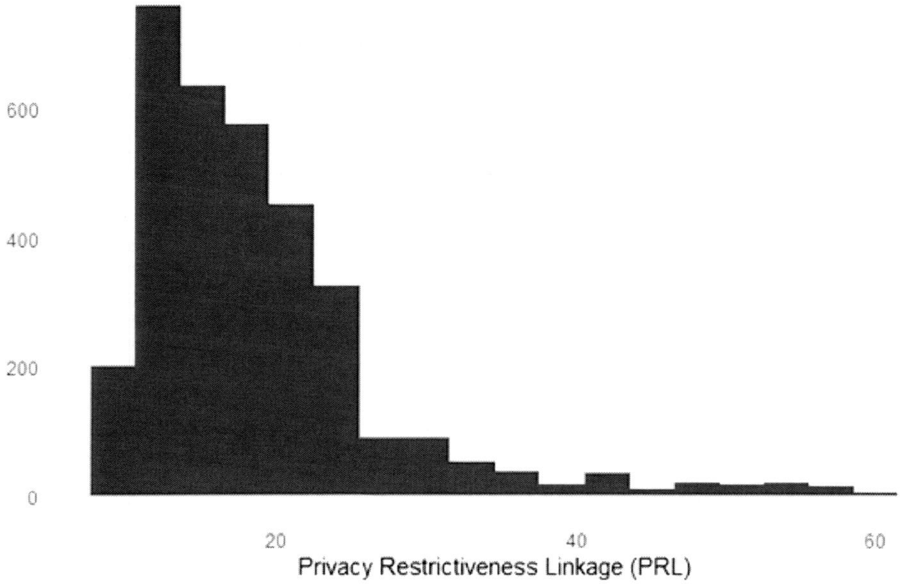

Figure 7. Distribution of PRL.

The composition of GOS makes it doubly useful in capturing costs associated with privacy law restrictions. Privacy laws impose explicit costs on firms through added forms of compliance that cost more to satisfy. Privacy laws also impose effective costs on firms by limiting the utility and usability of data. If consumer data is rendered less transferrable or has its range of uses limited, then that data becomes less monetizable and thus less valuable. These kinds of restrictions create market inefficiencies that lower firms' total output, effectively imposing additional costs on firms impacted by such laws. GOS can be broadly represented by the equation below.

$$GOS = Total\ Output - Intermediate\ Expenses\ - Compensation\ of\ Employees$$

Higher compliance costs result in higher intermediate expenses or higher compensation of employees, thus lowering GOS. Higher costs due to market inefficiencies lower total output, which also lowers GOS. Therefore, GOS should capture both kinds of costs associated with privacy laws. Additionally, an industry containing many multistate operations would report lower GOS due to duplicative costs of compliance with other states and the operational costs (captured by intermediate expenses and further compensation of employees) associated with discerning a patchwork system of 50 different privacy laws in place of one unifying federal law on consumer data.

Despite the advantages of GOS, ITIF's model still draws compromises due to issues in data availability. A key statistic of use for this model is industry-level trade data, in both goods and services, between U.S. states; however, to our knowledge, there is no freely available public dataset on this matter. Further, in economic census datasets collected by the U.S. Census, there is currently no publicly available data on the share of enterprises in each state that are multistate operations. For these reasons, we resort to proxies in calculating the final composite index PRL that serves as the model's predictor variable.

Regression Model

The purpose of this regression modeling is to measure the statistical relationship between the index of a state-year-industry's PRL and its GOS. This report constructs a multivariate linear regression model using the ordinary least squares (OLS) method of linear regression. The lead regression model detailing this relationship is below.

$$ln(\widehat{GOS})_{xyz} = \hat{\beta}_0 + \hat{\beta}_1 * PRL_{xyz} + \hat{\beta}_2 * GDP_{xy} + \alpha_y + \gamma_z + \varepsilon_{xyz}$$

$ln(\widehat{GOS})_{xyz}$ represents the response variable GOS as a natural log. GOS is taken as a natural log in order to model a log-linear relationship and help normalize the distribution of GOS for a data frame better suited for regression. This regression model, with results summarized in the following table, regresses a log-linear relationship by the OLS method in order to estimate the percentage change in GOS associated with a 1-unit change in the predictor variable, PRL. $\hat{\beta}_0$ represents the y-intercept estimate. $\hat{\beta}_1$ represents the coefficient estimate on the predictor variable PRL. $\hat{\beta}_2$ represents the coefficient estimate on the control variable state GDP.

α_γ represents yearly fixed-effects in which the model assumes errors in residuals are in part owed to unobservable variation within data between years but is constant between states and industries (e.g., national economic shocks that change between years but are of common impact on states and industries). γ_z represents industry fixed effects in which the model assumes errors in residuals are also owed to unobservable variation within data across different industries, as there are many factors that determine industry-specific performance that are together not easily captured by other controls. Lastly, ε_{xyz} represents residual error that varies for each fitted value.

Table 1. Regression table

	Coefficient Estimate	Standard Error	t-value	Pr(>ltl)
Intercept	13.27	0.10	132.8	< 2e-16
PRL	-0.00389	0.00115	-3.78	0.000737
GDP	1.025e-09	2.6e-11	39.4	< 2e-16

R-Squared: 0.734, Number of Observations: 3,984.

Comparisons to Bottom-up Modeling

This model differs from previous work from ITIF and others on modeling the costs of state privacy laws in that it employs econometric analysis. It is a top-down model whereby looking at a high- level residual in industry economic performance over time captures an aggregated change of multiple factors (compliance costs, market inefficiencies, duplicative costs, etc.). The top-down model gives strong insight into a total change in performance via loss in GOS, which estimates a total cost/economic burden incurred on states through the adoption of additional state privacy laws; however, since GOS is made of multiple components, ITIF's model is not able to discern exactly which components comprising GOS are changing and by how much. A model capable of identifying separate cost components with greater specificity can be better thought of instead as a bottom-up model. This is because a model like this would be identifying separate costs associated with added privacy laws and summing them up to derive a total cost borne by states. While data-constraints are present in the top-down model, a bottom-up model is especially constrained by the availability of data. A top-down model requires analyzing a response variable that encompasses multiple relevant factors in order to identify a statistical relationship, whereas a bottom-up model needs a unique dataset to identify costs for each line item included in the model. For example, increased legal costs through more lawsuits is captured in GOS due to increased intermediate expenses of legal services, which would incur a loss in GOS. However, there would be no way to identify what portion of a loss in GOS would be due to increased legal costs. In a bottom-up model, one would need a separate dataset capable of targeting increased legal costs associated with more lawsuits incurred by a change in a state's privacy laws, but such a model would be capable of identifying specific costs with greater precision. But given the lack of free and publicly available costs around specific economic burdens created by additional privacy law restrictions, a bottom-up model is less feasible. To address holes in a bottom-up model's demand for data, modelers would need to supplement their methodology with either survey data or suitable proxies. Survey data on self-reported costs on different restrictions induced by a change in state privacy law could help obtain information that is otherwise private; however, that data is only as effective as its survey. A 2019 Berkeley Economic Advising and Research report sanctioned by the Office of the California Attorney General conducts a similarly structure bottom-up model, supplementing holes in data with robust survey data taken from California firms reporting costs. Given the challenges inherent to conducting an effective and accurate survey, ITIF declines to supplement a bottom-up model with survey data. A bottom-up model also faces the challenge of identifying a state's costs for its businesses to comply with privacy laws set in other states. This model's main purpose is to quantify the cost of compliance with multiple states' privacy laws, and to model a hypothetical scenario wherein all 50 states have established their own privacy law, which is made possible by the calculation of SRS as a function of both in-state laws and (to a lesser degree by the deflator equation *d*) out-of-state laws. Capturing the costs associated with a system of multistate compliance in a bottom-up model would require information on the value of trade from businesses in state *a* to purchasers in state *b* (and to purchasers in state *c*, and so on). There is currently no dataset, to our knowledge, that covers this exchange to the specificity of NAICS industries. Therefore, without survey-data or access to a privately held database on industry-level trade between states, a bottom-up model lacks the ability to capture the cost effect imposed on firms by having to navigate a multistate system of divergent privacy laws. For these reasons, ITIF instead conducts the elaborated top-down econometric model presented in this report.

Nevertheless, a state's costs incurred by its own in-state privacy laws estimated by the top-down model in this report can be compared with a bottom-up model calculating only a state's costs due to in-state privacy laws (excluding out-of-state effects). ITIF constructs an example bottom-up model in order to compare its national estimate on the cost of in-state privacy laws against the estimates of the costs of in-state privacy laws projected by this report's top-down model. The methodology for this example of a bottom-up model follows ITIF's 2019 report "The Costs of Unnecessarily Stringent Federal Data Privacy Law," except it excludes the line item for data protection officers (DPOs), since a rule on DPOs was ultimately kept out of the CCPA. All calculations are based on both the number of enterprises by size in a state, the actual privacy laws passed in a state, and a state's share of national data-concerned industries.

Table 2. Comparing sample estimates of a bottom-up model

Line Item	AnnualNational Cost (Totaled among U.S. States) in 2020	Methodology
State Audit Costs	$189 million	0.5 percent of firms are estimated to be audited annually. Small enterprises (fewer than 20 employees) and nonprofits have estimated audit costs equal to $10,000. Medium-sized enterprises (between 20 and 500 employees) have estimated audit costs equal to $30,000. Large enterprises (more than 500 employees) have estimated audit costs equal to $60,000. Each state's total costs are calculated based on the number of firms by size and their number of in-state restrictions on privacy laws during 2021. National cost is taken as the sum of all state costs.
Cost of Database Administrators (Requirements on Updating and Maintaining Data Infrastructure)	$18.5 billion	Additional database administrators (DAs) would be needed to comply with requirements on updating and maintaining data infrastructures. Annual cost of a database administrator salary is $91,000. Small firms and nonprofits would require additional hiring on average of 0.05 new DAs, medium-sized firms on average wou ld hire an additional 0.1new DAs, and large firms wou ld on average hire an additional 1new DA. Each state's total costs are calculated based on the number of firms by size and their number of in-state restrictions on privacy laws during 2021. National cost is taken as the sum of all state costs.
Cost of Legal Enforcement (Lawsuits)	$1.4 billion	Due to the challenge of acquiring and preparing legal data between national and state agencies, this line item is proxied using ITIF's 2019 report estimate on the cost of lawsuits throughout the country due to enforcing data privacy laws. ITIF estimated a national cost of $2.7 billion due to a federal law applying to all states equally strict as CCPA. This statistic of $2.7 billion is scaled down to account for the actual number of privacy law restrictions in place within each state during 2021. Rescaling this statistic, in which state costs are scaled based on actual privacy laws rather than privacy laws equal to CCPA, gives a new sum across states equal to $1.4 billion.
Right to Access, Deletion, Data Portability,and Rectification	$3.5 billion	ITIF's 2019 report estimates data access,deletion, portability, and rectification requirements would cost the United States $7 .2 billion,wh ich assumes all states wou ld enact state laws equally strict to California's CCPA. This estimate is rescaled based on the actual laws passed by states through 2021, which gives a new estimate of $3.5 billion.
Productivity Loss in Online Services	$935 million	ITIF's 2019 report estimates the productivity loss in online services incurred by all states with equal privacy laws to CCPA would equal $1.9 billion nationally. This estimate is rescaled by each state's share of online services in the United States (proxied by national advertising share) and by their actual state privacy laws passed as of 2021, which gives a new estimate of $935 million.
Losses Due to Inefficienc ies of Less Data	$32.8 billion	ITIF's 2019 report estimates the national cost of economic losses due to market inefficiencies created by privacy laws restricting data would equal $71 billion.This estimate assumes that each U.S. state would have privacy laws equal to CCPA.This estimate is rescaled by each state's share of data concerned industries and by their actual state privacy laws passed, giving each state a new estimated cost. The sum of rescaled estimated costs among states equals $33 billion.

Line Item	AnnualNational Cost (Totaled among U.S. States) in 2020	Methodology
Losses Due to Inefficiencies in Advertising	$22.5 billion	ITIF's 2019 report estimates a national cost of $33 billion in economic value lost due to less-effective advertising inhibited by increased privacy laws. The $33 billion is scaled up relative to the growth in total advertising between 2018 and 2021, estimating a $46 billion loss nationally. However, this $46 billion estimate assumes all states have privacy laws equal to California's. State estimates on their share of loss due to ineffective advertising are rescaled based on their shares of the national advertising industry and by their actual set of passed state privacy laws as of 2021. The sum of rescaled state estimates for 2021 is equal to $22.5 billion.
Annual Total Cost of In-State Privacy Laws in 2021 (Bottom-Up Model)	$79.9 billion	Sum of all other line items in this sample bottom-up model.
Annual Total Cost of In-State Privacy Laws in 2021 (Top Down Model)	$95.3 billion	Using regression coefficients estimated from the econometric model in this report on PRL, each state's actual GOS loss due to PRL in 2021 is estimated, and out-state costs are subtracted from each state's total estimated GOS loss. The sum total of state costs due to in-state privacy laws estimated by the top down model is equal to $95 billion.
Difference in Estimates (Bottom-Up - Top-Down)	- $15.4 billion	The estimate on in-state costs from the bottom-up model is approximate ly $15 billion less than what is estimated by the top-down model.

This sample methodology on bottom-up costs helps provide, with greater specificity, estimates for economic burdens faced by states from their own in-state privacy laws. There is a notable discrepancy between these two estimates because a bottom-up model requires complete and accurate information regarding the factors influenced by privacy laws, which is nearly impossible given the complexity of the issue. As a result, costly line items concerning matters of compliance costs, both direct and indirect, and of market inefficiencies are likely to be missed or underestimated, explaining the difference in estimates. Regardless, the previous table helps demonstrate where, due to an increase in a state's own passed privacy law restrictions, some of the actual costs that amount to a loss in GOS come from and what they could amount to.

Time Horizon Model

Now that a statistical relationship is estimated between a state's change in PRL by 1 unit against a percentage loss in its GOS, ITIF's model can be extended to a scenario in which all states are assumed to pass some version of their own state privacy laws. States would adopt their own laws at different times, as some states would be less quick to adopt legislative changes than others. To model the time horizon over which each state would be estimated to determine their own set state privacy laws, ITIF uses the case study of data breach laws adopted by U.S. states. Each of the 50 states has its own version of data breach laws, but they have adopted those laws in different times. In total, between the first and last state to enact their own data breach laws, 15 years passed (between 2003 to 2018). From this example, ITIF constructs a time horizon model in which all 50 states enact (and settle) their own state privacy laws over 15 years.

Table 3. Annual state total costs of a SO-state privacy patchwork

			Years 1-5			Years 6-1O			Years 11-15		
State	Estimated Strictness of Privacy Law	Latest Year of Adoption	Total Costs	Costs Due to In-State Laws	Costs Due to Out-of-State Laws	Total Costs	Costs Due to In-State Laws	Costs Due to Out-of-State Laws	Total Costs	Costs Due to In-State Laws	Costs Due to Out-of-State Laws
AL	Low	15	$1.1B	$0.0B	$1.1B	$1.2B	$0.0B	$1.2B	$1.9B	$0.6B	$1.2B
AK	Low	10	$0.2B	$0.0B	$0.2B	$0.4B	$0.1B	$0.3B	$0.4B	$0.1B	$0.3B
AZ	Low	5	$2.9B	$1.1B	$1.8B	$3.1B	$1.1B	$2.0B	$3.1B	$1.1B	$2.1B
AR	Low	5	$1.0B	$0.4B	$0.6B	$1.0B	$0.4B	$0.7B	$1.1B	$0.4B	$0.7B
CA	High	5	$56.6B	$46.4B	$10.3B	$58.2B	$46.4B	$11.8B	$58.9B	$46.4B	$12.5B
co	High	5	$7.2B	$5.4B	$1.8B	$7.3B	$5.4B	$1.9B	$7.4B	$5.4B	$2.0B
CT	Low	5	$2.3B	$0.9B	$1.5B	$2.5B	$0.9B	$1.6B	$2.5B	$0.9B	$1.7B
DE	Low	5	$0.8B	$0.3B	$0.5B	$0.8B	$0.3B	$0.5B	$0.9B	$0.3B	$0.6B
FL	Low	15	$5.6B	$0.0B	$5.6B	$6.1B	$0.0B	$6.1B	$9.5B	$3.3B	$6.2B
GA	Low	5	$5.3B	$2.0B	$3.4B	$5.7B	$2.0B	$3.7B	$5.8B	$2.0B	$3.8B
HI	Low	5	$0.6B	$0.2B	$0.4B	$0.6B	$0.2B	$0.4B	$0.7B	$0.2B	$0.4B
ID	Low	5	$0.7B	$0.3B	$0.4B	$0.7B	$0.3B	$0.5B	$0.7B	$0.3B	$0.5B
IL	Medium	5	$9.2B	$5.1B	$4.1B	$9.6B	$5.1B	$4.5B	$9.8B	$5.1B	$4.8B
IN	Low	5	$3.3B	$1.2B	$2.0B	$3.5B	$1.2B	$2.2B	$3.5B	$1.2B	$2.3B
IA	Low	10	$1.1B	$0.0B	$1.1B	$1.9B	$0.7B	$1.2B	$2.0B	$0.7B	$1.3B
KS	Low	5	$1.5B	$0.6B	$1.0B	$1.6B	$0.6B	$1.0B	$1.7B	$0.6B	$1.1B
KY	Low	15	$1.0B	$0.0B	$1.0B	$1.1B	$0.0B	$1.1B	$1.8B	$0.6B	$1.2B
LA	Low	5	$2.0B	$0.8B	$1.3B	$2.2B	$0.8B	$1.4B	$2.2B	$0.8B	$1.5B
ME	Low	5	$0.5B	$0.2B	$0.3B	$0.5B	$0.2B	$0.3B	$0.5B	$0.2B	$0.4B
MD	Medium	10	$4.0B	$2.1B	$1.8B	$4.1B	$2.1B	$2.0B	$4.2B	$2.1B	$2.1B
MA	Medium	5	$6.0B	$3.3B	$2.7B	$6.3B	$3.3B	$3.0B	$6.4B	$3.3B	$3.1B
Ml	Low	5	$4.0B	$1.5B	$2.5B	$4.3B	$1.5B	$2.8B	$4.4B	$1.5B	$2.9B
MN	Medium	5	$4.0B	$2.2B	$1.8B	$4.2B	$2.2B	$2.0B	$4.3B	$2.2B	$2.1B
MS	Low	10	$0.5B	$0.0B	$0.5B	$0.9B	$0.3B	$0.6B	$0.9B	$0.3B	$0.6B
MO	Low	10	$1.6B	$0.0B	$1.6B	$2.7B	$0.9B	$1.7B	$2.8B	$0.9B	$1.8B
MT	Low	5	$0.4B	$0.2B	$0.3B	$0.4B	$0.2B	$0.3B	$0.5B	$0.2B	$0.3B
NE	Low	5	$1.2B	$0.5B	$0.8B	$1.3B	$0.5B	$0.9B	$1.4B	$0.5B	$0.9B
NV	Low	10	$0.9B	$0.0B	$0.9B	$1.5B	$0.5B	$1.0B	$1.5B	$0.5B	$1.0B
NH	Low	5	$0.6B	$0.2B	$0.4B	$0.7B	$0.2B	$0.4B	$0.7B	$0.2B	$0.5B
NJ	Low	5	$4.7B	$1.7B	$2.9B	$5.0B	$1.7B	$3.2B	$5.1B	$1.7B	$3.4B

			Years 1-5			Years 6-1O			Years 11-15		
State	Estimated Strictness of Privacy Law	Latest Year of Adoption	Total Costs	Costs Due to In-State Laws	Costs Due to Out-of-State Laws	Total Costs	Costs Due to In-State Laws	Costs Due to Out-of-State Laws	Total Costs	Costs Due to In-State Laws	Costs Due to Out-of-State Laws
NM	Low	15	$0.4B	$0.0B	$0.4B	$0.5B	$0.0B	$0.5B	$0.7B	$0.2B	$0.5B
NY	Medium	5	$19.8B	$11.4B	$8.4B	$20.8B	$11.4B	$9.4B	$21.2B	$11.4B	$9.8B
NC	Medium	10	$3.1B	$0.0B	$3.1B	$6.9B	$3.6B	$3.3B	$7.1B	$3.6B	$3.4B
ND	Low	5	$0.5B	$0.2B	$0.3B	$0.5B	$0.2B	$0.3B	$0.5B	$0.2B	$0.3B
OH	Medium	5	$7.6B	$4.2B	$3.4B	$7.9B	$4.2B	$3.8B	$8.1B	$4.2B	$3.9B
OK	Low	10	$0.9B	$0.0B	$0.9B	$1.5B	$0.5B	$1.0B	$1.6B	$0.5B	$1.0B
OR	Low	5	$1.9B	$0.7B	$1.2B	$2.0B	$0.7B	$1.3B	$2.1B	$0.7B	$1.4B
PA	Medium	5	$8.3B	$4.6B	$3.8B	$8.7B	$4.6B	$4.1B	$8.9B	$4.6B	$4.3B
RI	Low	5	$0.4B	$0.2B	$0.3B	$0.4B	$0.2B	$0.3B	$0.5B	$0.2B	$0.3B
SC	Low	10	$1.2B	$0.0B	$1.2B	$2.0B	$0.7B	$1.3B	$2.0B	$0.7B	$1.3B
SD	Low	15	$0.3B	$0.0B	$0.3B	$0.4B	$0.0B	$0.4B	$0.6B	$0.2B	$0.4B
TN	Low	5	$3.1B	$1.1B	$1.9B	$3.3B	$1.1B	$2.1B	$3.3B	$1.1B	$2.2B
TX	Low	10	$11.6B	$2.7B	$8.9B	$14.9B	$5.3B	$9.6B	$15.3B	$5.3B	$10.0B
UT	Low	5	$1.7B	$0.6B	$1.1B	$1.8B	$0.6B	$1.2B	$1.8B	$0.6B	$1.2B
VT	Low	10	$0.1B	$0.0B	$0.1B	$0.2B	$0.1B	$0.2B	$0.2B	$0.1B	$0.2B
VA	High	10	$9.3B	$7.0B	$2.3B	$9.5B	$7.0B	$2.5B	$9.6B	$7.0B	$2.6B
WA	Low	5	$4.9B	$1.8B	$3.0B	$5.2B	$1.8B	$3.3B	$5.3B	$1.8B	$3.5B
WV	Low	10	$0.4B	$0.0B	$0.4B	$0.6B	$0.2B	$0.4B	$0.6B	$0.2B	$0.4B
WI	Low	5	$2.6B	$1.0B	$1.6B	$2.7B	$1.0B	$1.8B	$2.8B	$1.0B	$1.9B
WY	Low	5	$0.3B	$0.1B	$0.2B	$0.3B	$0.1B	$0.2B	$0.3B	$0.1B	$0.2B
US			$209.3B	$111.8B	$97.5B	$229.6B	$122.1B	$107.5B	$239.3B	$127.1B	$112.2B

In that span, states are modeled to have passed their own laws during either the first five years (years 1-5), the second five-year span (years 6-10), or the last five years (years 11-15). If a state has already passed and settled its own state privacy laws as of 2021, then it is automatically modeled to have passed its privacy laws during the first five years. To simplify estimates over this time horizon of 15 years, states are modeled to adopt one of three possible levels of strictness in data privacy: high (in-state privacy laws= 10 [for calculation of SRS scores]), medium (in-state privacy laws= 4), and low (in-state privacy laws= 2). Using these totals for a state's number of in-state privacy laws, each state's SRS (and therefore PRL values) can be calculated over this hypothetical 15-year period. The following table demonstrates each U.S. state's estimated cost of a 50-state privacy law patchwork over the 15-year time horizon.

Small Business Estimates

ITIF estimates the costs that this 50-state privacy law patchwork would impose on small businesses by using the above annual costs per state over the 15-year time horizon. To do this, ITIF estimates the share of GOS loss in each state that would be borne by small businesses. For this extended exercise, small businesses are simplified as enterprises employing fewer than 50 people. This process requires the US. Census Statistics on U.S. Businesses tables, among which is the 2021 SUSS table "The Number of Firms and Establishments, Employment, and Annual Payroll by State, Industry, and Enterprise Employment Size: 2018." This source data provides both the number of enterprises by size for each state as well as the amount of payroll paid out from enterprises by size. Using this data, ITIF calculates the share of each state's total payroll paid out by small businesses. These shares serve as a proxy for each state's total GOS earned by small businesses. When the time horizon estimates a loss in GOS, small businesses are modeled to bear a loss equal to the proxy small business share of GOS times the total loss in GOS (equation below for state x during year y.

$$.Small\ Business\ Cost_{xy} = \left(\frac{Small\ business\ Payroll_x}{Total\ Payroll_x}\right) * GOS\ Loss_{xy}$$

However, this method of calculating the cost borne by small businesses assumes that estimated losses in GOS fall proportionally along firms by size as they would comprise total GOS. Burdens may fall disproportionately greater on small or large businesses depending on the specificities of laws enacted, which are not able to modeled in the time horizon model since the scenario assumed is hypothetical. Ahead is a time horizon of the annual costs by state borne by small businesses due to the 50-state privacy law scenario.

Table 4. Annual state small business costs due to a SO-state privacy patchwork

State	Estimated Small Business Share of GOS	Years 1-5 Total Costs	Years 1-5 Costs Due to In-State Laws	Years 1-5 Costs Due to Out-of-State Laws	Years 6-1O Total Costs	Years 6-1O Costs Due to In-State Laws	Years 6-1O Costs Due to Out-of-State Laws	Years 11-15 Total Costs	Years 11-15 Costs Due to In-State Laws	Years 11-15 Costs Due to Out-of-State Laws
AL	21.4%	$0.28	$0.08	$0.28	$0.3B	$0.08	$0.38	$0.48	$0.18	$0.38
AK	26.7%	$0.18	$0.08	$0.18	$0.1B	$0.08	$0.18	$0.18	$0.08	$0.18
AZ	19.1%	$0.58	$0.28	$0.38	$0.6B	$0.28	$0.48	$0.68	$0.28	$0.48
AR	21.7%	$0.28	$0.18	$0.18	$0.2B	$0.18	$0.18	$0.28	$0.18	$0.28
CA	20.0%	$11.38	$9.38	$2.08	$11.6B	$9.38	$2.48	$11.88	$9.38	$2.58
CO	22.8%	$1.68	$1.28	$0.48	$1.7B	$1.28	$0.48	$1.78	$1.28	$0.58
CT	20.2%	$0.58	$0.28	$0.38	$0.5B	$0.28	$0.38	$0.58	$0.28	$0.38
DE	21.3%	$0.28	$0.18	$0.18	$0.2B	$0.18	$0.18	$0.28	$0.18	$0.18
FL	20.7%	$1.28	$0.08	$1.28	$1.3B	$0.08	$1.38	$2.08	$0.78	$1.38
GA	18.7%	$1.08	$0.48	$0.68	$1.1B	$0.48	$0.78	$1.18	$0.48	$0.78
HI	23.2%	$0.18	$0.18	$0.18	$0.1B	$0.18	$0.18	$0.28	$0.18	$0.18
ID	28.9%	$0.28	$0.18	$0.18	$0.2B	$0.18	$0.18	$0.28	$0.18	$0.18
IL	19.3%	$1.88	$1.08	$0.88	$1.9B	$1.08	$0.98	$1.98	$1.08	$0.98
IN	18.7%	$0.68	$0.28	$0.48	$0.6B	$0.28	$0.48	$0.78	$0.28	$0.48
IA	20.5%	$0.28	$0.08	$0.28	$0.4B	$0.18	$0.38	$0.48	$0.18	$0.38
KS	21.5%	$0.38	$0.18	$0.28	$0.3B	$0.18	$0.28	$0.48	$0.18	$0.28
KY	19.1%	$0.28	$0.08	$0.28	$0.2B	$0.08	$0.28	$0.38	$0.18	$0.28
LA	23.5%	$0.58	$0.28	$0.38	$0.5B	$0.28	$0.38	$0.58	$0.28	$0.38
ME	28.2%	$0.18	$0.18	$0.18	$0.1B	$0.18	$0.18	$0.28	$0.18	$0.18
MD	22.3%	$0.98	$0.53	$0.48	$0.9B	$0.58	$0.48	$0.98	$0.58	$0.58
MA	18.5%	$1.18	$0.68	$0.58	$1.2B	$0.68	$0.68	$1.28	$0.68	$0.68
MI	21.2%	$0.98	$0.38	$0.58	$0.9B	$0.38	$0.68	$0.98	$0.38	$0.68
MN	18.5%	$0.78	$0.48	$0.38	$0.8B	$0.48	$0.48	$0.88	$0.48	$0.48
MS	22.4%	$0.18	$0.08	$0.18	$0.2B	$0.18	$0.18	$0.28	$0.18	$0.18
MO	19.4%	$0.38	$0.08	$0.38	$0.5B	$0.28	$0.38	$0.58	$0.28	$0.48
MT	36.8%	$0.28	$0.18	$0.18	$0.2B	$0.18	$0.18	$0.28	$0.18	$0.18
NE	22.6%	$0.38	$0.18	$0.28	$0.3B	$0.18	$0.28	$0.38	$0.18	$0.28
NV	22.1%	$0.28	$0.08	$0.28	$0.3B	$0.18	$0.28	$0.38	$0.18	$0.28
NH	24.8%	$0.28	$0.18	$0.18	$0.2B	$0.18	$0.18	$0.28	$0.18	$0.18
NJ	21.1%	$1.08	$0.48	$0.68	$1.0B	$0.48	$0.78	$1.18	$0.48	$0.78

Table 4. (Continued)

		Years 1-5			Years 6-1O			Years 11-15		
State	Estimated Small Business Share of GOS	Total Costs	Costs Due to In-State Laws	Costs Due to Out-of-State Laws	Total Costs	Costs Due to In-State Laws	Costs Due to Out-of-State Laws	Total Costs	Costs Due to In-State Laws	Costs Due to Out-of-State Laws
NM	26.6%	$0.18	$0.08	$0.18	$0.1B	$0.08	$0.18	$0.28	$0.18	$0.18
NY	19.3%	$3.88	$2.28	$1.68	$4.0B	$2.28	$1.88	$4.18	$2.28	$1.98
NC	20.0%	$0.68	$0.08	$0.68	$1.4B	$0.78	$0.78	$1.48	$0.78	$0.78
ND	26.3%	$0.18	$0.08	$0.18	$0.1B	$0.08	$0.18	$0.18	$0.08	$0.18
OH	18.6%	$1.48	$0.88	$0.68	$1.5B	$0.88	$0.78	$1.58	$0.88	$0.78
OK	23.3%	$0.28	$0.08	$0.28	$0.4B	$0.18	$0.28	$0.48	$0.18	$0.28
OR	24.7%	$0.58	$0.28	$0.38	$0.5B	$0.28	$0.38	$0.58	$0.28	$0.38
PA	19.4%	$1.68	$0.98	$0.78	$1.7B	$0.98	$0.88	$1.78	$0.98	$0.88
RI	24.9%	$0.18	$0.08	$0.18	$0.18	$0.08	$0.18	$0.18	$0.08	$0.18
SC	20.9%	$0.28	$0.08	$0.28	$0.48	$0.18	$0.38	$0.48	$0.18	$0.38
SD	27.3%	$0.18	$0.08	$0.18	$0.18	$0.08	$0.18	$0.28	$0.18	$0.18
TN	19.0%	$0.68	$0.28	$0.48	$0.68	$0.28	$0.48	$0.68	$0.28	$0.48
TX	19.2%	$2.28	$0.58	$1.78	$2.98	$1.08	$1.88	$2.98	$1.08	$1.98
UT	20.3%	$0.38	$0.18	$0.28	$0.48	$0.18	$0.28	$0.48	$0.18	$0.28
VT	20.9%	$0.08	$0.08	$0.08	$0.18	$0.08	$0.08	$0.18	$0.08	$0.08
VA	32.2%	$3.08	$2.38	$0.78	$3.18	$2.38	$0.88	$3.18	$2.38	$0.88
WA	19.8%	$1.08	$0.48	$0.68	$1.08	$0.48	$0.78	$1.18	$0.48	$0.78
WV	20.6%	$0.18	$0.08	$0.18	$0.18	$0.08	$0.18	$0.18	$0.08	$0.18
WI	21.5%	$0.68	$0.28	$0.38	$0.68	$0.28	$0.48	$0.68	$0.28	$0.48
WY	19.9%	$0.18	$0.08	$0.08	$0.18	$0.08	$0.08	$0.18	$0.08	$0.08
US		$43.38	$23.38	$20.18	$47.58	$25.48	$22.18	$49.58	$26.48	$23.18

Appendix B. List of Passed State Privacy Laws

State	Statute	Year	Reg. 1	2	3	4	5	6	7	8	9	10	11	12	13	14	15	16
AL	Alabama SB 318	2018	0	0	0	0	0	0	0	0	0	0	0	0	0	0	0	1
AK	Alaska Stat. § 45.48.010 et seq.	2009	0	0	0	0	0	0	0	0	0	0	0	0	0	0	0	1
AZ	Ariz. Rev. Stat. § 18-551 et seq	2006	0	0	0	0	0	0	0	0	0	0	0	0	0	0	0	1
AZ	HB 2154	2018	0	0	0	0	0	0	0	0	0	0	0	0	0	0	0	1
AR	Ark. Code §§ 4-110-101 et seq.	2005	0	0	0	0	0	0	0	0	0	0	0	0	0	0	0	1
AR	Personal Information Protection Act	2019	0	0	0	1	0	0	0	0	0	0	0	0	0	0	1	1
CA	S.B. 1386	2003	0	0	0	0	0	0	0	0	0	0	0	0	0	0	0	1
CA	S.B 24	2012	0	0	0	0	0	0	0	0	0	0	0	0	0	0	0	1
CA	SB 46	2014	0	0	0	0	0	0	0	0	0	0	0	0	0	0	0	1
CA	AB 1710	2015	0	0	0	0	0	0	0	0	0	0	0	0	0	0	0	1
CA	AB 964, SB 570, SB 34	2016	0	0	0	0	0	0	0	0	0	0	0	0	0	0	0	1
CA	AB 1130	2020	0	0	0	0	0	0	0	0	0	0	0	0	0	0	0	1
CA	California Consumer Privacy Act	2018	1	1	0	1	0	1	1	0	1	1	1	0	0	1	1	0
CA	California Privacy Rights Act	2020	0	1	1	1	1	1	1	1	1	1	1	1	1	1	0	0
CO	HB 1119	2006	0	0	0	0	0	0	0	0	0	0	0	0	0	0	0	1
CO	HB 18-1128	2018	0	0	0	0	0	0	0	0	0	0	0	0	0	0	0	1
CO	SB 190	2021	0	1	1	1	0	1	1	1	0	1	1	1	1	1	0	0
CT	SB 650	2006	0	0	0	0	0	0	0	0	0	0	0	0	0	0	0	1
CT	HB 6001	2012	0	0	0	0	0	0	0	0	0	0	0	0	0	0	0	1
CT	SB 949	2015	0	0	0	0	0	0	0	0	0	0	0	0	0	0	0	1
CT	SB 472	2018	0	0	0	0	0	0	0	0	0	0	0	0	0	0	0	1
CT	HB 5310	2021	0	0	0	0	0	0	0	0	0	0	0	0	0	0	0	1
CT	SB 1108 (Task force on consumer privacy)	2020	1	0	0	0	0	0	0	0	0	0	0	0	0	0	0	0
DE	HB 116	2005	0	0		0	0	0	0	0	0	0	0	0	0	0	0	1
DE	HB 247	2010	0	0	0	0	0	0	0	0	0	0	0	0	0	0	0	1
DE	House Substitute 1 for HB 180	2018	0	0	0	0	0	0	0	0	0	0	0	0	0	0	0	1
DE	Insurance Data Security Law HB 174	2019	0	0	0	1	0	0	0	0	0	0	0	0	0	1	0	1
FL	SB 1524	2014	0	0	0	0	0	0	0	0	0	0	0	0	0	0	0	1
FL	SB 1526	2014	0	0	0	0	0	0	0	0	0	0	0	0	0	0	0	1
GA	SB 230	2005	0	0	0	0	0	0	0	0	0	0	0	0	0	0	0	1
GA	SB 236	2007	0	0	0	0	0	0	0	0	0	0	0	0	0	0	0	1
HI	SB 2290	2007	0	0	0	0	0	0	0	0	0	0	0	0	0	0	0	1
HI	SB 2402	2008	0	0	0	0	0	0	0	0	0	0	0	0	0	0	0	1
HI	HCR 225	2019	1	0	0	0	0	0	0	0	0	0	0	0	0	0	0	1

(Continued)

ID	SB 1374	2006	0	0	0	0	0	0	0	0	0	0	0	0	0	0	0	1
ID	HB 556	2010	0	0	0	0	0	0	0	0	0	0	0	0	0	0	0	1
IL	HB 1633	2006	0	0	0	0	0	0	0	0	0	0	0	0	0	0	0	1
IL	HB 3025	2012	0	0	0	0	0	0	0	0	0	0	0	0	0	0	0	1
IL	HB 1260	2017	0	0	0	0	0	0	0	0	0	0	0	0	0	0	0	1
IL	Biometric Information Protection Act	2008	0	0	0	1	0	0	1		1	0	1	0	0	1	1	0
IL	SB 1624	2020	0	0	0	0	0	0	0	0	0	0	0	0	0	0	0	1
IN	SB 503	2006	0	0	0	0	0	0	0	0	0	0	0	0	0	0	0	1
IN	HEA No. 1197	2009	0	0	0	0	0	0	0	0	0	0	0	0	0	0	0	1
IN	HEA No. 1121	2009	0	0	0	0	0	0	0	0	0	0	0	0	0	0	0	1
IN	HB 2189	2020	0	0	0	1	0	0	0	0	0	0	0	0	0	0	0	1
IA	2007 S.F. 2308	2008	0	0	0	0	0	0	0	0	0	0	0	0	0	0	0	1
IA	2014 S.F. 2259	2014	0	0	0	0	0	0	0	0	0	0	0	0	0	0	0	1
IA	2018 S.F. 2177	2018	0	0	0	0	0	0	0	0	0	0	0	0	0	0	0	1
KS	Kan. Stat. § 50-7a01 et seq. SB 196	2007	0	0	0	0	0	0	0	0	0	0	0	0	0	0	0	1
KY	HB 232	2014	0	0	0	0	0	0	0	0	0	0	0	0	0	0	0	1
KY	HB 5	2015	0	0	0	0	0	0	0	0	0	0	0	0	0	0	0	1
LA	SB 205	2006	0	0	0	0	0	0	0	0	0	0	0	0	0	0	0	1
LA	SB 361	2018	0	0	0	0	0	0	0	0	0	0	0	0	0	0	0	1
LA	Insurance Data Security Law	2020	0	0	0	1	0	0	0	0	0	0	0	0	0	0	0	1
LA	HR 249	2019	1	0	0	0	0	0	0	0	0	0	0	0	0	0	0	0
ME	LD 1671	2006	0	0	0	0	0	0	0	0	0	0	0	0	0	0	0	1
ME	HP 672	2009	0	0	0	0	0	0	0	0	0	0	0	0	0	0	0	1
ME	LD 696	2019	0	0	0	0	0	0	0	0	0	0	0	0	0	0	0	1
MD	HB 208	2008	0	0	0	0	0	0	0	0	0	0	0	0	0	0	0	1
MD	HB 974	2018	0	0	0	0	0	0	0	0	0	0	0	0	0	0	0	1
MD	SB 30	2019	0	0	0	0	0	0	0	0	0	0	0	0	0	0	0	1
MD	SB 693/HB 1154	2019	0	0	0	0	0	0	0	0	0	0	0	0	0	0	0	1
MD	Personal Information Protection Act	2008	0	0	0	0	0	0	0	0	0	0	0	0	0	0	0	1
MD	Labor and Employment - Use of Facial Recognition Services - Prohibition	2020	0	0	0	0	0	0	1	1	0	0	1	0	0	0	1	0
MA	HB 4144	2007	0	0	0	0	0	0	0	0	0	0	0	0	0	0	0	1
MA	H 4806	2019	0	0	0	0	0	0	0	0	0	0	0	0	0	0	0	1
MI	SB 309	2007	0	0	0	0	0	0	0	0	0	0	0	0	0	0	0	1
MI	SB 223	2011	0	0	0	0	0	0	0	0	0	0	0	0	0	0	0	1
MI	HB 6406	2020	0	0	0	0	0	0	0	0	0	0	0	0	0	0	0	1

MI	Insurance Data Security Law	2021	0	0	0	0	0	0	0	0	0	0	0	0	0	0	0	1
MN	Minn. Stat. § 325E.61 and 325E.64 HB 2121	2006	0	0	0	0	0	0	0	0	0	0	0	0	0	0	0	1
MS	Miss. Code § 75-24-29 HB 582	2011	0	0	0	0	0	0	0	0	0	0	0	0	0	0	0	1
MO	Mo. Rev. Stat. § 407.1500 HB 62	2009	0	0	0	0	0	0	0	0	0	0	0	0	0	0	0	1
MT	HB 732	2006	0	0	0	0	0	0	0	0	0	0	0	0	0	0	0	1
MT	HB 74	2015	0	0	0	0	0	0	0	0	0	0	0	0	0	0	0	1
NE	LB 876	2006	0	0	0	0	0	0	0	0	0	0	0	0	0	0	0	1
NE	LB 835	2016	0	0	0	0	0	0	0	0	0	0	0	0	0	0	0	1
NV	SB 347	2008	0	0	0	0	0	0	0	0	0	0	0	0	0	0	0	1
NV	SB 186	2011	0	0	0	0	0	0	0	0	0	0	0	0	0	0	0	1
NV	AB 179	2015	0	0	0	0	0	0	0	0	0	0	0	0	0	0	0	1
NH	N.H. Rev. Stat. § 359-C:19 et seq. HB 1660	2007	0	0	0	0	0	0	0	0	0	0	0	0	0	0	0	1
NH	Insurance Data Security Law	2021	0	0	0	0	0	0	0	0	0	0	0	0	0	0	0	1
NJ	A 4001	2006	0	0	0	0	0	0	0	0	0	0	0	0	0	0	0	1
NJ	SB 52	2019	0	0	0	1	0	0	0	0	0	0	0	0	0	0	0	1
NM	N.M. Stat. 57-12C-1 et seq. HB 15	2017	0	0	0	0	0	0	0	0	0	0	0	0	0	0	0	1
NY	AB 4254	2005	0	0	0	0	0	0	0	0	0	0	0	0	0	0	0	1
NY	S 2605-D	2013	0	0	0	0	0	0	0	0	0	0	0	0	0	0	0	1
NY	Stop Hacks and Improve Electronic Data Security (SHIELD) Act	2019	0	0	0	0	0	0	0	0	0	0	0	1	0	1	0	1
NC	SB 1017	2009	0	0	0	0	0	0	0	0	0	0	0	0	0	0	0	1
ND	SB 2251	2005	0	0	0	0	0	0	0	0	0	0	0	0	0	0	0	1
ND	HB 1435, SB 2214	2015	0	0	0	0	0	0	0	0	0	0	0	0	0	0	0	1
ND	HB 1485	2019	1	0	0	0	0	0	0	0	0	0	0	0	0	0	0	1
OH	HB 104	2006	0	0	0	0	0	0	0	0	0	0	0	0	0	0	0	1
OH	Insurance Data Security Law	2019	0	0	0	0	0	0	0	0	0	0	0	0	0	0	0	1
OK	24 Okla. Stat. § 161 et seq., § 74-3113.1 HB 2245	2008	0	0	0	0	0	0	0	0	0	0	0	0	0	0	0	1
OR	SB 583	2007	0	0	0	0	0	0	0	0	0	0	0	0	0	0	0	1
OR	SB 574	2013	0	0	0	0	0	0	0	0	0	0	0	0	0	0	0	1
OR	SB 601	2016	0	0	0	0	0	0	0	0	0	0	0	0	0	0	0	1
OR	SB 1551	2018	0	0	0	0	0	0	0	0	0	0	0	0	0	0	0	1
OR	SB 684	2020	0	0	0	0	0	0	0	0	0	0	0	0	0	0	0	1
PA	73 Pa. Stat. § 2301 et seq. SB 712	2006	0	0	0	0	0	0	0	0	0	0	0	0	0	0	0	1

(Continued)

State	Statute	Year	Reg. 1	2	3	4	5	6	7	8	9	10	11	12	13	14	15	16
RI	HB 6191	2006	0	0	0	0	0	0	0	0	0	0	0	0	0	0	0	1
RI	SB 0134	2016	0	0	0	0	0	0	0	0	0	0	0	0	0	0	0	1
SC	SB 453	2009	0	0	0	0	0	0	0	0	0	0	0	0	0	0	0	1
SC	HB 3248	2013	0	0	0	0	0	0	0	0	0	0	0	0	0	0	0	1
SD	S.D. CODE 22-40-20 et seq. SB 62	2018	0	0	0	0	0	0	0	0	0	0	0	0	0	0	0	1
TN	HB 2170	2005	0	0	0	0	0	0	0	0	0	0	0	0	0	0	0	1
TN	SB 2005	2016	0	0	0	0	0	0	0	0	0	0	0	0	0	0	0	1
TN	SB 547	2017	0	0	0	0	0	0	0	0	0	0	0	0	0	0	0	1
TX	Acts 2007, 80th Leg., ch. 885, § 2.01. Amended by Acts 2009, 81st Leg., ch. 419, § 3.	2009	0	0	0	0	0	0	0	0	0	0	0	0	0	0	0	1
TX	Acts 2011, 82nd Leg., ch. 1126, § 14 (H.B. No. 300).	2012	0	0	0	0	0	0	0	0	0	0	0	0	0	0	0	1
TX	SB 1610	2013	0	0	0	0	0	0	0	0	0	0	0	0	0	0	0	1
TX	HB 4390	2020	1	0	0	0	0	0	0	0	0	0	0	0	0	0	0	1
TX	HB 3529	2021	0	0	0	0	0	0	0	0	0	0	0	0	0	0	0	1
TX	HB 3746	2021	0	0	0	0	0	0	0	0	0	0	0	0	0	0	0	1
UT	SB 693/HB 1154	2007	0	0	0	0	0	0	0	0	0	0	0	0	0	0	0	1
UT	SB 208	2009	0	0	0	0	0	0	0	0	0	0	0	0	0	0	0	1
UT	SB 193	2019	0	0	0	0	0	0	0	0	0	0	0	0	0	0	0	1
VT	S 284, H 254	2012	0	0	0	0	0	0	0	0	0	0	0	0	0	0	0	1
VT	H 513	2013	0	0	0	0	0	0	0	0	0	0	0	0	0	0	0	1
VT	S 73	2015	0	0	0	0	0	0	0	0	0	0	0	0	0	0	0	1
VT	S 110	2020	0	0	0	0	0	0	0	0	0	0	0	0	0	0	0	1
VA	Va Code § 18.2-186.6	2008	0	0	0	0	0	0	0	0	0	0	0	0	0	0	0	1
VA	§ 32.1-127.1:05	2011	0	0	0	0	0	0	0	0	0	0	0	0	0	0	0	1
VA	HB 2113	2017	0	0	0	0	0	0	0	0	0	0	0	0	0	0	0	1
VA	HB 2396	2019	0	0	0	0	0	0	0	0	0	0	0	0	0	0	0	1
VA	Consumer Data Protection Act	2021	0	1	1	1	0	1	1	1	0	1	1	1	1	1	1	0
WA	SB 6043	2005	0	0	0	0	0	0	0	0	0	0	0	0	0	0	0	1
WA	HB 1149	2010	0	0	0	0	0	0	0	0	0	0	0	0	0	0	0	1
WA	HB 1078	2015	0	0	0	0	0	0	0	0	0	0	0	0	0	0	0	1
WA	HB 1071	2020	0	0	0	0	0	0	0	0	0	0	0	0	0	0	0	1
WV	W. VA. Code § 46A-2A-101 et seq. SB 340	2008	0	0	0	0	0	0	0	0	0	0	0	0	0	0	0	1
WI	Wis. Stat. § 134.98 SB 164	2006	0	0	0	0	0	0	0	0	0	0	0	0	0	0	0	1
WY	Wyo. Stat. § 40-12-501 et seq.	2007	0	0	0	0	0	0	0	0	0	0	0	0	0	0	0	1
WY	SF No. 35, 36	2015	0	0	0	0	0	0	0	0	0	0	0	0	0	0	0	1

Table Key

Reg. 1	Creates privacy review body	Reg. 9	Private right of action
Reg. 2	Right of access	Reg. 10	Opt-in requirement age
Reg. 3	Right of rectification	Reg. 11	Notice/transparency requirement
Reg. 4	Right of deletion	Reg. 12	Risk assessments
Reg. 5	Right of restriction	Reg. 13	Prohibition on discrimination
Reg. 6	Right of portability	Reg. 14	Purpose/processing limitation
Reg. 7	Right of opt-out	Reg. 15	Biometric data collection restriction
Reg. 8	Right against automated decision-making	Reg. 16	Data breach law
Reg.## = 0	Law does not include restriction	Reg.## = 1	Law includes restriction

Acknowledgments

This report was made possible in part through financial support from TechNet. ITIF maintains complete editorial independence for all of its work. All opinions, findings, and recommendations are those of ITIF and do not necessarily reflect the views of its supporters. Any errors and omissions are the authors' alone.

About the Author

Daniel Castro (@CastroTech) is vice president at ITIF and director of its Center for Data Innovation. He writes and speaks on a variety of issues related to information technology and Internet policy, including privacy, security, intellectual property, Internet governance, e-government, and accessibility for people with disabilities.

Luke Dascoli is an economic & technology policy research assistant at ITIF. He was previously a Research Assistant in the MDI Scholars Program at the Mccourt School of Public Policy's Massive Data Institute. He holds a B.A. in Political Economy from Georgetown University.

Gillian Diebold (@gllliandiebold) is a digital media specialist and policy analyst at ITIF's Center for Data Innovation. She holds a B.A. from the University of Pennsylvania, where she studied Communication and Political Science.

About ITIF

The Information Technology and Innovation Foundation (ITIF) is an independent, nonprofit, nonpartisan research and educational institute focusing on the intersection of technological innovation and public policy. Recognized by its peers in the think tank community as the global center of excellence for science and technology policy, ITIF's mission is to formulate and promote policy solutions that accelerate innovation and boost productivity to spur growth, opportunity, and progress.

For more information, visit itif.org.

* * *

Robyn Boerstling
Vice President
Infrastructure, Innovation and Human Resources Policy

March 1, 2023

Representative Gus Bilirakis
Chair
Subcommittee on Consumer Protection and Commerce
Committee on Energy and Commerce
Washington, DC 20515

Representative Janice Schakowsky
Ranking Member
Subcommittee on Consumer Protection and Commerce
Committee on Energy and Commerce
Washington, DC 20515

Dear Chair Bilirakis and Ranking Member Schakowsky:

The National Association of Manufacturers welcomes the subcommittee's focus on data privacy. The NAM is the largest manufacturing association in the United States representing manufacturers in every industrial sector and in all 50 states. Manufacturing employs more than 13 million men and women, contributes nearly $2.81 trillion to the U.S. economy annually, has one of the largest economic impacts of any major sector and accounts for 55% of all private-sector research and development in the nation.[182] The NAM is the powerful voice of the manufacturing community and the leading advocate for a policy agenda that helps manufacturers compete in the global economy and create jobs across the United States.

Today's hearing "Promoting U.S. Innovation and Individual Liberty through a National Standard for Data Privacy" is an opportunity to further explore this important issue and assess the strong need for a federal data privacy standard. Manufacturers resoundingly support a federal data privacy standard that prevents a patchwork of state privacy laws and provides much needed legal clarity to support continued innovation and competitiveness.

Manufacturers are continuously developing innovative products and transforming the manufacturing process with the latest technologies. Data continues to be a critical source and biproduct of these breakthroughs and developments as modern manufacturing evolves. The Internet of Things (IoT) is continuing to transform manufacturing through billions of connected devices and advanced wireless infrastructure that allow for the transmission of vast amounts of data. Connected shop floors are generating data that industry is harnessing to improve efficiency, manage production activities, streamline repairs and safeguard plant security. Additionally, connected products utilize data to transform the consumers' experience in countless ways.

---

[182] https://www.nam.org/facts-about-manufacturing/.

Our nation's manufacturers support ongoing efforts to craft federal data privacy legislation that advances individuals' privacy while promoting U.S. innovation and industrial competitiveness. Without clarity from federal law, uncertainty will continue for our industry, causing manufacturers to sort through conflicting state privacy laws across the country. To provide greater legal clarity, federal privacy legislation should pre-empt state privacy regulations to resolve conflicting requirements in different states. A national approach to data privacy will strengthen businesses while supporting consumers.

Patchwork state privacy laws and unpredictable regulatory changes on data privacy are currently undermining the ability of organizations to manage privacy risks, protect consumers and make business decisions with the certainty they need. State-by-state privacy requirements create conflicts for manufacturers, their operations and their processes due to the interstate nature of data flows. They stall innovation by creating a regulatory burden that distracts from the development of next generation technologies and products. Manufacturers design and build security and privacy into their systems and products and it is often an extensive process to adjust those systems and products in the face of evolving data regulations.

Ongoing innovation requires flexibility, and any federal action on data privacy must be carefully balanced and thoughtfully implemented without sacrificing opportunities for economic leadership and progress. Businesses should be held accountable if they inappropriately utilize personal consumer data or violate a data privacy agreement. However, legislation that includes a private right of action should be constructed in a thoughtful way to prevent a legal dynamic that could encourage excessive legal challenges. Rather than innovating, companies could be focusing resources on unending legal challenges that the legislation unintentionally encourages.

Our companies are entrusted with vast amounts of data through diverse business interactions with customers, vendors, suppliers and governments. They understand that safeguarding privacy, protecting information and building consumer trust is a critical responsibility. Manufacturers support a data privacy policy that provides flexibility for innovation and advances U.S. economic growth and technological leadership. The NAM appreciates the work of the subcommittee and looks forward to engaging with you on this issue.

Sincerely,

Robyn M. Boerstling

Cc: Chair Cathy McMorris Rogers
U.S. House of Representatives
Committee on Energy and Commerce

Ranking Member Frank Pallone
U.S. House of Representatives
Committee on Energy and Commerce

* * *

The Honorable Cathy McMorris Rodgers
Chair
Committee on Energy and Commerce
U.S. House of Representatives
Washington, DC 20515

The Honorable Frank Pallone
Ranking Member
Committee on Energy and Commerce
U.S. House of Representatives
Washington, DC 20515

The Honorable Gus Bilirakis
Chair
Subcommittee on Innovation, Data, and Commerce
Committee on Energy and Commerce
U.S. House of Representatives
Washington, DC 20515

The Honorable Jan Schakowsky
Ranking Member
Subcommittee on Innovation, Data, and Commerce
U.S. House of Representatives
Washington, DC 20515

Dear Chair McMorris Rodgers, Ranking Member Pallone, Chair Bilirakis, and Ranking Member Schakowsky,

On behalf of The Leadership Conference on Civil and Human Rights, a coalition charged by its diverse membership of more than 230 national organizations to promote and protect the rights of all persons in the United States, we thank you for the opportunity to submit our views regarding online privacy. We ask for this letter to be entered into the record of the Innovation, Data, and Commerce Subcomittee hearing titled "Promoting U.S. Innovation and Individual Liberty Through a National Standard for Data Privacy" on March 1, 2023.

Technological progress should bring greater safety, economic opportunity, and convenience to everyone. And the collection of demographic data is essential for documenting persistent inequality and discrimination. But just as technology has created immense positive value by creating economic opportunities, facilitating civil rights advocacy, and adding new voices to our culture and public debate, it can also enable discriminatory conduct and give new tools to powerful institutions to entrench and exacerbate existing disparities. In 2014, The Leadership Conference, along with 14 signatories, released the "Civil Rights Principles for the Era of Big Data," (civil rights principles) calling on the U.S. government and businesses to respect and promote equal opportunity and equal justice in the development and use of data-driven technologies.[183] While the terminology has shifted from "big data" to "AI," the issues remain the same and the threats technology can pose to civil rights have only grown.

Recognizing this increased urgency, as well as the growing dispaiity between the vast amount of personal data available to companies, and the tiny amount of infolmation available to the public about how companies ai·e using it, in 2020, The Leadership Conference, along with a number of advocacy and civil rights organizations, released updated civil rights piinciples.[184] Those plinciples include ending high tech profiling; ensuring justice in automated decisions; preserving constitutional principles; ensming that technology selves people histodcally subject to disclimination; defining responsible use of personal infolmation and enhancing individuallights; and making systems transpai·ent and accountable.

Today, tens of millions of people ai·e without any kind oflegal protections for their personal data.[185] They ai·e discdminated against in housing, employment, credit, education, finance, and other economic oppoltunities, and they ai·e left in the dai·k about how their personal data is used.[187] As we have told this committee on multiple occasions, pdvacy rights ai·e civil rights.[188] Well-drafted comprehensive federal consumer privacy legislation like the Amelican Data Privacy and Protection Act (ADPPA) introduced in the last Congress will protect civil and humanlights; empower communities of color; ensure oppoltunities ai·e open for mai·ginalized populations; and ensure that companies, including "Big Tech," ai·e held accountable for the data they collect and use, especially when those actions impact individuals' lives.

The ADPPA, as it was voted out of the committee last Congress, contained impoltant provisions that served to address these issues. The legislation prohibited the use of personal data in a discdminatory manner in the provision of goods or services on the basis of protected chai·acteristics and ensured that these protections would be incorporated into the sectors that need them most through requirements to test algorithms for bias and measure potential impacts on equal access to and eligibility for housing, employment, credit, education, insurance, health cai·e, and public accommodations. It also preserved state civil rights lawsand other types of state laws that ai·e impoltant for the protection of consumers and marginalized communities. Strong data minimization requirements found in ADPPA fuither protected the rights of individuals by limiting potential data smveillance.

---

183 "Civil Rights Principles for the Era of Big Data," The Leadership Conference on Civil and Human Rights (Feb. 27, 2014), https://civilrights.org/2014/02/27/civil-rights-principles-era-big-data/#:~:text=Technological%20progress%20should%20bring%20greater,documenting%20persistent%20inequality%20and%20discrimination .

184 Press Release, "Civil Rights Leaders Announce Principles to Protect Civil Rights and Technology," The Leadership Conference on Civil and Human Rights (Oct. 21, 2020), https://civikights.org/2020/10/21/civil-rights-leaders-announce-principles-to-protect-civil-rights-and-technology/.

185 Thorin Klosowki, "The State of Consumer Data Privacy La:ws in the US (And Why It Matters), N.Y. Times (Sept. 6, 2021), https://wv.rw nytimes.com/wirecutter/blog/state-of-privacy-laws-in-us/.

187 "The Leadership Conference on Civil and Human Rights Views on Discussion Draft of The American Data and Privacy Act," The Leadership Conference on Civil and Human Rights (June 14, 2022), https://civilrights.org/resomce/letter-to-house-energy-and-collllllerce-committee-on-the-american-data-privacy-and- protection-act/.

188 "The Leadership Conference on Civil and Human Rights Views on Discussion Draft of The American Data and Privacy Act," The Leadership Conference on Civil and Human Rights (June 14, 2022), https://civilrights.org/resomce/letter-to-house-energy-and-collllllerce-committee-on-the-american-data-privacy-and- protection-act/.

Under the bill, consumers would have been able to hold companies accountable for data misuse through a private right of action. The Federal Trade Commission was given enforcement authority, and attorneys general and privacy agencies in eve1y state in the country were empowered to enforce ADPPA. Through these three layers of enforcement, consumers and our institutions would have been able to effectuate meaningful change and hold bad actors accountable.

These provisions are a key reason why The Leadership Conference endorsed the ADPPA. Any p1ivacy legislation moving fo1wai·d must include a prohibition on the use of personal data in a disc1iminato1y manner in the provision of goods or se1vices on the basis of protected chai·acteristics, the prese1vation of state civil rights laws and other types of state laws impo1 1ant for the protection of consumers, data minimization requirements, a piivate 1ight of action, and enforcement authoiity across the federal government and state governments.

We stand ready to work with Congress on policies that will protect civil 1ights, prevent unlawful discrimination, and advance equal oppo1 1unity. Should you require fuither inf01mation or have any questions regai·ding this issue, please feel free to contact Jonathan Walter, media and tech policy counsel, at walter@civilrights.org, Frank ToITes, civil rights technology fellow, at torres@civilrights.org. or Anita Bane1ji, senior director of the media and tech program, at banerii@civihights.org.

Sincerely,

Jesselyn Mccurdy
Executive Vice President of Government Affairs

September 26, 2022

The Honorable Nancy Pelosi
Speaker
U.S. House of Representatives
Washington, D.C. 20515

The Honorable Frank Pallone
Chairman
Committee on Energy & Commerce
U.S. House of Representatives
Washington, D.C. 20515

The Honorable Kevin McCarthy
Minority Leader
U.S. House of Representatives
Washington, D.C. 20515

The Honorable Cathy McMorris Rodgers
Ranking Member
Committee on Energy & Commerce
U.S. House of Representatives
Washington, D.C. 20515

The Honorable Jan Schakowsky
Chairwoman
Consumer Protection & Commerce Subcommittee
Committee on Energy & Commerce
U.S. House of Representatives
Washington, D.C. 20515

The Honorable Gus Bilirakis
Ranking Member
Consumer Protection &
Commerce Subcommittee
Committee on Energy & Commerce
U.S. House of Representatives
Washington, D.C. 20515

Dear Speaker Pelosi, Leader McCarthy, Chairman Pallone, Ranking Member McMorris Rodgers, Chairwoman Schakowsky, and Ranking Member Bilirakis:

We write to express deep concern about significant public safety consequences that could result if the American Data Privacy Protection Act (ADPPA, H.R. 8152) were to be enacted as currently drafted. Data privacy protections are critical for the safety of our citizens and our national security. Law enforcement also has a vested interest in data privacy as it directly relates to officer safety. Many law enforcement agencies have seen officers' personal data publicly exposed, and these officers and their families have been harassed and threatened as a result.

While strong consumer data privacy protections are needed, the ADPPA in its current form would likely have major negative consequences that would make it harder to investigate criminal activity. For example, in its current form, the ADPPA would likely complicate the private sector's ability to continue its ongoing efforts to cooperate and voluntarily share certain information with law enforcement throughout the course of a criminal investigation.

This legislation would also make common investigative tools unavailable or extremely limited. These tools are used successfully by law enforcement agencies around the country every day to investigate violent crime, human trafficking, child sexual exploitation, fentanyl and opioids trafficking, violent extremism, carjacking, kidnapping, and threats of mass violence that are made on social media. These tools provide the essential building blocks for generating leads, especially in the early stages of a critical incident, and there is simply nothing that can replace that capability for investigators. Some have grossly misconstrued how law enforcement uses these investigative tools to justify their elimination via the ADPPA. The reality is that law enforcement agencies have strict policies and procedures in place to mitigate the risk of misuse and abuse.

At a time when Congress is working to pass laws that support effective and accountable law enforcement and reduce violent crime, the ADPPA in its current form would make our jobs harder. It is a 21st Century reality that digital information generated by public and private entities is relevant to most criminal investigations. The ADPPA prevents law enforcement from obtaining publicly available information in a timely, lawful manner, which significantly jeopardizes our ability to rescue victims, protect communities, and prevent bad actors from exacerbating an already historic rise in violent crime. As currently written, this bill will make it more difficult for law enforcement to find critical pieces of information that are necessary to quickly generate leads and solve crimes.

Congress cannot push law enforcement's investigative capabilities back into the 20th Century as we try to address today's 21st Century criminal challenges. We strongly oppose the current version of ADPPA and urge the House to improve the bill to protect consumer privacy without weakening criminal investigations. Our organizations stand ready to work with you to achieve this balance.

Sincerely,

Association of State Criminal Investigative Agencies (ASCIA)
Federal Law Enforcement Officers Association (FLEOA)
Major Cities Chiefs Association (MCCA)
Major Count Sheriffs of America (MCSA)
National Association of Assistant U.S. Attorneys (NAAUSA)
National Association of Police Organizations (NAPO)
National District Attorneys Association (NDAA)
National Fusion Center Association (NFCA)
National Narcotics Officers' Associations' Coalition (NNOAC)
Sergeants Benevolent Association (SBA)

September 26, 2022

The Honorable Nancy P. Pelosi
Speaker of the House
U.S. House of Representatives
Washington, D.C. 20515

The Honorable Frank J. Pallone Jr.
Chairman
Committee on Energy and Commerce
U.S. House of Representatives
Washington, D.C. 20515

The Honorable Kevin O. McCarthy
Minority Leader
U.S. House of Representatives
Washington, D.C. 20515

The Honorable Cathy A. McMorris Rodgers
Ranking Member
Committee on Energy and Commerce
U.S. House of Representatives
Washington, D.C. 20515

Dear Madam Speaker, Mr. Chairman, and Representatives McCarthy and McMorris Rodgers,

We are writing on behalf of the Fraternal Order of Police (FOP) and the International Association of Chiefs of Police (IACP) to raise our serious concerns with current provisions in H.R. 8152, the "American Data Privacy Protection Act." Our organizations strongly support data privacy for all Americans. It is particularly critical to the safety of our officers whose personal information, if compromised, could put them and their families in jeopardy. However, we must be sure that we protect this personal data without negatively impacting the ability of law enforcement to conduct routine investigations.

Consumer data privacy protections are very important in this digital age, but in protecting personal data from unauthorized or unlawful access, we must be sure not to make it more difficult for law enforcement to conduct criminal investigations by accessing publicly available information from private sector entities who want to cooperate with law enforcement and voluntarily share information to assist in criminal investigations.

There are provisions in the bill as introduced that will negatively impact investigations by law enforcement and render many of the common tools these agencies currently use unavailable or too limited. Law enforcement agencies pursuing investigations into violent crimes like human trafficking, child exploitation, kidnapping, or threats of mass violence need these tools to generate leads and prevent potential harm to our citizens. For example, in the early hours following an abduction, access to publicly available data and the tools to quickly and efficiently search for this information is of the utmost importance to avoid tragic outcomes.

We live in a world of digital data and all of our lives are increasingly intertwined as we interact in publicly available virtual space. Because of this, law enforcement officers must be able to obtain publicly available information quickly and lawfully in order to protect the public, rescue victims, solve crimes, and prevent criminal actors form escaping justice. This legislation, as currently drafted, would jeopardize law enforcement's ability to do its job and it will put lives at risk.

On behalf of the members of the FOP and the IACP, the largest and most prominent labor and management law enforcement organizations in the country, we urge the House to work with law enforcement and public safety-oriented stakeholders to make the necessary changes to the legislation in order to preserve our ability to conduct effective investigations and protect our personal data.

Sincerely,

Patrick Yoes
National FOP President

Chief Dwight Henninger
IACP President

* * *

Mr. Bilirakis. So thank you very much, folks, even in the audience, for attending this meeting. I want to thank the ranking member and, of course, the ranking member on the full committee and the chairperson, Cathy McMorris Rodgers.

And, without objection, this subcommittee is adjourned. We appreciate all of y'all. Thank you.

[The information follows:]

* * *

Jessica Herron
Clerk, Innovation, Data, and Commerce
U.S. House Committee on Energy and Commerce
2125 Rayburn House Office Building
Washington, D.C. 20515
Via email
Wednesday March 29, 2023

Re: QFR Responses for Hearing Entitled "Promoting U.S. Innovation and Individual Liberty through a National Standard for Data Privacy," March 1, 2023.

Dear Ms. Herron:

Thank you for the invitation to appear before the Subcommittee on Innovation, Data & Commerce to testify during the March 1, 2023 hearing entitled "Promoting U.S. Innovation and Individual Liberty through a National Standard for Data Privacy."

Pursuant to the Committee's Rules, I have been asked to answer an additional question for the record, my response to which is attached.

Sincerely,

Alexandra Reeve Givens

Written Responses - Question for the Record, Alexandra Reeve Givens, President & CEO, Center for Democracy & Technology, for the U.S. House of Representatives Energy & Commerce Committee, Subcommittee on Innovation, Data, & Commerce, Hearing Entitled "Promoting U.S. Innovation and Individual Liberty through a National Standard for Data Privacy," March 1, 2023

The Honorable Diana Harshbarger

Question: As more and more connected technology devices are increasingly tracking human behavior and producing more and more data, do you think consumers should have ownership over this data?

Data ownership, while appealing in theory, is difficult to operationalize. One of the complicating factors is that data is a "non-rivalrous" good: copies of the same data can exist in multiple locations and be accessible by multiple people or entities, without necessarily jeopardizing each one's ability to make use of the data. For non-rivalrous goods, a property framework may not always be the best answer, particularly given how easy it is to copy data online. Further, allowing people to sell their data would benefit only the biggest online players, as large companies like Meta and Alphabet can surely afford to purchase the rights to use people's data from their significant user bases, while smaller start-ups would find that more difficult. And last, there is no guarantee that any particular piece of data would be worth more than a negligible amount, so it is unlikely that people would be compensated in a meaningful way. Large datasets are valuable because they allow for statistical analysis yielding insights about people or groups of people, but each individual data point, on its own, may not be worth much.

A more effective approach is to give people rights over data that pertains to them: rights to access, delete, correct, and port that data. These rights give people the ability to know what companies collect about them, and have the ability to correct it if it's wrong, delete it if they no longer want the company to have it, or port the data to another service provider. These rights have more meaning and value than the ability to own and sell data for fractions of a penny. They must, however, be enforceable, which is why a private right of action is such an important component of any federal privacy law (since the FTC and State Attorneys General are unlikely to prioritize these issues over other enforcement priorities).

However, the most important protections in any federal privacy law are data minimization and purpose limitation: prohibiting businesses and other entities from collecting more data than what is necessary to provide the service a person has requested. For example, an online retailer needs to collect customers' shipping information, payment details, contact information, and details about the product being sold. It does not need detailed demographic information about the customer or data about other websites they have browsed, and should not collect and retain that data (let alone share or sell it to unknown third parties, as can happen now).

To expand on this point, our hypothetical online retailer should not be allowed to sell its customers' purchase records to a data broker, which might then combine all of a person's purchase records, aggregated from various retailers, and any other information the broker can amass including location and demographic data, to create a detailed dossier of someone's online and offline life. Such a record is likely to reveal sensitive information about that person's likes and dislikes, health conditions, political opinions, religious affiliation, and more. When such records can be sold on the open market to any willing buyer (including large tech companies and foreign governments), they are ripe for exploitation and abuse. A data ownership framework is unlikely to meaningfully address these harms, but a robust federal law prohibiting such data practices can give consumers the protections they need.

Written Responses – Questions for the Record, Graham Mudd, President & Chief Product Officer, Anonym, Inc., for the Subcommittee on Innovation, Data, and Commerce, Committee on Energy & Commerce, United States House of Representatives, Hearing on Promoting U.S. Innovation and Individual Liberty Through A National Standard For Data Privacy, March 1, 2023

Attachment 1–Additional Questions for the Record

The Honorable Diana Harshbarger

As more and more connected technology devices are increasingly tracking human behavior and producing more and more data, do you think consumers should have ownership over this data?

Yes, I do believe that consumers should have more ownership and control over the data they generate – and that this issue will only become more important as Americans' use and reliance on connected devices deepens. Unlike physical property, data is infinitely replicable, which means it can be reproduced and shared with additional parties at very little cost. This means consumers can very quickly and easily lose any measure of control over their data. Without federal legislation in place, consumers have little assurance that data they generate and share with one party won't be shared with others and put to use in ways that may harm them. For example, in the digital advertising industry, data is a powerful asset, so there is a strong incentive for companies to share data with the platforms through which they advertise. As a result, advertising technology companies and data brokers build and maintain incredibly deep profiles of people' online and real-world behavior. These profiles can be used in ways that are counter to an individual's interests.

The Honorable Russ Fulcher

I wanted to ask you about the importance of ensuring the ability for businesses to continue to innovate. I want to give you more time to address the question below.

In the years since GDPR went into effect, we have seen the fall out in the EU. Large businesses continue to grow larger while small businesses and startups are becoming a rarity.

1. How can we ensure this does not happen within the United States?

Many would argue that GDPR was overly burdensome to small businesses, particularly relative to the potential privacy harms that these businesses are capable of inflicting. There are a number of potential lessons that can be drawn from GDPR, many of which are already addressed in the latest draft of ADPPA.

For example, the most significant compliance requirements should be focused on the entities whose data practices have the potential to affect the greatest harm. Data volume is one dimension to consider. For example, entities that collect data from many other companies to develop consolidated profiles on millions of individuals are worthy of more regulatory focus than small businesses who maintain information on a modest customer base.

The sensitivity of the data handled by an entity is another dimension to consider. Companies that handle health or financial information should reasonably be subject to stricter compliance requirements than businesses that handle de-identified or less sensitive data.

ADPPA recognizes both of these dimensions and requires more of companies that handle either large volumes of data or sensitive data than those which do not. For example, small businesses, as defined by ADPPA, are exempt from requirements to provide consumers with the right to request or correct their data, and from the requirement to establish a data privacy or security officer.

It's also important to proactively support small businesses in their compliance efforts. The ADPPA requires the FTC to develop a compliance program – this program should devote considerable resources to supporting small businesses.

In addition, Congress and regulatory agencies should encourage the development of technologies that support the adoption of privacy preserving practices (sometimes called "privacy-enhancing technologies," a.k.a. "PETs"). This can make privacy compliance easier for small businesses that don't have deep in-house privacy expertise. It also can level the playing field for small businesses that want to leverage data for analysis without compromising customers' privacy.

Thank you for your expertise. I know that the digital ecosystem runs on information, but sometimes it seems companies and data brokers are collecting more information than they need.

2. Can you explain what information companies are collecting, what information they are using, and if they aren't using everything, why collect more information than they are actually using?

It's difficult to answer your question about what is collected other than to say "everything." If a given behavior or attribute is digitally observable, then it is more than likely collected.

Without regulations in place, it is often the case that there are strong incentives to collect more information than might be immediately or obviously useful. This is because collecting and storing information is typically extremely inexpensive and unforeseen new applications for already-collected data are likely to arise in the future. For example, machine learning can be used to discover correlations that help a business make a prediction about consumer behavior that are far from obvious to humans.

Data minimization requirements, such as those included in ADPPA, provide a necessary incentive to reduce the collection, storage and transfer of data that isn't strictly necessary for an allowed purpose. These requirements can, and should, encourage companies to de-identify and anonymize data, which meaningfully reduces privacy risks while still supporting most applications and uses.

* * *

March 31, 2023

Jessica Herron
Legislative Clerk
Subcommittee on Innovation, Data, and Commerce
House Committee on Energy and Commerce
2125 Rayburn House Office Building
Washington, DC 20515-6115

Re: Jessica L. Rich's Responses to Additional Questions for the Record Dear Ms. Herron:

I want to thank the Subcommittee for inviting me to appear before it on March 1, 2023 to testify on the topic of "Promoting U.S. Innovation and Individual Liberty Through a National Standard for Data Privacy." It was an honor to testify, and your assistance both before and after the hearing was especially helpful.

Pursuant to the Rules of the Committee on Energy and Commerce, I am attaching my answers to additional questions for the record, in the required format.

Thanks again for your help, and please let me know if you have any questions.

Sincerely,
Jessica Rich
Of Counsel and Senior Policy Advisor for Consumer Protection
Kelley Drye & Warren LLP

Attachment 1—Additional Questions for the Record

The Honorable Diana Harshbarger

As more and more connected technology devices are increasingly tracking human behavior and producing more and more data, do you think consumers should have ownership over this data?

In theory, yes, consumers should own and control their data because of the adverse consequences that can result when that data is misused. However, one problem with an ownership model is that it would likely impose enormous burdens on consumers to manage their data and their privacy, including in each interaction they have with hundreds of companies. This could become completely unworkable, as we have learned from our experience with the notice-and-choice model for privacy. Indeed, the notice-and-choice model, while designed to give consumers more control over their data, ends up overwhelming them with hundreds of long and confusing privacy notices.

That's why there is so much support for the bipartisan ADPPA, which seeks to reduce these burdens on consumers and instead impose more duties on companies to follow responsible data practices, such as the duty to conduct privacy impact assessments; the duty not to discriminate; and restrictions on the use of sensitive data.

The Honorable Russ Fulcher

Building on our discussion in the hearing and specific to the American Data Privacy and Protection Act. In that act, certain entities are required to submit impact assessments to the FTC related to algorithms.

1. Currently, does the FTC have the ability to request information that would be included in the impact assessments using their own authority and also permit entities to submit such information in a manner that doesn't expose trade secrets?

Yes, the FTC has the authority to request a wide range of information (under the FTC Act and the FTC's Rules of Practice) in order to determine whether there have been law violations. The FTC also has the authority to conduct studies, such as the one it is current conducting on Pharmacy Benefit Managers (PBMs).

Many of these investigations and studies involve sensitive information and trade secrets, including (in addition to the PBM study) investigations and studies regarding merger and other antitrust issues; data security and privacy; and health products and health claims. The law and FTC rules allow companies to mark information as "confidential" (such as when it involves trade secrets) so that it receive special treatment and confidential handling. See here for a summary.

How would the FTC handle receiving all of these impact assessments if companies would be required to submit every assessment versus the FTC asking for it on their own accord?

Currently, the FTC obtains and reviews many third-party assessments, pursuant to its privacy and data security orders. While some of these assessments are automatically submitted to the agency, others are obtained by the FTC on request. In my experience, the FTC *does* frequently ask for and review even those assessments that aren't automatically submitted. Nevertheless, the assessment requirements under the ADPPA, which apply to any entity meeting a certain size threshold and not just those under an FTC order, would significantly add to the FTC's duties here. For the FTC to perform this work effectively, it would require more resources.

I wanted to ask you about the importance of ensuring the ability for businesses to continue to innovate. I want to give you more time to address the question below.

In the years since GDPR went into effect, we have seen the fall out in the EU. Large businesses continue to grow larger while small businesses and startups are becoming a rarity.

2. How can we ensure this does not happen within the United States?

Innovation is a hallmark of the US economy, and any privacy law enacted in this country should ensure that innovation continues to flourish. By necessity, that includes ensuring that small businesses can continue to compete and serve their communities.

One part of the solution is enacting a federal privacy law that sets a consistent standard, rather than forcing companies to navigate and develop costly compliance schemes for multiple different state laws. While compromise on preemption seems necessary in order to pass a federal law, the law still should try to achieve as much consistency as possible.

Another part of the solution is to limit the compliance costs on small businesses. Indeed, many existing privacy laws actually favor large companies, due to the high cost of compliance or because they focus unduly on limiting data-sharing with third parties (something large companies can avoid by keeping their functions in-house). The ADPPA attempts to avoid these effects by placing less emphasis on third-party sharing (in favor of more even-handed restrictions on data misuse) and by scaling down some of the duties for small businesses. For example, the bill reduces the burdens on small businesses when it comes to the data portability and correction, data security, executive responsibility, and audit and assessment requirements.

Chapter 2

Addressing America's Data Privacy Shortfalls: How a National Standard Fills Gaps to Protect Americans' Personal Information*

Committee on Energy and Commerce

Thursday, April 27, 2023
House of Representatives,
Subcommittee on Innovation, Data, and Commerce,
Committee on Energy and Commerce,
Washington, DC.

The subcommittee met, pursuant to call, at 2:02 p.m. in the John D. Dingell Room 2123 Rayburn House Office Building, Hon. Gus Bilirakis (chairman of the subcommittee) presiding.

Members present: Representatives Bilirakis, Bucshon, Walberg, Duncan, Dunn, Lesko, Pence, Armstrong, Allen, Fulcher, Harshbarger, Cammack, Rodgers (ex officio), Schakowsky (subcommittee ranking member), Castor, Dingell, Kelly, Blunt Rochester, Soto, Trahan, Clarke, and Pallone (ex officio).

Also present: Representatives Obernolte.

Staff present: Kate Arey, Digital Director; Michael Cameron, Professional Staff Member; Jessica Herron, Clerk; Nate Hodson, Staff Director; Tara Hupman, Chief Counsel; Sean Kelly, Press Secretary; Peter Kielty, General Counsel; Emily King, Member Services Director; Tim Kurth, Chief Counsel; Brannon Rains, Professional Staff Member; Lacey Strahm, Fellow; Teddy Tanzer, Senior Counsel; Hannah Anton, Minority Policy Analyst; Ian Barlow, Minority FTC Detailee; Waverly Gordon, Minority Deputy Staff Director and General Counsel; Daniel Greene, Minority Professional Staff Member; Tiffany Guarascio, Minority Staff Director; Lisa Hone, Minority Chief Counsel, Innovation, Data, and Commerce; Joe Orlando, Minority Junior Professional Staff Member.

Mr. BILIRAKIS. The subcommittee will come to order. The Chair recognizes himself for an opening statement.

---

* This is an edited, reformatted and augmented version of Hearing before the Subcommittee on Innovation, Data, and Commerce, of the Committee on Energy and Commerce, House of Representatives, One Hundred Eighteenth Congress, First Session, Serial No. 118–29, dated April 27, 2023.

In: Safeguarding Personal Information: National Standards for Data Privacy
Editor: Margaret K. Derosa
ISBN: 979-8-89530-698-7

Opening Statement of Hon. Gus M. Bilirakis, a Representative in Congress from the State of Florida

Again, good afternoon and welcome to the 36th hearing the U.S. Congress has held on privacy and data security over the last 5 years. I am using a bit of math there from one of our previous witnesses. As for the Energy and Commerce Committee, this will be our sixth hearing in the 118th Congress. We have now examined in depth how a Federal data privacy and security law can make us more competitive with China.

While a Federal standard is needed to protect Americans and balance the needs of business, government, and civil society, what happens when malicious actors like TikTok and the CCP, through ByteDance, exploit access to data, where the FTC's lines of jurisdiction and authority are and how that interplays with the comprehensive privacy law, the role of data brokers, and the lack of consumer protections over one's data, and, finally, our hearing today, which will examine how consumers may not be covered by sector-specific laws in a way that is consistent with their expectations.

The fact is that the data privacy and security concerns permeate across multiple areas within Congress, even in seemingly unrelated topics, which highlights just how important it is for us to work together across the aisle and across Capitol Hill to protect the American people.

In today's hearing we will discuss sectoral data privacy regimes like the Financial Sectors Gramm-Leach-Bliley Act; and the Fair Credit Reporting Act; and the healthcare's—health sector's Health Insurance Portability and Accountability Act, or HIPAA; the education sector's Family Education Rights and Privacy Act, FERPA; and, of course, the Children's Online Privacy Protection Act, COPPA, which this subcommittee knows very well, and the gaps in coverage that a piecemeal, sector-specific approach has created for consumers.

We will hear from the witnesses about how these gray areas for Americans also result in risks and uncertainty that businesses could better avoid if we had clearer rules of the road. This only gets more complicated as 50 different States move towards their own data privacy laws, meaning an increasingly complicated and confusing landscape for consumers and for businesses.

Having clear rules in place will protect Americans, particularly our kids, as well as fuel innovation in the American marketplace. Sounds good to me.

Each of the witnesses has a unique story to tell when it comes to these gaps, but the challenges are the same: Consumers think their data is protected, but the sector-specific law in place does not extend as far as consumers expect.

Mr. Codling, with REGO Payment Architectures, will discuss how it is possible to operate a payments infrastructure that has strong protections for children. REGO has filled the gaps that exist with the GLBA and COPPA by protecting all kids under 18. We appreciate that very much.

Ms. Vance, with the Public Interest Privacy Center, is a recognized expert in FERPA and kids' privacy. She will speak about how current gaps exist in educational privacy and child-specific laws that a comprehensive privacy law would cover.

Thanks very much for being here.

Mr. Britan, with Salesforce, helps clients collect data in a way that is compliant with the Federal sectors—sectoral laws and State privacy laws. His clients do business in every sector, and will speak to compliance burdens that the patchwork of State laws has created.

Thanks for being here.

Mr. Reed, with the App Association, will discuss how the piecemeal approach of State laws creates confusion for member companies. App Association members are regulated by all of the sectorspecific laws and must spend significant resources complying with all of the various State data privacy laws. That is so tough. It has got to be very difficult.

In closing, I want to thank all the witnesses for coming today. I also want to thank Chair Rodgers and the ranking member, Ranking Member Pallone, for all of the progress we have made so far and the continued commitment to get this done—we will get it done—as well as Ranking Member Schakowsky, who has made this effort a true bipartisan partnership. Thank you so much.

[The prepared statement of Mr. Bilirakis follows:]

Opening Statement of Chair Gus Bilirakis, as Prepared for Delivery, Committee on Energy and Commerce, Subcommittee on Innovation, Data, and Commerce, Hearing Entitled "Addressing America's Data Privacy Shortfalls: How a National Standard Fills Gaps to Protect Americans' Personal Information," April 27, 2023

Good afternoon, and welcome to the 36th hearing the U.S. Congress has held on privacy and data security over the last five years. I'm using a bit of math there from one of our previous witnesses.

As for the Energy and Commerce Committee, this will be our sixth hearing in the 118th Congress. We have now examined in depth how a federal data privacy and security law can make us more competitive with China. why a federal standard is needed to protect Americans and balance the needs of business, government and civil society. what happens when malicious actors, like TikTok and the CCP through Byte Dance, exploit access to data. Where the FTC's lines of jurisdiction and authority are and how that interplays with a comprehensive privacy law.... the role of data brokers and the lack of consumer protections over one's data .... and, finally, our hearing today, which will examine how consumers may not be covered by sector specific laws in a way that is consistent with their expectations.

The fact is that data privacy and security concerns permeate across multiple areas within Congress, even in seemingly unrelated topics, which highlights just how important it is for us to work together across the aisle and across Capitol Hill to protect the American people.

In today's hearing we'll discuss sectoral data privacy regimes — like the financial sector's Gramm-Leach-Bliley Act and the Fair Credit Reporting Act, the health sector's Health Insurance Portability and Accountability Act (HIPAA), the education sector's Family Educational Rights and Privacy Act (FERPA), and of course the Children Online Privacy Protection Act – COPPA – which this subcommittee knows well — and the gaps in coverage that a piecemeal, sectorspecific approach has created for consumers.

We will hear from the witnesses about how these gray areas for Americans also result in risk and uncertainty that businesses could better avoid if we had clear rules of the road. This only gets more complicated as fifty different states move towards their own data privacy laws, meaning an increasingly complicated and confusing landscape for consumers and for business.

Having clear rules in place will protect Americans, particularly our kids, as well as fuel innovation in the American marketplace.

Each of the witnesses has a unique story to tell when it comes to these gaps, but the challenges are the same: Consumers think their data is protected, but the sector's specific law in place does not extend as far as consumers expect.

Mr. Codling, with REGO Payment Architectures, will discuss how it is possible to operate a payments infrastructure that has strong protections for children. REGO has filled the gaps that exist with GLBA and COPPA by protecting all kids under 18.

Ms. Vance, with the Public Interest Privacy Center, is a recognized expert on FERPA and kids' privacy. She will speak about how current gaps exist in educational privacy and child-specific laws that a comprehensive privacy law would cover.

Mr. Britan, with Salesforce, helps clients collect data in a way that is compliant with the federal sectoral laws and state privacy laws. His clients do business in every sector, and he will speak to compliance burdens that the patchwork of state laws has created.

Mr. Reed, with the App Association, will discuss how this piecemeal approach of state laws creates confusion for member companies. App Association members are regulated by all of the sector-specific laws and must spend significant resources complying with all of the various state data privacy laws.

In closing, I want to thank all the witnesses for coming today. I want to thank Chair Rodgers and Ranking Member Pallone for all the progress we've made so far and their continued commitment to get this done, as well as Ranking Member Schakowsky who has made this effort a true partnership. I look forward to working with all of you on providing protections for Americans and certainty for businesses.

* * *

Mr. BILIRAKIS. Lastly, I want to recognize and thank a valuable member of our team, whose last day is tomorrow and has served as a technology fellow on our subcommittee, on our staff for this past year. We are really going to miss you, Lacey—Lacey Strahm. Lacey, your insights and contribution, particularly with the NIL, to the team have been invaluable over these past years. I really appreciate all your hard work. And don't be a stranger. We are going to miss you tremendously.

Ms. SCHAKOWSKY. Let's give her a round——

Mr. BILIRAKIS. Yes, why not?

[Applause.]

Mr. BILIRAKIS. Hey, Lacey, second thoughts? [Laughter.]

Mr. BILIRAKIS. No? I wish you would stay, but I understand.

I look forward to hearing from our witnesses today on providing protections for Americans and certainty for businesses.

So with that I will now recognize the gentlelady from Illinois, Ms. Schakowsky, for her 5 minutes for an opening statement.

Opening Statement of Hon. Jan Schakowsky, a Representative in Congress from the State of Illinois

Ms. SCHAKOWSKY. Thank you so much, Mr. Chairman. You know, you mentioned that we have been working in the subcommittee and the full committee for at least 5 years, talking about how are we going to protect consumers' data. And rather than things getting better, despite our being able to pass it out of the full committee, which was a tremendous achievement in a totally bipartisan way, I think consumers are increasingly, every day, concerned about their inability to protect their private information.

And you outlined some of the sectoral ways that consumers are supposedly protected but don't do the full job and don't fill the gaps. You mentioned healthcare, so—and I am really anxious to hear about that, among other things, because I think, at first, when HIPAA was put into place, the idea that doctors and hospitals would not be able to share information—there weren't so many applications out there that went well beyond that, and opportunities to go beyond that. But now we know that there are all kinds of apps that collect information and may share that, even sell that, about you and your health—one example of what we have to do.

You mentioned financial information. Now, you know, there were days where we just went to our banks, and we were pretty sure that that information wasn't going to be shared, and there were some protections. But we now know that there are retailers, for example, who have plenty of information when we do shopping online, and lots of our data, the—that leads back to all of our financial information becomes available.

And then you also mentioned FERPA, which is—I didn't actually know the acronym, but I am going to say it—it is the Family Education Rights and Privacy Act, for our kids. Well, you would hope that all of our—and we know that all of the information about our children isn't—is not protected right now. And for example, the student data. But children who attend private schools, they are not going to find that their information is protected. We know that there are a number of educational apps that our kids and, even as parents, that we are connecting them to, that may have lots more information about our children than we want. And that is always a primary concern for members of these committee—of this committee.

So I think I want to just conclude by going back to what we have already done. We have passed the American Data Privacy and Protection Act out of this committee, and it is time for us to return to that. If there are things that we still need to do, if we want to continue negotiations on various parts—but we passed a really good bill, and it is that that we ought to build on, that we ought to move forward on so that all those gaps that are now in protecting consumers' information, the information they do not want stolen, sold, the manipulations that are happening right now to our kids online, ourselves online—we can address this right now and get going once again on the ADPPA legislation and move forward as quickly as we can.

[The prepared statement of Ms. Schakowsky follows:]

Committee on Energy and Commerce, Opening Statement as Prepared for Delivery of Subcommittee on Innovation, Data, and Commerce Ranking Member Jan Schakowsky, Hearing on "Addressing America's Data Privacy Shortfalls: How a National Standard Fills Gaps to Protect Americans' Personal Information," April 27, 2023

A majority of Americans agree: consumers need comprehensive federal data privacy protections.

Existing sector specific federal privacy laws leave consumers vulnerable to invasions of their privacy.

HIPAA protects health information you share with your doctor or hospital, but not information collected by most mobile health applications.

Financial information you share with your bank has some protections, but not most payment data shared with retailers.

FERPA protects student data, but does not protect a child who attends a private school or when a child downloads and uses an educational app at home.

These laws leave large gaps in their protections.

Big Tech has stepped into those gaps to collect ever more personal and intimate data about us and our children.

Tech companies profit off of our habits, our finances, who we love, where we live, and our most sensitive health data.

Every time you browse the web or wear a smart watch, a tech company is tracking you.

They use this data to manipulate us, to addict us, and to keep us on their platforms so we can be fed more ads.

Or they sell the data to the highest bidder so that companies you've never heard of can build profiles of you.

Over the past few years, the DOJ charged three data brokers for knowingly selling lists of vulnerable Americans to criminal scammers.

These companies profited off defrauding elderly Americans and people with Alzheimer's.

Enough is enough.

We need protections for all Americans that put consumers back in control of their data. Americans are tired of feeling helpless online.

It is time to pass comprehensive federal data privacy legislation that protects consumers and fills the gaps in these sectoral laws.

* * *

Ms. SCHAKOWSKY. With that, I yield back, Mr. Chair.

Mr. BILIRAKIS. Thanks so very much. I appreciate it. And we are going to make a good bill even better.

I now recognize the chair of the full committee, Mrs. Rodgers, for her 5 minutes for an opening statement.

Opening Statement of Hon. Cathy Mcmorris Rodgers, a Representative in Congress from the State of Washington

Mrs. RODGERS. Thank you, Mr. Chairman. Good afternoon and welcome.

This is our sixth privacy and data security hearing this year. It gives us another chance to discuss our efforts to enact a comprehensive national standard. Currently, there are sector-specific Federal statutes on the books to protect data, ranging from healthcare to financial to youth-oriented laws.

While preserving those laws, the American Data and Privacy Protection Act passed out of committee with near unanimous 53 to 2 vote, and it included many safeguards to ensure activities in these various sectors remain governed by the appropriate State and Federal regulators. Many of these laws were crafted in this very hearing room over the last 30 years. The level of innovation and competition that resulted since then is amazing, and it represents some of the greatest accomplishments in American history.

That said, these technologies come with challenges that must be addressed. These companies have developed tools that interact to track Americans both online and offline, and they are also using their data to manipulate what we see and what we think. This is especially true for children.

I am very proud of our work last Congress to pass ADPPA out of committee. It included the strongest privacy protections for kids online. These protections have support from several stakeholders as being stronger than any proposals from any other Federal or State laws or proposals to date. It would make it illegal to target advertising to children and treats data about kids under 17 as sensitive. This means establishing higher barriers for the transfer of personal information.

This provision, along with the overarching data minimization provisions and the ability to delete personal information, will make it tougher for kids' personal identifiable information, like their physical location, to land in the hands of drug dealers, sex traffickers, and other evil actors attempting to find and track them.

It would also require assessments for how their algorithms amplify harmful content. This will keep them accountable for stories like the one reported by Bloomberg last week about Tiktok's algorithm continuing to push suicide content to vulnerable children.

Child privacy protection advocates, including many parent groups, are already on the record in support of a national data privacy standard. It is just one piece of protecting children online.

This is difficult to get right, but it is imperative that we do. Through many discussions with stakeholders, we determined that an underlying framework of protections must be strong and consistent, no matter the user, young or old. For this reason, any legislation to protect kids online must be rooted in a comprehensive national standard for data privacy and security to ensure there are broad protections. As long as there are regulatory gaps, companies will exploit them in order to monetize the data captured and refuse to do more to shield children from bad actors like cyberbullies, sex predators, drug dealers, and others trying to do harm. This can't be allowed to continue.

I can't emphasize this enough: We need legislation like ours that protects children from having their information harvested, like geolocation data—gives everyone the power to delete the information collected on them, and opt out of collection together—altogether, provides greater transparency over the algorithms these companies use to manipulate and amplify the information we see, and requires assessments for how algorithms harm children.

Last week, we had a hearing with the Federal Trade Commission. We raised concerns about the direction of the agency related to the unilateral rulemaking efforts. I believe the FTC should be the preeminent data protection agency in the world, but it needs to be at the direction of Congress.

I appreciate the work of the people in this room to ensure that we get this legislation right. Our efforts have shown us that the single best way to protect Americans in today's digital ecosystem is with a national privacy and data security standard, and the American people agree. More than 80 percent of Americans say that they are looking for Congress to act. It is our responsibility to ensure their data privacy and security, and to even higher levels of protections for their kids. It is time to rein in Big Tech.

[The prepared statement of Mrs. Rodgers follows:]

Opening Statement of Chair Cathy McMorris Rodgers, as Prepared for Delivery, Committee on Energy and Commerce, Subcommittee on Innovation, Data, and Commerce, Hearing Entitled "Addressing America's Data Privacy Shortfalls: How a National Standard Fills Gaps to Protect Americans' Personal Information," April 27, 2023

Good afternoon and welcome.

This is our sixth privacy and data security hearing this year.

It will give us another chance to discuss our efforts to enact a comprehensive national standard. Currently, there are sector-specific federal statutes on the books to protect data. ranging from health care, to financial, to youth-oriented laws.

While preserving those laws, the American Data and Privacy Protection Act passed out of Committee with a near unanimous 53-2 vote...

...and included many safeguards to ensure activities in these various sectors remained governed by the appropriate state and federal regulators.

Many of these laws were crafted in this very hearing room over the last 30 years.

The level of innovation and competition that resulted since then is amazing, and it represents some of the greatest accomplishments in American history.

That said, these technologies come with challenges that must be addressed.

These companies have developed tools that interact to track Americans both online and offline.

...and also they're using our data to manipulate what we see and what we think. This is especially true for our children.

I am very proud of our work last Congress to pass ADPPA out of Committee.

It included the strongest privacy protections for kids online — these protections have support from several stakeholders as being stronger than any proposals from any other Federal or State laws or proposals to date.

It would make it illegal to target advertising to children, and treats data about kids under 17 as "sensitive."

This means establishing higher barriers for the transfer of personal information.

This provision, along with the overarching data minimization provisions and the ability to delete personal information...

... will make it tougher for kids' personal identifiable information, like their physical location, to land in the hands of drug dealers, sex traffickers and other evil actors attempting to find and track them.

It would also require assessments for how their algorithms amplify harmful content.

This will keep them accountable for stories like one reported by Bloomberg last week about TikTok's algorithm continuing to push suicide content to vulnerable children. Child privacy protection advocates, including many parent groups, are already on record in support of a national data privacy standard.

It is just one piece of protecting children online.

This is difficult to get right, but it is imperative that we do.

Through many discussions with stakeholders, we determined that an underlying framework of protections must be strong and consistent no matter the user, young or old.

For this reason, any legislation to protect kids online must be rooted in a comprehensive national standard for data privacy and security to ensure there are broad protections.

As long as there are regulatory gaps, companies will exploit them in order to monetize the data captured...

...and refuse to do more to shield children from bad actors like cyberbullies, sexual predators, drug dealers, and others trying to do them harm.

This can't be allowed to continue.

I can't emphasize enough. We need legislation like ours that protects children from having their information harvested —like geolocation data...

...gives everyone the power to delete the information collected on them, and opt out of collection altogether...

...provides greater transparency over the algorithms these companies use to manipulate and amplify the information we see...

...and requires assessments for how algorithms harm children. Last week we had a hearing with the Federal Trade Commission.

We raised concerns about the direction of the agency related to their unilateral rulemaking efforts. I believe the FTC should be the preeminent data protection agency in the world.

But it needs to be at the direction of Congress.

I appreciate the work of the people in this room to ensure we get this legislation right.

Our efforts have shown us that the single best way we can protect Americans in today's digital ecosystem is with a national data privacy and security standard.

And the American people agree.

More than 80 percent of Americans say they are looking for Congress to act.

It is our responsibility to ensure their data privacy and security, to provide even higher levels of protections for their kids, and to rein in Big Tech.

I look forward to the testimony and I yield back.

* * *

Mrs. RODGERS. I look forward to your testimony, and I yield back.

Mr. BILIRAKIS. Thank you very much, Madam Chair. And now I recognize the gentleman from New Jersey, Mr. Pallone, for 5 minutes for an opening statement.

Opening Statement of Hon. Frank Pallone, Jr., a Representative in Congress from the State of New Jersey

Mr. PALLONE. Thank you, Chairman Bilirakis.

For decades we have sought to safeguard Americans' fundamental right to privacy with a series of fragmented sector-by-sector laws. Anyone with a smartphone, laptop, or tablet can tell you that we are not getting the job done. The alphabet soup of well-intentioned Federal privacy laws—HIPAA, COPPA, FERPA, GLBA— have failed to rein in the collection, use, and transfer of Americans' sensitive data. That is partly because they were not designed for our modern online economy.

FERPA, or the Federal Educational Rights and Privacy Act, passed in 1974. HIPAA, or the Health Insurance Portability Accountability Act, passed in 1996. GLBA, or the Gramm-Leach-Bliley Act, which addresses privacy within the financial sector, passed in 1999. And COPPA, or the Children's Online Privacy Protection Act, became law in 2000. So the phone wasn't released—or I should say that the iPhone wasn't released until 2007. In internet years, these laws are dinosaurs.

So today, health information is no longer confined to the relative safety of a doctor's filing cabinet. Fitness trackers monitor our heart rates, sleep patterns, and oxygen saturation levels. Health information websites provide diagnosis and treatment information on every possible medical condition. Mobile applications track dietary, mental, and reproductive health. But the HIPAA privacy rules only restrict the use and sharing of health information by healthcare providers, clearinghouses, and health plans. As a result, some of the most commonly used websites, apps, and devices have the green light to mine and use Americans' health information without meaningful limitations.

The lack of strong privacy protections threatens Americans' financial information, as well. Existing financial privacy laws largely do not apply to retailers and online marketplaces, nor do they provide protection from discriminatory algorithms.

Likewise, existing children's privacy laws leave vast amounts of children and teens' sensitive information unprotected. FERPA, the privacy law protecting educational records, does not apply to private and parochial elementary and secondary schools. It also doesn't apply to EdTech downloaded and used at home or in afterschool programs to supplement or complement children's schoolwork. And COPPA only restricts online operators from collecting data from children under the age of 13 without obtaining verifiable parental consent, but only under limited circumstances.

Children's data collected on sites like TikTok, Instagram, Google, Facebook, and Snapchat is not protected unless the site knows it is collecting information from kids under 13. So this honor system has become a get-out-of-jail-free card for Big Tech companies, which often claim that their services are intended for users 13 or older. But we know children are on these sites and apps. Sixty-four percent of children between 8 and 12 years old report watching online videos on platforms like TikTok and YouTube every day. Nearly one in five say they use social media every day.

So simply tweaking current child privacy laws will not sufficiently protect our nation's youth. That is because age verification is notoriously challenging and has proven to be ineffective. After all, children today are digital natives. They know how to bypass popups asking for their age or birth date and can enter these virtual playgrounds with little parental supervision and meager privacy protections.

So we also know that parents' use of the internet routinely provides information about their children, either directly or by inference. When a parent or guardian goes online to research and sign up for summer camps, family vacations, Little League teams, gymnastic classes, or a broad variety of other activities, they share data about their children, and that information is then used and shared for targeted marketing and other purposes. As a result, protecting kids and teens' privacy requires us to protect everyone's privacy.

So that is why we must pass a comprehensive privacy bill that closes the gap and enshrines Americans' right to privacy in law. We need a bill that reins in the overcollection of information by mandating data minimization. And we need a bill that puts all Americans back in control of how the data is collected, used, and shared.

Last Congress, as, you know, most of my colleagues have already mentioned, this committee overwhelmingly passed such a bill with broad bipartisan support. I am committed to getting a bill over the finish line, and look forward to continuing to work with Chair Rodgers and our subcommittee chairs to that effect.

[The prepared statement of Mr. Pallone follows:]

Committee on Energy and Commerce, Opening Statement as Prepared for Delivery of Ranking Member Frank Pallone, Jr., Innovation, Data, and Commerce Subcommittee, Hearing on "Addressing America's Data Privacy Shortfalls: How a National Standard Fills Gaps to Protect Americans' Personal Information," April 27, 2023

For decades, we've sought to safeguard Americans' fundamental right to privacy with a series of fragmented, sector-by-sector laws. Anyone with a smartphone, laptop, or tablet can tell you that we're not getting the job done.

The alphabet soup of well-intentioned federal privacy laws – HIPAA, COPPA, FERPA, GLBA – have failed to rein-in the collection, use, and transfer of Americans' sensitive data. That's partly because they were not designed for our modern online economy. FERPA, or the Federal Educational Rights and Privacy Act, passed in 1974. HIPAA, or the Health Insurance Portability Accountability Act, passed in 1996. GLBA, or the Gramm-Leach-Bliley Act, which addresses privacy within the financial sector, passed in 1999. And COPPA, or the Childrens Online Privacy Protection Act, became law in 2000. The iPhone wasn't released until 2007. In internet years, these laws are dinosaurs.

Today, health information is no longer confined to the relative safety of a doctor's filing cabinet. Fitness trackers monitor our heart rates, sleep patterns, and oxygen saturation levels. Health information websites provide diagnosis and treatment information on every possible medical condition. Mobile applications track dietary, mental, and reproductive health.

But the HIPAA privacy rules only restrict the use and sharing of health information by health care providers, clearinghouses, and health plans. As a result, some of the most commonly used websites, apps, and devices have the green light to mine and use Americans' health information without meaningful limitations.

The lack of strong privacy protections threatens Americans' financial information as well. Existing financial privacy laws largely do not apply to retailers and online marketplaces. Nor do they provide protection from discriminatory algorithms.

Likewise, existing children's privacy laws leave vast amounts of children and teens' sensitive information unprotected.

FERPA, the privacy law protecting educational records, does not apply to private and parochial elementary and secondary schools. It also does not apply to EdTech downloaded and used at home or in after school programs to supplement or complement children's schoolwork.

COPPA only restricts "online operators" from collecting data from children under the age of 13 without obtaining verifiable parental consent, but only under limited circumstances. Children's data collected on sites like TikTok, Instagram, Google, Facebook, and Snapchat is not protected unless the site knows it is collecting information from kids under 13.

This honor system has become a get out of jail free card for Big Tech companies, which often claim that their services are intended for users 13 or older. But we know children are on these sites and apps. Sixty-four percent of children between eightand twelve-years-old report watching online videos on platforms like TikTok and YouTube every day. Nearly one in five say they use social media every day.

Simply tweaking current child privacy laws will not sufficiently protect our nation's youth. That's because age verification is notoriously challenging and has proven to be ineffective. After all, children today are digital natives. They know how to bypass popups asking for their age or birthdate and can enter these virtual playgrounds with little parental supervision and meager privacy protections.

We also know that parents' use of the internet routinely provides information about their children, either directly or by inference. When a parent or guardian goes online to research and sign up for summer camps, family vacations, little league teams, gymnastics classes, or a broad variety of other activities, they share data about their children. That information is then used and shared for targeted marketing and other purposes. As a result, protecting kids and teens' privacy requires us to protect everyone's privacy.

That's why we must pass a comprehensive privacy bill that closes the gaps and enshrines Americans' right to privacy in law. We need a bill that reins-in the overcollection of information by mandating data minimization. We need a bill that puts all Americans back in control of how their data is collected, used, and shared.

Last Congress, this Committee overwhelmingly passed such a bill with broad bipartisan support. I'm committed to getting a bill over the finish line and look forward to continuing to work with Chair Rodgers on that effort.

* * *

Mr. PALLONE. And with that, Mr. Chairman, I yield back. But thank you and Chair Rodgers and Ranking Member Schakowsky for all that you are doing to push this national privacy bill and framework. I appreciate it.

Mr. BILIRAKIS. Good. Let's get this done. Now—thank you very much, I appreciate it, the gentleman yields back.

Our first witness is Morgan Reed, president of ACT–The App Association.

You are recognized, sir, for your 5 minutes.

Statements of Morgan Reed, President, Act–The App Association; Donald Codling, Senior Advisor for Cybersecurity and Privacy, Rego Payment Architectures, Inc.; Edward Britan, Vice President, Associate General Counsel, and Head of Global Privacy, Salesforce, Inc.; and Amelia Vance, Founder and President, Public Interest Privacy Center

Statement of Morgan Reed

Mr. REED. Chairman Bilirakis, Ranking Member Schakowsky, and members of the subcommittee, my name is Morgan Reed, and I am the president of the App Association.

The App Association is part of a $1.8 trillion global ecosystem that supports 6 million American jobs. Our members are often tiny companies but quite literally serve all 435 congressional districts. And most importantly, our member companies are building products that help your constituents manage their health, their finances, and their education.

For example, two companies—Thinkamingo in your district, Mr. Chair, and Kidz Learn in your district, Ms. Schakowsky—must manage the intersection between COPPA and FERPA and the gaps that exist. In healthcare our companies like Podimetrics help veteran warfighters manage their diabetic foot issues, and Rimidi gives doctors a platform to manage remote patient monitoring, all while dealing with HIPAA rules for both data portability, but also how to govern data that may be outside of HIPAA's very narrow scope.

But regardless of the regulatory silo, what our members hear from consumers is loud and clear: They want access to their information—health, education, and financial—in digital form, and they want to manage it on their smartphone. Moreover, they want all of that to happen in an environment that meets their expectations around privacy and security. This is a tall order, but one that is made more difficult by the lack of Federal privacy legislation, the current odd silos of privacy regulation that put parts of their personal data under HIPAA, others under FERPA, some under GLB. And what consumers feel like as a random mishmash really devalues the trust that we need in the system. And consumers need to trust our members are delivering the next wave of digital tools and services in a manner that protects privacy and secures data against bad actors. With this in mind, I want to focus on three concepts.

First, expanding HIPAA is a nonstarter. HIPAA is a portability and interoperability regime. It is right there in the name. The P stands for portability, not privacy. It is designed for insurers and providers as part of a narrow set of covered entities providing healthcare services to patients. Expanding HIPAA to all entities processing data with any connection to health—like grocery stores—under the concept of social determinants of health would turn the Office of Civil Rights into a second FTC.

Practically speaking, consumers don't need another FTC, especially when the staff of 72 that already oversees 6,000 annual complaints, many of them unrelated to privacy. And we also don't need grocery stores, mapping apps, and smart ag platforms to make all of their data interoperable with electronic health records, which is HIPAA's primary purpose.

But we can't shrug and walk away. Instances where digital health apps process or transfer sensitive personal data in ways that go against consumers' expectations are numerous. After the FTC entered a consent order with period trapping—tracking app Flo, we sent a letter to this committee arguing that the conduct of Flo is one of the most important reasons for a comprehensive privacy bill. But that privacy bill cannot be an outgrowth of a health record portability law. We need your bill to become law.

Number two, financial services go beyond Gramm-Leach-Bliley, and we need a risk-based framework to better empower consumers. Like HIPAA, GLBA only applies to a narrow, already defined group of entities. We need to, A, ensure that after financial data is passed from a GLBA-covered entity to the consumer, it is treated as sensitive PII; and B, provide a risk-based framework so that the financial services industry understands where their liability risks are and, most importantly, aren't, so that the industry can spur innovation.

Lastly, FERPA overlaps with the FTC Act and its child requirements under COPPA, resulting in uncertainty for parents, commercial industries, and the education institutions alike. We need to improve clarity and avoid making confusion worse. Some data is optout under FERPA but opt-in under COPPA. This helps no one.

We need to focus on ensuring that a Federal bill benefits all persons of any age and avoids convoluted fictions like adding a constructive knowledge threshold to COPPA, which will neither be constructive or add knowledge. And we need to modernize verifiable parental consent requirements currently in place so that parents and developers can actually make VPC work and make it harder for some to simply pretend that all of their audience is over 13.

Ultimately, privacy enforcers need better tools. When Tom Hanks' character was stranded on a remote island in the movie *Cast Away*, he used an ice skate to remove a tooth. What the FTC needs is not more ice skates, tools that don't fit the job and cause more pain than is necessary. The FTC and my members need a statute that specifically prohibits privacy harms resulting from processing, collection, and transfer that go against consumer expectations.

Thank you for inviting me to this important discussion, and I look forward to your questions.

[The prepared statement of Mr. Reed follows:]

Addressing America's Data Privacy Shortfalls: How a National Standard Fills Gaps to Protect Americans' Personal Information, Testimony of Morgan Reed, President, ACT | The App Association, before the U.S. House of Representatives, Committee on Energy and Commerce, Subcommittee on Innovation, Data, and Commerce

I. Introduction

We applaud this Subcommittee for holding today's hearing to examine the privacy risks— and the vast benefits—of activities involving the collection and processing of consumer data adjacent to the sector-specific federal privacy frameworks. Small businesses in the app economy lead the way in solving problems and protecting privacy in these areas.

ACT | The App Association is a global trade group for small and medium-sized technology companies. Our members are entrepreneurs, innovators, and independent developers within the global app ecosystem that engage with verticals across every industry. Today, the App Association represents an ecosystem valued at approximately $1.8 trillion and supports 6 million American jobs. Our members propel the data-driven evolution of these industries and compete against larger firms in a variety of ways, including on privacy and security protections.

Policymakers are appropriately curious and concerned about the privacy and security implications of data collection and processing around the edges of the Health Insurance Portability and Accountability Act (HIPAA), Gramm-Leach Bliley Act (GLBA), and Family Educational Rights and Privacy Act (FERPA). Given that the United States lacks an overarching, comprehensive privacy framework, the gaps between what consumers see as "health," "finance," and "education" are real. At the same time, this Subcommittee has also acknowledged that digital health, financial technologies (FinTech), and digital education tools provide expanded access to higher quality, more cost-effective services across these critical industries. The activity taking place in the penumbras around these silos is some of the most dynamic and beneficial economic activity the world has to offer, but the privacy and security sensitivities are also accordingly higher. They are the best reason for Congress to enhance federal privacy protections.

The layered applicability of the Federal Trade Commission (FTC) Act, FERPA, and HIPAA to real-life economic activity is deceptively complex. A comprehensive, risk-based privacy framework—like the American Data Privacy and Protection Act (ADPPA, H.R. 8152, 117th)—is the best option before Congress to clarify these complications, better protect consumers in and between the penumbras around federal privacy silos, and advance American digital economy competitiveness on the global stage.

We recommend Congress take the following into consideration as the Subcommittee continues its legislative work on comprehensive privacy legislation:

1. Simply "expanding" HIPAA is a non-starter.

- HIPAA is an interoperability regime, designed for an incredibly narrow set of "covered entities" providing healthcare services to patients. Expanding that list to all entities processing data with any connection to health—like grocery stores—would turn the Department of Health and Human Services (HHS) and its sub-agency, the Office of Civil Rights (OCR), into a second FTC, but one with a staff of 72 already overseeing 6,000 annual complaints and convert much of the economy into an interoperable system required to maintain data for audit purposes.

2. Financial services go beyond GLBA and need a risk-based framework to better empower consumers.

- Like HIPAA, GLBA applies to a narrow, already-defined group of entities. But unlike HIPAA, GLBA currently lacks consumer data access requirements. The outcome is that the GLBA silo sometimes traps financial information, making it more difficult for consumers to understand and control their information. A risk-based framework can make it clear to the industry what can be done and spur innovation.

3. FERPA overlaps with the FTC Act and its child privacy requirements, resulting in uncertainty for parents, commercial industries, and educational institutions alike.

- Instead of augmenting the risks these overlaps present by imposing age verification requirements or increasing data collection with a "constructive knowledge" threshold, a federal privacy law should modernize verifiable parental consent (VPC) requirements currently in place.

II. Health Insurance Portability and Accountability Act (HIPAA)

HIPAA Background

HIPAA and its concomitant Privacy Rule is one of the most misquoted or at least most misinterpreted laws on the books. Contrary to popular punditry, HIPAA is an interoperability regime, designed to help insurers, providers, and patients have access to electronic health records and support interoperability. Of course, Congress understood that enabling easier portability would create privacy concerns, but the "how" and "why" was left open so that Congress might pass a more comprehensive privacy law to deal with the issues. Specifically, when HIPAA first passed, it did not specify the kinds of privacy or security requirements the OCR should impose. Instead, the HIPAA statute included a "shot clock" provision implicitly authorizing what eventually became the Privacy Rule and the Security Rule, if Congress failed to authorize them directly within three years after HIPAA's initial enactment (by August of 1999).[1] That provision required OCR to send a report to Congress in 1997 with recommendations on how legislation governing health information privacy should look. Preemptively addressing future legislative gridlock, the statute further provided that, "If legislation governing standards with respect to the privacy of individually identifiable health information . . . is not enacted by the date that is 36 months after the date of enactment of this Act, the Secretary . . . shall promulgate final regulations containing such standards."[2] OCR finalized the Privacy Rule and Security Rule in 2003.

Congress should not defer entirely to agency rules like this again.

Scope and Summary of HIPAA

HIPAA applies to two classes of entity: covered entities (CEs) and their business associates (BAs). Similar to the General Data Protection Regulation's (GDPR's) classification of "controllers" and "processors," HIPAA directly applies to the "controller" analogue, CEs (health plans, providers that process insurance claims electronically, and clearing houses). This aspect of HIPAA's scope is notable. Most consumers would be surprised to know that the main touchstone for HIPAA's applicability to their health services is whether the provider processes insurance claims electronically. The "processors" in HIPAA parlance are BAs, which are only BAs to the extent they provide services on behalf of CEs but are liable for compliance with HIPAA via their contracts with CEs. Finally, HIPAA's provisions apply to CEs' and BAs' activities with respect to protected health information (PHI), which includes personally identifiable information (PII) that is created or received by a healthcare provider, among other entities; relates to past, present, or future physical or mental health or condition of an individual; the provision of healthcare to an individual; and that either identifies the individual or "with respect to which there is a reasonable basis to believe the information can be used to identify the individual."[3] The Privacy Rule generally allows CEs to use or disclose PHI for the purposes of "treatment, payment, and other routine healthcare operations."[4] With some caveats, the Privacy Rule only allows any other use or disclosure of PHI if the CE obtains the patient's

---

[1] Health Insurance Portability and Accountability Act (HIPAA), Pub. L. No. 104-191, Sec. 264, *available at* https://www.govinfo.gov/content/pkg/PLAW-104publ191/pdf/PLAW-104publ191.pdf.

[2] *Id.*, at Sec. 264(c)(1).

[3] 45 C.F.R. Sec. 160.103.

[4] 45 C.F.R. Sec. 164.506.

written "authorization."[5] Several administrative requirements also apply to CEs, including a requirement to provide individuals with written notices summarizing the Privacy Rule's provisions and patients' rights, along with contact information for someone at the CE who can handle privacy complaints and other communications. The Privacy Rule also requires CEs to designate a privacy official to develop and implement its policies and procedures and mandates disclosure—and therefore retention—of PHI for purposes of an OCR audit or investigation. Finally, CEs must obtain written assurance from BAs that they would use PHI only for the purposes permitted or required by contract, and "implement appropriate safeguards to prevent misuse of PHI."[6]

The App Economy Is Revolutionizing Digital Health

Several App Association members serve patients via BA agreements with CEs. That puts their core activities under the scope of HIPAA. For example, Rimidi provides a remote physiologic monitoring and clinical decision support platform for patients and their caregivers to manage a variety of chronic conditions. Similarly, Podimetrics provides a thermometric foot mat enabling caregivers to monitor patients at risk of developing diabetic foot ulcers (DFUs), identifying DFU development up to five weeks before they present clinically and preventing limb amputation. As digital health companies augmenting the caregiving services of healthcare providers, these member companies' activities are subject to HIPAA via BA agreements. Our member companies' digital health tools are only becoming more important for patients, consumers, and caregivers. With the current physician shortage of about 30,000 expected to increase to up to 124,000 by 2034;[7] healthcare costs spiking;[8] the efficacy of sensors and software that collect and analyze physiologic health data improving dramatically;[9] and the pandemic forcing patients to rely more generally on virtual care services, digital health tools are now an important fixture in American healthcare that can augment caregivers' reach and capabilities while controlling costs.

Some of our member companies provide services for clients and customers other than CEs subject to HIPAA, but nonetheless process sensitive PII with some connection to health. For example, App Association member Particle Health allows patients to receive and share their medical information digitally, seamlessly, and affordably. Importantly, Particle Health empowers consumers to make use of their health records both inside of the HIPAA umbrella and outside its borders. Particle Health's role in the digital health ecosystem is simple: Particle

---

[5] 45 C.F.R. Sec. 164.508.

[6] CONG. RESEARCH SERV., HIPAA PRIVACY, SECURITY, ENFORCEMENT, AND BREACH NOTIFICATION STANDARDS 6 (updated Apr. 17, 2015), *available at* https://crsreports.congress.gov/product/pdf/R/R43991.

[7] American Assoc. of Medical Colleges, "AAMC Report Reinforces Mounting Physician Shortage," press release (Jun. 11, 2021), *available at* https://www.aamc.org/news-insights/press-releases/aamc-report- reinforces-mounting-physician-shortage.

[8] "Lowering Unaffordable Costs: Legislative Solutions to Increase Transparency and Competition in Health Care," Hearing before the House Committee on Energy and Commerce, Subcommittee on Health, 118th Cong. (Apr. 26, 2023), *available at* https://democratsenergycommerce.house.gov/sites/democrats.energycommerce.house.gov/files/Ilyse%20Schuman_Witness%20Testimony_04.26.23.pdf.

[9] Aisha Malik, "Garmin launches a new FDA-cleared ECG app for the Venu 2 plus," TECHCRUNCH (Jan. 24, 2023), *available at* https://techcrunch.com/2023/01/24/garmin-new-fda-cleared-ecg-app-venu-2-plus/.

is the "Plaid of digital health."[10] If that comparison doesn't ring any bells, Plaid is the company that provides Venmo and other third-party financial services applications the programming interface to securely connect and transfer funds from a consumer's bank account to that specific payment app. Particle wants to serve the same function for digital health records, so that consumers have an easier, privacy-maximizing way to transfer their information from medical institutions to the various applications, platforms, and services they desire. Another company outside the scope of HIPAA, WeStrive, provides personal fitness trainers several digital tools to create programming for clients and monitor their progress. Consumers and trainers should be able to put sensitive health data to work with apps like WeStrive's, knowing that the law provides optimal privacy and security protections. WeStrive should not be thought of as failing to protect PII because bad actors in this space are culpable of privacy abuses, which reporting sometimes unfairly implies is the case with all digital offerings outside HIPAA. A federal privacy framework would better enable WeStrive to earn consumers' trust.

Health Privacy Abhors a Vacuum

Congress' decision in HIPAA to essentially defer entirely to HHS to create a health privacy regime has imposed avoidable costs on patients and would likely impose even greater costs on consumers in the general privacy context. As we noted in a letter to this Committee in 2021,[11] one of the most important reasons for Congress to enact a general privacy law is to enhance patients' privacy and security protections with respect to sensitive PII, especially as they relate to digital health activities outside the HIPAA umbrella. Congress' failure to act poses three related risks on this point: 1) that health privacy abuses are more likely to continue, undermining legitimate digital health offerings and weakening consumer trust; 2) that the FTC will continue to experience pressure to adopt overly expansive interpretations of its authority; and 3) that states will continue to take increasingly divergent approaches to health privacy outside the scope of HIPAA.

Without specifically arming the FTC with the authority to enjoin privacy harms, evidence suggests adverse headlines will continue, although the Commission is making use of its current tools. The FTC's recent consent orders show that it has prioritized punishing privacy and security abuses by digital health companies that may run afoul of FTC Act prohibitions on unfair or deceptive acts or practices. The FTC sought to enjoin health services companies outside the scope of HIPAA from telling their customers that they were not sharing their PII but doing so anyways for advertising purposes. For example, in one complaint, the FTC alleges that a company, "recognizing the sensitivity of this health information, . . . repeatedly promised to keep it private and use it only for non-advertising purposes such as to facilitate consumers' therapy,"[12] but then shared some PII with third parties for advertising. In another case, the FTC alleged that a period tracking app told its users that no PII would be shared with third parties

---

[10] *See* Matt Schwartz, "2020 Vision: Will Congress Have Foresight on Healthcare Privacy?" ACT | THE APP ASSOCIATION BLOG (Jan. 21, 2020), *available at* https://actonline.org/2020/01/21/2020-vision-will-congress-have-foresight-on-healthcare-privacy/.

[11] Letter from Morgan Reed, president, ACT | The App Association, to Hon. Frank Pallone, chairman, House Committee on Energy and Commerce, and Hon. Cathy McMorris Rodgers, Republican leader, House Committee on Energy and Commerce, Re: Fed. Trade Comm'n Settlement with Flo (Feb. 17, 2021).

[12] Fed. Trade Comm'n, *BetterHelp, Inc.*, FTC No. 202316, Complaint (released Mar. 2, 2023), *available at* https://www.ftc.gov/system/files/ftc_gov/pdf/2023169-betterhelp-complaint_.pdf.

but used software development kits (SDKs) that shared their PII with several advertisers.[13] Advertising and marketing are critical to making digital health tools accessible for consumers and patients, but it is equally important that digital health providers adhere to privacy representations as well as customer expectations.

At the same time, the FTC is also seeking to expand its current tools absent a new privacy law that would enhance penalties and clarify its authority specific to privacy and security. For example, although privacy experts have always distinguished between purposeful disclosures and data breaches, the FTC recently interpreted its Health Breach Notification Rule (HBNR) as a privacy rule. As then-Commissioner Wilson noted in a dissent, the statement expansively and awkwardly interprets a few aspects of the rule, including the definition of vendors of "personal health records" (PHRs), to which the rule applies.[14] She argued further that interpretations of a rule that differ in such a way from the text of its provisions typically require an administrative rulemaking procedure so that an agency can consider comments from the public. More fundamentally, the core of the HBNR is a requirement to notify affected consumers in case of a "breach of security," defined as "acquisition of [PHR identifiable health information] without the authorization of the individual."[15] There are two problems with applying this rule when a company purposely transfers data to a third party. First, such transfer is generally done under color of authorization by the affected consumer—in other words, the company has (erroneously but deliberately) inferred the consumer's authorization for its transfer. Characterizing the willful transfer by a company to a third party as a "breach of security"—which typically involves a malicious attack by a third party that thwarts the company's security measures—is at least an odd fit. The second problem with the interpretation is that it merely requires notice to the consumer for purposely transferring the data, instead of punishing the act of transferring the data. Going forward, a company could potentially comply with the broadly interpreted HBNR by simply notifying consumers after the fact that it has given their health information to Facebook. It could still be liable under Section 5 of the FTC Act as well, and that is the proper *current* law to apply in this scenario. But better than either option would be a privacy law that empowers the Commission to pursue and punish instances of purposeful onward transfer of health PII that is inconsistent with a company's own representations, the context of its relationship with the affected consumers, or data minimization requirements.

For a few years, states have steadily adopted new comprehensive privacy laws that differ in various ways from each other. However, in the wake of the Supreme Court of the United States' (SCOTUS') decision in the *Dobbs v. Jackson Women's Health Org.*, the gap between state approaches to privacy is widening at an accelerated pace. For example, Washington recently enacted a new consumer health privacy law, the Washington My Health My Data Act,[16] and a few other legislatures like Connecticut's and Maryland's are considering similar measures. Despite that legislators mainly sought to protect consumers against investigations

---

[13] Fed. Trade Comm'n, *Flo Health, Inc.*, FTC No. 1923133, Complaint (released Jan. 13, 2021), *available at* https://www.ftc.gov/legal-library/browse/cases-proceedings/192-3133-flo-health-inc.

[14] Fed. Trade Comm'n, Policy Stmt. On Breaches by Health Apps and Other Connected Devices, Dissenting Stmt. Of Comm'r Christine S. Wilson, FTC No. P205405 (Sept. 15, 2021), *available at* https://www.ftc.gov/system/files/documents/public_statements/1596356/wilson_health_apps_policy_statement_dissent_combined_final.pdf.

[15] 16 C.F.R. Sec. 318.2(a), 318.3(a).

[16] My Health My Data Act, Wash. House, HB 1155, 68th Leg. (2023).

into access to reproductive health services that are legal in Washington, the law does not address law enforcers' access to reproductive health data. Instead, it broadly proscribes collection, processing, or transfer by commercial actors of an exceptionally broad class of information that may relate to an individual's health. As noted above, even HIPAA allows for the collection, transfer, and processing of PHI for treatment, payment, and other routine operations. The My Health My Data Act prohibits any collection or transfer of consumer health data, with only two exceptions: 1) with consent of the consumer for "a specified purpose" and 2) to the extent *necessary* to provide a product or service the consumer has requested.[17] The prohibitions in this law appear to restrict WeStrive from improving its product to benefit consumers, or create a new data-driven feature that helps trainers and consumers reach their fitness or health goals. We agree with policymakers that the law should not allow app developers to create profiles on people using their sensitive PII in ways that contravene the context of the relationship they have with consumers or fail to gain their consent. However, only allowing two narrow bases for collection and transfer of consumer health data—including non-health information which can be used to extrapolate health-related information—would limit consumers' access to digital health tools. The answer to privacy and security risks involving consumer health data should not be to drastically limit consumers' ability to make use of them and incidentally sweep in non-health digital services in the process. The approach in ADPPA strikes a more reasonable balance that would punish privacy and security harms arising from collection and processing of health information—and impose reasonable data minimization requirements that mitigate unnecessary risks associated with the creation and maintenance of profiles—while allowing for product improvements, context-driven communications, and basic operations.

Information Blocking Rules

As part of the 21st Century Cures Act, Congress required HHS (via its National Coordinator for Health IT Policy or ONC) to prohibit entities subject to HIPAA from blocking a patient's access to their own protected health information (PHI).

The information blocking rules add further pressure on Congress to regulate privacy outside the scope of HIPAA because if they work as intended, they should empower patients to transfer their own PHI outside the HIPAA umbrella. CEs and BAs that collect and process PHI on behalf of patients worry about their own liability for transferring PHI to entities not subject to HIPAA, even at their patients' request. Entities subject to HIPAA tend to lack a detailed understanding of—and underestimate—the FTC's and state attorney generals' (AGs') enforcement practices regarding health privacy, but their concerns are not unjustified. Despite our Connected Health Initiative's (CHI's) suggestion for ONC to require privacy and security attestations by health apps receiving PHI on behalf of patients under the information blocking rules, ONC declined to adopt such a requirement. Requiring health apps and device companies to make those attestations would have equipped consumer protection enforcers with statements that could be matched against the companies' own conduct, setting up deception claims against companies behaving inconsistently with their representations. But ultimately, attestations would be a stopgap measure until Congress can enact a risk-based general privacy law that would prevent and penalize collection and processing activities involving health information that impose costs in excess of their benefits.

---

[17] *Id.*, Sec. 5.

HIPAA Is a Bad Fit for Digital Health Tools Provided Directly to Consumers

For example, some of the most important aspects of a general privacy bill are the requirements to respond to various kinds of consumer requests. One such requirement mandates that covered companies respond to verified consumer requests to delete PII pertaining to them. Although this protection should be limited by legitimate business or legal interests associated with maintaining PII, it is an important one in the general economy. However, the policy interest in allowing patients to request their healthcare providers to delete health information about them is generally weaker, while the policy interest in blocking such requests is stronger. A patient may want to delete addiction information about themselves in their health records, but that information may save their lives in the future. Thus, a central aspect of a strong consumer privacy regime probably should not even be a feature of patient privacy as applied to HIPAA CEs and BAs. Specific provisions aside, a regime like HIPAA designed around the patient-provider relationship is not well suited to consumer products. The main purpose of HIPAA is to ensure interoperability between health providers so that a patient can port their health records across providers. Thus, HIPAA is supposed to be a bulwark against the incentive for providers to block access by the patient in order to keep the patient's business, as well as the disincentive to invest anything in making health records accessible or readable by other providers. Consumer-facing products and services with health-related aspects are fundamentally different and appropriately require an approach more along the lines of what this Subcommittee is pursuing taking a risk-based approach to privacy and security protections. For this reason, we strongly support updated language in ADPPA that would clarify that PHI is exempt from ADPPA's requirements.

To the extent Congress wants to intervene to ensure interoperability between digital health services outside of HIPAA, we would recommend cosponsoring and forwarding the Better Interoperability for Devices (BID) Act (H.R. 1557). The BID Act would require the Food and Drug Administration to make recommendations to Congress as to how it could better allow for interoperability between medical devices inside and outside the HIPAA umbrella.

Federal Consumer Privacy Law Must Enable Healthcare Research and Necessary Processing Activities on Behalf of Consumers

Comprehensive privacy bills like ADPPA will likely include data minimization provisions. One aspect of the HIPAA framework that is appropriate for digital health tools outside of HIPAA is an allowance for those services to conduct health research and process payments and other healthcare functions on behalf of customers. To the extent federal legislation imposes data minimization restrictions on covered companies, they should appropriately allow for the use of covered data for research, especially "peer-reviewed scientific, historical, or statistical research," that "adheres to all relevant laws" governing such research, as ADPPA provides.[18] It is essential for a comprehensive federal privacy bill not to inadvertently hamstring legitimate medical research that currently benefits consumers and patients.

[18] American Data Privacy and Protection Act, Sec. 1(b)(10) (H.R. 8152, 117th Cong.).

III. Gramm-Leach-Bliley Act (GLBA)

GLBA Scope

GLBA applies to "financial institutions," which the regulation defines as entities engaged in any activity that is "financial in nature," or is "incidental to such financial activities as described" in the Bank Holding Company Act.[19] The FTC is the primary data security regulator of financial institutions under GLBA, which imposes security requirements, disclosure limits, and transparency requirements. GLBA authorizes two separate rulemakings, the Safeguards Rule (vested solely in the FTC) and the Privacy Rule (which four separate federal agencies maintain and enforce, divided up by entity type).[20] GLBA distinguishes between "consumers" and "customers" of financial institutions.

Consumers are individuals who interact with a financial institution, while customers are consumers who have an ongoing relationship with the financial institution.[21] For example, a person who applies for a loan from a financial institution—and therefore submits sensitive, non-public PII—is a consumer; but they only become a customer if they have an ongoing relationship with the financial institution.

The FinTech App Economy

The app economy activity in and around the scope of GLBA is robust. Our FinTech member companies are solving emerging and long-intractable problems for consumers. For example, Goalsetter provides a financial education platform for children, which allows kids to receive allowance or monetary gifts from friends, parents, and relatives, and/or spend money through the Goalsetter debit card. Another kids' digital wallet company, REGO, has gone so far as to patent the COPPA compliant opt-in protections in its Mazoola mobile wallet for kids.[22] Both of these FinTech apps put parents in charge and empower kids to learn financial literacy. With studies indicating that just over half of Americans are considered financially literate and only 24 percent of millennials understand basic financial concepts,[23] App Association members and companies like them are leveraging the power of smart devices and platforms to address this issue in privacy-protective ways.

Just as patients sought a remedy for better access to their records through the information blocking rules, concerns about customers' access to and portability of their financial information have punctuated financial services policy debates. The App Association filed comments on the Consumer Financial Protection Bureau's (CFPB's) statutorily required Section 1033 rulemaking[24] highlighting the need for more meaningful access by customers to their own financial information. As we noted in our letter, "[t]he opportunities for consumers

---

[19] 16 C.F.R. Sec. 314(b); Sec. 314(h)(1).

[20] 16 C.F.R. Sec. 314; 16 C.F.R. Sec. 313.

[21] 16 C.F.R. Sec. 314.2(b); Sec. 314.2(c).

[22] *See* MAZOOLA: A KIDS MOBILE WALLET POWERED BY PRIVACY, *available at* https://mazoola.co/.

[23] Kevin P. Chavous, "A Hand Up Or A Handout? Tackling America's Financial Literacy Crisis," FORBES (Feb. 3, 2022), *available at* https://www.forbes.com/sites/stopaward/2022/02/03/a-hand-up-or-a-handout-can- we-tackle-americas-financial-literacy-crisis/?sh=2258745fe251.

[24] Letter from Morgan Reed, president, ACT | The App Ass'n, to Hon. Rohit Chopra, Dir., Consumer Financial Protection Bureau, Re: Comments of ACT The App Association on the Consumer Financial Protection Bureau's *Request for Information Regarding Consumer Access to Financial Records*, Docket No. CFPB-2016-0048, 81 Fed. Reg. 83806 (Feb. 21, 2023).

in the open market are enormous. FinTech applications can improve consumer access to credit using data points that traditional lenders overlook; they can allow consumers to budget and receive personalized tips in real time; and they can send consumers sophisticated analytics tailored specifically to them and their goals."[25]

Unfortunately, "the current data access regime involves a mixture of informal credentials-based access agreements and formalized, token-based access agreements. This system is complicated to navigate for both consumers and third parties and often allows traditional financial institutions to impose their will regardless of consumer welfare."[26] These unnecessary levels of friction resulted in some FinTech companies playing fast and loose with consumer expectations, opting to "scrape" data from their banking screens in order to populate their apps.[27] Even though this was typically done to effectuate what the developers assumed was their customers' intent, it never involved actual notification to the consumer and consent, because it was done outside the managed lines of communication and contract. Just as the information blocking rules require electronic health records (EHR) companies to adopt open application programming interfaces (APIs), we also recommended that financial institutions enable safe, secure access—with appropriate data security and privacy guardrails—by customers to their own financial data via open APIs.

Having established the overwhelming policy interests in enabling consumers to access their own financial information and transfer it outside the GLBA umbrella, an equally important task is to ensure consumers continue to benefit from optimal privacy and security protections outside the scope of GLBA. The answer must be a federal, risk-based privacy framework.

IV. Family Educational Rights and Privacy Act (FERPA)

Scope of FERPA

FERPA's scope is not as narrow as it seems, and the gap it leaves is made smaller by the FTC's proactive approach. Similar to HIPAA and GLBA, FERPA also applies primarily to a specific class of entity—educational agencies and institutions—and a subset of personal information, "education records." The definition of education records, in turn, is tied to whether educational agencies or institutions are directing the processing or collection[28] and includes any information "directly related to a student." The two pillars of FERPA are 1) a requirement for schools allow parents access and review of their children's education records; and 2) a prohibition on schools from releasing students' education records without written consent of their parents, unless one

---

[25] *Id.* (citing AITE-NOVARICA, ALTERNATIVE DATA ACROSS THE LOAN LIFE CYCLE: HOW FINTECH AND OTHER LENDERS USE IT AND WHY, (2018), *available at* https://www.experian.com/assets/consumerinformation/reports/Experian_Aite_AltDataReport_Final_120418.pdf?elqTrackId=7714eff9f5204e7ca8517e8966438157&elqaid=3910&elqat=2; PWC, GLOBAL FINTECH REPORT 2019: CROSSING THE LINES HOW FINTECH IS PROPELLING FS AND TMT FIRMS OUT OF THEIR LANES, (2019), *available at* https://www.pwc.com/gx/en/industries/financial-services/assets/pwc-global-fintech-report- 2019.pdf).

[26] *Id.*

[27] Benjamin Pimentel, "Banks and fintechs agree: It's time for screen scraping to go. So what's next?" PROTOCOL (Oct. 5, 2021), *available at* https://www.protocol.com/fintech/fdx-financial-data.

[28] 20 U.S.C. Sec. 1232g(a)(4(A). Education records are materials that "contain information directly related to a student" and "are maintained by an educational agency or institution or by a person acting for such agency or institution."

of several exceptions apply.[29] Notably, FERPA's requirement to allow students' parents to access education records distinguishes it to some extent from other federal privacy silos and from state laws that apply adjacent to the federal laws. Observing shortcomings in the access requirements in GLBA and HIPAA, policymakers have sought to perfect the requirements in those contexts in ways that have not materialized as clearly under FERPA.

Notably, just as the HIPAA Privacy Rule refers to contractual entities working on behalf of CEs as BAs, the U.S. Department of Education's (ED's) rules promulgated under FERPA also create categories analogous to "business associate." The statutory provisions Congress enacted do not explicitly contemplate third-party companies providing digital education services using education records. However, schools routinely release education records to third-party education services companies—without incurring the requirement to obtain parental consent for disclosure—via the statutory exception allowing schools to provide such records to "school officials." ED's regulations spell out the relationship more concretely. To qualify for the school officials exception, schools must determine whether a third party "(1) performs an institutional service or function for which the agency or institution would otherwise use employees; (2) is under the direct control of the agency or institution with respect to the use and maintenance of education records; and (3) is subject to the requirements of Sec. 99.22(a) governing use and redisclosure of personally identifiable information from education records."[30]

The App Economy Is Thriving in Education Technology

Thinkamingo is an educational app company focused on getting kids excited about writing. Their app, Story Dice, helps give kids ideas for stories, while their apps Lists for Writers and Story Spark help kids lay out their story, build out their characters and plot points, and give them the tools they need to improve their overall writing and story structure. Through contracts with school districts, Thinkamingo provides these tools for students in the school context, which puts their activities under the scope of FERPA. But to the extent that the apps are available to kids and parents directly, COPPA and the FTC Act are the federal laws covering their privacy practices. Another member company, TORSH, provides a platform for teachers' professional development, enabling streamlined review, analysis, and management of classroom video clips.[31] The ability for schools to rely on digital tools like TORSH's is critical and increasingly important as we exit the pandemic.

COPPA Applies to Entities Subject to FERPA

It is difficult to address FERPA requirements without also covering the FTC Act and one of its subsections, COPPA, which regulates collection of PII about children under 13. There is no explicit carve-out from the FTC Act or COPPA for entities subject to FERPA. In fact, the FTC is adamant that COPPA applies readily to education technology companies, even when they are subject to FERPA via contractual relationships with schools.[32] However, COPPA rules do

---

[29] 20 U.S.C. Sec. 1232g(a)(1)(A); 20 U.S.C. Sec. 1232g(b)(1).

[30] 34 C.F.R. Sec. 99.31(a)(1)(i)(B).

[31] TORSH, POWER PACKED FEATURES DRIVE RESULTS, *available at* https://www.torsh.co/features/.

[32] Fed. Trade Comm'n, Policy Stmt. opf the Fed. Trade Comm'n on Education Tech. and the Children's Online Privacy Protection Act (May 19, 2022), *available at* https://www.ftc.gov/system/files/ftc_gov/pdf/Policy%20Statement%20of%20the%20Federal%20Trade%20Commission%20on%20Education%20Technology.pdf (FTC EdTech Policy Statement).

attempt to account for potential conflicts or incongruities between the two regimes. For example, COPPA's requirement for companies to obtain verifiable parental consent (VPC) prior to collecting PII from children does not apply "to the extent permitted under other provisions of law," (presumably, including FERPA's provisions).[33] This could lead to the two regimes applying slightly unevenly or confusingly, even though there might be good reasons for their overlapping structure, but the FTC has addressed the issue. Under FERPA, schools need not obtain parental consent for disclosing children's education records to educational apps on contract with the school. The FTC has clarified in a frequently asked questions (FAQ) section that an education technology company may rely on "consent obtained from the school under COPPA instead of the parent,"[34] when such collection is for the "use and benefit of the school and for no other commercial purpose."[35] Conversely, if the same children (if they are 12 or younger) sought to use the same educational apps outside the school context, the app must obtain VPC directly from those children's parents.[36] Thus, while the edges around sector-specific privacy laws may seem less regulated, in this case, more regulatory privacy barriers arguably exist under the FTC framework than under the sector-specific law.

The FTC's COPPA guidance for education technology companies emphasizes that students should not have to trade access to digital education services for their privacy.[37] This messaging addresses rapidly developing privacy concerns over the past three years, especially among parents, as the COVID-19 pandemic caused schools to move to a virtual model leaning heavily on digital tools. Parents worried that their children's mandatory use of those services would expose their children to undue privacy and data security risks, in an environment where no in-person alternative was available. Against this backdrop, the FTC sought to remind consumers and parents that the FTC Act—including COPPA—still applies to education technology companies. Most notably, the FTC reminded education technology companies that COPPA's prohibitions on 1) conditioning access to a service on a child disclosing more information than is reasonably necessary for the child to participate in an activity; 2) engaging in commercial activities like marketing, advertising, or other commercial activities unrelated to the provision of the school-requested service; 3) retaining PII about a child longer than reasonably necessary to fulfill the reason for which it was collected; and 4) failing to have procedures to maintain the confidentiality, security, and integrity of children's PII, *still apply* to education technology companies, even when they also comply with FERPA.

The FTC's and ED's separate jurisdiction over different kinds of entities help illustrate how they fit together. The FTC has jurisdiction over commercial entities—not schools—while ED has jurisdiction over schools receiving federal education funds. Thus, ED's enforcement mechanism is limited to punishing schools—not education technology companies directly—by withholding their federal education funds. Similarly, the FTC Act does not authorize the FTC to enjoin schools from activities that result in consumer harm related to privacy and security.

---

[33] 16 C.F.R. Sec. 312.5(c)(6)(iv).

[34] Fed. Trade Comm'n, Complying with COPPA: Frequently Asked Questions, N. COPPA AND SCHOOLS, Question N.1, (Jul. 2020), *available at* https://www.ftc.gov/business-guidance/resources/complying-coppa-frequently-asked-questions#N.%20COPPA%20AND%20SCHOOLS.

[35] *Id.*, at N.2.

[36] 15 U.S.C. Sec. 6501(9); Sec. 6502(b)(1)(A)(ii); 16 C.F.R. Sec. 312.5.

[37] FTC EdTech Policy Statement at 4, "Children should not have to needlessly hand over their data and forfeit their privacy in order to do their schoolwork or participate in remote learning, especially given the wide and increasing adoption of ed tech tools."

Where ED's jurisdictional limits suggest a gap in protections may exist, the FTC's guidance and policy statements make a strong case that federal privacy enforcers are holding education technology companies and schools accountable for privacy and security practices. Nonetheless, we have two suggestions as you consider updates to the FTC Act when it comes to children's and students' privacy:

1. Any amendments to or expansion of COPPA's protections to cover children up to 17 years old *should also modernize VPC requirements.* We have written extensively about the issues VPC present by shifting the onus for privacy protections to parents and consumers rather than companies providing services.[38] Expecting parents to provide credit card information, driver's license scans, or to call a 1-800 number to verify their identity for each online service with which their children interact is asking a great deal of today's parents. As the FTC itself has alluded to, parents now have little choice but to enable their children to make beneficial use of digital services. Requiring multiple redundant copies of their PII to exist in all corners of the internet their children may need to venture becomes a less workable concept with each passing day.
2. Any general consumer privacy legislation addressing kids' *privacy should avoid imposing age verification requirements or requirements that would require similar levels of data collection* to "verify" or "assure" a child's identity for age verification purposes. Similar to the issue described above, requiring detailed PII profiles on children to exist in multiple parts of the ecosystem with every company providing services a child may access introduces more serious privacy and security risks than are necessary. In fact, such requirements may conflict with other privacy provisions of a federal bill, especially those that apply to more sensitive classes of information like biometric indicators.[39] We also discussed this in testimony last year in the context of a privacy bill possibly moving COPPA to a "constructive knowledge" regime, which would require covered companies to compile much more granular profiles on children.[40]

V. Conclusion

Each of the federal privacy silos that exist today present unique challenges for this Subcommittee to consider as you continue to work on a comprehensive privacy bill. Although

---

[38] Letter from Morgan Reed, president, ACT | The App Association, to Hon. Maria Cantwell, chair, Senate Committee on Commerce, Science, and Transportation, and Hon. Ted Cruz, ranking member, Senate Committee on Commerce, Science, and Transportation, Re: Feedback/suggestions for improvement regarding the Kids Online Safety Act (KOSA) (S. 3663, 117th), *available at https://actonline.org/wpcontent/uploads/2023-03-01-ACT-KOSA-letter-Senate-Commerce-and-Sponsors-FINAL.pdf.*

[39] Eric Goldman, "Do Mandatory Age Verification Laws Conflict with Biometric Privacy Laws? – Kuklinski v. Binance," TECH. AND MARKETING L. BLOG, Apr. 8, 2023, *available at* https://blog.ericgoldman.org/archives/2023/04/do-mandatory-age-verification-laws-conflict-with-biometric-privacy-laws-kuklinski-v-binance.htm ("The invasiveness of [age verification] requirements could overwhelm and functionally moot most other efforts to protect consumer privacy").

[40] "Protecting America's Consumers: Bipartisan Legislation to Strengthen Data Privacy and Security," Hearing before the House of Representatives Committee on Energy and Commerce, Subcommittee on Consumer Protection and Commerce (comments of Graham Dufault, sr. dir. for public policy, ACT | The App Association).

COPPA applies to entities covered by FERPA, and the FTC Act overlays HIPAA, the sector-specific laws apply more narrowly than is often appreciated, causing gaps to appear wider than they are. As is often the case, the truth about activity around the federal privacy silos is both less shocking and more interesting than it appears at first glance.

These market activities happen to be some of the most important areas for consumers and job creation in the United States and are therefore worth preserving and strengthening with a federal data privacy and security law. We look forward to continuing to work with this Subcommittee on federal privacy reform in the 118th Congress.

Appendix: The App Economy in Your District

Majority

Chair: Bilirakis, FL-12

Since 2011, Tampa-based Thinkamingo is a husband-and-wife team working together to build family-friendly, education-focused mobile apps. Their apps range from interactive dice meant to take young writers to inspired storytellers to imagination-driven spy kits complete with virtual disguises, including a voice changer!

Vice Chair: Walberg, MI-05

Located in Jackson, Lean Rocket Lab is a coworking space and accelerator supporting businesses of all types by providing office space, education, mentorship, and pathways to funding for companies in a variety of industries. Their Manutech Incubator program and i4.0 Accelerators focus on startups creating devices and the software that powers them in manufacturing, transportation, data analytics, healthcare, and more.

Bucshon, IN-08

Located in Evansville and founded in 2016, anu is working to help people grow their own food through technology in order to create a more sustainable world and allow people to increase their food independence. With 11 employees, anu is building hydroponic farming systems that can grow anything from lettuce and other vegetables to any number of fruits or spices.

Duncan, SC-03

Topography Digital is a full-service software development company that focuses on providing services for small and medium-sized companies across industries looking to build or grow their digital presence or offerings. Their services include web and app development, drone programming, and cloud optimization.

Dunn, FL-02

TechFarms, founded in 2015 and located in Panama City Beach, has a singular mission: create a more technology-focused and vibrant entrepreneurial ecosystem in northwestern Florida. The team at TechFarms has created a collaborative coworking space for local business owners with the goal of lifting up the whole community.

Lesko, AZ-08

Founded in 2019, LiteraSeed is an early-stage digital health startup creating a visual way for patients to share their symptoms with their doctors. The product, called a "visual symptom report," focuses on helping those patients whose first language is not English and those with lower literacy levels to communicate with their doctors and better understand their medical records.

Pence, IN-06

Located in Muncie and founded in 1987, Accutech provides software solutions and services to those in the financial industry. Accutech's solutions include a wealth management platform, mobile applications that make opening an account easy, as well as a business intelligence dashboard.

Armstrong, ND-At Large

North Dakota-based Bushel built a digital ecosystem that powers APIs, apps, websites, and digital payment solutions to support agribusinesses and build digital infrastructure for the agriculture industry. Supporting more than 2,000 grain facilities with 40% grain origination in the United States and Canada, the Bushel platform strengthens relationships between grain processing facilities and farmers by enabling both to complete transactions quickly, safeguard important data, share information faster, and create a more complete picture of businesses.

Allen, GA-12

Zapata Technology is a veteran-owned Augusta-based cybersecurity company that provides critical cyber-secure infrastructure for the defense industry. Their products, offered globally, support persons in active duty with cybersecurity penetration testing, cloud computing and analytics, systems engineering and data integration, and custom software development.

Fulcher, ID-01

Located in Coer d'Alene, Chief Architect Software provides automated residential home design and interior decorating software for architects, builders, and designers. Through their suite of software products, industry professionals can create construction drawings and floor plans, get 3D renderings of interior spaces and elevations, and 360-degree panoramic renderings of whole buildings to better understand and craft design schemes unique to each building project.

Harshbarger, TN-01

Located in Kingsport, Code & Color is a digital marketing firm that offers software and design services and helps businesses grow through creative design. Their main services are clustered into marketing, design, websites, and mobile apps.

Cammack, FL-03

Founded in 2001, Atmosphere Apps is based in Gainesville and is a custom software development shop that works with clients through the design, development, maintenance, and integrations with other popular technologies. Atmosphere Apps also maintains their client's apps long after development ensuring the apps are always up to date with OS versions and compliance standards. While initially focused on clients in the health sector, Atmosphere is expanding its client base to include sales, media, and travel industries.

McMorris Rodgers, WA-05

Founded in 2017, Gestalt is a 31-person team working to bring healthcare into the 21st century by replacing microscopes and glass slides with automated, electronic, and digital workflows. They provide services related to pathology in the medical field to professionals as well as those in education or academic research from their HQ in Spokane.

Minority

Ranking Member: Schakowsky, IL-09

The one-woman team at Kidz Learn Applications has been developing iOS and Android mobile apps that provide educational content to children for the past decade. Kidz Learn Applications has developed over 20 apps with lessons ranging from math to vocabulary and even created a guide for educational, kid-friendly places in New York City for a day of fun for kids and adults alike.

Castor, FL-14

Located in Tampa nearly 200 employees, Accusoft, originally founded as Pegasus Imaging Corporation in 1991, focuses primarily on content processing through image and document cleanup while providing APIs and barcode collection through mobile apps. They also provide digital conversion tools that turn paper document and paper-based processes (often found in legal, financial, and health transactions) into customized digital processes based on each client's unique needs.

Dingell, MI-06

Founded in 2017 and headquartered in Kalamazoo, with two other offices in the state, SPARK Business Works is a custom software development and design firm. They help businesses of any size create an effective online presence that aims to improve each client's unique needs for the connected customer experience.

Kelly, IL-02

Based in Kankakee and founded in 2020, Pathfinder is a full-service creative marketing agency that helps their clients tell stories through web and mobile solutions. With 24 currently employed, their offerings include web development, graphic design, photography, and other digital marketing offerings.

Blunt Rochester, DE

Located in Wilmington, MightyCall is a cloud-based communications and customer service platform founded in 2013. Their virtual phone system is designed specifically for small businesses and remote teams making it easy for teams to connect from anywhere through mobile and desktop apps. Their apps provide unique features like call availability windows, scheduling services, and the ability to mask personal cell numbers, given that privacy is a core pillar of MightyCall's service.

Soto, FL-09

Originally founded as "Yelling Across Cubicles"—because it was essentially built as a digital walkie-talkie to be used in the workplace—Yac was founded in 2019 in Kissimmee. Since then, Yac has grown to include other functionalities including asynchronous meetings, voice messages, screen sharing and shareable links, all focused on making remote work more collaborative.

Trahan, MA-03

Founded in 1997 and located in Maynard, Fisheye Software focuses on building enterprise-level software that makes complex systems easier to understand. They provide services to a number of clients, both in the government and commercial systems, contributing to anything from data archiving to air traffic control or missile defense systems.

Clarke, NY-09

Since Stellar Health's founding in 2018, this Manhattan-based healthcare technology company has rapidly grown to over 200 employees and is providing connected health solutions to patients everywhere. Stellar Health helps deliver providers targeted recommendations to enable "value-based" improvements to care and financial performance to hospitals. This means that through Stellar Health's services, patients receive care faster and at a lower cost throughout the care chain.

Pallone, NJ-06

DealerApp Vantage, located in Piscataway, is the nation's leading native mobile app development company that specializes in automotive dealers. They have mobile app solutions aimed to fit all budgets and sizes, from small, single rooftop dealerships to some of the largest auto groups in the United States.

* * *

Mr. BILIRAKIS. Thank you. Thank you very much.

Our next witness is Donald Codling, senior advisor for cybersecurity and privacy for REGO, the REGO Payment Architectures.

You are recognized, sir, for 5 minutes.

Statement of Donald Codling

Mr. CODLING. Commerce Committee Chair McRodgers, Ranking Member Pallone, Subcommittee Chair Bilirakis and Ranking Member Schakowsky, and members of the subcommittee, thank you for inviting me to testify. My name is Donald Codling, and I am the senior advisor for cybersecurity and privacy.

For over 23 years, I worked in the FBI in various investigative programs focusing on international cyber crime and national cybersecurity operations. These programs particularly emphasize cybersecurity challenges that impact the global financial services, energy, and healthcare industries. I also served as the FBI's chairman of an international cyber crime working group that consisted of the heads of cyber investigative departments of Australia, Canada, New Zealand, the United Kingdom, and the United States. My experience in cybersecurity and the FBI have taught me to identify areas of cyber risk and assess its threats.

What we are now experiencing in the financial industry is the convergence of several trends that, though individually benign, will collectively cause unnecessary harm to our Nation's children.

The first trend is the rapid adoption of mobile devices by children under the age of 18. According to Statista, 97 percent of households with children under the age of 8 either have a smartphone or tablet that the children use exclusively.

Secondly, according to a report by Mastercard, the COVID–19 pandemic doubled consumer adoption of cashless payments.

Finally, the purchasing power of the under-18 demographic has significantly increased in recent years. The National Retail Federation reports that children influence 87 percent of a family's purchases, and preteens are spending their own money at over twice the volume compared to 10 years ago. Businesses know the enormous potential of the under-18 market. Yet this perfect storm of financial and technology trends is worsened because Federal laws and regulations have not kept up with the advent of a cashless society.

It is true that the Children's Online Privacy Protection Act of 1998 makes it unlawful for online companies to collect the personal information of children under 13. This is an opt-in process, while the parent must actively engage and agree to that data collection.

However, most fintech companies that provide financial services products to children adhere to the privacy protections of the Gramm-Leach-Bliley Act of 1999. Under GLBA, companies must offer an opt-out option for nonaffiliate data sharing.

But there is no opt-out option for affiliate sharing. This means the default setting for these websites and financial apps allows for the collecting and sharing of data between the ages of 13 and 17 for children with nonaffiliated third parties, unless the parent proactively opts out. In fact, there is often no ability for the parents to opt out of sharing of their children's financial transactions between affiliated companies.

Keep in mind that, according to a report by Superawesome, a London-based child privacy firm, by the age of 13, mobile applications have collected over 72 million data points from just one child. Though Federal laws are currently not adequate to make it unlawful for such behavior, it must be the responsibility of companies to take steps to protect our children's privacy. I am proud to be an advisor for REGO, who has developed the only certified COPPA and third-party GDPR-compliant financial platform for families and children of all ages. REGO is designed to be implemented as a white label offering for banks and credit unions, giving them the ability to provide a secure family banking platform that is fully integrated with their bank's brands and systems.

Since its inception in 2008, the core of REGO was built around the concept of data minimization, where the only information collected for children under 17 is the date of birth. That is it. REGO has created a family digital wallet experience that cannot function without the explicit consent and approval of the parent. This includes requiring parental approval for others to deposit money into the child's account or restricting children to purchase items only from parental-approved vendors, critical security features that many popular mobile payment apps do not have but should.

In my experience, no other financial technology company has child data and privacy protections so integrated into its foundational strategy except REGO. On behalf of REGO, we support the enactment of strong, comprehensive, and bipartisan Federal privacy legislation like ADPPA that includes strong data minimization and the data security standards and will update privacy laws to protect children. We believe that REGO is a perfect example of how you can create innovative fintech products and services that incorporate ADPPA standards and treat your users as customers instead of as products.

Thank you very much for giving us the opportunity to participate today. I look forward to your questions. Thank you.

[The prepared statement of Mr. Codling follows:]

U.S. House of Representatives Committee on Energy & Commerce, Subcommittee on Innovation, Data, and Commerce, Hearing on Addressing America's Data Privacy Shortfalls: How a National Standard Fills Gaps to Protect Americans' Personal Information," Prepared Testimony of Donald Codling, Rego Architectures, Inc. Senior Advisor for Cybersecurity & Privacy, April 27, 2023

Commerce Committee Chair McMorris Rodgers, Ranking Member Pallone, Subcommittee Chair Bilirakis, Ranking Member Schakowsky, and Members of the Subcommittee.

Thank you for inviting me to testify. My name is Donald Codling, and I am a Senior Advisor to Rego Payment Architectures, Inc. ("REGO") for Cybersecurity and Privacy. For over 23 years, I worked in the FBI in various investigative programs focusing on International Cyber Crime and Cyber National Security Operations. These programs particularly emphasized cybersecurity challenges that impact the global financial services, energy, and healthcare industries. I was the principal liaison officer to DHS US-CERT and ICSCERT for the FBI and was the lead supervisor for the Cyberstorm II and III national cyber exercises. I also served as the FBI's chairman of an international cybercrime working group consisting of the heads of Cyber Investigative Departments in Australia, Canada, New Zealand, the United Kingdom, and the United States.

Currently, I work as a CISO or CPO advisor to various FinTech companies, such as REGO. Using my experience in cybercrime, I advise companies' employees and Executive Management staff to craft a comprehensive cybersecurity and data privacy digital platform, combining core cyber hygiene, cyber threat intelligence, social media, and data privacy compliance tools.

My experience in cybersecurity and the FBI have taught me to identify areas of cyber risk and assess its threat. What we are experiencing now in the financial industry is the convergence of several trends that, though individually benign, will collectively cause unnecessary harm to our nation's children. The first trend is the rapid adoption of mobile devices by children under the age of 18. According to Statista, 97% of children under the age of 8 have either a smartphone or tablet they use exclusively. This is up from 41% in 2011. Secondly, the COVID-19 pandemic doubled consumer adoption of cashless payments, according to a report by Mastercard, citing 79% of survey respondents prefer contactless payments post-pandemic. Finally, the purchasing power of the under-18 demographic has significantly increased in recent years. According to a report by the National Retail Federation, 87% of a family's purchases are influenced by their children. In the same report, pre-teens are reported to spend their own money at over twice the volume as they did 10 years ago. Retailers, advertisers, and fintech companies know that the under-18 market is big business. However, what has not been in place is the legal framework to incentivize kids' privacy by design in the financial industry.

This "perfect storm" of financial and technology trends is exacerbated by the fact that federal laws and regulations have not kept up with the advent of a cashless society. It is true that the Children's Online Privacy Protection Act of 1998 (COPPA) makes it unlawful for online companies to collect and share the personal information of children under 13 without a parent's consent. This is an opt-in process, where the parent must actively agree to such data collection and sharing. However, most fintech companies that provide financial service products to children adhere to the privacy protections of the Gramm-Leach-Bliley Act of 1999 (GLBA). Under GLBA, companies must offer an opt-out option for *non-affiliate* data sharing, but there is no opt-out for *affiliate* sharing. This means the default setting for these websites and financial apps allows for collecting and sharing data of children 13-17 with non-affiliated third parties unless the parent proactively opts out. Of even greater concern, there is no ability for parents to opt out of the sharing of their child's financial transactions between affiliated companies.

How much data is being collected? According to a report by SuperAwesome, a London-based company that helps app developers navigate child-privacy laws, by the time a child reaches age 13, mobile apps have collected over 72 million data points from that one individual. What kind of data? Names, birth dates, email addresses, GPS location history, purchase history, likes, dislikes, behavioral profiles and more – all designed to deliver targeted ads – all without the parent's consent.

Though federal laws are currently not adequate to make it unlawful for such behavior, it must be the responsibility of companies to take steps to protect our children's privacy. I'm proud to be an advisor for REGO, who has developed the only certified COPPA and third-party GDPR compliant financial platform for families and children of all ages. Since its inception in 2008, REGO has invested millions of dollars to build the technological framework that not only protects and safeguards the data and privacy of kids, but a family digital wallet experience that cannot function without the explicit consent and approval of the parent. The core of REGO was built around the concept of data minimization, where the only information collected for children under 17 is date of birth, and only because the app stores of Google and Apple require it. Strict parental controls are applied to every aspect of the REGO experience, such as requiring parental approval for others to deposit money into their child's account or restricting kids to purchase items from only parent-approved vendors – critical security features that popular mobile payment apps do not have but should.

REGO was primarily designed as a white label offering for banks and credit unions, giving them the ability to provide a secure family banking platform that is fully branded and integrated into the financial institution. Through partnerships with banking core and technology providers, banks and credit unions can now more easily offer parents useful financial literacy tools with the comfort of knowing their children's data is not being collected or shared. Individual users can experience REGO by downloading Mazoola, an award-winning family digital wallet app that was built on the certified COPPA and third-party GDPR compliant platform.

In my experience, no other financial technology platform has child data and privacy protection so integrated in its core offering than REGO. That is only the result of over a decade of development, and a deliberate strategy to offer the most secure product regardless of the regulatory environment.

For these reasons, I am pleased to see recent bipartisan efforts to improve our nation's stance on protecting the data privacy of Americans, including our children. During her opening statements at the House Committee on Energy and Commerce on April 19, 2023, Chair Cathy McMorris Rodgers stated, "The American Data Privacy and Protection Act included the strongest internet protections for children of any legislation last Congress."

Ranking Member Jan Schakowsky, in the same hearing, added, "Most Americans worry about their data privacy and are concerned it is not being protected. I wanted to call attention to the American Data Privacy and Protection Act in which we say that we would require all data brokers to register…and with one push of a button, you can take yourself out."

Representative Kathy Castor remarked that, "The U.S. has fallen too far behind in prioritizing the protection of all people online, but especially young people. Because we do not have a national data privacy standard, we are currently stuck with this patchwork of state laws and narrow protections that leave a wide swath of our neighbors vulnerable to privacy abuses, including by data brokers."

I testify today, on behalf of REGO, regarding the importance of Congress passing comprehensive federal privacy legislation that will include updating privacy laws to protect children of all ages and in all circumstances. We support legislation that provides greater transparency to how our data is being used and the ability to control how that data is shared. Most importantly, we support legislation that provides a legal incentive and framework for companies to incorporate the kind of critical data protection processes and technologies to safeguard our children's data, especially as more young Americans are becoming active in the consumer marketplace at an earlier age. It was the sole purpose of protecting children's financial data and privacy that led to the creation of REGO. We sincerely hope to serve as an example of what can and should be done. We urge other companies to join us in our commitment to preserve the future safety of America's children.

Thank you again for giving me the opportunity to participate today. I look forward to your questions.

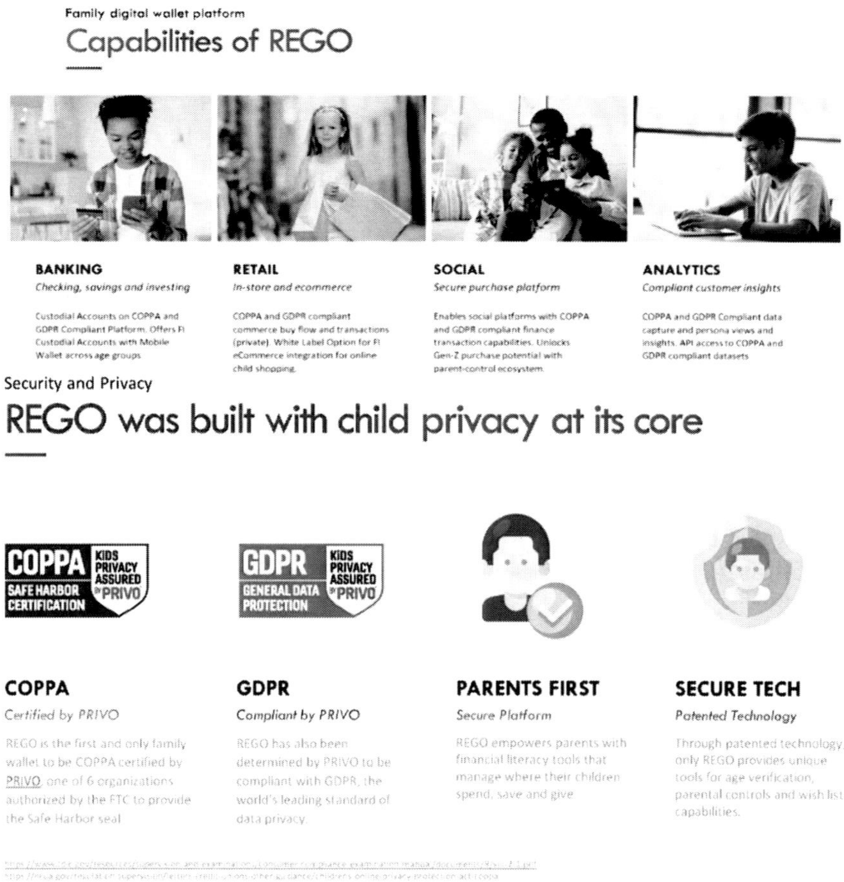

* * *

Mr. BILIRAKIS. Thank you. Next we have a witness, Edward Britan, from the head of global privacy for Salesforce.

You are recognized, sir, for 5 minutes.

Statement of Edward Britan

Mr. BRITAN. Thank you. Chairman Bilirakis, Ranking Member Schakowsky, and members of the subcommittee, my name is Ed Britan. I lead Salesforce's global privacy team, a team of professionals located across the U.S., Europe, and Asia Pacific regions. Thank you for this opportunity to testify. It is a privilege to be here today.

I am passionate about privacy and the urgent need for a comprehensive U.S. Federal privacy law. I have spent almost two decades focused on helping companies comply with global privacy and data protection laws, including roughly 2 years at Salesforce, 7 years at Microsoft, and 7 years helping a range of companies at Alston and Bird.

Global privacy laws have changed significantly during my career, with a particular inflection point being effectuation of the EU General Data Protection Regulation, GDPR, in May of 2018. Since then, comprehensive privacy laws frequently modeled on GDPR have passed all over the world. The U.S. is now one of the few developed nations lacking a comprehensive privacy law. The UK, Japan, Brazil, Kenya, and Thailand have all passed comprehensive privacy laws since the GDPR went into effect.

This is not to say that the U.S. has never been a thought leader in this space. In fact, the core concepts in GDPR and most other global privacy laws build upon ideas first introduced in 1973 in a report published by the Department of Health, Education, and Welfare, the HEW Report.

The HEW Report introduced rights to access, delete, and correct personal information, the data minimization inaccuracy principles, and restrictions on automated decision making. Further, it called for these concepts to be included in comprehensive Federal privacy legislation. Had the U.S. taken that action, our industry, a crucial driver of global innovation and economic growth, might not be facing the current crisis of trust that led our CEO, Marc Benioff, to call for a comprehensive Federal privacy law beginning in 2018.

But it is not too late for Congress to act. The world has advanced the concepts that the U.S. first introduced. Now, as we approach the 15th anniversary of the HEW Report, the U.S. can reassert its leadership by passing a comprehensive Federal law that builds on the current global standard and advances global privacy law for the next 50 years and beyond.

So why do we need a comprehensive Federal privacy law, and what should that law look like?

We need a Federal privacy law because privacy is a fundamental human right. It is also essential for preserving other human rights, such as life, liberty, speech, and freedom from discrimination. Polls show that a majority of Americans, regardless of political affiliation, strongly favor increased legal protections governing companies' use of personal information.

The right to privacy cannot be sufficiently protected by the current sectoral approach at the Federal level or by the individual State laws. The current U.S. sectoral laws are effective and influential, but they are not sufficient. Without comprehensive legislation, there are significant gaps in protection. For example, the Health Insurance Portability and Accountability Act, HIPAA, effectively protects data related to health conditions and provision of healthcare held—data held by providers and health plans. HIPAA fails, however, to cover health-related data that may be collected by noncovered entities such as through connected devices and online services that monitor and improve health and fitness.

States have sought to fill the national gap in privacy protection by passing comprehensive privacy laws of their own. Salesforce welcomes this development. These State-led efforts, which have taken place in red States and blue States, are important and demonstrate the need and demand for comprehensive privacy law.

However, one's level of privacy should not depend on their ZIP Code. Congress should be inspired to build upon these State-led efforts in setting a national standard which ensures that these privacy protections are held by all Americans. That Federal law should address core privacy principles, including transparency, individual control, data minimization, security, individual rights of access, correction and deletion, risk management, and accountability.

More specifically, the Federal law should include enhanced protections for sensitive data, children's data, mandatory data impact, and algorithmic assessments, prohibitions on using personal information to discriminate, the controller processor distinction, and restrictions on third-party targeted advertising.

Congress has made great strides toward passing a comprehensive Federal privacy law. Last year this committee passed the American Data Privacy Protection Act, ADPPA, by a resoundingly bipartisan vote of 53 to 2. While there are undoubtedly aspects of ADPPA that every stakeholder would like to change, ADPPA reflected a hard-fought compromise that would meaningfully protect privacy, increase trust in industry, and position the U.S. as a world leader on tech issues.

Salesforce welcomes the role of regulators in shaping responsible innovation. Presently, the world is looking to EU regulators and GDPR to write the rules of the road for emerging technologies like generative AI. With ADPPA, the U.S. has proposed important ideas that should be part of the global conversation.

The path to providing world-leading privacy protections for all Americans is clear. Now is the time for Congress to pass a comprehensive privacy law that builds upon the existing global standard and reasserts U.S. leadership on privacy and data protection. Thank you.

[The prepared statement of Mr. Britan follows:]

Written Testimony of Edward Britan, Vice President, Associate General Counsel, and Head of the Salesforce Global Privacy Team, Salesforce, Inc., before the House Energy & Commerce Subcommittee on Innovation, Data, and Commerce, Addressing America's Data Privacy Shortfalls: How a National Standard Fills Gaps to Protect Americans' Personal Information, April 27, 2023

I. Introduction

Chairman Bilirakis, Ranking Member Schakowsky, and members of the Subcommittee, thank you for providing me the opportunity to share my views on addressing gaps in U.S. privacy law through comprehensive federal privacy legislation. Comprehensive federal regulation of personal information is urgently needed to protect individuals, empower businesses, and advance responsible innovation.

My name is Ed Britan. I lead Salesforce's Global Privacy Team, a team of professionals located across the U.S., Europe, and Asia-Pacific regions. I have spent almost two decades focused on helping companies comply with global privacy and data protection laws, including the past two years at Salesforce, the seven years before that at Microsoft, and the previous seven years helping a range of companies as a lawyer at Alston & Bird, LLP.

U.S. Leadership in Privacy

Global privacy laws have changed significantly during my career, with a particular inflection point being effectuation of the EU General Data Protection Regulation (GDPR) in May 2018.[41] Since then, comprehensive privacy laws, frequently modeled on GDPR, have passed all over the world. The U.S. is now one of the few developed countries lacking a comprehensive national privacy law. The UK, Japan, Brazil, China, Kenya, and Thailand have all passed comprehensive privacy laws since GDPR went into effect.

---

[41] Regulation (EU) 2016/679 of the European Parliament and the Council of 27 April 2016 on the protection of natural persons with regard to the processing of personal data and on the free movement of such data, and repealing 95/46/EC (General Data Protection Regulation).

This is disappointing because the U.S. had been a thought leader in this space. In fact, the core concepts in GDPR and most other global privacy laws build upon ideas introduced in a 1973 report published by the U.S. Department of Health, Education and Welfare (the "HEW Report").[42] The HEW report introduced rights to access, delete and correct data, the data minimization and accuracy principles, and restrictions on automated decision-making. Further, it called for these concepts to be included in comprehensive federal privacy legislation. Had the U.S. taken that action, our industry, a crucial driver of global innovation and economic growth, might not be facing the current "crisis of trust" that led our CEO Marc Benioff to call for a comprehensive federal privacy law beginning in 2018.[43] But it is not too late for Congress to act. The world has advanced the concepts that the U.S. first introduced. Now, as we approach the 50th anniversary of the HEW report, the U.S. can reassert its leadership by passing a comprehensive federal law that builds on the current global standard and advances global privacy law for the next 50 years and beyond.

I am honored to have this opportunity to share with you the importance of passing a comprehensive federal privacy law and the features and concerns that such a law should address.

II. Why We Need a Comprehensive Federal Privacy Law

Salesforce Perspective

Salesforce is a cloud computing company offering customer relationship management (CRM) and other business-focused software to businesses, governments, non-profits, and other organizations around the world. Our online and mobile services help our customers connect with their customers, being consumers, employees or citizens. Our customers use our services to work with some of their most sensitive data, which is why trust has been our number one value since our founding almost 25 years ago. A loss of that trust would jeopardize our ability to continue innovating and remain competitive. Therefore, Salesforce is committed to continuously proving to our customers that we are trustworthy custodians of their data.

To that end, we have developed a comprehensive privacy and data protection program that accounts for the ever-evolving landscape of global data protection laws. But we do not stop there. We also build our products using privacy by design principles and educate our customers regarding how they can use our products responsibly.

Privacy Is a Fundamental Human Right

Beyond the business imperative, Salesforce recognizes privacy as a fundamental human right that is crucial to upholding other rights, such as freedom of life, liberty, speech and protection against discrimination. To this end, we apply legal requirements that further the fundamental right to privacy, including from GDPR and other laws, globally. For us, protecting privacy is not merely a business strategy, but a moral responsibility. We urge Congress to help fulfill this

[42] U.S. Dep't of Health, Education and Welfare, Secretary's Advisory Committee on Automated Personal Data Systems, *Records, Computers, and the Rights of Citizens* viii (1973), https://www.justice.gov/opcl/docs/rec-com-rights.pdf.

[43] Marc Benioff, Time for Silicon Valley to Get Behind a National Privacy Law, Politico (June 19, 2018), https://www.politico.com/agenda/story/2018/06/19/silicon-valley-national-privacy-law-000679.

responsibility by passing a comprehensive privacy law in the U.S. that applies to all Americans in all contexts.

Americans Are Demanding Privacy Protection Louder Than Ever

Americans want the government to hold companies accountable for how they process their personal information. This is borne out in a recent KPMG study in which 90% of respondents indicate that government has a role to play in ensuring accountability.[44] Further, this belief does not seem to vary significantly according to political party, as a recent Pew Research Center study indicates that a majority of Americans – regardless of political affiliation – strongly favor increased legal protections governing companies' use of their personal information.[45]

A Broad Federal Privacy Law Should Support Existing Sectoral Laws

The U.S. has not yet taken the same comprehensive approach to privacy as was recommended by the HEW report and effectuated with GDPR. Rather, privacy protection in the U.S. is sectoral and driven by issue-specific laws at the federal level. However, while U.S. law regulates privacy differently from the EU, these U.S. sectoral laws are also effective and influential. What is missing is comprehensive regulation of personal information that should support these sectoral laws.

Without such comprehensive rules there will be significant gaps in protection. For instance, the Health Insurance Portability and Accountability Act (HIPAA) protects data related to a physical or mental health condition, provision of health care, or payment, as processed by certain entities, including health care providers, health plans and health care clearinghouses. This excludes a vast amount of health-related data processed by non-covered entities, such as through connected devices and online services designed to monitor and improve health and fitness. A law carrying forward concepts from GDPR and recently-passed state laws would strictly regulate this data and the companies that process it.

Similarly, while the Fair Credit Reporting Act (FCRA) effectively regulates consumer reporting agencies that furnish consumer reports, it does not cover similar types of profiling conducted by other companies for other purposes such as delivering personalized content or conducting e-commerce. Such profiles could be used in ways that impact an individual's reputation and privacy and should also be regulated.

Following passage of GDPR in 2018, the states have been filling this gap in U.S. privacy law by passing comprehensive laws of their own. California was the first state to take such action with the California Consumer Privacy Act of 2018 (CCPA). Since then, comprehensive privacy laws have also been passed in Virginia, Colorado, Connecticut, Montana, Utah, Iowa, Indiana, and Tennessee. While CCPA focused on restrictions around sharing personal information with third parties, the eight states that have subsequently passed laws, as well as a subsequent California law amending CCPA, the California Consumer Privacy Rights Act (CPRA), more closely adhere to the global standard set into motion by the HEW report and effectuated with GDPR.

---

44 KPMG LLP, The new imperative for corporate data responsibility (2020), https://advisory.kpmg.us/content/dam/advisory/en/pdfs/2020/consumer-data-report-kpmg.pdf.

45 Pew Research Center, *Americans and Privacy: Concerned and Feeling Lack of Control Over Their Personal Information* (Nov. 15, 2019), https://www.pewresearch.org/internet/2019/11/15/americans-and-privacy-concerned-confused-and-feeling-lack-of-control-over-their-personal-information/.

Salesforce welcomes the passage of strong comprehensive privacy laws at the state level. These state-level efforts are important, as they demonstrate the need and demand for comprehensive privacy law. However, one's level of privacy should not depend on a ZIP code. Congress should be inspired to build upon these state-led efforts in setting a national standard which ensures that these privacy protections apply to all Americans.

III. What a Comprehensive Federal Privacy Law Should Address

Sensitive Data

The broad regulation of personal information should include enhanced protections for specific types of sensitive data, such as data related to race, gender, ethnicity, religion, disability, and health-related data not governed by HIPAA. Such regulation would be directly beneficial for promoting equality and civil rights by forcing companies to proactively identify, evaluate, and counter potential discriminatory impacts.

Emerging Technology – Mandatory Assessment

Salesforce has publicly raised concerns that certain types of technology, like facial recognition, currently pose a high risk of harm and discriminatory impacts, particularly for underserved communities. Because of these concerns, we don't offer facial recognition capabilities in our products.[46] But we continue to engage with these emerging technologies and have established guidelines for the responsible and ethical development of generative AI, which we're committed to following as the technology continues to advance.[47]

We believe that thoughtful regulation can enable development of appropriate safeguards that allow companies to responsibly innovate and unlock the economic and growth opportunities for themselves and for all Americans. In particular, we believe there's substantial value in performing data impact assessments and/or algorithmic impact assessments, as proposed under the American Data Privacy and Protection Act (ADPPA), when there's a high potential or risk of harm. We know that data sets used to train AI models are often discriminatory, and that unfortunately, discriminatory training data will yield discriminatory model outputs. To counter this, U.S. law should mandate that companies undertake assessments to purposefully and proactively identify and analyze data sets and how they will be used as a means to counter any latent discrimination or bias that may exist in the data.

Core Privacy Principles and Civil Rights

Salesforce strongly supports U.S. adoption of the core principles that underlie most global privacy laws, including GDPR. These principles, which were highlighted in the National Telecommunications and Information Administration's 2018 request for comments,[48] include

---

[46] Salesforce, Why We've Never Offered Facial Recognition (June 15, 2020), https://www.salesforce.com/news/stories/why-weve-never-offered-facial-recognition/.

[47] Paula Goldman, Generative AI: 5 Guidelines for Responsible Development, Salesforce (February 7, 2023), https://www.salesforce.com/news/stories/generative-ai-guidelines/.

[48] Notice and Request for Comments, Developing the Administration's Approach to Consumer Privacy, 83 Fed. Reg. 48,600 (Sept. 26, 2018) ("RFC").

transparency, control, data minimization, security, individual rights of access, correction, and deletion, risk management, and accountability.

Additionally, we believe that comprehensive federal privacy legislation should include provisions prohibiting the use of personal information to discriminate on the basis of protected characteristics. So we strongly supported inclusion in the ADPPA of "the first significant, nationwide expansion of civil rights protection in over a decade"[49] and would hope to see such protections included in future privacy legislation.

Controller/Processor Distinction

It is a current best practice in global data protection laws and regulations to make important distinctions between companies that decide how and why to collect and process personal data, who act as controllers of that data, and companies that provide services and process data on behalf of controllers, who act as processors of the data.[50] These distinctions date back 40 years and have been enshrined in GDPR and other leading data protection laws and regulations around the globe.[51] They are also reflected in the ADPPA, which recognizes that companies have different responsibilities when operating in different capacities. When companies focus on their role in handling personal data about individuals, they can more effectively identify and implement controls to help protect the privacy of those individuals.

In most global data protection frameworks, controllers and processors each have equally important obligations to ensure consumers' privacy. Controllers determine the purpose and means for collecting and using data, so they have direct responsibilities to consumers. For example, controllers are expected to disclose how they will use the data they collect and how long they will retain the data, and promptly respond to consumer requests to access or delete their personal information. Processors provide services to controllers under legal and contractual obligations that require them to only handle data at the specific direction of the controller, protect the data with adequate security measures, and allow controllers to meet their direct obligations.

For example, processors are contractually obligated to provide functionality within their services that enable controllers to honor consumer requests to access or delete their personal information. When Salesforce provides our software to our customers, we operate as a data processor, handling customer data on behalf of and pursuant to the instructions of those customers.

Encouraging Utilization of First Party Data

Companies shouldn't rely on third-party ad tech companies and third-party cookies to learn about their customers. Rather, we believe utilizing first party data obtained directly from customers is the best approach for customer engagement because this data exchange is known and expected by the customer, opens up the possibility for direct communication, and allows

---

[49] Bertram Lee, Federal privacy legislation the protects civil rights is critical for all Americans, The Hill (July 21, 2022), https://thehill.com/opinion/congress-blog/3568525-federal-privacy-legislation-that-protects-civil-rights-is-critical-for-all-americans/.

[50] Kate Goodloe, Why the Controller-Processor Distinction Matters to Privacy, Business Software Alliance (November 8, 2022), https://techpost.bsa.org/2022/11/08/why-the-controller-processor-distinction-matters-to-privacy/.

[51] Business Software Alliance, Controllers and Processors: A Longstanding Distinction in Privacy (October 12, 2022), https://www.bsa.org/policy-filings/controllers-and-processors-a-longstanding-distinction-in-privacy.

companies to build trusted relationships with customers through effective and transparent personalization. For example, marketers and salespeople can use a unified view of their first party data to honor an individual's contact preferences across internal systems and give the individual easy-to-use controls to manage and update their preferences. Customer success departments (who help customers implement and get the most out of their purchases) can be aware of recent purchases and tailor their support accordingly. Business departments can recognize what a person likes about a product to provide a personalized experience or enable internal development teams to determine what new features to prioritize.

Companies have more data than ever, and it's imperative that they're able to integrate it, analyze it, and understand it in a trusted and secure way. In an environment where a majority of individuals feel like they've lost control over how their data is used but still expect personalized experiences and engagement, these intentional first party interactions can build trust by delivering relevant, personalized interactions to individuals who have chosen to share their data. For example, individuals should be empowered to provide companies with clear instructions on how their data can be shared and used to create a better customer experience.

U.S. law should encourage these sorts of first party engagements. Such an approach is inline with global regulatory trends and market changes and would help to decrease reliance on less privacy protective third-party tracking techniques. It also allows consumers to more easily and effectively exercise their individual privacy rights. If consumers understand which companies process their data and how it will be used, they know who to contact to exercise their rights in a meaningful way.

IV. Conclusion

Congress has made great strides toward passing a comprehensive federal privacy law. Last year, this committee passed ADPPA by a resoundingly bipartisan vote of 53-2. While there are undoubtedly aspects of ADPPA that every stakeholder would like to change, ADPPA reflected a hard-fought compromise that would meaningfully protect privacy, increase trust in industry, and position the U.S. as a world leader on tech issues.

ADPPA not only lines up well against the global standard envisioned first by the US with the HEW report and effectuated by GDPR, but it would return the U.S. to its global leadership role, especially on impactful issues like algorithmic impact assessment, application of civil rights to data protection, and restriction of third-party targeted advertising.

Thanks to decades of work and the significant advancements made last Congress, the path to providing world-leading privacy protections for all Americans is clear. Now is the time for Congress to pass a comprehensive privacy law that builds upon the existing global standard and reasserts U.S. leadership on privacy and data protection.

* * *

Mr. BILIRAKIS. And last but not least, certainly not least, Amelia Vance from the founder and president of the Public Interest Privacy Center.

You are recognized for 5 minutes. Thank you.

Statement of Amelia Vance

Ms. VANCE. Chair Bilirakis, Ranking Member Schakowsky, Chair McMorris Rodgers, Ranking Member Pallone, and members of the subcommittee, thank you for inviting me to testify on the need for better child and student privacy protections.

My name is Amelia Vance, and I am president of the Public Interest Privacy Center; chief counsel of the Student and Child Privacy Center at AASA, the School Superintendents Association; and an adjunct professor teaching privacy law at William and Mary Law School. For the last decade I have focused exclusively in my career on child and student privacy.

Children require exceptional privacy protections. They are not yet equipped to weigh the potential benefits and risks of data collection and use. Gaps in Federal laws and a patchwork of State laws mean privacy protections for kids and students are outdated and confusing. Even when clear, these protections contain numerous loopholes that leave children unprotected from companies, predators, and other threats that endanger their health, support systems, and social development, and future opportunities.

Congress should enact baseline Federal privacy protections for all consumers that include additional protections for children and students that recognize children's unique vulnerabilities. Without proper privacy safeguards, children's lives and futures could be irreparably harmed.

I would like to focus my testimony today on a few key points: first, existing Federal law does not adequately protect children and students online; second, efforts by States has—have primarily created confusion and hampered efforts by schools, districts, and parents to protect kids online; and third, baseline consumer privacy law with special protections for children would be a meaningful step forward to protect kids online.

As discussed in the opening statements, two major Federal laws provide the bulk of privacy protections for children and students online: the Children's Online Privacy Protection Act, COPPA, and the Family Educational Rights and Privacy Act, FERPA. However, both of these have significant gaps that fail to provide children and students with the protections they deserve.

For instance, COPPA only applies when apps or websites collect data directly from children under 13. It does not protect children when websites or data brokers collect information about them. Even more concerning, most of COPPA's limited protections can be easily waived by one click of parental consent.

FERPA only directly regulates schools, not EdTech companies, saddling schools and educators with the burden of policing large companies and corporate data practices. This is an enormous problem, especially since those school vendors are responsible for more than half of student data breaches.

FERPA also only protects student information when EdTech is used in the classroom. The minute that a child goes home and stops using that app for homework, or the teacher suggesting it, FERPA protections go away and companies have free rein.

These are serious shortcomings in Federal law created in large part by lightning-fast growth in tech. Recognizing some of these issues, States have introduced and passed child, teen, and student privacy protections at an astounding rate. But even when these laws have been successful and have not created confusion, we are still left with a legal landscape riddled with far more gaps than many people realize. We need updated Federal data privacy protections.

ADPPA is a strong and important step forward. But when addressing general consumer privacy protections, it is critical to remember children are uniquely vulnerable to certain harms, and we must create meaningful protections to safeguard them. We have all seen recent headlines of dire consequences of insufficient privacy protections. For example, student information including detailed mental health and sexual assault records was posted online after a Minneapolis school district was hacked. The lives of these students are forever changed, and the worst moment of their lives may follow them every time someone Googles their name.

While increasing data security is one method, new protections must also minimize the data that is collected in the first place and ensure data is deleted when it is no longer necessary. Action to address these harms must be balanced with the real benefits that technology can provide to children learning and social connection. However, we need to make sure that those protections are rooted in a strong underlying, comprehensive consumer privacy law so children are still protected the day after they turn 13 and the day after they turn 18. Thank you so much.

[The prepared statement of Ms. Vance follows:]

Written Testimony of Amelia Vance, Founder and President, Public Interest Privacy Center, before the US House Subcommittee on Innovation, Data, and Commerce, "Addressing America's Data Privacy Shortfalls: How a National Standard Fills Gaps to Protect Americans' Personal Information," Thursday, April 27, 2023

Chair Bilirakis, Ranking Member Schakowsky, and Members of the Committee:

It is an honor to testify before you on the need for better child and student privacy protections. I am the President and Founder of the Public Interest Privacy Center (PIPC) and an adjunct professor of law at William & Mary Law School. I also run the Student and Child Privacy Center, housed at AASA, The School Superintendents Association. PIPC is a pending nonprofit that equips stakeholders with the insights, training, and tools needed to cultivate effective, ethical, and equitable privacy safeguards for all children and students.

The child and student privacy legal and practical landscape is undergoing rapid, continual change. While educators and school administrators grapple with understanding and applying new technologies and data sharing practices within the classroom, new child privacy protections are being introduced in federal and state legislation on an almost-weekly basis. Since 2014, over 140 state laws have been passed that attempt to close these gaps. What has resulted is a confusing, dense, and insufficient legal landscape that leaves parents thinking that their children are protected or that there are no laws at all. And, worse, the chaos and legal gaps leave children and students vulnerable to serious harm.

In my work over the past decade, I have worked on student and child privacy with parents, local and state education agencies, researchers, privacy advocates, civil rights advocates, data use proponents, and state and federal policymakers. These stakeholder groups can (and have) clashed regarding the appropriate balance of the use of data with sufficiently protecting privacy, but they all agree: current sectoral privacy protections are not sufficient to protect student privacy.

Today, I will share some of what I have learned in my work in this space, provide a brief overview of the current child and student privacy landscape, outline why children and students are particularly vulnerable to privacy risks, describe how current laws fall short in protecting children and students from privacy harms, and how a comprehensive consumer privacy bill could help close these gaps and create more safeguards for students and children.

Lay of the Land

Child and student privacy legal protections currently exist through a layered, often outdated, and hard to navigate patchwork of federal and state laws. The Children's Online Privacy Protection Act (COPPA) contains significant protection gaps. For example, it only applies to information *from* children under the age of 13 a surprise to many parents who think it applies to all information about their children and most of COPPA's protections can be, and often are, easily waived. The Family Educational Rights and Privacy Act (FERPA) provides additional privacy protections for students, but is particularly hard to understand and apply due to the additional rules that exist in statute, regulation, guidance, and other sources of law. Like COPPA, FERPA also includes significant gaps in privacy protections; while education technology is now used for attendance, personalized learning, student counseling, and other educational and administrative purposes, those companies are not directly regulated under FERPA; schools bear the burden of ensuring big tech's compliance, absent a state law. The state legal landscape is evolving at a near-impossible to follow rate, making it hard for stakeholders, including parents, schools, and companies, to understand and navigate.

Today, there is almost universal agreement among parents, educators, and policymakers at both the federal and state levels that children and students deserve better privacy protections. The next step must be to unite decision makers' understanding of what the current laws are, what gaps remain in the current legal landscape, what additional risks need to be addressed, what the possible legislative solutions are, and how to best implement those solutions without restricting children and student's access to safe online communities and opportunities.

Given this legal landscape and the vulnerabilities that remain, child and student privacy laws are long overdue for modernization and clarity, especially in light of the rapid rate of emerging technologies. However, just expanding those protections are not enough; our children deserve and need privacy protections both the day before *and* the day after they turn 18. A carefully and well-informed, comprehensive federal privacy law could help close these gaps and provide the safeguards that children and students have long-needed. However, we also know children are uniquely vulnerable to certain harms, and it is also important to create heightened protections that safeguard children from risks unique to them.

Children, Students, and Privacy Risks

Because students—especially younger children—are not fully equipped to weigh the potential benefits and risks of data collection and use, are more socially and physically vulnerable than adults, and lack experience in navigating social norms and knowing when to trust, they require special privacy protections. They also need to be protected from the more acute harms they are vulnerable to, such as opportunity loss and identity theft, that may not fully emerge until later in life.

Without proper safeguards, students' lives and futures may be irreparably altered by privacy invasions. Over the past decade, I've found that the concerns that are most often shared from parents, educators, policymakers, and students themselves can be categorized in the following ways:

Whether these risks are based on student privacy being violated or just the perception that it could be, these risks are generally what underpins child and student privacy controversies and dictates the content of child and student privacy laws, regulations, and policies. The perception of unethical or irresponsible practices due to misinformation or inadequate communication can result in a loss of trust, particularly in the student privacy context.

Risk	Definition	How these concerns might be raised
Health & Safety	Personal or otherwise sensitive information may be revealed that could endanger students.	Is a stranger or someone dangerous able to communicate with my child or learn where my child lives?
Over-Collection & Over-Surveillance	Over-collection and monitoring of student data and online activity can have chilling effects on students.	How much information is being collected about my child?
The Permanent Record	Records of events, specifically mistakes, may be retained	Will my child's mistakes be recorded forever?
	indefinitely, potentially leading to detailed profiles that negatively impact students' future opportunities.	
Loss of Opportunity	Student data can be used to make decisions about students and, specifically, can result in denials of opportunity.	What information will be used to make determine which opportunities my child doesn't have access to?
Equity Concerns	Students have varying access to devices or internet service, has implications for safeguards in place and monitoring that occurs.	What if the information is biased? What if it is used in an inequitable way? What if my child and I can't or don't have access to the information or technology?
Age-inappropriate Content	Students may access inappropriate websites and online content.	Is my child accessing content that isn't appropriate?
Social Harm	Revelation of personal and sensitive student information can result in stigmatization and cyberbullying.	Is my child being cyberbullied or stigmatized?
Commercialization	Companies may use student data to target students with advertisements and to build student profiles.	Are companies selling my child's data or targeting advertising to them?

When we don't properly safeguard against these risks, it can result in disastrous outcomes for students that can last long after they graduate. For example, recent data breaches in *Minneapolis* and *Los Angeles* school districts revealed sensitive information of both current and former students, including student disciplinary and health records. While increasing data security is one method of protecting against data breaches, minimizing the data that is collected in the first place and creating processes for deleting data when no longer needed can lessen the impact of these types of breaches.

The vast amount of data collected about children also poses a unique risk to children, potentially impacting their mental health, physical safety, and future opportunities. Especially in school, many children are unaware what is monitored and who may have access to their information.

For example, a national *survey* indicated that school monitoring negatively impacts student mental health because students are concerned about expressing their opinions or seeking out resources out of fear that their searches, identities, and opinions may be revealed to others without their consent. Students' sensitive information could be better protected by limiting this type of data from being collected, restricting who has access to the data, and providing students and parents with transparent policies.

Often, current child privacy law permits almost all protections of childrens' data to be waived by consent. This is a problem because companies face few restrictions on using data after receiving parental consent. For example, parents may rush through or not read a privacy notice and consent to their child's data being collected without understanding the potential consequences. Consent is not a panacea for adequate privacy protections: consent mechanisms alone may be insufficient if students and parents do not fully comprehend what they are consenting to due to the form in which the information is conveyed, or if students' opportunities to engage in learning or activities is conditioned on use of certain tools. Many educational activities take place without consent, and, in the educational context, obtaining meaningful consent might not be feasible. Therefore, it is vital for law to include underlying privacy protections that cannot be overridden by consent or that require a higher standard of consent where the risks are clear and consent is better informed, in order to protect the privacy and retain the trust and goodwill of students, parents, and educators.

These harms are certainly concerning for any parent and may spark a knee-jerk reaction that entails keeping their kids offline all together. However, in this day and age, robust technology use is not only a reality, but also a necessity in order to prepare young adults to navigate a digital world. Let's not forget that there are also many benefits that technology has provided for children. Unable to connect with their friends and communities in-person during the pandemic, young people relied on social media and other online tools to play, build community, explore their identities, and participate in civic and political forums. Many educational technology (EdTech) tools play a valuable and innovative role in a child's learning, digital citizenship prepares them for the adult world, and safe online interactions with their peers can create a vital sense of community. Online spaces can also be integral to fostering creative expression and providing resources related to health and well-being.

Allowing opportunities for youth online while mitigating risks is no small endeavor; it is entwined with children's well-being today and their opportunities tomorrow. In the same way we teach our children to look both ways before crossing the street, we must equip kids to make good privacy decisions for themselves. The most basic way technology changes society is through the choices that we make the choices that *our children* make about which technologies we adopt and reject, and how to wisely use the ones that are selected.

The current legal landscape, consisting of both federal and state level laws, does not adequately address these risks. While providing some privacy protections, significant gaps still remain.

Legal Landscape

Federal Laws

The Family Educational Right and Privacy Act of 1974 (FERPA) provides students with access to and transparency regarding their education records, and limits disclosure of education records by educational institutions to certain, limited circumstances listed in the statute.

However, FERPA has a critical gap in privacy protections. FERPA applies only to schools, and therefore its restrictions and requirements only apply directly to schools, and not to private sector organizations, including EdTech companies. However, EdTech companies can be indirectly regulated under FERPA. EdTech companies are generally only regulated by FERPA so far as the contract between the school and EdTech company includes FERPA protections something that is often a difficult burden for small schools to negotiate into contracts on their own.

In addition to FERPA, children's data is protected via the Children's Online Privacy Protection Act (COPPA), which restricts "online operators" from collecting data from children under the age of 13 without obtaining verifiable parental consent. COPPA generally only applies to online operators who target their services to children or who have actual knowledge they are collecting information from children. As you can imagine, this actual knowledge standard creates a confusion about whether or not data collection on many sites is actually covered. COPPA also does not provide any substantive rights to children or their parents regarding the data collected.

COPPA's only protection is to apply restrictions to data collection (by requiring consent) but once the data is collected, the company has no restrictions under COPPA to how it must use, process, or share, or refrain from using, processing, or sharing the data, and it does not afford any rights in the data.

There is also massive confusion around and problematic gaps in FERPA and COPPA's protections depending on where and for what reason an app is being used by a child: if an educational app is being used in the classroom or at the direction of a teacher for homework, the data being collected is generally protected under FERPA. However, the moment that that child starts playing with that educational app for fun or at their parents' behest, FERPA ceases to apply. At that point, it would be great if COPPA covered that gap; however, since COPPA allows parents to waive many of its protections via parental consent, parents may not realize that their child is now unprotected under both FERPA and COPPA.

Misunderstandings about the intersection of FERPA and COPPA also creates problems. For example, some EdTech companies have begun to shift their COPPA responsibilities for obtaining verifiable parental consent to schools, even though companies, not education institutions, are subject to and responsible for complying with the law. Lack of clarity on the intersection between the two laws has resulted in confusion, diffusion of responsibility, and evasion.

State Student Privacy Laws and Child Privacy

Since 2013, policymakers have introduced nearly one-thousand student privacy bills in all 50 states, and 41 states and Washington, DC, have enacted more than 130 laws, whose scope and effectiveness vary by state. Unfortunately, state-level student data privacy laws have been fragmented and variable, creating robust student data privacy protections in some states and insufficient protections. We've seen well-intentioned laws that have critical loopholes, and others that go too far and have overly-restrictive unintended consequences, which negatively impact student success and well-being.

For example, Louisiana passed a law that required parents to return a consent form to share any student data. Children of parents who forgot to return the form or chose not to, were excluded from consideration from the state scholarship fund. New Hampshire similarly passed a law with good intentions but negative unintended consequences when it banned the recording of classroom lessons. Classroom recordings are sometimes necessary for students with learning disabilities so they have the resources necessary to keep up with their peers. In an attempt to protect students, New Hampshire inadvertently took this resource away from the students who need it most.

As I noted in my Seton Hall Legislative Journal article, "Student Privacy's History of Unintended Consequences," many state level laws "were passed hastily in response to public fears or specific incidents, with little stakeholder input. Others neglected to clearly define the scope and requirements of the laws, resulting in confusion and anxiety." These state experiences with passing, implementing, and fixing student privacy laws may be valuable in informing the process of improving consumer privacy protections.

State Consumer Privacy Laws and Child Privacy

Utah's law includes children's privacy within its definition of "sensitive personal information," and states that controllers (covered businesses) may not "process sensitive personal data without *"processing the data in accordance with" COPPA.* If you are a covered business under Utah who collects information from children, but are not an online operator (or, if you have a website but don't collect data through your website), this is puzzling, because you are not required to process data "in accordance with" COPPA or to obtain parental consent since you are not an online operator. Similarly, Virginia's law also includes data collected from individuals under 13 in its definition of sensitive data, and requires businesses to not process "sensitive data concerning a known child, without processing such data in accordance with" COPPA. Like Utah, this is a bit confusing, because not all businesses that are covered under the VCDPA that collect/process child data are required to comply with COPPA. Accordingly, for businesses that are not online operators within COPPA's purview, collecting data "in accordance with" COPPA would likely look like normal data collection with no heightened protection, which undermines the purpose of these laws.

As mentioned above, these provisions are not always effective, and can be confusing, since COPPA only applies to online operators and the state consumer privacy laws apply to all businesses, regardless of how they collect information. Virginia and Utah's laws (and they are not alone) demonstrate both a misconception, and a gap when examining how state consumer privacy laws protect (or do not protect) children. The requirements in these laws seemingly try to create a heightened collection standard when it comes to child data, similar to the heightened standard (often opt-in, rather than opt-out consent) required to collect health data, biometric data, and other similarly sensitive data, but by tying this collection standard to COPPA, which only applies in the limited context of online data collection, it does not afford the robust protection it may appear to at first brush. Legislators need to remember that not all businesses are required to comply with COPPA, so the requirements to collect data in accordance with COPPA can be confusing or ineffective.

Finally, the safe harbor offered under some state laws (such as Virginia's) which deem businesses who "comply with the verifiable parental consent requirements of the Children's Online Privacy Protection Act (15 U.S.C. § 6501 et seq.)" to be in compliance with "any obligation to obtain parental consent" under the law may be more workable to blend COPPA and existing state law together in a way that understands what protections COPPA is already affording and where it does not afford protections.

Some of FERPA and COPPA's gaps are also filled by state consumer privacy laws that are being introduced and passed throughout the country and affording consumers in states who have passed such laws baseline privacy rights. Beyond simply being notice and consent regimes, which is largely what COPPA is and which often does not facilitate meaningful privacy protections, these state laws go a step beyond and provide more substantive, baseline rights to individuals.

The baseline rights appearing in state consumer privacy laws generally include the right to access information, the right to know what information is being collected, the right to delete information under certain circumstances, the right to opt-out of certain uses of information (such as using information for cross-context behavioral advertising or targeted advertising), and certain rights regarding sensitive personal information (such as the requirement for the business to obtain opt-in consent prior to collection or consent for certain uses of sensitive personal information). When these laws include new child privacy protections, they generally do so by placing COPPA-like restrictions on information collection from individuals under the age of 13, by providing safe harbors for companies that collect information "consistent with COPPA's requirements," or by including information of or related to individuals under the age of 13 in the definition of sensitive personal information.

Since these laws are based on a common misconception of COPPA's breadth, they do not adequately fill the gaps that exist under current law. However, because these laws apply to all individuals and do not set a floor for the age at which a consumer gains rights under the statutes (i.e., only afford individuals over 18 rights under the statute), these laws provide some additional protection to children via the substantive rights they afford to all consumers. Other than requiring notice of the company's privacy practices, and the right to review information collected (and in some instances, prevent further use), COPPA does not afford children (or parents on behalf of their children) significant rights in their data post-collection.

Another way that state consumer privacy laws tend to contemplate children is by including information of or related to individuals under the age of 13 in the definition of sensitive personal information. This means that the additional protections afforded to sensitive personal information under the law, which most often include opt-in rather than opt-out consent to collect and to use data for certain purposes, applies to children's data. In some ways, this is more protective than COPPA since COPPA only applies to information collection, and does not afford meaningful substantive rights or meaningfully restrict use or collection after consent to collection.

Some state consumer privacy laws say that if you are compliant with COPPA's verifiable parental consent (VPC) requirements then you also meet the requirements of the state law. However, the application of VPC can also be problematic. Obtaining VPC often involves using age verification methods, which can be easily circumvented by children. When applied, VPC may also lead to "age gating" the Internet and attempting to block certain content from children (which again, can be easily circumvented) instead of simply making the content more appropriate for audiences that may include children or younger individuals.

Instead of relying on restrictive systems that require opt-ins and parental consent, some states are moving toward a system where privacy protections are designed into the sites they expect children to visit.

Moving away from Notice and Consent to Underlying Protections: The Age Appropriate Design Code

In one of the first meetings of the *OECD's* expert working group to revise their recommendation on protecting children online, Baroness Beeban Kidron presented about the Age Appropriate Design Code (AADC) and put forth the question (paraphrased here) "What if kids didn't have to lie on the internet to be protected but also get access to services?" The

AADC is designed to enable children to do just that. It is built upon implementing additional safeguards that allow children to use the internet in an age and developmentally-appropriate way.

When introduced in 2020, the United Kingdom adopted the AADC, a detailed set of fifteen non prescriptive standards "*seek[ing] to protect children within the digital world, not protect them from it.*" The code establishes the *following fifteen standards* as a framing through which companies implement age appropriate design into their online services: best interests of the child; data protection impact assessments; age appropriate application; transparency; detrimental use of data; policies and community standards; default settings; data minimisation; data sharing; geolocation; parental controls; profiling; nudge techniques; connected toys and devices; online tools.

The EU's General Data Protection Regulation (GDPR) served as a foundation upon which the AADC is built. As explained in the *Information Commissioner's foreword* to the final Code, "The code is not a new law but it sets standards and explains how the [GDPR] applies in the context of children using digital services." This is a crucial point: the AADC's enhanced protections for children are based upon the foundation of privacy protections for everyone. These enhanced protections for children elevated the baseline protections to be more effective at protecting children because they accounted for children's unique vulnerabilities and need for additional protections. The US also needs a comprehensive privacy law upon which to build out additional protections for children.

The AADC includes various privacy safeguards by design and default to make the internet a safer place for children. For example, it protects the privacy of children's location data by requiring geolocation data collection be turned off by default in most circumstances and that geolocation be turned back off after a child has turned it on. It emphasizes just-in-time notifications to ensure that children are aware of what is happening while they are using the internet. It also prohibits the *use of dark patterns* to the detriment of children; limits profiling a child by default; requires businesses to think carefully and document decision-making about the privacy impacts of their services that are likely to be accessed by children; and calls for privacy policies to be available in terms that children can understand. Many of these child privacy protections should be represented in US privacy law, and not just to protect children.

Child Privacy-Specific State Laws

As with student privacy, policymakers have also attempted to close sectoral privacy law gaps by introducing additional state-level child privacy laws.

The U.S. Version of the Age-Appropriate Design Code

Following California's groundbreaking consumer privacy laws, California decided to innovate on child privacy too. Building off of the UK's AADC, the California Age-Appropriate Design Code Act (ADCA) mandates that businesses, as defined under the California Consumer Privacy Act/California Privacy Rights Act *(CCPA/CPRA)*, implement increased privacy protections by design for online services likely to be accessed by children. These laws are based on the acknowledgement that online engagement is a reality and baseline protections must be in place. UNICEF's "*Growing up in a Connected World*" report demonstrates this reality. They report that across the world, one in every 3 people online are kids and teens.

The ADCA requires covered businesses to either "estimate the age of child users with a reasonable level of certainty appropriate to the risks" or to "apply the privacy and data protections afforded to children to all consumers." This requirement alone has the potential to transform how everyone, including adults, experiences the internet. As was seen with the CCPA/CPRA, because of California's size and market power and because of the breadth of the law, even with its threshold requirements, this law could change online practices for companies throughout the US because of California's market power and size. The law may also raise the baseline standard for everyone who uses the internet or online resources because if businesses can't find a way to accurately identify children, the ADCA will effectively require them to treat everyone accessing their websites as a child, which resets the baseline and could result in content restrictions, limitations on personalization, and limited functionality for all website users, when these restrictions may only be appropriate for certain content that is unsafe for children.

However, some states are choosing a more restrictive approach, passing laws that place significant restrictions on certain websites and mobile apps, such as social media platforms, related to child users of these platforms, following the example of other countries like *China* and South Korea. For example, Utah's law applies to minors under the age of 18, and limits how and when children can use social media by setting a curfew that prohibits evening or early morning access, and requires parental consent for use, gives parents broad rights regarding access to accounts, and places use restrictions on social media companies related to children including prohibiting social media companies to display ads to children, target or suggest groups, products, posts, or services to children, and prohibiting the use of addictive design with child users.

While this law was passed with good intentions, blocking the internet from children instead of teaching them how to safely use the internet, or making the internet safer, would have more beneficial impacts, particularly since children historically figure out ways to bypass or circumvent age gates and access the content without consent (and in this case, past curfew). The law also treats all individuals under the age of 18 the same way, which overlooks that content that is safe and potentially beneficial for a 16 to 18-year-old is different from the content that is safe and beneficial for a four year old.

South Korea's law may actually be a case study in the problems with this approach. When South Korea passed the "Shutdown law" that banned children under the age of 16 from playing computer games between midnight and 6am, their government was, similarly to current U.S. concerns had some similar concerns to what we are hearing in the US now: worries about "*internet addiction*" that so bad, in some cases, that it led to people neglecting themselves or their children to "*the point of death.*" The paternalistic law *did not allow* parents the flexibility to choose to allow their child to play. However, South Korea repealed the law in 2021, choosing a more balanced approach that allows parents and guardians to "arrange approved play times" instead. South Korean Deputy Prime Minister and Education Minister said that, "In the changing media environment, the ability of children to decide for themselves and protect themselves has become important more than anything," and the government would, instead, "work with related ministries to systematically support media and game-use education at schools, homes, and in society so that young people can develop these abilities, and continue to make efforts to create a sound gaming environment and various leisure activities for children."

Other bills have proposed overly restrictive requirements that fail to consider the potential impact on schools and children. For example, some proposed solutions inadvertently undermine the goals of a bill by including censorship mechanisms restricting access to certain content.

These may discourage minors from seeking help and finding helpful resources that include personal stories from peers. Overly restrictive proposals may also undermine the abilities of schools to provide education using technology.

When it comes to safeguarding our children online, we commonly use two approaches. The first, encouraging our kids to wear their virtual seatbelts and take steps to stay safe while online. The second approach is to avoid the internet entirely or limit access only to occasions where there is parental supervision. Unfortunately, both approaches have significant drawbacks. They involve numerous gaps, can be easy for kids to get around, inappropriately place the onus on parents to adequately vet a technology's privacy practices, or rely on a large amount of additional data collection about families. These approaches also fail to adequately deal with additional risks, such as commercial exploitation of their data and excessive government surveillance.

A Comprehensive Law

Comprehensive consumer privacy laws provide necessary baseline privacy protections for all consumers, including children. By providing blanket rights for all consumers, we help close many of the privacy gaps in child and student privacy laws and make technology use much safer and beneficial for children. In the same way, the UK's AADC would not be effective if it were not based on the EU's general consumer protection code, the General Data Protection Regulation (GDPR).

While providing baseline privacy rights for all consumers, a general consumer privacy law does not completely close the gaps in child and student privacy laws. Since it does not fully address the specific child privacy risks that we have laid out and for that reason, additional privacy protections for children are necessary.

Businesses must also be transparent about what data they collect, how they use it, and how individuals can exercise their afforded rights.Transparency is a fundamental principle in many privacy laws, particularly because a lot of privacy laws are premised on the concepts of notice and consent. Transparency makes consumer consent more meaningful because consumers have clear notice. However, transparency may not be enough to ensure children are protected online.

The current model for providing transparency namely, providing a privacy notice requires individuals, including children, to be willing and able to engage with the organization's privacy information (source: *Data protection impact assessments*). In reality, children (and even some adults) will not read an entire privacy notice regardless of whether it is transparent and written in an understandable way. To ensure children are protected even if they do not engage with transparent privacy policies online, additional safeguards are needed. These additional safeguards may include measures such as meaningful use restrictions and limitations specifically targeted to alleviate specific harms to children, as discussed above, or additional processing restrictions including mandatory DPIAs before processing any child information.

Certain information processing activities pose different risks and harms to children than to adults, and it is important to recognize and account for additional potential impacts on children.

Conducting Data Protection Impact Assessments (DPIAs) and Algorithm Impact Assessments (AIAs) can help identify and assess a variety of risks, including risks that are unique to children. The UK Information Commissioner's Office (ICO's) DPIA framework set forth in the AADC lends a helpful framework, identifying several child-focused risks and potential impacts, specifically saying to consider "whether the processing could cause, permit, or contribute to the risk of: physical harm; online grooming or other sexual exploitation; social anxiety, self-esteem issues, bullying or peer pressure; access to harmful or inappropriate content; misformation or undue restriction on information; encouraging excessive risk-taking or unhealthy behaviour [sic]; undermining parental authority or responsibility; loss of autonomy or rights (including control over data); compulsive use or attention deficit disorders; excessive screen time; interrupted or inadequate sleep patterns; economic exploitation or unfair commercial pressure; or any other significant economic, social or developmental disadvantage." Due to the additional vulnerabilities of childrens, it is crucial that considering the likelihood and severity of potential risks and harms of processing on children at all ages and development stages is built into the evaluation process of online technologies in addition to the considerations for all consumers in a comprehensive law.

Once potential risks and harms to children have been identified through DPIAs and AIAs, those risks and harms can then be addressed with appropriate mitigation measures to better protect children. Additional security requirements, including mandated training and appointment of privacy and security officers, can be implemented to protect the rights of children. Data minimization requirements and additional protections for sensitive data, such as requiring affirmative express consent before transferring sensitive data about and from children, are especially critical to protect children from the potential negative impacts of collecting large amounts of sensitive data about and from children.

A comprehensive consumer privacy law should prohibit businesses from using manipulative design choices (dark patterns) to obscure or impair people's ability to exercise their rights. Dark patterns (referred to as "nudge techniques" in the AADC) can cause individuals, including children, to reveal more information than they would have if a website or platform did not push them to share additional information.

Children face additional unique risks from dark patterns when compared to adults. For example, dark patterns encouraging children to overshare personal information online may result in cyberbullying and dark patterns encouraging continued use of social media may result in amplified mental harms due to the tendency of children to be more susceptible to comparing themselves to others or viewing themselves under a microscope. Additionally, nudge techniques that encourage children to provide unnecessary personal data or to turn off privacy protective controls so that organizations can collect additional data from them goes against data minimization principles and can create a larger dossier of information related to children that can follow them for the rest of their lives.

However, manipulative design techniques can also benefit kids by gently encouraging them to stay engaged with healthy, productive, and learning-based content. For example, dark patterns or nudge techniques used in certain contexts may encourage children to share information that supports their health and wellbeing with appropriate parties to act on that information. Another potentially beneficial nudge specifically applicable to children may be techniques that encourage children to pause their activity online and step away from technology without losing progress to promote taking breaks in periods of uninterrupted screen time. In certain contexts, manipulative design techniques can be utilized in positive ways to promote childrens' wellbeing, encourage healthy habits, and encourage kid's engagement in productive activities. Because manipulative design techniques may benefit children when used appropriately, a comprehensive privacy bill should not ban them entirely. Rather, businesses should be restricted from using these techniques to keep individuals from exercising their rights, such as opting out of data collection.

A comprehensive and carefully crafted consumer data protection law can also add protections against entities and data practices less often considered to be harmful by regulating non-profits. Including non-profit organizations is useful for filling the gaps left by many existing sectoral privacy laws that do not apply to non-profit organizations.

A comprehensive consumer privacy law can also better protect data used for research. For background, many types of research—including education research—are controlled by Institutional Review Boards, which ensure that research is ethical and data is protected.

However, Institutional Review Boards are rarely equipped to evaluate privacy and security risks. Ideally, a comprehensive consumer privacy law could help remedy this gap by requiring additional privacy and security specific guidelines for research, with special attention to projects that are exempt from the review process.

In addition to raising privacy protections for all consumers, a comprehensive consumer privacy bill can carve out additional protections for children that fill the gaps in existing legislation. The law would ideally apply these additional protections when the covered entity knows the individual is under 17, without carving out different knowledge standards for some social media companies and large data holders.

Prohibiting targeted advertising to minors is a useful protection that can be provided by a comprehensive privacy bill. California's law provides this protection by allowing all consumers regardless of their age to limit the use of the "sale" and "sharing" of their data (with the "sale" and "sharing" of data generally understood to encompass the practice of targeted advertising). Specifically, California graduates the protections in this space by requiring opt-in consent from parents of children younger than 13 and directly from individuals age 13-16 in order to "sell" or "share" their personal information, and by allowing individuals over age 16 to opt-out of this practice.

Companies using targeted advertising exploit children's data to manipulate their decision-making to buying products or services, a particularly dangerous practice due to the increased vulnerability of children. This prohibition also fills gaps left by COPPA, where targeted ads are not prohibited as long as the provider has parental consent to collect and process a child's data. Additionally, the prohibition on transferring minor's data to third parties absent affirmative consent gives minors and parents control over how their data is used and limits the ability to use data for secondary purposes beyond what the data was originally collected for.

Among the provisions that require additional protections for minors, requiring large data holders to conduct yearly algorithm impact assessments that must describe, among other things, how the entity will mitigate harms specific to minors could be extremely beneficial. Requiring yearly algorithmic impact assessments to assess and mitigate potential harms to minors is a powerful tool to ensure that large data holders will think about the needs and specific vulnerabilities of children in designing and continuing to provide access to their services in safer ways for children. Entities must acknowledge the unique potential risks of algorithms to minors and plan accordingly to mitigate those harms.

Additionally, a comprehensive consumer privacy bill can create additional resources at the FTC dedicated to children and minor's privacy, including requiring the FTC to promulgate new

COPPA rules and funding a new Youth Privacy and Marketing Division. The FTC has limited resources to dedicate to protecting children because they are responsible for over 70 different laws. Adding a new division dedicated to children is useful to ensure compliance with ADPPA and its minor specific provisions.

Finally, rights provided to individuals are only meaningful if they can be enforced. A comprehensive consumer privacy law can fulfill this requirement by including a private right of action for individuals to enforce their rights. A private right of action provides specific benefits to children by filling gaps in existing legislation. Parents and children cannot sue businesses that violate COPPA and must rely on the FTC and state attorney generals to enforce their rights. A comprehensive consumer privacy bill that includes a private right of action gives parents, children, and all consumers more control over their data by allowing them to enforce their rights against businesses that fail to protect them.

Including Special Protections in a Comprehensive Consumer Privacy Law for Education

While it's the best next step in protecting children and students, it's important to note that a comprehensive consumer privacy bill on its own doesn't provide all the protections we'd like to see for children and students. Consumer privacy might not clearly address the relationship between schools and companies.

In the education context, consent is often not useful. Much student data collection, use, and sharing is involuntary: children are required to attend school, where they participate in activities that generate new data about them, such as completing online homework assignments.Under FERPA, schools are permitted to consent on behalf of parents–assuming specific privacy safeguards are in place–to enable nearly every aspect of tech-supported education, from keeping attendance records to grading exams. If this changed, any student whose parents have objected would likely be unable to use EdTech. Teachers may have to choose between creating and implementing multiple lesson plans for the same classroom or not using EdTech at all. This change would leave teachers not only ill-equipped to teach in a modern environment, but also coping with post-pandemic challenges like learning loss with resources of the 1980's. It is important to protect the ability of schools to use technology as core curriculum–the digital equivalent of a textbook–without permitting opt-outs. However, in order to ensure that companies are adequately protecting privacy, additional safeguards tailored to the education context are necessary. Even where consent may be appropriate, students and parents are often not in the best position to assess the benefits and risks of data collection and use; the burden of vetting the technology used by their child's school should not be placed on them.

One way to fix this is to include a federal version of the prominent state student privacy law regulating vendors, SOPIPA, in a comprehensive consumer privacy law. For example, a draft bill introduced by Representatives Polis and Messer in 2015 included the necessary nuance to deal with privacy in the education context, and was endorsed by most major education groups and the National PTA.

Conclusion

Children and students face many specific and acute privacy risks in this digital age. Despite policymakers' best attempts, we currently have a patchwork system of laws and protections that do not sufficiently protect children and students. Significant gaps remain in the federal laws and state laws are not successfully closing those gaps. A broader, general consumer-based approach, coupled with additional child-specific provisions, could be an effective best next step forward and a way to ensure that all children and students benefit from the opportunities provided by emerging technologies in a safer, more privacy-protective way.

* * *

Mr. BILIRAKIS. Thank you so very much, and excellent testimony by all of you. We appreciate it so much.

I will begin the questioning. I recognize myself for 5 minutes.

In the 1990s Congress responded to the rapid growth of online marketing tactics that targeted children by passing the Children's Online Protection Act mentioned many times, COPPA. In the decades since COPPA's enactment, unfortunately, we have seen far too many violation settlements between the FTC and Big Tech. Instead of protecting children under COPPA's guardrails, Big Tech has determined the value of exploiting kids' data is higher than the cost of FTC fines. In fact, they seem to operate their budgets to account for these fines. This is an unacceptable business practice, I think you all agree.

So this question is for the entire panel, but please be brief in your questions, because I only have a limited amount of time—in answering the questions. In your experience, what are the ways in which COPPA does not go far enough in its protection of children? And what are some circumstances where a parent might expect their child's data to be covered, but in reality it is not? Could you provide us with some concrete examples?

We will start from here, sir. Mr. Codling, please.

Mr. CODLING. Thank you, sir.

REGO protects the child's financial data, whether online or purchasing in a retail store, as an example. And part of its basic foundation is data minimization constantly, continuously. And quite frankly, sometimes that hasn't been super popular with the marketing folks. But the mantra has always been, "Do not collect more than the absolute necessary amount of data on that child in particular." Therefore, you don't have to protect something that you have never collected.

Mr. BILIRAKIS. Very good. Ms. Vance, please.

Ms. VANCE. As I mentioned, COPPA is limited to information collected from children, which I think many parents would be surprised by.

But there is also confusion about whether COPPA protects information when you have a label of "family-friendly" or "kid-safe." And many parents assume that, when they download an app or have their child access a website with those labels, it is protected not only from an appropriateness standard, but also from a privacy standard. And it, generally, is not.

Mr. BILIRAKIS. Yes, sir.

Mr. BRITAN. I think the greatest shortcoming with COPPA, as has already been mentioned, is that it only protects children of 13. Children 13 to 18 aren't protected under COPPA. It is also really hard to identify children. So the best way to protect children broadly is to pass baseline comprehensive privacy law that broadly regulates personal data of everyone, including children.

Mr. BILIRAKIS. I am happy to agree with that, sir. Mr. Reed, please.

Mr. REED. I will make this quick. Pretty much everything everybody else said, but I will say one aspect that has been phenomenally important: verifiable parental consent has to work for parents. Right now we call it the over-the-shoulder test. If the device has to go over the shoulder, come back to the parent, and they have to enter in something, the parent then says, "You know what, just go to the general audience app."

So as—we think your bill is really important because it protects people of all ages. Because when we are building the technology, if you make it too hard for the parent to use, then they won't always use it.

Mr. BILIRAKIS. Thank you. Congress needs to do—to once again respond to the new wave of online marketing tactics that fuel Big Tech's ad-based revenue stream and enact a comprehensive, as I said, Federal data privacy law—everyone is in agreement on that— to close these gaps. That is why we are having this hearing.

All Americans, no matter their age, deserve privacy protections, just as you said, sir. It is clear that privacy protections should not end when you turn 13.

So my last question, because I am running out of time, Mr. Codling, it seems like you already—you are already practicing a data minimization principle, as we included in last year's bill. It seems clear that REGO cannot only comply but continue to succeed if a comprehensive data privacy law is enacted. Is that accurate?

Mr. CODLING. Yes, sir. That is completely accurate.

Mr. BILIRAKIS. OK. You note in your testimony that REGO is the only certified COPPA-compliant financial platform for families and children. Can you explain what that certification means and what you have to do to—what do you go—how do you get that certification? How do you go through it?

Mr. CODLING. Yes, sir. It requires a very, very detailed audit where a third party—in our case, a company called PRIVO—is granted full access not only to our website, but our internal workings, our internal platform. They run tests of placing data in certain areas of an app, as an example, determine how that data is utilized, where is it stored, how is it processed, and, more importantly, how is it protected.

And that audit goes every single year. You look through any time there is a significant change in the app's performance or the app's features, it is run again through this audit, and we are told, "Yes, you are in compliance. Here are some areas you need to fix."

Mr. BILIRAKIS. So it is a valuable tool. How many companies are part of this, the certification program, now?

Mr. CODLING. I do not know that, sir, but we can certainly get you that——

Mr. BILIRAKIS. Yes, please get back to me on that.

Mr. CODLING. Yes, sir.

Mr. BILIRAKIS. All right. I appreciate it very much. Thank you.

All right. Now I recognize Ms. Schakowsky from the great State of Illinois for your 5 minutes of questioning.

Ms. SCHAKOWSKY. Thank you so much, and I really appreciate the testimony that we are hearing.

The—we had a hearing last week that dealt with data brokers who are buying and selling Americans' information. And I would like to focus first on healthcare information. And Mr.

Reed, let me ask you about that. So what kind of sensitive information do health apps have right now?

You know, we talked about what is covered, but what are the kinds of things that people ought to avoid, maybe giving it a little alert that their health data could be collected?

Mr. REED. Well, I think right now you are highlighting the problem by having this hearing and pushing for the Federal bill.

We actually operate under multiple State laws that have different perspectives. California has its own tweak on sensitive health information. The reality is, in many instances, it depends on the platform itself and the product itself. Generally, it is the State laws. And for a lot of our members, they have to abide by GDPR. But, as we—everybody has pointed out, it should be the United States Government that is also providing that insight.

Right now, too much data that people consider to be sensitive personal health information is available in conditions that I don't think people are aware of.

Ms. SCHAKOWSKY. What kind—can you describe what kind of an app would it be that people——

Mr. REED. Well, I think——

Ms. SCHAKOWSKY [continuing]. Should avoid?

Mr. REED [continuing]. One of the things that—the best example I can give is there is a very well-known website that has a portion of it that is COPPA that—I mean, sorry, that follows HIPAA and is a HIPAA-compliant entity, and another part of the website allows people to report their symptoms and have discussions about their symptoms and have a sense of community about it. But the information that they are typing into that website is available to be harvested for providing targeted behavioral advertising.

So I think that people oftentimes are misled by, as you said— heard earlier—by the names of the product in a way that can allow that data to flow to data brokers in a way that doesn't meet their expectations, and that harms the healthcare industry as well as the mobile app industry.

Ms. SCHAKOWSKY. I want to—your—in your testimony—maybe it is just really naive of me, but it says 97 percent of kids 8 and under. Was that the number?

VOICE. Yes.

Ms. SCHAKOWSKY. Are—either have a smartphone or a tablet.

Mr. REED. They have access to a smartphone or a tablet, right.

Especially nowadays, when schools are providing this technology as part of the curricula and the way that students are receiving their curricula.

So as Amelia Vance talked about, this gets very important on this overlay between what you are doing at school—you take your homework home—or for a growing community, for home schooling, what happens with that information? Does it meet the parents' expectations?

And I would go back to, for my industry, the key thing we need is trust. And when we don't have trust, nobody will buy our products. So it is important that there is a good Federal comprehensive privacy law that help us better eliminate the bad actors, and so that we are not pushed out and we lose that trust.

Ms. SCHAKOWSKY. I wanted to go to Ms. Vance about this issue too.

Just—I mean, of course, when I think about education now, kids, little kids, are online. I wonder if you wanted to add it to that— add to that, what we need to—how much more we need to do, and why this is a problem.

Ms. VANCE. Specifically related to data brokers?

Ms. SCHAKOWSKY. About children.

Ms. VANCE. About children in general? Yes, I mean——

Ms. SCHAKOWSKY. Especially——

Ms. VANCE. I think——

Ms. SCHAKOWSKY. I guess beyond the educational, but that they are on their phones.

Ms. VANCE. Absolutely. So as I think everyone knows by now, your phone is the computer in your pocket that tells everybody where you are, what you are doing, sometimes what you are thinking. And that is, of course, so much more sensitive when you are talking about kids who—their brains are still developing, they may post things or say things that they immediately regret or shouldn't have shared. And that information is already out there.

And particularly when we are talking about outside of the school context, when we are talking about the information coming from someone over the age of 13 or where there is another gap in COPPA, all of that is fair game for bad actors to take it and use it to market products, to potentially sell it, or otherwise——

Ms. SCHAKOWSKY. Let me ask one final question about kids.

Can we fully protect our kids' privacy if we don't also protect the parents' privacy?

Ms. VANCE. Absolutely, we need to protect parents' privacy. Just think of the last Amazon search you did, and the presents that you may have gotten your kids, or a workbook or a book about a learning disability. That information is incredibly sensitive, and so parental information needs to be protected, as well.

Ms. SCHAKOWSKY. Thank you.

Thank you. I yield back.

Mr. BILIRAKIS. Thank you for that question. It is so true. That is why we need the comprehensive bill, because one goes with the other. And so we are filling the gaps.

All right. Now I recognize the chairwoman from the great State of Washington, my friend Mrs. Rodgers, for your 5 minutes.

Mrs. RODGERS. Thank you, Mr. Chairman. A big thank you to all our witnesses for being here today.

I wanted to continue down this line about how we have these layered laws around privacy. We have the FTC Act, we have FERPA, HIPAA, other sector-specific laws, and kind of what Ms. Schakowsky was getting to, the ranking member: Americans think their data privacy is being protected, and yet there's many examples where it actually is not. And part of our goal with a comprehensive privacy bill is to address the gaps and make sure that people are protected, but also that innovation will thrive.

And, you know, this is our sixth hearing, as others have mentioned. It is also—it is just—we continue to feel like we—you know, I want to make sure—and I wanted to ask Mr. Reed about this— we celebrate the small businesses, the entrepreneurs, the innovators, and we want that competition to continue as we enact a national data privacy law.

So would you speak to what we have learned as far as the regulatory framework, and what resources do your members have to navigate not only this emerging patchwork of laws now that we see at the State level—the sixth State just implemented their own State law—but also the gaps in the other laws?

Mr. REED. Well, absolutely. And look, the reality is that, when you are a small business, trust is the most important thing that you can sell. Yes, your product has to work. Yes, it has to be a change element for the company or person who is buying it. But ultimately, nobody is going to use it if they don't trust you. And if you don't have the money to buy a Super Bowl ad, then you need to have an environment where trust is assumed. Therefore, having comprehensive privacy laws help.

And you talked about the State bills that have passed, but I don't know if you realize this: There are 289 currently introduced State privacy bills happening right now. I have a member of staff, my staff, who literally builds a State map of all of the privacy bills and how they are changing right now. We are happy to provide it for you.

The reality of that is that most of our members—and this is something superinteresting from an entrepreneurship perspective— my smallest member, including the ones in your district, are actually international businesses. They might only be 2 people, but they are selling mobile applications in 100 countries around the world. So having a bill that you pass mesh with GDPR is crucial for them to be able to innovate and sell globally while making domestically.

So from a tools perspective, I hope our trade association can help. That is my job, is to help them navigate it. But what you can do is provide them clear rules of the road that apply to the large companies that provide the infrastructure that we depend on, whether it is the platforms, whether it is the edge providers, whether it is our cloud computing services. If everyone in the food chain has the same set of rules, then small businesses can follow the rules in a way that gets them there.

Mrs. RODGERS. Thank you. I also wanted to ask you—because in your testimony you caution us on deferring entirely to the agency rules—Health and Human Services, HIPAA. As you know, FTC just announced their commercial surveillance rulemaking. It just— well, it was just weeks after we actually passed our bill out of committee last July.

But would you speak to your concerns around the FTC going its own way to establish rules in this space?

And do you think the FTC by itself has the ability to fill all the gaps created by these current——

Mr. REED. Well, the answer to your final—the last part of the question is no. And we just touched on it with the 289 State bills. The Federal Trade Commission can't issue the kind of preemption that we are absolutely going to need for small businesses to be able to manage their compliance.

Mrs. RODGERS. OK.

Mr. REED. We don't have 100-person compliance departments in order to do that.

Mrs. RODGERS. OK, thank you.

Mr. REED. So right off the bat, we can't do it.

Mrs. RODGERS. Thank you. I want to get to Mr. Britan too. I wanted to get to some of the new AI models that are—we see. We see reports every day about companies that are using AI, and there is—you know, and using reckless, transparent methods when they are incorporating AI into their products.

Just—would you speak to how risky some of the AI use is in processing of the data, in the heightened risk, and just how a data privacy law might help these new applications for AI? In 30 seconds, yes.

Mr. BRITAN. Absolutely, yes. There is no doubt that AI is powered by data, so the best way to ensure that AI is built responsibly is comprehensive regulation of data. And that is how the EU is presently looking at AI and regulating AI and examining generative AIs through the GDPR.

And so advancements in AI hold great promise, but they also highlight the need for a Federal comprehensive privacy law, so that the U.S. has a voice in how these technologies develop responsibly.

Mrs. RODGERS. I appreciate that. We will dig into that more.

Thank you, Mr. Chairman. I yield back.

Mr. BILIRAKIS. Thank you. And now I will recognize Ms. Blunt Rochester for her 5 minutes of questioning.

Ms. Kelly, I didn't see Ms. Kelly. Ms. Kelly, I will recognize you for your 5 minutes of questioning.

Ms. KELLY. Thank you, Chair Bilirakis and Ranking Member Schakowsky, for holding this important hearing this afternoon. It is critical that this subcommittee continues the discussions to ensure our Nation's laws provide adequate protections for Americans' personal information. So I want to thank the four witnesses for sharing your expertise.

As a chair of the CBC Health Braintrust, I am deeply concerned that sector-specific healthcare privacy law does not cover vast amounts of consumers' health-related data. Although many think their personal health data is secure, the reality is that consumers have few protections under the Health Insurance Portability and Accountability Act.

In fact, HIPAA does not provide privacy protections for health information, and only limits health data using and sharing by healthcare providers, healthcare clearinghouses, and health plans. This allows many health apps, websites, and devices to share information with a host of advertising companies and other uncovered entities. Reports confirm that some of this data transfers include terms like "HIV," "diabetes," and "pregnancy."

Common sense tells us that highly personal, intimate health information should be protected, regardless of the context in which that data is collected and used. Mr. Reed, I have a couple of yes-or-no questions for you. Does information about cardiovascular health become any less sensitive when collected by a fitness tracker rather than a cardiologist?

Mr. REED. No.

Ms. KELLY. Does information about a patient's symptoms become any less sensitive when collected by a website rather than a physician?

Mr. REED. No.

Ms. KELLY. Does information about reproductive health become any less sensitive when collected by an app rather than a gynecologist?

Mr. REED. No.

Ms. KELLY. Thank you for those quick responses. Lastly, Mr. Reed, is there any good reason why apps, websites, and fitness trackers shouldn't be required to safeguard consumers' sensitive health information and treat it with the same care as a physician? And please feel free to explain.

Mr. REED. This is the hard part. The legislation you are all proposing has important factors like data minimization and the right to delete. But when something is in your electronic health record and you are a physician, that information, it is really important that it not be deleted and the physician have the full totality of your record.

So we have to be very careful when we consider who the audience is for the product. A physician that doesn't know about your hypertension because you have deleted it might give you the wrong medication. So when we talk about it in that way, we have to look at it as, what does the physician need to know to treat you? And that is critical.

Separately from that, we also want fulsome data so that patients can treat themselves. By 2030 we will be 90,000 physicians short, and communities of color are more affected by that than anywhere else. At the same time, you see tools that allow the management of obesity and type 2 diabetes being absolutely critical to those communities.

So what we need—and your legislation helps to provide, the committee's legislation helps to provide—are some rules of the road for sensitive personal information. But I want to be careful that we don't suggest that what the doctor gets is covered in the same way, because the physician must know about your condition over time to properly treat you.

Ms. KELLY. Thank you for your response.

I also think it is important that any Federal privacy law we consider must strive to end data-driven discrimination. Simply put, any legislative proposal must strengthen civil rights protections by prohibiting discrimination using personal information. That is why last Congress I was proud to support the American Data Privacy and Protection Act, which prohibited covered entities and their service providers from collecting, processing, or transferring data in any way that discriminates or otherwise makes unavailable the equal enjoyment of any goods or services on the basis of race, color, religion, national origin, sex, or disability.

Mr. Britan, how would enhanced protections for specific types of sensitive data, notably data related to race, color, religion, national origin, sex, or disability, promote equality and civil rights?

Mr. BRITAN. Absolutely. We support those provisions of ADPPA, as well. And those types of protections will give individuals more power to control these sensitive categories of data and how they are used by companies. And I think giving individuals that power is what privacy law should be and data protection law should be all about, adjusting that power balance and giving power to people.

We also support the civil rights provisions that you mentioned that were included in the ADPPA around prohibiting discriminatory uses of data. That is a very important means to protect individuals, regardless of any actions they may take on their own behalf to protect their data.

Ms. KELLY. Thank you so much.

And again, thank you to all the witnesses, and I yield back.

Mr. BILIRAKIS. Thank you. I appreciate it very much, and I will— 5 minutes to Dr. Bucshon.

You are recognized for your 5 minutes of questioning.

Mr. BUCSHON. Thank you, Chair Bilirakis, for calling today's hearing.

Before coming to Congress I was president of a medical practice. I was a surgeon in southern Indiana and was acutely aware of how important it was to protect the health data and personally identifiable information of our patients and to comply with the requirements laid out in HIPAA.

As technology has advanced and society is gathering and utilizing ever greater amounts of data, it is very clear there are gaps in health data protections, as we have talked about some in this hearing. This committee needs to be thinking about the best ways to cover these gaps as it considers a national privacy and data security framework.

Interestingly, I was just with Chair Rodgers in Europe, and we met in Brussels with the EU. We did talk about this and about GDPR. And one of the things I want to make sure we avoid is the effect that we can possibly have on small and medium-sized businesses if we do the wrong thing here. So there is a fine line to be drawn.

Mr. Reed, in your testimony you mentioned cases where non-health information can be used to extrapolate health-related information that—and that putting extra restrictions on such information would limit consumers' access to digital health tools. I understand that concern and agree that we do not want to limit access to such tools, but I still believe private health information probably deserves greater protection than many other kinds of data. In fact, for the most part, it is the most monetizable data in the world, health information, in many people's estimation. By that I mean people get your data and they can make money with it, as people know.

Would it be feasible to require disclosures from an entity to a consumer if the entity does use or gather data to extrapolate private health information?

Mr. REED. So, Doctor, I think that is something that we continually work on. In your district there is a company called Anew that helps with——

Mr. BUCSHON. Yes.

Mr. REED [continuing]. Farm elements and agriculture. One of the problems we run into there is, as you know, under social determinants of health you could run into what they do, which is agriculture and food, being considered health data. So I agree with you.

And you are right, what we—we calculate that, if I get your full health profile, including key information, it is about $7 a person. It is the most valuable information on the black market possible.

Mr. BUCSHON. Yes.

Mr. REED. And so, completely right. I do think, though, we have to think about the totality and that we don't end up with grocery stores and the company in your district that provides agriculture technologies being there. So yes——

Mr. BUCSHON. What——

Mr. REED. Absolutely.

Mr. BUCSHON. Yes, what would be the biggest challenges implementing something like that, if we——

Mr. REED. Exactly, exactly what we just talked about: How do we make sure that it is sensitive information about you?

We look at things like physiologic data. Does it record physiologic data about you? We already have that. The FDA already explores these questions of collection of physiologic data. I think those are elements of it. But as you know, we have to preserve the ability to do research, as well. And whether it is through an IRB or other methodologies, we need to be very careful about not requiring such extreme data minimization that you can't do the research we need to do.

Mr. BUCSHON. Sure, I understand.

Mr. REED. Or cancer clusters, et cetera.

Mr. BUCSHON. And most research is de-identified information——

Mr. REED. Correct.

Mr. BUCSHON [continuing]. Anyway, right?

Mr. REED. Right. Well, you have to be very careful because, depending on which lawyer you talk to, the definition of de-identified is a moving line.

Mr. BUCSHON. I understand frequently you can extrapolate who it is, based on that.

Mr. Britan, you had comments on that, the same issue?

Mr. BRITAN. I would say the same thing, you know, and I would just say be on notice—notifying people of when that information is being used. We need a regime that protects the data—that protects data use for these purposes, regardless of whether an individual takes action to protect themselves and providing all these notices——

Mr. BUCSHON. Agreed.

Mr. BRITAN [continuing]. It has to be actionable, and I think people should be protected, regardless of whether they take action.

Mr. BUCSHON. Agreed. In fact, I would say the vast majority of people don't know that their health information is very, very valuable, and that it is one of the things that is at biggest risk of all of their privacy data. I am focusing on health here because I was a doctor.

Mr. Reed, are there any guardrails for the use or transmission of personal health information not covered by HIPAA that could protect users in these cases without limiting access to digital health tools?

So what can we—what should we do?

Mr. REED. So I think we are going to be a broken record on this entire panel. I think that we need to move forward with the bill that you have. There are some sections, section 702—I mean, sorry, 207—where there are elements that could affect doctors like you in terms of having to kind of double dip and be covered by both in a way that I don't think is helpful. But overall, I think comprehensive privacy reform that, as this panel has discussed, provides notice, provides actionable items, gives tools to the FTC when it is outside the domain of healthcare is the way to move.

Mr. BUCSHON. OK. As I said, the—even some of the EU people who we talked to, they didn't directly admit it, but you could tell by their comments that they do have the concerns with GDPR because of startups, small and large businesses—small and medium-sized businesses struggling to comply. And we want to avoid that situation here in the United States.

With that, I yield back.

Mr. BILIRAKIS. Thank you, Doctor. I now recognize Ms. Blunt Rochester for her 5 minutes of questioning.

Ms. BLUNT ROCHESTER. Thank you, Mr. Chairman, and thank you so much to the witnesses. Your testimony makes it abundantly clear that a comprehensive Federal data privacy law is desperately needed in this country.

Last year I was proud to support and vote out of committee the American Data Privacy and Protection Act, and I am ready to work with my colleagues on both sides of the aisle to get this bill passed and to the President's desk for signature.

While there are several gaps in our current sectoral privacy regulation system, I am alarmed by the rise of dark patterns, especially for children, and the use of health data without effective regulation. Over the last several years the FTC has detailed the ubiquity of dark patterns that misled consumers, as well as the misuse of health data on apps not covered by HIPAA.

To follow up on Ms. Schakowsky's questions, Ms. Vance, your testimony highlights the issues surrounding manipulative device design practices, often known as dark patterns, that are intended to trick people, including children, into making ill-informed choices. While deception isn't a new problem, deception and manipulation in the age of social media and mobile apps has changed the game. That is why I am planning to reintroduce the DETOUR Act, which would crack down on deceptive design practices that undermine user autonomy.

Ms. Vance, in your opinion, how pervasive a problem are dark patterns?

Ms. VANCE. I think we see across the internet that they are everywhere. Every, you know, smaller "no, I don't want this" button, every "no, I don't want to be smart when I don't subscribe to this newsletter," and sort of pushing people to stay on and keep on the apps and the games and the website, which is maybe good in the case of a math app and getting kids to read more but incredibly problematic in manipulating people against their will with no idea that it is happening.

Ms. BLUNT ROCHESTER. Yes. I have to tell you, I—for a while there I thought it was me, but I literally could not find these little X's to X out of things. I mean, I know I am not the only one now, and it is just ridiculous.

And, you know, are dark patterns especially pernicious when it comes to children's usage of online products?

Ms. VANCE. Absolutely. Children's brains are still developing, and they won't necessarily notice as easily as an adult might that they are being pushed in a certain direction or driven further down a rabbit hole of videos they are watching or monetization from games.

Ms. BLUNT ROCHESTER. Yes. Well, given the examples that you noted in your testimony, do you believe a comprehensive privacy bill that includes regulations on dark patterns is a more effective approach than a privacy bill that only protects children?

Ms. VANCE. Absolutely, especially since those, when they turn 18, go to higher ed, and that affects all of their futures.

Ms. BLUNT ROCHESTER. Yes.

Ms. VANCE. It is essential.

Ms. BLUNT ROCHESTER. Thank you.

And any other—Mr. Reed, I see you have got your hand up—on dark patterns?

Mr. REED. I think it is important to note that the issues you are talking about, about not being able to find the X, that actually hurts small businesses a lot.

If I have a mobile app, the numbers are very simple. If I build an application and I charge $1 for it on the store, I get 1 download for every 100 I get of an ad-supported application. But if you download my ad-supported application where I am using someone else to provide that ad, and you can't find the X, you stop using my app.

Ms. BLUNT ROCHESTER. So true.

Mr. REED. So the issue, as she points out, I don't care how developed your brain is, if you can't find that X, you stop using my product.

Ms. BLUNT ROCHESTER. Right.

Mr. REED. And so, as we clean up the industry, as we have this kind of legislation, it helps everyone do a better job.

Ms. BLUNT ROCHESTER. Yes, yes.

Mr. REED. Thanks.

Ms. BLUNT ROCHESTER. Thank you, Mr. Reed.

Mr. Britan, did you have something you wanted to share on dark patterns?

Mr. BRITAN. Sure, yes. I would just say Salesforce strongly believes that people should not be misled or tricked into making decisions based on dark patterns. I think the DETOUR Act would help in this regard, and the DETOUR Act as part of a comprehensive bill would be even better.

Ms. BLUNT ROCHESTER. Thank you so much.

And Mr. Codling, is there anything you want to share on dark patterns?

Mr. CODLING. Not directly with dark patterns, but as an example, because REGO is COPPA-certified, part of that certification process is to review the privacy policies, to look at the websites and specifically not allow certain dark pattern kind of behavior, to make the privacy policy age appropriate.

So there is one privacy policy for the parent and there is one for the child to say, here is what we are doing with your stuff and here is what we are not doing with it. It goes to your point, ma'am, about can I find the X quickly? Yes.

Ms. BLUNT ROCHESTER. Yes. Thank you so much. I have some additional questions that I will enter for the record for Mr. Reed, particularly on HIPAA and the health aspect of this, the health— I am on the Health Subcommittee, as well.

And so I will yield back the—actually, I don't have time to yield back, but I will yield back the time I don't have. Thank you.

Mr. WALBERG [presiding]. You always have time. You always have time to yield back.

Ms. BLUNT ROCHESTER. Thank you.

Mr. WALBERG. I thank the gentlelady, and I recognize myself for my 5 minutes of questioning.

And thanks so much to the panel for being here. This is a topic, as we have said, we must continue looking for solutions.

Children's privacy protections need to be updated. That is very clear. Whether at school or at home, there are significant gaps in how their information is protected. The pandemic and forced school closures made that even more clear. I am glad that there were so many online resources for parents and teachers and grandparents to turn to when their children were unable to go to school. Educational apps and websites offer immense benefits, and I would much rather my grandkids use them over social media. We at least can choose those apps.

But there are also very concerning reports of these apps and tools collecting and selling children's data for advertising. An article by the Washington Post last May reported that nearly 90 percent of educational apps and websites were designed to send the information they collected to advertising tech companies to help them predict potential buying habits of kids. Some EdTech platforms unnecessarily request access to students' cameras and locations.

And so I would ask for unanimous consent to include that article for the record.

Without objection, and I—hearing none, it will be included. [The information appears at the conclusion of the hearing.]

Mr. WALBERG. I serve on the Education and Workforce Committee, as well, which has jurisdiction over the Family Educational Rights and Privacy Act, or FERPA. I have also been an avid supporter on this committee for updates to COPPA and kids privacy overall. With at least a decade behind us since either of these laws were updated, neither of these laws reflect the realities of today's digital world.

Mr. Vance, there are clearly gaps and confusion on when and to what extent—excuse me, Ms. Vance—these two laws protect children's privacy. What is the result of this confusion for kids, parents, and schools, and how do we provide greater clarity?

Ms. VANCE. As Morgan was saying, they lose trust in vendors, in their schools, in other parents, in society itself. It undermines everything we do if we can't do the digital equivalent of step outside our front door without some harm potentially falling from the sky.

And so it is incredibly important that we have these comprehensive privacy protections, with heightened protections for children.

Mr. WALBERG. Mr. Reed, as I said, the explosion of digital education services is great, but I am extremely concerned how common and easy it is for apps to collect, store, and sell children's data.

In your testimony you indicated that COPPA and the FTC's guidance sufficiently holds EdTech and schools accountable for their privacy practices. But obviously, significant amounts of information about kids are being collected and sold by these tools every day. Where does the issue lie?

Mr. REED. I think, in the case of my testimony, I misspoke in the sense of sufficient, in the sense that they have authority over sufficient areas, but the gaps are huge.

One of the areas that creates the greatest concern—I think it is really important you talk about—is verifiable parental consent issues. I appeared before this committee, I think, in 2010 as a vociferous advocate for VPC. Unfortunately, verifiable parental consent has not taken the world by storm. And instead what you see is even limited amount of friction causes parents to basically say, "Well, use the general audience portion of the application."

One of our members actually provides—is a safe harbor and provides services to another person on this panel. And what they find is the cost of getting the parent engaged and to do these steps is oftentimes something the parent doesn't want to do. As I talked about earlier, we call it the over-the-shoulder problem. The moment the parent can say, "Oh, go to the Kids YouTube, it is too hard, go to regular YouTube," we have lost them. I testified multiple times at the FTC about this.

We need to have the platforms that are part of our ecosystem have more flexibility to provide either credentialing or flags to my members to say, "Hi. To the best of our knowledge, this user is a child. You need to behave in this manner when we pass that flag."

Unfortunately, right now you heard my fellow panelists talk about auditing. The platforms are not in a stage where they want to audit 1.5 million applications that are currently on their platforms. But if there were a way for the FTC to be more flexible in providing that flag, then that is something that the FTC, through your authority, can use to say, "Hey, you were provided this flag, you didn't use it, you didn't get rid of that information." It is a tool the FTC can use to get to what you want.

But merely expecting more from parents is not going to get the solution that you are after and that, frankly, all of your panelists are after.

Mr. WALBERG. Well, clearly, yes, we are—a comprehensive privacy law would fill many of the gaps we discussed today, but I also believe that we need to take another look at both FERPA and COPPA.

Thank you. My time is ended. I yield back, and now I recognize Representative Clarke.

Ms. CLARKE. Thank you very much, Mr. Chairman, and I thank our ranking member for holding today's hearing.

I would also like to thank our witnesses for being here to testify on such an important issue. Passing legislation to fill the gaps in current privacy laws is long overdue, and I remain committed to working with my colleagues across the aisle to pass a bill that protects all Americans' data.

Mr. Britan, in your testimony you cite the EU's GDPR as a driver of core privacy concepts like data minimization, the right to access, delete, and correct data, and guardrails on automated decision making. In your opinion, does the U.S.'s lack of a comprehensive national privacy standard inhibit our ability to lead or even participate in the global conversation on rights to data privacy and human rights?

Mr. BRITAN. Absolutely. And it is table stakes to enter those conversations. I believe we share these values with our allies all over the world, but at some point we have to demonstrate that through action.

Ms. CLARKE. Absolutely. I see you nodding your head, Mr. Reed. Would you like to add your position on that?

Mr. REED. I think Mr. Britan said it as well as any of us can, which is we need to demonstrate through action.

Ms. CLARKE. Very well. Mr. Britan, I would like to follow up and ask how the lack of a clear national standard will impact the U.S.'s ability to lead in data-intensive innovations like generative AI, quantum computing, and smart cities.

Mr. BRITAN. Salesforce welcomes regulation, and regulation is really important for ensuring that these new, innovative technologies are released in a responsible manner. Because if we release it in a way that reduces trust, it is virtually impossible to regain that trust.

And there's important global conversations happening right now. This is an amazing time for tech innovation, and the U.S. needs to be part of that conversation. In order for the U.S. to be an effective part of that conversation, we need comprehensive privacy law.

Ms. CLARKE. We can't be the weakest link, in other words. [Pause.]

Ms. CLARKE. Absolutely.

OK. Mr.—sorry—Ms. Vance, do any parts of COPPA require analysis of how algorithms may disproportionately cause harm to certain groups?

For example, some algorithms may show content that may be more dangerous if shown to children than the general population. Is there anything in COPPA requiring companies to look into how their algorithms affect children?

And what about FERPA?

Ms. VANCE. No, there is not in either law. And that is part of the reason why ADPPA was so exciting for me, because that is an invaluable and important protection.

Ms. CLARKE. Very well. Well, it is my position that comprehensive privacy legislation is long overdue and absolutely necessary for the U.S. to maintain leadership in a range of industries driving innovation. Our laws have failed to keep pace with revolutionary innovations, leaving Americans more vulnerable to discriminatory algorithms, invasive data collection, and cyber attacks. Increases in the amount of data available have earned—have created enormous and unprecedented consumer benefits. But we need legislation to ensure vulnerable populations are not—are, excuse me, are protected against discrimination, exploitation, and manipulation.

So I want to thank all of you for your expertise and bringing it to bear today in this—in today's hearing. We look forward to working with you as we move us into the 21st century, as I like to say.

And with that, Mr. Chairman, I yield back.

Mr. BILIRAKIS [presiding]. I appreciate that very much. Now I will recognize Mr. Duncan from the State of South Carolina for 5 minutes of questioning.

Mr. DUNCAN. Thank you, Mr. Chairman, for holding this hearing and the continued work that you are doing on this important issue. I want to ask all four witnesses—and I will start with Mr. Britan—from whom should we be protecting the data of American citizens? Who is the greatest threat here, is it Russian hackers, Communist Chinese, big American companies, identity thefts, predators?

And from your unique perspectives, who is the threat that we, as policymakers, need most to focus on to protect our citizens, especially kids and teenagers?

Mr. BRITAN. Those are all significant threats that I think a comprehensive privacy law would help us to address.

The greatest threat is going to be the one that we don't know about, and it is really hard to predict. And I think baseline protections that include data minimization and treating data as a potential liability and the reduction of data and managing data responsibly and in an organized fashion, understanding who has access to the data and that sort of data management capabilities is the best way to address all of those threats.

Mr. DUNCAN. OK. Mr. Reed?

Mr. REED. I think we have to be thoughtful. All of those are good, but there is a company in your district, Topography Digital, that does drone and a lot of other really cutting-edge technology. I think we have to realize that the biggest threat to the success of the companies in your district, like them, is the unexpected, for the loss of trust that happens.

So when we talk about threats from outside influences, what you really see is most of the data ends up in the hands of somebody who isn't going to do harm, just wants to make money off of it. But that destroys the trust and degrades the value of the systems we are providing.

So on the one hand, you absolutely should be focused on the international threats and the security, but we also need a comprehensive bill so that consumers know what to do and what the products are going to do to them, so they know if they are going to share the data. So it is the insidious ones that aren't there to harm, just there to make money off of it, that create the loss of trust sometimes.

Mr. DUNCAN. Yes.

Ms. Vance?

Ms. VANCE. I can't agree enough with my fellow panelists.

I would add anything that has the opportunity to destroy a child's future, whether it be information that data brokers are collecting and sharing with anyone who asks for it, or the use of that information by stalkers, parents with restraining orders, pedophiles, et cetera, that is really, I think, the greatest threat.

Mr. DUNCAN. Mr. Codling?

Mr. CODLING. Your question is excellent, sir, so I will split it into two areas. There is the criminal activity, and then there is the national security activity.

Criminal activity, cyber crime organizations, have become truly globalized. They have vertically integrated their capabilities to the state that they are as good as nation states, some of these criminal activities.

A national security standpoint, of course, you have got to be very concerned about the Chinese, Russians, Iranians, North Korea.

But a perfect example from a child's privacy protection standpoint, the worst-case scenario is something like TikTok or some other social media platform that can come in, aggregate the data that the child in this case is utilizing from the social media standpoint, and if that company platform also offered financial services capabilities, because those are affiliated companies that data is going to flow back and forth between those two. And Lord only knows where that stuff will end up.

So in my FBI career we spent a lot of time finding out where that stuff ended up.

Mr. DUNCAN. Yes.

Mr. CODLING. Typically, it was not in your home district. It was overseas someplace.

So just last week, TikTok made an announcement that they are very interested in working with large American retailers to allow individuals on the TikTok platform to purchase, buy, engage in commerce. To me, as an uncle, that is a nightmare. There is no good end of that with that particular company. I am not going to paint everybody in the same way.

It does scare me, because I can now build a complete data dossier on that individual as a young person and have now those last couple of little gaps filled in. I know who you are and what you are and what you have been doing since—pick an age. That is very, very concerning.

Mr. DUNCAN. Yes. OK. If Congress were to pass a Federal privacy law, what single provision would be the most essential factor in that new law being successful?

And I will ask Mr. Codling.

Mr. CODLING. I think having a comprehensive law, sir, puts the United States, to my—the panelists' opinion—back in the game. We should be the leaders. We were the leaders.

Mr. DUNCAN. Yes.

Mr. CODLING. We can be again.

Mr. DUNCAN. Let me ask Mr. Britan real quick. Mr. Britan, same question, yes. Eight seconds.

Mr. BRITAN. Yes, I think the key is to build these responsibilities and apply these responsibilities to the companies that process data, and ensure they are processing it responsibly.

I think the notice-and-choice regime has failed. It puts too much burden on the individual. We need a comprehensive law that comprehensively regulates data.

Mr. DUNCAN. Yes, identify the threat——

Mr. REED. I am going to say one word: preemption.

Mr. DUNCAN. Yes, yes, oh, yes. Identify the threat and then craft something to combat it. And you do that in football, you do that in war.

So I yield back.

Mr. BILIRAKIS. I thank the gentleman, and I will recognize Ms. Castor from the great State of Florida, and my fellow Tampa Bay resident. Go Rays.

Ms. CASTOR. Go Rays. All right. Thank you, Mr. Chairman, and thank you to all of our witnesses for being here to discuss data privacy.

I strongly support this committee moving forward expeditiously with a comprehensive data privacy law that protects the personal privacy of all Americans, and I have been particularly focused on the harms to children and just recently filed—refiled my Kids PRIVACY Act that was developed with advocates like you and parents and pediatricians from all across the country. And it is time to act. I was heartened last session that the committee included portions of the Kids PRIVACY Act in ADPPA, but we really need to move forward quickly.

And on kids, one of the things that we aim to do is raise the age. Right now there is—really, it is just kids 12 and under who are protected. Ms. Vance, is there any reason that we shouldn't give all adolescents a fighting chance here and protect their privacy by increasing the age?

Ms. VANCE. I think that is absolutely vital.

We also need to recognize, though, that teenagers have different needs, are at a different developmental stage. And so making sure we are taking that into account, as well, is really important.

Ms. CASTOR. That is why, in the Kids PRIVACY Act, I created a protected class, so it is not quite as stringent as COPPA, but the Children's Online Privacy Protection law right now, it is so outdated. When was it first adopted?

Ms. VANCE. In 1998.

Ms. CASTOR. In 1998. Think of all the technological changes since 1998 in this huge surveillance and data-gathering enterprise that exists right now. We have got to move now to update this.

You also, Ms. Vance, in your testimony highlight the fact—you kind of compare what the Europeans did in the GDPR, which is their privacy law, and then explained in your testimony that they followed on with an age-appropriate design code. So that is actually missing from

ADPPA. Do you recommend that the committee also begin to develop an age-appropriate design code? Some States have done this, as well, but—what is your recommendation?

Ms. VANCE. I think it definitely needs to be based on the foundation of a comprehensive consumer privacy law, and that is really what has led to a lot of the successes in the UK with their ageappropriate design code.

Obviously, the EU legal landscape versus the U.S. legal landscape is not the same. So there's a lot of details to work out, as California is finding out. But the principles, the underlying, you know, location, off-by-default, just-in-time notifications, consideration of different age ranges and what is appropriate, all of that are protections that should be here.

Ms. CASTOR. Isn't it interesting that some States are moving to banning social media outright? And it is such—it seems like, you know, it is appealing, it is kind of a—based upon all the harm that we know that it is causing to mental health, addiction, and things like that.

But wouldn't privacy protections come first, and then a design code to require that apps and platforms actually design their products with kids in mind? Isn't that the most important thing that we can do right now, and is—I don't know that banning social media is even—if that is even realistic. What do you think?

Ms. VANCE. I completely agree. We shouldn't punish kids for the bad actors, whether it be the companies, individuals on social media, or websites or apps. We should acknowledge we need to protect the spaces that they are going to go into.

We all know how innovative kids can be when it comes to getting around particular restrictions. And so it really is important to make the world that they are living in, that they are going to go into safe, no matter what website or what app it is.

Ms. CASTOR. And we have the ability and the authority to do that by passing new, modern laws that put the kids' interests first and direct that apps and platforms actually develop these with kids in mind, and then not allow them to target children with advertising. That is pretty basic in privacy laws that are being adopted across the country towards—for children, isn't it?

Ms. VANCE. Absolutely. Almost every one of the 140 State student privacy and child privacy laws that have passed in the past decade ban targeted advertising across the board for kids.

Ms. CASTOR. Well, I encourage the committee to move expeditiously, and I thank the witnesses and Ms. Vance for being here. Thank you.

Mr. BILIRAKIS. Thank you. I now recognize Dr. Dunn from the State of Florida for your 5 minutes of questioning.

Mr. DUNN. Thank you very much, Mr. Chairman.

At our last hearing I mentioned that the Chinese Communist Party seeks to sabotage freedom and democracy everywhere that it exists. And this mentality permeates throughout all of China's corporations, as well, including those that operate in America.

Despite American leadership and technology, we still do not have a comprehensive national privacy standard. Ironically, China does. However, China's privacy law, the personal information protection law, is in reality a national surveillance plan. Their law forces data sharing of every person and business in China with their government. Their law puts everyone's personal details at grave risk of government surveillance, and their law enables their government to individually target citizens for concentration camps, enslavement, and even death. It literally enables the Chinese Communist Party to target individuals who are a potential source for organ transplantation, and the government knows whose genetic codes match whose, and they will murder and steal organs at will. Thus, their law does not protect privacy at all. It gives all their data to the government. Most of all, it certainly doesn't keep China from hacking Americans' data.

I want to remind my colleagues and my fellow Americans of some of the largest data breaches in the last decade, all of which left millions, hundreds of millions, of Americans' data exposed.

[Chart displayed.]

Mr. DUNN. I refer you to the poster behind me, starting with Yahoo and going down to the final entry there, U.S. Government employees with security clearances, 20 million hacked.

The American Data Privacy and Protection Act is both a privacy bill and a cybersecurity bill, and we need both. Protecting Americans from privacy invasion by domestic and foreign companies is important. And when we choose to share our data voluntarily with them, the security of our data in that company is also essential. Information that is not secure cannot be private.

Without a comprehensive privacy standard, we can't stop Big Tech, the Communist Chinese Party, TikTok, or anyone else. When Big Tech and data brokers compile large troves of data, they are creating massive targets for malicious Chinese hackers and others. We cannot allow them to profit from our loss or inattention.

Mr. Britan, thank you for your testimony. You have spent the last two decades working on global privacy and data protection policies. In hindsight, what are the key Federal provisions you would recommend to protect Americans' data?

Mr. BRITAN. I think a strong Federal law has to have all the rights that were first introduced in the HEW Report that exist in GDPR and most global laws: the rights to access data, obtain a copy of data, to delete your data. I think that the—but that is not enough. That is the first step.

We couldn't—we can't—we shouldn't put the burden of protecting privacy entirely on individuals. I think what really sets ADPPA apart are the obligations it puts on companies to protect individuals, regardless of whether or not they exercise their rights. And those are obligations around mandatory assessments, obligations around corporate responsibility, and the duty—the duties that are included in ADPPA for companies.

Mr. DUNN. Excellent, excellent. So there are certain guardrails we think should be put—we talk about it as minimization of data, but guardrails on what data is being allowed to be collected and by whom. Can you comment on that, Mr. Britan?

Mr. BRITAN. Yes, absolutely. I think data minimization is—we view it as a good thing. It is not a new concept. As I mentioned, it is something that has existed since the HEW Report.

I think the key thing that ADPPA does is it forces data collection to be purposeful. It forces you to think about the data you are collecting and why you are collecting it, and have a strategy. And as you mentioned, that is going to be so critical for minimizing the data we have, ensuring we have it for the right purposes, ensuring that we have proper access controls around that data. That all has to be documented and analyzed under ADPPA, and that is going to be some of the best protection we have against the threats that you identified.

Mr. DUNN. Thank you very much.

Mr. Codling, in your testimony you mentioned that your experience with the FBI has informed your conducting cybersecurity assessments. What, in your opinion, is the most vital and vulnerable personal information the government collects on individuals?

Mr. CODLING. I am going to follow some of Mr. Britan's comments of data minimization, data minimization, data minimization, all day long. Then you have less material to defend. You have less material to be concerned about if you never collected it.

Data thieves are completely going to go after children's data, particularly their financial data. And the fact that you have a blank slate when you are a young person, data thieves, nation states can come in and destroy your credit before you even realize that you needed credit.

Mr. DUNN. Ah, the Equifax hack. Well, thank you very much to the entire panel for your time and testimony.

Mr. Chairman, I yield back.

Mr. BILIRAKIS. Thank you very much, Doctor. I will recognize now Mrs. Trahan for her 5 minutes of questioning.

Mrs. TRAHAN. Thank you. Thank you, Chairman Bilirakis and Ranking Member Schakowsky, for calling this important hearing. Today's meeting is just another example of the bipartisan consensus on this committee that the current laws governing the internet fail to protect users and our most sensitive information. And it further highlights the importance of passing a strong, comprehensive privacy law like the American Data Privacy and Protection Act, and doing so urgently.

As many of my colleagues on the committee are aware, I am deeply concerned about what the emergence and embrace of education technology means for privacy and data of our children. Students and parents rarely have the option to withhold consent when using education technology or providing their data for platforms and devices used by schools. That is why I unveiled draft legislation 2 years ago to detail concrete steps Congress should take to protect student privacy and rein in tech companies.

And I am grateful that, when this subcommittee met to consider ADPPA last Congress, the chairman and ranking member worked closely with me to improve the bill to specifically protect students, including an important clarification that EdTech companies are not exempt from the bill simply because they work with schools.

Ms. Vance, in your testimony you mentioned that EdTech companies must comply with FERPA only to the extent that schools negotiate those restrictions in their contracts. In your opinion, do you think it is right to place that burden on schools?

And do you believe they have secured sufficient privacy protections for their students in those negotiations?

Ms. VANCE. It is absolutely unfair to put that burden on schools, just as it is to put child privacy protections burden on parents. You often don't have a dedicated privacy person, security experts, and others who can adequately protect that. And whether a company is small or large, they have more personnel who can do that than an individual school.

Mrs. TRAHAN. Well, I couldn't agree more. I don't think superintendents or principals should be responsible for negotiating our kids' data rights with multibillion-dollar companies. And I certainly don't believe that parents should have to pore over school district contracts with EdTech service providers to understand where the protections negotiated by their schools are strong enough. At the end of the day, the burden should be on the companies to design their services with privacy at the forefront and minimize the data that they collect.

There is bipartisan agreement that data on minors should be considered sensitive data, but there are different views on how we should set standards for when a company knows a user is a minor. Ms. Vance, again, would you agree that, regardless of the company's size, a company should protect user data as sensitive children's data when the company targets and markets the products to serve K-through-12 students?

Ms. VANCE. Absolutely.

Mrs. TRAHAN. I agree. And we have discussed three circumstances where companies generally must take extra measures to protect kids data: first, in the school setting, where education records collected—excuse me, where education records collected by most schools are protected; second, when companies direct services towards children; and third, when companies have actual knowledge that users are children.

Are there other circumstances where you think companies should give heightened protection to kids' data, and can you explain how you think about those requirements?

Ms. VANCE. Absolutely. We briefly mentioned the UK's age-appropriate design code in a previous question. The creator of it asked a question on a working group I was in several years ago: What if kids didn't have to lie to be on the internet? What if they could have the same experience? And that doesn't mean making the internet kid-proof; it means I can say that I am a kid, I can say that I am a teen, under 18, and have tracking pixels and other things turned off.

Mrs. TRAHAN. Yes.

Ms. VANCE. And I think that isn't something that we have necessarily considered here. It doesn't have to be a kid-proofed internet or a Wild West. It can be a good place for kids to grow up in. Mrs. TRAHAN. Well, I share those concerns and that view of how the internet could be. And I think that there are important lessons here.

As our committee discusses the failures that exist in other laws, we always need to be on the lookout to strengthen the legislation that we work on and pass today. So I am grateful, certainly to the chairman and ranking member, members of the subcommittee, for their continued attention to these important issues, but really grateful for your expertise and bringing that to the subcommittee today.

I yield back.

Mr. BILIRAKIS. The gentlelady yields back. Now I will recognize the gentlelady from the State of Arizona, site of the NFL draft tonight.

I will recognize you for 5 minutes of questioning. Mrs. LESKO. Thank you, Mr. Chair.

Mr. Reed, according to a January 2022 report from the Information Technology and Innovation Foundation, the growing patchwork of State laws will cost small businesses at least $200 billion over the next 10 years. Given the differing levels of size and sophistication that businesses may have, how important is it to small businesses that a data privacy law is clear and consistent throughout all of the 50 States?

Mr. REED. It is absolutely essential for all the reasons you outlined. And I think what is most important about what you are trying to do is, it is not just the small businesses that will end up complying. It is all of the third parties that we depend on to build our products.

Software is built like Lego. We write something special, but it is built of parts from other things, whether it is a software development kit or any other tools that we need. When everybody has the same rules, it helps the small business build something unique and special out of the pieces that we all see out in the table.

Mrs. LESKO. Well, and related to that, my next question, followup, is if we keep the status quo and the patchwork of State laws continues to grow, how can we expect entrepreneurs to take risks and innovate? Will they?

Mr. REED. No. And a very good example during GDPR, which we have kind of all gotten to deal with, one of our members came to me and said, “Well, so for the past year I have had one of my programmers, a full FTE for an entire year, just going back through to make sure we complied with GDPR.” It is a five-person shop. Now it was—for a year it was a four-person shop. That means there were jobs they didn’t bid on, projects they didn’t build, innovations they weren’t able to put into it. And if I have to do that for 50 States, hire 50 different people doing a single year’s worth of FTE to comply, it is simply unworkable.

Mrs. LESKO. Yes, I can definitely see that.

The next question is to any of you: Is there a State data privacy law that this committee should look at that is a good example that we should either replicate or use parts of it?

Mr. CODLING. Yes, I will throw out California, because California Consumer Rights Act and California Consumer Privacy Act were leading edge. They actually said, “We have a problem, let’s tackle it. It may be a fight in the mud puddle, but let’s tackle it, and let’s move the ball forward.” So kudos to them. And several other States have followed suit with that.

Mr. REED. I am going to go in a different direction. Virginia and five other States—Virginia, Colorado, Connecticut, and others— have done bipartisan legislation that I think is worth looking at. Mrs. LESKO. All right, very good. One last question, and this is, quite frankly, to any of you: What changes, if any, should be made to the American Data Privacy Protection Act that we passed out of committee last Congress to make sure we put consumers in control of the data shared through their smart home systems?

Ms. VANCE. I think one of the really important things, as I mentioned, there is a lot of intangible privacy harms when it comes to kids, when it comes to all of us. And so making sure that we are really looking at protecting not only a physical safety issue, but also something that may happen down the road, the misuse of information that we don’t know yet is going to happen but history tells us it almost certainly will. So including more protections against those sorts of intangible harms would be invaluable.

Mrs. LESKO. OK. And does anybody have any input on specifically smart home systems?

[No response.]

Mrs. LESKO. No? All right. Well, thank you. Oh, Mr. Reed?

Mr. REED. Just that a smart home system is, at the end of the day, a way to collect data that should serve the consumer who buys it, right? I get a smart home system because I want to be able to answer questions in my kitchen. I want the Alexa when I say “Don’t forget that I need to buy milk” to do it. The question is, what is done with that data moving forward?

So I think, when we look at smart home systems, I think, as Ms. Vance said, there’s some physical security elements when it locks your door, when it shuts off your lights that are in question. But I think you should look at the totality of it, which is it is collecting data on you that should be used for the purpose that you want it to do—remind you to take out the garbage, play a song, not ship that data to somebody else, to a broker that you didn’t expect, that ends up shipping you something that you didn’t want.

So for that reason, I think smart homes are sensitive, but it is part of the larger picture of, “Hey, I am—I want a service,” and this is what you are doing with the data.

Mrs. LESKO. Thank you. Thank you for all of you coming here and spending hours with us. I appreciate it.

And I yield back.

Mr. BILIRAKIS. Well, I tell you what, you asked some great questions, Mrs. Lesko. Thank you very much.

I yield back—she yields back, and we are going to ask Mrs. Dingell to ask her—she has 5 minutes of questioning.

You are recognized.

Mrs. DINGELL. Thank you, Mr. Chairman. And I want you to know the NLF draft is in Detroit next year.

Mr. BILIRAKIS. Next year.

Mrs. DINGELL. The Debbie Caucus is cheering for the NFL. But thank you, Mr. Chairman and Ranking Member——

Mr. BILIRAKIS. That should be exciting. Am I invited? Am I invited?

Mrs. DINGELL. Well, did she invite you? I will.

Mr. BILIRAKIS. I will hold you to that.

Mrs. DINGELL. I will. Anyway, thanks for both you and Ranking Member Schakowsky for holding this important hearing, and this is a subject that is very important to me.

As I have highlighted at several of these hearings focused on privacy, we have got to ensure that consumers are the ultimate arbiter of the data while allowing companies to perform any action that consumers should reasonably expect from the use of a platform device or any other technology. And as we all know, but—we do, but too many consumers don't—many platforms are already collecting far more data than most consumers expect or know, and it is much to their detriment.

But we must also take into consideration how gaps in current privacy law have led to vulnerabilities, such as those presented by notice-and-consent regimes and their impact on consumer and industry behavior that we must ensure are addressed.

Neither a consumer that dutifully reads the terms of service of a platform nor one—and I think this is most people—that immediately click yes to this consent request currently have sufficient baseline privacy protections and availability of consumer choice in the current landscape. And I think it is crucial that Congress address this gap in any comprehensive privacy legislation we advance through committee and the Congress.

So notice and consent. To best safeguard America's sensitive information we need privacy by design, not privacy through popups. Unfortunately, our fragmented Federal privacy laws heavily rely on the failed notice-and-consent regime. As anyone who has ever opened up a checking account or filled out paperwork at a doctor's office or applied for a credit card online can tell you, notice and consent does not actually involve meaningful consent or consumer choice. It is simply impractical, especially online, where consumers may visit dozens of websites in any given day. And quite frankly, they want to get rid of the popup. They don't realize how it is impacting their life.

Mr. Britan, do existing privacy laws provide consumers with a meaningful opportunity to understand and say no to an entity's data practices?

Mr. BRITAN. Thank you for this question. I 100 percent agree with you that notice and choice has failed as a privacy regime. It puts too much burden on the individual. It is unfair to the individual. There is no—most individuals don't have the time or the wherewithal or the ability to find all the information they need to make meaningful decisions.

And individuals should be protected, regardless of the decisions they may or may not make. There need to be baseline protections. I think—that is not to say that notice and choice isn't helpful and that we should get rid of notice and choice altogether. I think it just should not be the end of the story. And there need to be clear obligations and protections that apply to individuals, regardless of any decisions they may or may not make.

Mrs. DINGELL. Thank you. I believe that we must move away from this failed approach and support data minimization.

By the way, I don't think most people know how much data they are giving away. I just think 98 percent of the people—and that may be generous—don't. But I think we got—the practice of only collecting, processing, and transferring data that is reasonably necessary, this is what I think we need to move to, and proportionate to provide or maintain a specific product or a service.

Mr. Britan, do you believe that all entities should be required to minimize the amount of data they collect on consumers by default?

Mr. BRITAN. I do. I think data minimization is a good thing. It is not a new concept. It is something that existed since the HEW Report in 1973. I think data collection should be purposeful. Companies should know the purposes for which they are collecting data and only collect the data that they believe they need to fulfill those purposes. This is—this sort of proactive, planful approach to managing data will produce better privacy results.

Mrs. DINGELL. Consumers are deluged with constant breaches of their privacy and trust: weather apps collecting and selling users' location data to the highest bidder; data brokers selling—and that is what—this is what people don't realize is happening—data brokers selling information collected from wellness apps about users' mental health conditions; and kids and teens' banking apps that collect sensitive data, name, birth dates, email addresses, GPS location history, purchase history, behavioral profiles, all about our Nation's youth.

Mr. Britan, without data minimization requirements in place, are companies incentivized to collect, process, and transfer user data that is not necessary to provide a specific product's services?

And does overcollection of data increase the potential impact of a data breach?

Mr. BRITAN. Absolutely. I think we need to shift the mindset of companies to, rather than thinking of data as an asset, to thinking of it as a potential liability. The more data you have, the more surface area you create for potential issues and—such as improper access or misuse of that data. So even seemingly innocuous data can produce significant impacts if it is combined with other data sets or used in different contexts than what were contemplated.

So yes, we need data minimization, and the more data you have, the more chances you have of a breach.

Mrs. DINGELL. Thank you, and I yield back with an invitation to Detroit for next year.

Mr. BILIRAKIS. Thank you very, very much. The gentlelady yields back, and I will recognize Mr. Armstrong for his 5 minutes of questioning.

Mr. ARMSTRONG. Thank you, Mr. Chairman.

Mr. Reed, COPPA imposes an actual knowledge standard on operators, meaning various duties are only imposed when an operator has information verifying that they are collecting or maintaining personal data on a minor.

ADPPA imposes a constructive knowledge standard on high-impact social media platforms that should have known the individual was a minor. Your testimony states that the constructive knowledge requirement may result in further data collection on all individuals, not just minors, in order to verify age. Can you explain that further?

Mr. REED. Sure. One of the problems that has existed from the initial step of COPPA was—remember, COPPA's initial purpose was—COPPA—was to prevent advertising to children. COPPA is a collection standard, right? If you collect the information, you need to first receive verifiable parental consent.

The problem when you start moving from an actual knowledge standard to a constructive knowledge standard is it essentially requires companies to start gathering more data on you to know whether or not—what the condition of it is. And I said earlier in my testimony here, one of the problems is that we aren't empowering some of the platforms that might be able to send a signal or add a flag as a way for our developers to have that information before we ever collect something. Instead, it puts us on the mouse wheel of verifiable parental consent, which the parents don't like, which leads to problems.

So overall, though, we think that ADPPA—can we say ADPPA now—ADPPA moves us in the right direction. But that is the thing to make sure, that we are not actually burdening parents with more, not less.

Mr. ARMSTRONG. Do you think there is any interaction between that and the First Amendment right to anonymous free speech?

Mr. REED. Well, not—we are focused here, instead of being on a constitutional law panel on apps. But absolutely, First Amendment is something that is critical to my members. They care about it. They talk about it. They send me emails about it. So absolutely, we need to make sure that whatever we are doing here around the privacy, that we do allow for anonymous speech in a manner that is—since the birth of our Nation and in the Federalist Papers.

Mr. ARMSTRONG. Your testimony also cautions against expanding the use of verifiable parental consent under COPPA, which you argue puts the onus on—of privacy protections on the consumers. Can you explain those concerns?

Mr. REED. Yes, that is exactly what we were just saying, that VPC essentially requires the developer to affirmatively identify that it is the parent that is providing the permission to do things. Once you are through that gate, you can do a lot, and that has its own questions.

As I know Ms. Vance testified in her testimony, once you are through that COPPA verifiable parental consent gate, your access and ability to use the child's data raises its own questions. So I think VPC is onerous on the small businesses who impose it, although there are good companies like PRIVO and others that provide solutions. But it is also onerous—it also creates uncertainty once you have gathered that data, especially if you have done it in a way that doesn't comport with PRIVO or other VPC safe harbors.

Mr. ARMSTRONG. Mr. Britan, this hearing is largely focused on sectoral privacy laws at the Federal level. But your testimony also states that Salesforce would welcome the passage of strong, comprehensive privacy laws at the State level. Does Salesforce support State privacy laws only in the absence of preemptive Federal comprehensive privacy law, or do you suggest that States should enact laws in addition to Federal privacy law?

Mr. BRITAN. I think States should continue to be the laboratories for democracy, but I think we need a strong national standard. We need to speak with one voice as a country. And I think that the States have done great work, and we have supported that work because it has advanced the fundamental right to privacy in ways that didn't exist previously. But I think ADPPA is objectively the strongest privacy bill I have seen in the United States, and so I think it would set a strong national standard.

Mr. ARMSTRONG. But we also already exempted—I mean, as part of ADPPA was, like, the Illinois Biometric Information Privacy Act. The case law that is produced from those laws is an important— it has to be a risk for this community. And one of the—to consider. You know, an Illinois Supreme Court case that was decided months after we actually voted on ADPPA fundamentally altered the legal ramifications in Illinois and, by extension, the ADPPA.

That court held that each scan or transmission of a biometric identifier or information constitutes a separate violation.

So you are working at White Castle. You have to open a cash register with your fingerprint. You do it 10,000 times. That is 10,000 unique individual counts that can be brought against you. So when we talk about national privacy, I mean, it just—how does—well, I will just ask you. How does Salesforce plan to mitigate for such compliance risks?

Mr. BRITAN. These are tough issues.

I think, on the issue of preemption, Salesforce understands that we need a Federal law. And we understand that preemption is one of the issues that is going to have to be a matter of compromise. And I think the compromise that was reached on ADPPA seemed reasonable. And if that is the compromise that has to be reached to get us a Federal law, that is—then Salesforce would support that.

Mr. ARMSTRONG. And I think—I mean, I can agree with that to some degree, except then you have a case that comes out exactly like this. And I just wonder how smaller businesses with less resources are going to be able to deal with it.

So I would love to, but I am out of time and they have called votes, so I will yield back.

Mr. BILIRAKIS. The gentleman yields back. I know they called votes. We are going to try to get through this so that we won't have to come back, but we are going to do the best we can.

I will recognize Mr. Allen for his 5 minutes of questioning.

Mr. ALLEN. Thank you, Chair Bilirakis, for convening this hearing, and I want to thank the witnesses for enduring this and talking about this important issue. I would like to follow up on Chair Rodgers'—the point she made in her questions about the dangers of tech companies recklessly testing their new AI models on the masses, specifically children.

Snapchat has a new feature called MyAI that integrates OpenAI's GPT technology into Snapchat's platform offering users which are on Snapchat, mainly teens, a new chat bot featured to interact with. This interaction can lead to hyperspecialized data sets on teens, including their thoughts, their questions, and their fears—namely, anything a teen would think to ask chat bots. Snapchat would own this data and plans to monetize it.

Mr. Britan, how should we think about data processing privacy in a world where users interact with chat bots on a wide array of topics?

Mr. BRITAN. Yes, I think the best thing that we can do is pass comprehensive privacy law. I know I sound like a broken record.

Mr. ALLEN. Yes.

Mr. BRITAN. But I think these advancements hold great promise. There is also great potential pitfalls. And I think AI is powered by data, and the best thing we could do to ensure responsible AI and responsible chat bots is to pass comprehensive law regulating data broadly. That is missing in the U.S.

Mr. ALLEN. Yes.

Mr. BRITAN. And in the absence of that law in the U.S., the rest of the world is looking at this issue and examining it and pushing for responsible regulation. I think the U.S. has a very important voice in that conversation and should be a part of that conversation, and can be if we pass ADPPA or a law like it.

Mr. ALLEN. Right. Well, we keep harping on data minimization. And certainly, this is the opposite of data minimization.

You know, as a Member of Congress, I am concerned that we should be about—I am concerned about what should be about AI-powered chat bots in the hands of our children. I have got 14 grandchildren, and I am worried about their interaction and the harm that this would do to their future. How valuable would this data set be to a business?

Mr. BRITAN. It is hard for me to speak. I have worked at Salesforce, and I have worked at Microsoft to primarily B2B company Salesforce, entirely B2B. So I haven't had in-depth experience with understanding the value of children's data at Salesforce. We do have some educational projects, but we don't sell any of the children's data related to those products. So I am happy to say I haven't had to examine that issue in my career.

Mr. ALLEN. And I assume you agree that this development makes a data privacy bill, which you said, even more timely.

And does everyone on this panel agree that this needs to be done as soon as possible?

Mr. BRITAN. Yes. I am not in the business of working—don't do children. I have three kids.

Mr. ALLEN. Yes.

Mr. BRITAN. I want them to be protected. We need a comprehensive privacy law to protect our kids.

Mr. ALLEN. Good. With that, is there anything that you would like to add that might accelerate this process as far as the Congress is concerned?

Mr. REED. Congressman, I think the most important thing that would be helpful on this is reminding the Members of Congress that the small businesses in their district are actually part of this. And the better that you can do a preemptive privacy bill that helps the small businesses, it has as much of an impact.

I have heard a lot of discussion about Big Tech, but the people that rely on the technology are the people in the factories, in the companies. In your district there is Zapata Technologies that does some military contracts and other work. They depend on a robust data system and a robust privacy system. So if you are talking to your members on the floor and want to make the case, don't make the case about regulating Big Tech. It is for the benefit of their small businesses and U.S. innovation, so that we can compete on the global scale.

Mr. ALLEN. Right. And I am in meetings, I am having meetings all week with small businesses from my district, and I am hearing the same thing.

So with that, I am out of time. Thank you so much for your time.

Mr. PENCE [presiding]. The gentleman yields back. The Chair now recognizes Congresswoman Harshbarger for 5 minutes.

Mrs. HARSHBARGER. I will be as quick as I can. Thank you all for being here.

You know, I believe it is tremendously important that we establish a single national standard, really, before Chair Khan and her posse have the opportunity to go rogue and create more disastrous regulations, which they are prone to do.

And I want to focus on the idea of creating a private right of action as part of any legislation this committee is considering. And one consideration when we create a private right of action is running the risk of differing interpretations in different court districts, which results in more confusion of the rules rather than more clarity.

So what can be done to mitigate some of these concerns with the private right of action so that our Federal standard brings real clarity to the regulated community?

And I guess I could start by asking you, Mr. Reed.

Mr. REED. Well, I think that we have all seen appropriate give-and-take on the question of private right of action. I think the main thing for small business is going to be not implementing a private right-of-action system that allows for what we call sue-and-settle, where you are going to send a letter to a small business, it is going to be for 50K. You talk to your attorney who is in your small town, they say, "I don't handle that stuff." And they say, "You know what, 50K? Just pay it."

Mrs. HARSHBARGER. Yes.

Mr. REED. So that is the part that we have to do. But I think the work, the bipartisan work that this committee has done to handle those questions, and hopefully some of their fellow members on the Senate side can get us through that hump by limiting it to a certain cadre of actions that can be taken.

Mrs. HARSHBARGER. Yes, I have been a small business owner. And so, you know, and having pharmacies, that leads me right into my next question.

You know, I have had pharmacies, and what we do is we have to get licensed in several States. And listen, every State has different rules and regulations for my profession. So I have learned that the most stringent regulation is the one we have to follow. It could be a Federal guideline from the FDA or it could be a State board guideline.

So if State data privacy standards are conflicting with the Federal standard, then companies may well have to listen to those, you know, stringent regulations. For example, you have talked about California, the blue State regulations, rather than the ones we set if there are conflicts. And so, you know, I don't want California telling me what I have to do in east Tennessee when it comes to how I practice pharmacy.

So how important is preemption in ensuring that we have clarity at a Federal level? And I go to you first, Mr. Reed.

Mr. REED. It is critical. And you raised an interesting point about levels. Some of the problems aren't levels, they are definitions. If one State says you call this data this, and this something else, or says——

Mrs. HARSHBARGER. Yes.

Mr. REED [continuing]. If you have a breach for a breach notification, you must immediately report. Others say you have to tell the police first. It isn't just that we have levels. I think too often when we discuss this issue, people say, "Well, one State can be a floor and another State"—and that doesn't create a ceiling. For small businesses, it might just be the definitions that are in that compliance regime that create the problem. It is not always about levels. So absolutely critical.

Mrs. HARSHBARGER. Mr. Britan?

Mr. BRITAN. Yes, we need to set a national standard for privacy. Privacy can't depend on ZIP Code, and we can't have more powerful States dictating rights for other States.

I think preemption is going to require compromise. But I think, at the end of the day, it has—it can't be a compromise that sets no level of preemption. It has to be a clear national standard that sets the rules of the road for the country.

Mrs. HARSHBARGER. Yes. You know, if there are carve-outs to get this on the President's desk, my question is what provisions of the framework should we absolutely refuse to concede? Anybody?

[No response.]

Mrs. HARSHBARGER. Or nobody.

Mr. REED. I think you have heard from everyone on the panel that data minimization is something that I don't think we can give up.

And I think that making sure that the exceptions—that whatever you have to give up doesn't do some kind of odd carve-out that puts small businesses on an unbeneficial footing.

We want to—we want privacy laws to apply to us. We want to abide—because that creates trust, and that helps us get from small businesses to big businesses.

Mrs. HARSHBARGER. It is almost like when you are audited by a PBM, and they ask for certain information. Don't give them any more than they ask for. It is just inviting more questions and more audits.

So with that, Mr. Chairman, I yield back.

Mr. PENCE. I thank the gentlelady. I now recognize myself for 5 minutes.

I would like to thank Chair Bilirakis and Ranking Member Schakowsky for holding this meeting, and all of you being here today at the end of the day.

You know, as the chairman already noted, this marks the 36th time Congress has had a hearing on the—on privacy in the last 5 years. I heard that a couple of hearings ago, and I was just shocked. I couldn't believe it. And here, really, we are talking—it is like a chipmunk in the wheel. We are just talking about the same thing over and over again, getting nothing done. And I don't think we are really getting the attention of Big Tech and those— the violators in this environment.

You know, like many of my colleagues have discussed today, our increasingly digital world leaves Hoosiers and all Americans in the dark about who has access to their information. It is striking to me how little the consumers back home know about how much of their information is being collected, shared with third parties, and monetized without their informed consent. And that really bothers me. What am I getting for all the information you are taking from me all the time?

Just as truth in lending—years ago I served on bank boards for many years—was enacted to protect consumers from bad actors manipulating a complex financial industry, Congress needs to enact similar protections for all Americans where no current protections exist, like for internet platforms that are becoming all but required to participate in modern society.

Unfortunately, this growth-at-any-cost mindset has led to more divisive interactions online and harmful rhetoric that is impacting social fabric.

There is nothing wrong with making money, but it seems to me that mass collection and sale of our information has become foundational to Big Tech's big business model, and now many other industries, as well.

Consumers deserve to have control over their information, how their information is collected, who has access to their data, the right to remove, private right of action, and where their data might be shared.

Mr. Britan, Axiom is commonly cited as one of the largest data brokers in the United States, collecting and selling information on hundreds of millions of Americans with whom they have no direct relationship. In the 12-month period preceding July 1st, 2022, Axiom reported receiving just 279 right-to-delete requests, despite at least 25 million American adults being eligible to make such a request under State laws.

One reason for this low participation rate could be that Axiom, like many of its peers, requires individuals to navigate a complex web portal in order to submit a relatively simple privacy request. It seems likely that data brokers have an incentive to make this process as difficult for individuals as possible. Even some of the non-Big Tech folks, it is difficult to get out of that.

Get—the question. What is your opinion—like—the gentlelady asked this—but the right-to-delete requests, especially for those directed at data brokers, what can we do about—should we treat the data brokers differently than others?

Mr. BRITAN. Absolutely, and I have supported a lot of the data broker legislation that we have seen across the country.

I think in order for the rights to be effective, people have to know who is processing their data so that they can make requests of those organizations. And I think that we need to make clear to people who has their data so that they can exercise their rights effectively.

I also think that we need to impose responsibilities on these companies that apply regardless of whether or not people take that action.

Mr. PENCE. Thank you.

Mr. Reed, though it was not mentioned today, we have discussed private right of action in past hearings. Without a well-defined private right of action in Federal law, how will consumers be able to actually enforce their right to delete and other important privacy rights?

I know you touched on that a moment ago, but what is the Federal way to do it?

Mr. REED. Well, I think right now, as you know, State AGs have power, and a bill like this would help them deal with it from a Federal—from a national perspective.

I think that we—the main caution that we would say—and we have supported the work that you guys are doing on this legislation—is to avoid making it so easy that we end up with a sue-and-settle system, which is hard on small business. But I think there are some ways to belts-and-suspenders this to put it into the hands of State AGs or other actions.

Mr. PENCE. Well, thank you for that. I hope we differentiate between the size of the folks involved.

And with that I yield back. I now recognize Mr. Obernolte for 5 minutes.

Mr. OBERNOLTE [presiding]. Thank you. Well, thank you very much for the hearing, and thanks to all of you for being here.

Mr. Reed, I would like to start with a question for you. First of all, very—I have a lot of respect for your organization. As an app developer myself, thank you for the good work that you do. You had some really interesting testimony about preemption and the need to take all of these disparate sectoral privacy standards and unify them under one universal rule at the Federal level. But I would like to ask kind of a followup question on preemption, because this is one of the big debates that we are having about the ADPPA here coming out of this committee, is the degree to which it should preempt State law.

So do you believe that we should fully preempt State law in the issue of digital data privacy, or do you believe that, as some States have requested that we do, that we merely establish a floor and allow the individual States to go above that floor in their requirements on privacy if they wish to?

Mr. REED. I think we need fully—a full Federal preemptive legislation. I think, without it, you cause international problems.

As I said earlier, tiny app developers will be in the international trade business. They will be selling their apps or making them available in 100 countries. So if the privacy laws aren't federally mandated across the board, then we have a problem even on international trade.

Secondarily, as you point out—and I said this earlier—there is this idea or conflagration of this idea that it is levels. But sometimes it is just the definitions. So I might do the right thing, but I call it one thing in one State and one thing in another. And that means the compliance costs for a small business go up, because I have to create separate documents to talk about separate regimes with slightly different definitions. It is not always about levels. Sometimes it is just about what you call it.

Mr. OBERNOLTE. Yes, I completely agree with you. You know, I think sometimes we forget about the fact that when we allow this patchwork of regulation to exist with 50 different laws and 50 different States, it is very destructive to entrepreneurialism because the people that have the regulatory sophistication to deal with that are the big companies that have offices full of lawyers. And the people that don't have the sophistication to deal with that are two people in a garage that have to pay lawyers by the hour. So I am— completely agree with you. I think that we have to be very careful about preemption. I think we need to decide what areas we are legislating in with our privacy bill, totally preempt within those areas, and then carve out the other areas to make it clear where States can act independently and where they can't.

And then, you know, just following up to that, I was in the California State Legislature. I was one of the leads in drafting the California Consumer Privacy Act, and I think it is very important that we avoid some of the mistakes that were made with CCPA. We got a lot of things right. We were under time pressure—without getting into detail—to get that passed, but there were some kind of unexpected consequences that arose after that.

One of the main ones was that, much to our surprise, we thought this was going to be an iterative process, and once we passed it we knew we were going to have things that were missed as it was implemented, and we thought we were going to come along in subsequent years and fix it. You know, we would have a fix-up bill that—the year after, another fix-up bill the year after that.

And what we had not anticipated is that when you create, even unintentionally, a regulatory landscape with winners and losers, all of the winners will then get together and try and prevent you from changing the rule the subsequent year, even if the rule was arbitrary, unintentional, or unfair. And that is just a fact of political life. And I had underestimated how much that came to play.

So that is why it is so important that you are here, because I think stakeholder engagement is how you guard against that. And so I think we need to be very careful and deliberate about that.

Another thing that I think we need to be very careful about is that we are very specific in our choice of language in the bill. When you allow ambiguity to creep into what should be technical terms, particularly when it comes to things like data minimization, you need to be very careful that you are specific about what you mean when you say the data that you collect has to be necessary. Or if you say that it has to be related to the core business of your company, you better define what that means.

If you use a technical term, you better very carefully define it, because otherwise you will find yourself in the situation that we were in of having to watch a roomful of lawyers argue in front of a judge about what the intent of the author was, and that is something that, you know, when we abdicate our responsibility as legislators to the judicial branch, it serves no purpose.

So I am hoping that we can avoid some of that—some of those complications this time around. And again, it is going to be through the engagement of stakeholders like the groups that you represent that we are able to get that done. So thank you very much for your testimony today, and we are looking forward to continuing to work with you to make sure we get this right.

So I will yield 5 minutes—do we have anyone else up?

Mr. BILIRAKIS. Do you want to close it?

Mr. OBERNOLTE. Sure.

Mr. BILIRAKIS. Close it. But you don't get it next time. [Laughter.]

Mr. OBERNOLTE. So I ask unanimous consent to insert in the record the documents included on the staff hearing documents list.

Without objection, that will be the order, and—as there is no one here to object.

[The information appears at the conclusion of the hearing.]

Mr. OBERNOLTE. I remind members they have 10 business days to submit questions for the record, and I ask the witnesses to respond to the questions promptly. I know you will.

Members should submit their questions by the close of business on May 11th.

Without objection, the subcommittee stands adjourned. [Whereupon, at 4:27 p.m., the subcommittee was adjourned.] [Material submitted for inclusion in the record follows:]

Subcommittee on Innovation, Data, & Commerce, Hearing Entitled "Addressing America's Data Privacy Shortfalls: How a National Standard Fills Gaps to Protect Americans' Personal Information," [April 27, 2023]

Documents for the Record

At the conclusion of the meeting, the chair asked and was given unanimous consent to include the following documents into the record:

1. A Washington Post article entitled, "Remote learning apps shared children's data at a 'dizzying scale,'" May 24, 2022, submitted by Representative Walberg.
2. A letter from the National Association of Federally-Insured Credit Unions, April 26, 2023, submitted by the Majority.
3. A letter from the California Privacy Protection Agency, April 26, 2023, submitted by the Minority.
4. A letter from Privacy for America, April 27, 2023, submitted by the Minority.
5. A letter from leading members of the U.S. startup ecosystem, April 27, 2023, submitted by the Minority.
6. A report from the Information Technology and Innovation Foundation entitled, "The Looming Cost of State Privacy Laws," January 2022, submitted by the Majority.
7. A letter from the Credit Union National Association, April 27, 2023, submitted by the Majority.
8. A statement for the record from U.S. PIRG, April 27, 2023, submitted by the Minority.
9. Written testimony from Mr. Edmund Mierzwinski to the Committee on Financial Services, February 26, 2019, submitted by the Minority.

Remote Learning Apps Shared Children's Data at a 'Dizzying Scale'

The educational tools used by students during the pandemic shared their information with advertisers and data brokers that could track them around the Web, an international investigation found

By Drew Harwell
May 24, 2022 at 9:00 p.m. EDT

Millions of children had their online behaviors and personal information tracked by the apps and websites they used for school during the pandemic, according to an international investigation that raises concerns about the impact remote learning had on children's privacy online.

The educational tools were recommended by school districts and offered interactive math and reading lessons to children as young as prekindergarten. But many of them also collected students' information and shared it with marketers and data brokers, who could then build data profiles used to target the children with ads that follow them around the Web.

Those findings come from the most comprehensive study to date on the technology that children and parents relied on for nearly two years as basic education shifted from schools to homes.

Researchers with the advocacy group Human Rights Watch analyzed 164 educational apps and websites used in 49 countries, and they shared their findings with The Washington Post and 12 other news organizations around the world. The consortium, EdTech Exposed, was coordinated by the investigative nonprofit the Signals Network and conducted further reporting and technical review.

What the researchers found was alarming: nearly 90 percent of the educational tools were designed to send the information they collected to ad-technology companies, which could use it to estimate students' interests and predict what they might want to buy.

Researchers found that the tools sent information to nearly 200 ad-tech companies, but that few of the programs disclosed to parents how the companies would use it. Some apps hinted at the monitoring in technical terms in their privacy policies, the researchers said, while many others made no mention at all.

The websites, the researchers said, shared users' data with online ad giants including Facebook and Google. They also requested access to students' cameras, contacts or locations, even when it seemed unnecessary to their schoolwork. Some recorded students' keystrokes, even before they hit "submit."

The "dizzying scale" of the tracking, the researchers said, showed how the financial incentives of the data economy had exposed even the youngest Internet users to "inescapable" privacy risks — even as the companies benefited from a major revenue stream.

"Children," lead researcher Hye Jung Han wrote, were "just as likely to be surveilled in their virtual classrooms as adults shopping in the world's largest virtual malls."

School districts and the sites' creators defended their use, with some companies saying researchers had erred by including in their study homepages for the programs, which included tracking codes, instead of limiting their analysis to the internal student pages, which they said contained fewer or no trackers. The researchers defended the work by noting that students often had to sign in on the homepages before their lessons could begin.

The coronavirus pandemic abruptly upended the lives of children around the world, shuttering schools for more than 1.5 billion students within the span of just a few weeks.

Though some classrooms have reopened, tens of millions of students remain remote, and many now depend on education apps for the bulk of their school days.

Yet there has been little public discussion of how the companies that provided the programs remote schooling depends on may have profited from the pandemic windfall of student data.

The learning app Schoology, for example, says it has more than 20 million users and is used by 60,000 schools across some of the United States' largest school districts. The study identified code in the app that would have allowed it to extract a unique identifier from the student's phone, known as an advertising ID, that marketers often use to track people across different apps and devices and to build a profile on what products they might want to buy.

A representative for PowerSchool, which developed the app, referred all questions to the company's privacy policy, which said it does not collect advertising IDs or provide student data to companies for marketing purposes. But the policy also says the company's website uses third-party tools to show targeted ads to users based on their "browsing history on other websites or on other devices." The policy did not say which third-party companies had received users' data.

The policy also said that it "does not knowingly collect any information from children under the age of 13," in keeping with the Children's Online Privacy Protection Act, or COPPA, the U.S. law that requires special restrictions on data collected from young children. The company's software, however, is marketed for classrooms as early as kindergarten, which for many children starts around age 4.

The investigation acknowledged that it could not determine exactly what student data would have been collected during real-world use. But the study did reveal how the software was designed to work, what data it had been programmed to seek access to, and where that data would have been sent.

School districts and public authorities that had recommended the tools, Han wrote, had "offloaded the true costs of providing education online onto children, who were forced to pay for their learning with their fundamental rights to privacy."

The researchers said they found a number of trackers on websites common among U.S. schools. The website of ST Math, a "visual instructional program" for prekindergarten, elementary and middle school students, was shown to have shared user data with 19 third-party trackers, including Facebook, Google, Twitter and the e-commerce site Shopify.

Kelsey Skaggs, a spokeswoman for the California-based MIND Research Institute, which runs ST Math, said in a statement that the company does not "share any personally identifiable information in student records for the purposes of targeted advertising or other commercial purposes" and does not use the same trackers on its student platform as it does on its homepage.

But the researchers said they found trackers not just on ST Math's main site but on pages offering math games for prekindergarten and the first grade.

Google spokesperson Christa Muldoon said the company is investigating the researchers' claims and will take action if they find any violations of their data privacy rules, which include bans on personalized ads aimed at minors' accounts. A spokesperson for Facebook's parent company, Meta, said it restricts how businesses share children's data and how advertisers can target children and teens.

The study comes as concern grows over the privacy risks of the educational-technology industry. The Federal Trade Commission voted last week on a policy statement urging stronger enforcement of COPPA, with Chair Lina Khan arguing that the law should help "ensure that children can do their schoolwork without having to surrender to commercial surveillance practices."

COPPA requires apps and websites to get parents' consent before collecting children's data, but schools can consent on their behalf if the information is designated for educational use.

In an announcement, the FTC said it would work to "vigilantly enforce" provisions of the law, including bans against requiring children to provide more information than is needed and restrictions against using personal data for marketing purposes. Companies that break the law, it said, could face fines and civil penalties.

Clearly, the tools have wide impact. In Los Angeles, for example, more than 447,000 students are using Schoology and 79,000 are using ST Math. Roughly 70,000 students in Miami-Dade County Public Schools use Schoology.

Both districts said they've taken steps to limit privacy risks, with Los Angeles requiring software companies to submit a plan showing how student information will be protected while Miami-Dade said it had conducted a "thorough and extensive" evaluation process before bringing on Schoology last year.

The researchers said most school districts they examined had conducted no technical privacy evaluations before endorsing the educational tools. Because the companies' privacy policies often obscured the extent of their monitoring, the researchers said, district officials and parents often were left in the dark on how students' data would be collected or used.

Some popular apps reviewed by the researchers didn't track children at all, showing that it is possible to build an educational tool without sacrificing privacy. Apps such as Math Kids and African Storybook didn't serve ads to children, collect their identifying details, access their cameras, request more software permissions than necessary or send their data to ad-tech companies, the analysis found. They just offered simple learning lessons, the kind that students have relied on for decades.

Vivek Dave, a father of three in Texas whose company RV AppStudios makes Math Kids, said the company charges for in-app purchases on some word-search and puzzle games designed for adults and then uses that money to help build ad-free educational apps. Since launching an alphabet game seven years ago, the company has built 14 educational apps that have been installed 150 million times this year and are now available in more than 35 languages.

"If you have the passion and just try to understand them, you don't need to do all this level of tracking to be able to connect with kids," he said. "My first beta testers were my kids. And I didn't want that for my kids, period."

The researchers argued that governments should conduct data-privacy audits of children's apps, remove the most invasive, and help guide teachers, parents and children on how best to prevent data over-collection or misuse.

Companies, they said, should work to ensure that children's information is treated differently from everyone else's, including by being siloed away from ads and trackers. And lawmakers should encode these kinds of protections into regulation, so the companies aren't allowed to police themselves.

Bill Fitzgerald, a privacy researcher and former high school teacher who was not involved in the study, sees apps' tracking of students not only as a loss of privacy but as a lost opportunity to use the best of technology for their benefit. Instead of rehashing old ways to vacuum up user data, schools and software developers could have been pursuing fresher, more creative ideas to get children excited to learn.

"We have outsourced our collective imagination and our vision as to what innovation with technology could be to third-party product offerings that aren't remotely close to the classroom and don't have our best interests at heart," Fitzgerald said.

"The conversation the industry wants us to have is: What's the harm?" he added. "The right conversation, the ethical conversation is: What's the need? Why does a fourth-grader need to be tracked by a third-party vendor to learn math?"

Abby Rufer, a high school algebra teacher in Dallas, said she's worked with a few of the tested apps and many others during a frustratingly complicated two years of remote education.

School districts felt pressured during the pandemic to quickly replace the classroom with online alternatives, she said, but most teachers didn't have the time or technical ability to uncover how much data they gobbled up.

"If the school is telling you to use this app and you don't have the knowledge that it might be recording your students' information, that to me is a huge concern," Rufer said.

Many of her students are immigrants from Latin America or refugees from Afghanistan, she said, and some are already fearful of how information on their locations and families could be used against them.

"They're being expected to jump into a world that is all technological," she said, "and for many of them it's just another obstacle they're expected to overcome."

* * *

April 26, 2023

The Honorable Gus M. Bilirakis
Chairman
Committee on Energy and Commerce
Subcommittee on Innovation, Data, and Commerce
U.S. House of Representatives
Washington, DC 20515

The Honorable Janice D. Schakowsky
Ranking Member
Committee on Energy and Commerce
Subcommittee on Innovation, Data, and Commerce
U.S. House of Representatives
Washington, DC 20515

Re: Tomorrow's Hearing: "Addressing America's Data Privacy Shortfalls: How a National Standard Fills Gaps to Protect Americans' Personal Information"

Dear Chairman Bilirakis and Ranking Member Schakowsky:

I write to you today on behalf of the National Association of Federally-Insured Credit Unions (NAFCU) ahead of tomorrow's hearing, "Addressing America's Data Privacy Shortfalls: How a National Standard Fills Gaps to Protect Americans' Personal Information." NAFCU advocates for all federally-insured not-for-profit credit unions that, in turn, serve over

135 million consumers with personal and small business financial service products. NAFCU and our members welcome the Subcommittee's review of this important issue.

As NAFCU has previously communicated to Congress, we believe there is an urgent need for comprehensive federal data privacy legislation that protects consumer data, establishes data safeguards, and recognizes the standards that have been in place for over two decades with the Gramm-Leach-Bliley Act (GLBA). In 2019, recognizing the importance of data privacy and the ongoing privacy debate, NAFCU issued a series of data privacy principles that calls for a comprehensive federal cybersecurity standard, the harmonization of existing federal data privacy laws, and the preemption of state privacy laws. As the Subcommittee works to develop muchneeded comprehensive federal data privacy legislation, NAFCU recommends you include the following elements as key aspects in any such proposal:

- *A comprehensive federal cybersecurity standard covering all entities that collect and store consumer information.* Uniformly strong cybersecurity is necessary to ensure Americans' data is adequately protected across the economy. Existing strong federal cybersecurity standards, like that contained in the GLBA, should be extended to the activities of all data collectors and processors exceeding certain reasonable thresholds.
- *Harmonization of existing federal laws and preemption of any state privacy law related to the privacy or security of personal information.* The current patchwork of federal and state data privacy laws generates incredible consumer confusion and significant compliance burdens while failing to address the most significant data privacy risks to Americans—those risks posed by unregulated or inconsistently regulated entities that collect, control, and process vast amounts of our data. Comprehensive federal data privacy legislation should responsibly build on the successes of robust, time-tested federal laws by extending the same robust data privacy standards across the economy and ensuring that already well-regulated entities, like credit unions, may confidently operate within their existing federal frameworks without fear of being subject to more than 50 different data privacy and security standards.
- *Delegation of enforcement authority to the appropriate sectoral regulator.* The National Credit Union Administration (NCUA) should be federal credit unions' sole data privacy and cybersecurity regulator. Allowing the NCUA, which is well-versed in the unique nature of federal credit unions and their operations, to continue to examine and enforce any privacy and cybersecurity requirements is the most efficient option for both credit unions and American taxpayers. Exposing credit unions and other already well-regulated entities to suits by states' attorneys general and private rights of action will dramatically increase compliance costs without providing a corresponding increase in consumer protection.
- *A safe harbor for businesses that take reasonable measures to comply with the privacy standards.* Comprehensive federal data privacy legislation should adopt principles-based requirements based on an organization's specific operations and risk profile and include a safe harbor for organizations that design and implement appropriate measures.
- *Notice and disclosure requirements that are easily accessible to consumers and do not unduly burden regulated entities.* Providing multiple data privacy disclosures and opt-

out mechanisms across multiple channels creates consumer confusion and unreasonable burdens for subject entities. A new privacy law should avoid conflicting or duplicative disclosure requirements by incorporating easy to understand language, like that consistent with the GLBA's disclosure requirements.

- *Scalable civil penalties for noncompliance imposed by the sectoral regulator that seek to prevent and remedy consumer injury.* Actual damages to consumers are too difficult to establish by evidence, and statutory damages for violations are incredibly ripe for frivolous lawsuits. Sectoral regulators alone should have the power to assess scalable civil penalties, which can then be used to remedy and prevent consumer harm in a meaningful way.

While NAFCU supports a national data security and privacy standard, we had some concerns about the American Data Protection and Privacy Act (ADPPA) that the Energy and Commerce Committee considered in the last Congress, including:

- *GLBA Exemption.* Through the GLBA, Congress defined robust federal data privacy and information security standards for the financial services industry and provided the NCUA and other federal financial regulators the means to create and maintain strong privacy and data safeguards. The ADPPA did not recognize these long-standing requirements by providing a GLBA exemption. Congress should recognize the strength and successes of the GLBA and other time-tested federal sectoral data privacy regulation, and the value of regulator-led regulation, by wholly exempting credit unions and other already closely-regulated entities.
- *Private Right of Action.* This legislation provided a private right of action which would allow individuals or states' attorneys generals to sue covered entities over potential violations allowing courts to determine the law. This means that different judicial interpretations will allow a consumer in California to have different privacy protections than a consumer in South Carolina, and credit unions will find themselves immediately and unnecessarily exposed to new and substantial compliance and legal risks.
- *Preemption of State Laws.* The ADDPA would preempt many state laws but then subsequently provided exceptions that undermine the preemption. This would perpetuate a patchwork of state and federal data privacy legislation and regulation. We believe Congress must leverage comprehensive federal data privacy legislation to expressly preempt all state data privacy legislation and regulation.

As your colleagues on the House Financial Services Committee tackle the Data Privacy Act, H.R. 1165, within its jurisdiction to improve the GLBA for financial services entities, we urge the Subcommittee to craft a workable GLBA expansion to those outside of financial services that may be handling consumer financial data. The GLBA has successfully served consumers, credit unions, and other covered financial institutions for nearly a quarter-century. Changes to the GLBA for those already covered by it must be viewed with a cautionary eye. While some modernization of the GLBA for financial institutions may be in store, the system has generally been a success and should be a model for other areas. Making the system work best means expanding financial data protection requirements outside of just financial services.

Retailers, merchants, and others that handle financial data should be subject to new requirements similar to those standards adopted for financial institutions. We urge the Subcommittee to work with your counterparts on the House Financial Services Committee to ensure a balance that recognizes existing law and the concerns of credit unions as Congress tackles the important issue of privacy reform.

NAFCU looks forward to continuing to work with you to address these concerns with consumer privacy. On behalf of our nation's credit unions and their more than 135 million members, we thank you for your attention to this important matter. Should you have any questions or require any additional information, please contact me or Lewis Plush NAFCU's Senior Associate Director of Legislative Affairs, at 703-842-2836 or lplush@nafcu.org.

Sincerely,

Brad Thaler
Vice President of Legislative Affairs

cc: Members of the Subcommittee on Innovation, Data, and Commerce

* * *

April 26, 2023

The Honorable Gus Bilirakis, Chair
The Honorable Jan Schakowsky, Ranking Member
Innovation, Data, and Commerce Subcommittee
House Energy & Commerce Committee
United States House of Representatives
Washington, DC 20515

Re: Innovation, Data, and Commerce Subcommittee Hearing: "Addressing America's Data Privacy Shortfalls: How a National Standard Fills Gaps to Protect Americans' Personal Information"

Dear Chair Bilirakis and Ranking Member Schakowsky:

The California Privacy Protection Agency (Agency)[52] writes to thank the Innovation, Data, and Commerce Subcommittee for highlighting the importance of protecting the privacy and security of personal information not currently covered by privacy laws in its hearing, "Addressing America's Data Privacy Shortfalls: How a National Standard Fills Gaps to Protect Americans' Personal Information."[53] But such protections should not come at the expense of

[52] Established by California voters in 2020, the California Privacy Protection Agency was created to protect Californians' consumer privacy. The Agency implements and enforces the California Consumer Privacy Act. It is governed by a five-member board that consists of experts in privacy, technology, and consumer rights.

[53] United States House of Representatives, Innovation, Data, and Commerce Subcommittee Hearing: "Addressing America's Data Privacy Shortfalls: How a National Standard Fills Gaps to Protect Americans' Personal Information" (April 27, 2023), https://energycommerce.house.gov/events/innovation-data-and-commerce-

existing rights. H.R. 8152, the American Data Privacy and Protection Act (ADPPA),[54] which the Agency opposes in its current form, seeks to significantly weaken the protections currently in place in the states, including safeguards Californians currently enjoy under the California Consumer Privacy Act, as amended (CCPA).[55] Instead, lawmakers should support legislation that sets a federal floor and encourages states to continue to take the lead to advance protections.

Supporting states' efforts to adopt legislation to address their own residents' needs is consistent with interoperability. For example, the CCPA directs the Agency to work with policymakers in other jurisdictions to ensure consistency in privacy protections.[56] And the Agency's CCPA regulations were carefully crafted to not contravene a business's compliance with other privacy laws, such as Europe's General Data Protection Regulation (GDPR) and consumer privacy laws recently passed in Colorado, Virginia, Connecticut, and Utah.[57] In addition to working with other jurisdictions to ensure consistent protections, the Agency is also in regular contact with state, federal, and international regulators to help ensure consistent enforcement of the law.

Nearly all federal privacy laws already allow states to adopt stronger protections, which California has done. Such additional protections have not prevented California from becoming one of the world's leading economies.[58] For example, The Health Information Portability and Accountability Act (HIPAA), the Gramm Leach Bliley Act (GLBA), and the Fair Credit Reporting Act (FCRA) all contain language that allow the states to adopt stronger protections.[59] The Telephone Consumer Protection Act (TCPA) and the Video Privacy Protection Act (VPPA) also allow for stronger state laws.[60] California has already adopted stronger protections in many of these areas, from the Confidentiality of Medical Information Act (CMIA), which is similar to, but broader than, HIPAA, and the California Financial Information Privacy Act (CFIPA), which was explicitly adopted to provide a higher standard of protections than GLBA.[61]

Furthermore, it's not clear that the ADPPA will create a single national standard, a purported justification for the bill's preemption language.[62] ADPPA seeks to preempt swaths of existing state privacy laws but allows covered businesses to develop their own compliance plans, to be submitted to the FTC for approval.[63] This safe harbor could lead to hundreds if not thousands of different compliance standards, causing confusion among consumers seeking to

---

subcommittee-hearing-addressing-america-s-data-privacy-shortfalls-how-a-national-standard-fills-gaps-to-protect-americans-personal-information.

[54] H.R. 8152 (2022), https://www.congress.gov/bill/117th-congress/house-bill/8152/text.

[55] Cal. Civ. Code § 1798.100 et seq.

[56] *Id.* § 1798.199.40(i).

[57] California Privacy Protection Agency, California Consumer Privacy Act Regulations, Notice of Proposed Rulemaking (July 8, 2022), https://cppa.ca.gov/regulations/pdf/20220708_npr.pdf.

[58] Office of Governor Gavin Newsom, *ICYMI: California Poised to Become World's 4th Biggest* Economy (Oct. 24, 2022), https://www.gov.ca.gov/2022/10/24/icymi-california-poised-to-become-worlds-4th-biggest-economy/.

[59] *See* 45 C.F.R. Part 160, Subpart B; 15 U.S.C. § 6807; 15 U.S.C. § 1681t.

[60] 47 U.S.C. § 227(f); 18 U.S.C. § 2710(f).

[61] Cal. Civ. Code § 56.10 et seq.; Cal. Fin. Code § 4051(b).

[62] Memo, from Committee Majority Staff, to Members, Subcommittee on Innovation, Data, and Commerce, re: Hearing Entitled "Addressing America's Data Privacy Shortfalls: How a National Standard Fills Gaps to Protect Americans' Personal Information" (Apr. 25, 2023), https://d1dth6e84htgma.cloudfront.net/IDC_Memo_American_Data_Privacy_Hearing_2023_04_27_1_bda35f1b5d.pdf?updated_at=2023-04-25T21:40:51.125Z.

[63] *See* Sec. 303-4.

exercise their rights. This could be particularly harmful to members of underserved communities that do not have the resources to navigate these varying procedures.

The ADPPA could certainly weaken existing protections. For example, the CCPA gives Californians significant protections with respect to automated decision-making (ADM), including the right to access meaningful information about the logic involved in automated decisions and the right to opt out of automated decision-making.[64] This would enable California to help rein in algorithms, such as those used by social media apps popular with young adults and children that play a role in targeting harmful content,[65] or generative AI and Large Language Models that are growing in popularity at an astronomical rate, which ADPPA does not address.

The ADPPA also seeks to prevent the states from strengthening privacy protections in the future. ADPPA was introduced before the Dobbs decision created new urgency for meaningful privacy protections.[66] Since ADPPA was introduced, California has already adopted new laws to protect reproductive privacy, including a bill that, among other provisions, prevents out-of-state law enforcement entities from obtaining information from California businesses about an abortion that would be legal in California.[67] This year, the California legislature is also considering a bill to protect data collected by certain reproductive health apps by the CMIA[68] and a bill that would restrict the tracking of consumers near family planning centers, among others.[69] Washington State appears poised to advance HB 1155, a reproductive privacy law with sweeping protections over this sensitive data. In contrast, ADPPA has not been meaningfully amended to address new concerns with respect to reproductive privacy.

Ten state attorneys general, including those in Illinois and New Jersey, criticized ADPPA's preemption language, and "encourage[d] Congress to adopt legislation that sets a federal floor, not a ceiling, for critical privacy rights and respects the important work already undertaken by states to provide strong privacy protections for our residents."[70] California Governor Newsom, Attorney General Bonta, Assembly Speaker Anthony Rendon, and members of the California Senate have also raised concerns about preemption language in the ADPPA.[71]

ADPPA represents a false choice: that strong federal protections must come at the expense of the states. Americans deserve both, a federal floor that allows states to adopt stronger protections. We look forward to working with you to promote and safeguard these protections.

Sincerely,

---

[64] Cal. Civ. Code § 1798.185(a)(16).

[65] Ben Smith, *How Tik Tok Reads Your Mind*, N.Y. Times (Dec. 5, 2021), https://www.nytimes.com/2021/12/05/business/media/tiktok-algorithm.html.

[66] *See, e.g.*, Alfred Ng, *Data Brokers Resist Pressure to Stop Collecting Info in Pregnant People,* Politico (Aug. 1, 2022), https://www.politico.com/news/2022/08/01/data-information-pregnant-people-00048988.

[67] 2022 Cal. Stat. 89 (AB 1242).

[68] AB 254 (2023).

[69] SB 345 (2023).

[70] Letter from Ten Attorneys General to Congressional Leaders (July 19, 2022), https://oag.ca.gov/system/files/attachments/press-docs/Letter%20to%20Congress%20re%20Federal%20Privacy.pdf.

[71] Letter from Governor Newsom, Attorney General Bonta, and the California Privacy Protection Agency to Congressional Leaders (Feb. 28, 2023), https://cppa.ca.gov/pdf/adppa_letter.pdf; Letter from California Assembly Speaker Rendon to U.S. House Speaker Nancy Pelosi (July 19, 2022), https://cppa.ca.gov/meetings/materials/20220728_item2_letter_assembly_speaker.pdf; Letter from Senator Tom Umberg et al. to U.S. House Speaker Nancy Pelosi (Aug. 9, 2022).

Ashkan Soltani
Executive Director

Cc: The Honorable Cathy McMorris Rodgers, Chair
The Honorable Frank Pallone, Jr., Ranking Member
Members, House Energy & Commerce Committee

April 27, 2023

The Hon. Cathy McMorris Rodgers
Chair
House Energy & Commerce Committee
2125 Rayburn House Office Building
Washington, D.C. 20515

The Hon. Gus Bilirakis
Chairman
House Energy & Commerce
Subcommittee on Innovation, Data, and Commerce
2306 Rayburn House Office Building
Washington, D.C. 20515

The Hon. Frank Pallone
Ranking Member
House Energy & Commerce Committee
2322 Rayburn House Office Building
Washington, D.C. 20515

The Hon. Jan Schakowsky
Ranking Member
House Energy & Commerce
Subcommittee on Innovation, Data, and Commerce
2408 Rayburn House Office Building
Washington, D.C. 20515

Dear Chair Rodgers, Chairman Bilirakis, Ranking Member Pallone, and Ranking Member Schakowsky:

Privacy for America is a coalition of trade organizations and companies representing a broad cross-section of the American economy. Our membership includes companies and trade associations in the advertising, travel, hospitality, media, financial services, data services, market research, and many other industries. We have long urged the creation of a single comprehensive, preemptive national standard for consumer privacy that supplements the existing set of sectoral and anti-discrimination laws already in effect in the United States.

As the House Energy and Commerce Committee Innovation, Data, and Commerce Subcommittee's ("Subcommittee") considers an approach to this type of comprehensive, preemptive law in its hearing on "Addressing America's Data Privacy Shortfalls: How a

National Standard Fills Gaps to Protect Americans' Personal Information," the Subcommittee should take a risk-based approach to such a law and balance consumer protection with the responsible use of data. This balance was absent from the American Data Privacy Protection Act ("ADPPA") as it stood at the end of the last Congress. We write to highlight several facts that we urge the Subcommittee to seriously consider during this hearing and its work going forward in an effort to appropriately calibrate a preemptive, comprehensive national privacy law for business and consumers across the United States.

- *Sectoral and anti-discrimination laws work to address data practices within their purview.* For decades the United States has maintained robust protections for data industries including health care, financial services, telecommunications, and education. It has also built up strong defenses against the misuse of data related to certain protected classes, including protections for children's data and protections against the use of data to discriminate against individuals in housing, credit, and employment based on characteristics like race and gender. These long-standing laws, with long histories of enforcement and complex compliance programs within responsible companies, should not be left by the wayside as Congress assesses how to address the modern data-driven economy.
- *The Privacy for America Framework provides the model approach for privacy legislation.* The Subcommittee can look to the Privacy for America *Principles of Privacy Legislation* ("Framework") as an example of how to strike an appropriate balance for national data standards.[72] The Framework defines certain uses of personal information as reasonable and others as per se unreasonable and thus prohibited.[73] The Framework prioritizes consumer protection while also allowing consumers and businesses alike to derive immense value from reasonable uses of data and access to a vibrant online ecosystem.
- *Congress should set a national standard when addressing potential gaps in privacy protections and not abdicate that power to the Federal Trade Commission.* When the Subcommittee considers approaches to a comprehensive privacy law to supplement the sectoral laws, a bedrock principle of that work must be to set a true, preemptive national standard. The regulation of the modern data-driven economy is best left to the democratically accountable legislative branch, not individual states or executive branch agencies. Personal data is collected and processed almost exclusively in interstate commerce and, accordingly, should be subject to a single national standard, not a patchwork of differing state statutes. Data collection and processing, therefore, should be established once through the clear authority granted to Congress by the American people and the Constitution.
- *Private companies should follow the law, not create their own.* When Congress creates a true national framework for data practices, no company should be allowed to interfere in the legitimate, responsible, data practices Congress has authorized. Just because one entity maintains a market position as an intermediary between consumers and publishers does not give it the right to prevent otherwise legally permissible and

---

[72] Privacy for America, *Principles for Privacy Legislation* (2019) https://www.privacyforamerica.com/overview/principles-for-privacy-legislation/.

[73] Framework at Part 1, Sec. 1(Y); Sec. 3: Sec 6(G)(c).

responsible data processing. This concern is especially true when those private actors choose to obstruct reasonable data flows in order to further their own financial goals to the inevitable detriment of their competitors. A federal law should ban such meddling.

- *Responsible data-driven practices deliver over $30,000 in value to each consumer per year.* Any comprehensive national privacy law needs to balance the costs to consumers and businesses against the increased consumer protections such a law may offer. And the costs of overzealous regulation could be immense, as studies have found that companies' data-driven practices keep $30,000 per year in the pockets of each consumer in the United States thanks to free and discounted entertainment, information, and other services.[74] Congress should not reach into consumer's bank accounts by imposing unreasonable restrictions on the data services companies that provide the backbone of many of these free and low-cost services that consumers desire. Consumers do not deserve a new $30,000 tax.

Thank you for your consideration of this letter on this important topic. We look forward to working with you as you continue to evaluate and develop approaches to preemptive, comprehensive, national privacy legislation that will properly balance consumer protection and the vital, efficient, and effective data-driven practices required for a growing and dynamic Unites States economy.

Sincerely,
Privacy for America

* * *

April 27, 2023

The Honorable Frank Pallone
Ranking Member
Committee on Energy and Commerce
2322 Rayburn House Office Building
Washington, D.C. 20515

The Honorable Maria Cantwell
Chair
Committee on Commerce, Science,
and Transportation
254 Russell Senate Office Building
Washington, D.C. 20510

[74] J. Howard Beales & Andrew Stivers, *An Information Economy Without Data*, 2 (2022), https://www.privacyforamerica.com/wp-content/uploads/2022/11/Study-221115-Beales-and-Stivers-Information- Economy-Without-Data-Nov22-final.pdf.

The Honorable Cathy McMorris Rodgers
Chair
Committee on Energy and Commerce
2125 Rayburn House Office Building
Washington, D.C. 20515

The Honorable Ted Cruz
Ranking Member
Committee on Commerce, Science, and Transportation
512 Dirksen Senate Office Building
Washington, D.C. 20510

Dear Chair Rodgers, Ranking Member Pallone, Chair Cantwell and Ranking Member Cruz:

As leading members of the U.S. startup ecosystem—entrepreneurs, startup founders, incubators, investors, accelerators, and support organizations—located in 26 states that serve individuals, businesses, schools, and governments in every state across the country and throughout the world, we write to urge you to pass a uniform, consistently-enforced, comprehensive data privacy law to create certainty for us and provide baseline protections for our customers.

We are creating new ways for individuals to learn critical skills, helping people to advance in their careers, assisting businesses in reducing emissions, improving health outcomes for at-risk populations, among so many other innovative contributions to advance society. We care deeply about our users, customers, and clients, respect their privacy, and invest heavily in keeping their data safe.

Unfortunately, the rapidly shifting landscape of state privacy laws makes it difficult for us to be confident that we are compliant with the letter of each law and leads us to spend considerable time and resources navigating these disparate, complex frameworks. In fact, new research shows that we each spend hundreds of thousands and forgo up to 20% of revenue on often duplicative compliance activities.[75] A uniform federal privacy framework would create clarity for us, streamline these costs, allow us to better serve our customers, and improve our competitiveness all while ensuring that our customers in each state have the same privacy protections. The resources we save could be put toward hiring more workers to grow our businesses, investing in R&D to improve our products, and supporting our communities.

Last Congress you came closer than ever to passing a federal privacy law. We encourage you to build on that momentum this Congress while keeping in mind the needs of startups. We need federal privacy law that:

Creates uniformity. Startups need a federal privacy law to preempt individual state privacy laws. Without preemption, a federal privacy law would merely be another law added to the patchwork and would not create certainty or ease compliance for us.

Limits bad faith litigation. A federal privacy law should be consistently enforced by expert agencies and limit opportunities for bad actors to exploit the high cost of privacy

[75] *Privacy Patchwork Problem: Costs, Burdens, and Barriers Encountered by Startups,* Engine (Mar. 24, 2023), https://static1.squarespace.com/static/571681753c44d835a440c8b5/t/6414a45f5001941e519492ff/167907440051 3/P rivacy+Patchwork+Problem+Report.pdf.

litigation to extract settlements from startups by bringing lawsuits even when startups have not violated the law.

Respects the resources of startups. Many of us have not yet raised formal funding rounds and instead rely on our personal savings or the revenue we generate. Even those of us that have raised outside capital have significantly fewer resources than our larger competitors. A federal privacy law must account for our resources and ability to comply.

Accounts for the tools startups use. We use multiple tools and services to build our companies. As you formulate a federal privacy law, you should keep in mind the interconnectedness of the startup ecosystem.

The startup community supports your efforts to create a uniform, consistently-enforced federal privacy framework to create clarity and establish protections for all Americans. We thank you for considering our views.

Sincerely,

1Huddle
6AM City, Inc.
Abstract
Airpals Technologies Inc.
Ardian Group, Inc.
Availyst
Bims Laboratories, Inc.
Black & Brown Founders
Boolean Girl
Broadside Digital
Bryght Labs
Carefully
Center for American Entrepreneurship
CitiQuants Corp.
Connector Labs
Courtam, Inc. dba People Clerk
Cover
Cranberry Queues Corp.
DAF.Financial, Inc.
Denver Angels
Ecobot
Educreations
Engine
Eskuad
Event Vesta, Inc
Free From Market
FundBlackFounders
Gaussian Holdings
Global Response Systems
Globalfy, LLC

Green Tech Coast
Gust
Hacom
hobbyDB
Hush
Infiltron Software Suite
Innovare
Institute for Energy and Sustainability, Inc.
IronCore Labs, Inc.
Libib
Linktree
ListedB
LiteraSeed, Inc.
Lumo
M1PR, Inc.
Max Borges Agency
Maxwell
Onfleet, Inc.
PILOT Inc.
PIE
Polyhedra
Productions.com
RAVN
Raydiant Oximetry, Inc.
Red Cap Ventures
Refraction, Inc.
Renee
Right to Start
Signals
STY Holdings
TaxCredit.ai
TheraTec, Inc.
Tostie Productions, LLC
Venntive LLC
Voatz, Inc.
WePower Technologies LLC

cc: Honorable Members of the House Committee on Energy and Commerce and the Senate Committee on Commerce, Science, and Transportation

* * *

April 27, 2023
The Honorable Gus Bilirakis
Chairman
Energy and Commerce Subcommittee on Innovation, Data and Commerce

United States House of Representatives
Washington, DC 20515

The Honorable Jan Schakowsky
Ranking Member
Energy and Commerce Subcommittee
on Innovation, Data and Commerce
United States House of Representatives
Washington, DC 20515

Dear Chairman Bilirakis and Ranking Member Schakowsky:

On behalf of America's credit unions, I am writing about your hearing "Addressing America's Data Privacy Shortfalls: How a National Standard Fills Gaps to Protect Americans Personal Information." CUNA represents America's credit unions and their more than 135 million members.

Credit unions strongly support the enactment of a national data security and data privacy law that includes robust security standards that apply to all who collect or hold personal data and is preemptive of state laws. We firmly believe that there can be no data privacy until there is strong data security. Securing and protecting consumer data is important not only for their individual financial health but as a further safeguard against rogue international agents and interference by foreign governments.

Data privacy and data security are major concerns for Americans given the frequency of reports of misuse of personally identifiable information (PII) data by businesses and breaches by criminal actors, some of which are state sponsored. Since 2005, there have been more than 10,000 data breaches, exposing nearly 12 billion consumer records. These breaches have cost credit unions, banks, and the consumers they serve hundreds of millions of dollars, and they have compromised the consumers' privacy, jeopardizing their financial security.

Stringent information security and privacy practices have long been part of the financial services industries' business practices and are necessary as financial institutions are entrusted with consumers' personal information. This responsibility is reflected in the strong information security and privacy laws that govern data practices for the financial services industry as set forth in the Gramm Leach Bliley Act ("GLBA"). GLBA's protection requirements are strengthened by federal and state regulators' examinations for compliance with the GLBA's requirements and robust enforcement for violations. Several of these significant regulatory requirements and internal safeguards include:

- Federal Requirements to Protect Information: Title V of the GLBA and its implementing rules and regulations require credit unions to protect the security, integrity, and confidentiality of consumer information.
- Federal Requirements to Notify Consumers: Credit unions are required to notify their members whenever there is a data breach where the misuse of member information has occurred or where it is reasonably likely that misuse will occur.
- Strong Federal Oversight and Examination: Under their broad-based statutory supervisory and examination authority, the National Credit Union Administration

(NCUA) and the Consumer Financial Protection Bureau (CFPB) regularly examine credit unions for compliance with data protection, privacy, and notice requirements.
- Strong Federal Sanction Authority: Under numerous provisions of federal law, credit unions are subject to substantial sanctions and monetary penalties for failure to comply with statutory and regulatory requirements.

While this extensive legal and regulatory examination and enforcement framework ensures that credit unions robustly protect consumers' personal financial information, this safety net only extends to financial institutions. As consumers' personal information is disseminated to third parties, those protections end and credit unions and their members are adversely impacted by the lax data security standards at other businesses. These loopholes must end and a comprehensive data security and privacy framework that covers all entities that that collect consumer information and is preemptive of state laws must be established and this standard must hold those who jeopardize that data accountable through enforcement.

With that in mind, we ask the committee to consider the following data security and privacy principles for any comprehensive framework:

- *New Privacy and Data Security Laws Should Keep GLBA Intact:* Congress should leave financial services' robust data and privacy requirements in place. Financial services and the healthcare industry are subject to federal data privacy laws. The GLBA and the Health Insurance Portability and Accountability Act (HIPAA) have protected American's PII for over two decades and should be left in place as financial services and healthcare and their respective regulators have developed regulations, guidance, and procedures for compliance.
- *Data Privacy and Data Security Are Hand in Glove:* Any new privacy law should include both data privacy and data security standards. Simply put, data cannot be kept private unless it is also secured. Congress should enact robust data security standards to accompany and support data privacy standards.
- *Every Business Not Already Subject to Federal Law Should Follow the Same Rules:* The new law should cover all businesses, institutions, and organizations. Consumers will lose if Congress focuses only on tech companies, credit-rating agencies, and other narrow sectors of the economy because any company that collects, uses, or shares personal data or information can misuse the data or lose the data through breach.
- *There Should Be One Rule for the Road:* Any new law should preempt state requirements to simplify compliance and create equal expectation and protection for all consumers. We understand that some states have strong security and privacy requirements. Congress should carefully examine those requirements and take the best approaches from state law, as appropriate. A patchwork of state laws with a federal standard as a floor will only perpetuate a security system littered with weak links. The federal law should be the ceiling and the ceiling should be high. Just like moving away from the sector specific approach, the goal should be to create a strong national standard for all to follow.
- *Breach Disclosure and Consumer Notification Are Important, But These Requirements Alone Won't Enhance Security or Privacy:* Breach notification or disclosure requirements are important, but they are akin to sounding the alarm after the fire has

burned down the building. By the time a breach is disclosed, harm could already have befallen hundreds of thousands, if not millions, of individuals.

- *Hold Entities that Jeopardize Consumer Privacy and Security Accountable Through Regulatory Enforcement:* The law should provide mechanisms to address the harms that result from privacy violations and security violations, including data breach. Increasingly, courts are recognizing rights of action for individuals and companies (including credit unions). However, individuals and companies should be afforded a private right of action to hold those that violate the law accountable, and regulators should have the ability to act against entities that violate the law.
- *Recognize This Issue For What It Is – A National Security Issue:* More and more, data breaches that expose consumer PII are perpetrated by foreign governments and other rogue international entities. The proceeds from these attacks are being used to fund illicit activity. The nature of these breaches alone calls for a strong federal response that ensures all involved in collecting, holding, and using PII do so with the security of the information of paramount concern. You simply cannot have data privacy unless there is data security.

On behalf of America's credit unions and their more than 135 million members, thank you for your consideration of our views and for holding this important hearing.

Sincerely,
Jim Nussle
President & CEO

* * *

April 27, 2023

The Hon. Gus Bilirakis
Chairman
House Energy & Commerce Subcommittee on Innovation, Data, and Commerce
2306 Rayburn House Office Building
Washington, D.C. 20515

The Hon. Jan Schakowsky
Ranking Member
House Energy & Commerce Subcommittee on Innovation, Data, and Commerce
2408 Rayburn House Office Building
Washington, D.C. 20515

Re: Hearing: "Addressing America's Data Privacy Shortfalls: How a National Standard Fills Gaps to Protect Americans' Personal Information"

Dear Chairman Bilirakis and Ranking Member Schakowsky:

Attached please find U.S. PIRG's statement for the record for your hearing on "Addressing America's Data Privacy Shortfalls."

It describes the inherent danger in preempting the states on page 2 in greater detail. We also believe it would be a mistake to exempt all entities covered by the Gramm -Leach-Bliley Act from your legislation and would be happy to discuss this further. Please let me know if you have any questions.

Sincerely,

Ed Mierzwinski
Senior Director, Federal Consumer Program, PIRG
edm@pirg.org

Testimony of Edmund Mierzwinski, Senior Director, Federal Consumer Programs, U.S. Public Interest Research Group, at a Hearing on Who's Keeping Score? Holding Credit Bureaus Accountable and Repairing a Broken System, before the U.S. House of Representatives, Committee on Financial Services, The Honorable Maxine Waters, Chairwoman, 26 February, 2019

Chairwoman Waters, Mr. McHenry, members of the committee. My name is Edmund Mierzwinski, Senior Director for Federal Consumer Programs at the U.S. Public Interest Research Group, which serves as the federation of state PIRGs, which are member-based, non-profit, non-partisan research and advocacy organizations around the country.

1. Summary

Thank you for the opportunity to testify today on the important matter of Fair Credit Reporting Act (FCRA) reform. The law was passed in 1970 and has been amended over the years. It regulates the activities of consumer reporting agencies (CRAs), commonly called credit bureaus. What is a CRA, or credit bureau? We like one court's description of the behemoth Experian as a "company that traffics in the reputations of ordinary people."[76]

We have prepared a rough timeline of some major consumer reporting problems that have led to state or federal policymaker reforms and enforcement actions by the Federal Trade Commission or Consumer Financial Protection Bureau. The list also includes enforcement actions by state attorneys general and consumer protection attorneys, who each play a critical role in reining in the CRAs. The timeline is attached as an appendix to this report. We hope it is helpful and I can answer questions about any of its items.

I first testified before this committee[77] on credit reporting mistakes in 1989, at a time when several states and the Federal Trade Commission (FTC) were conducting investigations and

---

[76] See https://caselaw.findlaw.com/us-9th-circuit/1209375.html.

[77] House Banking Committee, Subcommittee on Consumer Affairs and Coinage, Hearings on Fair Credit Reporting, 13 Sept 1989. (After the Gramm-Leach-Bliley Act of 1999, the full committee's name was changed to Financial Services Committee).

negotiating consent decrees with several large consumer reporting agencies[78] due to a troubling pattern of consumer complaints over both their mistakes and their recalcitrance and failure to correct the mistakes after consumers exercised FCRA-mandated dispute rights.

That 1989 hearing was the first real effort by Congress to rein in the credit bureaus since passage of the original act in 1970. Since then, Congress has continually conducted oversight and, in response to industry's indifference to the problems it causes for consumers seeking financial or employment opportunity, has enacted significant reforms in 1996, 2003 and 2010.

States Lead the Way

Critically, each federal reform was preceded by major accomplishments at the state level. A key part of my message today is that continued state leadership in all areas – from climate change to credit reporting and privacy and digital rights more broadly– is critical to the advancement of this nation's policies to improve consumer welfare, health and safety and liberty.

Numerous states emulated California's pioneering auto emissions rules, protecting the environment for us and future generations. As you know, those state rules are currently under administrative threat. The pioneering 2018 California Consumer Privacy Act is now under attack in the Commerce committees of both houses by a phalanx of powerful corporate interests led by Google, Facebook, Amazon and the telco/cable ISPs. If they win preemption of state laws, consumers and citizens lose, forever.

The big CRAs were early advocates of eliminating the right of states to protect their citizens. If the credit bureaus and banks had succeeded *in 1992* in their brazen House effort to reverse the FCRA's longstanding standard that the FCRA serve as a floor of protection, not a ceiling, and at that time 27 years ago successfully preempted all state laws related to credit reporting, we would not have nationwide free credit reports, we would not have access to our credit scores, we would not have identity theft protections, we would not have data breach notices, and we would not have the free nationwide credit freezes finally enacted in 2018.[79] Congress only acts to protect consumers after a disaster (cue 2008 financial collapse) or after several states act first. Industry's goal is to take state innovators and consumer cops off the credit bureau beat.

In this testimony, in addition to detailing the need for consumer reporting reform, we call on Congress to ensure that Equifax finally pays a price for its massive 2017 data breach affecting over 148 million consumers.

Finally, we offer our strong support to the two draft bills from Chairwoman Waters and other members, which are before the committee today. The first, a new version of the

---

[78] "Credit bureau" is a widely used colloquial term for Consumer Reporting Agencies regulated under the Fair Credit Reporting Act (FCRA) 15 U.S.C. § 1681 *et seq.* The so-called Big 3 bureaus, Equifax (formerly Retail Credit Company), Experian (formerly TRW) and TransUnion now qualify as Nationwide Consumer Reporting Agencies (15 U.S.C. § 1681a(p)) and face greater responsibilities under the act. Many other firms, including specialty CRAs offering check cashing and bounced check databases, employment background checks, tenant screening, medical insurance and other services are regulated under the act's definitions. However, the Big 3 continue to grow, with their recent acquisitions of competitors: for example, Experian acquiring Clarity Services, Equifax buying DataX and TransUnion buying FactorTrust, all in the last few years. The 3 smaller firms fashion themselves as alternative databases operating in the subprime space.

[79] In 1992, after Congressional consumer champions could not remove an amendment inserted in committee at the behest of the banks and CRAs, preempting all state laws under the FCRA, consideration of the Consumer Credit Reporting Reform Act of 1991, HR3596, was ended by a "House motion to rise" requested by consumer groups. See https://www.congress.gov/bill/102nd-congress/house-bill/3596.

Chairwoman's Comprehensive Consumer Credit Reporting Reform Act, is a response to the problems posed to all consumers by the failure of the consumer reporting system. That system is dominated by its Big 3 members – Experian, Equifax, and TransUnion – as self-appointed gatekeepers to financial and employment opportunity. Their lack of innovation and propensity toward mistakes perpetuates injustices and denies opportunity to many, especially lower-income consumers and people of color. The second bill, the "Protecting Innocent Consumers Affected by a Shutdown Act," will force the CRAs to lend a hand to the restoration of the financial lives of the government employees and contractors harmed by the recent extended shutdown. Since 1989, I have observed the arrogant attitude of the CRAs. They've always claimed that mistakes, let alone credit problems, aren't their fault; they simply report what they are told. It is literally the Bart Simpson defense: "It's not my fault." They won't change unless you make them. Passage of these two bills will make them change.

2. This Story Is About Consumers, Who Are Products, Not Customers, of the CRAs

This story is not simply about three big CRAs (credit bureaus) named Equifax, Experian and Trans Union. It is also about numerous specialty credit bureaus and also about numerous emerging companies that don't know or don't want to admit their products are consumer credit reports regulated under the FCRA.

It is also about the responsibilities of the creditors that voluntarily "furnish" information to CRAs.[80] Why do they do this? The theory is simple. If more credit files are available about more consumers and contain more trade lines (accounts) about consumer history, then the consumer reporting database will be more valuable to users. Most of the creditor-furnishers of information to the CRAs are also customer-users of the CRAs. The business customers gain the benefit of a larger database; they also have responsibilities as users of credit reports.

Yet, mostly it is about the plight of *consumers* whose financial and other histories are the subjects of credit reports, which are bought and sold without our consent. *We are not their customers; we are their product.* Note that this has not stopped the CRAs from developing a lucrative, multi-billion dollar marketing channel of subscription-based credit monitoring and identity theft protection products designed to play to our fears of low credit scores or imposters stealing our name.[81]

In reality those credit scores are low because the CRAs haven't been forced to do a better job protecting our files from misuse or to keep them accurate or to respond to us properly when we dispute the mistakes. Imposters prevail because of flaws in the credit granting system and debacles such as the Equifax breach that make financial DNA freely available. Instead of carrying out their statutory duties, the CRAs have persisted in ignoring them while simultaneously aggressively hawking a variety of over-priced self-help products.

---

[80] Furnishers did not have any duties until 1996 amendments. Duties to provide complete and accurate information are solely enforceable by regulators; private enforcement is available only when furnishers are notified of reinvestigation disputes (See FCRA Section 623, 15 USC 1681s-2).

[81] This lucrative channel includes identity theft protection and subscription credit scoring products. "The private research firm IBISWorld estimated that the U.S. market for identity theft services was about $3 billion in 2015 and 2016." See page 5, "Identity Theft Protection Services," U.S. GAO, March 2017, available at https://www.gao.gov/assets/690/683842.pdf.

In 2017, the CFPB fined Equifax $2.5 million; Transunion $3 million and Experian $3 million over deceptive marketing of credit monitoring products by offering deceptively marketing "educational" credit scoring products, not the scores actually used by lenders to make decisions. The CFPB also ordered Transunion to pay $13.8 million and Equifax to pay $3.8 million in consumer refunds for using bait and switch trial subscriptions.[82] If these products had the actual value affixed to the price ($19.99/month and up), they would be sold as stand-alone products that would jump off the shelves.

3. What Triggered Passage of the 1970 Fair Credit Reporting Act?

In 1968 Representative Clement Zablocki (WI) offered an unsuccessful amendment to regulate credit reporting during consideration of the original Truth In Lending Act. Hearings were then held by the Senate and House by Sen. William Proxmire (WI) and Rep. Leonor Sullivan (MO). The complaints that triggered Congressional interest focused on a variety of deprivations by credit bureaus but a key driver of the hearings was complaints about the Retail Credit Company's abusive investigations of consumers applying for insurance policies. The Fair Credit Reporting Act was enacted in 1970 and in 1975, Retail Credit Company changed its name to Equifax.

While the original act restricted the sale of reports to limited purposes, provided certain rights for consumers and imposed responsibilities on credit bureaus and credit report users (but not yet on voluntary "furnishers of information"), some consumer advocates withdrew support when the final law included an industry-supported amendment providing qualified immunity from state defamation laws.

Early Consolidation Led to Mistake Patterns and Lack of Compliance That Continue Today; Sloppy Practices Also Lead to Identity Theft

Following passage of the act and the acceleration of industrial computerization, local and state credit bureaus began a first major wave of consolidation that resulted in 5, then 3 national CRAs by the early 1990s. A series of early 1990s reports by U.S. PIRG, Consumer Union (now Consumer Reports) and certain non-aligned CRAs confirmed widespread complaints.[83] U.S.

---

[82] These enforcement actions were carried out under the first confirmed CFPB director, Richard Cordray. News release, CFPB, "CFPB Orders TransUnion and Equifax to Pay for Deceiving Consumers in Marketing Credit Scores and Credit Products," 3 Jan 2017, see https://www.consumerfinance.gov/about- us/newsroom/cfpb-orders-transunion-and-equifax-pay-deceiving-consumers-marketing-credit-scores-and-credit-products/ and News Release, CFPB, "CFPB Fines Experian $3 Million for Deceiving Consumers in Marketing Credit Scores," 23 March 2017, see https://www.consumerfinance.gov/about- us/newsroom/cfpb-fines-experian-3-million-deceiving-consumers-marketing-credit-scores/.

[83] James Williams of Consolidated Information Services, a New York area retail mortgage credit reporting agency, in 1991 analyzed 1500 reports from the three big bureaus and found errors in 43 percent of the files. It and other smaller resellers of consumer credit reports are regulated by the FCRA; they are also customers of the Big 3, which are also known as data repositories. Over time, the number of these resellers, which in the 1980s and 1990s had an important role in conducting manual underwriting (line-by-line human review of consumer credit reports) has dwindled and their business models have changed, under pressure from the CRAs. But they have produced at least one other study of accuracy. See, for example, Consumer Federation of America and the National Credit Reporting Association, "Credit Score Accuracy and Implications for Consumers," 17 Dec 2002, at https://consumerfed.org/pdfs/121702CFA_NCRA_Credit_Score_Report_Final.pdf. This detailed study of credit scores derived from over 500,000 consumer credit files also provides a useful history of other studies of credit

PIRG, through FOIA requests, found credit bureau complaints led all others to the FTC in the early 1990s.[84] The consolidation of databases written in different programming languages and non-standard reporting formats – along with lax enforcement of the law – certainly contributed to the problems identified by the FTC, state attorneys general, Congress and consumer groups.

The mistakes and problems we found in the early 1990s continued. In the mid-1990s, we documented the rise of identity theft, which left more consumers struggling with the credit report dispute process.[85] ID theft was fueled by the easy availability of Social Security Numbers and a security flaw in the credit granting process. An identity thief doesn't need to obtain your credit report (which requires you to verify a lot of identifying information, try it). The thief simply applied for credit in your name, with your SSN and his/her address. The retailer or creditor, a trusted third party to the CRAs, obtains your credit report and issues credit in your name, to the imposter using your SSN, at the imposter's address.

In 2013, the Federal Trade Commission found that 26% of consumers had at least one mistake that "might affect their credit scores" in one of their credit reports and 5% of all consumers had "errors on one of their three major credit reports that could lead to them paying more for products such as auto loans and insurance."[86]

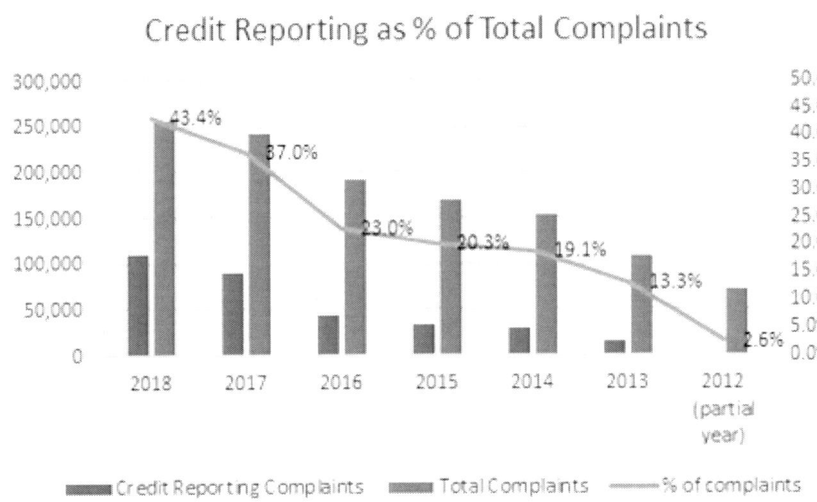

reporting accuracy and a discussion of the migration of credit and, especially, mortgage decision-making from manual to automated underwriting.

[84] See the following state PIRG reports: *Nightmare On Credit Street (Or How The Credit Bureau Ruined My Life): Case Studies Documenting Consumer Complaints and Recommendation For Amending the FCRA*, June 12, 1990; *Don't Call; Don't Write; We Don't Care,* 1991, which reviewed 156 consumer report complaints on file at the FTC and revealed that the average duration of complaints against a credit bureau was 22.5 weeks, or almost 6 months; and *Public Enemy #1 at the FTC,*" October 1993. Based on a Freedom of Information Act request, the 1993 report found that between 1990 and 1993, problems with credit bureaus was the leading cause of complaints to the FTC (30,901, 20.6%). *Public Enemy* also found that 44% of complaints concerned mixed files, and that among those, 64% involved the mixing of data with total strangers. We have published additional reports on consumer reporting errors, disputes and complaints in 1998, 2004 and 2014.

[85] See CALPIRG and U.S. PIRG, "Identity Theft: The Consumer X-Files," 1996, and "Identity Theft II: Return to the Consumer X-Files" and CALPIRG and the Privacy Rights Clearinghouse, "Nowhere to Turn: Stories from Identity Theft Victims," 2000.

[86] Federal Trade Commission, "In FTC Study, Five Percent of Consumers Had Errors on Their Credit Reports That Could Result in Less Favorable Terms for Loans," 11 Feb 2013, see https://www.ftc.gov/news-events/press-releases/2013/02/ftc-study-five-percent-consumers-had-errors- their-credit-reports.

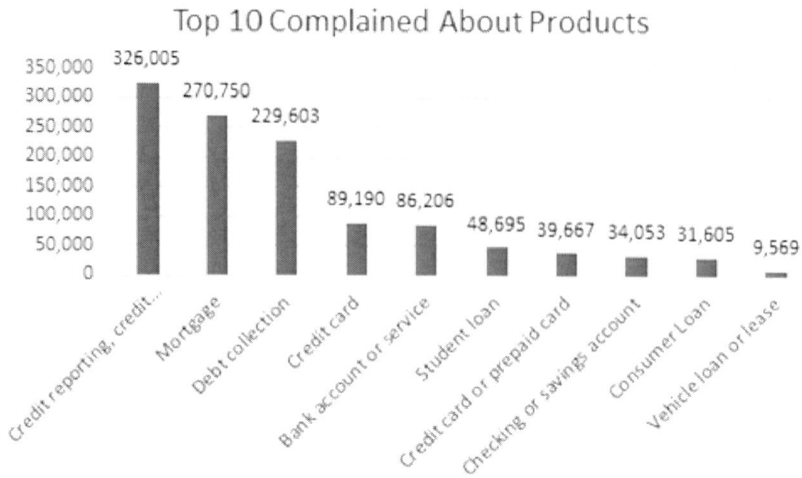

U.S. PIRG's regular reviews of the very important CFPB Public Consumer Complaint Database have most recently found the following, with 85% of all credit reporting complaints directed at Equifax, Experian and TransUnion.

The public CFPB Consumer Complaint Database is a critical tool for consumers, academics and other researchers and even competitors to make consumer financial markets work better.[87] Efforts by special interest groups to kill it must be rejected.[88]

4. The Failures of the FTC to Bring the CRAs to Heel over 40 Years

The Federal Trade Commission fought the credit bureaus with one hand tied behind its back from 1970-2010. The FTC had no or little rulemaking authority under the FCRA nor did it have supervisory or examination authority—the right to look inside the black box of CRA operations at any time to determine compliance and stop problems before the problems became worse.

Since 1970, we are only aware of one public civil penalty imposed by the FTC against the three CRAs for violating the FCRA. In 2000, in an action called Operational Busy Signal, the 3 were fined a total of $2.5 million for not having enough human staff to answer the complaint hotlines.[89] In 2007, under the FTC Act, not the FCRA, Experian subsidiaries were fined $300,000 for violating a consent decree issued in 2005 for deceptive marketing of its credit report monitoring subscription products.

Creation of the new Consumer Financial Protection Bureau, established by the Dodd-Frank Wall Street Reform and Consumer Protection Act of 2010, largely remedied these deficiencies.

---

[87] Since 2013, U.S. PIRG has released more than a dozen reports analyzing complaints in the database, on subjects including credit reports, and on categories of consumers, including the targeting of servicemembers by financial predators. See https://uspirg.org/page/usp/reports-cfpb-gets-results-consumers.

[88] Our June 2018 report, "Shining A Light on Consumer Problems: The Case for Public Access to the CFPB Complaint Database," summarizes why the database must remain open. See https://uspirg.org/reports/usp/shining-light-consumer-problems.

[89] In 2000, Experian and TransUnion were fined $1 Million and Equifax $500,000 for a total of $2,500,000 in the FTC's "Operation Busy Signal," for failing to comply withw a 1996 amendment to have adequate humans on hand to answer complaint calls.

The CFPB was given full rulemaking over 19 different consumer laws, including the FCRA.[90] The CFPB also has other authorities that the FTC lacks, including the right to impose penalties at any time[91] and supervisory or examination authority[92]—the right to look inside the black box of covered firms at any time to determine compliance and stop problems before the problems became worse.

The CFPB has exercised robust research,[93] examination and supervisory authority over the consumer reporting markets.[94] Yet, in one curious exception, with relevance to the Equifax breach, authority over CRA data security was retained by the FTC in Section 1031 of the Dodd-Frank Act. Title V of the Gramm-Leach-Bliley Act of 1999 had given the FTC authority to write rules establishing data security responsibilities for non-bank financial firms, including CRAs. Its data security rule is known as the "Safeguards Rule."[95] While the CFPB is reportedly pursuing an Equifax investigation and likely can defend its data security actions under its other authorities, it makes sense to transfer GLBA Title V authority to the CFPB, as recommended by the National Consumer Law Center in recent testimony before the committee.[96]

5. Equifax Showed Gross Indifference to Its Responsibilities to Protect Consumer Information; Its Data Breach Response Made Things Worse

Several Congressional committees have held hearings and/or issued staff reports detailing the Equifax breach. U.S. PIRG's own September 2018 report, "Equifax Breach One Year Later," summarized the following major problems:[97]

Had Equifax not been so careless, the breach may never have happened. Four months before the hacking, Equifax could have fixed a known security vulnerability in the widely-available and used Apache Struts open-source platform. Innumerable warnings from government security agencies and private experts were not acted on.

---

[90] The FTC retains joint authority over the FCRA, in addition, it retained a number of its own staff expert in the FCRA; annually the two agencies sign a Memorandum of Understanding concerning their shared FCRA duties.

[91] Although FTC can impose penalties for any violation of the FCRA or the Fair Debt Collection Practices Act, it can only impose civil penalties under either tits core authority under the FTC Act or its GLBA requirements after a firm is found to be in violation of an FTC-imposed consent decree.

[92] Congress gave the CFPB supervisory authority over banks > $10 Billion Dollars in asset size and over payday lenders, non-bank mortgage companies and private student lenders of any size. It also gave the Bureau, under Section 1024 of the Dodd-Frank Act, authority to write rules granting itself authority to supervise larger participants in other important financial markets. It has used the authority several times; notably, its first larger participant rule, in 2012, was over the consumer reporting markets. https://www.federalregister.gov/documents/2012/07/20/2012-17603/defining-larger-participants-of-the- consumer-reporting-market.

[93] See "Key Dimensions and Processes in the U.S. Credit Reporting System: A review of how the nation's largest credit bureaus manage consumer data," December 2012, https://www.consumerfinance.gov/data-research/research-reports/key-dimensions-and-processes-in-the-u-s-credit-reporting-system/.

[94] See "Supervisory Highlights: Consumer Reporting Special Edition," 2 March 2017 https://www.consumerfinance.gov/data-research/research-reports/supervisory-highlights-consumer- reporting-special-edition/.

[95] See https://www.ftc.gov/enforcement/rules/rulemaking-regulatory-reform-proceedings/safeguards-rule.

[96] See page 8, Testimony of Chi Chi Wu, National Consumer Law Center, House Financial Services Committee "Continuation of Hearing Examining the Equifax Breach," 25 October 2017, https://financialservices.house.gov/calendar/eventsingle.aspx?EventID=400866.

[97] Mike Litt, U.S. PIRG, "Equifax Breach: One Year Later: How to Protect Yourself Against ID Theft & Hold Equifax Accountable," 6 Sept 2018, available at https://uspirg.org/reports/usp/equifax-breach-one-year-later.

As explained in our report, the company also botched its response by:

- Delaying public notification for at least six weeks
- Setting up an online search tool that provided faulty results to those who used it about whether they were affected by the breach
- Initially understaffing its call center
- Initially including arbitration language that forced consumers to sign away their rights to a day in court
- Directing consumers to a fake website
- Failing to provide consumers full protection from new account identity theft -which it still hasn't done. (See Appendix A for a summary of Equifax's offerings to consumers in response to the breach and how they fall short of protecting consumers.)

Despite all the outrage and media attention last year, Congress has done little except make security freezes free, and even then, done so in a manner favorable to Equifax and the other CRAs, by preempting the right of states to enact stronger freeze protections going forward. Of course, the idea of the freeze didn't come from Congress, it came from 50 state freeze laws passed between 2003 and 2018. The idea of the free freeze also was jump-started by several free freeze amendments to existing state laws passed after the 2017 Equifax breach but before Congress passed S2155 in May 2018. That law created several minor consumer protections—but both the preemptive free freeze right and a military credit monitoring "right without a remedy" if monitoring was not provided were imperfect efforts. The comprehensive Waters CCRRA reform will cure both these problems. Congress should never preempt the states, especially at the behest of powerful special interests.

Also, critically important, Equifax has neither been held accountable nor paid a price for its breach. Further, this sensitive information, including Social Security numbers and birth dates, is still out there, with the potential to wreak havoc for the majority of consumers in perpetuity.

6. It Is Critical to Pass the Two Bills before the Committee Today

Finally, we offer our strong support to the two discussion drafts from Chairwoman Waters and her co-sponsors before the committee today. The first, the Comprehensive Consumer Credit Reporting Reform Act (CCRRA) of 2019, is a new version of the Chairwoman's longstanding effort to correct flaws in the consumer reporting system. It is a broad and thoughtful response to the problems posed to all consumers by the failure of the consumer reporting system, dominated by its Big 3 members as self-appointed gatekeepers to financial and employment opportunity. These firms have demonstrated for years that they lack the key incentives to do their jobs. Their failures perpetuate injustices that raise costs for nearly everyone and deny opportunity to many.

The second bill, the "Protecting Innocent Consumers Affected by a Shutdown Act," will force the CRAs to lend a hand to the restoration of the financial lives of the government employees and contractors harmed by the recent extended shutdown.

Since 1989, I have observed the bad attitude of the CRAs. They've always claimed that mistakes, let alone credit problems, aren't their fault; no, they claim "we simply report what we are told and if it is wrong, or negative, so what." They won't change unless you make them. The shutdown bill will make them take action to help people harmed through no fault of their own. The CCRRA addresses endemic problems in the consumer reporting system.

Title I of CCRRA: New Right of Appeal Critical to "Fixing the Dispute Process"

I will never forget the plea to the FTC by one of the consumers highlighted in U.S. PIRG's first report on credit bureau errors and failure to fix them. In 1990, the consumer asked: "It says "Item Remains, Confirmed By Source." What is this source!?"" A review of several narratives in the CFPB public consumer complaint database finds similar unanswered complaints from consumers continue today:

> "Experian states that the information remains…." [or] "Equifax completed the investigation yet this item still remains on my Equifax Credit Report " [or] "According to TransUnion 's updated credit file on XX/XX/2017 (# XXXX), XXXX # XXXX ... .. should be removed XX/XX/2017. As of XX/XX/2017, this item remains…." [or] "their responsibility must consist of something more than merely parroting information received from other sources…" [or] "I have asked Experian to provide the name of the data furnisher or third party source who verified this information so that I can contact them directly. Experian refuses to provide this information…" [or] "I have disputed this account several times online and in writing with no resolution. This account still remains on my credit report…"

So, the dispute system, despite efforts in 1996 and 2003 to fix it, is still broken. Title I of the CCRRA makes significant improvements. Most notably, for the first time, it establishes a right to appeal disputes. Title I also includes new matching procedures and other requirements to prevent disputed information from being routinely reinserted into consumer reports. Until now, greater weight has been placed on the opinion of "the source" furnisher than the consumer and less weight has been placed on whether an actual reinvestigation ever occurred, or whether the furnisher and CRA computers simply agreed that they both contained the same data, even if it was wrong.

Title II of CCRRA Limits the Use of Consumer Reports for Most Employment Decisions

Several states, including California, Colorado, Maryland and Oregon, and cities such as Chicago and New York have restricted the use of consumer reports for employment decisions. Further, the industry has admitted in testimony that it cannot show a relationship between a consumer's credit report and job performance.

Further, should any consumer be denied employment opportunity in a difficult economy due to a disputed item, or even an actual late payment, on a credit card?[98] The problem is harshest on persons of color and lower income consumers with "thinner" credit reports. Historically, their credit opportunities have not been extended from the national firms that

---

[98] See testimony of Chi Chi Wu, National Consumer Law Center, at a "Legislative Hearing on HR3149, the Equal Credit For All Act," Subcommittee on Financial Services and Consumer Credit, 23 Sept 2010, http://archives-financialservices.house.gov/Hearings/hearingDetails.aspx?NewsID=1355.

dominate the credit system. Should their job opportunities be similarly diminished by their credit reports?

Title III of CCRRA Improves Rights of Victims of Private Student Loan Borrowers

The title provides new protections for victims, including servicemembers and others, of unfair private student loan practices.

Title IV of CCRRA Makes a Variety of Changes to Rebalance the Reporting of Adverse Items

Credit scoring models prioritize the value of recent trade line information over much older information. Begrudgingly, under order by enforcement actions, the CRAs have also reduced the impact of non-predictive data, such as medical debt, and removed public records known to be full of misinformation. Yet, in general the CRAs have long resisted any changes to the types of information that they can collect or report or how long they can report it, even if it is now known to be non-predictive.

Title IV makes important changes to make reports more accurate and predictive. It shortens the reporting of certain bankruptcies from 10 to 7 years, eliminates reporting of certain public records and reduces the reporting of credit trade lines from 7 to 4 years, among other changes. It greatly reduces the impact of medical debt items, which are often mistaken due to bills that should be the responsibility of slow-pay insurance companies but are sent to collection under the consumer's name. Further, medical debt is the result of getting sick, or laid off, or losing insurance coverage, not due to a propensity toward "spending sprees." Both leading credit scoring models, FICO and VantageScore, a joint venture of the Big 3 CRAs, have already reduced or eliminated reliance on medical debt items.

Title IV also provides protection to victims of for-profit schools and other abusive practices.

Title V of CCRRA Establishes Oversight of Credit Scoring Models and the Use of Non-Traditional Data

Title V gives the Consumer Bureau clear authority to monitor and oversee the validity of credit scoring models to ensure that the often-opaque algorithms are accurate and predictive and do not introduce scoring factors that could violate the civil rights or fair lending laws. Further, Title V requires a Consumer Bureau study of the use of non-traditional data in consumer reporting. Alternative data is a shiny new toy you'll hear a lot about, but could have negative or unintended consequences, especially for some of the populations its proponents claim that it will assist.

Title VI of CCRRA Provides for Free Annual Credit Scores and Improves Requirements on Consumer Report User Firms to Promote Consumer Understanding of the Use of Reports and Scores

In the early 1990s the FTC proposed an interpretation that credit scores were, by definition, part of consumer credit reports that should be included in credit report disclosures[99] to

---

[99] The FTC did not have any rulemaking authority under the FCRA until limited authorities were granted in the 2003 FACT Act. In previous years, its views were described in often-amended "FCRA Interpretations" and through staff opinion letters.

consumers. Under an industry full-court press, it immediately reneged on this consumer-backed idea.

In 2000, following a joint campaign by realtors and consumer groups, California prohibited clauses in CRA contracts with users such as real estate agents that prevented them from showing credit scores to consumers. Since then, the veil over credit scores has gradually lifted. The CRAs have long-sought to monetize their disclosure, unfortunately also through deceptive marketing of "educational" scores, not the scores actually used by creditors.[100] It is past time to provide scores for free as part of the annual free report disclosure first required nationwide by the 2003 FACT Act. Section 604 of the CCRRA provides free credit scores in this and other circumstances.

Title VI also requires various users to provide consumers with additional information to improve their understanding of the consumer reporting system.

Title VII of CCRRA Bans Misleading and Unfair Consumer Reporting Practices

Even though we are not their customers, only their product, nothing has stopped the CRAs from developing a lucrative, multi-billion-dollar marketing channel of subscription-based consumer credit monitoring and identity theft protection products designed to play to our fears of low credit scores or imposters stealing our name.

Our credit scores are low because the CRAs haven't been forced to do a better job protecting our files from misuse or to keep them accurate or to respond to us properly when we dispute the mistakes. Instead of carrying out these statutory duties, the CRAs have persisted in aggressively hawking a variety of over-priced self-help products, often in an unfair or deceptive way.[101] Title VII would provide a variety of new protections against unfair and deceptive marketing of these products. Low-value versions of these products are often provided free after a data breach but consumers face a barrage of online and televised ads extolling the supposed virtues of upgrading to a $19.99/month, or even higher-priced, products. Section 703 gives the Consumer Bureau authority to restrict the prices of the subscription products.

Title VII provides additional protections to consumers with limited English proficiency and mandates by law that shopping around, for example, for a good deal on a new car, is not treated in credit scores as multiple applications for credit with multiple "dings" to a credit score. Further Section 707 establishes, for the first time, national registration of national and specialty CRAs to make it easier for the Consumer Bureau, FTC and consumers to hold them accountable.

---

[100] The CFPB used director Richard Cordray's bully pulpit very effectively to nudge more banks and credit unions to greatly expand the availability of free credit scores. Its most recent list is available: Skyricki, Irene, "A new list identifies more ways to access credit scores—for free," CFPB, 16 May 2018, at https://www.consumerfinance.gov/about-us/blog/new-list-identifies-more-ways-access-credit-scores-free/.

[101] For deceptive marketing of subscription products by CRAs, see news release, CFPB, "CFPB Orders TransUnion and Equifax to Pay for Deceiving Consumers in Marketing Credit Scores and Credit Products," 3 Jan 2017, at https://www.consumerfinance.gov/about-us/newsroom/cfpb-orders-transunion- and-equifax-pay-deceiving-consumers-marketing-credit-scores-and-credit-products/ and News Release, CFPB, "CFPB Fines Experian $3 Million for Deceiving Consumers in Marketing Credit Scores," 23 March 2017, at https://www.consumerfinance.gov/about-us/newsroom/cfpb-fines-experian-3-million-deceiving-consumers-marketing-credit-scores/.

Highlights of Title VIII of CCRA, Which Provides Additional Consumer Protections

The CRAs have long-imposed barriers on consumers fighting identity theft. Section 801 makes clear that there are a variety of ways a consumer can file a lawful identity theft affidavit, even if their local police do not take identity theft complaints. Most don't.

Section 802 makes improvements to the rights of protected or incapacitated consumers.

Section 803 improves statutory fraud alert rights for both consumers and active duty military personnel.

Section 804 corrects a CRA-driven provision in 2018 amendments that established a free national credit freeze right, but preempted states from providing additional, stronger protections. Section 808 corrects a separate 2018 amendment that provided servicemembers with free credit monitoring, but did not give them a remedy if the services were not provided.[102]

Title IX makes certain other amendments to ensure that the CRAs and other firms act in the public interest and under the law and requires the Consumer Bureau to complete rulemaking under the CCRRA within two years of passage.

6. Conclusion

This testimony and the attached timeline make an effort to describe how consumer reporting agencies have no incentives to sell accurate credit reports, so they do not. We also concur with the detailed testimony of my consumer and civil rights colleagues on the panel today, as well as the statements for the record submitted by a number of other consumer and civil rights advocates.

To protect consumers and ensure that markets work fairly, a combination of strong federal laws enforced by strong federal agencies must be accompanied by the right of states to respond more quickly to new threats in the marketplace. Further, full enforcement rights by state Attorneys General and local officials and strong private rights of action so that consumer protection attorneys can act as private attorneys general are also needed. The message is clear. Congress cannot solve every problem. Federal agencies cannot go it alone.

Going forward, we also look forward to working with the committee on newer and emerging problems of consumer protection, privacy and digital rights in the financial marketplace. For example, a large class of nearly unregulated data brokers sells products that are virtually identical to consumer credit reports, but not sold for "credit, insurance or employment purposes," so remain outside the protections of the FCRA. So-called lead generators sell lists of consumers, including to predatory lenders, derived from tracking their Internet activities. Pre-approved marketing decisions are being made, in real time, based on unregulated "e-scores" and look-alike consumers. Since the reports are not about a particular consumer, the firms contend their products are not regulated consumer reports.

As we point out on our "Digital Data and Consumer Protection Page:[103]"

---

[102] The provisions were included in S2155, a deregulatory proposal which became law as the Economic Growth, Regulatory Relief, and Consumer Protection Act (Public Law 115–174).

[103] See https://uspirgedfund.org/issues/usf/digital-data-and-consumer-protection-ensuring-fair-and-equitable-financial-marketplace.

"American consumers face new challenges and opportunities to their financial security as our economy is transformed by the convergence of digital media with "Big Data" technologies. Our use of mobile phones, social media, "apps," and other online tools have created new ways for us to spend, save and borrow money. Powerful forces are at work, however, that can undermine a consumer's ability to make the best choices and may place those already financially at risk even more vulnerable. The digital data-driven economy continually gathers vast amounts of information on individuals, online and offline, which is used to create a "profile" about our spending habits, behavior and our geo-location. These profiles can be "scored"—an invisible measure known only to the marketer and data brokers—that can determine whether we are offered high interest credit cards, payday and for-profit college loans and even what we may pay at retail and grocery stores. The uses of the information can be positive or, absent any regulation or meaningful protections, lead to discrimination, price manipulation or denied opportunity."

Thank you again for the opportunity to provide our views to the committee today. I look forward to your questions.

Appendix: Timeline of Significant Credit Reporting Events and Policymaker Responses

QUICK TIMELINE OF SELECTED CREDIT BUREAU (or CRA) EVENTS 1960s-TODAY		
Date	Problem/Policy	What Was the Problem; What was Response?
Late '60s	CRA Problem	Complaints grow about Retail Credit Corporation (now Equifax) insurance consumer report scandal
1970	Federal Response	Congress holds hearings on scandal; enacts Fair Credit Reporting Act to regulate companies selling consumer reports (called credit bureaus or CRAs)
1980s	RA Problem	First wave of consolidation of local/regional credit bureaus results in increase in errors in consumer credit reports
80s-early '90s	Both State/Federal Response	Responding to errors, investigations by state attorneys general and FTC result in CRAs brought under consent decrees, no fines
		-TRW (now Experian) signs multi-state and FTC consent order in 1991
		-Equifax signs consent orders with states (1992) and FTC (1996)
		-Trans Union signs consent orders with states in 1992 and FTC in 1994
1989	Federal Response	House Banking Committee (now FSC) holds first hearings in years on credit bureau errors
1991	CRA Problem	TRW (now Experian) incorrectly reports all citizens (3,000) of Norwich, VT area had failed to pay their taxes.
1992 - today	CRA Problem	By early 1990s, consolidations result in powerful gatekeeper "Big 3" national CRAs which now continue to acquire specialty competitors
1992	CRA Problem	Sponsors remove FCRA reform, HR3596, from floor action due to sweeping preemption provision demanded by banks/credit bureaus
Early 1990s	CRA Problem & Bad Policy Response	Use of non-transparent credit scores grows, FTC proposes FCRA interpretation that scores are part of credit reports; under industry pressure, reverses itself.
1992-1996	State Response	States led by Vermont and California enact comprehensive credit report reforms; 7 states provide annual free credit reports (VT, then CO, GA, MA, ME, MD, and NJ)
1994-today	CRA Problem	Rise of instant credit, easy availability of SSNs, other financial DNA, fuel rise of identity theft
1995-present	CRA Problem	Instead of improving compliance, CRAs respond to threat of errors/identity thieves by intensifying scare marketing of credit monitoring add-on products to consumers now fueling a $3 Billion/year marketing channel per GAO

(Continued)

QUICK TIMELINE OF SELECTED CREDIT BUREAU (or CRA) EVENTS 1960s-TODAY		
Date	Problem/Policy	What Was the Problem; What was Response?
1996	Federal Response	Congress finally passes Consumer Credit Reform Act (largely 1992's HR3596), imposes first duties on furnishers [creditors and debt collectors that provide information to credit bureaus] among other reforms. Limited preemption, primarily for new furnisher (bank) duties, to sunset after 8 years.
1998	Federal Response	Congress criminalizes identity theft, bureaus can now claim ID theft not our fault, "it's bad guys."
2000	Federal Response	Big 3 CRAs fined total of $2.5M (Experian $1M; Equifax $500k; TransUnion $1M) in Operation Busy Signal for failing to comply w/ 1996 amendment to have adequate humans to answer complaint calls
1998-2000	State Response	California realtors join consumer groups to win right for consumers to see their credit scores, previously prohibited by CRA contracts with user companies
2002	State Response	California enacts first data breach notice law
2003	State Response	California develops/enacts credit freeze protection right to deter identity thieves
2003	Federal Response	Congress passes FACT Act; limited bank preemption made permanent; annual free credit reports (but not free scores) included. Few identity theft fixes.
2003-2018	State Response	Following PIRG/Consumers Union model law, 50 states enact credit freeze and data breach notice laws to supplement omissions in FACTA.
2003	Consumer Action	Consumer protection attorney wins first case against a creditor-furnisher for failing to comply with FCRA in dispute investigation
2005	CRA Problem	Equifax spinoff ChoicePoint fined record $25M by FTC for selling credit reports to identity thieves
2005-2007	CRA Problem	Experian subsidiaries deceptively market subscription-based credit monitoring products by intentionally confusing them w/ free credit report by law
2005-2007	Federal Response	FTC places Experian under consent order in 2005 for deceptive marketing of subscription products, orders $300k penalty in 2007 for violating 2005 order under FTC Act
1970-2010	CRA Problem	FTC's lack of tools to enforce FCRA leaves consumers at risk of credit and job denial and identity theft as credit bureaus run amuck
2010	Federal Response	Dodd-Frank Act gives CFPB primary authority over FCRA and new tools to regulate/supervise/investigate/enforce violations of the FCRA
2012	Federal Response	In CFPB's first establishment of a "larger participant rule," agency begins examinations (supervision) of large Consumer Reporting Agencies
2012	Federal Response	Major FTC study finds 26% of consumers have errors on at least 1 report; 5% of consumers have a serious error that could cause denial of credit or higher costs for credit
2013	Federal Response	CFPB supervision results in CRAs sharing full consumer complaint files instead of 2-digit summary codes, w/ furnisher creditors in disputes, which advocates contend 1996 amendments had required for over 15 years.
1995-present	CRA Problem	Instead of improving compliance, CRAs respond to sloppy mistake-ridden reports/growth of identity theft by intensifying scare marketing of credit monitoring add-on products to consumers -now fueling a $3 Billion marketing channel, per GAO, even though consumers are their products, not their customers
2017	Federal Response	CFPB fines Equifax $2.5 million; Transunion $3 million and Experian $3 million over deceptive marketing of credit monitoring products by offering "FAKO," not FICO-like, credit scoring products. Also orders Transunion to pay $13.8 million and Equifax to pay $3.8 million in consumer refunds for using bait & switch trial subscriptions
2017	Consumer Action	Consumer protection attorneys win $60 Million jury verdict against TransUnion for falsely labeling 8,000 consumers as terrorists or drug traffickers.
2012-2017	Federal Response	CFPB releases "Key Dimensions report" and several "Supervisory Highlights" reports that document deficiencies in the Big Three CRAs' dispute systems, confirming findings in NCLC's 2009 Automated Injustice report

QUICK TIMELINE OF SELECTED CREDIT BUREAU (or CRA) EVENTS 1960s-TODAY		
Date	Problem/Policy	What Was the Problem; What was Response?
2014-2017	Both State/Federal Response	CFPB supervisory actions and a 31-state Attorney General settlement eliminate tax liens and civil judgements (often posted with inaccurate identifying information) from reports, raising credit scores for 12 million; and reduce the negative impact of medical debt on scores.
2015	CRA Problem	Data breach at Experian involving database used for T-Mobile customers affects 15 million consumers
2017	CRA Problem	Equifax breach: sloppy data security makes SSNs, other sensitive information for 148 million consumers available to outsiders
2019	Federal Response To Breaches	Still Waiting...
2019	Federal Response	Chairwoman Maxine Waters of House FSC Holds Important Hearing To Review Equifax Breach Response and Discuss Necessary Improvements To FCRA
Thanks to Chi Chi Wu of National Consumer Law Center for providing ideas.		
U.S. PIRG is responsible for any inaccuracies.		

* * *

Jessica Herron
Legislative Clerk
Subcommittee on Innovation, Data, and Commerce
House Committee on Energy and Commerce
2125 Rayburn House Office Building
Washington, District of Columbia 20515

Re: Morgan Reed's Responses to Additional Questions for the Record

Dear Ms. Herron,

Thank you for inviting me to testify on behalf of ACT | The App Association on April 27, 2023, at the hearing, "Addressing America's Data Privacy Shortfalls: How a National Standard Fills Gaps to Protect Americans' Personal Information."

Pursuant to the Committee on Energy and Commerce's Rules, I am attaching my answers to additional questions for the record in the required format.

Please let me know if you have any additional questions or if it would help for us to meet with Subcommittee staff as you continue your work on privacy legislation.

Sincerely,
Morgan Reed
President ACT | The App Association

The Honorable Kelly Armstrong

1. The Federal Trade Commission (FTC) advance notice of proposed rulemaking (ANPR) on "Trade Regulation Rule on Commercial Surveillance and Data Security" refers to "different kinds of consumers" and appears to consider employees as a type of consumer. The statement of Chair Khan regarding the ANPR also references "...tracking, collection, and analysis of consumer data in the workplace...," which seems to be a reference to employee data. The dissenting statement of then-

Commissioner Noah Phillips disagrees that the Federal Trade Commission Act confers jurisdiction on the FTC to "regulate any aspect of the employer-employee relationship that happens to involve data." It is evident that the employer-employee relationship is fundamentally different compared to a business-consumer relationship. An employer must process employee data for several purposes, including compliance with state and federal labor laws and other purposes related to professional activities. How would FTC action to regulate employee data impose challenges on the employer-employee relationship and existing laws governing that relationship?

I agree with the premise that the employer-employee relationship is fundamentally different compared to a business-consumer relationship. In our advocacy on privacy, the App Association has consistently urged lawmakers to ensure that however they decide to establish prohibitions on net harmful privacy conduct, those rules must respect the context of the business-consumer relationship. Employees' relationships with their employer are different enough from the business-consumer context that applying the same rules to both scenarios would result in awkward and ultimately harmful outcomes that policymakers would have to clean up later down the road. The contractual relationships at issue in these scenarios necessarily lead to differing privacy considerations. Whereas consumers pay companies for a given product or service (either monetarily or by allowing access to data about themselves), businesses pay employees for services in furtherance of the employer's production goals. Respect for context necessitates separate legislative—and regulatory—processes to consider the privacy issues that flow from these relationships.

The American Data Privacy and Protection Act (ADPPA) appropriately excludes "employee data" from the scope of "covered data." Likewise, the Federal Trade Commission (FTC) shouldn't seek to regulate privacy and security practices involving employee data under the same regime as consumer data. For example, mandating that employers respond to employee requests for access, deletion, or correction of data about themselves as if they were consumers of the company's products or services creates several obvious problems. An employee might disagree with their supervisor's characterizations of their performance and giving them a federally enforceable right to access any of their supervisor's communications about them or correct any of that information would obviously have a dramatically negative effect on the ability for businesses to operate. Although the FTC's Advance Notice of Proposed Rulemaking (ANPR) does not specifically ask questions about imposing requirements to respond to such consumer requests, any privacy framework policymakers ultimately pursue will likely include such requirements. Employers may also need to surveil employee activity—for example, to ensure safety or make timely adjustments to supply or staffing—in ways that would be inappropriate or at least communicated or conducted differently in the consumer-business context.

The Honorable Russ Fulcher

1. Does the ADPPA provide better and clearer guardrails on the use of data to allow for ensuring companies can engage in identifying for fraud protection, contractual issues,

and yet, provide avenues for these same companies to work with their partners by sharing user information?

Yes. Section 102 of ADPPA, which limits the data minimization principles in Section 101, appropriately allows for collection, processing, and transfer specifically for "fraud and identity fraud detection and prevention," and contractual issues.

2. I want to understand better data processing requirements of the ADPPA and again how it might differ from the GDPR. This is due to many B2B companies (like technology platforms) that work with application partners or other fulfillment partners. How does the service provider relationship with your companies work currently within the sectoral laws? Or is this not an issue?

There are lessons to be learned from how sectoral laws and the General Data Protection Regulation (GDPR) deal with the "controller"/"service provider" relationship. In general, the structure contemplated in the Health Insurance Portability and Accountability Act (HIPAA) appropriately delineates responsibilities between "controllers" (covered entities (CEs) under HIPAA) and "service providers" (business associates (BAs) under HIPAA). Under HIPAA, CEs are responsible for defining the scope of processing, collection, and transfer activities and communicating directly with patients about how they collect, process, and transfer protected health information. BAs may only process PHI provided to them through a CE via the contractual relationship they have with the CE and the contract defines the scope of what they are allowed to do with respect to that PHI. It is via that contract that HIPAA's requirements apply to BAs. This is a logical construct for privacy, and it works similarly in GDPR. Many of my member companies have operations that put them under a BA agreement and operations that put them under the FTC Act. Likewise, I have member companies that are "controllers" under GDPR for some of their activities, but "service providers" for some of their other projects.

Although the arrangements are complex, especially for small companies, having obligations flow via contracts through "controllers" to "service providers" is a better reflection of reality than making no distinction between those two categories.

3. Is there a worry over the lack of certainty for businesses in not having clarity over what obligations they will have to comply with when it comes to information collected from children that may not be protected under FERPA? Mr. Reed, how do your businesses view these challenges?

Yes, the legal landscape applicable to collection, processing, and transfer of children's data is complicated, whether the Family Educational Rights and Privacy Act (FERPA) applies or not. While the FTC has sought to clarify how FERPA and the FTC Act fit together, it is inevitable that the obligations that apply to education tech companies are ambiguous. In general, my member companies that provide education tools subject to FERPA pay closest attention to the Children's Online Privacy Protection Act (COPPA) with respect to any of their activities that fall outside the scope of FERPA.

COPPA does operate a little differently from FERPA since FERPA regulates school districts (as opposed to businesses and their relationships with consumers). For example,

COPPA's requirement for companies to obtain verifiable parental consent (VPC) prior to collecting PII from children does not apply "to the extent permitted under other provisions of law," (presumably, including FERPA's provisions). This could lead to the two regimes applying slightly unevenly or confusingly, even though there might be good reasons for their overlapping structure, but the FTC has addressed the issue. Under FERPA, schools need not obtain parental consent for disclosing children's education records to educational apps on contract with the school. The FTC has clarified in a frequently asked questions (FAQ) section that an education technology company may rely on "consent obtained from the school under COPPA instead of the parent," when such collection is for the "use and benefit of the school and for no other commercial purpose." Conversely, if the same children (if they are 12 or younger) sought to use the same educational apps outside the school context, the app must obtain VPC directly from those children's parents. Thus, while the edges around sector-specific privacy laws may seem less regulated, in this case, more regulatory privacy barriers arguably exist under the FTC framework than under the sector-specific law.

Ultimately, the takeaway for this Committee is that as it contemplates updates to children's privacy as part of ADPPA, there should be at least some focus on the burdens associated with VPC. As FTC Commissioners have pointed out, updates to privacy laws should avoid placing the burden on consumers wherever possible and instead place the burden of compliance on companies. VPC is an example of a requirement that places an inordinate burden on parents since it requires them to take seriously time-consuming steps to verify their identities with each and every service with which a child under 13 may interact. As a parent myself, I know that this is not a realistic burden to place on people as they seek to access educational services for their kids. And yet the current statute does not enable the market to provide VPC solutions in a convenient, organized way. It is often said that the notice-and-consent regime has failed because it doesn't fit real-world interactions between consumers and businesses. The same is true for VPC. A consumer privacy law can only ameliorate conditions for consumers to the extent it reflects reality and respects the ways consumers want to interact with and access digital goods and services.

* * *

May 27, 2023

Jessica Herron
Legislative Clerk
Subcommittee on Innovation, Data, and Commerce
House Committee on Energy and Commerce
2125 Rayburn House Office Building
Washington, DC 20515-6115

Re: Donald Codling's Responses to Additional Questions for the Record Dear Ms. Herron:

I want to thank the Subcommittee for inviting me to appear before it on April 27, 2023, at the Innovation, Data, and Commerce hearing entitled, "Addressing America's Data Privacy Shortfalls: How A National Standard Fills Gaps To Protect Americans' Personal Information."

Pursuant to the Rules of the Committee on Energy and Commerce, I am attaching my answers to additional questions for the record, in the required format.

Thank you again for your help, and please let me know if you have any questions.

Sincerely,

Donald Codling
Rego Senior Policy Advisor

Attachment —Additional Questions for the Record

The Honorable Kelly Armstrong

1. The Federal Trade Commission (FTC) advance notice of proposed rulemaking (ANPR) on "Trade Regulation Rule on Commercial Surveillance and Data Security" refers to "different kinds of consumers" and appears to consider employees as a type of consumer. The statement of Chair Khan regarding the ANPR also references "…tracking, collection, and analysis of consumer data in the workplace…," which seems to be a reference to employee data. The dissenting statement of then-Commissioner Noah Phillips disagrees that the Federal Trade Commission Act confers jurisdiction on the FTC to "regulate any aspect of the employer-employee relationship that happens to involve data." It is evident that the employer-employee relationship is fundamentally different compared to a business-consumer relationship. An employer must process employee data for several purposes, including compliance with state and federal labor laws and other purposes related to professional activities. How would FTC action to regulate employee data impose challenges on the employer-employee relationship and existing laws governing that relationship?

A. Thank you for your question. However, we do not possess the necessary subject matter expertise and thus are unable to provide a view to answer this specific question.

* * *

May 25, 2023

Jessica Herron
Legislative Clerk
Subcommittee on Innovation, Data, and Commerce
U.S. House of Representatives Committee on Energy and Commerce
2125 Rayburn House Office Building
Washington, DC 20515

Dear Ms. Herron,

I want to thank the Subcommittee for including Salesforce expertise and perspective in its April 27, 2023 hearing entitled "Addressing America's Data Privacy Shortfalls: How a National Standard Fills Gaps to Protect Americans' Personal Information." We hope that Members and staff found the hearing informative and helpful as they continue their work developing a national privacy standard. Please let us know if Salesforce can be of service in the future.

Pursuant to the Rules of the Committee, please find responses to questions for the record attached.

Sincerely,
Edward Britan
Head of Global Privacy
Salesforce

Questions for the Record

The Honorable Kelly Armstrong

The Federal Trade Commission (FTC) advance notice of proposed rulemaking (ANPR) on "Trade Regulation Rule on Commercial Surveillance and Data Security" refers to "different kinds of consumers" and appears to consider employees as a type of consumer. The statement of Chair Khan regarding the ANPR also references " ... tracking, collection, and analysis of consumer data in the workplace ...," which seems to be a reference to employee data. The dissenting statement of then-Commissioner Noah Phillips disagrees that the Federal Trade Commission Act confers jurisdiction on the FTC to "regulate any aspect of the employer-employee relationship that happens to involve data." It is evident that the employer-employee relationship is fundamentally different compared to a business-consumer relationship. An employer must process employee data for several purposes, including compliance with state and federal labor laws and other purposes related to professional activities. How would FTC action to regulate employee data impose challenges on the employer-employee relationship and existing laws governing that relationship?

In the U.S. we have a consumer-oriented privacy culture. The FTC should focus its ANPR on "Commercial Surveillance and Data Security" on protections for consumers. This will enable the ANPR and future rules stemming from it to gain more traction and be more effectively implemented.

There is a separate, well-developed field of employment law with which organizations must comply to protect employees. Salesforce believes that new employee-specific laws should be introduced to protect employee privacy. These laws could be enforced by the FTC with clear statutory guardrails to ensure that enforcement does not conflict with the existing employment legal structure.

Protecting employees in an ANPR primarily aimed at protecting consumers seems like a forced fit. Further, it would have unintended consequences in the employment context where obligations for consumer-facing companies and/or rights intended for consumers may come into conflict with data that employers need to maintain for legal compliance and/or to operate as an organization.

The Honorable Russ Fulcher

At our hearing in early March, we saw how the European Union is more characterized by economies that have large businesses continuing to grow, but with fewer startups as a result of the implementation of the GDPR. In a privacy briefing for my staff, a company privacy security officer noted how GDPR is putting more emphasis on businesses to explain how they are using consumer's data and subsequently, consumers receive more pop ups as a result. Compared to ADPPA which focuses more on data minimization as its base, do sectoral laws have notice and consent fatigue as well?

Notice and choice fatigue is real, and yes, this is an issue with the existing sectoral laws, which rely too much on opt-in or opt-out consent. Notice and choice places too much burden on the individual to protect their own privacy.

Notice, as envisioned by the GDPR's requirements around transparency, is good it helps to set expectations and enable individuals that are so inclined to act to protect their data. Choice or consent, however, has been used in problematic ways, such as when consumers are burdened with too many choices that are too granular or layered in nature. This often leads to consumers agreeing to things without fully understanding what they are agreeing to.

The intent of GDPR was to move away from notice and choice by making consent a much more difficult standard to achieve. However, it has unintentionally resulted in the opposite effect, as more companies have sought to apply simple pop-up consent experiences to demonstrate compliance.

That is not to say that there isn't a place for notice and choice. Giving people an ability to control how their data may be used is helpful. But that should not be the end of the story.

The sorts of obligations that ADPPA would impose on organizations, including the data minimization principles and impact assessments would protect people without forcing them to make complicated decisions that they may not entirely understand or have the time to address.

* * *

May 29, 2023

Jessica Herron
Legislative Clerk
Subcommittee on Innovation, Data, and Commerce
House Committee on Energy and Commerce
2125 Rayburn House Office Building
Washington, DC 20515-6115

Re: Amelia Vance's Responses to Additional Questions for the Record

Dear Ms. Herron:

I want to thank the Subcommittee for inviting me to appear before it on April 27, 2023 to testify at the hearing entitled "Addressing America's Data Privacy Shortfalls: How A National Standard Fills Gaps To Protect Americans' Personal Information."

Pursuant to the Rules of the Committee on Energy and Commerce, I am attaching my answers to additional questions for the record, in the required format.

Thank you again for your help, and please let me know if you have any questions.

Sincerely,

Amelia Vance
Founder and President
Public Interest Privacy Center

Ms. Amelia Vance

Attachment Additional Questions for the Record

The Honorable Russ Fulcher

1. Is there a worry over the lack of certainty for businesses in not having clarity over what obligations they will have to comply with when it comes to information collected from children that may not be protected under FERPA?

Yes, the lack of certainty for businesses regarding their legal obligations with regard to information collected from children is an important and concerning issue. The patchwork of sectoral laws that govern privacy in the US provide different, varying protections for the same information depending on the context in which the information is collected. For example, whether or not the same information collected from a child using the same educational app is protected by FERPA depends on where and for what reason that child is using the app. If a child uses an educational app at school or at home at the direction of a teacher, the data being collected is generally protected under FERPA. However, FERPA does not apply to information collected from a child using that exact same educational app in other contexts, such as when it has been downloaded by their parent or when the child has decided that the learning game is fun. This can leave the business operating the educational app in a difficult position where their legal obligations regarding a child's information changes depending on the context in which that child interacted with the app.

In addition to the harm that this can cause to children when the law isn't followed (or isn't sufficient), businesses that want to do the right thing are disadvantaged. A 2017 Carnegie Mellon University capstone project's interviews with edtech companies (attached) found that there was a "general lack of pressure or interest from their capital investors in data privacy," with investors simply "'checking-the-box' when it came to student data privacy."[104] This can create a monetary incentive for companies to do the bare minimum which sometimes includes not protecting the information collected by an edtech app used at home since it is unclear if the law applies.

In order to protect against unethical businesses taking advantage of any ambiguity or lack of clarity in the existing child and student privacy laws, we need a comprehensive privacy law that ensures baseline protections for all consumers. Not only will stronger privacy regulations protect vulnerable children and teens, they will also create a level playing field for ethical

[104] Disclosure: I was on the Advisory Board in 2016-2017 for this Capstone project.

businesses that prioritize privacy and security. Companies that invest in robust privacy security measures to protect our children's sensitive information deserve to have their efforts rewarded, rather than be undercut by competitors who are able to take advantage of lax enforcement or inadequate regulations.

Ms. Amelia Vance

The bipartisan American Data Privacy and Protection Act, introduced and passed out of this committee in the last Congress, is a strong and important step forward in not only better protecting everyone's privacy, but also in creating an even market for ethical companies that face a competitive disadvantage when they are doing the right thing.

I thank the Congressman for his question and will be happy to answer any further inquiries.

Building Effective Communications Around Student Data Privacy, an Analysis of Select K-12 Edtech Companies, Heinz College Systems Synthesis | Spring 2017

PROJECT TEAM MEMBERS
Joseph Babler
Flora Horvath
Daisy Huang
Elizabeth Martin
Mandi Prichard
Niels Smith

FACULTY ADVISOR
Andrew Richman

1. Executive Summary

As part of a capstone project of the Master of Science in Public Policy and Management (MSPPM) program at Carnegie Mellon University Heinz College, our team of six graduate students examined current practices of a select group of education technology (EdTech) startups in the K-12 space around student data privacy. Through a series of semi-structured interviews, we explored how each company develops public-facing communications regarding data use, privacy, and security policies. From analyzing the findings, the team garnered key insights and identified themes, which were used as a foundation for developing recommendations to the industry on building effective communications around student data privacy.

In Fall 2016, the Systems Synthesis Development Committee at Heinz College developed a broad problem statement for the team about student data privacy and commercialism in schools in the United States. This problem statement gave us a starting point for conducting a comprehensive literature review of over 135 articles and refining our project objective. After our initial research and consultation with our Advisory Board of subject matter experts, the team worked toward defining our project's objective, scope, timeline, and deliverables.

Employing a qualitative case methodology, we examined the current practices of a select group of emerging startups in the K-12 space, including how they develop public-facing communications regarding their data use, privacy, and security policies. Our intent was to find best practices regarding how emerging EdTech companies relay data privacy practices to the public and achieve meaningful transparency with stakeholders.

Using a merged database of companies that combined startup information from multiple sources, our team filtered 450 known EdTech startups down to a list of 120 EdTech companies and then selected 18 finalists based on criteria such as student data privacy risk, staff size, reputation, revenue growth, customer base, and value proposition. After a few weeks of standardized communications outreach and recruiting, six companies ultimately agreed to participate in our project, sitting for one to three hour-long interviews about their privacy practices and communications. After interviewing the companies, our team worked together to distill high-level commonalities across interviews, from which we gained the following key insights:

- Beyond complying with federal and state-level requirements, EdTech companies do not prioritize student data protections, as compared to customer acquisition and product development in their first five years.
- Due to factors such as limited resources and little demand from customers, EdTech companies do not establish formal strategies around public-facing communications about student data privacy for external stakeholders.
- Most EdTech companies use an open source, standardized privacy policy as a foundation for informing users about student data practices, which is customized as they scale up. Common practices include borrowing and/or adapting sections from competitors' privacy policies, as well as adding in sections based on customer demand and changes in federal or state-level requirements.
- Concerns about complying with privacy regulation and guidance do not seem to inhibit innovation at EdTech companies.

Although we garnered these insights from our data, the team believes that EdTech companies would also benefit from other recommendations. While most of the following recommendations were formed in the context of our small sample size of companies, they can inform and apply to emerging companies that come into the EdTech space.

- In a rapidly evolving industry landscape, the process of improving privacy practices and communications in EdTech companies should be dynamic, as opposed to one-time or periodic.
- As EdTech companies scale up, they should consider encouraging a shared responsibility for staying vigilant about changing technical standards across team members, instead of assigning this responsibility to one or two staff members. This will help increase engagement and awareness for data security practices across the company, as well as help instill a culture of respect for sensitive student data in staff.
- Instead of taking a piecemeal approach to developing privacy practices over time, young companies should consider building front-end processes and standards that guarantee evolutionary flexibility downstream.

- EdTech companies should resist collecting or storing unnecessary student data and establish strong internal controls to preclude doing so.
- EdTech companies should consider using strong and proactive public-facing communications about student data privacy as a product differentiator to stand out among competitors. Nimble adoption and understanding of new guidelines, technologies, and best practices can give initial adopters an important competitive advantage in the market.

Further, these cases offer important lessons for others within the EdTech ecosystem:

- For investors:
  - A theme emerged among these interviews about a perceived lack of meaningful interest about student data privacy from investors. Our team views this as a missed opportunity for everyone involved, and recommend that investors consider systematically assisting companies in ensuring strong privacy practices.
- For school districts:
  - School districts are the greatest force for our companies to change their privacy behaviors. Our team believes that more research needs to be done assessing school district capabilities across the U.S. for examining the technology that comes into their schools.

Our team submits that implementing these recommendations will benefit EdTech companies, their customers, and district and school-level stakeholders in this space. By employing a more proactive strategy to student data protection from day one, EdTech companies can position their vigilance as a key differentiator for their product, capture a broader market share, and share in the responsibility for protecting sensitive student data.

2. Introduction

2.1. Project Objective and Report Overview

The scope of our Systems Synthesis Project encompassed student data privacy practices of education technology (EdTech) companies that provide products, apps, or services for use by stakeholders in K-12 education. Our team interviewed six companies using a qualitative case study methodology that focused on public-facing communications on data use, privacy, and security practices. This group of companies includes a range of business models, from institutional to freemium (both for the institution and the consumer) as well as differing approaches to achieving user and revenue growth and articulating their value proposition. We synthesized the qualitative data from these case studies, distilling commonalities and key themes, and identified actionable recommendations to EdTech companies. Ultimately, our project's objective is to help nascent EdTech startups avoid communications missteps, establish trust with current and prospective customers, and build a dialogue about privacy practices between vendors and schools, districts, and other customers. This report presents the background and strategic context of student data privacy in the United States, discusses our research and data collection processes, presents our case studies, synthesizes our findings, and notes study limitations.

2.2. Advisory Board

Throughout our project's lifecycle, our team benefitted from the expertise of the following list of professionals and advocates from government, industry, nonprofits, and universities:

- Rachel Anderson, *Associate Director of Federal Policy and Advocacy at Data Quality Campaign (DQC)*
- Mark Luetzelschwab, *President of Eduphoric*
- Jim Siegl, *Technical Architect, Fairfax County Public Schools*
- Amelia Vance, *Policy Counsel, Future Privacy Forum (FPF)*
- Elana Zaide, *Associate Research Scholar at Princeton University's Center for Information Technology*

2.3. Project Methodology and Timeline

Our team began work on this project in Fall 2016 when the Systems Synthesis Development Committee at Carnegie Mellon University Heinz College developed a broad problem statement for our team. This problem statement gave us a starting point as guidance for reviewing relevant, evidence-based research and refining our project objective. We include the original problem statement prompt as Appendix 1 of this report.

To prepare, our team undertook a rapid literature review of available resources to familiarize ourselves with student data policy and the EdTech industry landscape.

We derived our research from a variety of source materials, including industry pledges and commitments driven by advocacy groups, state legislative activity (particularly concentrated in 2014-2015), and scholarly articles from EdTech industry trade journals.

In our review, we quickly identified a disconnect in communication between EdTech companies and their stakeholders (districts, parents, teachers, and students) regarding the collection, maintenance, and use of sensitive student data. Exacerbating factors involve unevenness in data literacy among stakeholders, an outdated legislative framework, and a series of headline-making scandals exposing EdTech companies misusing student data. In general, we found that many educators and parents are increasingly mistrustful of how EdTech companies amass and use data to track children, as well as commercialize students' personal information.

Figure 1 denotes a high-level timeline that our team followed for this project's thirteen-week life cycle, during which we presented three times to our advisory board. It identifies key meetings, research, and dissemination activities, as well as presentations to our advisory board members and policy community.

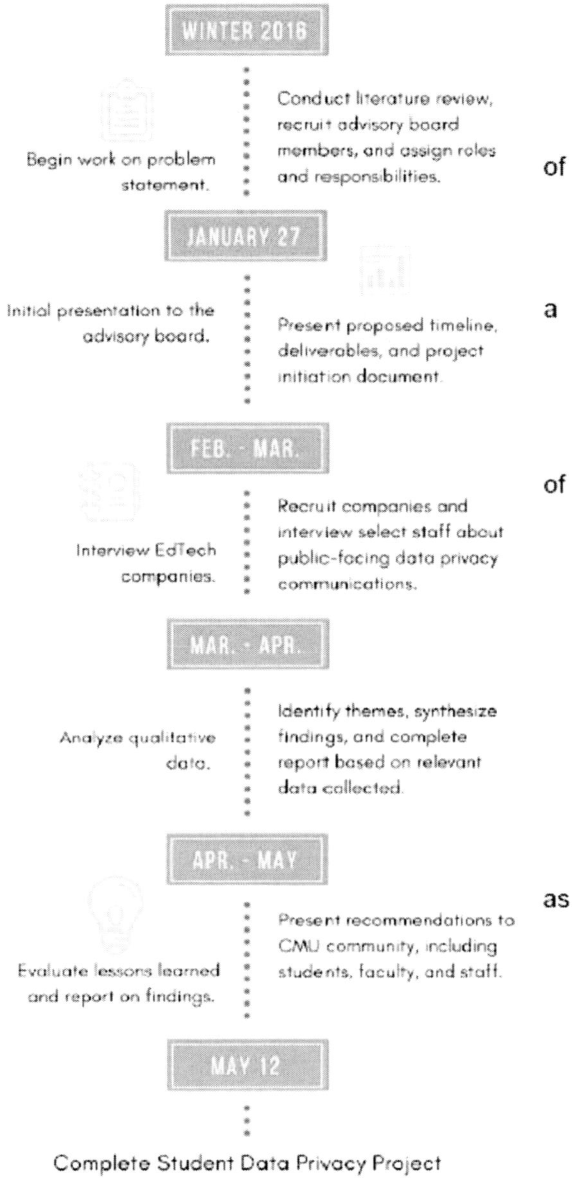

Figure 1. Project Timeline.

3. Strategic Context

3.1. History of Student Data Privacy

Before the mid-1970s, there was little regulation in the United States around schools sharing a child's information and records with third parties, with or without parental consent. Educational institutions could theoretically share records like enrollment forms, report cards, and disciplinary write-ups with the government, police, or vendors while also blocking parents from accessing those records.[105] At the state and federal level, education departments typically assigned a limited staff to generate basic statistical reports on basic data points, such as student enrollment, teacher characteristics, or education expenditures.[106] Teachers, administrators, and parents were able to effectively protect student records, as any data storage on servers was owned by school districts and stayed within a defined physical jurisdiction. As student record management has moved from paper-based systems to leveraging digital solutions, administrators at the district and school level have started collecting student data through a combination of the two methods. Big data capabilities have also emerged as a promising new method for collecting, analyzing, and communicating information about schools, teachers, and students within and across education management systems.[107] However, questions about the security, accessibility, and sharing of student data continue to concern IT leaders, with 64 percent of a recent leadership survey stating that it is a more important issue in 2016 than the previous year.[108]

3.2. Current Strategic Context

Fast forward to 2017, however, and big data capabilities in the education field have vastly expanded, with new digital learning tools utilizing algorithmic systems on thousands of comprehensive and varied indicators on their platforms.[109] Along with government agencies and nonprofit organizations, EdTech companies (e.g., Google Apps for Education) and consulting enterprises (e.g., Pearson and Mckinsey) have seized on business opportunities in analytics and associated technologies.[110] Through collection activities and commercial transactions on servers located outside of the district's physical jurisdiction, educators, researchers, and even parents have unwittingly released sensitive student data, such as students' *de facto* personally identifiable information (PII). With the advent of Software as a Service (Saas) based tools, schools are rapidly shifting to new technologies, such as cloud computing, to find off-premise data solutions that require significantly less up-front costs but grant EdTech vendors far more access to student data.[111] An evolving "surveillance culture" has emerged, in

---

[105] John Jennings. "1974: A Brief History of Student Data Privacy." Advancing K-12 EdTech Blog. https://www.skyward.com/discover/blog/skyward-blogs/skyward-executive-blog/february-2016/navigating-ferpa-and-p rotecting-student-data.

[106] Center for Digital Education. (2013) "Big Data and Analytics in K-12 Education: the time is right." *Houghton Mifflin Harcourt Center for Digital Education.* Retrieved from http://www.hmhco.com/~/media/sites/home/Teachers/Files/HMH-CDE_Issue%20Brief_DataAnalytics.pdf.

[107] Bradley Shear. (2015). "Ed Tech Must Embrace Stronger Student Privacy Data Laws." *The Journal.* Retrieved from https://thejournal.com/Articles/2015/05/28/Ed-Tech-Must-Embrace-Stronger-Student-Privacy-Laws.aspx.

[108] CoSN K-12 IT Leadership Survey. (2016). *Consortium for School Networking.* http://www.cosn.org/sites/default/files/CoSN%20K-12%20IT%20Leadership%20Survey%20Report%202016.pdf.

[109] Obama White House Archives. (2016). "Big Data: A Report on Algorithmic Systems, Opportunity, and Civil Rights." Retrieved from https://obamawhitehouse.archives.gov/sites/default/files/microsites/ostp/2016_0504_data_discrimination.pdf.

[110] Ibid.

[111] The Berkman Center for Internet & Society. (2013). "Working Roadmap: Student Privacy in the Cloud Computing Ecosystem." *The Berkman Center for Internet & Society at Harvard University.* Retrieved from https://cyber.harvard.edu/sites/cyber.law.harvard.edu/files/Berkman_Center_Student_Privacy_Working%20_Roadma p-June_2013.pdf.

which policymakers must carefully balance the sensitive intersection of education data and student privacy.[112] The fact that most information belongs to or relates to children only heightens the issues and sensitivities. Parents, advocacy groups, and other stakeholders in the education sphere share concerns over storing private student data on the internet, as third-party companies participate in data sharing processes, such as data mining, and sensitive student information, such as disciplinary records and disability information can fall into the wrong hands.

3.3. Legislative Landscape

In part, student data privacy has evolved into such a hot-button policy issue due to inadequacies in the legislative landscape. Simply put, there is no timely and comprehensive federal student privacy law. State legislators, school administrators, EdTech companies, and third-party vendors have struggled to interpret the Department of Education's role, which has led to varied and state-specific interpretations of the governance framework.[113] The Family Educational Rights and Privacy Act (FERPA) is the federal law that defines how and when educational institutions can disclose PII about students from their education records.[114] Signed into law by President Ford in 1974, FERPA provides outdated and scant guidance for protecting student privacy in 2017. For example, the legislation vaguely stipulates that only those with a "legitimate educational interest" should ever access a student's records, which school districts are left to interpret and enact as they see fit.[115] A complementary federal statute that governs schools on how they track, collect, and use student data is the Protection of Pupil Rights Amendment (PPRA). Like FERPA, it was signed into law in 1974, originally as a right of parent access to federally funded experimental materials, and was amended in 1978 to add parental consent for any educational institution collecting sensitive information from it students.[116] In 2002, Congress significantly expanded PPRA to limit schools' ability to both collect certain sensitive information from students, as well as disclose it for commercial purposes.[117]

Another important piece of legislation surrounding this issue is the Children's Online Privacy Protection Act (COPPA), which applies to children under the age of 13 and requires EdTech companies to obtain parental consent before obtaining PII from children for commercial purposes.[118] In 2012, the Federal Trade Commission (FTC) helped bolster several

[112] Faith Boninger and Alex Molnar. (2016). "Learning to Be Watched: Surveillance Culture at School. *National Education Policy Center at the University of Colorado, Boulder.* Retrieved from http://nepc.colorado.edu/files/publications/RB%20Boninger-Molnar%20Trends.pdf.

[113] David Raths. (2016). "The Patchwork of State Student Privacy Laws." *The Journal.* Retrieved from https://thejournal.com/articles/2016/10/13/the-patchwork-of-state-student-privacy-laws.aspx.

[114] Boninger and Molnar, 15.

[115] Ibid.

[116] i Lynn M. Daggett. (2008) "Student Privacy and the Protection of Pupil RIghts Act as Amended by No Child Left Behind." *UC Davis Journal of Juvenile Law and Policy.* https://jjlp.law.ucdavis.edu/archives/vol-12-no-1/daggett.pdf.

[117] Ibid, 56.

[118] "Talking about the Facts of Education Data with School Board Members." *National School Boards Education Center for Public Education and the Data Quality Campaign.*

elements of COPPA, including provisions for regulating new tracking technology.[119] One significant criticism of COPPA is its limited scope for protecting children under the age of 13, which can leave minors aged 13 to 17 with insufficient legal protection in their online activity.[120]

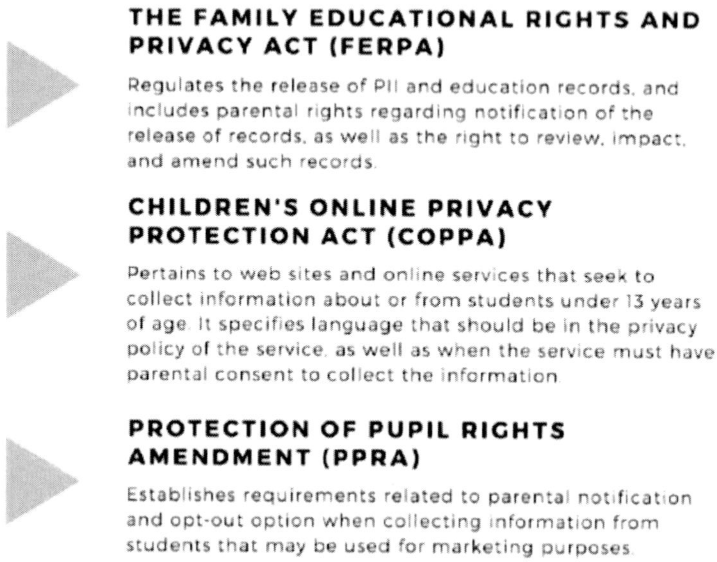

Figure 2. Guide to existing legislation.

Congress has attempted several times to overhaul these legislation and address student data privacy, most recently in 2015 when lawmakers introduced the Student Digital Privacy and Parental Rights Act that was ultimately not signed into law. In 2016, federal policymakers shifted toward enacting the newly reauthorized No Child Left Behind Act, known as the Every Student Succeeds Act.[121] In lieu of Congress introducing new legislation, the federal government has responded to state requests for clarification on FERPA guidance, e.g., in 2008 and 2011, when it released regulations defining the role of the state in using student data while maintaining privacy protections around PII.[122] These regulations likewise established specific provisions, including founding the Privacy Technical Assistance Center at the Department of Education, the creation of the Chief Privacy Officer position, and the implementation of penalties for certain kinds of privacy breaches.[123]

---

[119] Ibid.

[120] Caitlin R. Costello, Dale E. McNiel, Renee L. Binder. (2016). "Adolescents and Social Media: Privacy, Brain Development and the Law. Journal of the American Academy of Psychiatry and the Law Online. 44 (3), 313-321. Retrieved from jaapl.org/content/44/3/313.

[121] Data Quality Campaign Reports. (2016). "Student Data Privacy Legislation: A Summary of 2016 State Legislation." http://2pido73em67o3eytaq1cp8au.wpengine.netdna-cdn.com/wp-content/uploads/2016/09/DQC-Legislative-summar y-09302016.pdf.

[122] (n.d). "Talking about the Facts of Education Data with School Board Members." *National School Boards Education Center for Public Education and the Data Quality Campaign.* Retrieved from http://www.centerforpubliceducation.org/Main-Menu/Policies/Data-Privacy-Fact-Sheets-PDF.pdf.

[123] Ibid, 16.

3.4. State Legislative Activity and Challenges for EdTech Companies

As a result of federal privacy laws lagging behind the technology, state legislatures have passed a number of bills intended to regulate student data, particularly gaining momentum in legislative activity in 2014 and 2015. In 2014, states introduced and passed privacy bills focusing on state-level data collection and governing the federal government's responsibility, access, and oversight in this process.[124] In 2015, legislative activity shifted toward defining the data use and privacy activities of online service providers and vendors, as well as passing laws on supporting district's resource needs and staffing for student data privacy As a recent report from the Data Quality Campaign describes, "student data privacy bills adopt two main approaches: protecting privacy by limiting data use (a prohibitive approach) and protecting privacy by implementing data governance (a governance approach)."[125] In California, the Student Online Private Information Protection Act (SOPIPA), introduced in 2014 and enacted in 2016, is widely regarded as an effective, current, and all-encompassing bill for protecting K-12 student data.[126] Several states are seeking to replicate their own legislation on SOPIPA for regulating collection of K-12 student on websites, applications, and other technologies.[127]

EdTech companies have also proactively taken several steps to advocate for stronger student privacy protections, such as signing industry pledges and offering transparent privacy policies that protect children's personal information. While more robust privacy laws are expected in the near future, EdTech companies can, in the meantime, do more to address public concern about student data breaches or misuse, such as selling information for marketing purposes. In the absence of legal repercussions for such misuse, EdTech companies have provided robust privacy policies and adhered to best practices regarding parental consent and notification.

4. Literature Review Synthesis

4.1. Approach

Of the 135 articles our team read in the literature review, the majority focused on aspects of data privacy that were not directly relevant to the scope of our project. Overall, most of the results of our literature search focused on implications of FERPA, COPPA, PPRA, as well as other regulations. Much of the peer-reviewed work involved analysis and use of educational data to improve student performance through evidence-based interventions. Through our rating system described in appendix 5 of this report, we narrowed the results to 13 articles that provided the most useful background and concerns about successful data privacy practices and communicating data privacy to stakeholders in the K-12 education environment. This narrow

---

[124] Data Quality Campaign Reports. (2015). "Student Data Privacy Legislation: What Happened in 2015, and What Is Next." http://2pido73em67o3eytaq1cp8au.wpengine.netdna-cdn.com/wp-content/uploads/2016/03/DQC-Student-Data-Laws-2015-Sept23.pdf.

[125] Data Quality Campaign Reports. (2016). "Student Data Privacy Legislation: A Summary of 2016 State Legislation."

[126] Bradley Shear, "Ed Tech Must Embrace Stronger Student Privacy Data Laws."

[127] Ibid.

number of applicable articles to our research is evidence of the significant amount of work that remains to be done in this field.

4.2. Results

The selected articles fall into two categories: (1) those which discuss the best practices for protecting student data and maintaining data privacy, and (2) those which discuss successful communications practices on data privacy. Articles focusing on maintaining data privacy consistently suggest ensuring all employees who handle data be trained on use and privacy and that all organizations who use student data in any capacity are deeply knowledgeable about the applicable laws and regulations.

This literature review raised several salient concerns. First, there is no clearly established division of responsibility between schools and EdTech companies in regards to maintaining student data privacy. For example, one article discussed the ethics of the terms of service agreement that educators are forced to agree to when using some EdTech products and the limited bargaining power for privacy and security concerns that educators have with free apps or apps that do not directly contract with districts.[128] Another discussed the shift from school IT organizations to protect students to teachers, especially as teachers increasingly adopt digital devices, platforms, and apps in the classroom.[129] A number of articles published focus on the roles of school districts, school administrators, and teachers, but fewer cover the responsibilities and best practices of EdTech companies in the education sphere. This suggested to us a lack of synthesized awareness in the academic community to the practices of the EdTech sphere writ large.

Notably, and perhaps connected to the relatively minor coverage of EdTech company practices, several articles suggest a distrust of EdTech companies by researchers and school leaders, centered on the potential tension between ethical treatment of student data and the need for revenue generation to sustain the company. According to articles covering controversy around technology companies with privacy, researchers, parents, trade groups, and school administrators are primarily centered on the appropriate collection of data, sale of student data to third party groups, particularly for marketing purposes, and the potential for data breaches revealing sensitive student data.

The difficulty of communicating privacy practices is a known issue. One article specifically cited the closing of inBloom as the failure to communicate their data security and privacy protections in a way that convinced stakeholders of their commitment and effectiveness.[130] Similar issues cropped up for Google when a lawsuit was filed alleging that the company had violated federal and state laws by scanning and indexing emails of apps for education users.[131] There is a need to balancing transparency without overwhelming stakeholders–particularly parents and teachers□and there is a lack of guidance on how to do this successfully.

---

[128] Debbie Abilock, Rigele Abilock. "I Agree but Do I Know?: Privacy and Student Data." (2016) American Library Association.

[129] Dian Schaffhauser. "The hunt for data privacy in the classroom." (2016). THE Journal Magazine.

[130] Ben Kamisar. "InBloom Sputters Amid Concerns About Privacy of Student Data." (2014) Education Week.

[131] Benjamin Herold. "Google Under Fire for Data Mining Student Email Addresses." (2014) Education Week.

5. Methodologies

5.1. Literature Review

Working with a reference librarian at the Library of Congress, our team conducted a comprehensive literature review of periodicals, journals, and other written sources on educational technology and privacy written in the last five years. This involved pulling over 700 possible abstracts from multiple databases, including *Education Resources Information Center (ERIC)*, *Education Full Text* database, the *ABI/Inform Collection*, and *ProQuest Education*.

From this first pull, we further reviewed the list and ended with a narrowed list of 135 sources, an index of which can be found in appendix 5. The research team read and reviewed these 135 sources and an assigned team member graded each source using a pre-established quality scoring tool. The team generated the tool in an effort to identify the sources were most relevant to our research. Figure 3 gives an overview of our literature review process.

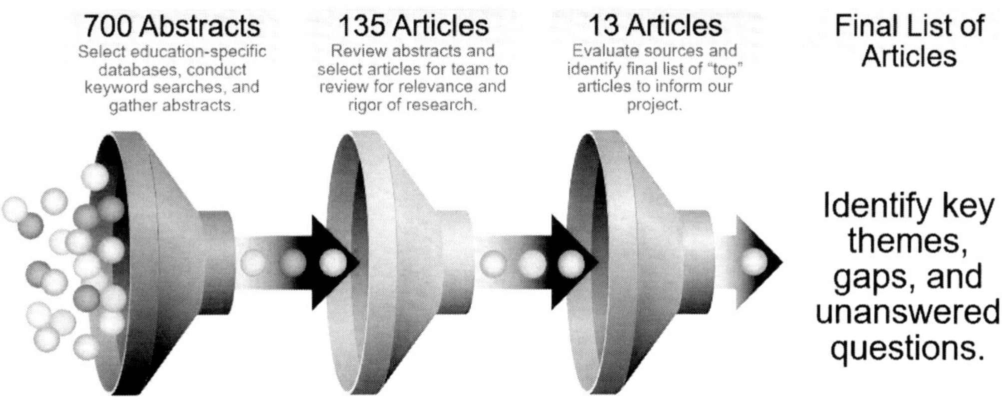

Figure 3. Literature Review Process.

5.2. Case Selection

After reading and discussing the gathered literature and conducting a series of informational interviews, we decided on a qualitative case study research method. These cases were intended to serve as the bulk of our primary research and reported findings.

To identify potential case companies, our team first defined our area of research as educational technology startups in the K-12 space that were old enough to have a meaningful customer base but still small and in the process of addressing privacy issues (generally less than 30 staff). We gathered a large list of 450 possible companies from multiple startup databases and removed any companies that did not fit our criteria. This process resulted in 120 potential companies that were individually analyzed by the research team along a range of criteria (see next section). The 120 companies were put into several tiers depending on how well they fit with our qualitative research goals, with the top tier comprised of the 18 startups that aligned with our research targets and goals.

5.3. Research Methodology

Once we had a target list of startups, we began reaching out to them through direct emails, social media (such as LinkedIn), and personal connections when possible. We explicitly offered to share our findings with the companies contacted as a means of incentivizing participation. After establishing first contact, we had brief (15-30 minute) introductory calls with various employees from the startup to explain our research goals and discuss their participation. Many startups did not respond at all to our inquiries, while a few decided not to participate once they spoke with us.

We conducted one-hour interviews with one to three staff members at each company that agreed to participate, along with examining and documenting any public records of the company. These interviews were conducted primarily over the phone with two members of our six-person research team. Extensive notes on the interviews were taken and results were discussed internally amongst the research. Figure 3 below shows our team's selection criteria and roadmap for finalizing the list of EdTech startups we interviewed.

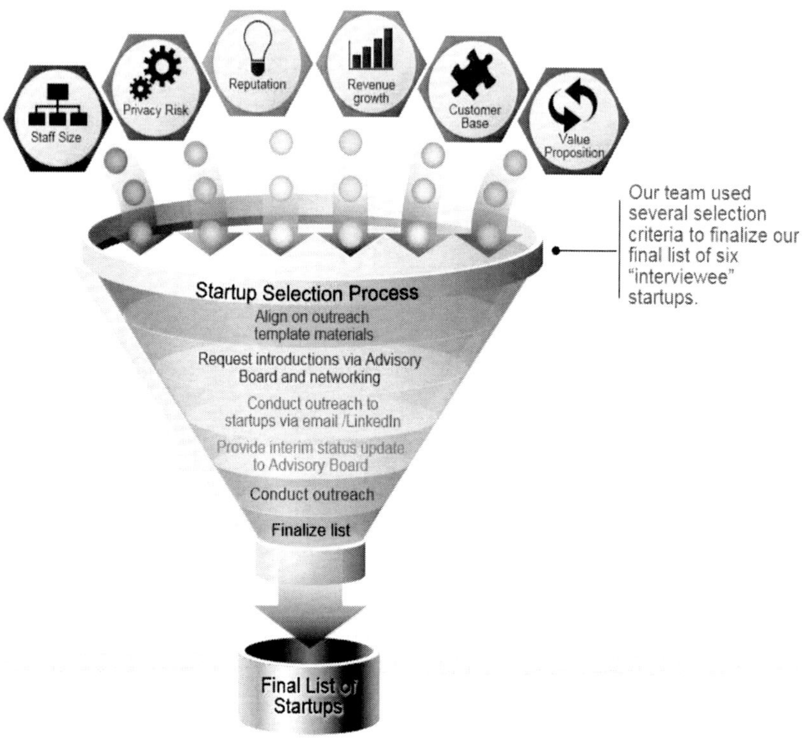

Figure 4. Process for Selecting EdTech Startups.

6. Cases

In general, these six companies were from all over the United States, with one international company who had a presence in the US market. They generally had no more than thirty staff. The ages of the companies varied but generally did not exceed eight years. Some of the products offered by these companies were used in a classroom, while others were used by the administration to somehow manage the school. They all had at least some clients, though some had been fully deployed for less than a year while others had been in business for multiple years.

To ensure the absolute protection of the companies who agreed to participate in our research, we have excluded write-ups of the individual case companies. This will protect their participation in our research and allowed these companies to speak candidly with us. The more robust, aggregated results appear in our findings and recommendations.

7. Recommendations & Conclusions

7.1. Conclusions

There is much about which to be optimistic. Educational technology is revamping schools and classrooms, changing the tools teachers have and the way students engage with learning. As a research team, we had the opportunity to explore just how dramatically and rapidly the landscape is changing, and we are all hopeful for the kinds of innovations it will yield. There are much larger issues of privacy and technology that exist well outside of the classroom concerning how we use technology and who gets access to our information. No special solution to these problems exist for the realm of education.

Broader debates about civil liberties will continue to have an impact on what kinds of tools end up in our classrooms. In the meantime though, work remains to be done on how privacy and technology intersect with our students. The companies we spoke with were all happy to follow guidelines, meet technical standards, and do what was asked of them to protect their customers' data. In that vein, below are our recommendations for educational technology companies that may just be starting out, investors, and further researchers on what *can* be done in the current technology environment.

7.2. EdTech Startups

- *View privacy practices as evolving and constantly improving:* Policymakers have implemented a variety of new legislation and regulations regarding privacy within the last five years; it is therefore important that company practices reflect these changes and acknowledge that their privacy practices may have to change as laws do. Additionally, security and privacy technologies and best practices are evolving, which will benefit companies who are able to nimbly and effectively adapt.
- *Keep track of changing technical standards:* Some of our companies were able to regularly keep up with changes in the industry to their (and everyone's) benefit. Sometimes this was done through an educational center, trade group, or other group of like-minded interests. Investors who focused particularly on the education technology market were good sources of changing standards and might prove a useful source for new companies. Certain CTOs we spoke with had deep experience in the industry and already had methods of tracking both policy and technical privacy standards as they

came to light. However it's managed, data security should be understood as a constant requirement.

- *Set good standards:* The majority of our startups made the major privacy decisions as they initially formulated their product. Most privacy decisions after the initial planning stages were limited and largely the result of outside feedback. This suggests that new companies□or companies launching new products□should think most critically and intensely about privacy during the initial phase. (For example, one of our case studies found part of its interest to schools was its ability to limit the collection of sensitive data relative to competitors.) This is not just a technical issue, but a policy issue of what kinds of information a company captures, who can manipulate that information, and where that information lives.
- *Do not collect or store unnecessary data:* This might not be as obvious as it seems. Several of the case companies we spoke with expressed the risks involved in collecting more data, particularly PII, than absolutely necessary for their product to function. A best practice is to be strategic and limited in data collection to minimize risk to the company and consumer. This involves drilling down to every field on a form, login for a product, or download for an app. Companies expose themselves to liability with each additional collected piece of information; new startups or product lines should gather the bare essentials to make a product work. Additionally, setting clear standards around data storage and deletion early on will create confidence in clients and easy standards to follow for staff.
- *Use privacy to differentiate:* Consumers generally are more aware of issues with their data security and the field of education is no different. One possible strategy for new EdTech companies is to sell not only their product but also their ability to keep limit data collection and increase security relative to their peers. Leading with good privacy standards as a marketable trait would be good for the underlying product and could help new companies attract more business relative to their peers.

7.3. Investors

Every company we spoke with discussed a general lack of pressure or interest from their capital investors in data privacy. Companies described investors as simply "checking-the-box" when it came to student data privacy. After an investor had made a decision to invest in one of our companies, the investor would do its basic due diligence and ensure that the startup did not run seriously afoul of any federal or state privacy standards, as well as being up-to-date on basic technical privacy standards. Because our companies are distributed across the United States and inhabit different parts of the EdTech space, this finding is likely particularly robust.

This lack of interest in privacy on the part of investors is a wasted opportunity for everyone involved. As our research found, new EdTech companies are particularly likely to need external support to navigate complicated and changing student privacy standards. Investors are uniquely exposed to these risks. The increased marginal cost to investors to offer technical and strategic advice to their investments is low relative to the benefit. EdTech investors can feel increased confidence that their investment is protected, while new startups can get much needed help in sufficiently prioritizing student data privacy.

7.4. More Research: School Districts

The moment when newer EdTech companies are most inclined to make significant technical or policy changes to their products to protect student data is when they are selling their product to a school or school district. The companies we spoke with generally described themselves as happy to meet whatever standards potential paying clients requested. And no other point in the development chain demanded or resulted in as much change at our case studies as when tried to get a new client.

There has been a flurry of lawmaking in the last decade at the state level; less discussed is how those state level laws will be met and enforced. It is an open question whether or not schools and school districts are uniformly well-equipped to be the arbiter of student data privacy standards for the whole of society. We suspect they are not. Given how widely resources can vary between schools within the same city, let alone the same state, our concern is that many schools lack the staff and other resources needed to effectively evaluate new technologies. New EdTech companies, unwittingly or not, could avoid the scrutiny that our case studies seemed genuinely happy to have.

However, these conclusions are beyond the scope of this effort. We encourage further work to be done into how successful and capable schools and school districts are at acting as the gatekeepers for their students' sensitive data.

8. Sources of Error and Limitations

8.1. Overview

Whenever possible, we tried to limit possible sources of error and ensure our cases were not an overly biased sample. However, there are several possible errors on the results we did produce and a variety of limitations on the reach of our conclusions. These are detailed below.

8.2. Sources of Error

While initially reaching out to companies, not every company responded or agreed to participate that we had initially chosen. One company said it was busy with a "product launch" while another cited an upcoming fundraising round. While most companies were ranked high on our scoring system (see appendix 6), it's possible that companies with serious difficulties or problems related to their privacy communications or standards simply opted themselves out of our review. This would skew the case studies we did toward companies that had not experienced problems, had better technological privacy solutions in place, and were generally more comfortable sharing this information with researchers. This might make our final conclusions seem more optimistic than they otherwise would be.

To ensure the privacy of the companies we interviewed and due to resources constraints, we did not record and transcribe our interviews. This fact prevented us from using well-known qualitative coding techniques to limit interview bias and interpretation in final results. To compensate for this we took generous notes during each interview, talked regularly across research teams to facilitate a common understanding, and collaborated closely on writing our final results.

Our interview questions were necessarily iterative and changed from company to company and interview to interview. While we collectively agreed on a mandatory set of basic questions□each two-person research team had the same original template to follow□follow-up questions, clarifications during the interview, and the natural course of conversation likely changed the tone and emphasis from interview to interview. Because our goal was not to generate final, authoritative results but instead get a general understanding of a wide swath of the educational technology field, this methodological choice made the most sense. However, it possibly introduced subtle but meaningful bias into the interviews and conclusions.

8.3. Limitations

Our use of a case interview methodology necessarily limited our findings. Because of the constraints on time and budget, generating, conducting, and analyzing a survey was not feasible. While we consciously wrote our conclusions to be suggestive rather than authoritative, we still may have over-generalized the lessons from our few cases to the broader field. We do not consider this research exhaustive, and our primary aim was discovery, hoping to cover ground that had not been well analyzed previously.

Our cases focused on a reasonably narrow developmental range□startups that were old enough to have some customers but not so old as to be very large in terms of staff size. This was a strategic choice of our research; we assumed companies any newer would not have enough to share and companies much larger would be generally less willing to speak with us in a candid way. Our hope in selecting this developmental range was to access companies that had already iterated some on their privacy communications and standards but likely were still contending with how to best move forward. This choice limits the external validity of our findings.

Our primary data□the case interviews with each company□depended on interviewees to be forward and honest about their companies and their issues with privacy practices. While we supplemented these interviews with public research, many of these companies were small enough or new enough to have little in terms of a public record. Ultimately, the extent which companies were willing share their information and struggles limited the extent of our research. Our team did not have the technical ability to do primary research into a company's inner workings, nor did we believe any companies would volunteer this type of access.

Appendix 1. Original Problem Statement

Prompt: Commercialism in the Schools & Student Data Collection

High-level Issue Definition: Big Data capabilities are revolutionizing marketing, which has become a billion dollar revenue stream for tech companies and marketing firms. Meanwhile, elementary and high schools in the U.S. are facing serious funding and accessibility to technology challenges in teaching their students. An evolving "surveillance culture" is developing in which schools are faced with a balancing act of assessing technology and allowing student data to be collected and commercially used, including de facto personally identifiable information (PII). Tech companies are opposing additional legislation to protect student data and many school districts, parents, other stakeholders are unaware of the extent their children's data is being used for marketing purposes to the children themselves. Should, and can, there be additional protections for young students? Can enforceable legislation be designed to protect students, and what information is needed? Should technology incentives that furnish devices for classroom and student use be regulated to protect students from marketing efforts?

Appendix 2. Proposed Project Timeline

Date	Activity	Description
Friday, January 27	Meeting	• Initial Advisory Board Meeting • Presentation of Project Initiation Document
January - March	Research	• Collection and analysis of relevant data from select EdTech companies
Friday, March 10	Meeting	• Second Advisory Board Meeting • Presentation of the project's interim status
March - April	Project Finalization	• Completion of report, findings, and recommendations on relevant data collected from select EdTech companies
Friday, April 28	Meeting	• Presentation of the project's final report, findings, and recommendations to the Advisory Board
April - May	Dissemination	• Submission of project findings to various conferences and exploration of other methods to distribute key findings to a wider audience
Friday, May 12	Presentation	• Presentation of the project's findings to Carnegie Mellon University community, including students, faculty, and staff

Appendix 3. One-Pager Sent to Prospective Companies

About Heinz College and the Master of Public Policy and Management Program (MSPPM)

The H. J. Heinz III College (Heinz College) at Carnegie Mellon University in Pittsburgh, Pennsylvania is a graduate college that consists of one of the nation's top-ranked public policy programs and information systems schools. The Master of Public Policy and Management Program (MSPPM) offers curriculum tracks in three locations, including Washington, DC (MSPPM-DC).

In the MSPPM-DC track, students take classes on campus in Pittsburgh in their first year and spend the second year in Washington, DC, working four days per week in full-time apprenticeships while completing degree requirements during weekday evenings. This integration of skill building with hands-on application, real-world experience, and networking creates a unique graduate school experience.

About the Systems Synthesis Project

In lieu of a master's thesis, MSPPM-DC students participate in a semester-long group project in the second year called the Systems Synthesis Project, where groups start with an unstructured problem, refine the scope, and then analyze, develop, and implement a solution. The Systems Synthesis Project delivers a capstone experience to students, which integrates core skills from coursework and builds hands-on problem solving, project management, and teamwork skills.

Our Systems Synthesis Project Proposal

- *Title: Building Effective Communications around Data Privacy Issues in the K-12 EdTech Industry*
- *Issue:* In the past two decades, big data capabilities have emerged as a promising method for collecting, analyzing, and communicating information about schools, teachers, and students within and across K-12 education management systems. Using online products and services, stakeholders (i.e., educators, parents, and teachers) must contend with a new information landscape, navigating complex questions about sensitive data. As thousands of online applications enter K-12 classrooms, there is an increasing lack of understanding between the education technology companies and the parents and students who wish to understand and protect themselves. In part, student data privacy has evolved into such a hot-button policy due to activity in state legislatures and a recent string of headlines involving high-profile companies and data privacy issues. Companies within the EdTech space have started facing criticism for a perceived lack of accessibility, transparency, and accountability in communicating their data use disclosure, privacy, and security policies to key stakeholders, i.e., schools, parents, and end users.
- *Approach:* We are using a qualitative case methodology to examine a group of 6-10 EdTech companies that meet the following criteria: (1) are 0-8 years old, (2) use click-through agreements for product delivery, and (3) offer educational services in K-12 classrooms. For each company, we will conduct a thorough analysis of public-facing communications strategy around data privacy, including interviews with staff and discussion of privacy practices.
- *Key Deliverable:* We will produce a 25-page report containing our findings, analysis, and guidance on communications best practices to help emerging EdTech companies successfully navigate messaging around data privacy. We will generate a one-page version of this report that contains our key takeaways, as well as a three-page executive summary version.
- *Timeline:* January - May 2017
- *Faculty Advisor:* Andy Richman

Appendix 4. Interview Template

Introductory Blurb

We would like to learn about your privacy policies and some of the practices you employ in implementing them. We are preparing a report in which, among other things, we will be briefing our advisory board, members of the Carnegie Mellon community, and various public policy decision makers, and NGOs working on privacy issues. We intend to make policy recommendations in our report that will include many of the issues our interview will address today so thank you again for the time you are giving our project today. It is very helpful.

Introduction/Professional Background (5-10 Minutes)

1. What led you to found [your company] and attracted you about the education technology industry in general?
2. What does privacy mean to you personally?
   a. What steps do you take to protect your own privacy?

Privacy Practices (20 Minutes)

1. Could you walk us through how your company established its privacy policies?
   a. How often do you revisit your privacy practices and why do you do so?

Possible Follow UPs

- Did you reference resources or outsource this task to someone else either to draft or review?
- Did you seek professional or legal advice when creating your formal policy?
- What specific changes have you made in your privacy practices since you were founded?
- With your investors, did you discuss privacy issues and to what extent? How important was it to them to have a comprehensive privacy standard?

Company-Specific Privacy Practice Communications (20 Minutes)

1. When it comes to your company, what is your outlook for announcing data collection and/or sharing practices, as well as any other changes to your customers?
2. Do you hire staff who handle data collection communications with customers?
3. Have you made plans if personal information were inadvertently disclosed?
4. How often do users reach out to you about privacy concerns and what are common issues?

Possible Follow UPs

- Generally speaking, what is the customer-preferred method for reaching out?
- What are the most common privacy concerns?
- Have privacy concerns prevented a customer from signing up for your service?
- How did you consider the accessibility of your privacy practices when making it, in terms of ease of obtaining and ease of understanding?
- If you signed a pledge to safeguard student privacy, is this information known to your users?
- What resources do you provide for users who have questions about your privacy policies?
- If there is a change in your privacy policy, do you alert your users? How so?

Company Specific Questions

(10 minutes)

Varies from case to case

Appendix 5. Literature Review Resources

Title	Last Name	First Name	Year	Publication
I agree, but do I know? Privacy and Student Data	Abilock	Rigele	2016	Knowledge Quest
The Privacy Problem: Although School Librarians Seldom Discuss It, Students' Privacy Rights Are under Attack	Adams	Helen R.	2011	School Library Journal
Guide to Data Privacy Issued for Parents	Armitage	Audrey	2015	Education Week
The Challenge of Data Privacy	Bames	Khaliah	2015	Education Leadership
Obama Tries New Tack to Collect Student Data	Baskin	Paul	2010	Chronicle of Higher Education
How Little Data Breaches Cause Problems	Bathon	Justin	2013	T H E Journal
Managing Student Identities in the Digital Era	Bjerede	Marie	2015	T H E Journal
Realizing Educational Rights: Advancing School Reform Through Courts and Communities	Blokhuis	J.C.	2014	Educational Theory
About This Report	Bushweller	Kevin	2014	Education Week
Microsoft Puts Privacy on Branding Agenda	Cavanagh	Sean	2014	Education Week
Ed-Tech Vendors Attend 'Boot Camp' for Data-Privacy Advice	Cavanagh	Sean	2015	Education Week
Google Commits to Pledge on Student-Data Privacy	Cavanagh	Sean	2015	Education Week
Privacy Protection	Cook	Glenn	2015	American School Board Journal
Privacy Concerns: The Effects of the Latest FERPA	Cossler	Christine	2010	School Business Affairs
Big Data Wants Your Students	Czuprynski	Christine	2015	American School Board Journal

Title	Last Name	First Name	Year	Publication
Ed Law: Technology weaves a tangled privacy web	Darden	Edwin	2015	Phi Delta Kappan
5 (Good) Ways to Talk About Data	Datnow	Amanda	2015	Educational Leadership
Indiana Data Network Draws Opposition	Davis	Michelle	2014	Education Week
New York Dumps inBloom; Now Must Find an Alternative	Davis	Michelle	2014	Education Week
TECHNOLOGY TRANSIENCE AND LEARNER DATA: Shifting Notions of Privacy in Online Learning	Dennen	Vanessa	2015	Quarterly Review of Distance Education
Partnership Books Data Privacy	Doran	Leo	2016	Education Week
Teaching Privacy in the Twenty-First Century	Edbrooke	Odette	2012	Social Education
Making the Right Commitment to Student-Data Privacy	Evans	Cameron	2015	Education Week
Student Privacy in the Age of Big Data	Ewbank	Ann	2016	Knowledge Quest
Replicating the Relationship between Teachers' Data Use and Student Achievement: The Urban Data Study and the Data Dashboard Usage Study	Faria	Ann-Marie	2014	Society for Research on Educational Effectiveness
#ED TECH	Farrace	Bob	2016	Principal Leadership
What it means when we talk student data	Fitzgerald	Bill	2015	Tech & Learning
Data-Privacy Training Lags Behind in K-12.	Flanigan	Robin	2015	Education Week
Managing School Social Work Records	Garrett	Kendra J.	2012	Children & Schools
Assessment Group Approves Privacy Rules for Student Data	Gewertz	Catherine	2013	Education Week
Privacy Group Pushes Parents To Opt Out of FERPA	Gilmore	Sara	2015	Education Week
Past, Present, and Future of Assessment in Schools: A Thematic Narrative Analysis	Green	Stephanie	2015	The Qualitative Report
Student Access to Technology and Its Impact on Achievement	Griffin	Jill	2013	Department of Educational Leadership, Southern Illinois University Edwardsville
Parents need access to education data and need to know it's secure	Guidera	Aimee	2015	Phi Delta Kappan
Schools Urged to Put a Higher Priority On 'De-Identifying' Student Data.	Harold	Benjamin	2015	Education Week
New Principles Aim to Guide Use, Safety of Student Data	Herald	Benjamin	2015	Education Week
Prominent Ed-Tech Players' Data-Privacy Policies Attract Scrutiny	Herald	Benjamin	2014	Education Week
Educators Hope Congress Provides Clarity, Support on Privacy Issues	Herald	Benjamin	2015	Education Week
President Obama Propose Student-Data-Privacy Upgrade	Herold	Benjamin	2015	Education Week
"Student Privacy Survey"	Herold	Benjamin	2014	Education Week
U.S. Outlines Data-Privacy Guidelines	Herold	Benjamin	2014	Education Week
Google Under Fire For Data Analysis of Student Emails	Herold	Benjamin	2014	Education Week
Ed-Tech Industry Weighs Impact of New Data-Privacy Laws	Herold	Benjamin	2014	Education Week
Major FERPA Overhaul Under Consideration in U.S. House	Herold	Benjamin	2015	Education Week
Draft bill on Student Privacy Raises Questions	Herold	Benjamin	2015	Education Week
Google Mines Student Data Outside Education Apps	Herold	Benjamin	2016	Education Week

(Continued)

Title	Last Name	First Name	Year	Publication
House Bill Aims to Increase Federal Role in Safeguarding Student-Data Privacy	Herold	Benjamin	2015	Education Week
Legislative-Advocacy Group's Model Bill Tackles Privacy of Student Data	Herold	Benjamin	2013	Education Week
Big Data' Research Effort Faces Student-Privacy Questions	Herold	Benjamin	2014	Education Week
Ferpa Primer: The Basics and Beyond	Hlavac	George	2015	NACE Journal
Navigating Student Data Privacy Laws	Holcomb	Carolyn	2015	Risk Management
Integrating Data Mining in Program Evaluation of K-12 Online Education	Hung	Jui-Long	2012	Journal of Educational Technology & Society
InBloom Sputters As Data Privacy Hits the Spotlight	Kamisar	Ben	2014	Education Week
Putting the Schools in Charge	Katzman	John	2012	The Education Digest
Data Messages	Kaufman	Daniel	2016	American School Board Journal
Craving Capacity	Kennedy	Mike	2016	American School & University
The Transformation of Schools' Social Networks during a Data-Based Decision Making Reform	Keuning	Trynke	2016	Teachers College Record
Aspirational Data Practices for Student Privacy	Kreuger	Keith	2015	School Administrator
Backtalk	Kreuger	Keith	2015	Phi Delta Kappan
New technology "clouds" student data privacy	Krueger	Keith	2015	Phi Delta Kappan
10 Steps That Protect the Privacy of Student Data	Krueger	Keith	2014	T H E Journal
10 Terms You Must Include in Contracts with Online Service Providers	Krueger	Keith	2014	T H E Journal
Let's Get Physical: K-12 Students Using Wearable Devices to Obtain and Learn About Data from Physical Activities	Lee	Victor	2015	TechTrends
Ethical and appropriate data use requires data literacy	Mandinach	Ellen	2015	Phi Delta Kappan
How Data Are Used and Misused in Schools: Perceptions from Teachers and Principals	Militello	Matthew	2013	Education Sciences
Bankruptcy Case Shines Spotlight on Data Privacy	Moiner	Michele	2014	Education Week
On the Block: Student Data and Privacy in the Digital Age□The Seventeenth Annual Report on Schoolhouse Commercializing Trends, 2013-2014	Molnar	Alex	2015	National Education Policy Center, School of Education at University of Colorado
In Data Area, Groups Push More Clarity	Molnar	Michele	2014	Education Week
Safeguard Use of Student Data, White House Report Urges	Molnar	Michele	2014	Education Week
FTC Acts to Protect Student Data in Ed-Tech Firm's Bankruptcy Case	Molnar	Michele	2014	Education Week
Florida Lawmakers Approve Student-Data-Privacy Bill	Molnar	Michele	2014	Education Week
FERPA and Homelessness: A Technical Assistance Tool for NAEHCY Members	N/A	N/A	2010	National Association for the Education of Homeless Children and Youth (NAEHCY)

Title	Last Name	First Name	Year	Publication
U.S. Department of Education's Proposed FERPA Regulations: Overview and Initial Analysis	N/A	N/A	2011	Data Quality Campaign
Call to Action: Clarify Applications of FERPA to State Longitudinal Data Systems	N/A	N/A	2011	Data Quality Campaign
Indiana Department of Education Notice of Procedural Safeguards	N/A	N/A	2010	Indiana Department of Education
Statistical Methods for Protecting Personally Identifiable Information in Aggregate Reporting.	N/A	N/A	2010	National Center for Education Statistics
Forum Guide to Data Ethics. NFES 2010-801	N/A	N/A	2010	National Forum of Education Statistics
Keeping Student Data Private	N/A	N/A	2014	T H E Journal
Manifold path to Happiness	N/A	N/A	2012	Times Education Supplement
Nonprofit Starts Campaign To Push Education as Priority	N/A	N/A	2015	Education Week
Parents Back Data Collection Depending on Its Use	N/A	N/A	2015	Education Week
Schools Gather more Data But for What purpose?	N/A	N/A	2015	Educational Leadership
Study: No Expectation of Privacy in Massachusetts Schools	N/A	N/A	2016	Information Management
Schools Putting Kids' SSNs at Risk	N/A	N/A	2010	Information Management
Surveying Encryption Practices of Technology Used Within Schools	N/A	N/A	2016	Common Sense Media
Keeping Student Data Private	N/A	N/A	2014	T H E Journal
Education Data Privacy: Seven Lessons Learned	N/A	N/A	2016	Tech & Learning
Education apps raise privacy concerns	N/A	N/A	2015	American School Board Journal
Guiding Questions for Data Analysis, by Reports	N/A	N/A	2015	Wake County Public School System (WCPSS), Data and Accountability Department
Forum Guide to the Teacher-Student Data Link: A Technical Implementation Resource. NFES 2013-802	N/A	N/A	2013	National Forum of Education Statistics
When Data Drives School Culture	N/A	N/A	2011	Leadership
All About The Data	N/A	N/A	2014	Tech & Learning
Big Data and Administrators: The Struggle to Store, Manage, and Analyze Data Safely	N/A	N/A	2015	T H E Journal
Law and American Education: A Case Brief Approach. Third Edition	Palestini	Robert	2012	Rowman and Littlefield Education
To Protect and Serve	Panter	Suzanna L.	2015	Knowledge Quest
Digital Youth in Brick and Mortar Schools; Examining the Complex Interplay of Students, Technology, Education, and Change	Peck	Craig	2015	Teachers College Record
States Working to Fill Privacy Gaps	Pik	George	2015	Information Today
Framing the Law and Policy Picture A Snapshot of K-12 Cloud-Based Ed Tech & Student Privacy in Early 2014	Plunkett	Leah	2014	Berkman Center for Internet & Society

(Continued)

Title	Last Name	First Name	Year	Publication
Assessment in the Kindergarten Classroom: An Empirical Study of Teachers' Assessment Approaches	Pyle	Angela	2013	Early Childhood Education Journal
Supporting assessment autonomy: How one small school articulated the infrastructure needed to own and use student data	Quartz	Karen Hunter	2014	Journal of Educational Change
Negotiating Access to Health Information to Promote Students' Health	Radis	Molly E.	2016	Journal of School Nursing
Beyond Teach and Hope: Moving from Data to Action	Regan	Kelley	2013	Teacher Education Quarterly
The Editor's Note: Mindful Privacy	Richardson	Joan	2015	Phi Delta Kappan
Promising Principles for Safeguarding Student Information	Robinson	Sharon	2016	Education Digest
Limitations and Analysis of FERPA Policies within Florida Public School Districts	Rogers	Sheryl D.	2012	ProQuest LLC
Amassing Student Data and Dissipating Privacy Rights	Rotenberg	Marc	2013	Educause Review
The Hunt for Data Privacy in the Classroom	Schaffhauser	Dian	2016	T H E Journal
Factors Influencing the Functioning of Data Teams	Schildkamp	Kim	2015	Teachers College Record
Pledge Reflects Ed-Tech Leaders' Concern for Student-Data Privacy.	Schneiderman	Mark	2015	Education Week
Online Student Collaboration and FERPA Considerations	Schrameyer	Alexander	2016	TechTrends
Ed Tech Must Embrace Stronger Student Privacy Laws	Shear	Bradley	2015	T H E Journal
Using data for decision-making: perspectives from 16 principals in Michigan, USA	Shen	Jianping	2010	International Review of Education
Proposed Data-Privacy Rules Seen as Timely for States	Sparks	Sarah	2011	Education Week
Guidance Offered on Guarding Student Privacy in School Data;	Sparks	Sarah	2010	Education Week
The Legal Implications of Surveillance Cameras	Steketee	Amy M.	2012	District Administration
Creating Anytime, Anywhere Learning for All Students: Key Elements of a Comprehensive Digital Infrastructure	Thigpen	Kamilla	2014	Alliance for Excellent Education
Student data privacy is cloudy today, clearer tomorrow	Trainor	Sonja	2015	Phi Delta Kappan
Putting Data Into Practice: Lessons from New York City. Education Sector Reports	Tucker	Bill	2010	Education Sector
Legal Implications of Using Digital Technology in Public Schools: Effects on Privacy	Tudor	Joanna	2015	Journal of Law and Education
State Lawmakers Ramp Up Attention on Student-Data Privacy	Ujifusa	Andrew	2014	Education Week
States Are Expanding Access to K-12 Data, Group Says	Ujifusa	Andrew	2014	Education Week
Hearing Weighs Student-Data Privacy Concerns	Ujifusa	Andrew	2016	Education Week
Star light, star bright	Vail	Kathleen	2015	American School Board Journal
Revisiting M.R.M. in Search of Legitimate Reasons for Limiting Student Privacy Rights	Walker	Kathryn	2015	Education & Law Journal

Title	Last Name	First Name	Year	Publication
Big Opportunities and Big Concerns of Big Data in Education	Wang	Yinying	2016	TechTrends
Privacy Concerns Often Ignored by Reformers	White	Jenni	2014	Education Week
Cyber Savvy: Embracing Digital Safety and Civility	Willard	Nancy	2012	Corwin; A SAGE Publications Company
Aligning the Effective Use of Student Data with Student Privacy and Security Laws	Winnick	Steve	2011	Data Quality Campaign
Determinants of online privacy concern and its influence on privacy protection behaviors among young adolescents	Youn	Seounmi	2009	Journal of Consumer Affairs
A 21st-Century Model for Teaching Digital Leadership	Young	Donna	2014	Educational Horizons

Appendix 6. Methodologies

Literature Review Methodology

In conducting the literature review, our team sought to gain an understanding of the material already available on this topic as well as formulate a novel research angle for our project's focus. We worked with our systems faculty advisor to narrow our scope to K-12 education in the United States, pertaining to the collection of student data.

The team worked with a librarian at the Library of Congress (LOC) to select discipline-specific databases, such as the *Education Resources Information Center* (ERIC), *Education Full Text* database, the *ABI/Inform Collection*, and *ProQuest Education*. The librarian advised the team on using Boolean operators in our search queries to optimize our search results, including the following,

- "student data privacy";
- "student record access";
- "student data" AND "privacy";
- "student rights" AND "privacy";
- (K-12* OR educat*) AND (privacy OR access);
- "student data" AND "education technology";
- "data" AND "education apps."

Team members filtered thousands of research citations generated by these queries by location, topic, and time frame in order to isolate sources that reflected the key themes or issues relevant to our team's research interests. This filtering process narrowed the results to about 700 abstracts. After reading each of the abstracts, the team further eliminated those that lacked relevancy.

In total, we selected 135 abstracts, listed in the appendix, for more detailed review, assigned them among team members, and carefully reviewed the articles based on factors like content, analytical rigor, credentials of authors, intended audience, and evidence-based methods. In our review, our team also tracked relevant references to other studies, articles, and compelling sources to locate others. We created a A-B-C-D quality scoring tool and included a description column for team members to provide rationale for scoring for each article. Our quality scoring tool assigned grades to articles based on factors such as relevance, audience, peer review, strength and rigor of research methods, and inclusion of anecdotal vs. evidence-based content.

Ultimately, our team used this information to produce a thorough review of the top-rated available research documents, which includes a detailed description of the list of studies that our team rated in the 'A' range, using our quality scoring tool. As mentioned in the preceding analysis, the body of literature is light on the education technology component.

Case Selection Methodology

In order to uncover the privacy communication practices of companies, we pursued a qualitative case methodology by examining a group of six EdTech companies. For each company, or case, we conducted a parallel analysis, including interviews with staff, primary analysis of data privacy practices, and examination of how the company communicates their privacy practices to key stakeholders.

Our case study methodology is broken into five parts: (1) creating a database of EdTech startup companies, (2) selecting the cases, (3) recruiting the companies, (4) executing research, and (5) analyzing the results from the case studies.

Creating a database of EdTech startup companies: To start the process, we needed to create a database of relatively new EdTech companies so that we would have a list of organizations that we could systematically research and contact. Our process for creating the database is detailed below.

1. The team downloaded lists of startup companies from relevant databases. The lists were then merged into an excel sheet and duplicate companies were removed, resulting in a file with 450 companies.
2. Not all of 450 of the companies fell into the EdTech category and thus needed to be filtered manually one by one. For our purposes, to filter only EdTech companies from the original 450 companies, we looked at the following criteria:
   - Is the company an EdTech company?
   - Do they operate in the United States?
   - Do they work with the K-12 market?

   Only companies that met the all three criteria remained on our list for a more in depth review in order to determine whether or not they would make good case study candidates. This resulted in a list of 120 EdTech companies that were based in the United States with a K-12 audience.

3. The team members each researched a portion of these 120 companies in a systematic way, filling in the information for the following pieces on each company:
   - Website and Privacy Policy: The website and privacy policy URLs
   - Year founded: The year the company was founded
   - Employees: The number of employees in the company

- Funding: The amount of funding given to the company to date
- Category: The EdTech segment they belonged to (games, adaptive learning, classroom management, etc.)
- Information Risk: The amount of PII collected by the company and how they used this information
- Entrance into schools: How these companies enter into schools (through teachers, students, administrators, etc.)

With these fields of information entered for each company, the team effectively created a brief snapshot of each organization and their characteristics.
Creating a purposive sample: Our research focused on several different types of companies and their place in the EdTech industry. Our standards for selecting the cases were as follows:

1. We wanted a good representation of the diverse EdTech startup landscape so we chose to pursue companies that varied from each other. No two companies were the same and differed in characteristics such as Category, Information Risk, Entrance in schools, etc.
2. From our database of 120 EdTech companies, we selected 18 as potential case study prospects. Although we only needed six, the team contacted all 18 companies because we expected that some would be unresponsive or unwilling to participate in our study.

Recruiting the companies: The success of our research was contingent on the participation of EdTech companies and the reliability of the information we received from them. The recruitment strategies we used are listed below:

1. To incentivize participation, our team committed to share copies of our final report, policy brief, general research deliverables, and other insights with the companies we examined. We anticipated that recently formed companies would appreciate the opportunity to learn more about how the industry discusses privacy issues with potential customers.
2. To protect our subjects, we anonymized the companies in our report and did not refer to them by company name. Although we took this step to protect their identities, we believe that some EdTech companies are unique to the point that they may still be identifiable.

Executing Research: Once our cases agreed to participate, we analyzed each case in an analogous way, detailed below.

1. Every case had two team members devoted to it, and team pairings differed from case to case (i.e., for six cases, each team member worked on two cases and had a different partner for each case). This ensured that ideas among the group cross-pollinated and that each case analyzed benefited from multiple perspectives.

2. Techniques of research and inquiry were broadly identical to ensure that the team maintained research fidelity across cases. The team met regularly to discuss progress and to confirm that we maintained consistency in our case methodology. However, there were instances in which each research team asked questions that applied to only that particular company and not others. Since we were explicitly relying our collective ability to pull multiple qualitative threads together, we did not want to severely limit any individual team's ability to fully analyze their case company.
3. For each company, or case, we used structured interviews with staff, primary analysis of data privacy practices (as much as possible), examination of how the technology is used in the classroom, and other kinds of evaluation. Through our interviews, we verified what kind of data storage and management practices exist at the companies we examined. When our technical knowledge fell short, we sought advice from experts in the community.

Analyzing the results: Upon completion of the individual company interviews, we generated a full final report to discuss our findings, as described below.

1. These findings are separated into two parts.
    a. The first part includes a reviews and analysis of each company case. The write-up of individual company cases was written by each paired research team, and it examined how the company deals with privacy concerns, exploring technical, legal, and policy dimensions of the issue as it relates to each case company.
    b. The second part of the final report synthesized the trends we all saw in all of our cases, the literature we have reviewed, insight from our advisory board, interviews we have done throughout the project, and our own reflections. This second part was a collaborative effort across the entire research team. We also discussed what we *do not* know and could not learn through this process, the pitfalls of our own methodology, and the questions that remain unanswered.

Index

T

U

V

W

Y